Nicolas Wa

THE WILLIAM MORRIS LIBRARY

THOEMMES

I would like to thank the William Morris Society for presenting me with the Peter Floud Award for 1991–1993. This greatly facilitated my research into Morris's political writings.

POLITICAL WRITINGS

CONTRIBUTIONS TO *JUSTICE* AND *COMMONWEAL* 1883–1890

William Morris

EDITED AND INTRODUCED BY
NICHOLAS SALMON

THOEMMES PRESS

Published in 1994 by

Thoemmes Press
85 Park Street
Bristol BS1 5PJ
England

ISBN 1 85506 252 6 : Paperback
ISBN 1 85506 251 8 : Hardback

Printed in Great Britain by Antony Rowe Ltd, Chippenham.

CONTENTS

INTRODUCTION

The least well-known aspect of William Morris's propaganda work for the socialist movement is his contributions to *Justice* and *Commonweal*. Yet between 1884 and 1890 he published almost 500 signed articles in these papers which included poetry, prose fictions, dialogues, lectures and numerous essays on contemporary politics. Few of the latter have been reprinted since they first appeared. The intention of this volume is to offer for the first time a chronological selection of these journalistic writings.

The origins of both *Justice* and *Commonweal* – two of the foremost socialist journals of the 1880s – can be traced back to the formation of the Democratic Federation in 1881 (it was renamed the Social Democratic Federation in 1884). This was originally a union of London Radical Clubs formed by H. M. Hyndman to promote a programme of progressive liberal reform. However, many radical members were driven away by Hyndman's socialistic tendencies and his outspoken opposition to the Irish Coercion Bill. They were replaced by left-wing enthusiasts such as Herbert Burrows, J. L. Joynes, Charles and James Murray, Andreas Scheu and Jack Williams. Under their influence the Federation passed a distinctly socialistic resolution at a conference held in May 1882. This was followed in the winter of 1882/3 by support for land nationalization, the appropriation of the railways and cumulative taxation. By this time the Federation was recognized nationally as a socialist body. Morris became a member of the Federation in January 1883 and was elected to the Executive as Treasurer later that summer.

The idea of launching a weekly socialist newspaper was discussed at a number of meetings of the Federation, held during the winter of 1883/4. The project was made possible by a donation of £300 made by Edward Carpenter who had been converted to socialism after reading Hyndman's book *England for All.* James McDonald recalled how the project was discussed with great enthusiasm. He particularly remembered one meeting where Hyndman outlined the aims of the new paper much to Morris's delight:

> ...he declared that humbug, political, social and scientific, would be exposed, art was to be emancipated (here Morris nearly shook his shaggy head off with approving nods) and the workers of the world would be united by means of a great free, independent Press! (*Thompson*: p. 313.)

The first edition of *Justice* appeared on 19 January 1884. Described somewhat awkwardly as 'The Organ of the Social Democracy' it cost a penny. Quarterly, half-yearly and annual subscriptions – including postage – were offered at 1s 8d, 3s 3d and 6s 6d respectively. Copies for distribution were sent out 'at the rate of 1s 3d per dozen'. These rates were largely included for form's sake as many copies were distributed gratuitously. Although the sale of the paper was pushed as hard as possible – with members of the Executive selling it in the streets – it was accepted from the start that it would be a loss-making enterprise. Morris wrote to his daughter Jenny at the time of the second issue of his fear 'that it will be a hard job keeping it afloat'. (*Letters*: II: p. 261.) This was a shrewd prediction as Carpenter's initial donation was rapidly exhausted and Morris was soon subsidizing the paper out of his own pocket.

It was a dispute over the editorial control of *Justice* that was one of the factors that led Morris to leave the Federation and found the Socialist League. Although Charles L. Fitzgerald was the original editor of the paper he was soon ousted by Hyndman. Having gained the editorship Hyndman insisted on exercising sole control of the paper and refused to be answerable in any way to the Executive. This soon became unacceptable to colleagues like Bax and Aveling who insisted that Hyndman relinquish editorial control. At first Morris attempted to mediate on the issue by suggesting to Hyndman that the Executive be given the power of veto over all the articles published. However, as time went on he became exasperated at Hyndman's refusal to compromise on the issue, and wrote to Joynes agreeing that the Executive's 'claim of control was obviously reasonable'. (*Letters*: II: p. 355.) It was this, along with Hyndman's parliamentary tendencies and political ambitions, that caused Morris and many other members of the Executive to leave the Federation and to found the Socialist League on 30 December 1884.

Morris was careful to avoid a similar dispute over the editorial control of the League's monthly paper *Commonweal* – the first edition of which was published in February 1885. In contrast to *Justice* the paper was clearly subtitled 'The Official Organ of the Socialist League'. In his 'Introductory' to the first edition Morris stated that the editor (himself) and the sub-editor (Edward Aveling) were 'acting as delegates of the Socialist League, and under its direct control: any slip in principles, therefore, any mis-statement of the aims or tactics of the League, are liable to correction from the representatives of that body.' (C: 1885: p. 1.)

The *Commonweal* – at the outset at least – was a more theoretical publication than *Justice*. In the first year of its existence Morris succeeded in attracting contributions by many of the most prominent socialists in England. Amongst those who wrote articles for the paper were Edward Aveling, E. Belfort Bax (who later became sub-editor of the paper), Thomas Binning, Frederick Engels, Frank Kitz, Paul Lefargue, Eleanor Marx Aveling, Andreas Scheu, George Bernard Shaw, Sergius Stepniak and Edward Vaillant. Many of these articles were distinctly Marxist in tone. In April 1885, for example, Morris published the first of a series of articles by Edward Aveling which was introduced as 'the first attempt to put the ideas of Marx...before the English people, in their own language'. (C: 1885: p. 21.) Morris's own analysis of Volume I of *Das Kapital* – written in collaboration with Bax – appeared as chapters 15 to 21 of 'Socialism from the Root Up' in 1887.

Generally, however, Morris left the exposition of scientific socialism to the theorists. His main intention during his early years as a journalist was to attract new recruits to the socialist movement. For this reason many of his essays were aimed at discrediting parliamentary politics. At the centre of his argument was an attack on the concept of 'constitutionalism' which he described in an early contribution to *Justice* entitled 'To Genuine Radicals' as 'nothing but a committee for arranging the affairs of the landowners and capitalists and their servants, or in plain English, their slaves, on the basis of servitude for the workers'. (*J*: 12 July 1884 : p. 5.)

He was often ingenious in his arguments against the constitutional system. For example, he interpreted the parliamentary machinations of 1884–85 over Irish Home Rule and Gladstone's Franchise Bill as indicating the break-up of the conventional parties and the imminent division of society into two opposed camps: on the one hand the extra-parliamentarists or the 'Party of the People' (basically the socialists and disillusioned radicals), and on the other the parliamentarists, a combination of the existing parties formed 'into one party of open conscious reaction'. (C: 1885: p. 54.) In an article entitled 'A New Party' he expanded on this idea and claimed that the new parliamentary grouping would 'be the strongest which our times have seen, and by whatever name it may be called, it will be the party of reaction grown conscious that firm and serious resistance must be made to the claims of labour...'. (C: 1885: p. 85.) Elsewhere he named this new political grouping 'the great Moderate Party' (C: 1885: p. 93.) and claimed it would 'be the final enemy of the Revolution'. (C: 1885: p. 101.)

Whether Morris seriously believed that a process of polarization was really taking place in Victorian politics is a matter of conjecture. Nevertheless the scenario had obvious propaganda value. By reducing politics to the level of reaction versus the people, he hoped to persuade the disillusioned middle-class reformers and the more intelligent working men to embrace socialism and be drawn towards 'the Party of the People'. In a series of articles which included 'Our Representatives', 'To Genuine Radicals' and 'Order and Anarchy', he appealed to the former by emphasizing the hypocrisy of parliamentary politics. To the working classes he was more direct, claiming that Parliament was redundant and that any support for palliative reforms was pointless. As he wrote in 'The Morrow of the Elections' 'the Radicals deceive themselves if they think they are likely to form a strong party in Parliament. For if they are progressive they must become revolutionary'. (C: 1886: p. 1.)

Despite this optimistic assessment of the drift of contemporary politics it would be wrong to suggest that Morris was oblivious to the inherent strength of bourgeois society. Although he was convinced at this time that capitalism was ultimately doomed by its own internal contradictions he appreciated that the middle-class would use every counter-revolutionary expedient at its disposal to postpone the revolution. For this reason he devoted many early essays to discrediting bourgeois ploys that could be used to temporarily retard the growth of class consciousness and frustrate the socialists' propaganda.

His main attack was directed against ameliorative reform which he regarded as the most serious counter-revolutionary ploy. The main criticism he levelled against the reformist movement – and in particular the skilled unionists – was that any improvements in living and working conditions that might be obtained were invariably gained by one group of workers at the expense of another. He was also conscious that cumulative ameliorative reform might lead to a process of embourgeoisement. As he put it, 'the whole system of palliation tends...towards the creation of a new middle class to act as a buffer between the proletariat and their direct and obvious masters'. (C: 1885: p. 61.) Such a class he feared would be 'formed out of the superior workers' and thus drive a wedge between them and their less fortunate colleagues. (C: 1886: p. 300.) This in turn would provide a barrier 'to stem the torrent of Socialism' (C: 1887: p. 1) for some not inconsiderable time if not 'guarded against sedulously'. (C: 1886: p. 300.)

Morris was also suspicious of bourgeois appeals to nationalism aimed at directing the workers' attention away from the class war by projecting them in conflict with their fellow workers on the continent. Many of his articles in *Commonweal* make reference to the possibility of the bourgeoisie deliberately precipitating Britain into a European war. This was a real threat in the 1880s as war-scares were frequently in the headlines of the middle-class press. In the short-term Morris believed a European war would be 'the most disastrous event that could cross the path of progress' delaying both the development of the international workers movement and the social revolution. (C: 1887: p. 9.) He recognized that the capitalist economy would be revitalized by the stimulus to trade and employment that would accompany military mobilization and that this would further disguise the imminent collapse of capitalism.

However, he was confident that a continental war would only be a short-term advantage to capitalism. As he put it in 'Facing the Worst of It', the war 'could not last forever; and quite apart from the more specially political results which might come of it, the time would come when some one would have to say, as Owen said after the end of the great war at the beginning of the century, "the war, our best customer, is dead".' (C: 1887: p. 60.) He predicted that a war would be followed by a commercial recession with falling prices, over-production, unemployment and rising discontent. This in turn would weaken the social framework and once more provide opportunities for the socialists.

A more long-term threat to social revolution was the potential new markets for British goods offered by imperialistic expansion in Africa, China and India. Morris acknowledged in *Commonweal* that if these countries could 'be opened up to commerce, and when opened up satisfy the expectations of the national pirates who are "on account" in this matter, the dissolution of our present system may be somewhat checked'. (C: 1887: p. 60.) As usual he attempted to cast a positive light on such a turn of events by arguing – not altogether convincingly – that any economic gains generated by the exploitation of these new markets would be accompanied by fresh demands by the workers. These 'would necessarily act as a spur to the competition of the gamblers, and make the pace faster and more furious; so that perhaps even the glorious hope of flooding Central Africa and China with trade "goods" which nobody wants, will turn out, when attained but Dead Sea apples to the capitalist'. (C: 1887: p. 60.)

In the early summer of 1886 Morris began to supplement these speculative articles with regular commentaries on contemporary politics. Although he had made some excursions in this area in *Justice* in articles like 'The Bondholders Battue', 'The Hammersmith Costermongers' and 'The Hackney Election', he had done so under Hyndman's strict editorial control. While his editorship of the *Commonweal* had freed him in this respect, the paper's initial appearance as a monthly had made topical comment impossible. As he wrote in the first report of the editors' published in August 1885: 'We are quite conscious that the *Commonweal* has not been a newspaper. As a monthly journal it could not assume this character.' (C: 1885: p. 66.) This difficulty was removed when the decision was taken to publish *Commonweal* as a weekly from 1 May 1886. Henceforth there was hardly an issue until 1890 in which Morris did not contribute his personal comments on Victorian politics under the titles of 'Notes on Passing Events' (1886) and 'Notes on News' (1887–1890).

The first issue to attract Morris's attention was the agitation for Irish Home Rule which occupied parliament extensively between 1885 and 1887. His contribution to the debate was made in a string of topical articles which included 'Ireland and Italy: A Warning', 'Independent Ireland', 'Home Rule or Humbug', '"The Law" in Ireland' and 'Law and Order in Ireland'. At first Morris encouraged the Socialist League to support Irish nationalism partly because it was a means of educating discontent at home and partly because he believed that the granting of Home Rule was necessary to 'clear the ground for sowing the seed of Revolution...in Ireland'. (C: 1886: p. 36.) As he wrote in one column of his 'Notes on Passing Events': 'It is only in the hope that through that independence she is groping her way to Freedom that to us Irish independance (*sic*) is worth thinking about.' (C: 1886: p. 73.)

As time went on, however, Morris began to lose his earlier confidence about the revolutionary potential of Ireland. He realized that the nationalists were not directing their hatred against their landlords and masters but against the English race. Without an awareness of the class war the granting of Irish independence would simply mean the founding of 'a nation fanatically attached to the rights of private property (so called), narrow-minded, retrogressive, contentious, and – unhappy'. (C: 1885: p. 87.) If Home Rule was granted under these circumstances the social revolution in Ireland could be seriously delayed: 'it seems likely that they [the Irish] will have to go through the dismal road of peasant-proprietorship before they get to anything like Socialism; and that road, in a country so isolated and so peculiar as Ireland, may be a long one.' (C: 1886: p. 43.)

The reason for this change in attitude was the experience Morris had on a lecture tour of Dublin in April 1886 at the height of the agitation. Indeed, he left England on the very day that Gladstone introduced his Home Rule Bill in parliament. It was on this trip that he came to appreciate that the religious antagonism between the Catholics and Protestants represented an additional barrier to the growth of class consciousness in Ireland. In 'Socialism in Dublin and Yorkshire', published in *Commonweal* in May 1886, Morris outlined his experiences in Ireland and concluded 'that at present the religious matter is the difficulty;...I cannot help thinking that when Home Rule is established the Catholic clergy will begin to act after their kind, and try after more and more power'. (C: 1886: p. 43.) He went on to made the astute observation that this would bring them into conflict with the Protestants whose religious feelings he described as 'dogmatic and not political'. (C: 1886: p. 43.)

Following this visit Morris became increasingly exasperated at the prominent position the Irish Question continued to occupy in parliamentary affairs. He rapidly abandoned his speculations on the likely course of events in Ireland in favour of attacks against the parliamentary parties' use of the issue to prevent consideration of events nearer home. In October 1887, for example, he wrote wearily 'that the Irish Question is a godsend to them [the parliamentary parties] simply *because* it blocks the way to the consideration of English matters'. (C: 1887: p. 321.) He was particularly annoyed at the way it enabled parliament to avoid facing the deepening economic recession. In 'What is to Happen Next?' – an article written after another abortive twist in the parliamentary tussle over Home Rule – he wrote: 'Peace with Ireland would not only have forced the consideration of their own economical condition, on the Irish themselves, but would have left nothing for us to consider in England, Scotland, and Wales, except our economical condition.' (C: 1886: p. 129.)

Morris had good reason for this complaint as the first half of the 1880s was a period of trade depression and high unemployment. Nevertheless, he was cautious in his attitude to this recession. While he saw it as another indication of the impending economic collapse of bourgeois society he did not underestimate the strength of capitalism. In 'Facing the Worst of It' he interpreted the recession as merely the first stage in a longer process of commercial decline: '...the downward tendency of commerce may and probably will be checked by recoveries of the nature of the rebounds from depression which were the rule for the last forty years before the depression of the six or seven years just passed set in, but far less complete and much shorter lived.' (C: 1887: p. 60.) Elsewhere he acknowledged that during these periods of recovery 'there may be an appearance of retrogression in our propaganda, as it will make a portion of the working class in this country 'contented' once more, who are now inclined to listen to our doctrines'. (C: 1886: p. 225.) However, he felt any recovery would be accompanied by a rise in trades union activity, which by gaining improvements in conditions would be of advantage to the socialists, for when the next depression came 'the discontent of the workmen will be much increased by their losing, or their dreading to lose, the advantages gained in the better times'. (C: 1887: p. 61.)

Morris's ambivalence about the trade depression also explains his view of the unemployment agitation orchestrated by the SDF in the East End. This campaign culminated in the famous Trafalgar Square riots of 8 February 1886 in which numerous shop-windows were smashed and the *Times* reported 'there was something little short of panic'. Morris's immediate response to the riots was an article published in *Commonweal* in March 1886 entitled 'Our Policy'. Here he made his much quoted remark that the events in Trafalgar Square looked 'like the first skirmish of the Revolution' (C: 1886: p. 17), a comment often used by critics to prove that Morris believed the revolution to be imminent. A closer reading of this article, however, reveals that it is an implicit attack on the programme of the SDF. In it Morris stated that although the latter's policy of inciting discontent amongst the unemployed had indeed created a revolutionary incident, 'that incident was practically aimless'. (C: 1886: p. 17.) It was pointless for the SDF to force the 'Gospel of Discontent' on the workers without first educating them in the aims of socialism: 'History teaches us that no revolts that are without aim are successful even for a time; even the failures (some of them glorious indeed) had a guiding aim in them, which only lacked completeness.' (C: 1886: p. 17.) As far as Morris was concerned education in organization remained essential for a successful revolution.

In fact Morris made little comment on the SDF's unemployment agitation. Instead he concentrated on discrediting the various schemes advocated by politicians to alleviate working class distress. Three policies aroused his animosity: emigration, the allotment scheme and the employment of women. The first of these was a well-established remedy for the ills of society. Between 1881 and 1890 no less than 3,259,000 people – 9.3% of the population of Great Britain and Ireland – emigrated. Morris saw emigration as an economic expedient: '...when private capitalists...egg on poor men to emigrate, their intention is only to get rid temporarily of *their* responsibility and trouble over the people thrown out of work by the system of artificial famine.' (C: 1886: p. 73.) He also suspected that the workers attracted to the idea of emigration were those with the most acutely developed class consciousness: 'If those who are most keenly stung by the evils of class domination, and at the same time have energy to resist them, leave the country which is the very forge of class domination, their desertion will surely put off the Revolution.' (C: 1885: p. 35.)

Joseph Chamberlain's allotment scheme – which aimed to provide small-holdings for the 'deserving' poor – aroused his particular wrath. From the start he described it as a 'swindle' whose aim was to prevent the growth of class-consciousness at a time of economic hardship. In *Commonweal* he urged his readers to look beneath the philanthropic rhetoric of its sponsor and understand that the measure – far from being an advantage to the workers – was socially divisive. He argued that by providing the land for the allotments the bourgeoisie were only encouraging the workers to spend their leisure growing sufficient food to raise them above the subsistence level and thus prevent them becoming a burden on the Poor Rates.

The issue of women's employment is more controversial as it raises questions about Morris's attitude to female emancipation. In 1886 an analysis of 600,000 wage-earners had revealed that the weekly wage received by women was half that paid to men. It followed, argued Morris, that 'the meaning of employing women and children to do work which men can do better...is simply the reduction of the wages paid to the adult male at the expense of the over-work and degradation of the weaker members of the household'. (C: 1886: p. 37.) He criticized the practice on the grounds that it enabled the capitalists to keep down their costs of production and reinforced the subservient position of women by forcing them to undertake work for which they were not suited.

It was this second point that led Morris to attack the 'women's rights' movement in his 'Notes on News' column in May 1887. He argued that the feminists, by projecting women as in competition with men, were merely reinforcing the dependence of women and thus hindering their emancipation. He urged the women's rights movement to accept as their motto the statement that 'As long as men are slaves, women can be no better'. (C: 1887: p. 172.) In the same article he made the following controversial statement: 'Under reasonable conditions of society every woman will be free to earn her own livelihood as every man will be, but for that very reason there will be no competition between the sexes; and women will neither get nor seek employment in work which men can do better than they can.' (C: 1887: p. 172.) Morris seems to have been oblivious to the fact that received prejudices concerning the 'correct' work for women were being used to justify their exploitation in the first place. It was reported in 1881 that the two occupations in which women outnumbered men were in domestic service and boarding-house keeping. Significantly, these are the first tasks women are seen performing in *News from Nowhere*! Despite his many penetrating insights into the nature of capitalism Morris failed to appreciate that assumptions about 'natural' and 'suitable' work for women were bourgeois myths.

Running concurrently with the Irish Question and the trade depression was the fight for free speech. After the split between the SDF and the Socialist League at the end of 1884 the two organizations developed a friendly rivalry as to who could maintain the most open-air pitches in London. One of the SDF's most popular gathering places was a long-established site on Dod Street in Limehouse which they used along with various other radical and religious groups. During the summer of 1885 their meetings at Dod Street began to attract the attention of the authorities and several cases of 'obstruction' were brought against their speakers. One of these, John Williams, refused to pay his fine and was sentenced to a month's hard labour. This was the beginning of a concerted campaign against open-air speaking by the authorities which by the time of the unemployment riots of February 1886 led to arrests being made virtually every week.

Throughout the period 1885 to 1887 the campaign for free speech was rarely absent from the pages of *Commonweal*. Morris himself contributed no less than five articles on the topic – 'Free Speech and the Police' (1885), 'Free Speech at Stratford' (1886), 'Free Speech in the Streets' (1886), 'The Abolition of Freedom in the Streets' (1886) and 'Coercion for London' (1887) – apart from numerous references to the latest developments in his regular news columns. In the light of his own commitment to open-air speaking it is easy to understand why he considered the issue to be of crucial importance to the socialist movement. Open-air meetings enabled speakers to make direct contact with the most oppressed and potentially discontented workers in a manner that was impossible through political literature, articles in *Commonweal*, or even formal lectures. Morris was very much aware of the value of personal contact and often defended this aspect of the propaganda against less enthusiastic colleagues like Bax.

The campaign for free speech also served as a means of encouraging discontent and winning popular sympathy to the socialist cause. Morris in his *Commonweal* articles emphasized that the persecution of the socialists for their advocacy of 'dangerous doctrines' was another indication of social disintegration. Directing his words at the radicals he argued that the laws under which the socialists had been prosecuted '...laid it down as a matter beyond doubt that no persons can meet in any part of the public highway, however little the traffic over the meeting-place may be, however little the inconvenience caused by the meeting may be, without committing that terrible crime, "Obstruction"'. (C: 1886: p. 161.) Elsewhere he pointed out that if the authorities were to be consistent in implementing these laws then they would be 'quite capable of accepting the challenge and getting rid of Temperance, Christianity, and Radicalism at one blow, in order to get rid of Socialism'. (C: 1886: p. 87.) The ultimate prospect – as he presented it in 'Free Speech in the Streets' – was Orwellian in its bleakness: 'They would clear the streets of coster-mongers, organs, processions, and lecturers of all kinds, and make them a sort of decent prison corridors, with people just trudging to and from their work.' (C: 1886: p. 137.)

The doubtful justice received by the socialist speakers led Morris to attack the whole legal and judicial system. On every possible occasion he harangued the police for their indiscriminate violence in breaking up open-air meetings and persecuting innocent bystanders; the magistrates for consistently accepted the word of a single police officer against any number of civilian witnesses; and the government for blatantly ignoring the spirit of the Law of Obstruction and using it instead as an instrument of repression. In his best article on the topic, 'Coercion for London', he skilfully brought all these criticisms together to argue that the government was undertaking a deliberate 'Coercion Campaign' in the capital. Addressing himself once again to the radicals – who were at the time rigorously opposing the Irish Coercion Bill – he urged them to recognize that the Irish Question and the free-speech campaign were aspects of the same tendency towards repression and should be faced with a united front. As he quite rightly pointed out, the Irish Coercion Bill once it became law would only '...enable any *two* magistrates in Ireland to sentence any one who is brought before them and whose looks they don't like to six months imprisonment. In London, any *one* magistrate has already got that power, and is on occasion not ashamed to exercise it.' (C: 1887: p. 153.)

Morris's main aim was to encourage discontent by exploding the myth of equality before the law. In this he was aided by the inconsistent actions of the authorities, a fact which he acknowledged with some satisfaction: '...no Socialist can help reflecting that these fools Matthews, Poland, Warren, and Co., are doing good propagandist work for us.' (C: 1887: p. 154.) His own attack concentrated on the class-based nature of British justice. Not only were 'respectable' individuals less likely to be arrested for obstruction than members of the lower classes, there was a vast discrepancy in their punishment when convicted: a well-to-do man had to pay a fine while a workman was sent to prison. Although an appeal system existed it required a guarantor to supply the costs – a sum forfeited if the appeal was unsuccessful. Morris referred sarcastically in one of his 'Notes on News' columns to '...the *Equal Laws* under which we *free* people live, which condemn these innocent men to a cruel punishment simply because they have no friends rich enough to be responsible for paying the expenses of the appeal if it chances to fail'. (C: 1887: p. 236.)

One other contemporary issue occupied Morris and the Socialist League during the summer of 1887: the campaign against Queen Victoria's Golden Jubilee. As E. P. Thompson has noted, this was the 'one campaign of the London Leaguers...to arouse their ready enthusiasm...and all elements of the League were able to unite in some effective anti-imperialist propaganda'. (*Thompson*: p. 497.)

Commonweal carried many reports on demonstrations of anti-monarchist feeling. In London a handbill – apparently written by Frank Kitz – was distributed to the crowds along the Queen's route urging the workers to dissociate themselves from 'the deification of a mean old woman who has had as much to do with the inventions of art as the man in the moon'. (*Socialists and the Jubilee*: 1887.) Although the bourgeois press chose not to acknowledge this agitation, it certainly reached the attention of the Queen for she noted in her journal '...the booing and hooting, of perhaps only two or three, now and again, all along the route, evidently sent there on purpose, and frequently the same people, probably Socialists and the worst Irish'.

Morris excluded from *Commonweal* any reference to the pageantry surrounding the Jubilee in order to emphasize 'the contempt with which all Socialists must necessarily look on the idiotic court ceremony'. (C: 1887: p. 204.) Nevertheless, his personal dislike of Queen Victoria – whom he dubbed 'the Empress Brown' – caused him to break his silence in an article published on 25 June 1887 entitled 'An Old Superstition – A New Disgrace'. Although he began by stating that he had no sympathy with the aspirations of middle-class republicanism, his main purpose was to expose the Victorian monarchy as a meaningless anachronism. He did this by contrasting it with the idea of kingship prevalent in feudal times. The feudal king, he argued, was integral to the social organization of medieval society. He had recognized duties such as the 'administration of affairs, the balancing of the various claims of the groups of the feudal hierarchy, [and] the assertion of the due rights of the great manor'. (C: 1887: p. 204.) However much these duties were neglected his existence meant something to the people. The rise of capitalistic society and parliamentary government had made the monarch redundant as a functioning entity. Instead the Queen had become the property of the bourgeoisie who had endowed her with the symbols of imperialistic unity and national pride and paraded her before the people as a colourful tonic for their economic ills. What does the monarch now represent, concluded Morris, but '...the Privilege of Capital, set on a background of the due performance of the conventional domestic duties; in short, the representation of the anti-social spirit in its fullness'. (C: 1887: p. 204.)

The summer of 1887 marked the beginning of a more retrogressive and defensive phase in Morris's work for *Commonweal*. This was the result of the gradual disintegration of the Socialist League and the increasing indications of the stability of the capitalist system. Faction fighting had been a feature of the Socialist League from the start. However, these ever-present rumblings of discontent came to the surface at the Third Annual Conference of the League held on 29 May 1887. A pro-parliamentary faction led by Bax, Donald and Mahon came out in open opposition to the anti-parliamentary stance adopted in the Constitution of the League. Bax's Croydon branch tabled a motion to amend the Constitution by adding the following sentence: 'Its objects shall be sought to be obtained by every available means, Parliamentary or otherwise.' (*Report of the Third Annual Conference of the Socialist League*: p. 12.) Morris countered this on behalf of the Hammersmith Branch by proposing that 'the question of agitating for and by Parliamentary means be not considered at this Conference and be deferred for one year'. (*Hammersmith Minutes*: 27 March 1887.) In the event both motions were withdrawn and the Conference considered a third resolution put forward by Mahon: that the League should utilize Parliament, local government and municipal elections as a means of 'spreading the principles of Socialism and organizing the people into a Socialist Labour Party'. (*Thompson*: p. 450.) Morris then moved an uncompromising anti-parliamentary amendment which was passed by the relatively narrow margin of seventeen votes to eleven.

This proved to be a hollow victory. Almost certainly the vote went in favour of the anti-parliamentarians not on the ground of principle, but, as Engels wrote to Sorge, because of 'Morris's threat to leave the League if any kind of parliamentary struggle be recognized in principle'. (*Thompson*: p. 453.) He added: 'as Morris covers the weekly deficit of the *Commonweal*, that outweighs all else by far.' (*Thompson*: p.453.) Following their defeat the parliamentary group refused to stand for election to the Council of the League. Instead, they organized a formal faction and used the Labour Emancipation League (which was affiliated to the Socialist League) as a base for their activities. Mahon soon tired of this approach and left the League at the end of the year along with his large band of supporters in the North. Bax and the Bloomsbury group (which included Binning and the Avelings) followed after a second defeat on the same issue at the Fourth Annual Conference in 1888. Their departure severely weakened the League and left Morris at the mercy of the growing group of anarchists on the League's Council.

Two important events in the autumn of 1887 were to have a bearing on the subsequent disintegration of the Socialist League: Bloody Sunday and the execution of the Chicago Anarchists. Bloody Sunday had its origins in a renewal of the unemployment agitation as a recession in the spring and summer of 1887 led to many idle men sleeping rough on the streets of the metropolis. Once again spontaneous marches of the unemployed became a familiar feature in the East End. Some of the leaders of the men began to organize meetings in Trafalgar Square under the symbol of the Black Flag. At first the police adopted a low profile at these meetings, but after one of the Black Flag processions had made its way through London to protest to the Lord Mayor on 14 October 1887, they suddenly moved in and dispersed the marchers with considerable brutality.

This action prompted Hyndman and the Social Democratic Federation to once again take up the cause of the unemployed. Meetings – now under the Red Flag – were held almost daily throughout late October and early November with hundreds of homeless men braving the cold and sleeping rough in Trafalgar Square in order to attend the next day's meeting. The presence of so many discontented workmen in the heart of the City led the authorities to clear the Square on 4 November. Four days later Sir Charles Warren, chief commissioner of the Metropolitan Police, banned all further meetings there on the dubious grounds that it was Crown property.

Morris still maintained an ambivalent attitude to this unemployment agitation. While he fully appreciated the workers' suffering – and indeed took part in several unemployment demonstrations – he remained convinced that it was futile to ameliorate the condition of the working classes within the existing framework of capitalist society. This latter view predominated in the *Manifesto* – signed by H. A. Barker but according to E. P. Thompson 'certainly written by Morris' (*Thompson*: p. 485–6) – which the Council of the League issued on 29 October 1887 in the midst of the agitation. While expressing sympathy with the predicament of the unemployed, the Council of the League distanced themselves from the SDF's campaign. Instead they made it clear that the suffering of the workers was a consequence of the capitalist system and that there could be 'no salvation for the unemployed but in the general combination of the workers for the freedom of labour – for the *Revolution*'. (*Manifesto*: 29 October 1887.)

As it turned out it was not the unemployment issue which finally precipitated the events of Bloody Sunday but an unlikely combination of Irish protest against coercion and British opposition to government repression in London. Before Sir Charles Warren's provocative ban on meetings in Trafalgar Square, the Metropolitan Radical Association had announced its intention of holding a demonstration there on Sunday 13 November 'to demand the release of Mr William O'Brien, MP, and other Irish patriots'. (*Times*: 14 November 1887: p. 6.) A circular was distributed to the various working-men's clubs in support of this meeting. It stated: 'Our brethren in Ireland are looking anxiously for help from the democracy of London, and it is in our power to assist them in their great national movement by large public meetings.' (*Times*: 14 November 1887: p. 6.) Just what response this appeal would have had without Sir

Charles Warren's ban is impossible to say. In the event the Metropolitan Radical Association soon received offers of support from both the SDF and the SL, thus realizing for the first time the triple alliance of socialists, radicals and Irish which Morris had done so much to encourage in the columns of *Commonweal.*

Morris's experiences on Bloody Sunday were representative of the treatment the marchers received. Along with the Hammersmith Branch of the Socialist League, he formed part of the contingent which assembled on Clerkenwell Green shortly before 2 o'clock that afternoon. Here the marchers, which a surprisingly sympathetic *Times* correspondent described as having 'the appearance of being respectable artisans' (*Times*: 14 November 1887: p. 6.), were addressed from a large cart stationed in the corner of the Green first by Morris and then by Annie Besant. Morris's speech reflected the general confusion over the purpose of the protest. After briefly expressing sympathy with the plight of O'Brien, he concentrated on the issue of free speech arguing that whenever the authorities attempted to deny the people this right '...it was their bounden duty to resist the attempt by every means in their power'. (C: 1887: p. 369.) Shortly before 3 o'clock the crowd was swelled to what a reporter on the *Daily News* estimated to be around 6,000 – a figure later described by Morris as 'an exaggeration' (C: 1887: p. 369) – with the arrival of the East Finsbury Radical Club and the Clerkenwell Branch of the SDF

The procession was formed shortly after 3 o'clock and set off briskly up Theobald Road, along Hart Street, and into Bloomsbury Street. However, when it reached the Bloomsbury end of St Martin's Lane the police – both mounted and on foot – charged in amongst the marchers striking out indiscriminately in all directions. Many were injured during this unprovoked onslaught and the marchers' attempts to reform the procession were ridden down by mounted police who made frequent use of their batons.

Morris was devastated by the suddenness of this attack. As he later wrote to Andreas Scheu, 'I shall never forget how quickly these unarmed crowds were dispersed into clouds of dust'. (*Thompson*: p. 490.) Somehow he managed to escape injury himself and struggled to Trafalgar Square where he was just in time to witness the calling out of the soldiers, the reading of the Riot Act by 'a sort of country-gentleman looking imbecile' (C: 1887: p. 369), and the arrival of a regiment of Guardsmen with fixed bayonets who proceeded to clear the Square. Later some 200 people were treated in hospital for the injuries they received in the assault. Three lost their lives.

The key to understanding Morris's subsequent reaction to the events of Bloody Sunday lies in his purist view of the revolutionary process. He believed that the economic and historical predicament of the proletariat was generating class-consciousness. It was the role of the socialists to aid this process by providing the workers with the organizational skills necessary to seize the means of production. However, he realized that in doing this there was a danger that the socialists might become the victim of their own propaganda. If they failed to distinguish between the mobilization of the proletariat for *political* rather than *revolutionary* ends it was possible that they might lose confidence in the working classes and substitute amelioration for education.

Morris refused to be affected in this manner by the events of Bloody Sunday. His immediate reaction was to write an article entitled 'London in a State of Siege' which appeared in *Commonweal* the following Saturday. He now knew that his optimistic assessment of the success of the League's socialist propaganda had been sadly misplaced. The men he marched with had displayed little evidence of class-consciousness or a will for revolutionary change. They had in fact lacked organization: 'I could see that numbers were of no avail unless led by a band of men acting in concert and each knowing his own part.' (C: 1887: p. 369.) On the other hand the bourgeoisie had displayed an impressive determination to defend their class interests. They had recognized the potential threat posed by the marchers and suppressed them with ruthless efficiency.

It was this conclusion which led Morris to lose his earlier confidence in the imminence of the revolution. A mere week after the publication of 'London in a State of Siege' he wrote in *Commonweal* that '...the struggle will be a long one, and must be carried on by us in a manner which will mean steadily and pertinaciously harassing the *apparently* all-powerful executive on all sides'. (C: 1887: p. 377.) A few months later he gave his readers a more detailed idea of the tough road that lay before them: '...passive resistance first, with the usual incidents of jail and fine and ruin, until our educational agitation has had its effect; then increase of reaction, increase of resistance...till at last the reactionary brute force of the executive finds itself helpless even in the hour of its triumph.' (C: 1888: p. 25.) Bloody Sunday did not cause Morris to lose faith in the revolution, as a number of early biographers have suggested, but to see his education programme in a considerably longer term perspective than he had done before.

Where Morris did miscalculate was over the political consequences of Bloody Sunday. At first he seems to have believed that the event would lead the radicals to socialism. By early 1888, however, it became clear that the radicals had instead turned towards parliament in an attempt, as Morris contemptuously described it, to gain 'free speech from the reactionists at the ballot box'. (C: 1888: p. 68.) In 'A Triple Alliance' – an article advocating the continuation of the spirit of co-operation between the radicals, Irish Nationalists and socialists – he attacked the parliamentary tendencies of the radicals directly, arguing that the pursuit of such a policy would simply lead to their being exploited by the existing parties for reactionary purposes.

It was not only the radicals who were attracted to parliament. Socialists like Bax and Shaw saw Bloody Sunday as a defeat, and their belief in the failure of direct social agitation greatly encouraged the movement towards gradualism which had already been much in evidence at the Third Annual Conference of the League. As Shaw wrote: 'Insurrectionism, after a two years' innings, vanished from the field.... In the middle of the revengeful growling over the defeat at the Square...the way was clear at last for Fabianism.' (*Fabian Tract*: No. 41.)

The other event which contributed to the disintegration of the League was the trial and execution of the Chicago Anarchists. On 3 May 1886, during a strike in Chicago, a fight between strikers and scabs had broken out outside the McCormick Harvester Works. The police were called, and as a group of strikers were running away from the scene they were fired on, many being wounded and four being killed. The American anarchists responded by issuing a circular calling on the workers to avenge this atrocity. The following evening a meeting was called in Haymarket Square in Chicago to protest at the action of the police. The meeting attracted three thousand people, but they dwindled away to a few hundred as a storm threatened to break over the city. At this point a detachment of 180 police advanced to the speakers' platform and ordered the crowd to disperse. A bomb was then thrown which exploded in the midst of the police, wounding sixty-six officers, of whom seven later died. The police responded by firing into the crowd, killing several people, and wounding over two hundred.

As the authorities were unable to identify the bomb-thrower they instead arrested eight prominent Chicago anarchist leaders. Under Illinois law anyone inciting a murder was deemed as guilty of the crime as if they had committed it personally. The evidence against the eight anarchists was consequently their ideas and literature. In fact only one of the accused men had been at the Haymarket meeting and he had been speaking on the platform at the time the bomb was thrown. Nevertheless they were all found guilty and sentenced to death. Their appeals to the Supreme Court were also refused, a decision which the *Times* applauded, praising the fact that the judges and juries in America 'draw no distinction between incendiaries of the platform and the Press, and the men who do their dirty work'. (*Times*: 12 November 1887.) Four of the convicted men – Albert Parsons, August Spies, Adolph Fischer and George Engle – were hanged in October 1887. Another, Louis Lingg, blew himself up in his cell by exploding a dynamite tube in his mouth. The three other men remained in prison where they served out long sentences.

Morris followed these events closely in *Commonweal* and even published biographies of the martyrs during the weeks after their death. His own comments on the affair were confined to interpreting the judicial murder of the anarchists as a further indication of the international tendency of capitalism to degenerate into reaction. In 'Free Speech in America', a comprehensive article published in *Commonweal* shortly before the anarchists' execution, he stated: 'They are persecuted for holding and expressing the opinions which we hold and express whether we call ourselves Anarchists or Socialists, and for applying those opinions to the events of the passing day and the oppression of the American workmen going on under their eyes.' (C: 1887: p. 324.) He added, 'We appeal, above all, to our Radical and Democratic friends...to remember that whether they may think our Socialist theories right or wrong, we claim at least equal liberty for all'. (C: 1887: p. 324.) Later he extended this argument a stage further, arguing that the martyrs had not died in vain, for by their unjust murder the American authorities had hastened the demise of their own corrupt society: 'You have sown the wind, you must reap the whirlwind.' (C: 1887: p. 361.)

The case of the Chicago Anarchists had serious consequences for the British socialist movement. The heroic manner in which the victims conducted their defence and faced the prospect of death had a strong psychological effect on many members of the Socialist League. Some influential figures such as Joseph Lane, Frank Kitz, Sam Mainwaring and Charles Mowbray, began to listen with increasing respect to the anarchists' case and even to look with sympathy on acts of terrorism and political assassination on the continent. By early 1888 these individuals, along with others with even more pronounced anarchist views like Tochatti and Charles, had become a recognizable group in the leadership of the Socialist League. Their position was greatly strengthened by the anti-parliamentary stance Morris adopted at the Fourth Annual Conference in May. This led to the suspension of the Bloomsbury Branch and a further shift towards the anarchists. Morris was far from happy at the outcome but accepted it which his usual philosophical resolve: 'We have got rid of the parliamentarians, and now our anarchists friends will want to drive the team. However, we have the Council and the *Commonweal* safe with us for at least a twelve-month, and that is something to be thankful for.' (*Thompson*: p. 509.)

The spread of factionalism amongst the socialists caused Morris to reassess the role of the Socialist League and of *Commonweal*. He had always believed that the most serious danger facing the movement was that its educational programme might be weakened by ideological disputes. The events of late 1887 and early 1888 confirmed his worst fears and led to a noticeable change in perspective. He abandoned all hope that the League could assume the leadership of the socialist movement. Instead he increasingly saw it as the educative and propaganda centre of purist revolutionary theory: existing within – but separate from – the wider framework of British socialism. After 1888 his attempts to convert the free-thinking members of the radical wing of parliamentary politics were gradually abandoned in favour of reconverting the various socialist factions to this purist view of the revolutionary process.

The first group Morris confronted were the parliamentary socialists. He opened the debate in *Commonweal* shortly before the League's Fourth Annual Conference by publishing a thinly disguised attack on the tactics of the parliamentarists entitled 'On Some "Practical" Socialists'.

Here he argued once again that the 'Practical' Socialists – a group he defined as those who were 'anxious that some step towards Socialism should be taken at once' (C: 1888: p. 53) – were pursuing a hopeless course in the light of the teachings of scientific socialism: 'it is utopian to put forward a scheme of gradual logical reconstruction of society which is liable to be overturned at the first historical hitch it comes to.' (C: 1888: p. 53.)

This article provoked an angry response from Binning who accused Morris of advocating 'Micawber' Socialism, that is, the politics of inaction. Instead he argued that 'Practical' Socialism should be aimed at the immediate relief of the poverty of the lower classes and at improving their social and political condition. Morris was genuinely surprised at the ferocity of this reply, and appended a short conciliatory paragraph to Binning's article: 'I should say my remarks were meant as words of warning to those, on the one hand, who are blind to the ideal which we have before us, and to those, on the other hand, who seeing and knowing that ideal, are afraid to put it before persons lest they should startle them too much.' (C: 1888: p. 61.)

Morris no longer felt any need to be constrained in his opposition to electioneering after the parliamentarists were defeated at the Fourth Annual Conference of the League. He emphasized the damage gradualism was doing to the educational propaganda. In particular he argued that the parliamentary socialists were being premature in their desire for legislative change: 'they have entered on this electioneering struggle with a people at their back not yet educated into a knowledge of the reasons for the wrongs which they suffer, or the remedies for them.' (C: 1888: p. 66.) He added that by committing themselves to parliament they were turning their backs on their real vocation: 'if propaganda by electioneering is practised by any body of Socialists they will have no time for any other means of propaganda.' (C: 1888: p. 66.) In one column of his 'Notes on News' published at the end of 1888 he asked: 'Is it worth the wear and tear for Socialists, who have so much work before them in merely putting before people the bare elements of their creed, to spend their energies, first in electioneering and next in the committee-room grind, in doing work which would be done quite as well, if external pressure were put upon them, by the Radicals and Secularists, who otherwise hinder the work of propaganda?' (C: 1888: p. 385.)

Morris was on less solid ground in his debate with the anarchists. In April 1889 James Blackwell initiated a discussion in *Commonweal* on 'Communist-Anarchy' referring sympathetically to a number of resolutions passed by the recent Anarchist Congress at Valencia. He argued that genuine anarchists were dedicated to 'the abolition of the principle of private property and of the exploitation of man by man' (*C*: 1889: p. 117), but believed that this could not be achieved while the individual was subject to any form of social control: 'Whilst the principle of authority exists, there will be no guarantee for the liberty of all members of society. The principle of authority...always degenerates into tyranny.' (*C:* 1889: p. 117.) Morris replied to Blackwell the following month, taking issue with the notion that a future society could exist without any form of social organization: '...if freedom from authority means the assertion of the advisability or possibility of an individual man doing what he pleases always and under all circumstances, this is an absolute negation of society, and makes Communism as the highest expression of society impossible.' (C: 1889: p. 157.)

It was an indication of Morris's growing isolation in the Socialist League that this reply aroused a storm of protest. In June 1889 he was obliged to publish no less than three letters criticizing his position. These were written by J. Armsden, H. Davis and an anonymous correspondent who signed himself 'An Anarchist'. Of these H. Davis's 'Anarchy and Communism: An Answer to William Morris' was the most telling. Defining himself as an 'Anarchist-Communist...because I will admit of no compulsion of man over man – because I would be free; and freedom cannot obtain where there *is* compulsion arising from authority' (C: 1889: p. 197), Davis went on to attack Morris for defending the need for authority. He claimed that in doing so he was accepting the contemporary bourgeois notion of the 'alleged imperfection of man'. (C: 1889: p. 197.) The anarchists, on the other hand, believed that men were by nature sociable and co-operative and that if the state could be destroyed they would naturally form voluntary groups working in complete harmony without recourse to authority of any kind.

Despite the moderation of Davis's argument – in which, for example, he made no mention of the violence that some anarchists advocated to achieve this aim – Morris remained totally convinced that 'man without society is not only impossible, but inconceivable'. (C: 1889: p. 261.) In a reply to Davis written after his return from the Paris Congress, he refused to change his position and argued that 'however much the unit of association may be divided, people will have to associate in administration, and sometimes there will be differences of opinion as to what should be done'. (C: 1889: p. 261.) Although the argument disappeared from the pages of *Commonweal* as Morris lost control of the paper it was undoubtedly one of the factors that led him to write *News from Nowhere*. It may also have influenced the later romances such as *The Water of the Wondrous Isles* and *The Wood Beyond the World* where he portrayed worlds where the absence of social control had made possible some of the more fanciful anarchist notions like the return to nature and free love.

Another reason why Morris wrote *News from Nowhere* derived from his increasing antagonism to schemes of centralized state socialism. Shortly after the opening of his debate with the anarchists he read Edward Bellamy's *Looking Backward*, a utopian fiction which was at the time attracting considerable attention in both England and America. Bellamy presented the transition to socialism as a slow but inevitable economic progression. Looking back from the year 2,000 he envisaged a situation in which all

America's capital assets had become concentrated into the hands of a small number of gigantic trusts who effectively controlled the entire economic life of the nation. At the appropriate time – when 'public opinion had become fully ripe' – these great trusts had handed over the means of production (without violence) to a 'single syndicate representing the people'. Morris was particularly annoyed at the way in which Bellamy portrayed the 'red-flag Socialists' as having hindered this development by frightening people with their revolutionary propaganda. In June 1889 Morris reviewed the book in *Commonweal*, concentrating on Bellamy's failure to appreciate the historical basis of the revolutionary process, and concluding by pointing out the inherent danger of presenting '...incomplete systems impossible to be carried out but plausible on the surface...to people ripe for change, but not knowing clearly what their aim is'. (*C*: 1889: p. 195.)

Nevertheless Bellamy's book had a significant influence on the growing Fabian movement. Although the Fabian Society had been formed in 1884 it was not until 1888–89 that it began to evolve a theoretical framework of its own. In 1889 a selection of articles by the most prominent advocates was published as *Fabian Essays*. Although initially printed in a limited run of 150 and not advertised in the press, this went through two editions in a matter of months and by the autumn of 1891 had sold over 27,000 copies. The authors advocated a gradualistic approach to social reform, arguing that through the permeation of existing parties and institutions sufficient socialistic measures could be passed to enable the transformation of society from within the executive. On 25 January 1890 Morris published a lengthy review of the book in *Commonweal*. He criticized the Fabians for both their failure to appreciate the economic basis of capitalistic exploitation and their refusal to accept the irreconcilable interests of the bourgeoisie and the working classes. He concluded by stating that even in the unlikely event that municipal socialism were ever to succeed '...though it should *logically* (perhaps) lead to the destruction of privilege and poverty, yet *historically* it may do nothing of the kind; and that at any rate is *not* Socialism, as it would still admit of the existence of competing classes'. (C: 1890: p. 28.)

The fragmentation of the socialist movement was not the only factor which contributed to the growing impotence of Morris's propaganda in *Commonweal.* There were also further indications of the inherent strength of capitalism. When trade began to recover slowly at the beginning of 1888 it had an immediate effect on both the unemployment agitation and the open-air meetings of the Socialist League. In *Commonweal* Morris found himself confined to meaningless rebuttals of the indications of economic recovery and even less useful speculations about the future prospects of trade.

More worrying still was that many of his earlier fears that imperialistic expansion might prove a long term barrier to the revolution seemed about to come true. During the first five months of 1888 the British obtained protectorates over Matabele, Sarawak, North Borneo and Brunei. At the same time the scramble for Africa was in full swing amongst the European powers with Britain in the South, Germany in the Cameroons, Portugal on the East Coast, and Britain, France and Italy fighting it out in the North. On 28 July 1888 Bax published an article on the partition of Africa in *Commonweal* in which he came to some very pessimistic conclusions about this development. After summarizing the contemporary position he made it clear what he considered this imperialistic expansion meant: '...*untold* mineral, vegetable, and animal wealth placed at the disposal of the modern commercial system; a new world of markets; *limitless* cheap labour; practically *boundless* territories for emigration....' His conclusion was utterly discouraging, for he speculated that the success of this exploitation was likely to lead to the 'dread possibility' of capitalism 'taking a new lease of life' with the result 'that the present stage would be prolonged in a slightly changed form even for another century'.

Bax's article worried Morris. In his 'Notes on News' column – published in the same edition of *Commonweal* – he took the unprecedented step of singling it out for special comment. Here he suggested that Bax may have overstated the advantages to be gained from imperialistic expansion. He even posed the question: 'whether the accelerated pace which the impulse of huge new markets would certainly give to competitive commerce would not go far to neutralize the advantages to capitalism of "opening up" Africa?' (C: 1888: p. 233.) However, Morris was unable to offer any evidence to support this view or to seriously challenge Bax's negative conclusions. Consequently as the months passed his criticisms of the capitalist exploitation of natives, the false jingoism generated by the various imperialistic campaigns, and his ridicule of colonial 'heroes' such as Stanley and Gordon became increasingly aimless and disheartened.

The revival in trade also meant that there were realistic chances of obtaining limited reform. People as diverse as Joseph Chamberlain, Randolph Churchill, Jesse Collings, Cardinal Manning and A. J. Mundella – often supported by the parliamentary socialists – were soon advocating specific measures for the improvement of working class conditions. The extension of the franchise through the passing of the Local Government Act of 1888 also made it possible for working class representatives to be elected to the new County Councils. Indeed the parliamentary socialists gained a notable victory when John Burns was elected to the newly created London County Council. Morris sensed a relaxation of the tension that had characterized the years 1885–87, and wrote despairingly that 'it is fashionable for even West-End dinner-parties to affect an interest' in socialism. (C: 1889: p. 194.) However, the success of the gradualists only increased his determination to stick to his own purist views, and he continued to dismiss reforms because they represented '*The improvement of the condition of the poor, at their own expense, for the peace and happiness of their masters*' [Morris's italics]. (C: 1889: p. 91.) He described the extension of the franchise as 'a farce' representing nothing more than 'the count[ing] of noses of unhappy people driven and cheated into voting for this or that form of the continuance of their own unhappiness'. (C: 1888: p. 196.)

Morris's refusal to abandon his purism was responsible for the Socialist League's failure to exploit the strikes which accompanied the emergence of 'New Unionism'. This was the one development in the late 1880s which offered the socialists the opportunity of encouraging discontent. From the collapse of the GNCTU until this time British trades unionism had been almost exclusively confined to skilled workers under the control of a far from revolutionary leadership. For this reason the unions were regarded with suspicion by many socialists, and early theoretical works such as Joynes's *Socialist Catechism* (1885) ignored them as potential revolutionary combinations. Morris's early view was characteristic of the general feeling. He saw the unions as appendages of the capitalist system: 'English unions are not prepared to accept the responsibilities of freedom...they are still contented with their position as a check on the masters – a check whose tendency is to ensure the existence of the employing class.' (C: 1886: p. 187.) He believed that by accepting this role they were actively divisive as their policies were sectionalist, aimed at raising one part of the working class at the expense of the other, and thus colluding with the middle class in encouraging the tendency towards embourgeoisement.

After 1888, however, there was an increase in unionism amongst the unskilled workers encouraged by the revival in trade. In the summer of 1888 the 672 women match-workers at Bryant and May successfully struck for better conditions backed by socialists like Annie Besant and Herbert Burrows. Morris followed this dispute closely, but while sympathizing with the women's plight he still viewed their success with cynicism: 'When one sees how small the gains to the girls are, how small their demands were, one is struck aghast at the miserable cheese-parings by which great fortunes are made....' (C: 1888: p. 233.)

A change in his attitude was to occur during August and September 1889 when the London dockers went on strike. At the outbreak Morris still held that strikes were hopeless because the workers were 'only acting in a scattered and skirmishing way, and can be crushed in detail'. (C: 1889: p. 265.) However, as the dispute progressed he was greatly impressed by the strikers' resolve and began to see their action not merely as another trade dispute but as a direct confrontation with the capitalists. In early September 1889 he devoted a complete article – 'The Lesson of the Hour' – to this idea: 'This is a strike of the poor against the rich...it gives us a dawning hope that they will be prepared to meet us half-way when the crisis comes.' (C: 1889: p. 281.)

This change in attitude came far too late to help the prospects of the League. Gradualists such as John Burns and Tom Mann had already begun to encourage the infiltration of the unions with the object of manipulating their leaders for political purposes. The League, still clinging half-heartedly to Morris's distrust of palliatives, was increasingly isolated. Although attempts were made to collect funds for the dockers and to distribute revolutionary literature at the dock gates such activities were largely ineffectual. The League's ambivalent attitude was summed up in October 1889 when the Council issued a directive – described by E. P. Thompson as 'the most pitiful in all its years of existence' (*Thompson*: p. 530) – stating that '...The Executive Council...desires to express its opinion that members of the League do not in any way compromise their principles by taking part in strikes, but asks them not to let the revolutionary propaganda suffer thereby'. (*Thompson*: p. 531.)

In reality this directive was hardly relevant as the League had effectively ceased to exist as a unified body. This was reflected in the declining fortunes of *Commonweal*. The success of the anarchists in the leadership battle had meant that the sound theoretical essays submitted by Binning, Mahon and others had been replaced by poorly written inflammatory articles with vague incitements to violence. At the same time the rising tide of gradualism and New Unionism had spawned a series of rival journals with a more direct appeal to the workers. These included the *Labour Elector*, Keir Hardie's *Miner*, the *Cotton Factory Times*, and (after 1889) the *Yorkshire Factory Times*. As early as 1888 the decline in sales and the difficulty of attracting sufficient copy had forced Morris to consider turning the *Commonweal* back into a monthly. More serious problems were encountered the following year when subsidizing the paper to the extent of some £500 a year threatened to become an intolerable burden. At Whitsun 1889 this forced him to withdraw his £1 a week salary guarantee to the staff and printers of the paper.

Despite these setbacks he was determined to keep the paper going as long as possible. Although he succeeded in retaining the editorship at the Fifth Annual Conference, the victory of the anarchists the following year enabled them to force both his, and his assistant editor Sparling's, resignation. They were replaced by Nicoll and Kitz who immediately turned *Commonweal* into an unequivocally anarchist organ. Despite this devastating blow, Morris still remained proprietor of the paper and continued to finance it and contribute to it in a limited way until November 1890. He almost certainly did this in order to ensure that *News from Nowhere* was published in its entirety.

During the last eighteen months of his association with *Commonweal* Morris largely abandoned any attempt to influence opinion. Over the period 1889 to 1890 his 'Notes on News' feature declined from a weekly page of contemporary political comment to an occasional paragraph on marginal side-issues such as the resignation of Bismarck and the death of the aged radical John Bright. His articles also slowed to a trickle. In 1890 his only significant contributions of this sort were short pieces entitled 'The Great Coal Strike', 'Labour Day', 'The "Eight

Hours" and the Demonstration', 'Workhouse Socialism' and 'Where Are We Now?' Instead the paper was filled by reprinting some of his lectures. 'Monopoly', 'The Development of Modern Society' and 'The Society of the Future' all appeared between March 1889 and his final split with the paper in the autumn of 1890.

Even in these 'posthumous' contributions to the paper he still refused to compromise his purist principles. In 'Where Are We Now?', a farewell article published in *Commonweal* on 15 November 1890, after assessing the recent progress of the socialist movement and expressing his disappointment at the tendencies towards anarchy and parliamentarism, he concluded by reiterating his belief in the fundamental aim of revolutionary socialism: 'I say, make Socialists. We Socialists can do nothing else that is useful, and preaching and teaching is not out of date for that purpose; but rather for those who, like myself do not believe in State Socialism, it is the only rational means of attaining to the New Order of Things.' (C: 1890: p. 362.) He was never to lose his conviction that it was essential to encourage a tradition of revolutionary socialist thought unsullied by theoretical disputes over methods.

Some idea of Morris's immense contribution to 'the Cause' can be gained from the impact his decision to withdraw from the active propaganda had on the Socialist League. Without his mediative influence the Council of the League fell completely under the control of the anarchists. One unnamed comrade, quoted by Mackail, described the resultant League as 'a romping ground of more than dubious characters...who, being suspected of relations with the police, drove the better elements away in disgust...'. (*Mackail*: II: p. 230.) Many of these disaffected ex-members later joined the Independent Labour Party (formed in 1893), while others concentrated on securing working class representation on the new County Councils and other local administrative bodies. With the anarchists in control of the Council the Socialist League rapidly disintegrated as a national body. The anarchists distrust of formal organization soon led to the provincial branches becoming isolated from London. This was a process that was accelerated after February 1891 when the London section reconstituted itself as the London Socialist League. E. P. Thompson claimed that this meant 'that the League, as a national organization, did not survive after February, 1891'. (*Thompson*: p. 587.)

Although Morris continued to fund *Commonweal* until the end of 1890, his departure had an immediate effect on the paper's fortunes. The first edition to appear after the Hammersmith Branch had severed its links with the League on 21 November 1890 carried a prominent notice announcing that henceforth the journal would appear as a monthly 'until we can tide over present difficulties'. (*C*: 1890: p. 372.) It went on to make an impassioned appeal for funds: 'We fear that the several appeals which have been made on behalf of 'Commonweal' have fallen flat because of their frequency. We are now hampered by want of premises, and still worse, want of money.... This is a final and urgent appeal. Surely the Revolutionary Socialists are not going to allow the common enemy to chuckle over the disappearance of a paper from the small list of those which appear in England to fight oppression and monopoly!' (*C*: 1890: p. 372.)

The reference to the loss of premises was pertinent. On returning to the status of a monthly the paper was transferred first to small premises in Great Queen Street and finally to a temporary address in Lamb's Conduit Street. The latter was in fact a tiny grocery store that was run by some of the remaining League members under the impressive – but entirely inappropriate – title of the Socialist Co-operative Federation. In December 1890 the *Commonweal* ceased to appear with the sub-title 'The Official Journal of the Socialist League' and instead described itself as 'A Journal of Revolutionary Socialism'. The following May it was printed on red paper as 'A Revolutionary Journal of Anarchist Communism'.

Without Morris's generous subsidies the paper was financed by voluntary subscriptions. With the membership falling away rapidly the paper was full of desperate appeals to its readers to renew their lapsed subscriptions. These appeals appeared incongruous in a paper which was at the same time advocating theft, arson, assassination and terrorism. Matters came to a head in February 1892 when six anarchists in Walsall were arrested and tried for manufacturing a high-explosive bomb. Although the whole affair was set up by Auguste Coulson – who styled himself a militant anarchist but was in fact a police informer – four of the anarchists were given prison sentences ranging from five to ten years.

Nicoll, the editor of *Commonweal*, rashly defended his comrades in an article entitled 'Are These Men Fit to Live?' which appeared in the paper on 9 April 1892. Although less inflammatory than some of the material published at the time, there was no doubt that Nicoll was urging the assassination of the judge who had passed the sentence on the men. This article came to the attention of the authorities, who raided the *Commonweal* office nine days later and seized the stock and printing press. It is possible that the police were acting on a tip-off as the next edition of the paper intended to expose Auguste Coulon's role in the conspiracy. Nicoll, along with Charles Mowbray the registered proprietor of the paper, was arrested and charged at Bow Street with incitement to murder. Mowbray's wife had died shortly before the arrest and Morris came before the Court personally to stand bail for £500 in order that Mowbray could attend her funeral on 23rd April. At his trial Mowbray convinced the court that he had disapproved of the article in question and had not been involved with *Commonweal* for some months. He was acquitted. Nicoll, however, was sentenced to eighteen months imprisonment. This verdict marked the end of the *Commonweal* as an effective propaganda tool, although it continued to appear spasmodically until the mid-1890s.

Morris's split with the Socialist League also led to changes in his own life. Although his withdrawal from the League did not shake his belief in revolutionary socialism it restricted his influence on the wider movement. Following the split the Hammer-smith Branch of the Socialist League was renamed the Hammersmith Socialist Society on 23 November 1890. The 'Statement of Principles' that Morris prepared to mark the new departure did nothing to address the problems that had beset his earlier propaganda for the League. Once again the familiar attacks on anarchism and parliamentarism were evident, and the propaganda aims differed little from those Morris had advocated in his earliest days in the movement: '...the object of the Society shall be the spreading of the principles of Socialism, especially by Lectures, Street-Meetings, and Publications....' (*Thompson*: p. 581.)

Although at first the propaganda work did continue with open-air meetings at Hammersmith Bridge, weekly Sunday lectures and monthly discussion forums at Kelmscott House, and even, after October 1891 the publication of a four-page monthly entitled the *Hammersmith Socialist Record*, the Hammersmith Socialist Society soon became an anachronism within the wider movement. As time passed it became more of a debating club than a revolutionary socialist society. Although many prominent figures spoke before the meetings at Kelmscott House the lectures were not confined to politics. When they ceased in February 1897, it was reported in the *Pall Mall Gazette* that 'of late years the Sunday evenings at Kelmscott Hall have been nearly equally divided between socialistic and artistic, historic or literary subjects...'.

Morris was never able to return to the active propaganda campaign following a bout of ill-health early in 1891. This was almost certainly brought on by the events of 1890 and a notable increase in the frequency and severity of his daughter Jenny's fits. Near the end of February he experienced a severe attack of gout, a complaint from which he had suffered for many years. On this occasion, however, the attack was accompanied by complications which were diagnosed as those of a serious kidney complaint. So debilitating was the attack that for some time he was unable to hold a pen. E. P. Thompson has postulated that this bout of illness 'may have represented the first onset of the diabetic condition from which he died'. (*Thompson*: p. 581.) The illness aged him immensely, as can be discerned from the surviving photographs taken during his last years. It also seems to have sapped much of the energy that had enabled him to sustain such a punishing schedule for so long. According to Sparling he even began to talk of dying.

Even so the 1890s were not entirely devoid of hope for Morris. One of the reasons why he had considered his own propaganda campaign had failed was that the Socialist League had been unable to organize the workers. Following 1890, however, there was increasing evidence that Morris had miscalculated the potential of the working classes. New Unionism continued to gather pace amongst the unskilled and semi-skilled workers, and many labouring men were elected to serve on local administrative bodies like School Boards and County Councils. The fact that Morris and the Hammersmith Socialist Society actively campaigned on behalf of these candidates, and were instrumental in approaching the SDF and the Fabian Society with the object of establishing a Socialist Federation, has occasionally led critics to suggest that Morris in his later years abandoned his earlier purist view of the revolution. There is little evidence for this. Lectures such as 'Communism' (1893) show no indication of a rejection of the need for revolutionary change. Indeed, the sentiments he expressed in one of his last letters on the subject, written on 9 January 1896, would not have been out of place in a lecture of 1885: 'I have not changed my mind on Socialism. ...Society (so-called) at present is organized entirely for the benefit of a privileged class; the working class being only considered in the arrangement as so much machinery. This involves perpetual and enormous *waste*, and the organization for the production of genuine utilities is only a secondary consideration. This waste lands the whole civilized world in a position of *artificial poverty*, which again debars men of all classes from satisfying rational desires.' (*Mackail*: II: p. 292.) What he did come to accept was that partial reform and parliamentary participation were likely to be features of the transitional phase before the revolution was possible.

Morris's disappointment at the failure of his propaganda campaign should not be allowed to detract from his influence on the socialist movement. When he joined the Democratic Federation in 1883 the vast majority of people in Britain had never heard of socialism. Yet by the time he died in 1896 socialist candidates had been elected to the London County Council, the Independent Labour Party had been formed, and Keir Hardie, John Burns and J. Havelock Wilson had succeeded in becoming MPs. Morris's part in promulgating socialism cannot be overestimated. Between 1883 and 1890 he was probably the most active propagandist in the whole country. In a seven year period he addressed over 1,000 meetings and was heard in person by as many as 250,000 people. His articles and editorials reached thousands more. As Thompson has written: '...every group of Socialists included some who had been converted by his words'. (*Thompson*: p. 602.) Many of these converts went on to play a prominent role in the subsequent development of the movement.

Morris's influence was also one of the reasons why the British socialist movement developed along different lines to those on the continent. In Europe socialist parties had gained a great deal of popular support in the 1880s. As early as 1869 the Socialdemokratische Arbeiterpartei had been established in Germany. This body, organized on Marxist lines, spawned similar Social Democrat parties in Belgium (1885), Austria (1889), Hungary (1890) and Bulgaria (1891). In Germany the Socialdemokratische Arbeiterpartei had polled 493,000 votes in 1877. By the time that Morris withdrew from the Socialist League in 1890 this had risen to 1,427,000 votes and had provoked Bismarck into passing unpopular anti-socialist legislation. By 1912 its support had risen to 4,239,000 and the party was only kept out of office by a coalition of various bourgeois groupings.

In Britain the revolutionary socialists were never to play such a prominent role in the working class parliamentary movement. Part of the reason for this was that the squabbles over tactics prevented the revolutionary movement from organizing the opposition to the bourgeois executive. Morris's role in this process was paradoxical to say the least. Although he worked harder than most to keep the movement together, his own purist beliefs and propaganda aims meant that throughout the movement's crucial formative years the revolutionary wing of the socialist movement was weakened by internal division. The split with the SDF not only fragmented the left of the movement; it led to the creation of the Socialist League, which was committed to a vigorous anti-parliamentary programme in opposition to both the gradualists and the trades unions. Of course it would be wrong to attribute this failure to Morris alone; H. M. Hyndman's opportunism and quasi-Marxist ideas contributed as well, as did the brief rise of anarchism in the late 1880s and early 1890s.

The result was that when parliamentary methods were adopted the initiative was taken by the more moderate elements in the movement. In 1888 the Scottish Parliamentary Labour Party was formed, followed five years later by the Independent Labour Party. When representatives of the latter along with the Fabians, the SDF and the trades unions came together in February 1900 to form the Labour Representative Committee, the leaders were able to pass distinctly moderate resolutions and avoid committing its supporters to either socialism or the class-war. This resulted in the SDF severing its links with the organization the following year and consigning itself to the fringes of British politics. The revolutionary wing of the socialist movement was never to establish a decisive influence over the Labour Party.

Nevertheless Morris's practical achievements in the movement were immense. He was in every sense of the word an activist. His lecture campaign of 1883 to 1890 remains one of the most impressive ever undertaken by a British politician. It deservedly brought him into national prominence as one of the most dedicated socialist speakers. His assessment of contemporary events in the columns of *Justice* and *Commonweal* reveals him to have been a perceptive political commentator. The insights he gained from this analysis were in many ways as important to the development of his mature political vision as his readings in theoretical socialism. In addition he almost single-handedly created a body of revolutionary socialist literature. This not only dramatised the reality of the revolutionary struggle but challenged bourgeois conceptions concerning the role of nineteenth century art. Although Morris failed to convince his contemporaries of the need for social revolution, his work stands as a testament to his implacable belief that there must be a better future for mankind. Until that future is achieved his lectures, articles and creative works will continue to be as relevant as when they were first written. As the prophet of a new order Morris remains unrivalled.

Nicholas Salmon
Buckinghamshire, 1994

TEXTUAL NOTE

The following articles from *Justice* were transcribed from a microfiche of the original papers held at the library of the London School of Economics and Political Science. Those from *Commonweal* were taken from original editions of the paper held at the same library. Both *Justice* and *Commonweal* can also be viewed at the British Newspaper Library, Colindale Avenue, NW9. All the articles have been reproduced in full with the exception of 'Dead at Last' which appeared in *Commonweal* on 17th March 1888. For reasons of continuity two unrelated paragraphs at the end of this article have been omitted.

CONTRIBUTIONS TO *JUSTICE*

1884

An Old Fable Retold

In the days before man had completely established his domination over the animal world, the poultry of a certain country, unnamed in my record, met in solemn conference in the largest hall they could hire for their money: the period was serious, for it was drawing near Christmas, and the question in debate partook of the gravity of the times; for, in short, various resolutions, the wording of which has not come down to us were to be moved on the all important subject, *'with what sauce shall we be eaten?'*

Needless to say that the hall was crowded to suffocation, or that an overflow meeting (presided over by working-class leaders) was held on the neighbouring dung-hill.

All went smoothly; the meeting was apparently unanimous and certainly enthusiastic, abundant wisdom was poured out on the all-important question, and the hearts of all glowed with satisfaction at the progress of the race of – poultry. The very bantam-*hens* were made happy by the assurance that their claims to cackling were to be seriously considered.

But when the hands of the clock were pointing to ten minutes to ten the excited audience, as they recovered from the enthusiasm produced by one of the great speeches of the evening, saw on the platform beside the chairman a battered looking and middle-aged barn-door cock, who they perceived was holding forth in a lugubrious voice, praising the career and motives of every advanced politician of the poultry yard. This bored the audience a good deal, but being used to it they stood it with patience for some time, till at last the orator's voice got rather clearer and louder, and he spoke somewhat as follows:– 'Sir, I know I have little right to air my own theories (cheers) after the remarkable and clear exposition of the rights of the poultry, which has been delivered in various ways on this platform to-night (loud cheers), but I am free to confess that one idea has occurred to me which seems to have escaped the more educated minds of our leaders to-night;- (cries of Oh, Oh) – the idea is this!' Here he stopped dead, and amid ironical cheers tried nervously to help himself to water from the long ago emptied decanter, then at last blurted out in a trembling, shrieking voice not without a suspicion of tears in it; 'In short *I don't want to be eaten at all*: is it poss–'

But here a storm of disapproving cries broke out, amongst which could be heard loudest the words 'practical Politics!', 'county franchise', 'great liberal party', 'municipal government for – Coxstead!' which at last all *calmed* themselves down into a steady howl of 'question, question!' in the midst of which the ragged, middle-aged cock withdrew, apparently not much more depressed than when he first stood up.

After his departure the meeting ended in all harmony, and a resolution was passed with great enthusiasm that the conclusions come to as embodied in the foregoing resolutions should be engrossed and forwarded to the farmer's wife (or widow was it?) and the head poulterer.

A rumour has reached us that while there were doubts as to the sauce to be used in the serving up, slow stewing was settled on as the least revolutionary form of cookery.

Moral: Citizens, pray draw it for yourselves.

JUSTICE, VOLUME 1, NUMBER 1,
19 JANUARY 1884, P. 2.

COTTON AND CLAY

The commission appointed by government to enquire into the sanitary condition of the weaving sheds where the delicious compound of filth called heavily sized cotton is worked up into cloth (?), says among other things: 'The amount of size used to a given weight of cotton warp could no longer be actually described as being from 50 to 90 per cent.; 100, 120, 150 per cent. of size is now not infrequently used. We conversed with one manufacturer, who admitted that to every 100 lb. of warp he put 200 lb. of size; another had gone as far as 230. In one factory visited by us the manufacturer weighed in our presence a piece of cotton cloth weighing 8 1/4 lb. and another weighing 4 1/2 lb. and remarked that the latter contained by far the larger amount of cotton.'

The commission, with touching fidelity to the doctrine of laisser faire, remarks elsewhere: 'Whatever natural regrets may therefore be felt at the decline of an ancient staple, they are as unavailing as if they were expended upon similar degradations that have long since taken place in silk and woollen manufactures.'

Unavailing indeed, while the profit-mongers are ruling the roast (sic)! But though we may smile at such barefaced and cynical rascality, it is no laughing matter. A working man of our acquaintance whose wife was a cotton-weaver a year or two ago tells us that she suffered terribly from rheumatism in the shoulders brought on by the damp air of the sheds where this filth is worked up; since steam has to be blown through them to soften the warps: he said also that when she got to work in the morning everything about her looms was dripping wet, the reeds and so forth rusty; and in consequence she necessarily made 'bad work' for the first few yards, for which serious deduction was made when the goods were taken to the warehouse; so that instead of making 20s. a week which would have been her normal wage as a 'four loomer', she would bring home no more than 14s.

Meantime, and while this race to fresh and hopeless savagery is going on, the *Textile Manufacturer* like his brethren of the Plutocratic press hymns the progress of the competitive commerce in an editorial attack on Professor Ruskin and (your humble servant) the Treasurer of the Democratic Federation.

What we have to remember is that these so called 'goods' are *forced* on poor and helpless persons and from that *force* come the riches of the manufacturers, the refinement of their sons, the peerages of their grandsons; if it were not for the poor who are *forced* to buy, and the poor who are *forced* to make it, this cursed heap of filth, (the words are used deliberately), would not be made at all.

JUSTICE, VOLUME I, NUMBER 2,
26 JANUARY 1884, P. 2.

ORDER AND ANARCHY

The Plutocratic Society which we Socialists are attacking, though an anarchy, is nevertheless an organized anarchy; an anarchy, too, which is sustained even by the efforts towards reform of those who are contented with it; as for instance the preachment of high morality and disinterested philanthropy among the well-to-do classes; the struggle of the Trades' Unions to keep up the wages of skilled artizans, while they admit the right of the masters to the sweating of labour, and are therefore still the slaves of the competitive market; the efforts of radical politicians to extend the franchise and improve the system of representation (?) while they are resolute to hand over the general welfare of the people to the tender mercies of *laissez-faire*: all the so-called progress, in short, which is so be-hymned in the plutocratic press of to-day, and the result of which will be but a bitter disappointment to the honest among the middle-classes themselves, since it means nothing but a widening of the basis of tyranny: all this is just the instinctive effort of the organization of commercial war; an insurance for the system of plutocracy, which perpetually strives to make good the prophecy, 'The poor ye have always with you'.

What kind of organization, then, have we Socialists to oppose to this terrible, this apparently inexpugnable organization, which is not only sustained by the greatest mass of material riches which the world has ever seen, but even makes use for its evil and destructive purposes of men's very virtues, of their aspirations towards freedom and social welfare?

Surely it is useless to meet it with the dignified measured efforts for redress which would befit free citizens living together with some approach to equality; for men living under such conditions the electoral arrangements which they themselves had agreed to might suffice for the expression of their opinions: how far we are from such a condition may be seen by the fact that in no constituency in England, Wales, or Scotland, has a working man candidate any chance of being returned except by the express leave and license, nay the strenuous efforts, of his capitalist masters, and he must be a sanguine man who thinks that universal suffrage would alter this while general opinion on the relations of capital and labour remain unchanged.

No, it is no use shutting our eyes to facts; we must remember that, in spite of fine words, in spite of the smoothness and varnish of modern life, and all the conveniences so easily obtained by the successful competitors in our hideous system of internecine war, we are not free citizens, but slaves.

Not as free citizens, then, can we organize ourselves; not as men prepared to ally ourselves from time to time with this or that body of politicians as they seem to agree more or less with our views and aims: we can have no allies among the governing classes; we can only have masters; let them bear the responsibility for their acts; do not let us be so tame as to shift any of it on to our shoulders.

Slaves are a necessity to the capitalist organization. Let the governing committee of capitalists feel that they are ruling discontented slaves, either of approval or disapproval of any of their acts. Meantime let us set about the great work of organizing and educating discontent, teaching the root doctrines of Socialism to every one we can reach, enrolling in the Socialist body every one who genuinely accepts those doctrines; making our voices heard as Socialists on every opportunity, but holding ourselves aloof from every movement which has not the furtherance of Socialism as its direct aim.

Such an organization would avoid that waste of power on side issues, which is the curse of popular movements in England; every member of it would feel that sense of brotherhood and support, that exaltation of soul which the holding of great principles in common with a mass of intelligent men, and their championship among people hostile and indifferent always gives to the initiated, changing doubt and shrinking into certainty and fearlessness.

It is true that this method is that of patience, that it would be pleasanter, and would seem easier to snatch a temporary victory every now and then by allying ourselves with those men to whom our hopes come in the form of fears. But we all know what such victories mean; how they do but breed a fresh set of enemies to revolution, by satisfying the outskirts of discontent on the one hand, and on the other by driving the over-sanguine into the cynicism caused by failure with the face of victory.

Surely it is no wonder if patience is required from those who further a cause whose final end is the happiness of the human race.

JUSTICE, VOLUME I, NUMBER 4,
9 FEBRUARY 1884, P. 2.

THE BONDHOLDERS BATTUE

The two fearful massacres which have taken place this week are but a continuance of that fatal succession of mischances which has dogged the policy of the Government in Egypt. To blame the miserable administration in Cairo for what has taken place is simply to eke out incompetence with meanness. Of course the Khedive and his advisers were half-hearted in supporting Baker Pasha, of course they are ready to intrigue with M. Barrère or anybody else. That is the nature of Orientals; especially when straightforwardness as in the case of Arabi ended in the disgusting butchery of Tel-el-Kebir. But the main responsibility for all these horrors inflicted upon the luckless Egyptians must rest with England; and it is high time that our people should understand what a fearful responsibility that is. For whatever we may say about our own Government, and there is plenty to be said from every point of view – this must ever by remembered that the monstrous blundering in Egypt like the shameful misgovernment in Ireland is due to the fact that Englishmen allow their rulers to do what they please in the name of the country.

The truth is that our entire action in Egypt has been shaped by a gang of international loan-mongers from the first outbreak of the soldiery under Arabi until now. The contention that the safety of the Suez Canal was in danger was a mere subterfuge. And when once we had beaten Arabi and had put up our puppet Tewfik nothing but a complete reversal of policy steadily carried out could relieve us from being Jew-ridden to the bitter end. Vacillation meant annexation or humiliation. That dilemma is before us to-day.

And who again is to blame for this? First and foremost, as everyone is saying, the Government. That hopeless incapacity to look facts in the face, and to gauge existing forces without bias which has always distinguished Mr Gladstone in external affairs, was never more fatally displayed than in this case. As we urged lately, every step taken has been directly calculated to make matters worse. What need was there to appoint a clique of financial hacks whose one object in life is to obey orders from international loanmongers to represent us in Egypt? Why allow Hicks to go to his fate in the desert without protest? On what grounds hesitate to employ Gordon in time, if he were to be employed at all? To obtain what advantage favour the hobnobbing of two such passed masters in intrigue as Nubar Pacha and M. Barrère? Granting that we were obliged to go to war for the bondholders, and to waste millions on butchering industrious peasants who only wished to be relieved from the grip of the usurers – even with such an admission thrown in, it might seem that England had thereby gained the right to consider her own people and the people of Egypt before anyone else. But we would neither leave the country alone, nor would we administer it in earnest when native Government had been rendered impossible by our action. For this Liberals and Radicals, we repeat, as the party in power are primarily responsible. The blood of those wretched fellahs is on their head. And, in a special sense, is this true of Mr Joseph Chamberlain and Sir Charles Dilke. But for their shameless disregard of every principle they professed when out of office, but for their determined efforts to silence any protest by Radicals in Parliament and in the country against their own infamous betrayal, we never could have been placed in the dangerous position which we occupy at this hour. We hope that even now some Radical member will have the pluck – very little is needed – to tell these men in plain language that they have sold out to the enemy, and that they have prostituted the principles of morality which they were placed in power to champion.

But though the ministers, being the ministers, are necessarily on their trial before the country, the

Conservatives have no right whatever to pose as their accusers. They themselves forced the wavering Cabinet into the bombardment of Alexandria and the fatal blunder of the conquest of Egypt. Why then did we not hear all this about the bondholders from the Tory benches which some of us at least never wearied of saying at the time? Why did not Lord Salisbury rise in the House of Lords and Sir Stafford Northcote in the House of Commons to challenge the expenditure of English blood and English money in the interests of bondholders and usurers? We all know very well. Because they wished for the war and taunted the Government with cowardice in not crushing a defenceless people. And the Government was weak enough and wicked enough to yield to this clamour.

What matters, however, which faction or what place-hunters ought specially to be denounced? It is the English people who must suffer for all this pusillanimity and greed. Can they not for once decide the matter for themselves? The situation is more dangerous even than it looks. Behind the growing probability of a widespread Mahommedan revival – an African and an Asiatic crescentade – lies the possibility of grave misunderstanding with France. Can any sober man honestly declare that the mass of the English people are interested in taking upon themselves a minor India and running the risk of rivalry with a great military nation? The thing is preposterous. Trade is bad, Ireland is far from pacified, social pressure is daily increasing at home, our army is overtaxed already, and Indian troops could not safely be used. But if all looked as flourishing as it now looks depressing, we ought equally to say that we do not intend to annex the country under any circumstances whatever. Yet to send troops now with the idea of leaving later is merely to go blindfold into unknown risks. Therefore we at any rate raise our voice against the dispatch of English or Indian troops to Egypt, knowing right well that such a step, if it is not to land us in disaster, can only be taken at the expense of an alliance, direct or indirect, with the banded military brigandism of Central

Europe. Let not Englishmen then, whatever may have been the fate of noble General Gordon, be deluded by a cry for vengeance, or an appeal to what, in this case at least, is a spurious patriotism. The workers have many accounts to settle nearer home, without allowing a Liberal government to promote reaction under the pretence of putting down slave-dealing, or to annex Egypt for the benefit of the upper and middle classes.

JUSTICE, VOLUME I, NUMBER 4,
9 FEBRUARY 1884, P. 4.

The Way Out
An Appeal to Genuine Radicals

There are doubtless many sincere Radicals outside the party phalanx whose war-cry is 'Our Leaders, Right or Wrong!' It behoves these sincere men to look round and consider their position, which they will find to be a sufficiently curious one; for as far as they have any power to carry out those reforms, the expectation of which gives the party its claim to existence, they are allied, whether they like it or not, first of all to the Whigs, that is to say to a kind of Liberals, who by virtue of their position among the privileged class are necessarily fossils, and next to the moderate Liberals, or Liberals simply, which ever you please to call them; that is to say, men possessed of property, but not of principles, whose consciences are just strong enough for them to dislike being called Conservatives, so long as they believe their property to be safe; but who will have to put up with being called reactionists about the time when their property seems to be in any danger. These politicians, who in fact are just hanging on till they see which way the cat is going to jump, are, of course, much the strongest party in our middle-class state, and since 1880 have had a good time indeed in dragging the conscientious Radicals who brought them into power through some of the dirtiest puddles in English history.

What is likely to be the fate of the Radical between these two allies? Well, first let us consider what sort of a Radical he is: he may be a mere Parliamentary Radical pinning his faith on the shufflings of the electoral system, and as wide an extension of free contract as humanity can stand, for the heal-all of every evil; or he may mix with his

Parliamentarism real disgust at our social short comings, and a sincere desire to amend them. In the first case he tends towards the Whig party or group, and will be sucked into it: or rather, putting names apart, he is really but a new Whig himself, and has no real aim in any direction. Well, as among the whole so-called Liberal party, the moderate Liberals are the strongest, so among the Radicals these Whig-Radicals or new Whigs are strongest: and they will find themselves, we may suppose, in a very dignified position; for the Whig party, since they are fossils, cannot die as long as the bourgeois constitution lasts.

One may say that each of these sections of the Liberal party has some power, and some prospects; but what is to be said of the conscientious social-reform Radical; what is his position among them all? Alas, he is the leavings of Liberalism, and will be used by all sections of it, and thrown aside by all as soon as he is no longer needed for party purposes: on all occasions when he brings his principles forward he will find that he is no longer a 'practical politician'; his feeble protests against sword-bible-and-shoddy policy, against Austrian Police Government in Ireland, and safe little stock-jobbers' wars, and the rest of it, will be quietly thrust aside, and he will be bidden to know his place and keep it.

So let him bethink himself what his Radicalism means to him more than that new Whiggery above mentioned; he may find that it means the hope of an intelligent and conscientious middle-class government for the benefit of – the middle class: in other words that in common with many worthy and moral people, he can see no other except the middle-class; which fact would seem as if he had brought about in a dream what we Socialists wish to bring about in reality, the extinction of classes; in that case, if what is bred in the bone won't come out of the flesh, let him make his dream as long as he can; only he may chance to have a rude awakening from it some day.

On the other hand he may, and I hope he will find his Radicalism means a real sympathy with democracy;

perhaps he thought before the advent to power of this last Liberal government that things were tending toward democracy, if only the Tories could be muzzled, slowly perhaps, but surely, under the guidance of such leaders as could be got; not over good leaders in themselves doubtless, nay not leaders at all, but fuglemen shoved on by a serious body of Radicals who were determined to obtain government by the people for the good of the people.

In that case what is he to do now that he is disillusionized of his Radical ideal, now that he finds that nothing of that kind was meant either by the fugleman or their shovers on? One thing he can do, and only one, he can clear his eyes and see whither the democratic ideal of his must lead him if he is true to it; he can already see that there is another class below the fugleman of the upper, and the shovers on of the middle-class; if he looks he will see that this class is in matters political treated as a voting machine, to be manipulated for the convenience of the players in the political game; and in social matters as a profit-grinding machine to be greased by palliatives into smooth working; if he looks a little closer he will see that the machine is wearing thin in places, and that it is not going to last; he will find out that the people will not endure for ever to be played upon, and exploited, or rather that they cannot endure it, but by mere necessity are being pushed on to the conflict with the now triumphant middle-class; he will see that all the old political parties have become mere names, and that the real aim of all of them is the same, insurance against a change of basis (or radical change) in our Society. This used to be called the Tory aim; let the conscientious Radical call it so now and call those who aim at it Tories; the name so used will include most of his old friends and leaders.

The upshot of it will be that the conscientious Radical will see when his eyes are cleared from the mist of words and names that there are but two camps; one is the camp of those who are the exponents of the change which is taking place; the other of those who are striving to insure Society against that inevitable change; if he chooses this latter he may remain a Radical in name to-day, but to-morrow will be called by his right name 'reactionist'; but if he chooses the former camp he will keep his Radical principles though he will have to undergo the shame of being called a Socialist.

My Radical friends, which will you keep, the name or the thing?

JUSTICE, VOLUME I, NUMBER 7,
1 MARCH 1884, P. 4

ART OR NO ART? WHO SHALL SETTLE IT?

The workman of the present day may well think that art is not a matter which concerns him much. To speak bluntly, he is not wealthy enough to share in such art (there is little enough of it, all told) as is going in civilized countries. His earnings are precarious, and his lodging precarious also, and, to boot, stowed away almost always in the dirtiest corners of our dirty cities; so that, at the risk of offending worthy people who are feebly trying to bestow some scraps of art on their 'poorer brethren', it must be said that the workman's home must be bare of art. Indeed, the attempt to bring beauty into such homes would be a task to break the heart of the most patient artist in Europe. That shabby gift of the crumbs that fall from the children's table must be taken back again, *for there is no such thing as cheap art*, and workmen can only buy what is cheap. On the other hand if the workman takes it into his head to go some day to the galleries of art that he may try to understand the raptures of us artists over the works of past ages, how does he speed on his educational errand? What does he find? – the door shut in his face on the one day in the week on which he could carry out his attempt to learn something from the study of his own property – the *National* Gallery say. It really does take an artist to understand the full force of this stupendous joke of the defenders of religion against common sense and common honesty.

It would exceed the limits of a newspaper article to show how far the workman is from having any share in art when he is at his work, but my workman friends, at least, know all about that; for even those who are engaged on making the wares which, in the wretched slang of would-be cultivation, are called 'art objects', have to work always as machines, or as the slaves of machines, and the 'organizers of labour' take good care that neither the quality nor the quantity of the art in these 'art objects' shall be too grand. Here, then, is the truth, which we artists know full well, that those who produce the wealth of civilized society have no share in art. So entirely are they cut off from it, that many, or most of them, it is to be feared, do not even know of their loss in this matter. Yet I am bound to assert here and everywhere that art is necessary to man unless he is to sink into something lower than the brutes. Middle-class supremacy has brought us to this at last, that such art as there is left is used (whatever its merits may be in each case) as a toy for the rich, while the workers are debarred from having any art, either in their work or their homes; that is to say that the workers are doomed by capitalism to live without the pleasure which is necessary to humanity.

Yes, middle-class supremacy! For things were very different all through the Middle Ages, from the 12th to the end of the 16th century, while the middle-class was being formed from the enfranchised serfs, yeomen, and craftsmen of the guilds. Throughout that period, at least, all manufactured goods, everything that admitted of ornament was made more or less beautiful; nor was the beauty charged for as a separate article, for all craftsmen were more or less artists, and could not help adding beauty to the goods they made. It is easy to see that this could not have happened if they had been working for the profit of a master. They worked, on the contrary, under such conditions that they themselves were masters of their time, tools, and materials, and, for the most part, their goods were exchanged by the simple process of the user buying from the maker. Under these circumstances it was a matter of course that a man, being master of his work should choose to make it pleasanter to himself by exercising on it that love of beauty which is common to all men till it is crushed out of them by the mere bitter struggle for life called competition for wages, and by subjection to a master who also is struggling for profit against other competitors. This system of a man working for himself leisurely and happily was infinitely better, both as regards the worker and his work, than that division of labour system which the profit-grinding of rising commercialism supplanted it by; but of course it is impossible to go back to such a simple system, even if it would not involve, as it would, a return to the whole hierarchical, or feudal state of society. On the other hand it is as necessary for the existence of art as it is for the well-being of the people otherwise, that the workman should again have control over his material, his tools, and his time; only that control must no longer be of the individual workman, as in the Middle Ages, but of the whole body of workmen. When the workers organize work for the benefit of the workers, that is to say of the whole people, they will once more know what is meant by art; but if this social revolution does not come about (but it must) art will assuredly perish, and the rich will have no more of it than the poor.

It is most important, therefore, for the workers to take note how capitalism has deprived them of art, for that word means really the pleasure of life, nothing less. I beseech them to consider it not a light thing but a most grievous wrong that their work should be barren of attractiveness and their homes of beauty; and I assure them that this wrong is not an accident, not the result of the carelessness and hurry of modern life, which a few well-meaning men of the middle-class backed by money can set right. It is not accidental, to be met by palliatives and temporary remedies, but it is the result of the subjection of the poor to the rich, and, at the same time, is the most obvious badge of that subjection. One thing only can amend it, the outcome of that class-struggle now happily in progress, and which will end by abolishing all classes.

JUSTICE, VOLUME I, NUMBER 9,
15 MARCH 1884, P. 2.

HENRY GEORGE

This eloquent and enthusiastic American writer and agitator has been among us for three months working hard to push what he believes to be the true remedy for our terrible social ills, some acknowledgement of which at least he has forced from the better part of the middle-classes. It is impossible not to feel sympathy and regard for a man of this kind, in whose most bitter attacks there is still an attractive kindliness, and whose earnest faith and simplicity cover over with a rude eloquence the grave mistakes which to others seem to lie at the foundation of all his teaching. It is indeed refreshing in days like these, when cynicism and contempt for all self-sacrifice are so often taken as the test-marks of the higher culture, to find a man who, rising from among the workers, throws the glamour of his own sincerity over the most callous and forces them to look into the misery around them, of which misery indeed many of the highly-critical and refined are the direct cause. For what he has done here in England we owe Henry George our sincerest thanks: he himself has earned our deep esteem. His book has stirred men and women of the middle-class to think of what must be called revolution as something possible and beneficent, and has even stirred some of them to act in a sort of way; ineffectual as their palliatives must be for the remedy of the wrongs which their class has created. It is not unlikely that a more logical and correct thinker, a more rigid economist would have failed where he has so far succeeded. People read between the lines of his book, not his economical errors, but his deep love of truth and his never-ceasing desire to benefit his fellow-men. The feelings were swept away by 'Progress and Poverty', the reason came limping lamely after to offer hopeless expostulation. And as with his writing so with his speaking. That winning frankness and genuine sincerity which ring through his every utterance have gone straight to the hearts of his English audiences on all occasions save when he was speaking at the would-be home of culture and refinement[.] If the land question at this hour is more clearly before the people than any other this is in great part due to Mr Henry George. No doubt he came at a favourable time as his book was published at a moment when it was likely to attract attention. Unless circumstances favour the writer or the orator his labour as all history shows is [in] vain for his own epoch. But this in no wise takes away from the merit of his work or detracts from the honour due to labours in the cause of the people. Granted that the depression throughout the country and the serious state of our agricultural industry helped Mr George to an attentive hearing, he never spared himself but strove as we are striving to stir an apathy which has lasted almost unbroken for over thirty years.

For ourselves we will confess that we looked with some misgiving to his visit now drawing to a close. Mr George's high qualities were themselves a drawback from our point of view. We feared – and the fear may still prove far from groundless – that the capitalists of this country wealthy, powerful, organized as they are, would make common cause with Mr George and, anxious to save the proceeds of their own still worse methods of plunder, would on the one hand show a tendency to throw the landlords overboard as Jonahs from a craft now owned and chiefly manned by themselves, and on the other would pit Mr George as the reasonable and moral reformer against the unreasonable and immoral revolutionists, of which we form a part. They have not done so. It is therefore unnecessary that we should here enlarge upon the grave differences which exist between Mr George and ourselves. We too desire to overthrow the landlord domination; we too have worked for years to get back the land for the people; we too are altogether at one with Mr George in his eloquent denunciations of the Ducal robbers who have rendered Scotland a wilderness, and the English garrison who have reduced the Irish to serfdom. In our own country also the grip of the land grabber is over us all; and commons and heaths of unmatched beauty and wildness have been enclosed for farmers or jerry-built upon by speculators in order to swell the illgotten revenues of some covetous aristocrat or greedy money-bag; while any real improvement in our great towns, where the lodging of the working class is an acknowledged disgrace to civilization, is rendered impossible by the fancy prices of land caused by competition ground rents. To every anathema which Mr George has launched against these cormorants of our health, happiness and comfort we heartily chant Amen. But we cannot finish, nay we cannot even begin, here. The worst enemies of the people to-day are those whom our 'Prophet of California' leaves untouched by his denunciations and unscathed by his sarcasm. To Mr George the robber of a hundred is a villain indeed: the dexterous annexer of many thousands may pass full pocketed on his way as a benefactor of his race. We cannot help thinking that their, to us, unexpected and surely impolitic treatment of Mr George should teach him a lesson; they have universally repudiated him; with the cynical impudence of attacked 'interests' they have called the ten commandments to their aid and have freely used the words theft and spoliation against one of the honestest men alive.

But our guest returns to his own people and our heartiest good wishes for the health and welfare of him and his go with him. However much and seriously we may differ from him, we feel that his enemies are ours also, and that his end like ours is the winning of a due share of happiness and refinement for the workers of the world; we English Socialists therefore give a hearty farewell to our friend and noble fellow-worker the American Henry George.

Justice, Volume I, Number 12,
5 April 1884, p. 4.

WHY NOT?

At a meeting of the Commons Preservation Society I heard it assumed by a clever speaker that our great cities, London in particular, were bound to go on increasing without any limit, and those present accepted that assumption complacently, as I think people usually do. Now under the present Capitalist system it is difficult to see anything which might stop the growth of these horrible brick encampments; its tendency is undoubtedly to depopulate the country and small towns for the advantage of the great commercial and manufacturing centres; but this evil, and it is a monstrous one, will be no longer a necessary evil when we have got rid of land monopoly, manufacturing for the profit of individuals, and the stupid waste of competitive distribution; and it seems probable that the development of electricity as a motive power will make it easier to undo the evils brought upon us by capitalist tyranny when we regain our senses and determine to live like human beings; but even if it turns out that we must still be dependent on coal and steam for force, much could still be done towards making life pleasant if universal co-operation in manufacture and distribution were to take the place of our present competitive anarchy. At the risk of being considered dreamers therefore it is important for us to try and raise our ideals of the pleasure of life; because one of the dangers which the social revolution runs is that the generation which sees the fall of Capitalism, educated as it will have been to bear the thousand miseries of our present system, will have far too low a standard of refinement and real pleasure. It is natural that men who are now beaten down by the fear of losing even their present pitiful livelihood, should be able to see nothing further ahead than relief from that terror and the grinding toil under which they are oppressed; but surely it will be a different story when the community is in possession of the machinery, factories, mines, and land, and is administering them for the benefit of the community; and when as a necessary consequence men find that the providing of the mere necessaries of life will be so far from being a burdensome task for the people that it will not give due scope to their energies. Surely when this takes place, in other words when they are free, they will refuse to allow themselves to be surrounded by ugliness, squalor and disorder either in their leisure or their working hours.

Let us, therefore, ask and answer a few questions on the conditions of manufacture, so as to put before us one branch of the pleasure of life to be looked forward to by Socialists.

Why are men huddled together in unmanageable crowds in the sweltering hells we call big towns?

For profit's sake; so that a reserve army of labour may always be ready to hand for reduction of wages under the iron law, and to supply the sudden demand of the capitalist gamblers, falsely called 'organizers of labour'.

Why are these crowds of competitors for subsistence wages housed in wretched shanties which would be a disgrace to the Flat-head Indians?

For profit's sake; no one surely would build such dog-hutches for their own sake: there is no insuperable difficulty in the way of lodging people in airy rooms decently decorated, in providing their lodgings not only with good public cooking and washing rooms, but also with beautiful halls for the common meal and other purposes, as in the Colleges of Oxford and Cambridge, which it would be [a] pleasure merely to sit in.

Why should any house, or group of lodgings, arranged in flats or otherwise, be without a pleasant and ample garden, and a good play-ground?

Because profit and competition rents forbid it. Why should one third of England be so stifled and poisoned with smoke that over the greater part of Yorkshire (for instance) the general idea must be that sheep are naturally black? and why must Yorkshire and Lancashire rivers run mere filth and dye?

Profit will have it so: no one any longer pretends that it would not be easy to prevent such crimes against decent life: but the 'organizers of labour', who might better be called 'organizers of filth', know that it wouldn't pay; and as they are for the most part of the year safe in their country seats, or shooting – crofters' lives – in the Highlands, or yachting in the Mediterranean, they rather like the look of the smoke country for a change as something, it is to be supposed, stimulating to their imaginations concerning – well, we must not get theological.

As to the factories themselves: why should there be scarcely room to turn round in them? Why should they be, as in the case of the weaving sheds of over-sized cotton, hot houses for rheumatism? why should they be such miserable prisons? Profit-grinding compels it, that is all: there is no other reason why there should not be ample room in them, abundant air, a minimum of noise: nay they might be beautiful after their kind, and surrounded by trees and gardens: in many cases the very necessities of manufacture might be made use of for beautifying their surroundings; as for instance in textile printing works, which require large reservoirs of water.

In such factories labour might be made, not only no burden, but even most attractive; young men and women at the time of life when pleasure is most sought after would go to their work as to a pleasure party: it is most certain that labour may be so arranged that no social relations could be more delightful than communion in hopeful work; love, friendship, family affection, might all be quickened by it; joy increased and grief lightened by it.

Where are the material means to come from for bringing this about? Fellow-workers, from the millions of surplus value wrung out of your labour by the 'organizers of filth';

screwed out of you for the use of tools and machines invented by the gathered genius of ages, for the use of your share of earth the Common Mother.

It is worth while thinking about, fellow-workers! For while theologians are disputing about the existence of a hell *elsewhere*, we are on the way to realizing it *here*: and if capitalism is to endure, whatever may become of men when they *die*, they will come into hell when they are *born*. Think of that and devote yourselves to the spread of the RELIGION OF SOCIALISM.

JUSTICE, VOLUME I, NUMBER 13,
12 APRIL 1884, P. 2.

THE DULL LEVEL OF LIFE

One of the chief terrors, real or affected, which afflicts the middle-class man in thinking of the chances of that 'Coming Slavery', which Mr Herbert Spencer so bewails, is a fear of the suppression of individuality. Our Socialist lecturers are all familiar with this objection which seldom fails to be raised at question time in meetings where those are present who have any claim to be considered educated. To us Socialists looking round on the present state of society the anxiety when genuine seems not a little ridiculous, considering the manner in which individualism founded on the gospel of commerce has guarded this precious jewel of individuality. Truly the mill-hand who is as much a part of the machinery of the factory where he works as any cog-wheel or piece of shafting is, need not be very anxious about the loss of his 'individuality' in a new state of things; the work-girl passing days and nights over her sewing-machine might be excused perhaps if she were willing to barter the said 'individuality' for the chance of a 'square meal' a-day: nay the banker's or lawyer's clerk, 'educated' as he is supposed to be, may be mean-spirited enough to find little solace for his life of mean drudgery in the contemplation of the theoretical 'individuality' secured to him as a prime blessing by the system of free contract. These and such as these pay a very heavy price indeed for that 'eager life of the world' that freedom from a 'low level of life' which the cant of the smug well-to-do man so glorifies nowadays; it does not need many words to show that the fear of death by starvation, which is the only motive to exertion that the anti-socialist can see, does certainly destroy individuality among the millions of ordinary workers; but it must be furthermore asserted that what breaks down *their* spirit, and reduces them to a dead level indeed, does also injure men of more exalted minds and rarer gifts. It is indeed the fashion to say that genius will break through all encumbering circumstances, and will even be bettered by struggling out of them: but is it really so? We know of those who have broken through the adverse circumstances, and have gained fame and honour and done useful work for the world, though their minds too often have been narrowed and their hearts soured in the bitter combat; but of those whom adverse circumstances have utterly crushed, of these and the loss to the world which has come of their misery we know and can know nothing.

So much for men of genius, while as to men of good ordinary gifts, those who may be called men of talent, it is the commonest thing for their special gifts, their 'individuality' to be thrust aside by the hideous waste of commercial war: which gifts if they were really considered and wisely organized would by means of due co-operation change the whole face of civilization and create happy lives to themselves and others. As it is what is their condition if they belong to the working-classes? We know very well that they are born and bred drudges, that they have just so much education bestowed on them as will not hinder them from drudgery profitable to their masters; that is their fate in the lump: and so besotted are we with the cant of individualism that the condition of even the prosperous working men is thought a fair result of all the thousands of years of the world's life: or if there is any further ideal about amongst the well-to-do, it aims no higher than a gradual improvement of these better off workers, which improvement is still to stop short of emancipation from drudgery; while below the better off must still be the terrible gulf of the residumn (*sic*). It is strange while this ideal satisfies people, that Socialism, aiming as it does at the total extinction of drudgery, should seem to anyone to be a threat against the development of individual talent or genius, which at the best at present is only possible to a few exceptionally lucky persons. The fear of this threat is of course in many places not genuine at all, and is only another way of putting the determination of the rich to keep down the poor; with such people argument is impossible: but to those who genuinely feel the fear, we may say finally that it is scarcely too bold to hope that in a state of society to which a class of drudgers is no longer necessary, education will not only be universal, but will be both more liberal, and wiser for all, than it is to-day for a few; and that it will be its function to develope (*sic*) any gifts which children or older people may have towards science, literature, the handicrafts, or the higher arts, or anything which may be useful or desirable to the community: furthermore that as it will be pleasant for those who possess such talents to use them, they will not deprive themselves of this pleasure merely because they are not driven to the exercise of their faculties by the fear of death by starvation.

It is a matter of course that these opportunities for the development of the higher faculties of the whole people will be founded, as hinted above, on the social use of that socialized labour aided by machinery which is in operation at present for the service of individual profit: how far machine production may be carried; to what extent it may at some time or other be limited by the increase of leisure, and ease of life, and the pleasure in useful work which we may expect to result from the development of Socialism, these are matters of speculation, on which different minds will have different hopes; but one thing is certain, that it will be one of the chief aims of a socialized state to limit pleasureless labour to the uttermost. The crushing weight of this pleasureless labour laid with such cruel indifference on our lives by the present anarchy is what individuality is languishing under; from Socialism it has nothing to fear, but all to gain.

To use the forces of nature by means of universal co-operation for the purpose of gaining generous and equal livelihood for all, leaving them free to enjoy their lives, and to emulate each other in producing pleasure for themselves and others is what Socialism aims at: the aim of middle-class individualism, to judge by the state of society which it defends so eagerly, would seem to be the creation of a shabby average of dull discomfort for a large class of the community, relieved only by a mass of dire misery on the one hand, and by idle and insolent waste on the other.

JUSTICE, VOLUME I, NUMBER 15,
26 APRIL 1884, P. 4.

A Factory as it Might Be

We Socialists are often reproached with giving no details of the state of things which would follow on the destruction of that system of waste and war which is sometimes dignified by the lying title of the harmonious combination of capital and labour: many worthy people say, 'We admit that the present system has produced unsatisfactory results, but at least it is a system; you ought to be able to give us some definite idea of the results of that reconstruction which you call Socialism'.

To this Socialists answer, and rightly, that we have not set ourselves to build up a system to please our tastes, nor are we seeking to impose it on the world in a mechanical manner, but rather that we are assisting in bringing about a development of history which would take place without our help, but which nevertheless compels us to help it: and that under these circumstances it would be futile to map out the details of life in a condition of things so different from that in which we have been born and bred. Those details will be taken care of by the men who will be so lucky as to be born into a society relieved of the oppression which crushes us, and who surely will be, not less, but more prudent and reasonable than we are. Nevertheless it seems clear that the economical changes which are in progress must be accompanied by corresponding developments of men's aspirations; and the knowledge of their progress cannot fail to rouse our imaginations into picturing for ourselves that life at once happy and manly which we *know* social revolution will put within the reach of all men.

Of course the pictures so drawn will vary according to the turn of mind of the picturer, but I have already tried to show in *Justice* that healthy and undomineering individuality will be fostered and not crushed by Socialism. I will therefore as an artist and handicraftsman venture to develope (*sic*) a little the hint contained in the journal of April 12th on the conditions of pleasant work in the days when we shall work for livelihood *and pleasure* and not for 'profit'.

Our factory then, is in a pleasant place: no very difficult matter, when as I have said before it is no longer necessary to gather people into miserable sweltering hordes for profit's sake: for all the country is in itself pleasant or is capable of being made pleasant with very little pains and forethought. Next, our factory stands amidst gardens as beautiful (climate apart) as those of Alcinous, since there is no need of stinting it of ground, profit-rents being a thing of the past, and the labour on such gardens is like enough to be purely voluntary, as it is not easy to see the day when 75 out of every 100 people will not take delight in the pleasantest and most innocent of all occupations; and our working people will assuredly want open air relaxations from their factory work. Even now, as I am told, the Nottingham factory hands could give many a hint to professional gardeners in spite of all the drawbacks of a great manufacturing town. One's imagination is inclined fairly to run riot over the picture of beauty and pleasure offered by the thought of skilful co-operative gardening for beauty's sake, which beauty would by no means exclude the raising of useful produce for the sake of livelihood.

Impossible! I hear an anti-Socialist say. My friend, please to remember that most factories sustain to-day large and handsome gardens, and not seldom parks and woods of many acres in extent; with due appurtenances of highly paid Scotch professional gardeners, wood reeves, bailiffs, game-keepers, and the like, the whole being managed in the most wasteful way conceivable: *only* the said gardens, &c., are say, twenty miles away from the factory, *out of the smoke*, and are kept up for *one member of the factory only*, the sleeping partner to wit, who may, indeed double that part by organizing its labour (for his own profit) in which case he receives ridiculously disproportionate pay additional.

Well, it follows on this garden business that our factory must make no sordid litter, befoul no water, nor poison the air with smoke. I need say nothing more on that point, as 'profit' apart it would be easy enough.

Next, as to the buildings themselves I must ask leave to say something, because it is usually supposed that they must of necessity be ugly, and truly they are almost always at present mere nightmares; but it is, I must assert, by no means necessary that they should be ugly, nay, there would be no serious difficulty in making them beautiful, as every building might be which serves its purpose duly, which is built generously as regards material, and which is built with pleasure by the builders and designers; indeed, as things go, those nightmare buildings aforesaid sufficiently typify the work they are built for, and look what they are, temples of overcrowding and adulteration and over-work, of unrest in a word; so it is not difficult to think of our factory buildings, showing on their outsides what they are for, reasonable and light work, cheered at every step by hope and pleasure. So in brief, our buildings will be beautiful with their own beauty of simplicity as workshops, not bedizened with tomfoolery as some are now, which do not any the more for that, hide their repulsiveness; but moreover, besides the mere workshops, our factory will have other buildings which may carry ornament further than that, for it will need dining hall, library, school, places for study of various kinds, and other such structures; nor do I see why, if we have a mind for it, we should not emulate the monks and craftsmen of the middle-ages in our ornamentation of such buildings, why we should be shabby in housing our rest and pleasure and our search for knowledge, as we may well be shabby in housing the shabby life we have to live now?

And again, if it be doubted as to the possibility of getting these beautiful buildings on the score of cost, let me once again remind you that every great factory does to-day sustain a palace (often more than one) amidst that costly garden and park aforesaid out of the smoke, but that this palace, stuffed as it is with all sorts of costly things, is for one member of the factory only, the sleeping partner - useful creature! It is true that the said palace is mostly, with all it contains, beastly ugly; but this ugliness is but a part of the bestial waste of the whole system of profit-mongering, which refuses cultivation and refinement to the workers, and therefore can have no art, not even for all its money.

So we have come to the outside of our Factory of the future and seen that it does not injure the beauty of the world, but adds to it rather; on another occasion, if I may I will try to give a picture of how the work goes on there.

JUSTICE, VOLUME I, NUMBER 18,
17 MAY 1884, P. 2.

INDIVIDUALISM AT THE ROYAL ACADEMY

To a Socialist hoping for a speedy change in the basis of society a visit to our picture exhibitions is not altogether lacking in encouragement, though to a serious artist who has not conceived hopes of revolution it would surely be most discouraging: for here also are signs of that coming bankruptcy of our present society, tokens of which are forced upon us so plentifully from the economic and the political side of things; it is with a certain exultation that one walks through the wild jumble of inanity that clothes the walls of the Royal Academy to-day, when one thinks that the dominant class the commercialist, noble and non-noble, who have deprived the people of art in their daily lives, can get for themselves nothing better than this for the satisfaction of their intellectual craving for beauty. Two or three men of genius, mostly outside the Academy, and a few of talent, half of whom also seldom if ever exhibit there, this handful is all that can show any attempt at the highest form of intellectual art which does not deserve the contempt of all serious and honest lovers of beauty; and all the while the golden shower rains down fast from the centres of profit-mongering on the army of incapables who make up the rest of the painters of pictures, or at least on many of them, and those by no means the least incapable.

On entering the National Gallery, or any other gallery of ancient pictures, the first thing that must strike the eye is the general beauty of colour, in spite of the pictures not being meant to be seen in juxtaposition: next, when we go near them we cannot fail to note the workmanlike method and certainty of their execution; there you have in brief the two qualities absolutely necessary to make a work of art in picture-painting, beauty of colour, beauty of execution; now bear in mind that the individuality of these old painters was influenced by at least the amount of co-operation which tradition gives, and also mostly be direct co-operation akin to that of the gilds in the less intellectual arts: with this in your mind go into the Academy Exhibition which is, by the way, of the same quality as the exhibitions of the last 15 years barring the brilliant exceptions of a few really fine pictures that have been shown in the course of those years. Well, what are the first things that strike you if you are unprejudiced? First that the general colour is bad, nay mostly frightful; next that the execution is essentially unworkmanlike, a mere vague haphazard scrabble. And next, what is there to redeem this essential failure? Indeed that is hard to say; for bad as the colour of these works is, and unsatisfactory as their execution, it is on a pretence of originality of colour or tone, it is on some cleverness and readiness of execution that they must base their claim to be considered at all. The painters of the old pictures had prescribed to them religious subjects which were still thoroughly believed in; or classical subjects whose incidents in the fervonr (*sic*) of the re-birth of learning they passed from hand to hand and accepted as realities with child-like faith; though all were not inventive or imaginative, many were, and the common-place minds accepted their position and shared the gifts of the greater minds with the humility of the true artist, who is determined at all events to turn out something which shall be beautiful and pleasant. All that is changed now, and individualism reigns supreme among our painters: that is to say, that while some plagiarize in the coolest way from the works of those that happen to be most in fashion; others, and these are the cleverest, disregard their own real talents and pretend to an originality which they have not, straining in competition for the guineas of the Manchester patron: giving him (and the world) as little work as they possibly can for the said guineas: everybody must at least pretend to be a master: for, look you, it no longer *pays* an artist to work hard to correct the faults which he himself cannot fail to recognize: it doesn't do to depend on the intelligence and love of beauty of the public; for bourgeois rule has forced the public into ignorance of beauty and vulgarity of mind; it is that which you must appeal to for a livelihood – or at least for a fortune. Therefore if you are weak in drawing, daub away with a pallet-knife and praise vagueness and formlessness as the one thing to be aimed at: if you have no eye for colour, paint with London mud and swear that colour is the degradation of art; or with mauve and magenta, emerald green and snuff colour, and sneer at those who really understand colour as affected mediævalists. This in short is the game to be played, to elevate your defects into the standard for all art: great shall be your cash-reward if you play it well: yet even then mere clever unscheming vulgarity may bear off the bell from you. In plain words, corruption has eaten out the higher arts almost entirely, and I repeat that it is common for artists to prostitute their talents such as they are, not to popularity, which would be respectable comparatively, but to fortune-hunting: the ignorant public I have been mentioning is not the simple, uneducated public, but the cultured and guinea-shedding public, and there is no limit to its gullibility; for in fact it likes to be gulled.

Grievous indeed that art should be used as a stalking horse for such proceedings; unbearable to an artist, if we did not see revolution beyond it, and a clean sweep of all that folly. Surely it must be said that if the coming change in the basis of society were to make an end of all this sham and half-sham art without any hope of a new art arising from it the loss would not be great; but that if, as I confidently believe, it will sweep the sham art away and give us good hope of a new art arising from a society founded on the equality of labour, there will be no loss, but immeasurable gain.

JUSTICE, VOLUME I, NUMBER 19,
24 MAY 1884, P. 4.

WORK IN A FACTORY AS IT MIGHT BE II

In a recent article we tried to look through the present into the future and see a factory as it might be, and got as far as the surroundings and outside of it; but those externals of a true palace of industry can be only realized naturally and without affectation by the work which is to be done in them being in all ways reasonable and fit for human beings; I mean no mere whim of some one rich and philanthropic manufacturer will make even one factory permanently pleasant and agreeable for the workers in it; he will die or be sold up, his heir will be poorer or more single-hearted in his devotion to profit, and all the beauty and order will vanish from the short-lived dream; even the external beauty in industrial concerns must be the work of society and not of individuals.

Now as to the work, first of all it will be useful, and therefore honourable and honoured; because there will be no temptation to make mere useless toys, since there will be no rich men cudgelling their brains for means for spending superfluous money, and consequently no 'organizers of labour' pandering to degrading follies for the sake of profit, wasting their intelligence and energy in contriving snares for cash in the shape of trumpery, which they themselves heartily despise. Nor will the work turn out trash; there will be no millions of poor to make a market for wares which no one would choose to use if he were not driven to do so; every one will be able to afford things good of their kind, and as will be shown hereafter, will have knowledge of goods enough to reject what is not excellent; coarse and rough wares may be made for rough or temporary purposes, but they will openly proclaim themselves for what they are; adulteration will be unknown.

Furthermore machines of the most ingenious and best approved kinds will be used when necessary, but will be used simply to save human labour; nor indeed could they be used for anything else in such well-ordered work as we are thinking about; since, profit being dead, there would be no temptation to pile up wares whose apparent value as articles of *use*, their conventional value as such, does not rest on the necessities or reasonable desires of men for such things, but on artificial habits forced on the public by the craving of the capitalists for fresh and ever fresh profit: these things have no real value as things to be used, and their conventional (let us say sham) utility value has been bred of their value, as articles of exchange for profit, in a society founded on profit mongering.

Well the manufacture of useless goods, whether harmful luxuries for the rich or disgraceful make-shifts for the poor having come to an end, and we still being in possession of the machines once used for mere profit grinding but now used only for saving human labour, it follows that much less labour will be necessary for each workman; all the more as we are going to get rid of all non-workers and busy idle people; so that the working time of each member of our factory will be very short, say, to be much within the mark, four hours a day.

Now next it may be allowable for an artist, that is one whose ordinary work is pleasant and not slavish, to hope that in no factory will all the work, even that necessary four hours work, be mere machine-tending; and it follows from what was said above about machines being used to save labour, that there would be no work which would turn men into mere machines; therefore at least some portion of the work I mean, would be pleasant to do; the machine-tending ought not to require a very long apprenticeship, therefore in no case should any one person be set to run up and down after a machine through all his working hours every day, even so shortened as we have seen; now the attractive work of our factory, that which was pleasant in itself to do, would be of the nature of art; therefore all slavery of work ceases under such a system, for whatever is burdensome about the factory would be taken turn and turn about, and so distributed would cease to be a burden, would be in fact a kind of rest from the more exciting or artistic work.

Thus then would the sting be taken out of the factory system; in which as things now are the socialization of labour which ought to have been a blessing to the community has been turned into a curse by the appropriation of the products of its labour by individuals, for the purpose of gaining for them the very doubtful advantages of a life of special luxury and often of mere idleness; the result of which to the mass of the workers has been a dire slavery, of which long hours of labour, ever increasing strain of labour during those hours, and complete repulsiveness in the work itself have been the greatest evils.

It remains for me in another article to set forth my hopes of the way in which the gathering together of people in such social bodies as properly ordered factories might be, may be utilized for increasing the general pleasure of life and raising its standard material and intellectual; for creating in short that life rich in incident and variety, but free from the strain of mere sordid trouble, the life which the individualist vainly babbles of, but which the Socialist aims at directly and will one day attain to.

JUSTICE, VOLUME I, NUMBER 20,
31 MAY 1884, P. 2.

WORK IN A FACTORY AS IT MIGHT BE III

I have tried to show in former articles that in a duly ordered society, in which people would work for a livelihood and not for the profit of another, a factory might not only be pleasant as to its surroundings, and beautiful in its architecture, but that even the rough and necessary work done in it might be so arranged as to be neither burdensome in itself or of long duration for each worker; but furthermore the organization of such a factory, that is to say of a group of people working in harmonious co-operation towards a useful end, would of itself afford opportunities for increasing the pleasure of life.

To begin with such a factory will surely be a centre of education; any children who seem likely to develope (*sic*) gifts towards its special industry would gradually and without pain, amidst their book learning be drawn into technical instruction which would bring them at last into a thorough apprenticeship for their craft; therefore, the bent of each child having been considered in choosing its instruction and occupation, it is not too much to expect that children so educated will look forward eagerly to the time when they will be allowed to work at turning out real useful wares; a child whose manual dexterity has been developed without undue forcing side by side with its mental intelligence would surely be as eager to handle shuttle, hammer, or what not for the first time as a real workman, and begin making, as a young gentleman now is to get hold of his first gun and begin killing.

This education so begun for the child will continue for the grown man, who will have every opportunity to practice the niceties of his craft, if he be so minded, to carry it to the utmost degree of perfection, not for the purpose of using his extra knowledge and skill to sweat his fellow-workman, but for his own pleasure, and honour as a good artist. Similar opportunities will be afforded him to study, as deeply as the subject will bear, the science on which his craft is founded: besides, a good library and help in studying it will be provided by every productive group (or factory), so that the worker's other voluntary work may be varied by the study of general science or literature.

But further, the factory could supply another educational want by showing the general public how its goods are made. Competition being dead and buried, no new process, no detail of improvements in machinery, would be hidden from the first enquirer; the knowledge which might thus be imparted would foster a general interest in work and in the realities of life, which would surely tend to elevate labour and create a standard of excellence in manufacture, which in its turn would breed a strong motive towards exertion in the workers.

A strange contrast such a state of things would be to that now existing! For to-day the public, and especially that part of it which does not follow any manual occupation, is grossly ignorant of crafts and processes, even when they are carried on at their own doors; so that most of the middle-class are not only defenceless against the most palpable adulterations, but also which is far more serious, are of necessity whole worlds removed from any sympathy with the life of the workshop.

So managed, therefore, the factory by co-operation with other industrial groups will both provide an education for its own workers and contribute its share to the education of citizens outside; but further, it will, as a matter of course, find it easy to provide for mere restful amusements, as it will have ample buildings for library, school-room, dining hall, and the like; social gatherings, musical or dramatic entertainments will obviously be easy to manage under such conditions.

One pleasure – and that a more serious one – I must mention: a pleasure which is unknown at present to the workers, and which even for the classes of ease and leisure only exists in a miserably corrupt and degraded form. I mean the practice of the fine arts: people living under the conditions of life above mentioned, having manual skill, technical and general education, and leisure to use these advantages, are quite sure to develope (*sic*) a love of art, that is to say, a sense of beauty and an interest in life, which, in the long run must stimulate them to the desire for artistic creation, the satisfaction of which is of all pleasures the greatest.

I have started by supposing our group of social labour busying itself in the production of bodily necessaries; but we have seen that such work will only take a small part of each worker's time: their leisure, beyond mere bodily rest and recreation, I have supposed some would employ in perfecting themselves in the niceties of their craft, or in research as to its principles; some would stop there, others would take to studying more general knowledge, but some – and I think most – would find themselves impelled towards the creation of beauty, and would find their opportunities for this under their hands as they worked out their due quota of necessary work for the common good; these would *amuse* themselves by ornamenting the wares they made, and would only be limited in the quantity and quality of such work by artistic considerations as to how much or what kind of work really suited the wares: nor, to meet a possible objection, would there be any danger of such ornamental work degenerating into mere amateur twaddle, such as is now inflicted on the world by fine ladies and gentlemen in search for a refuge from boredom; because our workers will be thoroughly educated as workers and will know well what good work and true finish (not trade finish) mean, and because the public being a body of workers also, everyone in some line or other, will well understand what real work means. Our workers, therefore, will do their artistic work under keen criticism of themselves, their workshop comrades, and a public composed of intelligent workmen.

To add beauty to their necessary daily work will furnish outlet for the artistic aspirations of most men; but further, our factory which is externally beautiful, will not be inside like a clean jail or workhouse; the architecture will come inside in the form of such ornament as may be suitable to the special circumstances. Nor can I see why the highest and most intellectual art, pictures, sculpture, and the like should not adorn a true palace of industry. People living a manly and reasonable life would have no difficulty in refraining from overdoing both these and other adornments; here then would be opportunities for using the special talents of the workers, especially in cases where the daily necessary work afforded scanty scope for artistic work.

Thus our Socialistic factory, besides turning out goods useful to the community, will provide for its own workers work light in duration, and not oppressive in kind, education in childhood and youth. Serious occupation, amusing relaxation, and mere rest for the leisure of the workers, and withal that beauty of surroundings, and the power of producing beauty which are sure to be claimed by those who have leisure, education, and serious occupation.

No one can say that such things are not desirable for the workers; but we Socialists are striving to make them seem not only desirable, but necessary, well knowing that under the present system of society they are impossible of attainment – and why? Because we cannot afford the time, trouble, and thought necessary to obtain them. Again, why cannot we? *Because we are at war*, class against class and man against man; all our time is taken up with that; we are forced to busy ourselves not with the arts of peace, but with the arts of war, which are briefly, trickery and oppression. Under such conditions of life labour can but be a terrible burden, degrading to the workers, more degrading to those who live upon their work.

This is the system which we seek to overthrow, and supplant by one in which labour will no longer be a burden.

JUSTICE, VOLUME I, NUMBER 24,
28 JUNE 1884, P. 2.

TO GENUINE RADICALS

In spite of Irish Coercion Acts, wars against freedom in South Africa and Egypt, emigration swindles, Cobden Club dinners, and the ceaseless hypocrisy of a bogus monarchy, there still exists a Radical party in this country. With the parliamentary leaders of that party, or the phalanx of factory lords which supports it in the hope that such a party may still mean *reasonable liberty* – to sweat the workers at its pleasure; with these we have nothing to do, not even to warn them of the change which is coming over the face of European civilization.

But beyond and besides these there are all those whom they have led into their pinfold of so-called practical politics, wherein they were to be comfortable for ever – if the laws of supply and demand would allow it. It is to this crowd of men, by no means interested in the continuance of the present state of things, but who are tacked on to the skirts of those lords of commerce who are interested in nothing else, that we have a word or two to say. We address ourselves to the political working men, to whom Radicalism seems an advanced creed; who think that by persisting in pushing it at the polling booth and public meetings they will somehow gain good education for their children, a steady and tolerable livelihood undisturbed by disgraceful wars abroad, or ruinous commercial crisis at home, in a word decent life and self-respect: to these, I say, to whom Radicalism has come as the best and most advanced opinion, and who at present know nothing beyond it, we are bound to say and shall do so again and again that they have thrust themselves into a blind alley with nothing but a blank wall at the other end. What are you going to get by remaining mere Radicals? that is what we ask: 'We are going to get universal suffrage.' Yes, you are, but your leaders won't ask for it, or let you do so if they can help it.

'We are going to abolish the House of Lords'[.] Well, you think so, and so do I, but your leaders are going to *reform* that august body; worth taking trouble about isn't it? 'We are going to abolish the monarchy?' I have no doubt about it; but don't tell your leaders of your intentions – not yet – you know you were over hasty with Sir Charles Dilke; you must *permeate* your leaders with your advanced opinions; and when you have done so – excuse me, you must first *have* opinions – you will find that you have got no leaders – and do not want them.

And again, when you have gained Universal Suffrage which at the present *Radical* rate will I should think take you about 150 years, and have by means of it abolished (in another 150 years) the House of Lords, and then the monarchy in another 150, what will you do then? 'Then we shall all be citizens and free!' Yes indeed, as free as the citizens of France are now for instance, who have no hereditary rulers; France, a country which your leaders look on as a commercial concern which is a dangerous rival to England in the markets; but which you should look at as a country sustaining so many millions of fellow-workers, who are not as contented with their *freedom* as you expect to be with yours, when you have abolished your hereditary rule.

'Yes, but by the way we intend to abolish monopolies.' All of them? 'Yes certainly.' My Radical friends, you will abolish monopolies when you know what they are; but I don't think your leaders will give you very accurate information on that point, for they themselves are one and all monopolists.

I am sure that you long for freedom, that you wish to live easily, comfortably, reasonably, without overwork, or the oppression of sordid anxiety for your livelihood; and I must tell you that your leaders, that body of rich and educated people from whom you choose your representatives in Parliament, *cannot* wish to gain this kind of freedom for you, though they may think they do; for their position of riches and cultivated leisure, their dominion in other words, depends on your ignorance, your overwork, your sordid anxiety for a livelihood. We Socialists know that this is so, that there is a necessary and unceasing war between you and your *Masters*, whom you send to Parliament to represent you; and it is this knowledge and neither inborn wickedness nor Tory bribes that forces us in the columns of *Justice* to take up a tone of implacable resistance to the sham popular government, which, whether it is called Liberal or Conservative, is nothing but a committee for arranging the affairs of the land-owners and capitalists and their servants, or in plain English, their slaves, on the basis of servitude for the workers.

Well, I know that you Radicals are angry with us Socialists for disturbing the course of *practical politics* and *reasonable reform*; but go on being Radicals a little longer and see what will happen; only try to make Radicalism real and progressive, take part in affairs yourselves, and don't look on while your leaders pretend to work for you; press them on such points as free education, and the eight hours working day; push them on to attacking the railway monopoly, the vested interests of property in typhoid or cholera, and you will find that you will either force them into avowed Conservativism of the modern cynical type, which allows that slavery is bad for the working man, but will uphold it all the same, or into nameless groups of philanthropical varnishers; you will either force them into avowed tyranny or conscious and obvious hypocrisy, and they will be leaders who in either case can only lead people who are conscious of their slavery. And then when you have unmasked your leaders and are led by principle and not by place-hunters, and are on the way at least to gaining those good things above mentioned, and many others, the Radical party, what of it was worth anything, will be merged into the Party of the People, those whom we now call SOCIALISTS.

JUSTICE, VOLUME I, NUMBER 26,
12 JULY 1884, PP. 4–5.

The Housing of the Poor

Let us on this matter be sure of one thing that as long as there are *poor* people they will be poorly housed; those of our philanthropists who have really dealt with the subject practically have no doubt about that; and consequently all their endeavours are turned to one end, trying namely to get the 'poor' a little less disgracefully housed than they are at present; what they hope to accomplish is very little indeed, and they are so well aware of the difficulties of their accomplishing even this little, that they are terrified at the expression of any hope of realizing a higher standard of comfort in this matter of housing than their most miserable palliation of the evil; because they cannot help feeling that the hope of Revolution must consciously or unconsciously underlie the hope of a somewhat higher standard, and that when this becomes obvious, as it soon must, the dominant class will shudder back from the whole subject, and bring to an end even the niggardly attempts of the 5 per cent. philanthropists. In case it should be said that I exaggerate the humility of the hopes of these latter good people, I refer to a letter written by the most practical of them, Miss Octavia Hill, to the *Pall Mall Gazette* in the past spring, in which she actually allows herself to say that after all it is not so bad as one might think for a whole family to live in one room; by a *room* of course meaning the ordinary 12ft. sq. hutch of an east end house.

Now while we may well feel too stern of mood when we think of the life-long tortures of the 'poor' to laugh even sardonically at such a limitation to the hopes of the philanthropist, I wish our friends to accept my assertion that Miss Hill is a well intentioned, disinterested and kindly person, for in that very fact lies the force of her words as an indictment of our present society; she, a good and eminently practical woman, with plenty of experience as to the extent to which it is possible to move the rich to help, and how far it is possible to use that help for the benefit of the 'poor', is forced to reduce her standard down to this point, lest the spectre of *confiscation* should rise to bar the way against her.

That she is quite right to dread that spectre the behaviour of the present hole-and-corner Royal Commission has doubtless already told her; but we will leave her household paradise of one room for a while, nor will we much concern ourselves with the standard of decent housing held out by those huge masses of brick and mortar, which are rising up in various parts of the town to compete for the workman's scanty shillings against the closeness, squalor and huddled make-shift of the ordinary landlord; bare, sunless, and grim bastilles, are these and look like embodied night-mares of the hopeless thrift of the wage-slave; we will leave them also, and try to give our *masters* the philanthropists some idea of what we consider decent housing for the working classes.

It might be advisable, granting the existence of huge towns for the present, that the houses for workers should be built in tall blocks, in what might be called vertical streets, but that need not prevent ample room in each lodging, so as to include such comforts of space, air, and privacy as every moderately-living middle-class family considers itself entitled to; also it *must* not prevent the lodgings having their due share of pure air and sunlight, necessaries of life which the builders of the above mentioned bastilles do not seem to have thought of at all. This gathering of many small houses into a big tall one would give opportunity for what is also necessary to decent life, that is garden space round each block. This space once obtained, it would be a small matter to make the gardens far more beautiful, as they would be certainly far more cheerful, than the square gardens of the aristocratic quarters of the town now are; it would be natural to have cloisters or covered walking or playing places in them, besides such cheap ornaments as fountains and conduits. Inside the houses, beside such obvious conveniences as common laundries and kitchens, a very little arrangement would give the dwellers in them ample and airy public rooms in addition to their private ones; the top story (*sic*) of each block might well be utilized for such purposes, the great hall for dining in, and for social gathering, being the chief feature of it.

Of course it is understood that such public rooms would not interfere with the ordinary private life of each family or individual; they would be there for use, if any one wished to use them, as they quite certainly would, for the avoidance of waste and the fostering of reasonable pleasure. I cannot be expected to forego the hint that these houses will be in no degree bare or prison-like: many cottages of the 10s. per week agricultural labourer that I have seen avoid that fault at any rate, and I can't see how it is possible that the city craftsman, with his habit of work and almost instinctive general capacity, should err on that side, if he had any starting point of hope given him, and proper leisure from mere bread-winning toil. I am quite sure that due co-operation among the men of diverse crafts who would inhabit these houses would make them not merely comfortable and pretty, but beautiful even.

The possession of space and pure air, with the determination not to live in the midst of ugliness, which relief from anxiety and overwork would give our mechanics, who are ingenious and ready-witted still in spite of their slavery, would supply the stimulus for such town-houses being made proper dwellings for human beings, even in the transition period between the anarchy of to-day and the social order which is to come. A fair portion of the earth's surface, due leisure for the exercise of thought, ingenuity, and fancy; that is all we ask for making our dwellings healthful, pleasant, and beautiful. Yes, that is *all!* Ah, fellow-workers, it is no use asking our *masters* for these necessaries: they *cannot* give them to us; there they sit in the Royal Commission asking – the Lord knows who – whether we have got these good things now, and whether if we have not got them we want them!

Understand this clearly, as long as labour, that is the lives of strong and deft men; is a *commodity* which can only be bought when it yields a profit to the non-worker, we cannot be allowed to use the earth to *live on* like men; it is all wanted for us to *work on* like machines; and just as much of the produce of our work will be given to us as will keep the *machines* going.

Workmen of England, you are just now agitating or being agitated for the purpose of obtaining the suffrage for some of you who have not had it before; this you do, I am ready to believe, with the ultimate intention of getting the suffrage for all adult persons. This agitation may be worth the trouble if you make up your minds that when you get the suffrage you will vote that you shall be machines no longer, and see that your vote is carried out. For what is a machine? Is it not a force of labour which has no control over its labour, but must be set a-going by a master?

Fellow-workers, what you have to do is to determine that you will be men, not machines, and will have full control as a body over your own labour, that you will organize it for the good of each of you and all of you. If you determine on this whatever it may cost, and it is worth any cost, you will obtain it, with the suffrage or without it: if you do not so determine, you may get the suffrage, but it will be given to machines; and then as to this matter of housing you can at the best only be housed as careful masters house their machines. Alas! I fear that many of you will be housed as *careless* masters house them.

JUSTICE, VOLUME I, NUMBER 27,
19 JULY 1884, PP. 4–5

SOCIALISM IN ENGLAND IN 1884

Some three years ago anyone who had predicted the new birth of Socialism in England would have been looked upon as a dreamer, if not crazy; whatever hopes democracy had were centred on the more advanced wing of the Liberal party, which had just carried that queer composite body to victory almost in spite of itself: many words need not be wasted in the columns of *Justice* in talking of the speedy disappointment of any hopes for the party of the people which had been founded on that Liberal victory, and to those of us who had most faith in progress as an idea, the outlook seemed to be nothing better than a dreary waste of perpetual Whig-Liberal rule, feeble and pedantic, except where coercion was dealt out with a *liberal* hand to the Irish, desperate at the new disappointment which fell on them with the accession to power of the 'great Liberal party'. This seemed the outlook, I say, only relieved by the helpless grumblings of a few Radicals who really meant what they had said while the Tories were still in power, and a still fewer irreconcilables, who were at heart Socialists.

That the outlook is now so different may be partly due to the disappointment caused by the cool way in which the Liberal leaders swallowed all their promises; the party of the people could not be looked for in that direction, among the men (and they were Radicals too) who cheered coercion to the echo, and seemed rejoiced to find that they had not deserved the jeers of their Tory opponents, but could be as good Jingoes as the best when occasion served. But though this disappointment might have taken some men out of the Liberal camp, it would have but landed them as disgusted non-politicals, if there had not been forming another party for them to join and in which they might be actively useful;

Socialism was not dead in England in spite of all appearances to the contrary, and the Democratic Federation by its out-spoken resistance to coercion in Ireland, and later by its courageous, though abortive, protest against the abolition of the right of asylum in England, had earned the right of being considered the one organization which cherished the rights of the people. With that object in view it was impossible for it to stop short of a direct declaration of adhesion to the principles of Socialism, which declaration it made by the publication last year of the manifesto 'Socialism made Plain', which has since been so widely distributed.

It does not seem too much to say that the consequences of this step will be of the greatest importance; it is true that many thoughtful middle-class men were turning to Socialism in this country as the only scheme that gave any hope of escaping from the corruption of society which they have felt so bitterly, and that no blindness of our rulers or carelessness of our literary leaders would long have kept them from the serious study of Socialism; but such a school of thinkers might long have remained a school of cultivated thinkers only, to whom the social revolution would have been but a happy dream.

The hope of the speedy advent of that Revolution is now being instilled into thousands by the action of the Democratic Federation, and Socialism is rapidly becoming something more in this country than a speculative philosophy; its practicability is being tested by our propaganda, by the preaching of this real gospel to those that do indeed in their own persons need a new gospel, if their children are not to sink lower in the scale of humanity than any generation of Englishmen yet born. True it is that their very need for revolution, the depth to which the slavery of competition for subsistence wages has eaten into them, so to say, makes it harder for them to conceive of any possibility of a change; yet undoubtedly the *hope* is spreading, and even far more speedily than some of us would have thought possible a little time ago; and it is clear that when the *hope* is once received into the hearts of the mass of our people, the beginning of the new day is at hand.

Here then is a very different state of things from that which existed in the first days of the present Parliament. The Tory party destroyed; the Liberal party a mere set of groups only held together by a more than half hypocritical respect for Mr Gladstone; the foundations of a European war carefully laid by the contending factions, neither of which have any other idea of policy than simply drifting; an agitation against the Constitution set agoing as a piece of political tactics, which may be found more difficult to manage than some at least of the Liberal leaders think – that is the outlook of ordinary politics.

Meantime Society is permeated by an uneasy feeling that all is not quite right; if it were not so serious it would be ludicrous indeed to note the feverish anxiety of our philanthropists both personally and as a body to prove that their nostrums are really of *some* use. 'Society' is sick, and like the devil under like circumstances, would fain be a saint.

It is not wonderful that intelligent middle-class men should be deeply struck by all this and should find themselves Socialists almost without knowing it. As I have said, if their adhesion to the cause were all, there would be little chance of a speedy and *orderly* Revolution in England; it would come indeed, but most probably with spasms of mere misery and starvation emphasized by hunger riots; the intelligent determination of the workers to put an end to wage-slavery and capitalism by nationalizing all the means of production and exchange is the one thing necessary for carrying on a *civilized* revolution.

There are cheering signs on all sides that this will not be lacking to us in England. Those whom Socialism once gets hold of show a real devotion to the cause which may well be called 'religious'. One thing they have to add to that devotion, and we shall be on the road to victory; that one thing is *organization*. I hope our comrades will excuse me giving this one hint on the occasion of the Democratic Federation commemorating its fourth year of existence.

JUSTICE, VOLUME I, NUMBER 30,
9 AUGUST 1884, P. 4

Uncrowned Kings

Most people who profess Liberal opinions doubtless please themselves by thinking that the reign of absolutism is at an end in this country, that for us kings are done with, since the live image or puppet of a so-called constitutional monarchy is capable of performing no more dreadful function than that of boring itself and all those with whom it comes into contact, and of providing a constant centre of hypocrisy and corruption for the rich classes, if indeed any thing could make that corruption worse which seems now rapidly approaching its climax, and carrying us on toward revolution.

Nevertheless though the old kingship may be dead, at least in England, we may perhaps have in these latter days fashioned a new kingship, not the less dangerous because it is not so obvious and brutal as the old one. Some of our Positivist friends not long ago were hugging themselves on what seemed to them, not so wrongly, the tendency of modern democracy to personal government; of modern democracy, that is, under class domination – a morally corrected essence of which is the political ideal of Positivism. In truth we Socialists may well take note of three kings who have ruled the sheepish multitude within the last thirty years of more or less reformed parliamentary government, and bear in mind how futile its boasts of reasonable freedom have been within our own immediate knowledge. Palmerston, Beaconsfield and Gladstone; when one failed, another must be chosen, we could not do without a king: the two first are dead, and we may pass them by, the first with merely the sense of shame which the mere mention of Palmerston's name calls up to us at the thought of the disgraces we let him drag us through; as to the second, we Radicals or ex-Radicals can scarcely escape another touch of shame at the memory of our helplessness as we watched the moves of his fantastic game, doubtless as amusing and profitable to him as it was bewildering and fruitless to us. However let that pass, since both these two are dead; the one who is alive, Mr Gladstone, is as a personality a more complicated problem than either of the others, I mean for the study o[f] the dramatist or novelist: with which study we need not trouble ourselves, for to us as people who want to get on he simply represents a certain amount of obstruction, not so much because of his genuine Conservative instincts which lead him to make for ever just such concessions as may seem to serve to bolster up our present system o[f] slavery, not so much for this, because the course of events will inevitably reject such concessions, and force on the real demand for revolution; rather he is obstructive because of the stupefying influence of his kingship which stops people's qualms of conscience, relieves them of their sense of responsibility, and gives them just one duty to fulfill (*sic*) – shouting out for their leader; a leader too who for many years past has been careful of one thing at least – not to lead.

Surely Mr Gladstone's hearers of last Saturday must have been as one is in a dream, when one sets out to see some great cathedral or temple of the Gods, and finds it nothing but a jerry-built Little Bethel; but then (so strange is the compulsion of dreams) has to persuade oneself that after all it is all right. In sober earnest this clinging to the personality of a mere politician; a man by his very profession bound to humbug at least his followers, and often, as in Mr Gladstone's case, himself also – it is this refinement of flunkeyism which makes one almost despair of getting anyone who bears any party name to look at realities, and try to deal with them himself.

I have appealed to Radicals in these columns before, I do so again now, and beg them to lay aside this worship of names; to accept *themselves* a little responsibility for themselves, for the dreary wretched lives which they and their brethren lead: to ask themselves if they have all they want except the franchise; all that a man ought to want, and how they are going to get it; to ask themselves if they really think that a reformed House of Lords, whatever that may mean, or an Elected Second Chamber, with the First Chamber to help them, would or could give them anything of what they want. I entreat them to ask themselves why they are dirty, ignorant, ill-fed, ill-clad, ill-housed, and when they have found out, or rather when they have gained an inkling of it, or even before, let them ask Mr Gladstone why they are all this, why they are *slaves*, and if he can't tell them, let them try to do without him, and go elsewhere for leading. Only I warn them let them have plenty of leaders, all knowing the way, all with one tale in their mouths, and let them take care that these said leaders *lead*. I think they will then take the road towards Social Revolution.

JUSTICE, VOLUME I, NUMBER 34,
6 SEPTEMBER 1884, P. 4

THE HAMMERSMITH COSTERMONGERS

The case of the Hammersmith costermongers has already been briefly alluded to in *Justice*: it is what is commonly called a 'hard case', a phrase however which means very different things according to the position of those to whom it is applied, meaning to some people the loss of a hundred pounds or so, which everyone can see they ought not to lose, but which loss will only inconvenience them; while to others it means the loss of livelihood; which latter loss is to be dreaded by the Hammersmith costermongers, especially if the other local boards imitate the conduct of the Hammersmith magnates. The facts if the readers have not noticed them are briefly these: the costermongers have been used from time immemorial to hold a curb-stone (*sic*) market in King Street on Saturday evenings, obviously to the inconvenience of the mass of the people about, who are quite poor enough to be forced to follow out one part of a maxim of bourgeois political economy and buy in the cheapest market. The Hammersmith Board of Works has in its wisdom deemed that the general public is seriously damaged by the busy, but as a rule quite orderly, crowd, which this curb-stone (*sic*) market attracts, and has taken the opportunity of the recent opening of the tram-line to order the costermongers to clear their barrows away, and after some preliminary skirmishing in which they pressed the Kensington magistrates (in vain) to impose serious fines or imprisonment on the one or two cases tried, have instructed our old acquaintance Mr Besley to take out 16 summonses in the Hammersmith Court against these poor men as a beginning of the serious attack on them. Meanwhile defenceless as the costermongers might seem to be, they have bestirred themselves, and our friend Mr Applebee has canvassed the whole of the shopkeepers in King Street for their opinion as to this so-called nuisance of [a] curb-stone (*sic*) market: the result of which has been that while scarcely anyone has ventured to declare openly for the tyranny of the Board, a few have to be reckoned as neutrals, and by far the greater number have declared that they at least are not inconvenienced by the 'nuisance' aforesaid. It is needless to say that the Board does not trouble its head about all that, and a body of useful, industrious and orderly men are in a fair way to be taught by ruin the meaning of the word 'freedom' as applied to the lives of those who have not by birth, or by force and fraud, acquired the privilege of making other people do their work for them.

The Hammersmith Board have distinguished themselves as tyrants in a small way; and I must say that it is with special shame and indignation that one protests against this notable piece of Bumbledom, when one considers how poor the prize is for which the costermongers are striving; the privilege of being allowed to pick up the crumbs that fall from the children's table: in truth Hammersmith High Street is a sad enough sight on a Saturday evening, both buyers and sellers; and 'tis not to be wondered at that Bumble and Co. want to get rid of it; 'Sweep it away into the back streets, and let us forget it! Who is responsible? Not we!'

Fellow workers, if we could only instil some hope of getting out of this dismal skinflint poverty into such men as these who are intelligent and energetic enough, if they could but see the hope; if we could only first raise their discontent and then organize it, Bumble might have a rough awakening one of these days.

Justice, Volume I, Number 36,
20 September 1884, p. 3

AN APPEAL TO THE JUST

There are doubtless many worthy people who shudder at the word Socialism, who, nevertheless wish sincerely to see the condition of the people bettered, and who generally console themselves when they hear of any of the horrors of our capitalist civilization by thinking, 'well, at any rate, things are getting better steadily'. Ask them how they are getting better, and they will answer you with, 'the general spreading of education', 'the growth of liberal ideas among the working-classes', and such-like vague stuff. Ask them how soon they think this gradual amelioration is likely to abolish poverty for all but the vicious and idle, and they will answer with vague commonplaces again; for the truth is their hope is a languid one. Amidst whatever anxieties a bourgeois family may lie under, they are themselves comfortable in condition; and, in truth, have never quite realized that there is any class that is 'uncomfortable', or in plain words overworked, half-starved, and laden with deadly anxieties. Yet it must be supposed that they really do wish, as abovesaid, to reduce the misery and poverty which in a mechanical way they know to be the yoke-fellow of modern progress, and some of them may perhaps begin to think what the differences are between riches and poverty, or, if you will, between well-to-do life and poverty. And when they do, they will presently realize the existence of a vast class living under perpetual oppression and injustice, who are now being educated, in a way, but at all events enough to enable them to read the words of those who are discontented like themselves; and surely they will in time be able to see that this discontented class may be a danger to their comfort and refinement, and that they had best turn their attention to dealing with that discontent before it is too late; and then when they do so they will find out that their vague remedies to have effect at some vague future will be utterly useless, that it will be utterly impossible to make the discontented believe in their being intended to remedy their lot. Whither then will they find themselves obliged to turn to prevent civilization from slipping back from the very doubtful point it has already gained? Where lies any hope for re-construction, and hope for to-morrow even? With the Socialists only; with the much-maligned Socialists, whom they have loaded with all kinds of nick-names and accused of having no thought of anything but destruction.

Even to-day, while the two parliamentary factions are splitting straws over an insufficient Franchise Bill based on no principle, while the different sections of the Liberal party are pulling some one way and some another, some nervously anxious that the question of an hereditary second chamber shall be shelved, and others hotly trying to press it on for immediate solution, (hopelessly enough if they only knew): while the most advanced of the non-Socialist politicians have a vague idea that these political reforms will work not as instruments to gain social advancement, but by a kind of magic will better the condition of the people with nothing further done; while all those sword strokes in the air are going on, the Social-Democratic Federation is preparing an agitation for demanding immediate physical amelioration for those who need it most. It is attacking the cruel farce of *educating* starving children; it is attacking the very heart of misery and degradation in calling on legislation against overwork; it is attacking the poverty growing heavier on our hands every day, by calling for the State to employ for the benefit of the common weal those poor people whom the ferocity of commercial war forbids to earn their own livelihood, or add any wealth to the community.

All these things indeed *we* believe will lead towards Socialism; towards fresh, and ever fresh demands on the part of the workers till all classes are abolished: but if as our Radical friends think at present, our Socialist ideal is impractical and unfeasible, they must admit that in forcing on the attention of our rulers these matters of physical amelioration we are doing their work as well as our own: if when these are attained to, the people becomes contented and asks no more, but turns a deaf ear to our further agitation, they, the Radicals, will have been proved right and we wrong, but the step will at least have been gained. But if on the contrary, as we believe, the attainment of these matters still finds us Socialist agitators at work and listened to, and the step forward has proved to be another rung on the ladder which leads to the realization of our ideal of the common weal founded on the equality of labour, surely it will turn out to have been a foolish thing for those who called themselves advanced politicians to have played the part of reactionists in the first step towards the new order of things. Only I think before we come to that, as I have said before in these columns, we shall have converted all the real Radicals, and those that are left will turn out to be only peculiarly stupid Tories, masquerading in the cast-off clothes of the extinct Whigs.

JUSTICE, VOLUME I, NUMBER 39,
11 OCTOBER 1884, P. 4

THE LORD MAYOR'S SHOW

It would be a hard-hearted person indeed who could either object seriously to or look sourly upon the Lord Mayor's Show as a holiday pageant, an afternoon brightening-up of the hideous and sordid streets of the 'Great Wen', as Cobbett called it; and considering the depths of the degradation of all spectacular art at the present day, it would be too cruel to criticize the spectacle of last Monday from an artistic point of view, even if the columns of *Justice* were the best place in which to do so. But since the Fathers of the City have thought good in one part of their show to call attention to an episode of London history, the murder of Wat Tyler, it may be worth while for the sake of the practical moral to recall to our readers the story of which that murder was the climax; all the more as it has become a sort of nursery tale in which the figures of the wise and pious kingly youth, the sturdy loyal citizen, and the ruffianly agitator have been made to stand out against a dark background of foolish and ignorant armed peasants, knowing not what they asked for.

We will take our tale from that marvellous gallery of pictures of the past, which a contemporary, the aristocratic priest, John Froissart, wrought for us. Priest and Queen's Chaplain though he was, his Gothic love of incident prevents his prejudice from damaging his account of facts too much. Besides it seemed to him so natural that such things should be, that he never thinks of softening any enormity of the lordly tyranny which he served; *hypocritical* tyranny was the invention of a later age.

Says he:– ...'I will speak thereof as it was done, as I was informed, and of the incidents thereof. There was an usage in England and yet is in diverse countries, that the noble men hath great franches over the Commons, and keepeth them in servage: that is their tenants ought by custom to labour the lords' lands, to gather and bring home their cornes, and some to thresh and to fanne, and by servage to make their hay, and hew their wood and bring it home: ...and there be more of these people in England than in any other realm.... These unhappy people began to stir saying, why should they be kept so under like beasts; the which they said they would no longer suffer, for they would be all one.'

In short they objected to exploitation by means of serfdom. The worthy cannon then tells us of the 'imagination of a foolish priest in the county of Kent, called John Ball', who on Sundays after mass used – in fact to hold open air meetings. Into his mouth Froissart puts simple and noble words by no means out of date at present, beginning thus; 'Ah ye good people, the matter goeth not well to pass in England, nor shall do till every thing be common, and there be no villians nor gentlemen, but that we all be united together'. John Ball was imprisoned by the Archbishop, but soon came out again by no means cured of his 'imagination'. The men of the home counties rose, saying that they would march on London, where they hoped to be well received, 'and would so do to the King that there should not be one bondman left in England'. They were 60,000 strong led by John Ball, Jack Straw and Wat Tyler, 'who', says Froissart, 'was indeed a tiler of houses, an ungracious person'. The King's mother the Princess passing through their bands as she came from Canterbury received no sort of harm from them: the townsmen of Rochester were, says Froissart, 'of the same secte' and received them well; they forced the captain of the Castle and some other men-at-arms to go with them as their leaders, and sent from Blackheath where they encamped, Sir John Newton the Captain of Rochester to lay their grievances before the King; the result of which was that the King held a parley with the leaders from his barge off Rotherhithe, but nothing came of it; so they marched into London where they met with no resistance from the citizens; 30,000 of whom, says Froissart 'were of their own sect'. There they broke open the Marshalsea Prison and pillaged the Savoy, the palace of the Duke of Lancaster, the King's uncle, who was as unpopular as need be: otherwise they did little damage, considering how rough the times were.

The Mayor, Sir William Walworth was ready to attack them, but the King and his court were panic-stricken and found the good old plan of temporizing and lying the most convenient. The Earl of Salisbury and the wise men about the King said; 'Sir, if ye can appease them with fairness it were best, and to grant them everything that they desire'.

So a proclamation was issued that they should all draw together to a fair plain place called Mile-end, whereas the people of the city did sport them in the summer season? There the King and his lords met them and asked what were their grievances, 'And such as understood him said, "We wish that ye make us free for ever, and that we may be no more bond, nor so reputed". "Sirs", said the King, "I am well agreed thereto; withdraw you home to your own houses, and leave behind you of every village two or three; and I shall cause writings to be made and seal them with my seal, the which they shall have with them, containing everything that ye demand; and to the intent that ye may be the better assured I shall cause my banners to be delivered into every bailswick, shire and county."'

These promises broke the neck of the rebellion; the country people took their papers and banners and went home happy we must suppose with those very immaterial guarantees. But their leaders knew their masters better and dared to try to hold matters together still; and the next day (Saturday) the rebels met together on Smithfield some 20,000 strong, thither also came the King and his lords from Westminster, intending, as Froissart says, to leave London, but halting at St. Bartholomew's Church on sight of the rebels. Wat Tyler, seeing the halt, spurred up to the King; Froissart with mediæval minuteness gives a strange dramatic dialogue between the two; which was ended by the coming up of the Mayor with a small following secretly armed. It was then pretty much a word and a blow, Walworth unhorsed Wat with a sword stroke on the head, and one Standish or Cavendish, a squire of the King's, finished him with his sword as he lay on the ground. The angry people, seeing their leader fall, advanced with bent bows, but the King met them again boldly enough, promised all redress, and offered himself their captain; and the rebels uncertain and leaderless again began to disperse. Meanwhile the 'party of order' had been drawing to a head, and a large body of well-armed men, seven or eight thousand, came on the field. The King, says the chronicler, prevented a general onslaught of the knights and men-at-arms on the now broken people, but their leaders and spokesmen were forced to deliver up the banners and letters of redress they had received, which latter were torn up before their eyes, and the whole host was dispersed.

John Ball and Jack Straw were hunted out and slain, and their heads with Wat Tyler's stuck on London Bridge.

Then came the reaction of which Froissart tells with great naiveté. The king made a progress through Kent, at every town and village the ring-leaders were hunted out and dealt with; the letters promising redress were torn up solemnly before the people, and the great peril for the privileged was got over. Froissart leaves no doubt in our minds as to how that peril struck him; for he connects this rising of the Kentishmen with the revolt of Ghent, and the rising of the 'unhappy people with the iron mallets at Paris.' But all these things were but as the stirring among the dry bones, terrible as they semed (*sic*) to the rich of that period, and it took a long course of economic events before the power of privilege was even shaken.

Meantime we need make no mistake about the cause for which Wat Tyler and his worthier associate John Ball fell; they were fighting against the fleecing of the people by that particular form of fleecing then in fashion, viz.: serfdom or villeinage, which was already beginning to wane before the advance of the industrial gilds. We need not grumble therefore if the sword of St Paul in the city arms is sometimes innocently taken for Wat Tyler's instrument of martyrdom, however little the worthy city fathers may like the construction we should put on that legend. Nor will we say that he and John Ball died for nothing, however doleful is the story (an oft repeated one) of the stout men of Kent breaking up half in fear and irresolution, half deluded by the lies and empty promises of their masters, to whom, as ever, any course seemed good that enabled them to keep the people down.

JUSTICE, VOLUME I, NUMBER 44,
15 NOVEMBER 1884, P. 2

THE HACKNEY ELECTION

The Hackney Liberals have returned Professor Stuart by a sufficiently large majority, and the Liberal press has been engaged in singing the praises of the new member, who it seems is the very pattern of a useful politician and much advanced thinker; this may be, but if a man is to be judged by his utterances we take the liberty of thinking all this jubilant praise a little overdone. If Professor Stuart has very advanced opinions he at least did not venture to put them forward even before such a very Radical constituency as Hackney; in point of fact so-called 'fair trade' and so-called free-trade seem to have been the issues joined at Hackney; and, ably as this subject was treated in *Justice* in a late number, we may in passing once more call attention to the fact that for the workers this is just a battle of Kites and Crows. They may be sure that whether the landlords tax their victuals in order to gain higher rents by means of protection, or the capitalists lower their wages, and land them in such terribly bad times as the present by means of free trade, they will be fleeced all the same until they make up their minds to take matters into their own hands.

We cannot help lamenting that the Hackney Radicals, who have lately issued so Democratic a programme, should have been so blinded by the excitement of an electoral contest as not to see this fact. Nothing could have been more common-place and unsatisfactory than Professor Stuart's election speeches; he is obviously taking his place in the House of Commons as an advocate (one might hope the last new one henceforward) of *laissez faire*, and if the Hackney Radicals interpret Radicalism thus, we can only say that they have been converted to Whiggery with strange swiftness and completeness. It must be supposed however that this is not quite the case, but that in the first place they were terrified at the idea of their being represented by such an extinct monster as a protectionist Tory; and that in the second place they were a little doubtful as to whither their Radicalism would lead them in the long run. Now as to the first fear, we must say that even supposing the said queer monster had been returned, it would not have damaged Radicalism so much as the watering down of the present very feeble Radical party in the House by such a man as Professor Stuart, who *laissez faire* principles (?) are rapidly becoming as extinct as landlord Protection itself; and it is disappointing indeed that the Hackney Radicals could see no other course open to them than voting for a man who does not hold their views. If they had no candidate whom they could vote for with a clear conscience, why should they have voted at all? Abstention from the poll accompanied by a protest so distinct as to make it obvious that the abstention was organized, and was the result, not of political languor, but of political insight, would have read a sharp lesson to those politicians, so-called Radicals, who are hanging about waiting to see how the cat will jump.

As to that last matter we must once again assure our Radical friends that there is no doubt about it, and that if Radical is to mean anything else than Whig 'writ large', it must mean some one who claims full political power for the people, *in order* that it may be used by them for dealing with the social questions which really concern them.

Amongst other signs of the times we may draw our Radical friend's attention to the fact that the *Pall Mall Gazette* has turned towards this view the half eye which it could spare from overlooking its grand jingo enterprise, and even quoted with approval Henry George's statement that the late election in America had destroyed the two old parties there, and that a new party was springing up in their place whose business it would be to solve the social questions of the day.

Yes, that is it; it takes no prophet to see that Society will presently wake up and find the Whigs extinct, the Liberals extinct, the true Radicals rapidly becoming Socialists and facing a party which will have been forced to drop its mask; which may be called Tory or what you will, but which proclaims at last without hypocrisy its real maxim, '*Keep them Down*'.

JUSTICE, VOLUME I, NUMBER 46,
29 NOVEMBER 1884, P. 4

PHILANTHROPISTS

As the word 'philanthropist' is pretty often used in the columns of *Justice*, it may be worth while to write a short chapter on the natural history of this species of man, with as little bitterness or even grumbling as may be; though it must be admitted that 'their ways and their manners' are often not a little trying to those who are doing their best to get the 'poor' to understand the real causes of their poverty, so that they may themselves attack the disease instead of sitting hopeless while others feebly palliate its worse symptoms.

Well, the Philanthropists may, first of all, be broadly divided into two kinds, the old and the new, or the uneconomical and the economical; the first give, I think, with some pleasure in the act of giving, with pity also, and perhaps are able to imagine the transient pleasure which their gifts may confer on the poor wretches that receive them; they have of course no other hope than this transient good done to individuals, for the bitter words of the Judæo-Christian chronicler, 'The poor ye have always with you', convey to their minds no taunt against their own privileged comfort, but are accepted in all good faith as a statement of providential fact, at which neither the poor nor the rich have any right to repine. These good souls are clearly survivals from the alms-givers of the mediæval Church, and sometimes have a share of the imaginatively pious generosity of the days before the rise of Capitalism drove both Catholics and Protestants into mere hypocrisy; doubtless, if ever they have heard of Socialism it has only been [to] shudder at its wickedness; nevertheless we have no call to class them as enemies, and may pass by them easily, if for no other reason, yet at least because they are nearly extinct and have no principles to impress on society, and no power to impress them if they had them.

The other kind of Philanthropist, the economical kind, may again be sub-divided into two varieties, the first may be called the preaching Philanthropists and are the money-bags of the species, giving sums which, though not very large relatively to the profits which they have squeezed out of labour, look comfortable enough to a man of moderate means; but it seems to me that they take it out in preaching: unlike the almsgivers of past times to whom suffering was suffering and to be alleviated however it had been incurred, these men are stern moralists, and from amidst their luxury preach the virtues of Stoic philosophy to the artizan and the labourer, the minute and (individually) helpless portions of the great profit-grinding machine of Labour; temperance and thrift are the gods which they set up to be worshipped by the wage-slaves whose hard earnings they themselves waste in vulgar ostentation and aimless degrading luxury. From the unfathomable depths of their stupidity they have fished up the idea that the 'lower classes' can be 'raised', that is, made permanently serviceable as machines to be depended upon, by holding out to them the hope of comfort founded on thrift and temperance, by which they mean if they knew it, as they probably do not, a life degraded by the meanest pinching niggardliness. It is almost incredible that these preachers should venture to preach to working-people and expect to be believed; but it is thought by some that they are mostly not so much conscious hypocrites, as very specially callous and stupid rich men soaked through and through with middle-class prejudice.

There remains the second variety of the economical kind of philanthropists, who might be called philanthropists proper. I am sorry to have to say of them that they to a great extent accept the doctrines of the preacher philanthropists; sorry, because they often work hard and disinterestedly at their wizened scheme for the regeneration of Society: as a rule they would do anything towards raising the condition of the workers which would not involve an encroachment on the profits of the capitalist; they have made up their minds that the basis of society cannot be altered; and this, coupled with the fact that their well-intentioned work brings them face to face with the wretchedness of our society, drives them into a despairing callousness which not seldom places them in an attitude very like hostility to the people whom they mean to help: in short their desperate efforts to ignore the great fact of the antagonism of classes makes that fact the clearer to those who have eyes to see. Their ideal of comfort and decency is so low that they are ready to accept as tolerable a state of things that would be intolerable except to a slave class; their making the best of it sometimes goes so far (to my certain knowledge) as to praise as rather pleasant places those parts of Stepney and Bethnal Green which are not quite the worst: their self-satisfaction at the minute palliatives of the misery which they work is absolutely sickening to a Socialist, who knows what kind of life the workers might obtain for themselves, if the hope of the destruction of profit-mongering could once take a hold of them.

We many of us have experienced the bitter hostility of these philanthropists to Socialism, which in point of fact they realize as the foe doomed if successful to make an end of their occupation; a foe which would quite change that class on which they try their benevolent experiments, and which they look upon meantime as a necessary appendage of capital, would convert it into an all-powerful organization that would at last absorb all society, and become nothing less than the State.

And yet, though these well intentioned people look upon us as their enemies, I don't think we need accept the position; we must at least take what we can get from them; take for instance as an instalment of a decent London the parks and gardens which their efforts have done much to get for us. What we would press upon them is that they should get a higher ideal before them than turning the life of the workers into that of a well-conducted reformatory or benevolent prison; and that they should understand that when things are done not *for* the workers but *by* them, an ideal will present itself with great distinctness to the workers themselves, which will not mean living on as little as you can, so as not to disturb the course of profit-grinding, but rather living a plentiful, generous, un-anxious life, the first quite necessary step to higher ideals yet.

Let the philanthropists think of this and allow some foresight to pierce their armour of callousness, and then we think many of them, those of them who are not mere 'orderers about' and busy bodies, would look towards Socialism as a faith which would give them a fresh and more hopeful career; we could find plenty for them to do.

JUSTICE, VOLUME I, NUMBER 49,
20 DECEMBER 1884, P. 2

Contributions to *Commonweal*

1885

INTRODUCTORY

We beg our readers' leave for a few words in which to introduce to them this Socialist journal, *The Commonweal.* In the first place we ask them to understand that the Editor and Sub-Editor of *The Commonweal* are acting as delegates of the Socialist League, and under its direct control: any slip in principles, therefore, and mis-statement of the aims or tactics of the League, are liable to correction from the representatives of that body.

As to the conduct of *The Commonweal*, it must be remembered that it has one aim – the propagation of Socialism. We shall not, therefore, make any excuses for what may be thought journalistic short-comings, if we can but manage to attract attention to the study of our principles from those who have not yet thought of Socialism, or who are, as often happens, bitterly hostile to them through ignorance; or if we can help those whose feelings are drawing them towards the cause of the workers, but who need definite instruction as to its aims and methods. To awaken the sluggish, to strengthen the waverers, to instruct the seekers after truth; these are high aims, yet not too high for a journal that claims to be Socialistic, and we hope by patience and zeal to accomplish them.

It is our duty to attack unsparingly the miserable system which would make all civilization end in a society of rich and poor, of slaves and slave-owners. In all its details we must attack it; but in doing so we shall avoid mere personalities, not for the sake of escaping the accusations of bad taste and bitterness, which doubtless will in any case be flung at us, but because it is illogical to attack those men, monstrous as their position is, who are themselves mere helpless wheels in the terrible machine of modern commerce. To attack such persons, unless they put themselves forward as the representatives of the system, implies the belief that the decency or benevolence of their conduct would usefully palliate the evils of that system; an implication against which we protest from the outset.

The Commonweal will only deal with political matters when they directly affect the progress of the Cause. We assume as a matter of course that a government of privileged persons, hereditary and commercial, cannot act usefully or rightly towards the community; their position forbids it; their arrangements for the distribution of the plunder of the workers, their struggles for the national share of the exploitation of barbarous peoples are nothing to us except so far as they may give us an opportunity of instilling Socialism into men's minds, or of organizing discontent into Socialism.

We invite from all, Socialists or others, free discussion of anything we put forward, in the belief that even an uninstructed attack may elicit useful information which might otherwise have lain dormant.

Our articles will, for the most part, be of an educational nature: there will be a series on historical revolutions, expositions of the scientific basis of Socialism, and contributions from men of various nationalities.

Lastly, a word of appeal, to the workers chiefly. It is not only that whatever we say is professedly directly in their interest: much more it is that through them alone, through the slaves of society, we look for its regeneration, for its elevation from its present corruption and misery. We cannot pretend to think that they, the workers, as yet know much of the principles of the cause that rests upon them, or their own cause, in fact. We beseech them to help us in spreading knowledge of those principles amongst their fellows, that as we believe they will now find us honest, so their support may make us resolute, patient, and hopeful – in a word, successful in our efforts for the furtherance of the cause we have at heart.

COMMONWEAL, VOLUME I, NUMBER 1,
FEBRUARY 1885, P. 1

THE WORKER'S SHARE OF ART

I can imagine some of our comrades smiling bitterly at the above title, and wondering what a Socialist journal can have to do with art; so I begin by saying that I understand only too thoroughly how 'unpractical' the subject is while the present system of capital and wages last. Indeed that is my text.

What, however, *is* art? whence does it spring? Art is man's embodied expression of interest in the life of man; it springs from man's pleasure in his life; pleasure we must call it, taking all human life together, however much it may be broken by the grief and trouble of individuals; and as it is the expression of pleasure in life generally, in the memory of the deeds of the past, and the hope of those of the future, so it is especially the expression of man's pleasure in the deeds of the present; in his work.

Yes, that may well seem strange to us at present! Men to-day may see the pleasure of unproductive energy – energy put forth in games and sports; but in productive energy – in the task which must be finished before we can eat, the task which will begin again to-morrow, and many a to-morrow without change or end till *we* are ended – pleasure in that?

Yet I repeat that the chief source of art is man's pleasure in his daily necessary work, which expresses itself and is embodied in that work itself; nothing else can make the common surroundings of life beautiful, and whenever they are beautiful it is a sign that men's work has pleasure in it, however they may suffer otherwise. It is the lack of this pleasure in daily work which has made our towns and habitations sordid and hideous, insults to the beauty of the earth which they disfigure, and all the accessories of life mean, trivial, ugly – in a word, *vulgar*. Terrible as this is to endure in the present, there is a hope in it for the future; for surely it is but just that outward ugliness and disgrace should be the result of the slavery and misery of the people; and that slavery and misery once changed, it is but reasonable to expect that external ugliness will give place to beauty, the sign of free and happy work.

Meantime, be sure that nothing else will produce even a reasonable semblance of art; for, think of it! the workers, by means of whose hands the mass of art must be made, are forced by the commercial system to live, even at the best, in places so squalid and hideous that no one could live in them and keep his sanity without losing all sense of beauty and enjoyment of life. The advance of the industrial army under its 'captains of industry' (save the mark!) is traced, like the advance of other armies, in the ruin of the peace and loveliness of [the] earth's surface, and nature, who will have us live at any cost, compels us to *get used* to our degradation at the expense of losing our manhood, and producing children doomed to live less like men than ourselves. Men living amidst such ugliness cannot conceive of beauty, and, therefore, cannot express it.

Nor is it only the workers who feel this misery (and I rejoice over that, at any rate). The higher or more intellectual arts suffer with the industrial ones. The artists, the aim of whose lives it is to produce beauty and interest, are deprived of the materials for their works in real life, since all around them is ugly and vulgar. They are driven into seeking their materials in the imaginations of past ages, or into giving the lie to their own sense of beauty and knowledge of it by sentimentalizing and falsifying the life which goes on around them; and so, in spite of all their talent, intellect and enthusiasm, produce little which is not contemptible when matched against the works of the non-commercial ages. Nor must we forget that whatever is produced that is worth anything is the work of men who are in rebellion against the corrupt society of to-day – rebellion sometimes open, sometimes veiled under cynicism, but by which in any case lives are wasted in a struggle, too often vain, against their fellow-men, which ought to be used for the exercise of special gifts for the benefit of the world.

High and low, therefore, slaveholders and slaves, we lack beauty in our lives, or, in other words, man-like pleasure. This absence of pleasure is the second gift to the world which the development of commercialism has added to its first gift of a propertiless proletariat. Nothing else but the grinding of this iron system could have reduced the civilized world to vulgarity. The theory that art is sick *because* people have turned their attention to science is without foundation. It is true that science is allowed to live because profit can be made of her, and men, who must find some outlet for their energies, turn to her, since she exists, though only as the slave (but now the rebellious slave) of capital; whereas when art is fairly in the clutch of profit-grinding she dies, and leaves behind her but her phantom of *sham* art as the futile slave of the capitalist.

Strange as it may seem, therefore, to some people, it is as true as strange, that Socialism, which has been commonly supposed to tend to mere Utilitarianism, is the only hope of the arts. It may be, indeed, that till the social revolution is fully accomplished, and perhaps for a little while afterwards, men's surroundings may go on getting plainer, grimmer, and barer. I say for a little while afterwards, because it may take men some time to shake off the habits of penury on the one hand and inane luxury on the other, which have been forced on them by commercialism. But even in that there is hope; for it is at least possible that all the old superstitions and conventionalities of art have got to be swept away before art can be born again; that before that new birth we shall have to be left bare of everything that has been called art; that we shall have nothing left us but the materials of art, that is the human race with its aspirations and passions and its home, the earth; on which materials we shall have to use these tools, leisure and desire.

Yet, though that may be, it is not likely that we shall quite recognize it; it is probable that it will come so gradually that it will not be obvious to our eyes. Maybe, indeed, art is sick to death even now, and nothing but its already half-dead body is left upon the earth: but also, may we not hope that we shall not have to wait for the new birth of art till we attain the peace of the realized New Order? Is it not at least possible, on the other hand, that what will give the death-blow to the vulgarity of life which enwraps us all now will be the great tragedy of Social Revolution, and that the worker will then once more begin to have a share in art, when he begins to see his aim clear before him – his aim of a share of real life for all men – and when his struggle for that aim has begun? It is not the excitement of battling for a great and worthy end which is the foe to art, but the dead weight of sordid, unrelieved anxiety, the anxiety for the daily earning of a wretched pittance by labour degrading at once to body and mind, both by its excess and by its mechanical nature.

In any case, the leisure which Socialism above all things aims at obtaining for the worker is also the very thing that breeds desire – desire for beauty, for knowledge, for more abundant life, in short. Once more, that leisure and desire are sure to produce art, and without them nothing but sham art, void of life or reason for existence, can be produced: therefore not only the worker, but the world in general, will have no share in art till our present commercial society gives place to real society – to Socialism. I know this subject is too serious and difficult to treat properly in one short article. I will ask our readers, therefore, to consider this as an introduction to the consideration of the relations of industrial labour to art.

COMMONWEAL, VOLUME I, NUMBER 3,
APRIL 1885, PP. 18–19

UNATTRACTIVE LABOUR

For our purpose of considering the relations of labour to industrial art, the wares made at the present day, the articles made for the market that is, may be divided into two classes – those that have some pretensions to be considered ornamental, and those that have not. The latter, I suppose, is much the larger class; but at any rate the important thing to remember is that there is this difference. Now it seems to me necessary to understand that everything made by man must be either ugly or beautiful. Neutrality is impossible in man's handiwork. But in times past, before the commercial age, it did not follow that a piece of handiwork was ugly because it did not aim at being ornamental; it had a certain use, which it fulfilled, and at the same time, without apparent effort of the maker, it was beautiful. *It grew so*, one may say, exactly as a piece of Nature does. That is far from being the case now. In the wares which are made for utility only, it is rare that you find any beauty of form; they have a natural tendency to grow ugly, like a London starveling has. Even in the commonest things, such as fences in fields and other simple agricultural appliances, except for a few survivals, matters which have accidently clung to old traditions, ugliness is the rule. An ordinary house, or piece of furniture or of attire, is not only not beautiful, it is aggressively and actively ugly, and we assume as a matter of course that it must be so. And if we have a mind for any beauty (or pretence of it), we must make a definite effort; we must give our orders for an ornamental article to be made for us. And I may say, in passing, that, order as we please, we cannot always get our order executed. The sense of beauty and power of expressing it, under the present circumstances, is one of the rarest of gifts, so that the ordinary public have to put up with such pretence to beauty as the so-called ornamental class of wares can furnish to them. Therefore, while the rich man, by spending much money, can gather about him a certain amount of beauty, and while the man of moderate means may be able to attain the same end by taking an infinitude of trouble, the working man, who has no time to take trouble and no money to enable him to dispense with it, must put up with the lack of beauty altogether. Here, then, is a strange thing, that whereas in the pre-commercial ages we had beauty without paying for it, it has now become an article of the market, and, like most other market articles, is so shamefully adulterated that we can scarcely buy it even for our money.

I know that to many people this will seem a small matter, because only those (and how few they are!) who can make their surroundings decent can understand the full horror, the dullness and poverty of life which it involves. For my part, having regard to the general happiness of the race, I say without shrinking that the bloodiest of violent revolutions would be a light price to pay for the righting of this wrong.

For this is not a matter of accident, but springs from the the (*sic*) form which the slavery of the many has taken in our days. It is but one of the consequences of wage-slavery. Until that wage-slavery was completed and crowned by the revolution of the great machine industries, there was some attractiveness in the work of the artisan. There is now none, or next to none; and the reason why the ornamental wares above-mentioned are so adulterated is because the very ornament itself is but a part of the machine labour, made to sell, and not for use, whether it be done by human machines or non-human ones. It is no exaggeration to say that our civilization has destroyed the attractiveness of labour, and that by more means than one: by lengthening the hours of labour: by intensifying the labour during its continuance; by the forcing of the workmen into noisy, dirty, crowded factories; by the aggregation of the population into cities and manufacturing districts, and the consequent destruction of all beauty and decency of surroundings; by the levelling [of] all intelligence and excellence of workmanship by means of machinery, and the consequent gradual extinction of the skilled craftsman. All this is the exact contrary of the conditions under which the spontaneous art of past ages was produced. Our forefathers of the Middle Ages worked shorter hours than we do (even since the passing of the Factory Acts) and had more holidays. They worked deliberately and thoughtfully as all artists do; they worked in their own homes and had plenty of elbow room; the unspoiled country came up to their very doors and, except in their dreams of hell – if even there – they could have had no conception of the glories of the Black Country or South Lancashire, which I heard a famous demagogue the other night enumerating among the blessings of peace, such peace as he could conceive of. Finally, all their work depended on their own skill of hand and invention, and never failed to show signs of that in its beauty and fitness; it was even thought wrong to cheat people by adulteration of goods, so that (strange to say) good work was creditable to the worker.

Thus the development of the commercial system crowned by the revolution of the great machine industries has deprived us of the attractiveness of labour, and as far as it could of the beauty of the earth. What, then, has it left us? The hope of revolution, of the transformation of civilization, now become on the face of it a mere corruption and curse to the world, into Socialism, which will set free the hands and minds of men for the production and safeguarding of the beauty of life.

I have said that our mediæval forefathers worked shorter hours than we do; but yet they worked far too long, and of course suffered from their special form of slavery, that is serfdom, and other arbitrary violence of the privileged classes, and their chances of successful rebellion were pretty much *nil*. It was necessary that they should struggle upwards till they formed a middle-class and created commerce with its proletariat doomed to ceaseless unattractive dull labour, in place of the old yeoman and craftsguildsman with his pleasant easy-going work. Nevertheless, it is that proletariat only that can make good the claim of workmen to their share of art, without which no art can live long.

It is no real paradox to say that the unattractiveness of labour which is now the curse of the world will become the hope of the world. As long as the workman could sit at home, working easily and quietly, his long hours of labour mattered little to him, and other evils could be borne. Those evils, too, were visible and palpable to everyone and external to their lives; and the remedies were not far to seek. Peace instead of violence, equal rights before the law, these were things which people might hope their very masters would try to win for them.

But now that labour has become a mere burden, the disease of a class, that class will, by all means, try to throw it off, to lessen its weight, and in their efforts to do so they must of necessity destroy society, which is founded on the patient bearing of that burden. For there is no longer, as in the days of feudal violence, any means of relieving them of the burden while our present society exists. True, their masters, taught prudence by fear, will try, are trying, various means to make the workers bear their burden; but one after the other they will be found out and discredited. Philanthropy has had its day and is gone; thrift and self-help are going; participation in *profits*, parliamentarism and universal suffrage, State Socialism will have to go the same road, and the workers will be face to face at last with the fact that modern civilization with its elaborate hierarchy and iron drill is founded on their intolerable burden, and then no shortening of the day's work which would leave profit to the employer will make their labour hours short enough. They will see that modern society can only exist as long as they bear their burden with some degree of patience, their patience will be worn out, and to pieces will modern society go.

And I repeat, that to my mind the unattractiveness of labour, which has been the necessary outcome of commercial industry, will have played a great part in this revolution; the price which commercialism will have to pay for depriving the worker of his share of art will be its own death.

COMMONWEAL, VOLUME I, NUMBER 4,
MAY 1885 (SUPPLEMENT), P. 37

ATTRACTIVE LABOUR

In what I wrote last month I tried to make it clear that under the wages-system labour is bound to be unattractive as well as excessive in quantity and underpaid. The creation of surplus value being the one aim of the employers of labour, they cannot for a moment trouble themselves as to whether the work which creates that surplus value is pleasurable to the worker or not. In fact in order to get the greatest amount possible of surplus value out of the work, and to make a profit in the teeth of competition, it is absolutely necessary that it should be done under such conditions as make (as I wrote in my last) a mere burden which nobody would endure unless upon compulsion. This is admitted on all hands, nay is loudly insisted on by anti-Socialists. The necessity for the existence of class distinctions as a means of compelling people to work is always present in their thoughts; and no wonder, since the only type of worker that they can conceive of is the worker of to-day, degraded by centuries of forced labour, wearisome and hopeless. To such a man, indeed, ever fresh and fresh compulsion must be applied at any cost, at any risk, until the string breaks with the strain. It is no wonder that the bare idea of the destruction of the hierarchy of compulsion terrifies those who rejoice in our modern civilization. But for us whose business is leading people towards the destruction of that hierarchy, who believe that men's morals, aspirations, and what not, are made by their material surroundings, there is no room for fear of the consequences of revolution. We do not *fear* for the transformation of civilization, we *hope* for it; nay it is an assured hope for us which consoles us for the disappointments and griefs of the passing day, which makes 'life worth living' for us; and my reason for writing this is to do my best to quicken that hope in the minds of our comrades. For that purpose I want if I can to give a very slight sketch of attractive labour which, of course, I presuppose is to be done not for the profit of a master, but for the production of wealth for the use of ourselves and our neighbours.

I can see, without much straining, labour going on under quite the reverse of the circumstances which surround it at present, and yet the world none the poorer for it. It would, one might think, be possible in the first place for a man to choose the work which he could do best; which if he were a healthy constituted man in mind and body, would mean from the outset that his work would be no longer a mere burden to him, since everyone likes to do what he can do well; there is at least some pleasure in such work. This choice of work would not be difficult; for though it may seem under our present profit-ridden conditions that people have little choice in such matters, are listless and don't care what they do, so they can but live by it pretty easily – this state of mind is artificially produced by commercial tyranny. People's innate capacities are pretty much as various as their faces are; but individual character and varied capacity are not cherished by the system which tends to get rid of skilled labour altogether. If a man would live now, as a part of industrial economy, he must submit to be the hundredth part of a machine and swallow any longings he may have to exercise any special faculty.

But in a reasonable community these varied capacities would be looked out for and cultivated; the industrial arts would be an essential part of all education, and not only would they be taught gradually and easily to children, and as a part of their pastime, but grown men also would have opportunities for learning more than one craft. There would be no reason for forcing them to practice one craft only all their lives long. Nay many, or most, men would be carrying on more than one occupation from day to day. Surely almost everyone would wish to take some share in field or garden work besides his indoor occupation, even if it were no more than helping to get in the harvest or save the hay; and such occasions would become really the joyous and triumphant festivals which the poets have dreamed of them as being, and of which pleasure there is still some hint or, it may be, survival in *barbarous* countries. But besides such obvious change in work as this, there could certainly be found useful outdoor occupation whereby a person could vary his or her indoor work; helping, for instance, in the work which has to do with the transit of foods. It needs but people to turn their attention to life and not to profit-scraping to find such opportunities.

This matter of fitting people's work to their capacities and not, as now, their capacities to their work, would be the most important reversal of the present system of labour. And though my hint about it has been put in a few words, I beg our readers to consider what a difference it would make in labour if it were carried out. It is not too much to say that the difference would be immeasurable; labour so set about would not differ in degree from our present labour but in kind. But to complete the change, two other elements are necessary: leisure and pleasantness of external surroundings. I need not say much about the first, it may be thought, since among the better-off part of the workers the struggle with the employers about the length of the working-day has been going on so long, and in our own times, so obviously; though even with these it has been and is being fought on the assumption that the wages-system is to endure for ever – that the hierarchy of compulsion is necessary and the shortening of the day's labour has really meant a mere raising of wages.

As for real leisure in work I am afraid I must say that working men do not know what it means; their work being generally an anxious, strained hurry of drudgery, varied by what the natural repulsion to such slavery is sure to bring about as a reflection of it, a listless dawdling through the day, when owing to the due driver not being to the fore they are able to indulge in it. Both of these miseries are miles apart from the way of working when people are not working for wages, but for the wealth of the community: the work would be done deliberately and thoughtfully for the good's sake and not for the profit's sake, but cleanly and briskly too, under the influence of hope and the looking, not to next day's drudgery, but this day's further pleasure by men saying, 'Let us get through with this job, and then on to the next piece of our life'. In work so done there is no slavery; whereas ordinary work now is nothing but slavery. It is only a question whether the slaves shall be idle or industrious. Perhaps on the whole, looking at the effect on the community, they had better be idle.

Work so done, with variety and intelligently, not intensified to the bursting point of the human machine, and yet with real workmanlike, or rather artistic eagerness, would not be a burden, but an interest added to life quite apart from its necessity; with such work to do we might even bear with equanimity as a temporary evil, some of the discomforts of our town life, though surely not the dreadful squalor which the hierarchy of compulsion condemns us to to-day. But there is no reason why we should bear with the discomforts; it is, for instance, only the necessity for making a profit that compels us to the wretched and even ridiculous want of elbow-room, which is the universal rule in factories.

The crowding up of factories into huge towns, or congeries of towns, is a thing which we shall refuse to bear when we work voluntarily and for the purpose of leading happy lives. A great deal of work is still done on the workshop rather than the factory system. There is no sort of need for these workshops being heaped together in the mass of disorder and misery which we call a big town. Centres of a manageable size would afford all the necessary elements of life and refinement and movement when all were educated and had the leisure which alone can make education valuable, and had the intelligence which, pretty equally distributed among every knot of men and women, would not be repressed by sordid misery. The only thing which makes huge centres desirable to the privileged few at present, is the fact that the lives of the greater part of men are wasted in drudgery. On the other hand, where associated labour on the large scale was necessary, and the factory system in its fullest organization had to be used, each of those factories highly improved as to the means of production, as it would be, should be itself a town. It should be no mere phalangstery on a philanthropical basis, arranged for the passing an existence somewhat better indeed than our helpless wage-slaves of the mill now live, but bare of the real joys of life; but it should contain in itself all the resources for a refined and well-occupied life – at once manly, restful and eager. There is no reason why it should not be beautiful itself, and the country about it might well be a garden. When we were working for our own wealth, and not the waste of others, we should surely think it well in spending part of our work on housing ourselves decently, and on taking care that we left behind our work no signs of the haste, bred by the terror of ruin and starvation, in the shape of smoke and ash-heaps and all the unutterable filth which now disgrace our manufacturing districts and distinctly brand the work done there for what it is – work done by helpless slaves for helpless masters.

But work done under such conditions as I have been trying to sketch out would, I am sure, be attractive to all except the exceptions, the monsters of vagabondage and loafing who are now bred by the excessive overwork which is the general lot of the workers or by the privileged idleness of the rich, and whose descendants might last through a few generations, but would soon melt into the general body of people living in the happy exercise of energy.

By such work and such a life we should be set free from intestine warfare among ourselves for the nobler contest with Nature, and should find that she also, when conquered, would be our friend, and not our enemy.

COMMONWEAL, VOLUME I, NUMBER 5,
JUNE 1885 (SUPPLEMENT), PP. 49–50

SOCIALISM AND POLITICS (AN ANSWER TO 'ANOTHER VIEW')

A friend, R. F. E. Willis, whose letter we publish, seems inclined to answer the question, 'Shall Socialists enter the Parliamentary struggle?' in the affirmative. The question is such a serious one that I make no excuse for answering our friend at some length.

I must admit that as a matter of policy it might be prudent to affect a belief in the Parliamentary method of revolution, even if we did not really believe in them, and this all the more in the face of the coming election, which has aroused such hopes in the minds of Democrats – hopes likely to be disappointed, even on the mere Democratic side. But I am convinced that all such dishonesty is sure to fall back on the heads of those that practise it, and that it is no use enrolling recruits who do not really agree with us, and will fall away before the first sincere declaration of our principles. Therefore I think that Socialists ought not to hesitate to choose between Parliamentarism and revolutionary agitation, and that it is a mistake to try and sit on the two stools at once; and, for my part, I hope that they will declare against Parliamentarism, as I feel assured that otherwise they will have to retrace their steps at the cost of much waste of time and discouragement.

I now ask our friend – what is the object of Socialism? Do we not hope to see society transformed, to be changed into something quite different from what it now is? On the other hand the object of Parliamentary institutions is the preservation of society in its present form – to get rid of defects in the machine in order to keep the machine going. Liberal legislation (and there is no other, for the Tories are forced to legislate liberally when they are in office) means yielding what is absolutely necessary to popular demands in the assured hope of hushing those demands, so that the fleecing of the people may not come to an end.

Let us take the Factory Acts instanced as an example by our friend, and see how the thing works. It was necessary (as it still is) to our capitalist manufacture that the auxiliary labour of women and children should be employed, so as to keep down the cost of production by lowering the wages of adult males. But in the earlier years of the great machine industry, the monstrous abuses in the employment of women and children, which could no longer be hushed up, threatened the existence of that employment. Necessity therefore compelled the manufacturers to submit to the palliation of these abuses, so that now the burden of this still shameful labour is lightened, and thereby the system is saved – which means that the wives and children of our factory workmen cheapen labour for the manufacturers at the expense of their own husbands and fathers. Meantime there is still left a large mass of 'auxiliary labour', untouched by the Factory Acts, which will remain till Socialism has transformed our civilization.

On the other hand, therefore, the slavery of the better-off workers, though lightened, is confirmed. On the other, the fringe of labour, *which is absolutely necessary to our present system of manufacture*, is left untouched or even changed for the worse.

This is the regular course of Parliamentary legislation, which acts like a doctor trying to heal his patient by attacking the symptoms and letting the cause of disease alone. In short, for the purpose for which it is intended, the support of the class-state, Parliamentary legislation is valid, otherwise it is a delusion.

I should like our friend to understand whither the whole system of palliation tends – namely, towards the creation of a new middle class to act as a buffer between the proletariat and their direct and obvious masters; the only hope of the bourgeois for retarding the advance of Socialism lies in this device. Let our friend think of a society thus held together. Let him consider how sheepishly the well-to-do workers to-day offer themselves to the shearer; and are we to help our masters to keep on creating fresh and fresh flocks of such sheep? What a society that would be, the main support of which would be capitalists masquerading as working men! Shall the ultimate end of civilization be the perpetual widening of the middle classes? I think if our friend knew as well as I do the terrible mental degradation of our middle-classes, their hypocrisy, their cowardice, their joylessness, it would scare him from attempting to use their beloved instrument of amelioration – Parliament.

It is a new Society that we are working to realize, not a cleaning up of our present tyrannical muddle into an improved smoothly-working form of that same 'order', a mass of dull and useless people organized into classes, amidst which the antagonism should be moderated and veiled so that they should act as checks on each other for the insurance of the stability of the system.

The real business of Socialists is to impress on the workers the fact that they are a class, whereas they ought to be Society; if we mix ourselves up with Parliament we shall confuse and dull this fact in people's minds instead of making it clear and intensifying it. The work that lies before us at present is to *make Socialists*, to cover the country with a network of associations composed of men who feel their antagonism to the dominant classes, and have no temptation to waste their time in the thousand follies of party politics. If by chance any good is to be got out of the legislation of the ruling classes, the necessary concessions are much more likely to be wrung out of them by their fear of such a body, than they are to be wheedled and coaxed out of them by the continual life of compromise which 'Parliamentary Socialists' would be compelled to live, and which is deadly to that feeling of exalted hope and brotherhood that alone can hold a revolutionary party together.

Commonweal, Volume I, Number 6,
July 1885 (Supplement), p. 61

FIRST GENERAL MEETING OF THE SOCIALIST LEAGUE

Sunday, July 5, 1885

HELD AT 13 FARRINGDON ROAD, LONDON, E.C.

The first General Conference of the Socialist League will be remembered with pleasurable feelings by all that took part in it. It was a day of heartiness and good feeling; of realization of hopes and the planning for future work. Whether the organization founded in December last, and having its second birth, as it were, on Sunday, July 5, 1885, is to exist until the principles it works for are understood and accepted of men – whether it will ever be merged in a larger, wider, more international body; whether those gathered together on that Sunday will see in their time anything more than the lessened darkness of the sky before the dawn of the better day that is to come; whether any of them will be able to sing *Nunc dimittis* ere they depart – these are but secondary questions. The one thing of primary importance is that a veritable Socialist body is in existence, and is at work in England, the home of capitalism.

A genuine enthusiasm marked from first to last all that was done. Even the dry details of business reports were signals for cheering. In an assembly of men and women holding pronounced and advanced views, considerable differences of opinion upon points of detail and even, now and again, on larger questions, was assured. But even where the difference was marked enough to be called a divergence, all discussion was carried on with kindliness and generosity. In one thing the Conference was unanimous – its earnestness for Socialism, its eagerness to do everything for the furthering of the cause.

And now the League is thoroughly on its feet. Its Council and officers have been chosen. The inspiration of our first gathering together is yet strong upon us. Our work lies before us. The hideous monstrosities, cruelties, and blasphemies due to capitalism, assail our every sense. Our fellows lie supine, or if they struggle at all, so fight they as those that fight the air. To work, then!

COMMONWEAL, VOLUME 1, NUMBER 7,
AUGUST 1885, P. 65

A NEW PARTY

It would undoubtedly be futile to prophecy as to the immediate results of the forthcoming general elections, or to wager which side may get the majority; but whichever does come uppermost in the struggle, certain tendencies in the elected and the electors are likely to develop in a manner which can fairly be judged of, without pretence to the gift of prophecy, by noting the signs of the times at present; and it is not out of place, even in a Socialist paper, to look into these tendencies, since some of our friends are so anxious to try their luck in the game which is going on at St Stephens, hoping that they may be allowed to remain Socialists even in the midst of the House of Commons.

It was easy to foresee that when the Tory Ministry came in it would make some attempt to dish the Liberals, though perhaps not quite so easy to foresee their eagerness in that amusement, and still less the speedy revolt of their own friends against it. Coercion in Ireland is turning out as much of a stumbling-block to the Tory party as it was to the Liberals. Lord Randolph Churchill is not to have it all his own way after all; there are Tories who are bent on trying what chance they have of preserving something more of Toryism than its name. There is apparently likely to be as wide a split in the Tory party as there has been for some time past in the Liberal. This has somewhat changed the aspect of affairs. A week or two ago it seemed as if it were a mere struggle between the Liberals and the Radicals, and that the latter depended for their chance of forming a strong party in the next Parliament on the success of the Tories in the elections; that a large Liberal majority would defer the hopes of the Radicals.

But now behold disunion in the hitherto united party, and such a state of parties, such a condition of party strife as seems to a Socialist to offer a most splendid opportunity – for leaving it alone. The 'collective wisdom' is falling into chaos quite fast enough without our help.

And yet, it may be said, from out of that chaos something will emerge. Will that something be as favourable to our hopes as the chaos itself? Ought we not to try to bring out of the confusion something which will at all events approach nearer to Socialism than anything which has yet called itself a party?

Well, I think the Liberal split and the Tory revolt against overdoing dishing are merely superficial tokens of the creation of a new party which is now going on. Old Toryism, though not at an end in the country generally, has confessedly no chance of a majority in Parliament. Liberalism as a party had fulfilled its programme, and has nothing left to do. Radicalism is itself divided between the last dregs of the 'Manchester school' and the new democracy, with some form of land nationalization as one of the planks of its platform.

'There are no solid parties, then?' says the Parliamentary Socialist. 'Let us go in and make a party and sway Parliament in a Socialist direction.'

True, there is as yet no solid party, but I repeat there is one forming, which I believe will be the strongest which our times have seen, and by whatever name it may be called, it will be the party of reaction grown conscious that firm and serious resistance must be made to the claims of labour for equal rights for all. Read the serious articles in the *Standard* and the *St James' Gazette* on this subject and you will recognize how different they are from the ordinary artificial tongue-in-the-cheek Tory articles. Sensible men of all the *bourgeois* parties are beginning to be alarmed and to see that the business cannot be played with, that Parliament must not be allowed to dally with its true function of seriously considering the best means of upholding our present economical and social conditions, and of using those means in the teeth of all opposition, all sentiment.

The party which this instinct (for such it is) will form will not deal in sensation; it will be peaceful, considerate, philanthropical; it will rally to it all 'reasonable' and 'practical' men who have to do with public matters; it will doubtless make large concessions to the cries of distress which will swell year by year, and so gather to it more and more the 'good' men of the comfortable classes, while it will put down coolly and remorselessly anything which openly wears the token of danger. It will, in a word, *govern* us, and will do so as the committee of that Hierarchy of Compulsion which, under various disguises of free trade, personal freedom, and the like, is the one enemy which we Revolutionary Socialists have before us.

And outside this party, what will there be in Parliament to resist it? Nothing but a scattered discontent, which will be helpless there, discredited by all *respectable* persons, who will point to the good deeds of the 'party of order', and protest most energetically against any interference with those who are so busy making people happy and 'contented'. Any attempt to deal with such virtue and consistency from a revolutionary standpoint will be absolutely useless until the Revolutionary Socialists have stirred up and organized the discontent outside Parliament – until the workers have become conscious that their interests must be opposed to those of the governing classes, however anxious the latter may seem to be, or may really be as individuals, to promote their happiness and content; and when that time comes, what need will there be for Parliamentary agitation?

Meanwhile, once more it seems to me that the new party will soon raise its head up, and will put an end to puny opposition in Parliament. It will govern so reasonably and strongly that no one outside our ranks will have a word to say against it. Should that discourage us? By no means; it will unite the suffrages of all respectable people by aiming at bringing about peace by every means except the only one possible – the abolition of classes. It will have a great success, and be blessed by the whole *bourgeois* world, and – will lead us into Revolution.

With its respectable march let us have nothing to do, nor affect to think that it can serve our cause otherwise than by that repression which it will assuredly try. Let all *our* efforts be directed towards giving it something to repress.

COMMONWEAL, VOLUME I, NUMBER 8,
SEPTEMBER 1885 (SUPPLEMENT), P. 85

IRELAND AND ITALY
A WARNING

Mr Parnell has been celebrating his triumphs in the past Parliament, and it may be said also those that are to come in the future one; he and his supporters also fully believe in the complete organization of the party, which will be strong enough not only to return 85 members this autumn, but also to compel every accepted candidate to sign a solemn pledge to submit to party discipline. Doubtless Mr Parnell is strong, and he and his are quite justified in their cries of victory. The English Parties cannot conceal their terror: Tory is calling to Whig, Whig to Liberal, to stand firm at last, since now the enemy is really upon them; but all the time they are, like the troopers in 'Old Mortality', 'looking over their shoulders as if they liked the road behind them better than the road before'. In all probability Mr Parnell will have his way, and, as he says, this coming Parliament will be the last in which the Irish representatives will sit at Westminster.

Well, this is revolutionary, and we revolutionists rejoice in it on those grounds, and in the blow which it will deal at the great Bourgeois Power – the British Empire: also it may well be that Ireland must become national before she can be international. Yet we must ask ourselves what is to come next; will Ireland ruling herself be progressive, revolutionary that is, or reactionary? Will Socialists find their work easier in the Parnellite Ireland than now? Will Michael Davitt be a dangerous rebel then as he is now? There is no doubt as to the answer to those questions if we are to go no further than Mr Parnell would have us; the fullest realization of his programme would bring Ireland to pretty much the state of things which Liberal reformers want to realize in England as a bar to the march of Socialism which they have at last heard of, and are beginning to fear. An improved landlordism founded on a wider basis and therefore consolidated; that would lead, it seems to me, to founding a nation fanatically attached to the rights of private property (so called), narrow-minded, retrogressive, contentious, and – unhappy.

I ask Irishmen to consider a somewhat parallel case, that of Italy. Italy as well as Ireland had an unconquerable yearning for national independence, which swallowed up all other aspirations; in the teeth of all difficulty she conquered her independence amidst the best wishes of generous-minded men of all parties. How our hearts burned within us as we heard of the exploits of her patriots; surely revolution for the world was drawing near, thought some of us who did not know what the new revolution was to be, as we followed the heroism of Garibaldi and the lofty morality of Mazzini.

Italy triumphed and became 'free' and united; those noble deeds accomplished that at least. What, then, has been the gain? I will not say nothing, but I will say something very small compared with all the energy, enthusiasm, and self-sacrifice that brought it about, very small compared with the high-wrought hopes that went before it. For whatever the gain was, it was confined to the bourgeoisie, and the proletariat did not share it, has not shared it.

In the midst of the richest gifts of nature and art, cradled by the history of the world, exists a population of which the following words can be said without contradiction: 'According to some the average pay (of the labourers) runs from 3d. to 4d. a day, according to others to 7d., without making any allowance for loss of time either through bad weather of ill-health. For this pittance they have to work like galley-slaves, and out of it such of them as have families must provide food for their children and keep a roof of some sort over their heads. The utmost that a labourer can earn *with the help of his family*, says Signor Arcozzi Manio, a large landowner, is equal to little more than 10d. a day. Their food' – but one need not go into that; it is obvious that their food must be the food of beasts in quality and less than theirs in quantity. 'The population engaged in agriculture is estimated at eight and a quarter millions, of whom a million and a half at the most' (one can guess what that qualification means) 'are landed proprietors, the remainder being farmers, metayers, and labourers.' It is added that the lot of the proprietors and farmers if not brilliant, is at least tolerable; the said proprietors being mostly small ones it must be understood, peasants for the most part.

Such then are the *free* workmen of Italy while as a nation under her Constitutional King and Liberal Parliament, she ambitiously strives to snatch here and there some rag of stolen territory which may help her to get a share of the world-market from the older European firms, and keeps on foot a goodly army of warlike idlers to that end. Italy is free and united, and is almost a 'great power', while the mass of her population is living, to speak bluntly, in abject slavery.

Here then is a warning to Irishmen if they will take it; they can see what the barrenness of the programme of driving out the Teutons has led to in Italy; can they think that a similarly barren programme of driving out the Saxon will lead to anything better in Ireland?

If the sword of Garibaldi could have led the workers of Italy to a condition of things under which what they produced would have been their own to live upon, the Austrians and their kingly and grand-ducal deputies would have been suppressed as they are now, and no 'foreigner' could govern them against their will; but the places of the Austrian tyrants would not have been taken by the great collective tyrant Capital, who prevents poor people from eating, and murders them with 'pellagra' or famine-fever as it has been called in Ireland, a tyrant who has no heart to be softened, no soul to be moralized, in spite of Mazzini and the Positivists.

If only the Irish could take this lesson to heart, and make up their minds that even if they have to wait for it, their revolution shall be part of the great international movement; they will then be rid of all the foreigners that they want to be rid of. For my part I do not believe in the race-hatred of the Irish against the English: they hate their English *masters*, and well they may; and their English masters are now trying hard to stimulate the race-hatred among their English brethren, the workers, by all this loud talk of the integrity of the Empire and so forth. But when once the Irish people have got rid of their masters, Irish and English both, there will, I repeat, be no foreigners to hate in Ireland, and she will look back at the present struggle for mere nationality as a nightmare of the charmed sleep in which Landlordism and Capitalism have held her so long, as they have other nations. To the Irish, therefore, as to all other nations, whatever their name and race, we Socialists say, Your revolutionary struggles will be abortive or lead to mere disappointment unless you accept as your watchword, WAGE-WORKERS OF ALL COUNTRIES UNITE!

COMMONWEAL, VOLUME I, NUMBER 9,
OCTOBER 1885, PP. 86–87

ON THE EVE OF THE ELECTIONS

By the time this paper is published, the country will be in the thick of the elections; indeed it may be possible to get some idea by that time as to their possible result, but it must be admitted that before the first few come off, any prophesy on this can be little more than mere guessing.

It seems to me, however, that one may set aside the chance of an actual Tory majority, and that the chances lie between a Liberal majority large enough to swamp the united (?) Tories and Parnellites and a majority too small to carry the Liberal party through in the teeth of such a combination.

We Socialists, I think, need not be over anxious as to which of these events will take place. In the first case of an overwhelming Liberal majority, the Parliament will certainly be one of inaction; although the Parnellites will not have it all their own way, yet they will be strong enough to hamper the Government terribly if they do not give way to their demands. Apart from the Irish Question, it will be the aim of the Government not to stir anything which might divide the Party; some slight and 'safe' concessions will probably be made to the demand for Social Reform, and for the rest as near nothing as may be. A Great Whig Liberal majority will exhibit to the eyes of those that can see, more clearly than ever heretofore, 'the Representatives of the People' engaged in their natural function of holding together with as little change as possible, the mass of suffering, injustice and chicanery which is dignified with the name of Orderly Society.

Whether the Radicals revolt and break up the party or not in this case, this spectacle of the incompetency of Parliament for anything except repression, will be advantageous to the cause of Revolution; but in the other case of the Tories and Parnellites together outnumbering the Liberals, though the consequences may not be more disruptive of Parliamentary government, they will probably be more dramatic. For not only will some attempt at the solution of the Irish Question be forced on Parliament, but also the Radicals will most likely be driven into forming a separate party, and the Great Moderate Party, upon whose advent I have speculated before, and which I believe will be the final enemy of Revolution, will be definitely formed. Perhaps some of our Radical friends will be surprised when they see who will adhere to it amongst those whom they have considered their own special champions.

Meantime something may be learnt from all the late speech-making and maundering, besides what has been already noted in these columns. And first it must surely strike a Socialist (or indeed anybody else) how strong the tendency is, in our representative system, towards personal government.

What hopes, for example, were hung on Mr Gladstone's appearance! How he was not only to undo the harm done by Mr Chamberlain's impatience (save the mark) but also to give spirit and meaning to the whole Liberal attack. There was the man; we were all to wait for him: then we should see!

Well, now the oracle has spoken what has it said? Commonplace and twaddle enough; that we expect as a matter of necessity, just as the ancients expected the verse of the Delphic oracle. What else? An indefinite and indeed oracular bid for the Irish support, received by Mr Parnell with solemn, one would almost think ironical courtesy and an awkward request to state more definitely what concessions to Home Rulers Mr Gladstone would be prepared to make.

And next? A declaration against the disestablishment of the churches, English and Scotch; a declaration made necessary in a sense by the obvious dissatisfaction of the Moderate Party, but which taking into consideration the tone of the speech in which it was made, must show clearly to all not blinded by party tactics that Mr Gladstone has ratted to the Conservatives. Nevertheless, if one is to believe the Liberal and Radical papers, Mr Gladstone is still the trusted leader of the Party of Progress. Little as a Socialist can sympathize with the hopes of the so-called Radicals, one cannot help hoping, however, for the sake of manliness, that there is some muttered protest in the Radical ranks; but if there is it is inarticulate.

And to think that persons apparently reasonable, should accept as a proposition having any reason in it that the matter of disestablishment has not yet been long enough before the nation to be made a matter of Parliamentary discussion. Surely when the great Liberal leader said that, a twitch, that might have grown into a sardonic smile but for special self-command, must have come into the solemn mask which has so long been shown to the public.

Worthy people of England, that are so proud of your Representative Government, take note once more how the Parliamentary Machine has been once again used, as it always will be, to sweep aside inconvenient questions. To check all aspirations towards progress; never to pass any law, however much desired by everybody, till the whole country has grown sick and tired of the subject; and then only to pass half of it, so that it becomes worse than useless – that is, it seems, the business of your Representative Parliament that governs you. When will you learn to do your own business yourselves?

COMMONWEAL, VOLUME 1, NUMBER 11,
DECEMBER 1885, P. 101

CONTRIBUTIONS TO *COMMONWEAL*

1886

A Letter from the Pacific Coast

We have received an interesting letter from San Francisco relative to the labour question and especially to the conference lately held there, in which the main subject of discussion was the Chinese labour question. Our correspondent's letter is as follows:

'1035 Post Street, S. F., California, Dec. 9. '85.

'*Dear Comrades*,– We last night adjourned from the 'Trades and Labour Organizations Convention' which had, with an interval of two days, been sitting since last Monday week. A full report is in course of preparation, of which you will undoubtedly receive a copy, but this is not yet ready, and I am anxious that you should receive at least an outline of the proceedings in time for your January issue. I am sending you copies of the *Daily Report* which, though a capitalistic paper, has given the gist of the speeches with commendable fairness. A study of such copies will give you a general idea of the work and temper of the convention, but it may be useful to English readers if I add the following as explanatory notes.

'In the first place we consider that we have gained a most decisive victory over the politicians, who have hitherto been the curse of the labour movement in this city. They, having obtained control of the District Assembly of the Knights of Labour, appointed themselves an Executive Board, and summoned the convention. They originally intended to run it as a political convention, and for that purpose threw out the credentials of the Socialist organizations. The convention by an overwhelming vote defeated them in this, and, if you will note that the names I have underlined are those of the Socialists, you will see what a significant part we played.

'The line we have taken throughout is briefly this. We have leaned greatly on the Declaration of Independence, which declares this to be a government of and for the people, and that all are entitled to life, liberty and the pursuit of happiness. I may, perhaps, say here that I feel now convinced that this is invariably safe ground to take with an American audience. We accordingly declared that, the will of the people on this coast having most unequivocally declared for the expulsion of the Chinese, the people were bound to be true to themselves, and to enforce compliance with their demand. Everyone, however, of our speakers declared (and we had the ear of the audience throughout) that the Chinaman was our brother-slave; that we had no quarrel with him, and that not one drop of his blood must be shed; that the crime lay with the property owners, the employers who make profit out of the Chinese, and the officials who refused to execute the demands of the people. These we recommended as personally responsible. We adopted the same line of personal responsibility of officials to the people in our handling of the Convict Labour and Hard Times questions, in which last, of course, we got in plenty of work, every speaker being distinctly Socialistic, and an audience of some 1500 having the whole question laid before them in the clearest and most thorough manner.

'Having had for six nights an audience of 1500 to 2000 people, we have, I believe, conclusively shown that we Socialists are the power in the labour movement on this coast, and we have for the first time got the Trades Unions, who are now in course of federation, in sympathy with us. This I consider an incalculable gain.

'I may add that a careful study of the proceedings, and of the audience – which was throughout a most orderly and intelligent one – has convinced me that the people are far more advanced than I for one had imagined. The feeling against the wealthy and the police is, I am also certain, intensely strong. It has, however, modified my judgement on the Chinese question; for I have honestly held the belief that there would be this winter at least an attempt to drive the Chinese out of this city by force, and have further considered it a sacred duty incumbent on us to make at least an attempt to direct the storm against those who deserve that it should fall upon them. I now incline to the opinion that there are large masses who recognize that the cause of hard times lies far deeper than the Chinaman, and that they will wait till they can settle this question upon broader and sounder principles. If we have accomplished this we have, as I am sure all English comrades will admit, done good work.'

This on the whole is satisfactory and reassuring, especially considering the sinister rumour of a plot for the massacre of the Chinese which was published in the English press some weeks ago, and which now appears from information since received from America to have been one of the breed of plots instigated by the police for the benefit of the capitalists. Our correspondent being present at the Convention would have a much more accurate impression of its tendency than any newspaper report could give, as he would understand the significance of what was said there in comparison with the utterances of former times.

Nevertheless, if anything can be said on this side of the Atlantic which might strengthen the hands of the American Socialists in pointing out to the workers their real enemy, it ought to be said; so as an International Revolutionary Socialist, I venture to make a few remarks, premising for the information of our English friends that a law has been passed restricting the importation of Chinese labour (apparently made that it might not be carried out) and that this law is systematically disregarded by the capitalist officials, so that our American friends are only exercising their ordinary rights as citizens in calling on the government to see that the law is carried out. It must also be remembered that whereas the European immigrants, Irish, German, or Scandinavian, speedily mingle with the general population, and so do not affect the standard of livelihood permanently by the lower standard which they bring over with them, the Chinese do no such thing, but remain Chinese in America, a community within a community.

Now I must say it would be difficult to exaggerate the crime of the capitalists in their importation of Chinese labour; done as it was for profit, quite regardless of the welfare of either Chinese or American workmen. I fear, indeed, that some of the individuals of that order (of capitalists) who were engaged in the transaction, would give an ugly grin at the weakness of anybody supposing that they *could* think of anyone's welfare except their own and their families'. But the preamble of the resolution passed at the Convention pointed out very truly that the expulsion of the Chinese would by no means solve the labour question in America, and if our comrades there can only drive that home hard enough, so that American workmen can really understand it even amidst the sufferings caused by the immediate and special attack on their standard of livelihood, then the labour question in America will have entered into a new phase.

For this crime is being committed everywhere and always in civilization by Capital; nor can it help committing the crime as long as it exists. Neither preaching nor terrorism will make it refrain from this: it is not an accident, but an essential condition of its life to drive down wages to the lowest point possible. Foiled in one direction it will try it in another, and will in the long run always succeed as long as it has life in it.

The Chinese workmen are only doing what every workman is *forced* to do more or less, that it to compete with his fellows for subsistence. It is true that the Chinese are *forced* by capital into being more obviously the enemies of their fellow-workmen than is usually the case, but that is only a surface difference; it is more dramatic, that is all. Every working-man is *forced* into the same false position of contest with every other working-man until he becomes a Socialist, and is conscious of his being naturally the *friend* of every workman throughout the world, and until he does his best to realize the consequences that should flow from this friendship.

The Chinese workmen are no more guilty of the suffering which their competition causes than are the women and girls who in London are starving the male adult tailors; are being *used* to starve them one should say – used against their own husbands, brothers and sweethearts.

It would be miserable indeed in this Chinese matter if, as too often happens, the instruments should receive the suffering due to those who have used them; who indeed in their turn are but the instruments of the long centuries of oppression which we may surely hope are now drawing to a close. If the American workmen can see this, and abstain, as we may well hope they will, from playing into the hands of their real enemies by attacking their fellow wage-slaves the Chinese, they will deserve well of the Brotherhood of labour, and will show that they understand the motto: *Wage-workers of all countries unite!*

COMMONWEAL, VOLUME 2, NUMBER 13,
FEBRUARY 1886, P. 13

OUR POLICY

The recent 'disturbances' as the word goes, the stir in the dry bones of labour, is a strange phenomenon to most people, and even to us, who have been working towards a change in the basis of Society, is unexpected; amidst the routine of our ordinary educational work we have been surprised, as it were, by something which, whatever else may be said of it, does look like the first skirmish of the Revolution.

The riot, or whatever it may be called, of February 8th, though a small matter in itself, became of importance because it has got to be a fixed idea in the heads of – well – most men, men of all classes, that the English workman had at last been brought to the point of incapacity of expressing his grievances by anything more threatening than an election riot; which expressed nothing at all except a certain pleasure in a 'rough and tumble', joined perhaps to the irritation which comes of the indigestion of the 'lower classes', an indigestion bred of garbage-eating, and want of fresh air and leisure.

But here was a crowd composed in the main, in spite of the watch-stealing, which was the work of professional thieves on the look out for plunder, of genuine working-men, who were angry, or excited, or miserable enough to cast off their habitual fear of consequences for an hour or two, and indulge in a threat to the Society which had made them the lower classes; as to the details of that threat I will not say much. I have no doubt that the shoeing-horn to the riot was the 'truly gentlemanly' behaviour of the fools at the Carlton Club, who took for granted the axiom above stated, that a crowd of the English 'lower classes' will stand anything, and threw jeers and milk-cans at them accordingly. However, let that pass. Apart from what actual plunder there was, the wrecking of shops to carry the contents away, the proceedings of the crowd seemed like a sort of gigantic practical joke against the tyrant – Sham Society. A joke mingled with threatening, embittered by anger and contempt; characterized by the English tendency towards brutality masked by good humour, which is so apt amongst our countrymen to accompany the first stages of a great tragedy. These seem to me to have been the outward aspects of this strange, and, in spite of all drawbacks, most memorable scene.

What was the meaning of it? At bottom misery, illuminated by a faint glimmer of hope, raised by the magic word *Socialism*, the only hope of these days of confusion. That was what the crowd represented, whatever other elements were mingled with it.

What has come of it? The first outcome was on the Tuesday and Wednesday following, a panic at first sight quite inexplicable. There were no mobs in the streets, no placards threatening revolution, no processions – 'no nothing' in short, – and the respectabilities were terribly afraid. Such abject cowardice has perhaps seldom been so frankly shown as was shown by the middling bourgeoisie on those two days. Whatever were they afraid of? Of nothing? No; they were afraid of their own position, so suddenly revealed to them as by a flash of lightning; their position as a class dominating a class injured by them, and more numerous than they. No doubt this insight into the depths of Society will be of service to the dominated class; who will also remember the terror it caused, after their masters have forgotten it.

As another result: the money which was coming into the Mansion House Fund very slowly, is now coming in in sacksful. I would wish to be as fair as possible to the richer classes; and I must say, therefore, that I think this comes partly from people's consciences being touched by the distress now at last become visible to them; yet partly also, I think, from fear. 'Let us show them how kind we are, it may keep them quiet!'

What will come from these 'disturbances'? First, some palliative measures. That is the regular course of events in England of late years; every reform has been blindly resisted till obvious violence has been brought to bear upon the question. Witness the Irish 'difficulty', which has made great steps since I heard John Morley in St James's Hall, before the Westminster electors in 1880, declare that Home Rule was a subject inadmissible of discussion. Well, furthermore, these palliatives must necessarily take the form of an interference with the sanctity of the labour market; an artificial raising of wages by authority, which in its turn will be a spoke in the wheel of our commercial system, will hasten its disruption, in other words, will tend to bring on Revolution.

Another thing may happen, at first sight very unpleasant to us of the Socialist League. We may be suppressed; practically at least, if not formally. It is true that just now cool-headed people of the middle-classes rather smile at the ravings of the *Telegraph*. And yet I think that those ravings are prophetic. Already something or other, probably the Leicester strike riots, has forced the government to turn back on its resolution of letting the speakers at the Demonstration alone, and they are now on their trial.

Well, what will be the result of that attempt at the suppression of opinion? Of course, opinion cannot be suppressed; we shall find means of disseminating our opinions; but repressive interference with us will make those opinions a kind of mystery, a thing to conjure with. The upper-classes will, of course, look upon that mystery as a hateful but also a fearful thing; on the other hand the lower-classes will be eager to know what this Socialism is, which professes to be altogether in their interest, and which the upper classes think so dangerous that no man must know anything about it if it can be helped. Repression will attract the working-classes to us. Opinion which must be suppressed is Revolutionary; under such conditions fear and hope are abroad, the mere dramatic situation forces people into enquiry, action is dreaded and is hoped for; the

Socialist Party will become a political force when all these things happen.

Now I should like to say a few words with the utmost seriousness to our comrades and supporters, on the policy of the Socialist League. I have said that we have been overtaken unprepared, by a revolutionary incident, but that incident was practically aimless. This kind of thing is what many of us have dreaded from the first, and we may be sure that it will happen again and again while the industrial outlook is what it is; but every time it happens it will happen with ever-increasing tragedy. It is above all things our business to guard against the possible consequences of these surprises. At the risk of being misunderstood by hot-heads, I say that our business is more than ever *Education.*

The Gospel of Discontent is in a fair way towards forcing itself on the whole of the workers; how can that discontent be used so as to bring about the New Birth of Society? That is the question we must always have before us. It is too much to hope that the *whole* working-class can be educated in the aims of Socialism in due time, before other surprises take place. But we *must* hope that a strong party can be so educated. Educated in economics, in organization, and in administration. To such a body of men all the aspirations and vague opinion of the oppressed multitudes would drift, and little by little they would be educated by them, if the march of events should give us time; or if not, even half-educated they would follow them in any action which it was necessary to take.

To forge this head of the spear which is to pierce the armour of Capitalism is our business, in which *we must not fail.*

Let we ask our comrades to picture to themselves the consequences of an aimless revolt unexpectedly successful for the time; we will even suppose that it carries with it a small number of men capable of government and administration, though that is supposing a great deal. What would be the result unless the people had some definite aim, however limited?

The men thus floated to the surface would be powerless, their attempts at legislation would be misunderstood; disappointment and fresh discontent would follow, and the counter revolution would sweep they (*sic*) away at once.

But, indeed, it would not even come to that. History teaches us that no revolts that are without aim are successful even for a time; even the failures (some of them glorious indeed) had a guiding aim in them, which only lacked completeness.

This educational process, therefore, the forming a rallying point for definite aims is necessary to our success; but I must guard against misunderstanding. We must be no mere debating club, or philosophical society; we must take part in all really popular movements when we can make our own views on them unmistakably clear; that is a most important part of the education in organization.

Education towards Revolution seems to me to express in three words what our policy should be; towards that New Birth of Society which we know must come, and which, therefore, we must strive to help forward so that it may come with as little confusion and suffering as may be.

One word to Socialists who do not belong to the League. I think there is a tendency abroad towards holding aloof from union on insufficient grounds. I do not urge formal union between those who really disagree as to principles, or the tactics which follow from them, since this results in quarrelling instead of the friendly difference which might otherwise be. But when the principles and tactics held are practically the same, it seems to me a great mistake for Socialist bodies to hold aloof from each other. The present is no time for the formation of separate societies, whether central or local. Habitual and organized intercourse is necessary to the education I have been speaking of; no independence is sacrificed by this intercourse, and propaganda is made much easier by it. I appeal, therefore, to all who agree with us, individuals, local bodies, or central ones, to give up the mere name of independence in order to attain its reality, and to join our League so that we may show a firm front to the common enemy in these troublous yet hopeful times that our coming on us.

COMMONWEAL, VOLUME 2, NUMBER 14,
MARCH 1886, PP. 17–18

SOCIALISM IN THE PROVINCES

I am asked by some comrades to give a brief report of my lecturing tour to Sheffield, Liverpool, and Norwich. I do so, therefore, believing it of some use to give the impressions of a Londoner as to our prospects in other parts of the country.

I gave two lectures at Sheffield on Sunday February 28th, in the Secularist Hall: both were well attended, although I was told that the religious rancour which runs high in Sheffield would keep many people away from the Secularist Hall. Both lectures were well received, the evening one, the more plain-spoken and less historical of the two, particularly so: indeed I have never stood before a more sympathetic audience; and it seemed to me that the interest in the subject had much increased since I was last in Sheffield about a year and [a] half ago.

On the day following, I attended a private meeting of about thirty sympathizers, called to discuss the possibility of starting a definite Socialist body. Of course I went as an advocate of the League. I found much interest in the subject amongst these friends, also some doubts and hanging back from that step of association, a step undoubtedly harder to take in a provincial town where people are so much more known and as it were ticketted (*sic*) than in London. The doubts had reference, some to the religious question, but mostly I think they turned on our repudiation of the Parliamentary method, the reasons for which I did my best to explain. However it was determined to set on foot a Socialist body, of which I hope we shall hear more soon; as undoubtedly several will join it who are both intelligent and eager to do something. Sheffield, I was told, is a specially good town for open-air meetings; and those who gather at them have every reason for listening to speaking which offers a remedy for the present state of things, as labour is very badly off there, and as far as I could make out from what I heard, political matters are sufficiently mixed up. It is worth noting in relation to the matter of would-be Parliamentary Socialism, that an advanced Radical association with a semi-Socialistic programme, which had been established in the town, was swept away by the General Election, the Radicals belonging to it joining the regular party, as they are pretty sure to do under such circumstances.

From Sheffield I went to Liverpool and delivered my lecture at the Concert Room in Nelson Street, on March 2nd. The hall was crowded with an audience mostly of working men, who not only listened with very great attention, but took up all the points which they caught and understood with very hearty applause. After the lecture I had the group round the platform eager to ask questions, which one always encounters in these more northern towns, and there could be no doubt of their eagerness to learn. It is much to be regretted that the League has no branch at Liverpool: although the members of the Workers' Brotherhood are doubtless intelligent and in earnest, they seem to shrink from the full consequences of the change which they advocate: I must ask them to excuse my pressing on them the advisability of their forming themselves into a branch and rallying to them energetic people from the working-classes. From all that I saw and heard at Liverpool, half-a-dozen, nay two or three energetic and uncompromising men pushing our principles there would soon have a following, especially if they spoke quite roughly and plainly to their listeners whether working or middle-class men.

On the 8th March I went to Norwich and lectured to a very good audience, some 800 I should think, at the Victoria Hall. Again the audience was mostly working-class, and was or seemed to be quite in sympathy with the movement. There was no opposition except from a clergyman, who I was told was a worthy man; he however only said that he disagreed, without giving his reasons.

It was strange to me for once to be preaching Socialism in a city like Norwich, with its beautiful architecture and strange half-foreign old-world aspect. But from all I can learn its seems as likely a place as any in England for the spread of Socialism. The working-classes there are in a sad plight; the old weaving industries are fast perishing; the modern industry of mechanical shoe-making is hard pushed by foreign competition, and the 'hands' are terribly exploited. Like all other industrial towns its 'reserve army of labour' or something more than that is all but disbanded. The magnates of the town have been forced to give them some employment, but it is a good illustration of the helplessness of the authorities in such a crisis that they are chiefly setting them to tumble the hillocks into the holes on Mousehold Heath, a rough uncultivated tract of land near the city and which now belongs to it, and where these sturdy bodies are producing under the bourgeois organizers of labour nothing at all, except – ugliness, and literally, platitude.

I had the pleasure, which was a real pleasure and not a mere conventional one, of meeting our branch before the lecture. And here there was no room for the regret one felt at Liverpool, for they seemed just the men wanted in such a place, with their hearts in the business, and with no thought of compromise, thoroughly understanding the futility of Parliamentary agitation. Here again they told me there was good opportunity for open-air work, and they intended to set about it as soon as the weather permitted.

Altogether it is not as a partisan but as an observer that I say that every where people are willing and eager to listen to Socialists, and that the doctrines will take root; and as a last word I appeal to all who are not afraid of the expression of opinion, to help us, whether they call themselves Socialists or not. Some of those who are better off, if their position or their sensitiveness, whatever that may mean, prevents them from joining us, or working actively, can at least help us with money; and let them remember that these people who want to know about that Socialism which is beginning to stir the world, and which offers them a remedy for their hardships and degradation, are poor and daily growing poorer. Some day they will assuredly *move* in a way which will shake everything and overturn much: surely it will be better even for you well-to-do people if they have an aim and a policy in their movement. And to help them to this is our purpose; therefore in our turn we ask help of all thoughtful people.

COMMONWEAL, VOLUME 2, NUMBER 14,
APRIL 1886, P. 30

EDITORIAL

In laying before the Socialist public the first number of our new departure, we feel that a few special words are likely to be looked for from the editors.

Now, as we understand the policy of the Socialist League, it aims at education and organization towards action when the fitting moment arrives.

When that action is set on foot it will have nothing less for its aim than the taking over by the workers of all the means of producing wealth, to be used for the benefit of the community, that is to say, for the benefit of each and all of those who compose it; in other words, the realization of a new society with equality of condition for its basis. Before we can attain to this it is necessary that the mass of the workers should understand this much at least, that nothing short of this will deliver them from the ills they now groan under, that anything short of this though it may change the number of their masters or their position to each other, though it may take from one group of them to give to another, will leave them under masters still, will still leave them slaves to arbitrary authority.

But it will be said to us: 'Do you believe in a sudden leap into this new society, as the result of a consecutive and logical change, with no experiments, no attempt at temporary amelioration of the lives of the workers?'

No; we believe in no such an impossibility: a time of transition there must be, and many will accept the incompletest transition as the realization of their hopes: experiments there will be, and many will refuse to acknowledge their failure even in the teeth of obvious facts. Attempts at bettering the condition of the workers will be made, which will result in raising one group of them at the expense of another, will create a new middle-class and a new proletariat; but many will think the change the beginning of the millenium (*sic*). All these things will and must be; the question for us is, what share shall we take in them?

Whatever our share in them may be, we believe that these attempts, this transitional condition, will be chiefly brought about by the middle-class, the owners of capital themselves, partly in ignorant good-will towards the proletariat (as long as they do not understand its claims), partly with the design both conscious and unconscious, of making our civilization hold out a little longer against the incoming flood of corruption on the one hand and revolution on the other.

We believe that the advanced part of the capitalist class, especially in this country, is drifting, not without a feeling of fear and discomfort, towards State-Socialism of the crudest kind; and a certain school of Socialists are fond of pointing out this tendency with exultation, as presaging the early triumph of the Cause of the People, and are looking forward to the time when we shall be 'All Socialists' in the sense that Krapotkine (*sic*) uses the phrase in the chapter under that title in his 'Words of a Rebel'. Well, we also exult in this change of front of the middle-classes, not because we wish to become All Socialists on these terms, but because it is good that the attempts and failures should be made, the new officialism of the transition period foisted on the world by the dominant class, which has no other function but self-preservation. We rejoice to see Bourgeoisdom digging its own grave amidst the blunders and blind stumbling that Socialists might otherwise be driven into.

But though we rejoice in this and though we admit that it is good that partial changes should take place, since they cannot be final, or the condition of things they bring about be long enduring, what have we to do with helping them on, save by steadily enunciating our principles?

Can we pretend to push forward some measure which we know is impracticable or useless, loudly crying out on practicality meanwhile? Can we who preach the downfall of hypocrisy make friends with the compromise which we despise? Can we who preach freedom, fetter our souls from the outset by cowardly acquiescence with a majority which we know is wrong? A thousand times no!

Again we are but a few, as all those who stand by principles must be until inevitable necessity forces the world to practise those principles. We are few, and have our own work to do, which no one but ourselves can do, and every atom of intelligence and energy that there is amongst us will be needed for that work; if we use that energy and intelligence for doing work which can be done just as well by men who are encumbered with no principles, we waste it; and we had then better confess ourselves beaten, and hand over our work to others who understand better what a party of principle means. Whatever of good may go with the stumbling, compromising kind of Socialism, let it be done at least by those who *must* do it; do not let us do their work as well as our own. We *must* wait and they must act; let us at least not confuse our ideas of what we are waiting for by putting a false issue before ourselves.

But there is another thing besides Bourgeois stumbling into State Socialism, which shows which way the tide is setting, and that is the instinctive revolutionary attempts which drive them into these courses. What is to be said about these? They are leaderless often, and half blind. But are they fruitful of nothing but suffering to the workers? We think not; for besides the immediate gain which they force from the dominant class as above said, they are a stern education for the workers themselves. And however bitter that education may be, it surely is not so much worse than the periods of quietude they have had to endure; the worst thing that we have to dread, though every day now it is less to be dreaded, is that the oppressed people will learn a dull contentment with their lot, and give their masters no more trouble than may come of their dying inconveniently, and being terrible objects to look at or to speak to while they live: the rudest and most unsuccessful attempts at revolution are better than that, though *that* is what is chiefly aimed at by middle-class social reformers.

With all genuine revolutionary attempts, therefore, we must sympathize, and must at the least express that sympathy, whatever risk its expression may subject us to; and it is little indeed if we can do no more than that.

The *Commonweal*, then, will steadily continue to put forward the principles of International Revolutionary Socialism; will deprecate all meddling with parliamentary methods of 'reform'. Constitutionalism means the continuance of the present system; how can Socialists, therefore, who aim at abolishing the system, support its support? Will all revolutionary movements the *Commonweal* will sympathize as it always has done, and will not accuse the people of rashness for doing what they have been forced to do, or of blindness for making the only protest against their wrongs that they are able to make.

In few words, our function is to educate the people by criticizing all attempts at so-called reforms, whose aim is not the realization of equality of condition, but the hindering of it; and by encouraging the union of the working classes towards Revolution and the abolition of artificial restraints on life. The true aim of the people of this epoch is to learn how to live, and to assert their right to do so in the teeth of all opposition.

Commonweal, Volume 2, Number 16,
1 May 1886, p. 33

INDEPENDENT IRELAND

Mr Gladstone's measure has at last seen light, and it must at least be said of it that under the circumstances it has been accepted joyfully by the people whom it was chiefly meant to serve: the Irish at least are pleased. This is an improvement on the character of most measures of reform, which usually rather err in defect than in excess of that ancient vice and modern virtue, cowardice; and which consequently discourage friends while they fail in conciliating enemies. To find the irreducible minimum has been Mr Gladstone's aim, and according to the verdict of both friends and foes he has succeeded. A simple-minded man might have expected the Radicals, at any rate, to be pleased at this, but he will by this time be disillusioned. Some of them do indeed eat the leek thus presented to them by the Celtic champion with a tolerably good grace, but a great many insist on being thrashed before eating, which grace before meat they are, I think, not likely to lack.

The fact is these worthies were quite prepared to give Ireland Home Rule so long as Humbug accompanied it, so long as the grant of it did *not* enable the Irish to manage their own affairs; and they seem to have hoped (not perhaps without some reason) that Mr Gladstone would contrive this trap for their benefit. It would indeed have been a triumph for modern bourgeois legislation to have been able to say, 'We have done what you wanted, we offer you Home Rule, and now you won't take it'. And that would have been quite in its manner too. But they have been disappointed and are forced to face a measure which the Irish believe will make them practically independent, and whether the bill passes or not, there is no doubt that they will not now accept anything less than it. This is grievous enough for our Federation-of-the-Empire friends, but if they are Radicals to boot, what are they to do? Mr Chamberlain sees that he cannot, as yet, join the Tory-Whig coalition, and consequently, in spite of the almost unanimous agreement of the London Liberal press, including the once anti-Jingo *Echo*, which now sees the error of its ways, he will probably have to content himself with looking on at a Gladstone triumph and a Whig protest, without sharing in either. The bill will pass the Commons either now or after a coalition muddle, or else the Irish will in some way or other rebel.

Under these circumstances it is not worth while to look into the details of Mr Gladstone's bill, even if such matters could concern Socialists at all. It means the Independence of Ireland and not the sham Federation which the greater part of the Liberal Party intended it to mean. This is clearly shown by the fact that while Radicals cry out on injustice to the Irish in excluding them from the Westminster Parliament, these themselves will by no means accept the honour if they can help it, as they perceive it to tend towards Federation. One remedy at least they might have, of the kind known to the unthirsty horse when brought to water; they need not drink of the stream of honour and consideration flowing from Westminster; in other words they may stay at home and mind their own business, which they will sorely need to do. For the rest, the bill is a specimen of the usual Constitution-building, and is full of safeguards against dangers which, when they come near will send the said safeguards flying into space. We need not heed all that; the Irish people accept it, the Whigs reject it: that is enough.

But what is this new parliament to us Revolutionary Socialists who see no panacea in parliaments of any kind? Well, first the Irish (as I have some reason to know) will not listen to anything except the hope of independence as long as they are governed by England; no, not even to the most elementary propositions about the land, which concern them most and nearest – they can see nothing else than an Ireland freed from that government. They are, as it were, demoralized by a long war, and will likely enough confirm the prophecies of their enemies by floundering wofully (*sic*) amidst their difficulties, when they have their own affairs to manage. But it is only by finding out what a parliament is like that they can know what a worthless instrument it is towards helping the community to a decent life; and they will have to meet those difficulties themselves and be responsible for their manner of dealing with them, instead of letting their responsibilities lapse into the willing hands of England. They will then surely begin to find out that English rule was so disastrous to them, not because of the difference of race between the governors and the governed, but because a crude form of arbitrary authority was practised on the 'inferior race'; because England represented landlord and capitalist oppression, which, to say the truth, would not have lacked a representative even if she had not been paramount in Ireland.

Home Rule for Ireland is not of itself necessarily a revolutionary measure, but it will clear the ground for sowing the seed of Revolution; and that all the more as the problem in Ireland is simpler than elsewhere, owing to its being chiefly an agricultural country. The patience and good humour of the people may help its new rulers to stave off the great change which shall make Ireland free by freeing all its inhabitants; and their terrible apprenticeship in misery may help in restraining them from claiming that decent and happy life which it will be easier for them to get for the claiming than it is to most peoples; but the claim will certainly be made, and can only be crushed by a bourgeois England triumphant over its enemy - *The People.*

COMMONWEAL, VOLUME 2, NUMBER 16,
1 MAY 1886, P. 36

SOCIALISM IN DUBLIN AND YORKSHIRE

I have to say a few words of another lecture tour, which I hope may be of some interest to our readers. I started on the night of Thursday 8th April, made memorable by the introduction of the Home Rule Bill and Mr Gladstone's speech, which more by token I found awaiting us on our landing next morning at Kingstown. The next day I addressed an audience mostly of 'ladies and gentlemen' at the Molesworth Hall, on the 'Aims of Art'. There were a few workmen scattered among the audience, and our comrades of the Dublin Branch put in an appearance, and two, I think, spoke in the discussion which followed. I fear that the 'ladies and gentlemen' were disappointed with what I was forced to lay before them, which, as a matter of course, included advocacy of Socialism as a necessity for the new birth of art.

The next day I attended the 'Saturday Club', and opened a debate on 'Socialism: what it is'. The audience, mostly of working men, was a large one, and naturally somewhat excited by the affairs of the week. I had no reason, however, to complain of my reception. Plenty of assent and dissent was expressed, with cheering vigour on both sides. I spoke for some forty-five minutes, and was well listened to. One slip I unwittingly made by mentioning Sackville Street, which is popularly known as O'Connell Street, a name which the authorities refuse to accept. A great to-do followed this blunder, which, on a hint from the chairman, I corrected with all good will, and so was allowed to go on, with cheers. A rather poor debate followed my speech, for the attackers of Socialism didn't know anything about it, and the first would-be defender claimed it as the 'crystalisation (*sic*) of Christian ethics', which opened the door to a great deal of rather rampant theology. This in its turn seemed to excite the audience considerably, and brought out the bigotry which one certainly expects to find in an Irish audience. An incident finished the evening, which, as it was magnified by some of the papers into a 'riot', I may as well mention. The chairman closed the debate by calling on me to answer, but the audience had not had enough, or some one was wanting to speak out of whom they expected some sport, so they got out of hand, and made some noise for 600 people; but after singing 'God Save Ireland', and finding the chairman firm, they quieted down in about a quarter of an hour, and listened peaceably enough to my answer, which was shorter than it otherwise would have been. Whatever disturbance there was, it was not directed against the representative of Socialism.

On the Sunday I met the members of the Branch at comrade Schumann's rooms, and had a very satisfactory evening. It is clear that at present the religious matter is the difficulty; but I cannot help thinking that when Home Rule is established the Catholic clergy will begin to act after their kind, and try after more and more power, till the Irish gorge rises and rejects them. The Protestant religious feeling being dogmatic and not political, is hopeless to deal with. Meantime, open-air meetings are not possible for us in Dublin – at least till we are much stronger in numbers. The Branch has taken action very judiciously, through comrade Schumann, in the glass-blowers' strike and the importation by the masters on false pretences of Danish workmen, who have behaved very well in the matter, and show all appreciation of the solidarity of labour.

On the Saturday I lectured in the hall of the Branch on the 'Political Outlook'. The audience, mostly working men again, seemed for the most part heartily with me, and the meeting turned out quite a success.

Of course, though I saw many people in Dublin (and many of them, by the way, not far from Socialists), my short stay in one place in the country could not add much to my power of judging of our chances of success there. It is a matter of course that until the Irish get Home Rule they will listen to nothing else, and equally so that as soon as they get Home Rule they must deal at once with the land question. On the whole, I fear it seems likely that they will have to go through the dismal road of peasant-proprietorship before they get to anything like Socialism; and that road, in a country so isolated and so peculiar as Ireland, may be a long one. On the other hand, it will lead them straight to ruin unless they can keep out of the world-market – which they can scarcely do. Undoubtedly the Irish are bent on doing all they can to further Irish manufactures, however artificially, and to that end are sure to drive new railways through the country, and so to stimulate that production for profit which throws the peasant into the hands of the usurer, and makes peasant-proprietorship a miserable make-shift – a piece of reaction leading nowhere, save *down* the hill. So that after all things in Ireland may go quicker than we now think.

So much for the Irish journey. On Saturday the 17th, I went by invitation of the Leeds and Bradford Branches to Shipley, and there lectured at the Co-operative Hall on 'The Political Outlook'. The hall was not so full as it should have been, considering that Shipley is a very Radical place; I was unlucky, probably, in tumbling into the middle of the Bradford election; amidst such an audience also, a rational view of the Parliamentary system was not likely to be popular. However, I was well listened to, and with a good deal of assent. I gave myself up as a stalking-horse to some Radical rhetoric at a 'free-and-easy' after the lecture, not much to anybody's edification I fancy, flowery vagueness being the staple of these gentlemen's remarks; nor where they so anxious for any information that I could give them as for the enunciation of the venerable platitudes that make the stock-in-trade of a Radical becoming a Whig by the force of circumstances.

The next day, Sunday, I lectured at the Temperance Hall in Bradford to a full audience, very attentive, and who caught the points well, and seem pleased by the attack on Bourgeoisdom. A few questions were put, but, as usual, clearly not by those who were thinking most of the lecture. In the evening we had a meeting of the Leeds and Bradford Branches, partly convivial and partly business, where I had to try to clear up a few difficulties as to principles and tactics which had occurred to two or three members, though everything went in the friendliest manner possible.

On the Monday I lectured in Leeds, and found the audience rather heavy to 'spring', partly, perhaps, because though there were a great many people present, over 600 I should think, the hall was too large for the audience, who were, however, very attentive at least, and cheered heartily at the necessary expulsion of one gentleman (said to be an employer of labour) who (or rather the alcohol in whom) tried to prevent my being heard. Once more those who really wanted to ask questions were prevented by vague or cavilling speeches, quite outside the four corners of the lecture.

I took leave of the Branches in the committee-room here, and had no difficulty in accepting the assurance that though they had not a very numerous membership, their members were all real, and did actual work; indeed, they were clearly working very hard, and in spite of all drawbacks with much success.

In dealing with these centres of the great industry, one is apt at first to be disappointed with the reception of Socialist principles, but it is to be remembered that those that one comes across personally in a hurried visit are the would-be progressive leaders who generally belong to the aristocracy of labour in its most limited sense, foremen and the like, who as to their material needs are comfortably off, and suppose that it will last for ever; such men, unless they have special intelligence and aspirations, are generally the narrowest of Whigs. Again, the constant weight of drill in these highly organized industries has necessarily limited the intelligence of the men, and deadened their individuality, while the system is so powerful and searching that they find it difficult to conceive of any system under which they could be other than human machines. Nevertheless, the average intelligence is high, and when they once find time to understand what the stealing of labour means, that very drill will make them move in a mass, and then-, then, Mr Self-made Man, you must turn to and work once more, an equal amongst equals.

Meantime, we are really getting on in these places. Two years ago, when I lectured at Bradford, the place seemed hopeless to me; the one or two concerts whom I – I will not say made, but perhaps helped on that occasion, in conjunction with one or two at Leeds [I managed] to make, must be congratulated on the results of their steady courage and hard work.

COMMONWEAL, VOLUME 2, NUMBER 17,
8 MAY 1886, P. 43

Our Representatives

The past week of parliamentary and party strife has been sufficiently barren of interest to the ordinary observer. No one has expected anything new to be said about the Home Rule Bill, and no one has been disappointed. The Disarming Bill was carried, as every one knew it would be, and the votes pro and con were very much what was expected. Accordingly, the thing which usually happens in a dull interval of an exciting period has happened now. People having few additional facts to go on have been turning guesses at facts into facts, and disputing about them as vigorously as if they had really happened.

As an addition to this amusement, a violent sham quarrel about nothing at all has been got up by the *Pall Mall Gazette* against Mr Chamberlain. That journal is almost entirely on Mr Chamberlain's side in the Home Rule matter; it has been one of the most unsparing opponents of the Bill; and might have seen, if it did not, in Mr Chamberlain a thick and thin supporter of its favourite fad of imperial federation and the deification of the central parliament of the empire. But all this is not enough, and an attack must be made on him on grounds difficult enough for a simple person to see. Mr Chamberlain's conduct in the Irish business is attackable enough from various sides; but that the most spiteful attack should come on him from a friend, or at least an ally, is quaint indeed. If it means anything more than a newspaper sensation, it must point to the utter want of faith in the Liberal-Radical party, whose leaders in the press and in Parliament are hitting out wildly in the hopes of attracting some applause somewhere from some section or other of that once respectable drilled phalanx.

Nor can Mr Chamberlain be congratulated on any success in keeping his temper. His attack on the meeting of the Liberal and Radical Council seems to show that their hint of censure has been taken as a deep cause of offence; though, perhaps, like the servant-maid in Dickens, he has only been 'showing them what kind of a temper he keeps' – a mode of striving for his own way familiar enough to the ex-master of the Caucus. For the rest, his appeal in his letter for political gratitude for past services, to shield him from censure on present blunders, would be feeble argument indeed if the rank and file had not got so used to leadership – by the nose.

Quarrelling among once allies has been diversified by a good deal of watering down of strong utterances against enemies when the latter have raised too much of a storm around the speech-makers. Lord Salisbury having put forward some alternative to Home Rule, found no difficulty in proclaiming the necessary Tory scheme of coercion, carried on, if necessary, to extermination of the rebellious race. But, frightened at the sound of his own words, he has tried to explain all that away into paternal government for Ireland, and the attainment for it of all the blessings 'which in this island we have for a long time been privileged to enjoy'. *We?* Landlords and fundlords, it must be supposed, who indeed have had no bad time of it in Ireland either.

Of course there is nothing in this vague nonsense; but that his lordship thinks it necessary to explain away his tall talk does mean something: he is looking towards the Whigs and Whigizing of Radicals, it is but part of the same operation as the quarreling (*sic*) of the old allies – namely, the tendency for all reaction to run together into the Moderate Party. Sheer Toryism can now only work through hypocrisy – that is, Whiggery, alias dying Constitutionalism confronted with young Revolution.

Even the bold Major Saunderson was anxious to 'explain', much as if a man using the word 'damned' with reference to an adversary, were to point out that he did not intend a theological assertion. Lord R. Churchill, however, stood to his guns, and asserted the constitutionalism of rebellion in the teeth of the 'sacro-sanctity of assemblies' ingeniously enough, whatever may be said about his ingenuousness. Poor Constitutionalism! that has to be supplemented by Revolution!

The respectabilities that followed Lord R. Churchill – Gladstonite and other, including Mr Gladstone himself – did not accept this view of Constitutionalism; their respectability rang hollow enough since they were driven into using war-like metaphors in the usual unreal and meaningless manner; in spite of which all that was said made clear once more that brute force is the real cement of all sham society, and that it will breed force as a solvent of its tyranny. It is a pity indeed that such a discussion should have had no better occasion than the carrying on on one side of the old habit of refusing the Irish the rights of citizenship, and on the other an attempt to put the Irish landlords in the right, whatever means they may try for the upholding of their monstrous oppression.

The 'negotiations' for patching up that broken jug, the Liberal Party, and all the lies, half-lies, contradictions, evasions, and the rest of the brood of party tactics may be passed over in unrespectful silence. Thus the game of 'representation' goes on, and outside it the people live and die – live miserably and die before their time, and the veil of words, and sham intentions, and half intentions, and the self-interest of the rich now grown mild and fatherly – in words – dulls the sound of that

> Lamentation and an ancient tale of wrong,
> Like a tale of little meaning though the words are strong;
> Chanted from an ill-used race of men that cleave the soil,
> Sow the seed, and reap the harvest with enduring toil.

How long will it last? 'Our time' think our Representatives. Well, some of them are old men, but some scarcely middle-aged, and 'he who lives will see'.

Commonweal, Volume 2, Number 20,
29 May 1886, p. 68

NOTES AND QUERIES
PRACTICAL SOCIALISM

A friend who says that he quite understands the theory of Socialism, [h]as some questions on its 'practical application':-

> (1) Will there be any shopkeepers or public[–]houses in the new state of society, and if not how are things to be exchanged? (2) Will there by any money used? (3) Who will superintend workmen in factories, etc.? 'These', says our friend, 'are questions I am constantly asked, and am unable to give a satisfactory reply to; I want to see a plan as it were of the new state of Society.'

When the plan is visible the new state of Society will be realized, it cannot be visible before. As to questions 1 and 2, it must be pointed out that the essence of the new Society is that both the production and the distribution of goods will be carried on for the benefit of the community, instead of as now for the gain of individuals at the expense of the community. Of course there will be distributors of goods (which goods will, I hope, include drinks, as we shall it is to be hoped be able to enjoy ourselves without bestiality on one side, so shall not need total abstinence ritual on the other). A dozen 'plans' for such distribution might be made, but none of them would be of any particular value. We shall follow the 'plan' which we find to be necessary and useful. Money will be used if necessary, as it may be at first, but will only be used as counters representing so much labour. As to question 3, the answer is those who are fit to superintend will do so, and will do it willingly as it will be easy for them, since they are fit for it; the workmen whom they direct will also follow that direction willingly, as they will find out that doing so will make their work easier and more effective; also on *every* workman will rest a due share of responsibility, he will not be as he is now a mere irresponsible machine.

Our friend also wants some information about the revolutionary movements in other countries. He will find a good deal in the *Commonweal* on this head. As to the differences of opinion amongst Socialists, these must exist, but it is surely a mistake to further their crystalisation (*sic*) into *parties* with names attached to them that by no means always mean the same thing. There is no difference whatever between the aims of the English and the Foreign Socialists, the different shades of opinion are represented in all countries, and all share this aim, the destruction of the system which robs the workman of the fruits of his labour, which robbery our friend says the field labourers he talks with can see clearly. This last fact is better news than even he perhaps thinks. He says also that he cannot get them to 'organize'. Let him try his best in the confidence that the course of events will force them to do so.

COMMONWEAL, VOLUME 2, NUMBER 20,
29 MAY 1886, P. 71

Instructive Items

The eight hours movement in America has not been the failure it is so loudly proclaimed. It is found, by actual computation, that nearly half-a-million have gained the eight hours system; that another half-million are working under the nine hour rule, and that not less than a million besides have succeeded in shortening the hours of labour in one shape or another. The fourteen and fifteen hours men have cut off two or three hours; the Saturday half-holiday men have largely gained their object, and the early closing and Sunday closing movements have been successful in most places.

'What should I go to see in Europe?' writes Lady Hester Stanhope, from the wild solitary home she has made for herself among the high lands of Palestine. 'Nations worthy of their chains, and kings unworthy of ruling. Before long, your old Continent will be shaken to its foundations. All therein is worn out; the kings found no dynasties, they fall, borne down by death or dethroned for their faults, and degenerate as they succeed each other; the aristocracy, soon to fade from the world, will give place to a wretched and ephemeral Bourgeoisie without strength or vigour; the people alone still retain character and some virtues. Tremble, if they ever realize their own strength!'

Even in the villages and little towns of the country, as well as in the great centres of labour, employment is lacking. Bampton-in-the-Bush and Lechdale, two such towns on the upper waters of the Thames, have their share of this trouble I find. Some farmers that I was amongst in a second-class carriage between the two places amongst others gave me information (by their talk between themselves) on this point. At last the conversation took the following turn: 'I was sorry', said the youngest man present, 'that they couldn't do anything for that man who had cut his fingers off and came for medical relief.' 'Well, you see', said another, 'we have to be very particular about such cases, or they would make up all kinds of stories.' 'He ought to have taken care of his fingers', quoth a third, a white-headed man of the small parrot-nosed, broad-faced type, with self-satisfied arched eyebrows, which proclaims the unfeeling fool without any admixture, and is common among well-to-do bourgeois in our moral country. Said the younger man: 'He will have to pay a doctor to cure him out of 11s. a week.' 'He ought to have belonged to a club', said parrot-nose. The younger man said: 'Well he didn't, and it's a hard case.' 'He ought to have', said parrot-nose again; 'he could easily have paid up weekly.' Therewith the train stopped at a station, and the party broke up, not much dispirited at the idea of the maimed labourer and his position between the poor-law and civilization.

COMMONWEAL, VOLUME 2, NUMBER 21,
5 JUNE 1886, P. 79

FREE SPEECH AT STRATFORD

A meeting was held at Stratford last Saturday on the same ground as on the former week. Comrades Aveling and Morris spoke for the League, and Messers. (*sic*) Ellis (of the Peckham and Dulwich Radical Club) and Rose (Whitechapel Liberal Club) also spoke. A solid and attentive audience at once came together as soon as the first speaker began; about 300, I should think, was the number of the actual meeting. Our two Radical friends spoke well and strongly on the right of free speech, and the audience was obviously in complete sympathy. At the close of the meeting, which lasted an hour, comrade Aveling called for a show of hands in favour of free speech generally, and of maintaining it on that spot, and all hands were help up. The police did not interfere, although there were many about and in the crowd in plain clothes, and an inspector came up to the skirts of the meeting several times to take note of our proceedings.

It must have been clear to all those present that there was no real obstruction caused by the meeting; and it should be the opinion of all those interested in free speech that it is most important to keep up the meetings here. Most meeting-places, except those held in parks or on commons, are attackable on the same grounds as this is. Nor will it do merely to challenge the police to remove bodies speaking there other than Socialists. In their zeal for getting rid of Socialist meetings, the Respectables are quite capable of accepting the challenge and getting rid of Temperance, Christianity, and Radicalism at one blow, in order to get rid of Socialism. All those, therefore, who care at all about the expression of advanced opinion should take warning, and remember that it is no use standing aside to be eaten up last. Any excuse will be made use of in order to clear the streets altogether of everybody but proletarians hurrying to and from their daily toil and sauntering fine ladies and gentlemen. To make the world outside Respectability one huge prison is the darling wish of the Respectables, from Matthew Arnold the pensioner down to some petty vestry tyrant at Stratford. Sweet alliance of the Superfine and the Bumble! Lovers of freedom, combine to overthrow this alliance, which is dangerous though ridiculous.

COMMONWEAL, VOLUME 2, NUMBER 22,
12 JUNE 1886, P. 87

HOME RULE OR HUMBUG

It would be but waste of time to go through all the election addresses of even the principal leaders of parties which have been put before the public during the last few days; but those addresses, and the reception of Mr Gladstone on his journey northward, seem to foreshadow the nature and issue of the coming contest, and a few words seem desirable about it. Mr Gladstone has definitely given up his Bill, and takes his stand on the principle of a parliament for Ireland. It is clear that this may mean compromise - that he is prepared to accept something less like independence than the Bill intended; but it may not mean anything more than electioneering vagueness, trying to make the sweep of the net as wide and inclusive as possible, – a dangerous manoeuvre, but which will always be tried at elections, and by Mr Gladstone.

The point is, whether the Irish people are prepared to accept anything less like independence than the Bill; or rather, will the march of Parliamentary events compel them to do so. The Chamberlainites have the power, perhaps, of forcing them to accept a compromise. The immediate purpose of Mr Gladstone's declaration of the death of the Bill is an olive-branch to Radical dissentients. If they accept it as a body, the whole Liberal-Radical party (outside Lord Hartington's Whigs) will be pledged to shaving down the measure for the new Parliament to something less than the defunct Bill. The Irish, at all events their central group, will shrink from the attitude of irreconcilability if the shaving down is not very flagrant, especially if it gives them, as it almost certainly will do, an immediate opportunity for carrying on the agitation. Unless, therefore, the Chamberlainites are dead against any real Home-Rule, they will give up their present opposition to Mr Gladstone, and leave their Tory-Whig friends in the lurch.

It is much to be hoped that they will not take this course, for in their coming into the Gladstonian camp again lies the real danger to the success of Irish independence. Whether Mr Gladstone is strong enough to win in the elections or not, he will at least have at his back a minority strong enough in opposition to prevent the passing of a measure intended for the complete shelving of the question, which would have to be enforced by the usual method by which English gifts are presented to Ireland – coercion, to wit. But on the other hand, a majority of men merely pretending to support Home Rule, joined to the usual amount of waverers, might so dally with the question as practically to draw us back again into the trouble from which we have seemed to be emerging. A firm and strong minority would educate people somewhat: a sloppy majority would wear them out and make them languid as to the whole subject.

Meanwhile it is observable that no party *professes* to intend shelving the question; and further, that in spite of all the bluster of the Tory press, the Tories are beginning to see the impossibility of dragooning Ireland in the future, and are loudly disclaiming coercion. Even the *St James's Gazette* is driven to this retreat, and talks about Lord Salisbury's 'unguarded moment', – the moment in which he very frankly expressed the intentions or hopes of the Tory party as regards Ireland; intentions which would have to become those of Whigs and Jingo-Radicals if they were to succeed in getting support enough to impose their schemes on that country. This looks very like throwing up the sponge. Things have come to this point, that even those who, if they could, would coerce Ireland by any and every means, including a scheme of depopulation, which Lord Salisbury is now driven to disavow, perceive that the thing is impossible in the face of the gathering instinct of the English people against their forcible benevolence in favour of the landlords.

It is becoming impossible then to impose the rule of the English bureaucracy in its worst form on Ireland. What alternative is left then to the reactionists in dealing with her? Apparently, to involve the whole question in a hopeless, lawyer-like muddle, so as to sicken people of it, and to get up the old cry of the impossibility of dealing with the Irish. This is what is being attempted; and, on the whole, Mr Gladstone's answer to it must be considered an effective one, and none the less so because of its simplicity; he has for once thrown off all finesse, and puts the broad question before the country of Home Rule or Humbug; it was necessary to do this in order to break through the network of evasions, intrigue, and compromise that the end of last Session had woven round the question. It is no use prophecying (*sic*) as to the result of the elections, but if they go against Home Rule this simplifying of the present issue will give force and distinctness to the powerful opposition which, as above said, is the alternative to a success at the polling booths.

One may say about the Radicals generally, looking at them from the Socialist point of view, that they may be divided into two sections. The first are the pedantic Radicals with certain party shibboleths on their tongues, and in their hearts bitter hostility to everything which seems to interfere even temporarily with the party game which they are playing. Between them and us there is and must be mere war; they will not even listen to us. They look upon us with more hatred than they do upon the Tories, for without the latter they could not carry on their game. But besides these pedantic Radicals, there is another Radical section who are on the look out for progressive ideas, and are the representatives of advancing Democracy. These may, and often do, oppose us as inconvenient impracticable persons, who interfere with what they have learned to consider progress, but they are not really unfriendly and are willing to hear us, and when they have done so they will find, many of them, that they are Socialists after all.

Well, the Chamberlainite Unionist Radicals, many of whom are quite fanatical in their opposition to Home Rule, do on this occasion represent to us the hostile pedantic Radicals, while those who are championing Home Rule represent our Radical friends, who are waiting to be told what Socialism really is, or at any rate waiting to find out what it is, and who when they have found out will become Socialists. As Socialists, therefore, we are bound to wish the utmost success to those who can at least see that it is necessary for Ireland to take her own affairs into her own hands, whatever the immediate results may be. To the pedantic Radicals, the new Jingoes, we need scarcely wish ill-success, for as things are going they are getting themselves deeper into the mire at every step.

COMMONWEAL, VOLUME 2, NUMBER 24,
26 JUNE 1886, PP. 100–101

A LETTER FROM SCOTLAND

On Tuesday 22nd I found myself at Arbroath, a pleasant stone-built town of some 20,000 inhabitants on the German Ocean, the original of 'Fairport' in Scott's 'Antiquary', the remains of a magnificent church and abbey dominating the homely houses. The industry practised there is sail-cloth making, and it is in a very dismal condition at present. There was much suffering there in the past winter. In a walk that I took with my host (a Free Kirk minister and a Socialist), we got into conversation with a field-labourer who was resting from his job of harrowing at a field's end. I should premise, for the benefit of our English readers, that Scotch field-labourers are hired by the half-year, and receive their 'meal-and-milk', lodging in a 'bothy' – or a not too luxurious pig-stye – and a sum of money. This friend, who was a brisk and intelligent young man, told us that wages were low, and that he was now receiving £9 for the half-year, instead of £12, which he used to receive. He also told us, perhaps unnecessarily, that he could not save out of this splendid salary. I was told afterwards that wages had fallen back to what they were ten years ago, at which time they had risen suddenly. A foreman, a friend told us, was now getting £28 per annum, which used to be the wages of a full private labourer.

In the evening I lectured to an audience of upwards of 600 very attentive persons, mostly of the working-class. They cheered me heartily, and took up the points well. There was a goodly attendance on the platform of the committee who had organized the meeting, and who were chiefly co-operators. Questions being asked for, I only got one, from the irrepressible temperance champion, which was received with some laughter. In fact, the meeting was rather huddled up at the end, as there was no gas and the light began to fade into the mid-summer twilight, which is all the darkness of those northern regions at this time of year. A fair amount of literature was sold.

On the 23rd I lectured at Edinburgh, in the Oddfellows' Hall, for the committee which is the fag-end of the Industrial Remuneration Conference of last year. We expected but a poor attendance, as there were several meetings of parliamentary candidates going on in the city; but after all it turned out well, the attendance being better than at any previous lecture. Again the audience seemed sympathetic – nay, enthusiastic. I asked for questions in writing, dreading the meandering speech which usually accompanies spoken questions. I got quite a pack of cards of them; and the answers were well received. A clergyman was in the chair, another (our friend Mr Glasse, who made a Socialistic speech) moved the vote of thanks, and a third seconded it. This last gentleman poked some heavy ecclesiastical fun at me, interlarded with buttery compliments. Once for all, I must ask our comrades to forgive me for receiving votes of thanks, on the ground that I could not help it. The sale of literature was good. I had a short but pleasant interview with the members of the Branch afterwards. They seemed rather depressed; lack speakers, and so find it difficult to make much way; but are getting a few new members, in spite of the slackness of their propaganda. They told me that a branch of the Social Democratic Federation started, apparently with good prospects, early this year or late last (I forget which), had quite disappeared after a few weeks' existence. One comrade said that in talking to fellow-workmen they would agree with everything that he said in favour of Socialism, but could not be brought further than this passive adherence. On the other hand our comrades are making most commendable efforts to push the *Commonweal*, and with much success. The news-shops take it and sell it, too, and they are also getting newsboys to sell it; so that propaganda of some sort is going on, only our comrades feel the want of public and obvious propaganda. I should add, the University Society, who have a good deal retreated from their position, at all events in appearance, are starting a kind of progressive debating society, appealing to trades' unionists and co-operatives to join it, which our comrades intend to use for their own and other people's education.

The 24th I gave the same lecture at Glasgow. A wet evening, meetings of candidates throughout the town, and again apprehensions of a failure; but again a good audience, perhaps rather more in assent than at Edinburgh; a somewhat overwhelming amount of questions, the answers to which were very well received. A sprinkling of Ruskinians were there, somewhat inclined, I fancy, to take exception to the roughness of the opinions: indeed, the mover of that (terrible) vote of thanks said as much, and was somewhat cheered.

I may here remark that it seems to me that the Scotch are much given to 'lion-hunting', and that therefore it is necessary for a Socialist who wants to get at the facts to discount a certain amount of the enthusiasm with which he is received, if he happens to have any reputation outside Socialism. Still enough remains in these cases to show that there were many in the audience who really agreed. At Glasgow there was a good sprinkling also of Land Restorers; but these, I think, are beginning to see out of the narrow close in which Henry George has hedged them.

The 25th I lectured at Dundee, and had much such an audience as at Glasgow, only that they lacked the instruction that our Branch has, with all drawbacks, given to the Glasgow folk, and therefore did not seem so ready to take up the points. Trade is very slack at Dundee; the jute business nearly gone, Indian competition having destroyed it. I was told that there are few places where the difference between the classes is more felt than it is at Dundee. I much regretted that I could not stop there and get to know some of the workers. Our comrades here (Glasgow) ought to make a push to get up a branch at Dundee.

I meet the Branch to-day, and in the evening lecture again. Tomorrow I lecture at Bridgeton, a suburb of Glasgow. But I send this off to be in time for the current number, and will give an account of whatever else happens next week.

Commonweal, Volume 2, Number 25,
3 July 1886, pp. 105–6

THE SEQUEL OF THE SCOTCH LETTER

On Sunday 27th June I lectured on the 'Political Outlook' at the Waterloo Rooms, Glasgow, the same place where my Thursday's lecture was given; this was under the auspices of the Branch, and our comrade Muirhead took the chair. There was a larger attendance than on the Thursday; howbeit several got up and went out almost as soon as I began: it seems there was some mistake as to my subject, as there was a religious meeting elsewhere on the premises, and some of the proper audience thereof had wandered into our hall. Moreover I suspect that some found themselves 'caught' by my title, and expected the lecture to refer to the present election instead of the wider subject which it dealt with. The audience was over 600, I should think, and was attentive and sympathetic. Instead of the cut-and-dried, meaningless vote of thanks, our comrades arranged to try the effect of a resolution, which was thus worded: 'That all political action which does not aim at placing the entire means of production in the hands of the community, to be used by it for the equal benefit of all, is totally inadequate to raise the present labouring classes to the level which they have a right to claim as human beings.' Comrade Glasier put this resolution in a very able speech, and it was seconded by Mr Cunninghame; and to my surprise no one proposed an amendment, or spoke against it: some half-dozen hands were held up against it; the rest, for. We afterwards appealed to the audience to make their resolution good by joining the League, and got some names at any rate. Mr Bennet, once editor of the *Radical*, who said he had come in late by misadventure, made a sympathetic speech at the end of the meeting. The literature sold well.

The last lecture was on Monday 28th, at Bridgeton, the east end of Glasgow, and so speak plainly a most woeful abode of man, crying out from each miserable court and squalid, crowded house for the abolition of the tyranny of exploitation. But here we did not score a success. There were election meetings going on all about us; and I fear that our audience was just *not* that which we wanted – to wit, the poor folk of the district, who, if they only knew it, do so sorely need showing what it is that has doomed them to their special form of hell-upon-earth – one of the worst forms in existence, I should think. The audience was about 200, in a large hall, but entirely on our side. The monotony of acquiescence was only broken by an eager religionist, who turned his question-time into a kind of sermon addressed to us, which the audience listened to rather impatiently. A clergyman who elicited from me the answer that service as well as actual production of commodities conferred the title of good citizenship upon a man, seemed satisfied that this admission safe-guarded his craft in future society; but as he did not openly champion that position, it was not discussed. Comrades Glasier and Greer moved and seconded a resolution, the wording of which has escaped my memory, but which was rather more complete in its Socialism than the one of Sunday, and no hand was held up against it. Several names were taken for the Branch before we left the hall.

This was the end of my work; but I should mention that I had a long conference with the Branch on the Sunday, and must say that though circumstances prevent their propaganda from being showy, it is sound, and especially that there seems every chance of their developing the sale of *Commonweal*. I must add that the Branch of the Social Democratic Federation is on very friendly terms with them, and that they co-operated heartily in trying to make our meetings a success; and the members that I came across were very cordial to me.

Altogether the condition of opinion in the Scotch towns that I have visited is encouraging. It must be remembered that it was a bad time of the year for the kind of work I had in hand; to which must be added the much more important stumbling-block of the most exciting election-time of our days; and yet the halls were mostly well filled, and the audiences more than attentive – almost enthusiastic – and as above said, two of them passed Socialist resolutions. In short, not to make too much of outward tokens, one could not help feeling that the ideas of Socialism are taking hold, and that people are beginning to feel the hollowness of that kind of politics in which all reforms pass by those who need them most. Nor will the attachment to puritanic religion, which has been held up as such a bug-bear to us, be a very serious barrier to Socialism; the one or two appeals to it which were made in my hearing were received decidedly coldly. The Scotch, it seems, no longer care to mix religion with their politics, whatever influence genuine feeling, or habit, or respectability may have on them in the matter. I was told that when Henry George appealed to their old puritanic feeling on the occasion of his last visit, it fell very flat indeed; and I was not surprised to hear it, after my own small experience herein. Here, then, is good hope of harvest, and once again the labourers are few. Let us hope that will mend before long, and that Scotland will not be the last in the Revolution.

COMMONWEAL, VOLUME 2, NUMBER 26,
10 JULY 1886, P. 114

What is to Happen Next?

The elections are over with the result of a Parliament that comprises a majority of more than a hundred against Home Rule, although the Tories are in a considerable minority as regards a possible (?) combination between the Whigs, Jingo-Liberals, Parnellites, and Gladstonians or British Home Rulers. It would be idle not to admit that this is a success of the Reactionists, and a success unexpected by most persons. Moreover, it would certainly have been a great advantage to the Socialist propaganda if the ground had been cleared of a question which very naturally excites political passions deeply, and at the same time has only an indirect bearing on our great object, the destruction of monopoly and exploitation. Peace with Ireland would not only have forced the consideration of their own economical condition, on the Irish themselves, but would have left nothing for us to consider in England, Scotland, and Wales, except our economical condition: unless some scare of a Russian war could have been set on foot by our 'rulers'.

But though it is most necessary to face the fact spoken of in our last issue of the powerlessness of the political working-men under our present system, it may not be amiss to emphasize the other point mentioned therein; to wit, the humbug of our electoral arrangements; otherwise, well-intentioned people might be genuinely discouraged at the apparent desertion of democratic opinion by the working-classes in the just past elections. If Hercules is knowable from the sight of his foot, according to the classical proverb, Mr Dell's figures in the *Daily News* of July 13th, are worth at least something in this direction as to the vote of the boroughs outside the metropolis. According to these figures, 512,415 Home Rule votes produced 50 members, while 512,415 Tory and Jingo votes made 97 members. Every one really knows that this is but a specimen of the juggling of our Representation, and in itself disposes of the pretence of looking on the elections as they are now conducted as a test of opinion.

Admitting this juggle then, it may be said, for the encouragement of those that are discouraged by the would-be popular vote of the 'New Democracy', that even from their point of view it is not so bad after all. Let them further consider the influences brought to bear on the workmen voters, influences which must bear heavily on the average of men. The confusion caused by the desertion of their leaders, Mr Chamberlain the Ransomer, Mr J. Bright the Tribune of the People, Mr Jesse Collings the Allotter; the raising of the No Popery cry; the threat of Irish labourers flooding the English labour market, the mere hint of which is enough to alienate many a voter, who hasn't grasped the idea that *one* method of keeping the Irish in Ireland would be to allow them to cultivate Ireland. It might surely have been foreseen that such things as these brought to bear upon men *forced* into narrowness and ignorance by the invariable course of their labour and their lives, would be hard indeed to resist; and that they have been resisted as widely as they have been, should, when we come to look upon the matter seriously, give us good hope of even the average material of the 'masses' on whom we depend for the body of assent which must be the first step towards the new Society.

Meantime, the past few days have developed an idea, founded, perhaps, on the considerations above mentioned, that Mr Gladstone though he is beaten need not resign. The *Pall Mall Gazette* distinguished itself by suggesting that Mr Gladstone should gather up all the different opinions on Home Rule, and frame a measure which should satisfy everybody from Mr Chamberlain to Mr Parnell. Mr Labouchere thought that as the Tories would after all be in a minority, Mr Gladstone might hold office for the rest of the year, and bring in a Home Rule Bill in the spring session. But as he was clear that such a bill would be defeated, not seeing, as the sapient *Pall Mall* does, how Yes and No could be reconciled, it is hard to see what, from his point of view, could be gained by merely putting off the evil day, except the satisfaction of appetite for loaves and fishes for a short time. The plain truth is that no mechanical contrivances will hold together even the semblance of a Liberal party. The Whig-Tory party has triumphed, and though probably the name of coalition will be avoided in forming the new government, it will really be a coalition; but this will be a coalition not depending on temporary circumstances, but on the open admission of the fact that Whig and Tory no longer indicate real party differences, much less any ghost of a difference as to principles.

A Whig-Tory Government it will be, then, from the first, and, as to the Irish business, will plainly be inexpugnable. Nay, in other matters also it will be strong, because the fear of playing into the hands of the Separationists will always be present to the minds of the Jingo-Liberals whenever they may be inclined to assert their liberty. They have begun by letting themselves be made the tools of the Whig-Tory party, and they must play out their part to the end, – unless any of them should repent and swallow Home Rule after all, which is by no means impossible.

As for the Irish party, it is difficult to see what amongst ordinary parliamentary tactics they can take to. As long as they are in close alliance with the Gladstonian party their old game of parliamentary obstruction must be in abeyance: nor, indeed, was it ever anything more than a protest against the shelving of the Irish question. The position of tail to the Gladstonian party, or even head of it under Gladstone, would not be a very exciting one for them; but they will have to accept it unless they take one other course. Is it possible that when they see that the Westminster Parliament is determined not to yield to their just demand, then they should leave it to do as it will, and return to Ireland and there sit to give help and counsel, if nothing else, to the Irish people? It may be said that this would precipitate mere violent coercion on the English part; but what then? Are not the English preparing for veiled coercion at least? Will they not be driven to use that? And might it not be well to strip the veil from the ugly thing and show it for what it is? Might it not be well to say, 'Since you must govern us, and against our consent; since you can no longer pretend not to know what we want – govern us, then! And take on yourselves the responsibility for the government! We have besought you, argued with you, taught you, warned you – in vain. We will do so no longer; we have no more to do with you. Take your own course, and find out for yourselves that Ireland is not England.' Such a voice as this would ring throughout all history, if only it could be uttered. But it is not likely to be. The cause of Irish Independence will most probably have to be dragged through all kinds of pettiness and intrigue before its true aim, the happiness of the Irish people, becomes visible.

COMMONWEAL, VOLUME 2, NUMBER 28,
24 JULY 1886, P. 129

FREE SPEECH IN THE STREETS

The police-war against the open-air speaking of the Socialists is being carried on with much vigour this year, and cannot fail even at this stage of it to be noticed by the general public. As this number of the *Commonweal* may, like other numbers, come into the hands of many who are not Socialists, it is not untimely to say a few words on this subject; especially since it is one of great importance to *us* and not unimportant to people generally, even in these days of Dilke-Crawford trials and the coming Tory Government.

For the information of those who have not followed the course of the attacks made on us, I should premise that we were first interfered with at Stratford for speaking on a triangular piece of ground, where a meeting of 600 persons can be held without in any way interfering with the traffic, either foot or vehicular, and where the houses on one side at least are practically out of earshot of the speaking, certainly on days when there is any wheel traffic (our meetings there were held on Saturdays). One of our speakers was arrested there last year, but on his proving before the magistrate that there was no real obstruction to either foot-passengers or vehicles, the charge was dismissed, and we held other meetings there without being meddled with. It is worth while mentioning that a leading Radical of the neighbourhood on being appealed to for help in a demonstration which it has been proposed to organize apropos of this station, declined on the grounds that it had drawbacks as a meeting-place (every place has except the parks) and that there was a place further on that we could use without interference; but it turns out that the place in question is private property, a piece of ground awaiting building operations, and from it, therefore, we could be turned off at any time.

About the same time that we were interfered with at Stratford, the Social Democratic Federation were attacked at Kilburn.

At Bell Street, Edgeware Road, our speakers and those of the Social Democratic Federation had been in the habit of addressing the public on Sundays for eighteen months without any interference on the part of the police; but on Sunday July 4 one of our speakers was arrested, and the two following Sundays two more, together with one of the Federation.

This spot is certainly not so defensible as the piece of waste at Stratford, being a street merely; but there is very little traffic in it on a Sunday, and all Socialist speakers have sedulously kept the footways clear. Whatever inconvenience, therefore, there has been to the public in our meetings, must have been to the occupiers of dwelling-houses in the street; but for eighteen months no complaint has been made. That the inhabitants should suddenly wake up to the unbearableness of our meetings without any promptings from without, looks a little like a miracle, which perhaps the police authorities can explain. On the whole, it must be said of Bell Street that it is somewhat more inconvenient, though but a little more, than Dod Street, where last year public feeling compelled the police to yield.

At the Harrow Road our speakers were 'moved on' some weeks ago and a better place suggested to them by the police; but they were not left in peace there. On July 3 a speaker of ours was summoned for addressing a meeting there and since then meetings have been interdicted. This station is much the same sort of place as the piece of ground at Stratford.

Now we do not claim to be allowed to hold *demonstrations* on these or such-like places, but only our ordinary weekly meetings, held for instruction in our doctrines and discussion of them; these from the nature of them cannot be very large, the same kind of people (often I should hope the same people) week after week; persons who attracted at first by seeing *something* going on, listen, and find it worth while to come again; on the whole, in fact, serious people with some political proclivities. Our Radical friend above-mentioned, was clearly thinking of the Stratford station as a place for holding an excited political meeting on a subject specially interesting at the time; in short, an actual demonstration; whereas our meetings are educational in their character.

It must be remembered, too, that apart from our wishing to extend the field of our operations, and to get at people that might be shy of entering a lecture-room, we *cannot* always get a lecture-room for either love or money. We are strictly boycotted. This was the case in Stratford, and in the district of Bell Street also; at the latter place our Branch being turned out of several rooms after a lecture or two simply on the grounds of our being Socialists. In such districts, therefore, if we are not allowed to speak in the open-air we are gagged, and this although, at the latter place at least, the whole of the population in the streets are enthusiastically in our favour.

As to the causes which have impelled the police against us, I believe that they are complex. There is the natural wish to keep the streets as clear as may be: no one can have a word to say against that, except that there may be cases where the greater advantage may override the less. Only I have noted of late years a growing impatience on the part of the more luxurious portion of society of the amusements and habits of the workers, when they in any way interfere with the calm of their luxury; or to put it in plainer language, a tendency on their part to arrogant petty tyranny in these matters. They would, it they could, clear the streets of everything that may injure their delicate susceptibilities, although all this roughness and squalid stir is but the wrong side of the system which gives them their superior position. They are ashamed of these coarsenesses, though they are not ashamed to be the perpetual pensioners of those whom they force into them, and to live on their unpaid labour. They would clear the streets of costermongers, organs, processions, and lecturers of all kinds, and make them a sort of decent prison corridors, with people just trudging to and from their work. It is impossible but that this feeling should influence the police, who are their immediate servants; and I do not doubt that they truckle to it, apart from the question of Socialist or non-Socialist.

At the same time no one who has noticed the way in which street-corner meetings have been dealt with by them can doubt that they have, to say the least of it, shown a strong bias against Socialists, in spite of all plausible arguments to the contrary. It is quite clear that if they are allowed to indulge in this prepossession, and to act up to the letter of the law in one case while they let it alone in another, they can clear the streets of Socialists while leaving religious, temperance, and other *respectable* meetings to flourish as they may; and moreover a very little exercise of the bias may do all that is necessary, as, *eg.*, to let the gospel preacher have his full hour and *then* move him on, while the Socialist is accosted after ten minutes. Such things as this can be done, and so plausibly put before the public that it is humbugged into believing the police to be merely the champions of free circulation in the streets, while in reality they are lending themselves to mere party purposes.

What we Socialists ask for is not to be interfered with in cases where the holding of a meeting is no real inconvenience to the neighbourhood. We do not believe that the existing law was intended to interfere with such meetings, or that it should be strained in that direction against any bodies of men – religious, temperance, secularist, or others; at the same time we claim to be treated no worse than any of these. If, on the one hand, the police are ambitious to draw the reins of discipline tighter, and to turn London into a model city in such matters, do not let them attack the others through us, because we are a new sect and therefore accounted dangerous. On the other hand, if the authorities consider it necessary to suppress the preaching of our doctrines as dangerous, do not let them sneak behind a mere police order for the regulation of traffic, but attack us in front for our spoken or written utterances which are before the public everywhere. The public can then choose whether they like to see prosecutions for opinion going on in England at the end of the nineteenth century.

For the rest, we appeal to all reasonable people not to allow the streets to be deprived of all life or pleasure at the dictation of wealthy pedants and pleasure-seekers. The workers have not too many intellectual pleasures. Their homes are dull and narrow at the best; for many the streets are their only drawing-room. It may be questionable whether setting their brains to thinking over 'dangerous' doctrines is really so dangerous as driving them back into brutality by constant repression. It is perhaps worth while to sacrifice some of the decorum of the streets for the sake of some extra education in these days of political ferment. On the other hand, if there are any who think it possible to quench the expression of great principles that are at work throughout all civilization by petty police persecution, they will find themselves mistaken. In short, the public have to make up their mind whether the police small be their servants or their masters. In order that they may escape the danger of the latter event they must bestir themselves and look at what is being done without prejudice against the Socialists because of their doctrines.

COMMONWEAL, VOLUME 2, NUMBER 29,
31 JULY 1886, P. 137

MR CHAMBERLAIN'S LEADER

Parliament has met for a ceremonial, and done about as much as it would have done if it had met for the despatch of business – nothing, to wit. But besides that, the two parliamentary groups that represent anything like principle and at the same time have any power in Parliament, have also met, and each has done so much at least as to announce its policy in the present state of things. The Parnellites have met in Dublin, and the Jingo-Whigs in Devonshire House; and the conclusions come to by both parties are certainly encouraging to those who wish to see an end of all parties, since they point directly to the further disintegration and final impotence of parliamentary government.

The Parnellites had obviously a very simple course to take: they had merely to state that they had not changed their minds at the bidding of the English shopkeeper terrified into a special exhibition of spite. They have taken that course, and have announced 'that no measure offering less legislative or executive control over Irish affairs than that contained in Mr Gladstone's Bill can be accepted as a settlement of the Irish national question'. They would have betrayed their trust if they had said less than this, and no one supposed that they would say less. But they go further, and hint in terms by no means obscure that the rents are not likely to be forthcoming, and point out that the first and simplest measure of pacification must be the suspension of evictions. There is no doubt that the whole of non-Orange Ireland will support them in the war which they have declared. It is to be hoped under the circumstances that the Irish will not by rash outbreaks give the Government the opportunity of renewing direct and flagrant coercion: that would simplify their position very much. If the Irish 'fight cunning', the position of the Government will be a very intricate and difficult one, unless, as is possible, they make up their minds to dish the Gladstonians by bringing in a real Home Rule Bill.

That they might do, if it only depended on themselves and their declared Tory following, who would but curse and follow; but they have to reckon also with the Whig-Jingo group, who are not under their leadership, though they are allies to be trusted, in the Irish matter at least; and *they* cannot allow serious concessions to be made, as their doing so would really mean opening the door to Mr Gladstone again, and it is quite clear from what took place at Devonshire House that they are determined not to do that.

It really affords curious matter for reflection on the stability of mere party names and the influence that they still have over the mechanical cohesion of a party long after that party has lost its principles, that some of the Liberal papers, notably the *Daily News*, affect to look on Lord Hartington's speech at Devonshire House as an indication of the healing of the breach in the so-called 'Liberal Party'; whereas it was the plainest statement of the irreconcilability of the split, – a definite tender of help to the Tory party so long as the latter would do its duty in opposing Mr Gladstone and Home Rule. The 'Liberal Party' can only be united by the Gladstonites declaring definitely against Home Rule; and doubtless many of them are longing to do so. Mr Alderman Cook, for instance, will probably not lack his reward, but will be returned for East Birmingham as a convert to the cause of Chamberlainism and no surrender. If Mr Gladstone were to die, or if he were to give up the parliamentary game, as he is not likely to do; or if he were to argue himself out of his present position of the Friend of Ireland, as it is to be feared he may do – this kind of reunion of the Liberal party would certainly take place; and then the world would wake up and find itself Whig. Apart from the *people*, who have an inconvenient craving for food once or twice in the twenty-four hours, not easy to satisfy at present, there would be a glorious Whig world, in which contention would be dead, or would only be represented by a feeble Radical spray beating against the firm rock of Whiggery.

For as between the solid political parties the matter stands thus: the Liberals, the Radicals even, though some of them, like Mr Bright and Mr Chamberlain, had coquetted with the Irish party at one time or another, had no thought of granting Home Rule to Ireland; Mr Gladstone became converted to the necessity of granting it; one may well wonder why; possibly he may have seen the necessity of providing a new battle-field for the old Liberal and Conservative faction-fight; or again, he may have wished to atone for the Soudan massacres by making peace with Ireland; or, strange as it may seem to a non-professional politician, the elections of 1885 may have made him see for the first time that the Irish were almost unanimous in claiming Home Rule. Anyhow, he was converted, and bade his party be converted also; and most of them obeyed, since they were overawed by his appeal to the generosity and justice of the *People*; an appeal to which the People would probably have responded if they had had votes or dared to use them. But 'the Party', the Parliamentary hacks, wire-pullers, etc., were converted against their wills, and though doubtless they are sorry that they have been thrust out of power, they will not be sorry to come back to power by the help of the 'Unionist Liberals' as Home Rulers so modified that the Irish will not know them as friends.

This, then, is the chance of Lord Hartington and his friend and follower Mr Chamberlain, that they may 'unite' the Liberal party by taking away all reason for its existence, or, may not one say, by 'uniting' it to the Tory party. For let us be clear about one thing, that except for this revolutionary question of Home Rule and its consequences, which has so strangely become a question for 'practical' politicians, there is nothing which can be debated in

Parliament concerning which the recognized factions have any serious difference of opinion, or on which at least they can differ seriously as to action. The Irish Question once resolutely shelved, the peace of the kingdom of heaven would descend on St Stephens, except for a few Radicals, whose grumblings no one would heed, and who, if they were not blind, would have to declare themselves either Whigs or Socialists.

Let us hope that those who declare themselves the latter will also have the wits to come out of the Constitutional Parliament, and join the People, who were never intended to have anything serious to do with that august body, nor ever will, till the day when they destroy it.

COMMONWEAL, VOLUME 2, NUMBER 31,
14 AUGUST 1886, P. 153

THE ABOLITION OF FREEDOM OF SPEECH IN THE STREETS

The trial of the Socialists which ended on Friday 13th was not so well reported by most of the newspapers as some ordinary petty larceny case would have been; the *Pall Mall Gazette*, for instance, which was so hot about the Dod Street affair last year, not even noticing it till the last of the three days. Nevertheless, it is a matter of importance to the public generally, and not to Socialists only; for both the counsel for the prosecution and the judge laid it down as a matter beyond doubt that no persons can meet in any part of the public highway, however little the traffic over the meeting-place may be, however little the inconvenience caused by the meeting may be, without committing that terrible crime, 'Obstruction'. And the penalty for committing this crime is a fine which only a well-to-do person can pay; that is to say, for this crime a well-to-do man has to pay a fine, and a workman is sent to prison, there to be treated exactly as a felon is treated. Now apart from the preposterous exageration (*sic*) of a slight offence, and the punishing it as severely as if it were a crime, let all persons who are interested in making any cause popular by bringing it home to people who are too poor, too busy, or too shy to enter a hall, – let all such, I say, mark that they cannot any longer hold meetings in any public place except the parks (*at present* they are open to them) without rendering themselves liable to the above-stated penalty.

In giving his evidence on Thursday 12th Sir Charles Warren was very particular in asserting that it was obstructions and not meetings that his police interfered with, and he declined to accept the word 'meeting' from the counsel who was eliciting his evidence; but now it is clear that all meetings are obstructions when held in a public place, and it is Sir Charles's duty to see that they are at once dispersed. And this not in London only, in one town or another, but throughout the length and breadth of the British Islands. Furthermore, it is not only the police who have it in their power to prevent any one obnoxious to the Government opening their mouths to speak in the open air, but it seems by last week's trial that any person can take out a summons against the persons so offending. Thus a political, religious, or temperance meeting is at the mercy of the first cantankerous person, neighbour or otherwise, or of a political or ecclesiastical enemy. In other words, it is a mere phrase without truth to say that freedom of speech exists in this country.

Last year when this very thing seemed to be threatened by the action of the police at Dod Street, the whole of the public who were not openly mere reactionists were prepared to help in sustaining the right of free speech; whereas now, when the affair has entered into a far more important and threatening stage, they seem to be apathetic. The probable reason for this is that Mr Saunders foolishly let out what the real reason was for the police persecution, whereas the present attack has been made with a cunning which reflects much credit on the police and authorities as pupils in the school of Castlereagh. The dry official answers of Sir Charles Warren in the witness-box the other day left little to be wished for from this point of view.

But indeed the question for the non-Socialist bodies who may wish to address their fellow-citizens in the open air is not now, as it was last year, whether they will allow the Socialists to be crushed without helping them, but whether they will allow themselves to be crushed. They must understand that it is not a matter of the relative suitability of the corner of Bell Street as compared with other meeting places. Once more, all meeting in any public place except those specially set apart for it (if there be any such) is contrary to the law.

All who are on the side of progress may be well assured that if they do not take up the matter now the mere reactionists, who are the common enemies of us all, will look on with a grin of pleasure, possibly not unmingled with surprise, while the other progressive bodies stand by to see the Socialists persecuted. This is, in fact, their revenge for Dod Street, or rather, their counter-stroke in the war for the free expression of opinion.

To speak plainly, we Socialists are not such fools that we do not understand the matter. Sir Charles Warren was put into Colonel Henderson's place after the Trafalgar Square riots that he might make a stroke on us by driving our propaganda out of the streets. The authorities probably would have no great wish to suppress the religious meetings, or those of Radicals or Secularists even; but if it must be done in order to get rid of us – well, it must; 'and let's hope', would be their thought, 'that they won't notice it or care about it much'.

It only remains to be said that if they do not notice it, so much the worse for them, and to repeat that such petty persecution will not get rid of the discontent of the poor, nor of the only remedy for it – *Socialism.*

COMMONWEAL, VOLUME 2, NUMBER 32,
21 AUGUST 1886, P. 161

MISANTHROPY TO THE RESCUE!

A paper read by Mr Wordsworth Donnisthorpe at the Fabian Conference has been printed in the *Anarchist*. It excited much interest at the time when it was read, and aroused no little indignation in the minds of some of the Socialists that heard it; but printed, it does not seem a very remarkable piece, being simple an example of the ordinary pessimistic paradoxical exercises which are a disease of the period, and whose aim would seem to be the destruction of the meaning of language. Thus Mr Donnisthorpe declares himself an evolutionist, but his evolution simply runs round the circle; and in fact what he really means is the ordinary assertion that no condition of things but the present one is really natural and enduring; or, to put it in another way, that slavery is a necessity and that the latest development is the best, as it is the most veiled and therefore the safest for the slave-holder. This is indeed the due conclusion for the secretary of the Liberty and Property Defence League to arrive at; but it is a little curious that some people should have been ensnared by his not very ingenious fallacies, and supposed that he was covertly supporting some advanced doctrine or other. To these I commend his concluding sentences: 'The best system that I could bethink myself of if my opinion were asked would be the system of private property. To every man the fruits of his labour. If this view was adopted a state of things would arise exactly like what we have now,' etc. 'To every man the fruits of his labour.' Might one make bold to ask Mr Donnisthorpe what are the fruits of the labour of a duke, a shareholder, or a lawyer? The worst enemy of the non-producing classes would scarcely grudge them the fruits of *their* labour – nothing, to wit. If Mr Donnisthorpe is not misreported, this sentence is a curious one to come from a man who affects such exactness of thought.

But indeed all these abstractions of Mr Donnisthorpe's are but Politics in the Moon. In spite of his dyspeptic pessimism, human beings will always take interest in one another, and will have some sort of common aspirations; even, what doubtless will be a frightful word to Mr Donnisthorpe, some religion, some bond of responsibility to each other. It is impossible for no other relations between men to exist long save those between the bester and the bested, the slave and the slave-holder; society will arise and grow in spite of all calculations founded on a one-sided view of men's struggles for self-preservation: nay, it exists now outside the world held together by those arbitrary rules which are sustained for the upholding of private property, and which Mr Donnisthorpe really means when he speaks of liberty; and indeed it is just that rudimentary and as yet vague society of well-wishers, into which people are attracted by the interest in each other as human beings, which holds the world together until it shall be forced into a completer society by the march of economical events. It is true, as Mr Donnisthorpe says, that the working-classes are degraded, though whether they are more degraded than their degraders is another matter; but it is not because they produce that they are degraded, but because they are kept poor by arbitrary rules in favour of property. But poor as they are, they now have before them the prospect of getting poorer, while at the same time they are growing less ignorant; or say the luxury of keeping masters to employ them is getting so expensive that it threatens to ruin both master and man, and that while the masters have no way of escape, the men have a simple one – to wit, the getting rid of their masters. This they are beginning to learn, and when they get more perfect with their lesson, and come to understand that they can produce without the help of the lookers-on who pocket so large a part of their product, in spite of all abstractions, and in spite also of misanthropical prophecies they will insist on having 'the fruits of their labour'. Nay, they will be forced to take steps to having them from the breakdown of that very slave-system of which Mr Donnisthorpe is such a sedulous supporter. That slave-system is at best preparing widespread commercial ruin, and thereby is performing the last action that it is capable of; it is expending the last force that it has in giving force to the new order of things; it is putrid, but still useful – as dung.

Let us, then, take to heart some of Mr Donnisthorpe's taunts, and use them for what they are worth. He tells us in a great many words, considering the simplicity of the statement, that if the workers can take over the artificially protected property of the useless classes they have a right to do so, and sarcastically cheers them on in the attempt. It is our business to accept the challenge; and we may at least thank him for not hypocritically deprecating the use of force as a wickedness and immorality in the ordinary fashion of the day. But though the day of change will come at last, surely it will come the quicker if we take to heart those taunts aforesaid. True it is that it is the surroundings of the workers acting on exactly the same material as that of the useless classes which has produced their degradation; but it is possible for men who have once had a religion implanted in them to make that surrounding overcome the others – at least for the practical purposes of revolution. It has been seen over and over how a religion, a principle – whatever you may chose (*sic*) to call it – will transform poltroons into heroes, by forcing men to make the best of their better qualities and making the excess of what they have got in them that is good supply the defects of their lacking qualities. So I think we may, in spite of Mr Donnisthorpe, each one of us, make ourselves good enough for revolutionists, though in this generation we may fall short of perfection. Yet I admit that it is a difficult thing to do, for it means giving a sense of responsibility in greater or less degree to a great many people; so once more let us take warning by the enemy, and remember that the Religion of Socialism which our manifesto speaks of does call upon us to be better than other people, since we owe ourselves to the *society* which we have accepted as the hope of the future.

COMMONWEAL, VOLUME 2, NUMBER 33,
28 AUGUST, P. 172

THE PARIS TRADES' UNION CONGRESS

Mr Burnett has written an article to the *Pall Mall Gazette* in which he has given his views of the International Trades' Union Conference recently held in Paris. Considering Mr Burnett's position and that of the English trades' unions at present, this is a document of some importance, and it would be well to understand what the drift of it is. He writes as a trades' unionist, and clearly is anxious to establish the superiority of the English workman over the French, who from his point of view is more backward as being less of an unionist, and also as being worse paid than his English brother. As to the latter point I need say nothing, save that Mr Burnett's figures help to confirm the Socialist view of the general industrial depression all over the world. For the rest, he speaks of the French trades'-unionists as belonging to the Possibilist section of the Socialists, who, I must remind our readers, are the most backward section of the party, being sorely tainted with opportunism, and aiming at mere State Socialism; so that I must assume that the French trades' unionists, though they may go further in a Socialist direction than the English do, are nevertheless not amongst the most advanced of French workmen. As for the resolutions for which the English delegates refused to vote, it is true, as Mr Burnett states, that some of the measures they indicate have been in force in England for some time; but the two most important of them are the claims for an international minimum of wages and for a maximum of eight hours for the day's work, which of course have not been touched here. However, Mr Burnett states that the English delegates would have affirmed their assent to them, 'but for the first clause, which required the workmen of the different countries represented to urge their respective governments to open negotiations for the purpose of concluding international conventions and treaties concerning the conditions of labour'. Now the neutrality of the English delegates on these terms does seem, as the *Cri du Peuple* calls it, 'grotesque', because these resolutions imply the continuance of the present state of things otherwise, and can only be carried into effect by the existing machinery of government; so that to a plain man the meaning of the neutrality seemed to be, 'Yes, we agree to these measures, but we do not want to have them carried out'.

Of course to us Revolutionary Socialists the resolutions seem to approach to a solution of the labour question; and to try to carry them as an instalment of our claims seems a more than doubtful step, as it is possible that after a long agitation they might be yielded to by the masters, who, though they would then be in a worse position perhaps, would still be the masters; labour would not be emancipated, while the workmen would be 'contented' by the concession – *ie.*, put off from the real issue.

But, also of course, the neutrality of the delegates was not based on this objection: they were not afraid of *State* Socialism, but of Socialism. Nor, indeed, can we pretend to be surprised that they were not prepared to vote on this point with the other delegates, who were all avowed Socialists of some shade or other. Mr Burnett's phrase of 'the English unions depending for their advancement upon themselves' is a mere phrase, and really means the reverse of what it seems to mean. It means that the English unions are not prepared to accept the responsibilities of freedom, that they are still contented with their position as a check on the masters – a check whose tendency is to ensure the existence of the employing class. But it is clear from Mr Burnett's article that they are shaken somewhat, as the following quotation from it shows decidedly: 'It was felt that with so strong a Socialistic feeling now manifesting itself in England, it was not possible to stand on the high ground of three years ago, as if no such feeling existed.'

There is a certain weight in these words, coming from Mr Burnett, whether we look upon him as 'Chief Correspondent to the Labour Bureau of the Board of Trade', or as a trades' union delegate: in both capacities he is bound to be *very* cautious. We may fairly hope that three years from this time the trades' unions will not be 'sitting on the fence', but will be in the lists, and on the right side there.

COMMONWEAL, VOLUME 2, NUMBER 35,
11 SEPTEMBER 1886, P. 187

AN OLD STORY RETOLD

It is told of Matthias Corvinus, King of Hungary – the Alfred the Great of his time and people – that he once heard (once *only?*) that some (only *some*, my lad?) of his peasants were over-worked and under-fed. He took the matter to heart, being, as kings go, a just man, besides being more valiant than they mostly were, even in the old feudal days. So he called together such lords and councillors as he deemed fittest, and bade busk them for a ride; and when they were ready he and they set out, over rough and smooth, decked out in all the glory of attire which was the wont of those days. Thus they rode till they came to some village or thorpe of the peasant folk, and through it to the vineyards where men were working on the sunny southern slopes that went up from the river: my tale does not say whether that were Theiss, or Donau, or what river. Well, I judge it was late spring or early summer, and the vines but just beginning to show their grapes; for the vintage is late in those lands, and some of the grapes are not gathered till the first frosts have touched them, whereby the wine made from them is the stronger and sweeter. Anyhow there were the peasants, men and women, boys and young maidens, toiling and swinking; some hoeing between the vine-rows, some bearing baskets of dung up the steep slopes, some in one way, some in another, labouring for the fruit they should never eat, and the wine they should never drink. Thereto turned the King and got off his horse and began to climb up the stony ridges of the vineyard, and his lords in like manner followed him, wondering in their hearts what was toward; but to the one who was following next after him he turned about and said with a smile, 'Yea, lords, this is a new game we are playing to-day, and a new knowledge will come from it'. And the lord smiled, but somewhat sourly.

As for the peasants, great was their fear of those gay and golden lords. I judge that they did not know the King, since it was little likely that any one of them had seen his face; and they knew of him but as the Great Father, the mighty warrior who kept the Turk from harrying their thorpe. Though, forsooth, little matter was it to any man there whether Turk or Magyar was their over-lord, since to one master or another they had to pay the due tale of labouring days in the year, and hard was the livelihood that they earned for themselves on the days when they worked for themselves and their wives and children. Well, belike they knew not the King; but amidst those rich lords they saw and knew their own lord, and of him they were sore afraid. But nought it availed them to flee away from those strong men and strong horses – they who had been toiling from before the rising of the sun, and now it wanted little more than an hour of noon: besides, with the King and lords was a guard of crossbowmen, who were left the other side of the vineyard wall, – keen-eyed Italians of the mountains, straight shooters of the bolt. So the poor folk fled not; nay, they made as if all this were none of their business, and went on with their work. For indeed each man said to himself, 'If I be the one that is not slain, to-morrow I shall lack bread if I do not work my hardest to-day; and maybe I shall be headman if some of these be slain and I live'.

Now comes the King amongst them and says: 'Good fellows, which of you is the headman?'

Spake a man sturdy and sunburnt, well on in years and grizzled: 'I am the headman, lord.'

'Give me thy hoe, then', says the King; 'for now shall I order this matter myself, since these lords desire a new game, and are fain to work under me at vine-dressing. But do thou stand by me and set me right if I order them wrong: but the rest of you, go play!'

The carle knew not what to think, and let the King stand with his hand stretched out, while he looked askance at his own lord and baron, who wagged his head at him grimly, as one who says 'Do it, dog!'

Then the carle lets the hoe come into the King's hand; and the King falls to, and orders his lords for vine-dressing, to each his due share of the work: and whiles the carle said yea and whiles nay to his ordering. And then ye should have seen the velvet cloaks cast off, and mantles of fine Flemish scarlet go to the dusty earth, as the lords and knights busked them to the work! So they buckled to; and to most of them it seemed good game to play at vine-dressing. But one there was who, when his scarlet cloak was off, stood up in doublet of glorious Persian web of gold and silk, such as men make not now, worth a hundred florins the Bremen ell. Unto him the King with no smile on his face gave the job of toing and froing up and down the hill with the biggest and the frailest dung-basket that there was; and thereat the silken lord screwed up a grin, that was sport to see, and all the lords laughed; and as he turned away he said, yet so that none heard him, 'Do I serve this son's son of a whore that he should bid me carry dung?' For you must know that the King's father, John Hunyad, one of the great warriors of the world, the Hammer of the Turks, was not gotten in wedlock, though he were a king's son.

Well, they sped the work bravely for a while, and loud was the laughter as the hoes smote the earth and the flint stones tinkled and the cloud of dust rose up; the brocaded dung-bearer went up and done, cursing and swearing by the White God and the Black; and one would say to another, 'See ye how gentle blood outgoes churls' blood, even when the gentle does the churl's work: these lazy loons smote but one stroke to our three.' But the King, who worked no worse than any, laughed not at all; and meanwhile the poor folk stood by, not daring to speak a word one to the other; for they were still sore afraid, not now of being slain on the spot, but this rather was in their hearts: 'These great and strong lords and knights have come to see what work a man may do without dying: if we are to have yet more days added to our year's tale of lords' labour, then are we lost without remedy.' And their hearts sank within them.

So sped the work; and the sun rose yet higher in the heavens, and it was noon and more. And now there was no more laughter among those toiling lords, and the strokes of the hoe and mattock came far slower, while the dung-bearer sat down at the bottom of the hill and looked out on the river; but the King yet worked on doggedly, so for shame the other lords yet kept at it. Till at last the next man to the King let his hoe drop with a clatter, and swore a great oath. Now he was a strong black-bearded man in the prime of life, a valiant captain of that famous Black Band that had so often rent the Turkish array; and the King loved him for his sturdy valour; so he says to him, 'Is aught wrong, Captain?'

'Nay, lord', says he, 'ask the headman carle yonder what ails us.'

'Headman', says the King, 'what ails these strong knights? Have I ordered them wrongly?'

'Nay, but shirking ails them, lord', say he, 'for they are weary; and no wonder, for they have been playing hard, and are of gentle blood.'

'Is that so, lords', says the King, 'that ye are weary already?'

Then the rest hung their heads and said nought, all save that captain of war; and he said, being a bold man and no liar: 'King, I see what thou woulds't be at; thou hast brought us here to preach us a sermon from that Plato of thine; and to say sooth, so that I may swink no more, and go eat my dinner, now preach thy worst! Nay, if thou wilt be priest I will be thy deacon. Wilt thou that I ask this labouring Carle a thing or two?'

'Yea', said the King. And there came, as it were, a cloud of thought over his face.

Then the captain straddled his legs and looked big, and said to the Carle: 'Good fellow, how long have we been working here?'

'Two hours or thereabout, by the sun above us', says he.

'And how much of thy work have we done in that while?' says the captain, and winks his eye at him withal.

'Lord', says the Carle, grinning a little despite himself, 'be not wrath with my word. In the first half-hour ye did five-and-forty minutes' work of ours, and in the next half-hour scant a thirty minutes' work, and the third half-hour a fifteen minutes' work, and in the fourth half-hour two minutes' work.' The grin now had faded from his face, but a gleam came into his eyes as he said: 'And now, as I suppose, your day's work is done, and ye will go to your dinner and eat the sweet and drink the strong; and we shall eat a little rye-bread, and then be working here till after the sun has set and the moon has begun to cast shadows. Now for you, I wot not how ye shall sleep nor where; nor what white body ye shall hold in your arms while the night flits and the stars shine; but for us, while the stars yet shine, shall we be at it again, and bethink ye for what! I know not what game and play ye shall be devising for to-morrow as ye ride back home; but for us when we come back here to-morrow, it shall be as if there had been no yesterday and nothing done therein, and that day's work shall be nought to us also, for we shall win no respite from our toil thereby, and the morrow of to-morrow will all be to begin again once more. Therefore, if ye are thinking to lay some new tax or tale upon us, think twice of it, for we may not bear it. And all this I say with the less fear, because I perceive this man here beside me, in the black velvet jerkin and the gold chain on his neck, is the King; nor do I think he will slay me for my word since he hath so many a Turk before him and his mighty sword!'

Then said the captain: 'Shall I smite the man, O king? or hath he preached thy sermon for thee?'

'Smite not, for he hath preached it', said the King. 'Yet when another hath spoken our thought, our thoughts are born therefrom, and now have I another sermon to preach; but I will refrain me as now. Let us down and to our dinner.'

So they went, the King and his gentles, and sat down by the river under the rustle of the poplars, and they ate and drank and were merry. And the King bade bear up the broken meats to the vine-dressers, and a good draught of the archer's wine, and to the headman he gave a broad gold piece. But when the poor folk had all that under their hands, it was to them as though the kingdom of heaven had come down to earth.

In the cool of the evening home rode the king and his lords. The king was distraught and silent; but at last the captain, who rode beside him, said to him: 'Preach me now thine after sermon, O king!'

'I think thou knowest it already', said the king, 'else hadst thou not spoken in such wise to the Carle; but tell me, what is thy craft and the craft of all these whereby ye live, as the potter by making pots and so forth?'

Said the captain: 'As the potter lives by making pots, so we live by robbing the poor.'

Again said the king: 'And my trade?'

Said he 'Thy trade is to be a king of such thieves, yet no worser than the rest'.

The king laughed.

'Bear that in mind', said he, 'and then shall I tell thee my thought while yonder Carle spake. "Carle", I thought, "were I thou or such as thou, then would I take in my hand a sword or a spear, or were it only a hedge-stake, and bid others do the like, and forth would we go; and since we would be so many, and with nought to lose save a miserable life, we would do battle and prevail, and make an end of the craft of kings and of lords and of usurers, and there should be but one craft in the world, to wit, to work merrily for ourselves and to live merrily thereby."'

Said the captain: 'This, then, is thy sermon. Who will heed it if thou preach it?'

Said the King: 'They who will take the mad king and put him in a king's mad-house, therefore do I forbear to preach it. Yet it *shall* be preached.'

'And not heeded', said the Captain, 'save by those who head and hang the setters forth of new things that are good for the world. Our trade is safe for many and many a generation.'

And therewith they came to the king's palace, and they ate and drank and slept, and the world went on its ways.

Commonweal, Volume 2, Number 36,
18 September 1886, pp. 197–198

THE REWARD OF 'GENIUS'

It is a very common incident at a debate on Socialism for an opponent or doubter to take up the cudgels on behalf of 'brain-work' as opposed to hand-work. Even before you avow yourself a Communist (as I have to do), such a questioner is anxious about the future of brain-work in the transitional stages of Socialism. Though this subject has been ably treated before in these columns, I will nevertheless venture on a few plain words in addition to what has been said; which I hesitate to do the less because I have had some small experience of hand-work, though not of the most laborious kind, and abundance of experience of 'brain-work', so-called.

Our objectors dwell upon diverse aspects of their anxiety for the future of the brain-workers. Some, for instance, seem most exercised on the question of what is to become of the men of genius when Socialism is realized; but I must beg them not to let this anxiety destroy their appetites or keep them awake at night, for it is founded on a perhaps popular, but certainly erroneous, conception of that queer animal the man of genius, who is generally endowed with his full share of the predatory instincts of the human being, and can take remarkably good care of himself. Indeed, I can't help thinking that even under a Socialistic condition of things he will pull such long faces if he doesn't get everything that he wants, and will make matters so uncomfortable for those that he lives amongst if he falls short of his ideal of existence, that good-natured and quiet people will be weak enough to make up a purse (or its equivalent) for him from time to time to keep him in good temper and shut his mouth a little. I must further say, though, that they *will* be exceedingly weak if they do so, because they will be able to get out of him all the special work he can do without these extra treats. For the only claim he has to the title of a 'man of genius' is that his capacities are irrepressible; he finds the exercise of them so exceedingly pleasant to him that it will only be by main force that you will prevent him from exercising them. Of course, under the present competitive system, having been paid once for his work by getting his livelihood by it, and again by the pleasure of doing it, he wants to be further paid in various ways a great many times more. Neither under the circumstances can I blame him much for this, since he sees so many people for doing nothing paid so much more than he is, except in the matter of pleasure in their work. But also of course, he won't venture to claim all that in a Socialist society, but will have at the worst to nibble at the shares of those who are weak enough to stand it. So I will in turn dismiss *my* anxiety, with the hope that they will not be so weak as to coddle him up at their own expense, since they will have learned that so-called self-sacrifice to the exactions of those who are strong in their inordinate craving and unmanliness does but breed tyrants and pretenders.

But furthermore, I do not see, and never could see, why a man of genius must needs be a man of genius every minute of his life. Cannot he work as well as ordinary folk in some directions, besides working better than they in others? Speaking broadly, all men can learn some useful craft, and learn to practice it with ease. I know there may be exceptions; just as there are cultivated people who cannot be taught to write (the late Dean Stanley was one, for instance); but they must be considered as diseased persons, and the disease would die out in a generation or two under reasonable conditions of life. In short, the 'man of genius' ought to be able to earn his livelihood in an ordinary way independently of his speciality, and he will in that case be much happier himself and much less of a bore to his friends, let alone his extra usefulness to the community.

As to the comparative wear and tear of 'brain-work' – the work of the man, for instance, who is occupied in the literary matters – the theory of our objectors, apart from their strange ideas of the usefulness of this craft, is that he works hard – harder, they will often say, than the hand-worker. Well, if he works under bad sanitary conditions, doesn't get fresh air or exercise enough, no doubt that does exhaust him, as also if he works too long or is harassed in his work by hurry and anxiety. But all these drawbacks are not special to his craft; all who are working otherwise than in the open air work under the first of these disadvantages, and all wage-earners work under the last of them. There is any amount of humbug talked about the hard work of the intellectual workers, which I think is mostly based on the fact that they are in the habit of taking regular and, so to say, socially-legalized holidays, which are supposed to be necessary to their health, and we may admit are so, but which the 'non-intellectual' workers have to forego, whether they are necessary to *them* or not. Let us test the wear and tear of this intellectual work very simply. If I have been working at literary work for, say, eight hours at a stretch, I may well feel weary of it, although I have not felt it a mere burden all along, as probably I should have done if I had been carrying a hod of bricks up and down a ladder; but when I have knocked off, I can find relaxation in strong physical exercise – can, for example, take a boat and row for a couple of hours or more. Now let me ask is the hodman after *his* eight hours' work fit for a couple of hours mental work as a relaxation? We very well know he is not so fitted, but rather for beer and sleep. He is exhausted, and I am on the look out for amusement. To speak plainly, I am only changing my amusement, for I have been amusing myself all along, unless I have added disadvantages to my work which are not essential to it.

And again, has not the hodman's work dealt in some way with his brain? Indeed it has. I have been using my brain, but not exhausting it; but though he has not been using his, he has been exhausting it by his hand-work done at a strain, or else he ought to be able to take the mental relaxation corresponding to my bodily relaxation. In truth, whereas at present the hours of the intellectual worker are really always shorter than those of the hand-worker, the very reverse ought to be the case, or in other words the wear and tear of the hand-labour is far greater.

But our objectors have not as a rule got so far as to consider this matter from the wear and tear side of it. They think that the superior workman should have extra reward because he is superior, and that the inferior must put up with being worn and torn in the service of this divine right. That is their superstition of divine right in this business; but also from the economical point of view they consider that it is necessary to bribe the superior man, for fear that you should lose his talent. What I have said of the man of genius being compelled to work by his genius applies to all superior workmen in greater or less degree, and disposes of the *need* of a bribe. You need not bribe the superior workman to be superior, for he has to work in any case (we must take that for granted), and his superior work is pleasanter, and indeed easier, to him than the inferior work would be: he will do it if you allow him to. But also if you had the need you would not have the power to bribe, except under a system which admitted of slavery – *ie.*, tormenting some people for the pleasure of others. Can you bribe him to work by giving him immunity from work? or by giving him goods that he cannot use? But in what other way can you bribe him when labour is free and ordinary people will not stand being compelled to accept degradation for his benefit? No, you will have to depend on his aptitude for his special work forcing him into doing it; nor will you be disappointed in this. Whatever difficulties you may have in organizing work in the earlier days of Socialism will not be with the specialists, but with those who do the more ordinary work; though as regards these, setting aside the common machine-work, the truth of the matter is that you can draw no hard and fast line between the special workman and the ordinary one. Every workman who is in his right place – that is, doing his work because he is fit for it – has some share in that 'genius' so absurdly worshipped in these latter days. The 'genius' is simply the man who has a stronger speciality and is allowed to develope (*sic*) it; or, if you please, has it so strongly that it is able to break through the repressing circumstances of his life, which crush out those who are less abundantly gifted into 'a dull level of mediocrity'. It is a matter of degree chiefly.

I am afraid, therefore, that our anti-Socialist objectors will have in the future – I mean under a social arrangement – to put up with the misery of not having more than they need forced on them in return for their occupying themselves in the way which pleases them most, and with the further misery of seeing those who are not so intellectual as themselves doing their work happily and contentedly, and not being deprived of their due food and comforts because their work is less pleasing and exciting than that of their luckier fellows. No doubt this will be hard for the geniuses to bear (though harder still, I suspect, for the prigs or sham geniuses); but if there be any truth in the old proverb that 'other peoples' troubles hang by a hair', the rest of the world – *ie.*, all except a very few – will bear it with equanimity. Indeed they well might, if they consider in those happier days what enormous loss the world has suffered through the crushing out of so much original talent under the present system; for who can doubt that it is only the toughest and strongest (perhaps the highest, perhaps not) of the geniuses that have not been crushed out. The greater part of genius, shared in various proportions by so many millions of men, has been just wasted through greed and folly.

COMMONWEAL, VOLUME 2, NUMBER 37,
25 SEPTEMBER 1886, PP. 205–206

The Moral of Last Lord Mayor's Day

The Lord Mayor's Show has come and gone, and it may be supposed that many respectable people, including probably the city magnates who formed part of the procession, are easier in their minds that it is well over. But perhaps they will not on reflection be thoroughly reassured. The procession was far from being a triumphant one, and was escorted by hoots and groans all along. The success of the police in preventing a demonstration was only partial, since a huge meeting was held and harangued in Trafalgar Square, in spite of Sir Charles Warren's proclamation, besides the large meeting in Hyde Park held together by members of the League in spite of the pouring rain. All this is not very like a police triumph. But the most significant fact is that the allies counted on by the police, judging by Colonel Fraser's letter, entirely failed them. It goes without saying that the Kenny and Kelly gang were nowhere, and that the Liberty and Property Defence League might as well have saved themselves the expense of printing and circulating the handbill which was plentiful in the city on the 8th, and which was practically an incitement to the crowd to attack the Socialists. All this was a small matter, but what was important was that the crowd everywhere were in sympathy with the Socialists; and it must be said this is a very important fact, and shows that the propaganda of the past year has produced its effect. The middle-class – the respectables – certainly expected it to be all the other way, and the press has shown its disappointment clearly enough, though some part of it has tried to hide its uneasiness at the affair. The *Standard* probably expresses the general feeling on the matter, and the tone of its article is regret that the police did not stop the meeting at any cost, because authority has received a blow from what took place – as indeed it has. The *Pall Mall* admits the collapse of authority. The *Daily News* loses its respectable head from sheer peevishness, even to the extent of allowing itself to publish the following remarkable sentence: 'The spirit in which they [the Socialists] conduct their agitation is a good deal more important than their principles.' Really, Mr Bourgeois, 'even for your own purposes', you should try not to be so empty as that. Socialist principles, whether they are right or wrong, profess to deal with a subject no less than the whole of human life; and however rude and offensive we, the present agitators, may be in our agitation, those principles will be discussed, whether they are acted upon or not, long after the world has got rid of such passing matters as us and our rudeness.

A very few words upon, not the cause of this demonstration, but its occasion. The *Daily News* ends its article by saying, 'Socialism is one thing, and the prevention of the threatened winter's sorrow at the East End is quite another. Those who doubt it have only to read the resolutions carried at Trafalgar Square yesterday.' Yes, that is true, but nearly in the inverse sense that the *Daily News* means it. The steps suggested by those resolutions, or rather the action of the Government which the whole agitation is meant to force on, would certainly do something towards 'preventing the winter sorrow'. But, let alone the very little that the Government could be forced to do for poor people, even the whole of the resolutions do not mean Socialism or anything like it, though they *do* mean an attempt to palliate present poverty. An attempt, it must be said, which, even as a palliative, is bound to fail, because it is a palliative that looks towards Socialism. No bourgeois government could carry out the measures claimed by these resolutions, even if they would; and certainly none will try to do so, or can be forced to try, so long as they are a constitutional government and not a revolutionary body.

Nevertheless the crowd in Trafalgar Square did not draw, and had no chance of drawing, any nice distinctions. They were there supporting the Socialists in general, who they believed were trying to raise them from the terrible condition in which they are, and they were at least in a fair way of understanding that they are poor because the masters of the police and soldiers are rich. The net gain of this strange Lord Mayor's Show is that, as far as it goes, it has struck a blow at bourgeois authority, and that it has emphasized the class distinctions which rob us all of our due life. That at least is something. Until people find out either by learning to see it, or by instinctive feeling, that there is a class war going on, and great change for the better is impossible. When the poor begin to know that they are poor not by irremediable accident, but because they are robbed by a useless class who can be got rid of, the beginning of the end is at hand.

Commonweal, Volume 2, Number 45,
20 November 1886, p. 265

MR JAWKINS AT THE MANSION HOUSE

Lord Salisbury, in his speech at the Mansion House, did in some respects only strengthen somewhat the words of his colleague, Lord Randolph Churchill. Like him he tried to bury dangerous Jingoism decently. It was pretty much the old story: 'Sir, you have called me a liar, you have pulled my nose, you have kicked me downstairs, now beware, lest you rouse the sleeping lion!'

As to Ireland again, he, like the other, declared for stiff support to landlordism, and hinted at coercion; and his only contribution to the stock of news of Government intentions, was his assertion that no discretionary powers had been given in the matter of eviction to his bum-bailiff Buller. It is hardly worth while criticizing his speech on these points therefore; it was, of course, only natural that he should praise the valour of the Bulgarian people, whose independence he had done his best to prevent; nor did any one for a moment expect he would have anything to say on the subject of Ireland; but, perhaps, some persons were curious to see how far he would endorse the Tory Democracy of Lord Randolph Churchill; on that side their minds may now be at rest, he has taken the position of Mr Jawkins, of the firm of Spenlow and Jawkins in Dicken's 'David Copperfield'. Mr Spenlow can now show his good-will by making any amount of promises dependent on Mr Jawkins consent, which privately he knows will be withheld. Three acres and a cow, embraces to Jesse Collings, free education, local self-government, railway reforms, besides many another blessing dim in the distance; all these you shall have for the asking, my friends, if only Jawkins will consent. Well, and what says Jawkins to all this fine flower of reform? Hear him: 'But, in truth, as far as domestic affairs are concerned, *the whole interest of home politics* is absorbed in the consideration of that one Irish question.' (Hear, hear.) Thus does Jawkins put down his foot, and crush mercilessly the fairy fabric of Radical hope, tinged even with a slight suspicion of Socialism, raised by the kindly Spenlow. The firm is certainly a convenient one; and, moreover, it is likely to last as long as such conspiracies usually do, because, in fact, the Salisbury-Jawkins woodenness is really and truly the thing which all respectable people are asking for. Do not let us forget that not only are the Hartington-Whigs and the Chamberlainite Radicals supporting this man, but that practically the Gladstonian Radicals have come to the same conclusion, as was shown by the Leed's Conference, whose dullness on every question except the Irish one, which had got to be their party war-horse, was pointed out in this journal so lately. Strange to say (since Lord Salisbury said it) it is true that 'as far as domestic affairs are concerned, the whole interest of home politics is absorbed in the consideration of that one Irish question'. That is, it is true of the Constitutional machine which we have made a god to rule over us; that is about the measure of its capacity for managing the affairs which we, fools that we are, have handed over to its management; whatever there is which is dealing with the real problems of life is outside that machine, which is absolutely helpless for 'considering' them even; and when it has considered them will find it can get no further.

Surely on that day, if never before, that wooden Tory-Whig might have 'considered' something besides the Irish question; or even in his dim mind might have 'considered' that that question owed its absorbing interest to its being at bottom part of the great question now being thrust into the faces of all Governments by the workers: 'What do you want sitting there, while we who made you are miserable and degraded?' There sat that dull man, that party politician, amongst the City magnates, who found their wine tasted better because they were drinking it in their joy of having escaped being rolled in the mud by the half-starved population of London; amongst the shops barricaded against 'domestic affairs'. Why, the ball-cartridges were scarcely out of the pouches of the soldiers who had come to take a part in a 'domestic affair'; and yet he had nothing to say about it, and the servile mob of respectabilities had the baseness to cheer him for his evasion. Yet, indeed, no one expected him to say anything about the condition of this frightful centre of our empire of force and fraud, and all the misery of which, after all, its misery is but a sample. Any why did they not expect him to do so? Because he is the leader of a Parliamentary party; and really, when one thinks of the absurdity of his position, which, once again, necessitates his ignoring the real questions of the day, one has to restrain one's indignation against the cruel stupidity of the man by steady determination to do one's best to abolish the system. Besides that, there is a danger that one's readers might think that he who attacks one party leader is condoning the others for their blindness and evasion. Lord Salisbury is only doing after his kind; and even the Jawkin's (*sic*) business will most certainly be repeated by the Government which will supplant him, though it may not take quite such a grotesque form as the present one. That, after all, is mostly due to the other member of the Tory-Whig firm of Spenlow and Jawkins.

Commonweal, Volume 2, Number 45,
20 November 1886, pp. 268–269

THE TEN COMMANDMENTS

Amongst the articles in the '*Mall Pall Gazette*' (*sic*) occur some that express sad trouble about the ten commandments. These are always of a peculiar character, so that it is safe to assume that they are written by one person; and that person's function seems to be to repress the excesses of those contributors to the journal who are Socialistic in tendency. It is not the business of the *Commonweal* to criticize literature, so we may leave the style of the above-said contributor alone; but his anxiety as to the fate of the ten commandments in a future state of society, which is shared, doubtless, by many well-to-do people, is a little curious, considering the life they live in the present one; and therefore we may be allowed to ask which of the ten commandments it is he is so anxious about, since it may be assumed that it is not one or more of the theological ones. Should we be hazarding too much if we were to guess that it is the sixth, which is likely to be not much heeded when Imperial Federation is well on foot, and the lives of various niggers stand in the way of its success? Or, indeed, is it ever heeded, seeing how short the life of the workers is, compared with that of the idlers, and considering how manufacturers have to be compelled by fear of fire rather than by fear of ignominy, to take the most ordinary precautions against the *accidental* death of their men? Or is it the tenth? It is true that coveting a man's goods is only a small part of the process of taking them away from him; and it is so inbred in us under our 'Society' of Artificial Famine, that we don't heed that our bourgeois morality is specially constructed to justify us, or a few of us, in keeping our neighbours poorer than they should be in order that we may grow rich through their poverty. Still the commandment is an important one, and worth anxiety. But commercial morality, that of to-day, is an organized system of coveting our neighbour's goods; therefore the writer in question may let his anxiety go by the board on that score, since the commandment is already broken as much as it can be. Nor, surely, need anxiety for the future of the eighth keep him awake at nights; 'tis quite done with now, since not only are many poor devils compelled to steal for a livelihood (and I doubt if the Jewish lawgiver had *that* in his mind), but that which compels them to do so is the unceasing robbery of the poor by the rich, which is so habitual that it has not only become legal, but is the very bond of our Authoritative sham-Society, the basis of 'law and order'. It may be said that this is the commonplace of Socialism, and so it is; but if the writer in the *Pall Mall* can give any other explanation of the miseries of our society of rich and poor let him do so, and not shelter himself behind a superstitious regard for an ancient rule of life, which he and his have long ago ceased to practice, but the words of which they use to evade the problems of civilization, by throwing them in the faces of people even more ignorant than themselves – people who suffer from the misfortune of superstition rather than the crime of cant. To these, who are unhappily ignorant, we Socialists say that in the true society which we are striving to realize, honesty and mutual respect will become so habitual that the very meaning of these commandments will have grown dim to us.

COMMONWEAL, VOLUME 2, NUMBER 46,
27 NOVEMBER 1886, P. 276

IS TRADE RECOVERING?

We are being told by the middle-class press at present, that there are signs of the passing away of that depression of trade which nobody denies is real enough. Now, non-Socialists will doubtless look on Socialists who dread this recovery of trade as likely to calm down the present agitation as very dreadful persons; but I would ask them first to remember that the realization of Socialism means to us a new and happy world; and considering how frightful are the sufferings of a large part of civilized populations, and how still more frightful is their degradation even in prosperous times of trade, we are surely justified by our point of view in thinking the speedy advent of Socialism worth paying a heavy price for. Furthermore, those of us who study history and believe in the evolution of the race, cannot doubt that Socialism can only be realized by the rotting away of the system which it is getting ready to supplant. No amount of preaching, of enthusiasm, or of devotion even, will induce the workers, with whom the worlds' future lies, to accept and to act upon mere abstract propositions of what they have a right to aspire to; necessity must push them on before they can even conceive of the future of equality and mutual good-will which we *know* awaits them.

When the working-classes become conscious of the struggle which is always going on between them and the classes which live upon their labour, then they will be able and ready to face the dangers of the action which must come before the realization of the new order of things; the dangers, the added miseries, the load of responsibility which must attend such action; then, and not till then. And necessity only can make them conscious of this struggle.

The classes that live upon the labour of the workers, if they are not conscious of this, yet act instinctively as if they were. They act as if they knew that the consciousness of the class-struggle were being forced upon the workers. Except for a few poor-law and charity organization pedants, no one *in public* ventures to speak of the working-classes with the brutality which I am old enough to remember as the common manner of talk about them. All kinds of philanthropical schemes are set on foot for their supposed benefit by the richer classes, from the building of goody-goody people's palaces up to schemes which are a kind of demi-semi-Socialistic. The aim of all this philanthropy is undoubtedly to make it somewhat easier for the workers to live – as wage-slaves; and possibly many of the philanthropists believe that they are acting thus of their own free-will; but as a class they [are] not so doing, necessity is compelling them on the one hand to keep the poorest slaves quiet by hope of charity in some form or another; and on the other to give all opportunity possible for the better paid workers to rise into the capitalist class. To make the basis of exploitation as wide as possible, to interest as many as possible in the plunder of labour, is the aim of all middle-class dealings with the workers which are not mere demented folly. It is clear that this attempt at diverting the aspirations of the workers into the channel of mere individual self-interest has not the same chance of success when times are bad and trade slack, as in periods of commercial prosperity; and if that prosperity should when it came turn out to be steady and continuous, Socialism would become a mere 'pious opinion'; because the pleasure and excitement of the gambling for livelihood which would be open to all the better-off workmen, would blind them to the degradation of their condition and the sordidness of the desperate struggle. In short, the class-struggle would tend toward the creation of a new class formed out of the superior workmen, just as our present middle-class has been formed out of the guild-craftsmen and freedmen of the Middle Ages.

To counteract this tendency is the main business of Socialists at present. To assert the necessity of the wage-workers, not only of all countries but also of all conditions, to unite; to refuse to admit any distinction between skilled and unskilled, employed or unemployed, must be our answer to the bourgeois attempt at building up a new middle-class. And Socialists must consider that if that tendency becomes a fact and the new class does grow up, it will show that we have been mistaken in supposing that the present system was rotting to its end. It would mean that Socialism was put off not for fifty years, but for centuries.

Therefore, at the risk of being accused of want of sympathy with suffering, and inhuman party spirit, we are bound to hail the signs of the rotting away of commercialism, the depression of trade and confusion of politics, just as an oppressed people hails the war which is to set them free. It is unheard of and impossible that birth should take place without struggle and suffering; but in spite of that we long for the birth.

As for the recovery of trade with which we are threatened, the signs of it are not very obvious as yet. Probably in many cases it is simply a matter of speculation, as the *Cotton Factory Times* of November 26 tells is the case with the apparent recovery in that industry; in others it simply means that the stocks have been somewhat worked off, and so give opportunity for beginning fresh over-production. An account to hand of the final report of the Commission on the Depression of Trade makes no boast of recovery, and is not very heroic in its proposed remedies. After having admitted that 'there is a tendency in the supply of commodities to outrun the demand', they say, 'that the great object to be aimed at is to diminish the cost of production, so far as it can be done consistently with the maintenance of sound quality and good workmanship'. Has it occurred to these Gothamites that the only way of reducing the cost of production is by reducing the labour used in producing, and under our present system that can only be done by lowering wages. What these curious persons propose is to remedy over-production by producing more on the one hand, and by decreasing our power of consumption on the other.

The ridiculous position of these Commissioners is an indication amongst others numerous enough, that a recurrence to the roaring times of trade is unlikely to happen, or at least if it did, the recovery would speedily be followed by a deeper depression. That means that the state of trade will go from bad to worse, until at last the workers will be forced to take the organization of labour into their own hands, and make an end to our system of usury and robbery. That is the apparent logical conclusion to be drawn from passing events; nevertheless, disturbing influences *may* put off the day of change; and I hold that the above-mentioned possible tendency toward a new lower middle-class is even now visible as one of them, and must be guarded against sedulously. Therefore, we should set our faces sternly against any proposal which seemed likely to benefit one part of the workers, while it left the other out in the cold, however specious its form might be; and at the same time we should above all things put forward complete equality of condition as our ultimate end[.]

COMMONWEAL, VOLUME 2, NUMBER 49,
18 DECEMBER 1886, P. 300

'THE LAW' IN IRELAND

The Government has struck its stroke and we are to have another State trial on behalf of law and order. Unless a miracle of jury-packing is performed the accused will be acquitted, or at least the jury will not agree; so it is hard to see what the Government can gain unless they are prepared to go head over ears into coercion. Meantime not only are the Tory and other definitely reactionary papers jubilant at this exhibition of firmness, but all the Liberal Press approves with the single exception of the *Pall Mall Gazette*, to which must be added that Mr Labouchere at Birmingham spoke strongly and generously of Mr Dillon 'as one who had come forward to protect the poor and humble Irish against the exactions of the vilest set of Shylocks that ever existed'; and was by no means scared of the illegality of Mr Dillon's action.

It is perhaps not certain that this apparent withdrawal of the Liberal party from the Irish alliance is as serious as it looks, because it may mean nothing more than the usual conventional twaddle that Parliamentary people are wont to indulge in; but whether it is merely this kind of petty lying, or a serious attempt to back out of a difficult position and surrender the Gladstonian fort to the enemy, it is discreditable enough to the Liberal party. In the first place these virtuous people are in a mighty hurry to condemn the accused before they have been heard; for, to take the matter on the lowest grounds, is it so sure that the Plan of Campaign is illegal? As the *Pall Mall* leader writer very reasonably points out, just the same kind of decisions as the Judges have made in Mr Dillon's case the Judges gave in cases of combination between workmen in the militant days of Trades Unionism.

But we Socialists at least need not trouble ourselves about the legality of proceedings which are necessary acts of self-defence against mere greed and tyranny. And pray what suggestion of action less determined than the Plan of Campaign has the *Daily News*, for instance, to suggest to the tenants whom Lord Clanricarde and others have made up their minds to ruin? It is at least a plan, and has been successful, in some instances at least, in bringing the landlords to such reason as is implied by their taking all they can get and not trying for more. Once more see how very tender the conscience of constitutionalists is! It is the threat against such very doubtful property as the second skin of a cat which has frightened these useful allies of the Irish people. Where will the Liberal 'Justice to Ireland' be when property is seriously threatened there?

Indeed it seems probable that the Irish question is drifting into a new phase, which will for a time throw the Irish on their own resources, until both they and *the people* of England, Scotland, and Wales have begun to learn the true lesson for the oppressed, *Property is Robbery*. Surely the events now taking place in Ireland should teach them something in that direction. I have said that the Plan of Campaign may not turn out to be illegal; but I admit that that will only mean its finding a loophole whereby to evade the law. The law which allows rack-rent and backs it up with the full force of the executive is quite blind to any ruin which may be the result of it. Lord Clanricarde and the other shabby tyrants have, according to law, full right to squeeze the uttermost farthing out of their luckless tenants; and we may be sure of one thing, namely, that if any check is put on that right by laws made by our bourgeois government it will mean just the same kind of kindness which is accorded to sufferers on the rack, who are recovered from their fainting in order that they may be racked again. Those tormented by the rack of usury have sometimes to receive the cup of cold water so that they may live to be squeezed once more for the benefit of the usurers. The latter years of the Irish question must have taught the

Irish peasants that in the eyes of English law they are people whose function it is to pay landlords, and who must be helped to do so, sometimes by coercion, sometimes by Acts of Parliament made apparently in their favour, really in favour of the landlords.

When they have got rid of their last illusion, whlch (*sic*) would seem to be that an English Constitutional party can help them, the day of their redemption will be drawing near.

COMMONWEAL, VOLUME 2, NUMBER 50,
25 DECEMBER 1886, P. 305

CONTRIBUTIONS TO *COMMONWEAL*

1887

EDITORIAL

With this number there is begun a new volume of the *Commonweal*. For two years it has managed to appear regularly and keep before the public a consistent, unflinching exponent of International Revolutionary Socialism. Difficulties of many kinds have had to be surmounted, and in the future we may confidently look for a hardly less arduous endeavour as the price of a continued and useful existence.

During the two years that have elapsed since the *Commonweal* was founded the cause of Socialism has made great strides. In every country of the civilized world there is a definite, strong, and increasing Socialist party; while the influence of the untiring propaganda of its advocates is markedly shown in every popular political and social movement. From all directions come tidings of good cheer; everywhere and all the time commercialism, making desperate but futile efforts to regain its ground, contesting vainly every vantage point, is being beaten backward toward the precipice of final destruction.

In the warfare against class-rule and social wrong the *Commonweal* has borne and will bear its full part. Though there are signs of victory on all hands, and the end of the struggle approaches, yet no strain must be relaxed, no effort cease. Again and again have popular movements been wrecked, because at some period of promise their supporters failed in their vigilance or neglected their labour.

We call upon all men who desire to see the solution of the great problems that befront the labouring people to help us in our task. What we can do shall untiringly be done, but there exist a thousand places into which the light of Socialism has not penetrated, millions of men whom it has not reached. Everyone can help in some way to spread the light. Let each one do his best. Circulate the *Commonweal*, push Socialistic literature, speak a word in season and out of season for Socialism. Let pass no opportunity of helping on the overthrow of capitalism and the substitution for it of a system of united free labour and fraternal enjoyment.

COMMONWEAL, VOLUME 3, NUMBER 51,
1 JANUARY 1887, P. 4

WORDS OF FORECAST FOR 1887

The war-rumours are solidifying and it cannot be denied that there is great probability of this year seeing the long-threatened war which will embrace all the nations of Europe. There have within the last few days been stories of alliance between Germany and Russia. This seems at first sight highly improbable, considering the strong race animosity between the Slav and the Teuton, and also the difficulties which dealing with Austria would offer to both the great reactionary states; because Austria, if not used as the tool of Germany against Russia, would probably in the case of a successful expedition of the two great robbers, have to submit to the doom of partition.

One thing may be noted in reference to this rumour about Russia, that it points to the fact that there are two developments of the European struggle possible – the one springing from the forward impulse of Russian aggression in the East, the other from Bismarkian or German bourgeois aggression in the West.

As regards the effects of such an alliance on the popular movement. At first sight it would seem to be the most disastrous event that could cross the path of progress, meaning little less than crushing the various and often-disappointed aspirations of the nineteenth century with the weight of a new influx of the post-feudal absolutism which has survived into our epoch; but on the other hand it may be hoped that it would stir up a fresh force of resistance from all the elements which tend towards liberty, and that the struggle would develope (*sic*) in the proletariat a more definite consciousness of what real liberty means, so that the onrush of a mere reactionary current might be met with the rising flood of revolution, and the attempt, even if partially and temporarily successful, might inflict a mortal wound on the Bourgeois World.

In the other contingency of war beginning in the West, it is a matter of course that Germany, with what allies she can muster, would fall upon France. As we said in last week's issue, in that case Germany would probably hope for England as an ally; but obviously the best method for Germany to gain that advantage by would be to involve this country in a quarrel with Russia, which might possibly, although not necessarily, develope (*sic*) into direct hostility with France. It is absolutely necessary, therefore, for Socialists to watch the situation carefully and closely so as to avoid any possibility of their being dragged into a false position by the recrudescence of jingoism which is quite certain to be one result of even the advancing shadow of a European war.

It ought not [to] be forgotten that for some time past there has been a steady attempt on the part of the bourgeois press to embitter public feeling in this country against France. If Germany attacks France, she will attack her not as the enemy who is plotting a war for the regaining of Alsace and Lorraine, but as the dangerous home of revolution – a country whose proletariat may at any moment unite actively with their brethren the German proletariat – which is the real danger to the monstrous absolutism bound together in slavery (for the time so successfully) by the ceaseless care and energy of the Prince of blood and iron.

Our readers must not think that in mentioning these matters we are merely smiting the air. It is true that a rumour published one day in the papers is discredited the next; but then as often as not it is reasserted on the day after that, and certainly the general tone of the news everywhere, joined to what Socialists must know of the economical necessities of the European states, betokens the coming of the great war, in spite of the fact that our English press has little time for the consideration of European affairs in face of the eagerness with which the public fall on tidings of the wretched intrigues and petty squabbles, party and personal, of the Tory, Unionist, and Gladstonian factions.

COMMONWEAL, VOLUME 3, NUMBER 52,
8 JANUARY 1887, P. 9

FACING THE WORST OF IT

Though we Socialists have full faith in the certainty of the great change coming about, it would be idle for any one of us to attempt to prophesy as to the date of the realization of our hopes; and it is well for us not to be too sanguine, since overweening hope is apt to give birth to despair if it meets with check or disappointment. Although the oppression and robbery of the past and the present is preparing a certain revenge in the future, yet history has shown us over and over again that retribution is halt-foot; or perhaps, to put it with as little metaphor as language will allow of, great revolutions have to wait till the force which is to destroy the old order and create the new is so overwhelming that there is no chance of any real or serious reaction marring the effects of the hopes and necessities which make great revolutions.

There are two streams of the force which is creating the new order of things, and which, already visible to thoughtful persons, will one day rise into a great flood-tide of change visible to every one, and make a new world. On the one hand the system under which we now live and which is, we are firmly convinced, the last development of the oppression of privilege, is of its own weight pushing onwards towards its destruction. The energy and ceaseless activity which made its success so swift and startling are now hurrying it towards its end; there is no turning back possible, no pausing for the tide of that commerce which bears all life with it in the present; it is not only that its goal is ruin, but the goal is now within sight. Yet though the energy which is now sweeping onward to the sea of destruction cannot falter, yet it may itself create checks – eddies, to keep up the metaphor – in which we now living may whirl round and round a long time. So, that we may not be disappointed and be taken unawares, it is well to consider what these may be.

At the same time, although commercial ruin *must* be the main stream of the force for the bringing about [of] revolution, we must not forget the other stream, which is the *conscious* hope of the oppressed classes, forced into union and antagonism by the very success of the commercial system which their hope now threatens with destruction. The commercial or capitalistic system is being eaten out by its own energy; but that energy may on the one hand create partially new conditions for it, yet, on the other hand, in doing so it will stimulate the energy which is consciously attacking it; and these attacks will be more powerful than its struggles to resist its coming fate, the eddies in the stream above said.

As for these, let us look a little closer to see what form they are likely to take.

First, the downward tendency of commerce may and probably will be checked by recoveries something of the nature of the rebounds from depression which were the rule for the last forty years before the depression of the six or seven years just passed set in, but far less complete and much shorter lived. We are threatened with such a recovery at present, and there may be some foundation for the threat, of course if it is realized we shall have plenty of discourses addressed to us of the 'I told you so' kind, and the advocates of the capitalists who have any power of pen or tongue will be jubilant and noisy. We Socialists, however, need not trouble ourselves much about their joy, because such a period is sure to be fruitful of disputes between the trades' unionists and the capitalists; and it will be our business to stimulate and support the claim to a higher standard of livelihood which the brisker business and consequent bigger profits of the manufacturers will enable the workmen to make with success. The period of recovery will certainly be followed by another depression, and the discontent of the workmen will be much increased by their losing, or their dreading to lose, the advantages gained in the better times; so that after all even this apparent check to the progress of the disintegration of the present system will but lead us so much nearer to revolution by making clearer to the workers the antagonism which exists between them and the thief-class – the employers.

Such recovery as above mentioned would come in the ordinary condition of things, and would mean simply an emptying more or less of the shelves of the salesman. But recovery may come from another and more dramatic cause – to wit, the great European war with which we are now threatened. Such a war would give a great stimulus to trade while it lasted; just as if half London were burned down, the calamity would be of great service to those who were not burned out, – all this, of course, applying only to the idiotic system of rewarding labour under which we now suffer, and having nothing to do with a system in which work means production or service of some sort to the community.

But 'good' as the war might be for trade, it could not last for ever; and quite apart from the more specially political results which might come of it, the time would come when some one would have to say, as Owen said after the end of the great war of the beginning of the century, 'the war, our best customer, is dead'.

Then would come the inevitable reaction, and what between falling prices, and crowds thrown out of employment, and the certain disappointment and disgust which would attend the exhaustion of the finish of the struggle, our present thief-society would receive a rude shake, which one might hope it would scarcely recover. But whether that were so or not, at least the inflation of the war-time would be far more than counterbalanced by the depression of the following peace. Only the most short-sighted of the capitalists can pray for war in the times we are now in, one would think, because behind the brilliant 'respectable' war stands its shadow, revolution.

And yet though they may dread war, still that restless enemy of the commercial system, the demon which they have made, and is no longer their servant but their master, forces them into it in spite of them; because unless commerce can find new capacities for expansion it is all over, or will be in a very few years; the partial and brief recovery of trade before mentioned is too insignificant to be worth much notice; the one thing for which our thrice accursed civilization craves, as the stifling man for fresh air, is *new markets;* fresh countries must be conquered by it which are not manufacturing and are producers of raw material, so that 'civilized' manufactures can be forced on them. *All wars now waged, under whatever pretences, are really wars for the great prizes in the world-market.* And certainly if the countries, the chances for whose monopolization (distant chances too) are now leading Europe into a war the end of which no one can foresee, can be opened up to commerce, and when opened up satisfy the expectations of the national pirates who are 'on the account' in this matter, the dissolution of our present system may be somewhat checked. Yet, on the other hand, this very success would stimulate the cut-throat competition of the commerce-gamblers; and once more, since of their plunder they would only yield to the workers as much as the latter compelled them to yield, whatever 'prosperity' might follow such enterprises, would, now that the idea of Socialism has taken root amongst the workmen of Europe, be accompanied by fresh demands on their part; and these demands again would necessarily act as a spur to the competition of the gamblers, and make the pace faster and more furious; so that perhaps even the glorious hope of flooding Central Africa and China with trade 'goods' which nobody wants, will turn out when attained but Dead Sea apples to the capitalist.

These three chances of checking the onward course of capitalistic commerce to its annihilation, are the only visible ones I think: – 1st, The lessening of stocks and consequent slight temporary recovery; 2nd, A great European war, perhaps lengthened out into a regular epoch of war; and 3rd, The realization of the hopes of important new markets, which hopes are the real causes of hostility between nations. How far they might act as checks on Socialism it is not possible to foretell; but that they will not be unmixed advantages to Capitalism is, I think, certain, nor is there anything about the possibility of their happening which need discourage us. Probably none of them would have much influence in checking the growing tendency towards the union of the workers in England. Certainly they would have no power to break that spirit of union which already exists among the great nations of the Continent.

Besides these obvious resources of the system we are attacking, there are less obvious possibilities about which one may speculate, perhaps with some profit; these more speculative possibilities point to attempts of Capitalism at avoiding its doom, which would lead to more ruin and suffering than are likely to be involved in even those above-mentioned. I have not space to call our reader's attention to them at present, so I will end by saying that our part as acknowledged and organized Socialists is, while we watch keenly the development of the causes whith (*sic*) would lead to the destruction of the present system, even if there were no acknowledged Socialists at all, to do all we can to aid the *conscious* attacks on the system by all those who feel themselves wronged by it. It is possible that we may live to see times in which it will be easier than now for the labourer to live as a labourer and not as a man, and there is a kind of utilitarian sham Socialism which would be satisfied by such an outcome of times of prosperity. It is very much our business to meet this humbug by urging the workers to sustain steadily their due claim to that fullness and completeness of life which no class system can give them. The claims of non-Socialist workmen go little beyond the demand for a bigger ration, warmer coat, and better lodging for the slave; and even Socialist workmen, I think, are apt to put their claims too low, at least in this country; for, indeed, one must say with a sense of shame in one's own better luck not possible to express, that the conditions under which they live and work make it difficult for them even to conceive the sort of life that a man should live.

COMMONWEAL, VOLUME 3, NUMBER 58,
19 FEBRUARY 1887, PP. 60–61

FIGHTING FOR PEACE

Our contemporary, the *Cotton Factory Times*, has an article on the Lanarkshire riots and the position of the men there which is worth noting, as showing the kind of prejudices and superstitions which will have to be removed from the minds of the workers before they can attain to that complete union and perception of the interests of labour by which alone they can meet the organization of capital on equal terms: and this is the more worth noting, as the *Cotton Factory Times* is an excellent paper, and really devoted, according to its lights, to the interests of labour.

Our contemporary does not seem to have understood the meaning of these riots, or the necessities of the men who made them. They were distinctly hunger-riots, that is to say the expression of the despair of men driven into a corner, dying by inches of starvation: and we may be sure that such events will, at the rate we are now going, become common and increase in misery and terror, unless the workers become conscious of their present position and its remedy: their position being to speak plainly that they have to pay the piper in the game of cut-throat competition played by their masters, who are themselves *forced* by the rules of the game to *force* their men to accept the very lowest wages possible. The result of this famine-test of wages (for that is what it is) must be such misery as we now see in Lanarkshire coupled from time to time with the incident of open revolt: the riots of the other day are a hint to the masters that the wages they now offer are *impossible* of acceptance.

Surely our contemporary if it had known all the circumstance[s] would scarcely have blamed the miners for not making provision for a rainy day. Alas! it is always a rainy day with these poor people, unless when it is worse; a life of days like the three in the ballad:

> The first day it was wind and weet,
> The nexten day it was fire and sleet;
> The third day it was birley-banes,
> Knocked the little birds' nebs against the stanes.

But what provision can be made against 'birley-banes' when even the better days are so bitter?

Here are some questions for our contemporary: How much is it possible to save out of a (precarious) income of 12s. 6d. a week? If it be possible to save anything out of such a pittance without being actually starved to death, why should a man be put to such torture and degradation as this saving involves, when we all know that he actually produces more than enough to keep him in comfort, unless his labour be utterly wasted? Again, can the getting of coal be carried on gainfully in Lanarkshire? If it cannot, why is it carried on? And if there is a due gain in it, why are the getters starved?

These are the kind of questions which the working-men who profess to be organized must ask and have answered if their organization is to be of any use: they must not fight against capitalism blindly, as they mostly do now, but be conscious of the nature of the fight, and especially must have a definite aim *to end it*. Our contemporary is very far from this. He says, *eg*.: 'A fair stand-up fight between capital and labour with no striking below the belt frightens no one. The best men win, after which both sides can be as friendly as before, with no bitter memories to cherish.'

Well, well, if I had but 12s. 6d. a week as the 'reward' of hard and repulsive labour, I think I might be bitter without drawing on the resources of 'memory'. But in fact the fight between capital and labour on the Lanarkshire terms *ie*., the capitalist with his money resources to stand by on, and the miner with the three choices of 12s. 6d. a week, death, and the workhouse, is about as fair (if we are to keep up the metaphor of the ring) as the champion against a London errand boy. And again, the writer speaks cheerfully of these 'fair' fights; can he possibly think that a condition of industry to which they are necessary (and frequent) incidents can be a stable one? These 'fair fights' are but incidents, skirmishes, or battles in the continuous war on which all industrial society is founded at present. Like all other wars it must one day come to an end by the exhaustion of one or other of the combatants: either the workman must be subjugated into a hopeless slave, receiving such housing, clothing, and rations as it may be convenient for his master to give him (and for that matter it could not be less than the 'reward' of a Lanarkshire miner), or the capitalist must disappear altogether, and his privilege of usury be a thing of the past; and that whether he be the boss of a big business, or a small shareholder in a 'co-operative' store.

Now I will ask our trades' union friends which of the two results of the struggle they are fighting for? The have no choice, it must be one or the other, or indeed is there a choice even between those two results? Is not the final subjugation of the workman impossible? Even now, even when the strikers are least conscious of it, their limited and local fight is really, as I have said, a part of the great labour war: but when they do become conscious of what the end of that war is, to wit, the abolition of private property in the means of production, the inequality between the two combatants will be no longer against them, but against their masters, and the war will soon be over. On the other hand, although the end must come, yet if the workers remain unconscious of what they are striving for, it will probably be long delayed through a period fertile of misery and degradation to the workman, and terror and degradation to the master, and will be brought about at last by the mere break up and ruin of our capitalistic system involving inconceivable horrors of starvation, aimless violence, repression, and revenge.

The choice of these two alternatives gives the reason why sober, thoughtful, and peaceable men, even when they themselves are not pinched by the present system, when they have once learned the economic truths of Socialism are so eager in the Revolutionist propaganda: it is for peace they are working, not war.

COMMONWEAL, VOLUME 3, NUMBER 59,
26 FEBRUARY 1887, P. 68

WHY WE CELEBRATE THE COMMUNE OF PARIS

The 'moons and the days' have brought us round again to the anniversary of the greatest tragedy of modern times, the Commune of Paris of 1871, and with it the recurring duty for all Socialists of celebrating it both enthusiastically and intelligently. By this time the blatant slanders with which the temporarily unsuccessful cause was assailed when the event was yet fresh in men's minds have sunk into the dull gulf of lies, hypocritical concealments, and false deductions, which is called bourgeois history, or have become a dim but deeply rooted superstition in the minds of those who have information enough to have heard of the Commune, and ignorance enough to accept the bourgeois legend of it as history.

Once more it is our duty to raise the whole story out of this poisonous gloom and bring it to the light of day, so that on the one hand those who are not yet touched by Socialism may learn that there was a principle which animated those who defended revolutionary Paris against the mingled dregs of the woeful period of the Second Empire, and that that principle is still alive to-day in the hearts of many thousands of workers throughout civilization, and year by year and day by day is growing in strength and in the hold it has of the disinherited masses of our false society; and on the other hand that we Socialists may soberly note what went on in this story, and may take both warning and encouragement from its events. I have heard it said, and by good Socialists too, that it is a mistake to commemorate a defeat; but it seems to me that this means looking not at this event only, but at all history in too narrow a way. The Commune of Paris is but one link in the struggle which has gone on through all history of the oppressed against the oppressors; and without all the defeats of past times we should now have no hope of the final victory. Neither are we yet sufficiently removed in time from the events to judge how far it was even possible to avoid the open conflict at the time, or to appreciate the question as to what would have become of the revolutionary cause if Paris had tamely yielded itself up to the perfidy of Thiers and his allies. One thing, on the other hand, we are sure of, that this great tragedy has definitely and irrevocably elevated the cause of Socialism to all those who are prepared to look on the cause seriously, and refuse to admit the possibility of ultimate defeat. For I say solemnly and deliberately that if it happens to those of us now living to take part in such another tragedy it will be rather well for them than ill for them. Truly it is harder to live for a cause than to die for it, and it injures a man's dignity and self-respect to be always making noisy professions of devotion to a cause before the field is stricken, on which he is to fight in the body. But with the chance of bodily sacrifice close a-head there come also times of trial which either raise a man to the due tragic pitch or cast him aside as a useless and empty vapourer. To use a transparent metaphor, on the march to the field of battle there are plenty of opportunities for the faint-hearted to fall out of the ranks, and many will do so whose courage and devotion were neither doubted by others nor by themselves while the day of actual battle was far distant. So such times of trial are good because they are times of trial; and we may well think that few indeed of those who fell sixteen years ago, who exposed themselves to death and wounds at all adventure, were mere accidental braggarts caught in the trap. Of those whose names are well known this was far from being the case, and who can doubt that the nameless multitude who died so heroically had sacrificed day by day other things than life, before it came to that?

Furthermore, it must surely be rather more than doubtful to all thoughtful men if the mere exercise of every-day and civil virtues, even when directed towards the social end, will suffice to draw the world out of its present misery and confusion. Consider the enormous mass of people so degraded by their circumstances that they can scarcely understand any hope for their redemption that can be put before them in peaceful and constitutional times. Yet these are the very people for whom we are working; and are they to have no hand in the work, then? Is it to be once more according to the degrading Positivist motto, 'everything *for* you, nothing *by* you?' Meanwhile in these people, unless we Socialists are all wrong, there are seeds of manly and social feeling, capable of large development; and surely when the time comes that their hope will be made manifest, as it was in the time of the Commune, and will lie before them for their hands to take, they will then have part in the work indeed, and by the act of doing so will at once raise themselves out of the slough of degradation into which our false society has cast them and in which it keeps them. The revolution itself will raise those for whom the revolution must be made. Their newborn hope translated into action will develope (*sic*) their human and social qualities, and the struggle itself will fit them to receive the benefits of the new life which revolution will make possible for them. It is for boldly seizing the opportunity offered for thus elevating the mass of the workers into heroism that we now celebrate the men of the Commune of Paris. True they failed in conquering immediate material freedom for the people, but they quickened and strengthened the ideas of freedom by their courageous action and made our hope of to day possible; and if to-day any one doubts that they were fighting for the emancipation of labour, their enemies at the time had no doubt about the matter. They saw in them no mere political opponents, but 'enemies of society', people who could not live in the same world with them, because the basis of their ideas of life was different – to wit, humanity, not property. This was why the fall of the Commune was celebrated by such hecatombs sacrificed to the bourgeois god, Mammon; by such a riot of blood and cruelty on the part of the conquerors as quite literally has no parallel in modern times. And it is by that same token that we honour them as the foundation-stone of the new world that is to be.

Commonweal, Volume 3, Number 62,
19 March 1887, pp. 89–90

Law and Order in Ireland

The Coercion Bill and the attempt to drive it through Parliament is really a matter of great simplicity, although the whirl of party politics has made it seem somewhat intricate. It is the mere 'outward and visible sign of the inward and spiritual grace' of that Conservatism, Toryism, or Reactionism, whichever you please to call it, to which all the respectability of Parliamentary life gravitates, and which has engulfed not only the grave and portentous Philistinism of the once Tribune of the People, John Bright, but also the gathering ambition and vague aspiration to do something remarkable of Joseph Chamberlain; besides many other luminaries of a lesser order, some of whom have been set down as Radicals, and perhaps thought themselves to be so, but surely only because other people called them so.

However, even this outward and visible sign is a serious thing, not only for Ireland but for England also, and must at the outset be admitted to be far more serious than any other Coercion Bill, not because of any speciality in its provisions, nor even because it is to last permanently (which may mean perhaps as long as next year), but rather because it is to be enacted in the teeth of the disapproval of a great part of the *English* population. That is to say that the ordinary Englishman supposed that former measures of coercion were passed to restrain a band of plotters and miscreants in Ireland from injuring the ordinary peaceful law abiding people there, who had no sympathy with their doings. Therefore, though some of the more advanced politicians might oppose such measures on principle, and others because they thought there was no special need for such strong measures, yet the greater part even of those who usually take some interest in politics would pass such matters by with the vague idea that it was a necessary step to take against Fenians and moonlighters, and other rebels, as unreasonable as only Irish can be. All that is changed now, and it is only in Parliament that any one pretends to think that the Coercion Bill is directed against a minority of the Irish people. It is, however vaguely by some persons, felt to be what the *Pall Mall* called it the other evening, a declaration of war against Ireland; to say to a part of the Empire: 'We are going, not to suspend, but to abolish your civil rights by the strong hand, and let us see what you dare to do in resistance to this violence', is to admit that such people are in rebellion against the central authority, and are perfectly conscious of their solidarity as against it; and if they had, I will not say any chance of success, but any opportunity, they would make that manifest by rising in armed revolt against the central tyranny, and to a large part at least of the peoples of England, Scotland, and Wales, that rebellion seems a righteous one; to how large a portion no general election will make clear to us, but rather the march of events.

It is a pity indeed that agitation on a really large scale cannot be at once set on foot, so as to show the reactionists that they are rashly playing with fire; but though it can scarcely be doubted that a genuine poll of the country would give a large majority against landlord-magistrate law in Ireland, yet it is hopeless to expect a serious expression of opinion at all in proportion to the dissatisfaction that doubtless exists, still less any expression of opinion which would mean a serious threat of 'Don't try that on again!' The politically minded part of the workers who can claim to have any approach to organization, have unhappily been organized to be at the beck and call of their leaders at election time, and also to forbear even the mildest agitation unless the wire-pullers give the sign. They have been so debauched by allowing themselves to be treated as the mere machinery of a Parliamentary party, that now when the time comes that even that organized hypocrisy, their party, would be glad of their help they can do but little; at the best they can but show that they exist as dissatisfied persons in some numbers, which the reactionists know already, but any genuine strong and fierce outburst of feeling from them is scarcely to be expected when one thinks of the deep respectability of the gentlemen that lead them.

However, what can be done must be done, and that out of Parliament. The Bill will certainly be passed. The Radical Unionists, all but two or three, will have a sop thrown to them by the withdrawal of the clause for changing the venue of the bigger trials, which was probably put in to be withdrawn, as also perhaps was the 'permanency' of the bill, which, however, these precious Democrats have swallowed so sweetly. And then the Reactionists will have their way in Parliament, as is but natural, and all one can hope is that the country will wake up after the bill is passed; though it is no use hoping that anything more will come of that but a dissolution and general election. Home Rule may follow that, though of course only a compromise Home Rule, and the ground will be cleared so far for the question of property in Ireland – and elsewhere. The day of the Tories proper has passed with this Coercion Bill. Tomorrow the Liberals in the English Parliament will have to be dealt with, criticized, and resisted. The day after it will be the turn of the Dublin Parliament. Let us hope that true social feeling in Ireland will not have exhausted itself in combining to defeat the English landlords, but will rise with the new condition of affairs and demand freedom not only for the tenants but for all.

COMMONWEAL, VOLUME 3, NUMBER 65,
9 APRIL 1887, P. 113

COERCION FOR LONDON

It may be thought that the patriots who are so eager for the unity of the British empire that they want to use artificial means to make it more specially uncomfortable to live in one part of it than it is elsewhere, are taking unnecessary trouble; that the coercionists are such enthusiasts in the art of coercion that they are hunting it when they have already got it.

It is true that there is a pleasure in making a special and blatant demonstration of success, but it is a pleasure that has to be paid for by the opposition that the attempt to make it stirs up. The wise are contented with having the substance and letting the shadow take care of itself, especially if they have to fight for the shadow when they have got the substance peaceably and easily.

One is compelled by recent events to look on the subject from this point of view. Ireland is to have an extra dose of coercion, but London has already got enough for all practical purposes. A Bill is being put forward and opposed, with great fervour on each side, which, when it becomes law, will enable any *two* magistrates in Ireland to sentence any one who is brought before them and whose looks they don't like to six months' imprisonment. In London, any *one* magistrate has already got that power, and is on occasion not ashamed to exercise it.

It is perhaps worth while to tell over again a short story of the manner in which the coercion machine in London is set a-going, as it can be done in so much fewer words than the Langworthy case.

One Sunday there were, as usual, Socialist meetings going on in Hyde Park near the Marble Arch, during and after which various salesmen were proposing, as usual, to sell

Socialist papers outside the park (selling inside being forbidden). The police had for some time past hustled and bullied, and even run in, these Socialist salesmen, although the sellers of other newspapers were not interfered with. On the occasion in question, after the Socialist meetings were over, the crowd, much increased by the news of the high-handed proceedings on former Sundays, poured out through the gate close by, being as a matter of course largely composed of mere Sunday strollers attracted to the Socialist platform – non-combatants, most of them, in the battle of opinion between Socialism and Bourgeoisdom. Well, these people, who would else have gone about their business quietly, were immediately set upon by the police *à la* Donnybrook, and a rough-and-tumble ensued, of the kind which the timid citizen of to-day looks at with pleasure – from a window, and in which you may find yourself half-throttled on the way to the police-station without being conscious of what has led you to that expedition, otherwise than that a policeman tried to knock you down and that you tried to stand upright: such an entertainment being obviously a good occasion for any one of an inventive turn to exercise his capacity for romance as a police-court witness.

The result of this police battue was a pretty good bag, although the police acted rather as the foreigner in Leech's woodcuts, who shoots the foxes and the owls instead of the pheasants, and got hold of more of the above-mentioned non-combatants than Socialists. These 'rioters' being brought up before Mr de Rutzen, were prosecuted by the Government jackal Mr Poland, the farcical nature of whose opening speech no one, now Dickens is dead – more's the pity – need attempt to render.[1] The farce was continued by various policemen giving what is facetiously called 'evidence', and more accurately 'swearing the leg off an iron pot'; and Mr Rutzen, in virtue of his position, wound

[1] I don't know, though; the author of 'Cashel Byron', though he wouldn't do it with the richness of Dickens, might deal with such a case – *why* doesn't he!

up with the grand joke of the whole entertainment by saying that since Mr Poland did not press the case as one of riot, he would treat it as a mere assault on the police, and would be so kind as not to send the accused for trial, but would – Fine them 10s. and caution them, thinks the unsuspecting 'cultivated' person, rejoicing in the security of property and person in this civilized and 'free' country. No – sentence them, two Socialists (one of whom had not been present in Hyde Park) and five non-Socialists, to six months' hard labour!

This was the end of the first act of the farce called 'Justice' in this happy land: though such a finish of the Hyde Park Sunday saunter might well be looked on by the luckless persons who were rash enough to try it as a tolerable tragedy in its way.

However, the farce is not done yet. The convicted persons may appeal to a bench of magistrates – if they can. That is, if they have money or friends with money; otherwise they must bear the six months' torture of an English jail as well as they can; even if they have been convicted of assaulting the police when they were miles from the spot.

Two of the Socialists, our friends Williams and Pole (which last was the absent man), appealed at once and found bail; and two of the non-Socialists subsequently appealed, one of whom, at least, found bail. The other three must lie in prison for six months, unless Mr Matthews extends his 'mercy' to them – (a lawyer's mercy!).

'But why didn't they also appeal?' says the well-to-do inhabitant of a 'free' country. Because they must find bail for their appearance at Westminster on July 16th. Not so difficult, you think? Yes, but the bail *must be liable to the expenses of the appeal if it is rejected*, which in plain terms means that if an ordinary working-man is arbitrarily convicted by a magistrate and sentenced to such a terrible punishment as six months' hard labour, no matter how preposterous the behaviour of the magistrate may be, the working-man *cannot* appeal. The rich man *can* defend himself, the poor man *cannot*.

This is the meaning of there being the same law for rich and poor, of justice never being sold in this country, and the like damned hypocritical twaddle. Justice is *always* sold in this country.

The answers to questions asked in Parliament have enriched the farce with other good jokes. Mr Matthews had the boundless impudence to declare again (for he has done it before) that he did not know what part the Government had taken in the prosecution – he is a useful article at the price certainly!

Mr Stuart Wortley refined on the Jorkins business in a manner that shows his fitness for office in the most satisfactory manner, and in short, the answers to questions on this matter illustrate the great leading farce of Parliament as well as need be.

It would be unfair also to leave off without complimenting the so-called labour representatives on their 'masterly inactivity' in this matter. Years ago, before the possibility almost of labour representatives was thought of, what an advantage their presence in the House would have been considered! What a row one would have thought such men would have made about such treatment as De Rutzen's of men of their own order! – and now, mum is the word. A London middle-class member, Mr Pickersgill, and a Scotch landowner, Mr Cunninghame Graham, have taken upon them the duty of Messrs the Labour Representatives, who should have made the row - such a row that they ought by this time to be all sitting in the Clock Tower.

Space fails me as to the progress of the affair at Kennington, but it is all a part of this same Coercion Campaign; and no doubt it is well thought of by the magistrates to refuse protection to harmless citizens against hired roughs, since all Socialists are not athletes, and there is a double danger in carrying deadly weapons. The preposterous charge against a physically weak man, like our comrade Blackwell, of attacking the police violently, is seemingly the sort of thing that Socialists must expect to meet with at present.

In conclusion, grieved as we must all be at the torture to which innocent men are being subjected, no Socialist can help reflecting that these fools, Matthews, Poland, Warren, and Co., are doing good propagandist work for us. People generally have some idea of fair play, and the spectacle of such blatant injustice as has been recently exhibited, has to my certain knowledge moved to indignation people not particularly favourable to Socialism. It is still more important that the working-classes should have a further instance of what law means under our system – a cunning instrument for the oppression of the poor by the rich.

COMMONWEAL, VOLUME 3, NUMBER 70,
14 MAY 1887, PP. 153–154

THE REWARD OF LABOUR
A DIALOGUE

Persons: An Earnest Enquirer, an East-end Weaver, a West-end Landowner

Scene: Outside a philanthropical meeting on Social Science.

Earnest Enquirer. Excuse me, gentle – h'm, gentle*men*! neither of you seem quite comfortable after the noble sentiments showing the harmony that should exist between the rich and the poor, and the inculcation of altruism, and self-sacrifice on *both* sides, which we have heard in there. You, sir (*to the Weaver*), whom I take to be a soldier in the noble army of industry, seem discontented; a little sour – sulky even, if I may say so. And you, sir (*to the Landowner*), you also (again a million apologies!) seem sulky: although, probably because of the restraint which the refinement of hereditary culture and habits of command makes easy to you, I can't think why.

Landowner (somewhat languidly). Not at all. I assure you I was much interested. The subject is a very interesting one; I heard much which I did not know before. (*Lapses into thinking of something else.*)

E. E. Were you puzzled?

L. No, I quite agreed with it all.

E. E. All? Was it all alike then?

Weaver (with a grin). Pretty much.

E. E. Eh! what's that? Would you answer me a question or two, my friend?

W. Well, yes, so long as it's not chaff and you really want information. You began as if you were going to chaff me openly, and him slyly. Now, you know, you said I was sulky, and perhaps I am; anyhow I know I am irritable because of my liver (you'd know why if you was me); and being irritable, I can't stand chaff. So if you do chaff me, since I'm not big enough to hit you, I shall be off.

E. E. Well, thank you. I really didn't mean to chaff you; one must begin somehow, you know. (*To L.*) And you, sir, will you answer me a question or two?

L. Well - yes; though I have a suspicion of what you are driving at. Begin with this good man; I am curious to hear what he has to say; he looks thoughtful and intelligent. (*Aside.*) Might get something out of him; looks like an ultra-Radical – perhaps a Socialist; and we're all expected to be so damned original in the House now.

E. E. (To W.) You heard that gentleman who moved the vote of thanks just now, and who spoke so – well, so elegantly on the compensation which the working classes have for their apparently inferior position; and how necessary it was for the progress of civilization that there should be this division of labour and life; and what a noble position it was for the workers to hold; and how the slight sacrifices they had to make they ought to make cheerfully and almost as a matter of religion, that new religion of Humanity, considering their position as the foundation of all the culture, thought, light and leading which is the glory of Humanity. What did you think of all that?

W. What's the use of asking me such questions as that? I shall go away at once if you haven't got something more than that to say to me.

L. (to W.) My dear sir, if you would but pay a little more attention to such speeches as that which this gentleman is speaking of, it would be a very good thing for you.

W. Think so? Do you know what he meant by it?

L. Yes, I think I do.

W. (to E. E.) Do you know what he meant by it?

E. E. No, I think I don't.

W. Well, I think I do. Besides, it ain't quite new to me, you see. But that's neither here nor there; don't waste your time by asking me what I think of a vote-of-thank's speech, but ask me something about my work and my earnings, and the sort of way I live in.

E. E. Well, well, I was going to, but allow me a little explanation, I want to find out something about that compensation which our altruistic friend in there did apparently think was due to you for your apparently inferior position; which, indeed, so far as I can see, is abundantly apparent to me. Your clothes are old, worn, and when they were new they were bad; you're not very clean, you don't speak like an educated man (though I perceive in you some of the intelligence which this educated man here spoke about so patronisingly) and worst of all you don't look properly grown or healthy; you are stunted, sallow, and ugly – there, don't bounce out at me! I cannot fail to see that some compensation is due to you, if all this, as I suppose, is the result of your being the foundation of the progress of civilization, and a bearer of the palm branch of martyrdom for the behoof of the religion of Humanity. No, no, don't go! That vote-of-thanks speech will stick in my memory, as meaningless words often will, when they are spoken according to art. What I want to get at is how you get that compensation above spoken of. So here goes for my definite questions. What is your occupation?

W. I am a silk weaver.

E. E. Is that difficult? Does it take skill to do?

W. Well, you wouldn't ask that if you had seen a weaver at work, taking care that his pattern doesn't work out longer or shorter than it should; mending half-a-dozen of the fine silk threads of the warp, for instance.

E. E. As difficult as a barrister's work, for instance?

W. I'm sure I don't know – it's not so easy as lying, at any rate. But don't get off the subject.

E. E. Is it a useful occupation?

W. It seems so. People will have silk; and why not since they can? It is pretty stuff and clean, and wears well. Didn't you notice that lady at the back of the platform, the young and pretty one, who went to sleep during the lecture, and how nice she looked in her new silk gown. Well, I wove her gown.

E. E. Well, your work is useful and requires skill; let's see on what terms you carry it on. How many hours a day do you work?

W. As many as I can. That's none too many as things go I assure you!

E. E. You mean to say that you are sometimes out of work?

W. Sometimes!!

E. E. And you take all the work you can get? You're not one of those lazy ones of which I have heard a good deal?

W. Now I want to keep my temper, and I really think you don't believe that 'good deal' you have heard.

E. E. Well, no I don't. But tell me, would you work eight hours a day if you could?

W. Eight hours! I shouldn't get a job if I didn't put it through as quick as I could; ten at the very least.

E. E. Well, now as to payment. Suppose you worked ten hours a day all the year round except Sundays, how much would you earn?

W. From 35s. to 40s. a-week.

E. E. Say £90 a-year?

W. No, I *won't* say £90. Haven't I just told you that I've got to sit and look at my loom many and many a-day? I should think it a good years' work in which I got nine months full employment. I'll say £60 if you like – and don't I wish I may get it, year in and year out!

E. E. Have you got a family?

W. Wife and five children

E. E. Do they make anything?

W. My wife gets a job now and then weaving plain silk or winding, and one of the lads is a half-timer in a shoe-shop; it don't come to much altogether; £75 a year, since we must put it in the grand style, will cover it all.

E. E. H'm, well (*aside:* Poor devil!)[.] Rent's cheap, I suppose in the East-end, since you are all working-men there?

W. (in sudden wrath) No, it's *not*, I pay £26 a-year for my house; how much do you pay for yours?

E. E. Well, never mind.

W. Yes, I know; and then the whole of my house together isn't as big as your drawing-room.

E. E. Well what sort of a house is your house?

W. Good enough for me, I suppose; it's a weaver's house.

L. (with sudden interest) Dear me, I should like to see it; it must be quite curious.

W. Should you? Well I shouldn't like you to see it; it isn't fit for a gentleman.

E. E. (to L.) Excuse me, sir, let me have our friend to myself; think about the sort of questions I am likely to be asking *you* presently. (*To W.*) Well, certainly I haven't come to the compensation which we all think you have a right to claim as a representative of that noble army of labour we all praise so highly – especially at election time.

COMMONWEAL, VOLUME 3, NUMBER 71,
21 MAY 1887, P. 165

THE REWARD OF LABOUR
A DIALOGUE

Persons: An Earnest Enquirer, an East-end Weaver, a West-end Landowner

SCENE*: Outside a philanthropical meeting on Social Science.*

E. E. (continuing to W.) But I am a stranger in London, and will you believe it, don't know what the East-end of London is like; but I have heard of so much being done for the benefit of the East-end, People's Palaces, Mosaic pictures, and the like, that I suppose by now it is quite a pleasant place; that small and squalid as your house is, you can get out of it at once into fresh air, pleasant gardens, roomy squares; and that it is well supplied with libraries, baths, and, in a word, all the benefits of civilization - (*aside*) whatever that may mean.

W. Well, sir, you suppose a great deal. What's the use of building a People's Palace in Hell, or putting up a Mosaic picture on the walls of the devil's scullery. If the parsons are right about that job, and some of us do happen down there, we shall beat Old Scratch; for he will scarcely be able to make it so nasty that we shan't think we have got back again home. Excuse me, I told you that I was a bilious subject.

E. E. No excuse needed; I must get on, and indeed make an excuse to you for what I am going to say. Perhaps both I and this frock-coated, shiny-hatted gentleman here were after all wrong in thinking you intelligent; perhaps that's only a show – eh, Mr Landowner? – to cover that dangerous discontent of the inferior part of the lower orders, which is getting to be so prevalent; and ain't you perhaps stupid, unable to seize hold of your advantages; – there, I don't want to hurt your feelings, I am only speaking of you as a type of a large body of men.

W. Never mind my feelings, I shan't get in a rage; I'm used to you now. Well, I'll answer as a type, and say I'm no stupider than other people, high as well as low; and at all events I am able to do my *work* – come!

E. E. (aside.) Well, the secret of the compensation to the working classes for their inferior position does rather elude my grasp, certainly; like trying to hold an eel when one hasn't sanded one's hand. Well, let's try once more, and try the moral side of things. (*To W.*) As I understand, we have got so far: you are a skilled workman, not stupid especially, you produce useful things, and yet you are poor; for that is the word we use, Mr Landowner, to express a condition of life that you know nothing of, so that the word doesn't carry much meaning in it for you; nor as much as it should for you either, Mr Weaver, because *you* don't know what being rich is, or what a soft and comfortable life it means, in spite of the moralists. However, I will just tell you both what being poor means, so that henceforth you, Mr Landowner, may attach some meaning to the word, and you, Mr Weaver, may understand partly what the word rich means. To be poor is to live in perpetual anxiety about satisfying the very simplest wants, and to have all kinds of wants besides which you have no chance of satisfying. Do you understand that, Mr Landowner? – no, scarcely yet, I am afraid. Well, it can't be helped – he who lives will see. And now to my search for compensation again. You are, as it seems, skilful, industrious, useful – and poor. Yet, perhaps, you may be compensated even for that; for you know that according to the story, in ancient times the philosophers, whom you may look upon as a kind of reasonable parsons, were poor as well as useful, but they had their compensation in being much honoured and respected. Let us hope that it is the same with you, and that you are looked upon with a sort of veneration because you add so much to the wealth of the community and take so little from it.

[A faint smile is observed to play on the features of the Landowner, who has been listening a little lately].

W. Yes, I thought we should get to the chaff again, or else where have you been dug up from to ask such a question? A working-man honoured and respected! Yes, when he's a working-man representative. But look here, as to the respect I'm held in, I don't want to be vague, so I ask you to take the trouble to notice the way in which a policeman (a public servant, mind you) speaks to an East-ender and a West-ender; that will enlighten you as to the respect paid to me as a philosopher; and as to those of ancient days, 'tis hard to understand; and apart from it being as the old woman said, 'a long way off and a long time ago', I can't help suspecting that some of them were dodgers. Excuse me again, I am but a weaver, and therefore ill-bred.

E. E. Well, it comes to this, then, that you're skilful, industrious, useful, poor, and despised – one of the lower class?

W. Just so – a working-man.

E. E. Why?

W. Why? Because I'm a working-man.

E. E. Well, well, can't we get any further than that with our reason?

W. No, *not yet*. However, here is this gentleman, an educated man, an MP, who has of course considered this sort of thing. Begin upon him now. And since he has stood by and listened to me, perhaps he won't object to my doing the same by him.

E. E. By all means stay, and if you can set him a-going when he sticks by a word in season, *I* shan't grudge you. (*To L.*) Well, sir, now for it! And I like the prospect of questioning you. You are burly and healthy looking; your step is firm, your eye bright, your features well cut. If it were still the old slave-times of the world, and our friend the weaver and you were by the fortune of war offered to me for sale, I think I should prefer speculating in you. You would last longer, for one thing. – Now, without further preamble, tell me what is your occupation?

L. I am a landowner.

E. E. Yes, I know that. What does that mean as to the work of it? What do you do?

L. Do? Well – why – well, I manage my estates.

E. E. *You* manage them? And pleasant work too, since they are yours. But is your statement quite accurate? Come now, on your honour, as an English gentleman.

L. Well, you understand; my lawyer does, and my steward, and my bailiff, and –

E. E. Yes, I see. Well, what else do you besides – not managing your estates?

L. (with hesitation) Well, you heard what the weaver said, I sit in Parliament.

W. (sotto voce) O Lord! That's what he *does*!

E. E. Well, I needn't follow up the enquiry further on that line, as it's clear that that trade, when successful, consists not of doing anything, but preventing things from being done. Do you do anything else?

L. Well, I suppose you won't call shooting doing anything?

E. E. Well, it doesn't do much service to others – not even the partridges.

L. Or horse-racing? At anyrate that's as useful as stock-jobbing.

E. E. I am happy to be able to agree with you.

W. And stock-jobbing isn't so bad as sweating.

E. E. Hilloa, my friend! That subject would lead us further, before we have done with it: let me stick to the honourable member's usefulness.

W. Like the breeches to the legless man!

E. E. (To L.). Well, all this – shooting, horse-racing, yachting, and the like – we had better not trouble ourselves as to its details; it can all be called by one generic name, can't it?

L. Yes; you mean amusement, I suppose.

E. E. You have said it. So that your work consists in your amusing yourself?

L. Yes (*sadly*) – or boring myself.

E. E. What are you paid for it?

L. Eh, what's that? – paid for it?

E. E. Yes, paid for it: you can't feed and clothe yourself on the game you shoot; it wouldn't pay powder and shot, I doubt. Shall I put it in another way? Who keeps you?

L. Keeps me? I keep myself, or course. My father used to keep me; he couldn't get a decent Government place for me.

E. E. Well, never mind your family history: we can guess at it. I must put my question another way, since you *will* be so obtuse. What do you get?

L. Oh, you mean my income? Well, my rent-roll is ten thousand a-year; but it doesn't come to much after all outgoings. First there's –

E. E. Excuse me; never mind those details, I am not a tax-gatherer. What's your income, all deductions made?

L. (blurting it out). Six thousand a-year – there!

E. E. Well, and what do you think the reward for doing nothing ought to be?

W. (eagerly). Nothing.

E. E. Yes, but I didn't ask you. What do you say, Mr Landowner?

L. Nothing.

E. E. Well, well, this is sad. You get £6000 a-year for doing nothing, for which our friend here thinks you ought to have nothing, and you have nothing to say to it. Your position is a strange one. Where does your £6000 a-year come from?

L. From my property, of course.

E. E. Where does that come from?

L. Come, come! you want to know too much. Suffice it, the property is mine, and that I came by it legally.

E. E. Well, I might press you on that point; but as I know that you are your father's son, as the saying goes, I had rather ask the questions I might ask you, as to where the property comes from, of a self-made man – that is, a man who has made money; which means he has 'collected' it. But now, suppose me to be a man from another world, and answer me this: You live softly and comfortably, you can have everything you want, even to the point of the satisfaction of your desires boring you, and you do nothing useful.

L. (interrupting.) Does any one?

E. E. What, not the men who supply you with food? Well, perhaps they don't, if that's all they do.

L. Well, you know what I mean.

E. E. No, I'm damned if I do – unless 'tis 'nothing' once again. But you interrupted me with your meaningless pessimism. I say you do nothing, and for that you have and spend the livelihood of a hundred silk-weavers. You take a great deal out of the stock of wealth of the world, and put nothing into it. As an inhabitant of another world, allow me to ask, don't people look down upon you, jeer at you for this?

L. Certainly not; I am much respected, looked up to – liked even.

E. E. Why?

L. Well, I'm a good-natured sort of fellow.

E. E. You should be that at least, considering your easy life. But I wonder are you very clever? Perhaps a poet; – no, of course not: you would have let me know *that* long ago – but *are* you very clever?

L. Certainly not a poet, not even an inarticulate one; and not specially clever, I admit. But look here, if I were, I shouldn't be respected any more: I am respected because of my property, my position.

E. E. Well, I haven't much else to ask you; but tell me this: If you were employing two workmen, and one did his day's work well and straightforwardly and ate workman's victuals, and the other you had to feed on venison and champagne, and his day's work came to nothing, would you respect the second workman more than the first – as his employer, you know?

L. Of course not; but you see I'm not in the same position as the second workman. You see, my dear sir, the complexity of civilized society – in short, your question is quite wide of the mark.

W. Oh, oh!

E. E. I must put the case otherwise, then. Here is a man (*pointing to Weaver*) who works hard and usefully and is paid for it with £60 a-year and contempt; and here is another (*pointing to L.*) who does nothing at all and is paid for it with £6000 a-year and respect. As an earnest enquirer, I ask if you can tell me *why*?

L. These inequalities are necessary for the maintenance of society.

E. E. But it seems to me that it is an injustice, a gross one. Don't you really think so too? Come, try to throw away caste prejudices, and answer me like a man.

L. Well, perhaps it is – in the abstract.

E. E. Then injustice is necessary to the maintenance of society – why?

L. Because there must be rich and poor or there would be no society.

E. E. That is saying the same thing in other words. Again I ask, why?

L. I know it always will be so, that's all.

W. Then it's a bad look-out – that's all.

[*While they have been talking, a small crowd has gathered about them, under the impression that an open-air meeting is going on. Enter to them a policeman, under the same impression, who pushes through the ring, and, seeing the Weaver, catches hold of him and gives him a rough shake, and says, 'Come,* YOU *get out of this'. Exit Weaver, hurriedly, glad to get off so lightly. Then policeman turns round to Landowner, who is very nicely dressed, touches his helmet, and says, 'Shall I get you a cab, sir?' Landowner nods and moves off to meet the cab, and the small crowd disperses. Earnest Enquirer walks off slowly, soliloquising.*]

E. E. I must try to find out *why*; for as the weaver said, 'tis a bad look-out. Society *should* mean something else than organized injustice; and somewhere there ought to be the germs of a society of which no one need ask the question, 'Why does it exist?'

Commonweal, Volume 3, Number 72,
28 May 1887, pp. 170–171

'COMMON-SENSE SOCIALISM'

The first word of the above title is usually a sort of danger signal to the wary reader to avoid boredom and confusion. 'Common-sense' as applied to knotty questions usually meaning the ignoring of the main issue, or the putting forward of a remedy difficult to apply and useless when applied. This is so well understood by persons with not more than the average amount of time for throwing away on futile and foolish literature, that the title of this book will probably prevent many people from looking into it at all. This is a pity, although before the end of the book the author justifies this well-grounded fear – a pity, because two-thirds of it or more, which is devoted to the criticism of the present state of things, and the remedies proposed by non-Socialists and semi-Socialists, is on the whole clearly put and well reasoned. The author points out the growing discontent, the insufficiency of the reward of labour; the futility as remedies of thrift and temperance, of preaching Malthusianism, of land nationalization, peasant proprietorship, etc. But then having condemned capitalism by showing its inevitable results, and having condemned all the 'tinkering' methods of reform which we Socialists know so bitterly well, he puts forward his own nostrum, which, after all this labouring of the mountain, turns out to be one of the smallest and feeblest of mice every brought forth. The competition, which he sees very clearly to be producing a condition of industrial production which will end in a dead-lock, is to be checked artificially; and how? By regulating the hours of labour in factories where machinery is used!

For he expressly excepts field labour, the building trades, etc., which etc., by-the-by, must include at present at least, the labour of the coal-hewers and our hapless friends the chain-makers.

It is true he adds to this 'remedy' some sort of semi-Georgeite land-tax (having argued well and clearly against Mr George in an earlier chapter), and the restriction on heritage usually advocated by those who take up that form of tinkering, as also a tax on speculation; but he does not seem to set any great store by these latter remedies, his great invention being the limitation of the day's work in machine-using factories and workshops.

What lies at the bottom of this curious aberration seems to be an ingrained tendency in the author to utopianism. Mr Kempner seems incapable of conceiving of the class-struggle, or the historical evolution of industrialism, or of understanding that the real point at issue is when and how the workers shall emerge from their condition of pupillage and be masters of their own destinies.

In spite of all this the book may be recommended to young Socialists, as the destructive part of it is, once more, clear and well-reasoned, and the would-be constructive part so feeble that it is scarcely possible that anybody could be misled by it, or attracted to it.

It is worth while to note apropos of the attempt some persons make to draw a hard and fast line between Socialism and Communism, that Mr Kempner uses the latter word in the sense that it is used in the 'Manifesto' of Marx and Engels, of 1847. A Communist is with him one who advocates the communization or nationalization of the raw material and instruments of labour and distribution.

COMMONWEAL, VOLUME 3, NUMBER 75,
18 JUNE 1887, P. 197

'Common-Sense Socialism.' By H. Kempner. (Swan Sonnenschien and Co.)

AN OLD SUPERSTITION – A NEW DISGRACE

As was said last week, the contempt with which all Socialists must necessarily look on the idiotic court ceremony of the week has prevented anything more than a mere hint being given in the *Commonweal* about the Jubilee. And besides this, Socialists feel of course that the mere abolition of the monarchy would help them little if it only gave place to a middle-class republic; such an one, for example, as that which butchered so many thousands of citizens at Paris in 1871 and now in 1887 grown respectable and liberal, still blocks the way to all progress in France, and holds out a hand to the corruption of society there. Nevertheless, now the monstrous stupidity is on us (for I am necessarily writing before the event), one's indignation swells pretty much to the bursting-point, and I really must take advantage of my position to relieve my feelings, even at the expense of being considered somewhat old-fashioned. And we must not after all forget what the hideous, revolting, and vulgar tomfoolery in question really means nowadays, or how truly its hideousness and vulgarity of upholstery symbolizes the innate spirit which has forced the skinny twaddle on a nation that is in the habit of boasting (how vainly!) of its practicality. Such a ceremony would once have meant something very different to what it does now. Time was when the central figure in the procession from palace to Abbey would have been a man or woman whose personality would have been felt, though acting according to the ethics and maxims of feudality. The central figure in the procession would at the worst have been also in the centre of the feudal warriors gathered for the battle, and not seldom in the centre of the enemy's host. The administration of affairs, the balancing of the various claims of the groups of the feudal hierarchy, the assertion of the due rights of the great manor (scarcely yet a country) – all these would have been the duties of the central figure of a great royal procession; and no monarch of England, not even the worst of the Angevines or the most faineant of the Plantagenets could altogether neglect such duties; they had to do the deeds of men and women, however faulty or perverse, and not the deeds of a gilt gibbie-stick; they were each of them a part of the public, and an active part too.

All that is as dead as King Harold now. The nucleus of that grievous mass of flunkeyism which has been a disgrace even to disgraceful London (although the coolness with which her duties are neglected is from time to time noticed by the public and the press) is on the whole considered as a satisfactory representative of what she does represent; so satisfactory that we are called upon to take part in a set of antics in her honour compared with which a corobbery of Australian black-fellows is a decent and dignified performance.

What is it then that this central figure does represent? Not the feudal hierarchy, dead centuries ago; nor the queer pedantic divine-right-of-kings, whose struggle with the bourgeois divine-right of parliamentary majority played such an important part in developing the supremacy of that bourgeoisie. No, it does not represent these extinct superstitions, but, superstition as it is itself, it represents commercial realities rather: to wit, jobbery official and commercial, and its foundation the Privilege of Capital, set on a background of the due performance of the conventional domestic duties; in short, the representation of the anti-social spirit in its fulness is what is required of it.

That is the reason why the career of the present representative is, in spite of those few grumblings aforesaid, so eminently satisfactory. It has been the life of a respectable official who has always been careful to give the minimum of work for the maximum of pay, to keep the public well at arm's length, and to abstain from any fantastic act of generosity, which might have been taken as a precedent in the future. All this has been expected of it and it has performed it in a way which has duly earned the shouts of the holiday-makers, the upholsterers, fire-work makers, gasfitters and others who may gain some temporary advantage from the Royal (but shabby) Jubilee Circus, as well as the deeper-seated applause of those whose be-all and end-all is the continuance of respectable robbery. For us Revolutionists it is clear that the gibbie-stick line of conduct is better than one with some show of human interest in it would have been; so that we have nothing to complain of. The more reaction is stripped of sentiment the better for us.

One word before this loathsome subject of the Jubilee is consigned to its due dust-heap. Fifty years ago the country was yet in the throes of that unorganized but formidable insurrection which followed on the industrial revolution, and the reckless greed of those benefitted by it – the capitalists, to wit. That insurrection was damped down by the commercial successes which so much increased the number and power of the definitely middle–classes, so that twenty-five years ago a survivor of the discontent of 1837 might well have thought that all was over. But unbridled competition has forced the pace more than any one could have guessed it would; fifty years is gone, and once more we have 'discontent' amongst us, if not wider spread than before, yet at least deeper seated, and with no apparent staving-off remedy before it except Mr Chamberlain's feeble attempts at peasant-proprietorship. And even this vulgar Royal Upholstery procession, trumpery as it is, may deepen the discontent a little, when the newspapers are once more empty of it, and when people wake up, as on the morrow of a disgraceful orgie (*sic*), to find dull trade all the duller for it, and have to face according to their position the wearisome struggle for riches, for place, for respectability, for decent livelihood, for bare subsistence, in the teeth of growing competition in a society now at last showing its rottenness openly.

COMMONWEAL, VOLUME 3, NUMBER 76,
25 JUNE 1887, P. 204

THE BOY-FARMS AT FAULT

The silly season in the newspapers is beginning briskly with a rain of letters from distressed parents concerning their troubles in dealing with their male children home for the holidays. This is a kind of twaddle which is always recurring: this well-fed, well-housed bourgeois on the hunt for some artificial trouble or another, some sham grievance, since he has no real ones, except his own inherent stupidity and vacancy; but on this occasion there is, if the said bourgeois only knew it, a moral to be drawn. I can imagine the 'boy', 'the enemy of the human race', as Dickens called him, retorting on his injured parent somewhat in this style:

Father. Well my lad, haven't you nearly had enough of it?

Son. Enough of what, Pa?

F. The holidays, my lad, the holidays.

S. No, Pa.

F. Because if you haven't, I have. No answer? Now you're sulking.

S. Well what *am* I to say? You're always badgering me.

F. There, there! Say something that isn't mere peevishness. I can see that *you* are sick of the holidays or else you wouldn't be like that.

S. Very well; I will then. Why do you want me back at the boy-farm? What have I been doing that's wrong?

F. Boy-farm! What do you mean by that impudence? As to what have you been doing; that's just it. You've been doing nothing, while here I am feeding, clothing and housing you, and having you expensively educated (not that I suppose you learn anything) and then you come home and kick your heels about, and do nothing but gorge and make a noise.

S. *(with a grin)* What do you do, Pa, when you're *not* having a holiday?

F. *(seeming to swallow something and turning very red)* Why, I do business and make money for you.

S. *(rudely)* O ah! I know what that means; precious hard work that is, isn't it?

F. *(with dignity)* Yes it is; as you'll know when you grow up and have to face the troubles of life.

S. *(with increased rudeness).* Come, I say, Pa, how much will you take to don't? (*sic*) I remember you taking me to your office last Christmas holidays when I was to be measured for a suit of clothes; and there I sat all the morning, and as I hadn't a book to read I fidgetted (*sic*), and you nagged me; so I said to myself now I'll just take notice of what the governor does. Well, first you read the newspaper and warmed your front at the fire; and then you didn't read the paper and warmed your back; and then you were crusty with me; and then one of the junior clerks came in to ask you a question and you were beastly rude to him and I wonder he didn't punch your head for you (I heard him say he should like to as he passed me). And then you went and talked to the senior clerk, that little dry grey old chap; and you were civil enough to him, and I could see that you were rather afraid of him and that he did all your business; and then that chap came in that dines at home sometimes, and he was deuced smartly dressed, and he asked you to come to lunch at two o'clock; and you said you couldn't, and hitched your head over your shoulder at me; and he said, 'Oh, never mind! bring the shaver along'. And you were sulky, but you said 'All right', and he said, 'Well, I must go and order lunch'. And then you sat down and wrote a letter, and that took you a quarter of an hour; and then you were crusty and told me not to sniff, and you stood and warmed your back again; and all the time the clerks were scribbling away as hard as they could, and chaps kept coming into the office and talking to the head clerk about business; and the head clerk came to you with some papers and a gentleman, and I heard you say 'damn it' to yourself; but you were mighty politeful to him; and you went away with him and were away for half-an-hour; and then you came back and said 'Come along and don't sniff'. And then you went with me to an awfully swell place to lunch where there were lots of flunkeys in blue coats and orange-coloured plush breeches, and then we had lunch with that other chap and another chap; and it was a mortal gorge and very jolly; only you and the other chaps would talk about Russia and France and Austria; awful rot, don't you know, like Mr Toots and the other fellow in 'Dombey'. So that took till four o'clock, and the other fellows asked you to come and play at whist with another fellow, and you couldn't because you had to take me to the tailor's; and then you took me back to the office and the head-clerk said something to you, and you didn't pay much attention to him; and then you said to me 'Come along and don't sniff', and so we went home and you couldn't eat much for dinner, and Ma said, 'I'm afraid you're not well dear'. And you said 'I've had a very tiring and anxious day in the city, my dear'. So I suppose that sometimes you have a less tiring day than that; and if that's the case I think you are soon tired.

F. Well what do you mean by all that rigmarole I should like to know? Are you qualifying yourself to write a realistic novel, pray?

S. Bosh! You know what I mean. You're always bullying me about the holidays and say I do nothing in them; and all the time you do nothing in the days that ain't your holidays.

F. You're a young fool and don't understand these things.

S. And then you are always saying that you are spending money on me. Well, I should like to know who spends money on you, since you don't do anything to earn it? – not even Latin prose.

F. Ah, well, you will be wiser one of these days when you have sons of your own.

S. (grinning). Come, Pa, turn to and make me wiser now by telling me how it is that you can't stand me doing nothing and boring people through the holidays, and you keeping me gratis all the while; and there you are all the while doing the same thing, and being kept gratis; and you would be very much surprised if they were to send you off to a man-farm and try to get something out of you in the way of work – a big strong chap like you.

F. Come, I'm not going to stand this any more.

S. Very well, then, why did you begin bullying me? You may think yourself very lucky to have such jolly long holidays. Why, the other day when you came on that chap who was carpentering upstairs, and he was having a nap after his dinner – my! how you did bullyrag him for resting twenty minutes! and he looked sheepish as though he had been caught doing wrong. I say, I wonder why *you* don't look sheepish,

F. Just take yourself and your wonder out of the room. I never heard such a parcel of impudent rubbish as you've been talking now you *have* found your tongue.

S. Very well, then, why did you begin bullying me?[*Exit.*

F. Really! I wonder what will happen to that boy. Suppose he should turn Socialist when he grows up!!!

COMMONWEAL, VOLUME 3, NUMBER 81,
30 JULY 1887, P. 241

BOURGEOIS VERSUS SOCIALIST

Without wishing to carry on the debate any further which has been going on in the *Commonweal* between comrade Bax and Mr Bradlaugh, it is natural that we should *print* a few words on it, as it is clear that there must have been a good many words *said* on the subject.

In the last paper, Mr Bradlaugh complains that there has been no real debate on the question will Socialism benefit the English people?[1] Perhaps after all this is likely to be the case in all so-called debates where the disputants differ as to principle: clearly they must take some things for granted or they would stick fast from the first. This debate is now the third I have noticed carefully, and in all the three the disputants on either side, though in all cases very able persons, seemed, so to say, to find it hard to get at each other and strike the big stroke. However, one thing they can do and should do, if they are to claim any success; each may at least state what his position is; and though this is specially incumbent on the one who takes the affirmative or positive side, yet even the one who takes the negative side must not be so wholly negative as not to show the basis of his objections: he must not be a mere objector, but must object on principle.

Now it seems to me that in this debate our friend Bax has stated his position quite clearly, and to every one not prepared from the first to pick holes in his statement, quite unmistakably. Mr Bradlaugh, on the other hand, has done nothing but make objections, some of them merely verbal

1 By the way, when I was last lecturing in Scotland I got on more than one occasion 'a dressing' for using the word English in too inclusive a sense (though I meant no harm by it). Perhaps the same thing would happen in Wales – let alone Ireland.

and frivolous, others rather what I should call debaters' objections – the sort of thing which catches cheers in an oral debate; and some, no doubt, the objections of the kind which naturally occur to a person prejudiced against a change in the basis of society. Bax has been under the disadvantage of having in his second paper to follow Mr Bradlaugh through the whole string of questions which he thought proper to put, so that his restatement of his position had to be deferred to his last paper, which was somewhat languidly replied to by Mr Bradlaugh; of whom in truth I fear it must be said that he does not take much interest in the whole subject. In fact throughout he has not really been attacking Socialism, but rather has been desperately defending a statement which he stumbled on in his anxiety to be considered 'practical', that there may be or is an essential difference in the economic basis of life between the various countries that make up civilization; and he has also been fighting against the admission that modern production compels the aggregation of capital. It is hardly worth while arguing seriously against either of these queer pieces of perversity; but it is really strange to find a man of ability who has not been struck by the international character of modern capitalism, and who cannot grasp the argument that if capitalism is international, the foe that threatens it, the system which is put forward to take its place, must be international also. As to the other point, which, though not an essential one for the general argument, Mr Bradlaugh defends very stoutly and returns to more than once, the denial of the tendency toward aggregation of capital under our present system, what *can* one say but that it is one of the commonplaces of the day that competition forces people to produce cheaply, and that you can only produce cheaply by producing on a large scale? Anybody who doubts this and has money to throw away had better try it in practice – as I have done. Mr Bradlaugh in his last paper taunts Bax with not being able to bring more instances of this generally admitted fact; I may perhaps be allowed to give another, as coming under my own notice. Textile printing used to be done wholly by means of blocks on long tables, and there used to be a great many small businesses of this kind, employing down to as few as ten or a dozen men; but when the cylinder machine was perfected, and a man and two boys at one machine could do the work of 200 blockers and their attendant 'tearers', these businesses had to shut up, as they could not find work for even one machine. Again, in my small business I am obliged to refrain from doing certain kinds of weaving I should like to do because my capital can't compass a power-loom. But really there is no need to multiply examples to prove what is patent: one can only stand aghast at Mr Bradlaugh's hardihood in denial.

In short, Mr Bradlaugh thinks Socialism an unpractical matter, and therefore cannot bring his mind to bear upon it sufficiently to conceive of it. He has not even tried to understand what Socialists mean by monopoly, and says, though rather guardedly, that he sees no class in the country which has the monopoly of the means of production. Again, one can only say that if he were a manual workman he would soon find out whether he could work for his livelihood without paying the tribute demanded by the monopolist; nor would he be long in doubt as to the fact that his master was not an individual but a class, when he sets to work to try how much more reward he could get for his labour from Peter than he could from Paul.

It is a pity that Mr Bradlaugh will not try to understand his Socialist opponents, but in this matter he acts pretty much as the ordinary bourgeois does, and shows the usual persistency in reading incidents characteristic of the present condition of things into the future. At the bottom of all this lies, not, it may be, a want of information as to the mere facts of history, but an entire incapacity of understanding their significance and their continuity; in short, a practical denial of the doctrine of evolution. To persons of this turn of mind the class struggle in the past is nothing more than a confused contest, with no steady, though often unconscious, aim in it; to such persons at some arbitrary point determined by the interest, prejudice, or taste of the individual, all that contest comes to an end, and Society, which has been ever changing through so many thousands of years, is at last stable, though it lacks no element of revolution which the last epoch of change had, but holds them all, possibly changed in form but certainly not in essence. To such persons it is a kind of theological proposition that the status of Society consists of a great middle-class with an unnecessary encumbrance above it in the shape of the aristocracy, and a necessary encumbrance below it in the shape of a proletariat. The presence of the workers cannot be wholly denied, because they are there before our eyes, weaving, metal-working, building, and the rest of it; but they are not looked upon as a class with common interests, which force them to act together even against their wills, but as a series of accidents; they are a mere collection of potential middle-class persons, or failures from the middle-class.

And what is to be done with these abnormal persons? That is not a question which presses for solution, think our readers who sustain the orthodox holiness of bourgeoisdom. To reduce the numbers of the successive generations of them, and to raise the wages of those that would be left – that were good if it could be done, but it doesn't much matter, because, whether or no, Society is stable on its present basis (established by the Reform Bill of 1832).

It is true that some glorious but dim vision floats before the eyes of these 'practical' persons of a time when the whole of these accidental misfortunes in a human form shall, by the exercise of thrift and Malthusianism, be absorbed into the great middle-class, cleared by that time of its upper encumbrance, and a bourgeois paradise will supervene, in which every one will be free to exploit - but there will be no one to exploit. How the great middle-class will then live, deponents say not; but the setters forth of this doctrine are happy in the fact that their Socialist opponents are not in the habit of asking them many questions as to *their* Society of the future. On the whole, one must suppose that the type of it would be that town (surely in America and in the neighbourhood of Mark Twain) that I have heard of, whose inhabitants lived by taking in each other's washing.

COMMONWEAL, VOLUME 3, NUMBER 82,
6 AUGUST 1887, P. 252

A NOTE ON PASSING POLITICS

The Gladstonians are very naturally triumphant at the Northwich election, and the Tories as naturally have been attempting to explain away their defeat; which, however, taken in conjunction with the other bye-elections (*sic*), does seem to an onlooker to mean the extinction of the Chamberlain party, the absorption into definite Toryism of Lord Hartington and a few other nobodies (*sic*), and in short, the defeat of the revolt in the Liberal party against Mr Gladstone, who seems destined to have one more triumph before he dies. To some ardent Liberals the way seems so direct to Liberal victory that the *Pall Mall Gazette* urges the Gladstonians to force on a dissolution by means of obstruction at once. That no doubt would be good tactics for them if the party were really what the writer of the article in the *Pall Mall* seems to think it – a party with principles and a steady aim. As it is, one may be quite sure that they will attempt nothing so revolutionary or anti-respectable as that: their advent to power will come by a longer road, with many more turns in it. For the respectable part of them have no very burning desire to pass a real Home Rule measure, and indeed don't think much about that or anything else except the mere party triumph. However, doubtless in the course of time we shall see a Liberal ministry in power again, with somewhat more pretensions to Radicalism than a ministry has had yet, and with the mandate to pass a Home Rule Bill. The said Bill will also, of course, be one of compromise; but we may suppose that it will do something to give the Irish question a little rest, though with its accompanying Land Bill it will not be so easily settled, even temporarily, as some people seem to suppose. But a truce once made with the Irish troubles, what will the new Gladstonian government do next? That is the rub. It will be expected to do something, and if it values its life must try hard not even to appear to do anything. To appear, I say, because, except as regards the franchise, the instrument of parliamentary democracy, there is no longer anything for that democracy to do. There may, and probably will be, a sharp fight in Parliament over the franchise, which will split up the party once more and give the Whig-Tories another innings; but when that is over and the democratic sword sharpened duly, where will be the enemy to be smitten by it? Doubtless there will be a new Allotments Acts (*sic*), a Leasehold Enfranchisement Act, and other devices for dividing the power of our landlord masters without lessening it; and also doubtless some rubbish about perpetual pensions and the cultivation of grouse-moors and the like. But all this will be but using the newly-whetted democratic sword for cleaving a pat of butter instead of a helmetted (*sic*) head: it will be doing nothing. Nevertheless it will have an appearance of doing something and will lead to the death of more than one 'Liberal' ministry, if constitutionalism lasts as long; so that what between disgusting real democrats with really doing nothing, and terrifying respectability with seeming to do something, the Gladstonian party is likely to have a rough time of it, and may well pray for a continuance of the Irish quarrel, in which they have managed, after a deal of standing on alternate feet, to take up a position apparently not (to their thinking) too dangerous to constitutionalism.

Meantime, after all the Tory Government is not going to die tamely; they have plucked up heart to pass the Lords' amendments to the Land Bill and proclaim the National League, and seem to be going to put their foot down; probably because they perceive that their Chamberlainist friends are of no value to them, and that they must play their last card of attempting to drive the Irish people into violent action, which might turn the respectability of the Liberal party against Home Rule again. Fortunately they are probably too late once more; the mind of the ordinary person not pledged to the cause of reaction is getting used to the idea of Home Rule, and any outbreak on the part of the Irish that is not systematic will be looked on as a mere incident in the struggle.

Some measure of Home Rule is now certain; and all we Socialists can hope is that it will not be too long in coming; for what we want now is a professedly popular government in power, which, face to face with the real question of the day – whether labour is to be free or the slave of monopoly – will not be able to deal with that question, because it and the parliament which has produced it are and must be essentially the guardians of that very monopoly.

COMMONWEAL, VOLUME 3, NUMBER 85,
27 AUGUST 1887, P. 276

IS LIPSKI'S CONFESSION GENUINE?

So Lipski has confessed and all is right, 'he has been brought to a frame of mind that has enabled him to make the reparation', says the *Daily News*. Bourgeois justice and the Home Secretary are triumphantly vindicated. Thus, doubtless, thought the 'respectable' world on Monday morning.

There is nothing to be surprised at in Lipski's confession. Indeed, it was just what was to be expected; those who have never believed in his guilt have no need to do so now, the evidence is entirely against such an hypothesis; but that under the circumstances the world should be given to understand that he has confessed, and 'admitted the justice of his sentence', was absolutely essential to the stability of the government, of the system of capital punishment, and to the credit of our judicial machinery generally. What goes on within the walls of a prison is known only to those in the swim of the bureaucratic trade, and we do not pretend to decide dogmatically with respect to the origin of the document. We need only call the reader's attention to the fact that the bureaucrat is by the necessities of his profession a liar, skilful or unskilful; the value of official disclaimers is proverbial.

Who knows what kind of cajolery or even threats might not have been employed, since the occasion was so urgent and so much was at stake?

In connection with this it is well to remember that the witches who were burnt in the seventeenth century almost always confessed their guilt, and 'admitted the justice of their sentence' – or were said to have done so. It must not be forgotten, moreover, that Lipski, who came from Russian Poland, remembering that in his own country a confession of guilt is necessary before a condemned criminal can be executed, and that there torture is admitted to be used on occasion to extract such a confession, might have a confused idea that the same thing might happen here, and seeing his case was hopeless and that he had to die, submitted to what he might think was a general formula for the sake of dying without unnecessary worry.

Anyhow the document bears upon it the stamp of ungenuineness. Lipski says that he had not begun to search for money before Miriam awoke and alarmed him. Does it seem likely that a man not being a maniac would murder a woman for fear of discovery, simply because she had found him in her room, and before he had committed any crime?

He says the aquafortis he swallowed had no effect on him. Is this probable?

He didn't know how his arms were abraded, and did not feel it at the time. Is this probable if the statement next above is true?

These objections lie on the surface of the confession, but no doubt other discrepancies will occur to other searchers into the document. Under any circumstances the main point to be remembered is that *the evidence on the trial* was insufficient for a jury to convict upon if undirected by the judge, and bearing in mind the maxim so often put forward by those who boast of the immaculate nature of English law, that a doubt should be interpreted in favour of the accused.

COMMONWEAL, VOLUME 3, NUMBER 85,
27 AUGUST 1887, P. 276

ARTIST AND ARTISAN AS AN ARTIST SEES IT

I have nothing to object to in our comrade's remarks, but a word or two may be pardoned in explanation of the fact that an artist is looked upon as a gentleman (a sort of one), and sometimes receives a certain portion of the respect accorded to that class, which, however, is dealt out so much more liberally to the mere money-maker in other trades; to the landowner, manufacturer, contractor, stockjobber, or what not; in short, it is dealt out to members of the proprietary class exactly in proportion to the obviousness of their living by *owning* wealth and not *creating* it. In other words the less pretence they make to be more than mere thieves, the more they are honoured.

However, let that pass, as it must be admitted that the artists when they gain the point at which they receive any recognition from the public at all, do as hangers-on share in the plunder won by the class to which, if our workmen friends knew it, they are admitted somewhat *grudgingly*. Now, it must be admitted by all thoughtful people that the conventional flattery of the intellect, which is conventionally supposed as a separate and specially worshipful quality, to be the main-spring of the artist's capacity, is both stupid and harmful. But, like all the rest of our conventionalities, it is founded on history; it is a birth of the individualist commercial system which we are at work combatting to-day, with good hope of seeing it disappear. It is that system which has divided the old craftsman into two, artist and artisan. For, before the rise of capitalism in the sixteenth century, the artisan did not differ in kind from the artist; all craftsmen who made anything were artists of some kind, they only differed in degree, and only a few of those who had very special gifts of hand and brain have so much as left their names behind them. No one knows, *eg.*, the name of the man who designed Westminster Abbey, although it rose up amongst the King's Court, and doubtless was talked about enough in its time; and meantime every joiner or mason or blacksmith was doing his share of work towards the pleasure which our comrade feels is necessary to the life of man, and never dreaming of receiving any special reward for the beauty or invention in his work; although doubtless he did receive the unconventional and genuine praise and thanks of his neighbours for it, just as he gave it to his neighbour craftsmen. With the growth of the historic sense which is a gain of the present century, with the knowledge of the continuity of history which we have now learned, we have come to a conscious knowledge that the intellect of man works co-operatively and collectively; but although the workmen of the Middle-Ages were not conscious of this fact, they were happier than we are in this respect, that they practised that co-operation in their production of beauty; whereas we, as long as we are under the domination of the profit-grinders, cannot do so; and the result follows which I have so often spoken of, that art is a skinny drowsy skeleton amidst the stir and enormous riches of modern civilization; and that too in an age, which as I have just said, has discovered that it was the collective people, and not a few miraculous individuals who have produced all worthy, that is all genuine, art in the past. I say when art is hopeful and progressive there is plenty of it for every one, and every one is in some sense an artist, and those who produce beauty are not demi-gods but men, and all can understand them; it is only when beauty produced by man becomes rare that we take to deifying its producers. There is little that is mysterious about the plagiarists and compilers of the Augustan age of Rome; the authors of that mass of platitudinous rubbish, that fresh flowing well-spring of stupidity, are well known and amply ticketted (*sic*). But modern research has made Homer a dim and doubtful shadow to us, while it has added clearness to our vision of the life of the people of that time, who were the real authors of the Homeric poems. Beowulf, the first and the best poem of the English race, which they bore hither across the seas with them, has no author but the people. No other authors has the splendid literature of our Scandinavian kinsmen, the best tale-tellers the world has seen, through whom we can to-day live with the people of Northern Europe in the tenth century, and know them, not as puppets of chivalry romance, but good fellows such as our living friends are to-day. Again, along with William Cobbett, contrast the dungeon-like propriety of St Paul's, the work of a 'famous' architect, with the free imagination and delicate beauty of the people-built Gothic churches, that were raised by masons who had no architect over them, and who did their work for the reward of a free life, and needed no fame as an extra; and then consider how the people build. In short, our comrade will understand me when I say that what we want is to extinguish not the artist, but the mere artisan, by destroying the flattery-craving flunkey in the one, and the brutal toil-worn slave in the other, so that they may both be men; in which case they must be artists in one way or other, that is, they must take an interest in life.

Meanwhile, I cannot see that any extra reward should be given to a man for following an 'intellectual' calling. If he does his work in it well, it is more pleasurable to him than a 'non-intellectual' one, and why should he be paid twice over? If he does it ill, let him be pulled out of it in the gentlest way possible, and learn to do what he *can* do. A poet doesn't need paying for his poetry (he is not paid much now), because he will write better poetry and not worse if he has an ordinary occupation to follow. As for the other mere artists, a painter for instance, I admit that he will probably have to stick to his painting if he has to do it well; but then he should be paid not for the 'intellectual' part of his work, but for the workman's part of it; finishing up everything properly, doing everything as well as it can be done in all respects. This will take something out of him. But the exercise of his 'intellect' will take nothing; it is mere play.

The long and short of it is this, a decent life, a share in the common life of all is the only 'reward' that any man can honestly take for his work, whatever it is; if he asks for more, that means that he intends to play the master over somebody. When the workers have made up their minds to be free, he won't get that, so he may make himself easy, and get amusement out of his work as he can, if he is a 'superior person'. Well, I end as our comrade, with the word 'equality', which will one day become a real thing and no mere word, and so cure all our troubles.

COMMONWEAL, VOLUME 3, NUMBER 87,
10 SEPTEMBER 1887, P. 291

FREE SPEECH IN AMERICA

Our readers will see that meetings to protest against the cold-blooded judicial murder of the seven Chicago prisoners are to be held within the next fortnight. Since this number of the *Commonweal* may come into the hands of persons who have not read other numbers and who have but a vague idea of the bearings of the whole case, or as is most likely, have been prejudiced by the misrepresentations of the press – the stark lies of the American capitalistic press, the careless lies of the English – it may be well to state briefly what the real crime of these men is in order that it may be determined whether their execution would be an act of justice or a crime.

These seven men are condemned to death for being present at a meeting called to protest against the murderous attack on a demonstration of workmen on strike by the police and the hired swashbucklers of the capitalists. At that meeting a bomb was thrown which killed and wounded several policemen. The police fired on the meeting, and the workmen defended themselves, and the capitalist government took this opportunity of hatching an accusation against our comrades, brought them to trial and condemned them in the teeth of the evidence. On their appeal they have been kept in prison for more than a year and re-condemned by a court which is practically the same as the first one. These men are really condemned for supporting the workmen in their strike and for speaking out their opinions on the vile, miscalled 'Society' of America and civilization generally. They are persecuted for holding and expressing the opinions which we hold and express whether we call ourselves Anarchists or Socialists, and for applying those opinions to the events of the passing day and the oppression of the American workmen going on under their eyes. Their persecution is an *in terrorem* measure directed against freedom of speech in America; and it will be a disgrace to the British workmen, whatever their politics may be, if they do not express themselves clearly and emphatically on this attack on the liberties which the United States have been supposed to guard so jealously, but which it would seem are but a one-sided affair after all. We appeal, above all, to our Radical and Democratic friends who are now trying to destroy the base anti-Irish prejudice once so current in this country, not to consider men outside the pale of fair-dealing because they express revolutionary ideas; and to remember that whether they may think our Socialist theories right or wrong, we claim at least equal liberty for all, and that amidst the present welter of politics in which reaction is struggling so hard to lift up its head, if we do not guard the liberties we have won with the utmost care and jealousy we shall find them encroached on day by day till at last Radicals will have no more doubt than Socialists that they are the slaves of the rich and powerful in all senses.

COMMONWEAL, VOLUME 3, NUMBER 91,
8 OCTOBER 1887, P. 324

Practical Politics at Nottingham

The orthodox Liberals have had a great field day at Nottingham under very brilliant circumstances, all things considered; the democratic portion of the population of England, Scotland, and Wales, and it is even hoped the voters in general who have any claim to be considered Liberals, are prepared to accept Home Rule for other people though they have scarcely begun even to think of it for themselves. This acceptance of Home Rule for Ireland, by everybody who could ever possibly accept it, is so universal that there are no shades of opinion on the subject; the unspoken (nay, sometimes the spoken) word when people meet now is, 'You are a Home Ruler and a beast!' 'You are a Unionist and a rascal!' Argument is at an end, and people, dog-sick of the question, would be much relieved if it were possible for a thousand champions a-side to meet on Wimbledon Common, or some other suitable place, and there fight it out to the death like Clan Chattan and Clan Quhele of old days; but since civilization and the natural desire to best one's opponent at no expense to oneself forbids such a proceeding, all people are looking forward with disgust to the long spell of Parliamentary tactics, which will on this occasion as on other similar ones in modern times, take the place of 'point and edge' with small advantage to the public generally.

Such a condition of things was, I repeat, most favourable to the occasion, which was certainly made the most of. Mr Gladstone exhibited himself for the worship of the faithful, which was poured forth on him in the most abundant measure, so that he must have thought it worth while indeed to be a statesman. He exercised the art of oratory if not to the fullest, yet at least as far as need be; the art, I mean, which consists of spinning out two or three sentences of meaning into speeches getting on for two hours long, so that the audiences mostly were thoroughly delighted. Indeed, those of them who had memories capable of resisting the wear and tear of five or six years might have employed the leisure which the great man's flow of speech-words afforded them in blessing their stars and their leader that it was not they but their adversaries this time who were trying to wield the great net of Coercion, with the certainty of their knocking themselves into the water with it. Some of them might also have remembered the roars of joy with which pure Liberal meetings received the news of their present ally Mr Parnell's arrest and imprisonment; and probably Mr John Morley was now and then pensively thinking of the evening, when before the electors of Westminster in 1880 he put down his foot on Home Rule in such a clear, brief, and convincing speech, that everybody in the hall, except a few grumblers and Irishmen, shouted for joy.

However, let pardon be given to those who have changed their opinions in the right direction, and let us hope that such changes will be common during the next few years among political men. It is at least satisfactory to see that Mr Gladstone is doing no backsliding in this Irish matter, that he who is exceedingly slow to perceive that the enemy must be attacked in front has at last seen it. All that he has to do now is to set his political wits to work to get rid of the Tory majority in the house before some portion of his men, the really anti-Radical part, who much outnumber the Radical, swing in the other direction, and carry him along with their impetus. Don't let him dally with the crisis as he dearly loves to do, like a too artistic angler, who having a good fish on his line plays him showily to show his art, and loses him in the end.

Well, the Irish Question disposed of, what other schemes of reform had this enthusiastic multitude of delegates and notabilities, sitting in the good town of Nottingham, where, forsooth, they might have some rather serious thoughts suggested to them by the locality and its industries. I remember I was there some six years ago, and trade was booming then. I was told, I don't know with how much truth, that an ordinary twister-in, or lace-weaver, could earn £6 a-week; prosperity was great, and the horrible red-brick blue-slated shanties of a prosperous Midland town were effacing the last remains of the beautiful crocus-meadows, for which the town was once famous; and any hints I ventured timidly to give as to how long this prosperity might last, were received with the contempt which prophecies deserve. Whereas, now it would seem by the weekly trade reports as if the population, high and low, would soon be reduced to living on taking in each other's washing.

Well, as to the reforms to be taken in hand after the carrying of Home Rule, the Liberal Conference at Nottingham has been what its members call bold indeed: venturing to go in for disestablishment of the Welsh Church; the abolition of plural votes, by means of having all the elections on one day, shortening the period of residence which qualifies a voter; free education (important this, at any rate); local option (this also important – for the vote); London government, allotments for labourers (*ie.*, permission to them to pay their own poor-rates); and what is called 'free-land' – *ie.*, all obstacles removed which might stand in the way of Mr Wynans or his like buying up all England to turn it into a deer forest.

All this, which is heralded in the Liberal newspapers as an 'advanced programme', in all the dignity of extra large type, is indeed quite as far as anyone could have expected the Liberal Party to go as a body – *ie.*, with the leave of Mr Gladstone and its other bosses; and one must admit that most of these reforms will have to be done, whether they greatly matter or not. But it is not much wool for so great a cry; and when one thinks that this is received as an 'advanced programme' with a regular flourish of trumpets by the party which considers itself the popular party, in righteous opposition to the Tories or reactionists, one cannot help noting how much of an accident it has been that the Liberals have been driven to make peace with Ireland, and that Home Rule once gained the Liberal Party will have performed its functions to the very end, and must either make its exit or must go about with the brains knocked out of it. And that all the more as the Tory Party is quite capable of dishing the Liberals on all these great reforms, and probably will do so.

And meanwhile the trades unions are crying out for a Labour Party, have declared for land nationalization, and have their faces turned towards Socialism; and all over the country workmen are asking themselves why they are in a position of inferiority to those who do not work. The authorities in London are as afraid to let workmen speak their minds there as the Irish authorities to let the Irish speak, and a terrible winter of misery and want of employment is opening out before us.

Of all these things the Nottingham delegates took as much cognisance as though they were living in another planet. These things, since they concern the daily life and happiness and misery of the working classes, are, forsooth, 'not within the scope of practical politics'.

Query – What are practical politics? Answer – Vote-catching for election time, so that *we* may be in and *you* may be out.

COMMONWEAL, VOLUME 3, NUMBER 94,
29 OCTOBER 1887, P. 349

Honesty is the Best Policy; or, The Inconvenience of Stealing

[A Dialogue *between* Mr James Brown, *a business man, and* Mr Olaf Evans, *a kind of artist and literary man; neighbours.*]

Scene – *A Suburban Highway, tending townward.*

Evans (*turning round as* Brown *catches him up on the road*). Well, Brown, you look in a deuce of a hurry this morning.

Brown (*sulkily*). And you look as if you have no need to hurry.

E. No, I havn't (*sic*) – because I must write my own books and paint my own pictures myself – but don't be in such a hurry, old man; its a long time since I have had a talk with you, although we live next door but one to each other.

B. (*testily*) No, no, its all very well for you, who have all the day before you to loaf in, to take it easy; but I must get on to my business, and catch the 'bus.

E. Come now, Brown! You know well enough that your clerks don't want you; and they can't idle, because they have got old Jackson to drive them; and he does it as a pleasure and not as a duty. You will only be in the way when you get there.

[Brown's *sulkiness visibly increases; but he slows down, and they walk on side by side for a little, but without talking,* Evans *whistling 'The Last Rose of Summer' very much out of tune.*

B. Well, now, why don't you talk, Evans, since you have kept me here lounging along with you: and there you go mooning along, pretending to be pondering over your novel, or your picture, and really thinking about nothing.

E. Well, you see, I like human company even when it doesn't talk. But what were *you* thinking about Brown?

B. (*very testily*). You.

E. Curious! I was thinking about *you*, and wondering what had put you out so this morning; because you are generally rather a cheery kind of a bird.

B. Well, I admit that I *am* in a bad temper – there.

E. Or rather you were; but since you have made up your mind to tell me all about it you are beaming as usual. Well, 'out of the abundance of the heart the mouth speaketh'; abound my friend, abound!

B. Well you know, Evans, you may think it a little thing, but there's that jolly little garden of mine, all spoilt this morning. You know, the square piece between the trees.

E. Hilloa! who's done that? One of your Tory friends been spiting you these brisk political times, like Mr Whiteley's desperate enemies?

B. Well you see, it's the pears. They have come after them; you know, that jargonelle tree close by.

E. Come after them? Yes, and got them too, I suppose – boys, I should think.

B. Every blessed one – no, no! it *isn't* boys, its blackguards; blackguards I tell you. No one can keep any fruit for them in this beastly hole.

[*Here he uses the resources of the English language in a manner too emphatic for our printer to render with the resources of type.*]

E. My dear Brown, calm yourself, when its done you all the good it can! I suppose these blackguards had no pears and wanted some, and had no money to buy them with. Blackguards seldom have any money, I notice. It often happens so to me.

B. No, blast them! They had spent it all in beer.

[*The resources of the English language drawn on again.*]

E. Doubtless; and the pears would come refreshing to them after hot-coppers – if blackguards ever *have* hot-coppers!

B. Refreshing! Don't be a fool! Don't you know that they would sell 'em and buy more beer with them, blast them!

E. Touching instance of the Marxian formula, C-M-C! Never mind me, Brown, my mind wanders a little sometimes. But I say, really, don't let it put you out so, for you can easily buy some more pears, and much better ones; you're not a blackguard, and you have got plenty of money, and the ones that were gone were no great shakes after all. And then they won't be wasted, somebody will eat them; and look here, it quite squares with your dignified position as a leading Radical in the neighbourhood to grow fruit for the public benefit. By Jove! an idea seizes me. Suppose you put up for Parliament here next election, you might get a good deal of popularity by this affair if you managed it properly. But since the pears were what they were, perhaps you will give people the gripes; but even then that's a kind of revenge for you at the worst, even if the stealers exchange their commodity pears, for money wherewith to buy the commodity beer; *some one* will get the gripes.

B. Now look here, Evans, you think yourself damned clever with your chaff; but you know very well I don't care about the value of the pears, but one does want to know what becomes of one's own fruit. And when you talk of the gripes and the beer and all that; that's just what I say. It damages me and doesn't do any good to them. That's what always comes of stealing. And as to the pears being wasted, I know my garden is wasted; why my wife had tears in her eyes when I fetched her out before breakfast to look at the damage those damned blackguards had done; all those single dahlias broken down and all, and she doesn't care about flowers anything like as much as I do! Damnation!

E. Poor Mrs Brown!

B. Now there you go! You won't understand me! they are welcome to the fruit. Next year I'll have it all picked and put in baskets before the door in the open street with a placard over them, 'Blackguards are requested to partake of other people's property; scoundrels are begged to accept what other people have worked for'.

E. A very proper thing to do! and won't do your popularity any harm. People will take in your pears much quicker than your jokes, though they are not bad. If only you understood where they would lead you if you followed them up properly.

B. What I mean is this, and I'm sure when you think fit to be serious, you will agree with me; that in stealing it isn't so much the shifting of the property from one man to another, especially if he is a rich man, that is so bad, as the confusion and nuisance of it, and its waste and destruction, and the heart-burning and hatred it causes. In short, as I said, it does harm both to the stealer and the stolen-from; in short, it is bad all round.

E. Isn't even good for trade?

B. Of course not. (*Pompously*.) Nothing is good for trade except steady production, and honest dealing in the things produced. But, Evans, I really wonder at a decent man like you, and very good-natured fellow, being so flippant about such a beastly, miserable, destructive, inconvenient vice as stealing. The more I think of it the more I hate it: it is simply the worst form of war. Come, my dear fellow, be serious.

E. I assure you I'm as serious as possible, and quite delighted to hear that you hate stealing, since I quite agree with all that you have been saying about it.

B. (*mollified*.) Well, I thought you would.

E. Yes; and what you have been saying makes me bold to say something to you in return: that since you hate stealing, you ought to do your best to get rid of it altogether.

B. Well, so I do, don't I?

E. Do you? How, pray?

B. Why, I look sharp after my property; don't allow anyone that I have to do with to be backward with their accounts; don't put temptation in anyone's way; whilst at the same time I must say for myself that I am liberal in my dealings – give my servants good wages, and my clerks too, though you did sneer at me about old Jackson; who, I must tell you, is a very useful person, and a precious good screw he gets from me. In short, I'm none of your sloppy, indulgent, weakly good-natured persons like – like –

E. Like me, eh?

B. Well, don't take offence; but you are, rather, you know, ain't you? But look here, Evans, it don't do, you know – that sort of thing; you do much more harm by it than good. Now I really take trouble with the people I have to deal with, and both by example and by looking sharply after them and treating them justly (and they know when they are justly treated, bless you!) I do hope I make them honest persons. I hold that a man has no right to have property unless he accepts its responsibilities and takes that kind of trouble: and it is a trouble, mind you. Now you –

E. But do you never try to do anything to keep yourself from stealing?

B. There, there! you are at it again! – never serious for two minutes together! But you needn't look penitent; I wasn't offended, my dear fellow,

E. Well, but I am not penitent at all; but I am somewhat discouraged, because I was deadly serious, and was going to beg you to help me and others to put an end to stealing, both other peoples' and our own.

B. Evans, what do you mean?

E. Since you did really seem to hate stealing so, and since I know you are an honest man enough at heart, I was going to ask you to join the Socialist League, to which I belong –

B. Evans! Evans!

E. And the object of which is to get rid of all stealing for good and all.

B. Get rid of all property, you mean! But I never knew that you were a Socialist; – I am shocked, I am shocked! And the Socialist League, too! Well!

E. How you fly out at a man! How should you have known I was a Socialist? If ever I began to talk about the wrongs of the working class, or the stupidity of our system of production, you would take me all cross, and think I was only talking Ruskinism; and then you would shut me up with some Radical aphorism, and get excited about Gladstone, and not listen to one word I had to say. And I didn't like to push myself forward, as if I were a person of any importance.

B. Well, only to think of it! And let me tell you, Mr Socialist, when you call me a thief, I call you a coward for not telling me before.

E. (*penitently.*) Well, it was rather cowardly. But now you see I've done it; so you need not twit me with it. And I won't be cowardly any more about it; and I'll speak at the open-air meetings about here, instead of at the East-end only.

B. What! you a street-preaching demagogue too! – go about advising people to rebellion and murder and all that?

E. No; I advise them not to steal or let others steal. Come, I say, I don't mind your hard words, but just think it over about joining us.

B. NO!!!

E. Well, here we are close to the Straightway and the 'bus. Let's make peace, at any rate; and come in this evening and have a pipe, and convert me, if you can, to the ways of peace, righteousness – and stealing: and forget about your garden.

B. Well, I will come in, but no Socialist politics, if you please. Well, I promise to come.

E. Well, we won't talk politics. I'll read you the manuscript of my last poem, on the Birth of the Bruce: it isn't very long.

B. (*dubiously.*) All right, all right. Now I must be off: [the] 'bus is just going to start. (*Exit on 'bus.*)

E. (*to himself*). Well, I've caught him properly. Because, don't you see, when he comes in and sees my MS. on the table, he will be anxious to put off the evil half-hour of the reading, and he will be glad to let me begin to talk of Socialism or anything else rather than read my poetry to him. And when I once begin he will presently get hot and argue; and even if I don't sow a seed or two in him (and really he is a very good fellow) at all events it will be good practice for me against my next open-air speech.

Commonweal, Volume 3, Number 95,
5 November 1887, pp. 356–357

HONESTY IS THE BEST POLICY; OR, THE INCONVENIENCE OF STEALING

[A Dialogue *between* Mr James Brown, *a business man, and* Mr Olaf Evans, *a kind of artist and literary man; neighbours.*]

PART II

Scene – *A Room in* Mr Olaf Evan's *house, a good deal littered with odds and ends of art and literature; pipes and tobacco, and materials for grog on the table; in a conspicuous place a rather large bundle of MS.*

Brown. Well, you see I've come.

Evans. Yes, and thank you for coming. Do you know, this morning you were very nearly quarrelling with me. However, let us hope the Bruce will mend all that.

B. (*hastily, and looking furtively at the MS.*) Oh yes, I was glad to come and have a talk with a neighbour.

E. Well, light up, and let me mix you a glass of grog before I begin.

B. (*taking his eye from the MS, and looking hard into a corner of the room.*) Oh, thanks, thanks, presently; I'm not in a hurry.

[*Lights his pipe and smokes busily.*]

E. How is business?

B. So-so; it's the old story. I have got to do twice the business to make half the money that my father did.

E. How do you account for that?

B. Competition; things must be sold cheap or down you go.

E. A good thing for the country though, especially for the working-classes.

B. Well, I'm not so sure of that; to tell you the truth, taking them all round, I don't think they are so much better off; if they get nominally higher wages they don't get such constant employment, and some don't get higher wages. There are the clerks now – do you call them part of the working-classes?

E. Well, yes, as things go. They certainly don't belong to the proprietary classes.

B. Well, I tell you that they are not as well off as they used to be, by a long way; I can get a steady going German who knows three languages thoroughly for 30s. a-week or less. Some years ago there would have been a fight for such a youth at the price.

E. Still, to have things cheap ought to be a benefit.

B. Well, *I* don't want them cheap. And look here, if things go on at this rate I shall have to sell my business at what it will fetch, and live as well as I can on the interest of what I have saved. I can't go on for ever slaving for 2 1/2 per cent. And what I shall do other people will do, and are doing. Capital will be withdrawn from business wholesale, and then a nice mess your working-men will be in with nobody to employ them.

E. H'm – well *now* shall I mix for you – and begin the business of the evening?

B. Oh, we needn't be in a hurry, there's plenty of time. Let us talk.

E. Very well, I'm agreeable; only I hope we shan't quarrel.

B. I don't think we shall. You are in a reasonable humour now, I can see, and inclined to listen to people when they talk on subjects that they understand better than you.

E. Yes, there are many business matters I don't understand. I'll ask you a question or two presently.

B. Do; and one thing I can easily make clear to you, that an employer of labour doesn't lie on a bed of roses in these days. Everything that's done now must be for the benefit of the working-classes; as to the middle-classes, the real back-bone of the country, the real working-classes, mind you, they may take care of themselves.

E. Well, they can do that pretty well, I think.

B. How, I should like to know, with prices falling and wages rising on all hands?

E. But I though you said you could get clerks (who we are agreed are working-men) cheaper than you used to do.

B. Not in proportion to the profits I make.

E. Well, let that pass; for I want to raise your spirits by showing you how the middle-classes can take good care of themselves, and in fact do do so. Only I think you must abandon your ideal of their *all* retiring from business, and *all* living on the interest of their savings.

B. Well, I warn you that you trades' unionists and Socialists may drive us to that if you don't take care.

E. If we could only drive you to trying it! but it won't go quite in that way, I fear. But I admit that many of you can retire without bringing the whole thing about your ears, and can so take care of yourselves; while the rest of you take care of themselves by going down to their offices and looking at their clerks, and doing other laborious work for four hours a-day when they are not holiday-making.

B. Now, Evans, you are getting unreasonable again; talking about matters you don't understand.

E. Excuse me, Brown, my questions, the answers to which are to enlighten my ignorance, are just going to begin. What are you going to live on when you retire disgusted with 21/2 per cent profits, on what I imagine to be a biggish turnover?

B. (*rather crustily*) On my earnings.

E. On what you have made?

B. Yes, of course, on the money I have made.

E. Oh! I didn't know you made money, I thought you made soap.

B. Yes, of course. I manufacture soap, but I make money.

E. Manufacture – to make with the hands – soap is a cheapish article. What a lot of soap you must have made with your hands to live on your earnings in the style in which you live! You must be one of the cleverest men alive; I am quite proud of your acquaintance, Brown.

B. Here comes these nonsensical paradoxes again! However, go on, go on.

E. Paradoxes? Don't you make the soap with your hands then?

B. Why, you *know* I don't, not an ounce. Go on with your questions.

E. But you *manufacture* many tons of it?

B. Why, of course I do. How could I live else?

E. And who does make the soap with his hands which you *manufacture*?

B. With *his* hands? Why, I employ over 500 men at my works.

E. Oh! I see! But I can't understand how soap is so cheap then. Because as those men make the soap and you don't, and you I suppose are only a kind of hanger-on or parson to them, of course they must live as comfortably as you do, and like you can retire from business when they are tired of slaving for small profits! How *can* it be done?

B. (*who has mixed for himself, with a grin.*) Well, I answer you to keep up the game, because of course you know better than that; the men in my works, the mere workmen, get from 18s. to 30s. a-week.

E. Ah! they need some other people to take care of them then, as long as that lasts. But I want to get at what your *manufacturing* means in modern speech, since it seems its etymology goes for nothing. You doubtless see to the men's work, superintend the mixing and boiling, and whatever goes on there.

B. I can't say I do; the foremen and managers of the departments do that.

E. And what style do they live in? Can they retire on

their earnings? Not that I much care though if they cannot, since the other men cannot.

B. Well, they get £2 and £3 a-week, and the managers more.

E. Well, the soap being made must be sold. Who sells it?

B. It is travelled; the travellers sell it; and then there are the clerks and old Jackson.

E. And could they retire from business and live on their earnings?

B. You heard what I said about the clerks; as for the travellers, no, of course not. Old Jackson might, he has always been a close man; I think he's warm. But look here, or course I know what you are driving at, Evans, and you must admit that I've kept my temper *well.* Come, now, ask me what I do.

E. Well, I ask it.

B. I'll tell you. First I find the capital, that you understand; and since you must admit that that is necessary, if I'm not to be paid for that what am I to be paid for? Well, then there is my risk consequent on my allowing my property to be used for the production of wealth; then am I to be paid nothing for superintending such a vast affair? And then remember in these days of sharp competition what a job it is to look after the markets and keep pace with the march of commerce. I tell you it's a regular war with the other manufacturers. I say that I earn my money *well*, much better than if I helped to make a few tons of soap every week; all the more as it's the machines that do it, much more than the men. (*Getting hot.*) I heartily wish it was all machines and no men; such a bother as we have with them.

E. Shall I tell you a little fable, Brown?

B. Oh, go on – go on!

E. Well, once upon a time the lion and the other carnivorous beasts went a-hunting,[1] and had good sport; and at the end of the day they met to divide the spoil, the

[1] This illustration is taken from Proudhon's 'What is Property?' The fable an ancient one, as might be expected.

lion in the chair. The chairman bade the carcases (*sic*) be separated into four equal portions, besides the guts and other offal, which was put in a heap by itself. Great expectancy there was among the beasts: the leopard purred and waved his tail; the bear rolled about jovially; water ran from both sides of the wolf's mouth; the jackals whined happily; – the fox, though he smiled a good deal, as his custom is, was the only one that seemed uneasy. 'Friends', said the chairman, 'here is the wealth which our united labour has produced; I thus apportion it according to the sacred rights of property: the first is mine because I am called lion; the second because I kindly allow you to live; the third because of my strength, beauty, and nobility, without which the world were a dull place indeed; as for the fourth, let him touch it who dares; but yonder heap of offal you may divide it amongst you as you please; but if you follow my advice you will consume it with thrift and temperance.' So said the lion; and the other beasts, like the law-abiding citizens they were, declared themselves contented. – Well, Brown, it seems to me that the lion managed to take good care of himself.

B. Again I see what you are driving at; but I don't think much of your fable as applied to a captain of industry.

E. Well, you see, Brown, all fables have their weak places, this amongst others. As you have noticed, I suppose, the lion probably did a good share of the hunting, being in that respect quite unlike the captain of industry. But, to leave [the] fable and come to your statement of what you do, you say you *find* the capital: yes, pretty much as those – individuals – found your pears last night. And as to the risk you run in employing what you have *found*, I daresay they run some risk in turning these *findings* into the universal equivalent. As to your payment for superintending such a vast affair, you as good as told me that Jackson in the office and the managers at the works did that: so at any rate don't take too much – the lion's share – for that service. There remains your payment for that war with your brother soap-boilers which you told me about, which I admit under the circumstances seems necessary: yet don't you think it rather rough on those that *make* the soap that they should have to pay for that incident of its *manufacture*?

B. Rough on them – what do you mean? What have they got to do with it?

E. Nothing, I admit.

B. Well, you have got some preposterous utopian nonsense in your head, so you had better bring it out at once, since we have got on this unlucky subject again.

E. My utopianism drives me to wishing that the word 'manufacture' could be used in its original sense, and that there should be no occasion for using it in its modern sense.

B. Well, you see the fact that it has so changed its sense ought to show you how much more important in the production of wealth is the direction of labour than the labour itself.

E. (*softly, as if to himself.*) H'm: the foreman couldn't retire, nor the managers at the works; Jackson might, perhaps, and you certainly could, – a sliding-scale of usefulness at all events from the foreman downwards: the men who do most get least.

B. You are getting rude again, Evans.

E. I am afraid I shall get ruder presently. I really must say that the – individuals – who – did business – in your pears have a right to claim the title of manufacturers – so far as they went.

B. (*emphatically, but not angrily.*) Meaning that I'm a thief.

E. Well, you are not a thief – morally – not at present; because, till you have heard all I have to say and thought about it, you know no better. But it does seem to me that your very respectable business of *manufacturing* soap really means stealing soap and selling it, and sticking to the plunder. I admit by the circuitous process of robbing the people who make it.

B. Yes, I thought we should come to it again. However, go on.

E. Well, in for a penny in for a pound. This morning you called stealing the worst kind of war – a beastly miserable destructive vice. Isn't your account of what business is coming to proof positive of that? See what a market you are bringing your pigs to! You have achieved complete success is producing wares marvellously cheap, and the result is, if it stops there, that the workmen, take them all round, are none the better for it; and as for yourselves, the employers, you are threatening to give up employing, because that war which forces you to crush out the life and individuality of your workmen bids fair to ruin yourselves – the conquered conquered and the conquerors undone. All that comes of stealing.

B. Well, Evans, I see I was wrong to think that you were not in earnest. But since you acquit me of the moral guilt of theft – and you must remember, by the way, that here I am in my position, and even supposing I wanted to get out of it, how can I – since you admit what you do admit, why do you use such hard words?

E. Why, in the first place, though I acquit you personally of moral theft, I don't acquit your class: that upas-tree of *Cant* which overshadows the whole middle-class in this country, and, for aught I know, throughout all civilization, and poisons every action of our lives, and makes our pleasures, our art, our literature, our would-be aspirations even, sickening to any one who can think of an honest world,– is not this a symptom of our guilt? Year by year we of the middle-classes, as we are getting more and more conscious of what ought to be, are getting more and more hateful and contemptible to ourselves and others – building up wrath against the day of wrath. How will the change come? What horrors may you and I live to see? Yes, that is the reason why I use hard words – or plain words – or bitter words, if you will: because I feel them and cannot help it. But, apart from the moral side of things, as to the material 'inconvenience', there –

B. There, I admit at once that if you are right in condemning the system as dishonest the 'inconvenience' of it – that is, the necessary disturbance and misery – is of course much worse than that which results from what we call stealing now, we respectables. Spasmodic stealing disapproved of by society in general we could almost afford to pass over without notice (when are gardens had not been just spoilt by it); but continuous stealing, approved of by respectability, authority, and religion, – well, if that really is the basis of our classes to-day, I must as an honest man who tries not to be a fool admit that no price would be too high for ridding ourselves of that: riot, ruin, civil war, revolution, would all be a cheap bargain. But you must convince me class society is so founded.

E. I will try to do so. Meantime I can't tell you how glad I am that we have got as far as we have done. When a man can see that the occasional theft of the product of labour is a joke to the theft in one lump of the whole of the raw material and instruments which alone allow labour to be, it is not difficult to argue with him. – Well, old fellow, it's too late now to begin on that 'Birth of the Bruce'; so have another glass of grog, and then we'll say good-night in peace and quietness: though it *did* seem rather like a quarrel at one time.

Commonweal, Volume 3, Number 96,
12 November 1887, pp. 364–365

London in a State of Siege

Sir Charles Warren has kept his promise and prevented the meeting organized by the Radical Clubs. From the military point of view he has been eminently successful, and deserved to be so, and it is now proper that we should make him a peer of the realm and Commander-in-Chief of the British forces, if he will kindly consent to waive the title of Emperor or three-tailed Bashaw or whatever else is the proper nick-name of a supreme and irresponsible ruler. Sir Charles, I repeat, made his military dispositions admirably, and revolutionists should study them, since they have had a little piece of real war suddenly brought to their notice. The 'Square', *ie.*, the sunken space, was guarded by foot-policemen four deep, whose business was simply to guard it and who had orders not to stir from their posts; outside these were strong bodies of horse-police who took careful note of any incipient gathering and at once scattered it.

This defence was ample against anything except an organized attack from determined persons acting in concert and able to depend on one another. In order that no such body should be formed and no such attack be possible, the careful general had posted strong bodies of police, with due supports to fall back on if necessary, about a radius of about a quarter of a mile of the Square, so that nothing could escape falling into the meshes of this net.

Into this net then we marched. The column in which the comrades of the League were, started from Clerkenwell Green in company with the Patriotic Club and some of the East-end clubs, including a Branch of the SDF. I see the correspondent of the *Daily News* estimates this column at 6000, but I think that is an exaggeration. Anyhow, we marched in good order through Theobalds' Road, and up

Hart Street, crossing Oxford Street and Shaftesbury Avenue without attack from the police, but we had no sooner crossed the latter street and were about to enter the Seven Dials streets to make our way to St Martin's Lane, than the attack came, and it was clearly the best possible place for it. The divergence of the streets would confuse any procession which had lost its rallying point; the side streets and the width of the thoroughfare at the spot gave a good opportunity for a flank charge, and at our rear was the open space of Shaftesbury Avenue to allow a charge in that quarter to finish us up after the attack on front and flank. It was all over in a few minutes: our comrades fought valiantly, but they had not learned how to stand and turn their column into a line, or to march on to the front. Those in front turned and faced their rear, not to run away, but to join in the fray if opportunity served. The police struck right and left like what they were, soldiers attacking an enemy, amidst wild shrieks of hatred from the women who came from the slums on our left. The band instruments were captured, the banners and flags destroyed, there was no rallying point and no possibility of rallying, and all that the people composing our once strong column could do was to straggle into the Square as helpless units. I confess I was astounded at the rapidity of the thing and the ease with which military organization got its victory. I could see that numbers were of no avail unless led by a band of men acting in concert and each knowing his own part.

What happened to us happened, as I hear, to the other processions with more or less fighting. An eye-witness who marched up with the western column told me that they were suddenly attacked as they came opposite the Haymarket Theatre, by the police rushing out on them from the side streets and immediately batoning everybody they could reach, whether they resisted or not. The column, he said, was destroyed in two minutes, though certainly not quite without fighting; one brave man wrapping his banner torn from the pole round his arm and facing the police till he was hammered down with repeated blows.

Once in the Square we were, as I said, helpless units, especially as there were undoubtedly a good many mere spectators, many of them club gentlemen and other members of the class which employs Warren. Undoubtedly if two or three hundred men could have been got to make a rush on the cordon of the police, especially at the south-east corner the crowd could have swarmed into the Square, and if the weakest of the columns could have reached the Square in order this could easily have been done. But the result would probably have been a far bloodier massacre than Peterloo; for the people, once in the Square, would have found themselves in a mere penfold at the mercy of the police and soldiers. It is true that as matters went, there seemed very little need for the appearance of the latter, so completely were the police, horse and foot, masters of the situation; and the great mass of the people also round the Square was composed of Radicals, very angry it is true at the horrible brutality with which they had been treated by Warren's men, but by no means strung up to fighting pitch. So that I was fairly surprised, the crowd being then quite quiet, to see the Life Guards form at the south of the Square and march up towards St Martin's Church with the magistrate at their head (a sort of country-gentleman-looking imbecile) to read the Riot Act. The soldiers were cheered as well as hooted by the crowd, I think under the impression that they would not act as brutally against the people as the police: a mistaken impression, I think, as these gorgeous gentry are just the helmetted flunkies of the rich and would act on their orders just as their butlers or footmen would. A little after this a regiment of the foot-guards made their appearance with fixed bayonets, and completed the triumph of law and order.

Sir Charles Warren has thus given us a lesson in street fighting, the first point of which is that mere numbers without organization or drill are useless; the second, which ought also to be noted, is the proper way to defend a position in a large town by a due system of scouts, outposts, and supports.

We Socialists should thank our master for his lesson, and so pass on from considering the military aspect of the case to its civil aspect. Warren has won a victory, but on what terms! It is clear from what is above printed that he would not have been thoroughly successful if he had not had a free hand given him: if he had not attacked citizens marching peaceably through the streets in just such a way as banditti might do, destroying and stealing their property, they would have been able to claim their right of meeting in Trafalgar Square in such a way that nothing but sharp shot and cold steel could have dealt with them. London has been put under martial law, nominally for behoof of a party, but really on behoof of a class, and *war* (for it is no less, whatever the consequences may be) has been forced upon us. The mask is off now, and the real meaning of all the petty persecution of our open-air meetings is as clear as may be. No more humbug need be talked about obstruction and the convenience of the public: it is obvious that those meetings were attacked because we displeased the dominant class and were weak. Last Sunday explains all, and the bourgeois now goes about boasting that he is the master and will do what he likes with his slaves. Again, the humbug is exposed of the political condemnation of coercion by Act of Parliament in Ireland, when here in London we have coercion without Act of Parliament; and the feeble twitterings of the *Daily News* will be received with jeers by the triumphant Tories.

And the greatest humbug which Sunday's events have laid bare is 'the protection afforded by law to the humblest citizen'. Some simple people will be thinking that Warren can be attacked legally for his murderous and cowardly assaults of Sunday. I say Warren, because 'tis no use beating the *stick* that beats you. Some perhaps will think that there may be a chance of his getting a few years penal servitude for inciting to riot and murder. But these persons forget that he has been *ordered* to act as he did just as he *ordered* his brigands, and that Salisbury and Co., who *ordered* him have done so at the *orders* of the class which they represent. They have made the laws, but have never intended to keep them when inconvenient. It has now become inconvenient to keep them – and in consequence we must think ourselves lucky to be *only* beaten by the policeman's baton if the bourgeois don't like us – lucky to get off the six months' or twelve months' imprisonment which is likely to accompany such an *accident*. In short, the very Radicals have now been taught that slaves have no rights. The lesson is a painful one, but surely useful to us boastful Englishmen: nay, in the long run it is necessary.

Commonweal, Volume 3, Number 97,
19 November 1887, pp. 369–370

INSURANCE AGAINST MAGISTRATES

The meeting held in the Memorial Hall on November 18th will do good service if the protective League inaugurated by it keeps to its promise (as I see no reason for doubting that it will) of helping all persons without distinction of opinion who 'get into trouble' in their endeavours to defend freedom of speech. Stewart Headlam in his speech on that occasion said nothing less than the bare truth when he said that no poor man had any chance of obtaining justice in a magistrate's court, – in which, by the way, he would doubtless have included the Middlesex Sessions if he had had any experience of Judge Edlin. No better instance of the necessity of some corporate protection for the victims of the law could be given than what happened on the morning of the meeting, when nine prisoners convicted by Ingham's drum-head court-martial were able to appeal against the unjust and malignant sentences pronounced against them by an ancient piece of incompetence, no doubt inspired by orders from headquarters. I believe none of these poor men would have been able to appeal but for the responsible bail provided for them chiefly through the efforts of Mrs Besant, whose untiring energy and devotion throughout the whole affair will surely win her a place in the hearts of all working men. It has been stated in these columns before, but may as well be stated again, that no one can appeal from a magistrate's decision unless he can find two sureties who will bind themselves to pay the costs of the appeal if rejected; – where can a poor man find such sureties, who may have to pay £50 in case of failure?

The struggle for mere freedom of speech (whatever it may lead to) will certainly be a long and arduous one. Even the present idiotic Tory Government will not be easy to get rid of; and though it is possible that a Liberal Government would treat us better, at least for a while, because the Liberals may be forced to take the matter up and come in on it, yet such a trifle as a mere change of ministry will not cure the gangrene of the law-courts; nor will it have much influence on the reaction which is obviously setting in and which is the necessary accompaniment to the no less obvious progress of revolutionary ideas. The struggle will be a long one, and must be carried on by us in a manner which will mean steadily and pertinaciously harassing the *apparently* all-powerful executive on all sides. The League which the *Pall Mall Gazette* has set on foot will, if it performs its functions duly, take up one side of the attack, and will assuredly do good service. All Socialists will be glad to see Mrs Besant's name on the committee as an earnest of due fulfilment of its promises; and although 'votes of thanks' are not in favour amongst us, it would be unfair and ungenerous not to acknowledge the great services which the *Pall Mall Gazette* has done to the popular cause throughout this agitation. Well-to-do people especially should join this League, and help it both with their money, for a good deal of that will be necessary, and also by sending in their names as persons to be relied on for bail and sureties of the prisoners taken in the war for Freedom of Speech.

Commonweal, Volume 3, Number 98,
26 November 1887, p. 377

THE LIBERAL PARTY DIGGING ITS OWN GRAVE

For months past the Gladstonian Liberals have been protesting loudly against Coercion in Ireland, and the speeches of the 'distinguished' amongst them have been filling columns on columns of the papers. They have just had a splendid opportunity of striking a great blow against Coercion in London. We need not ask how they have used that opportunity, that would be a joke; but it may be profitable to point out some possible consequences of their gross stupidity in throwing it away. It is their business as political Liberals to get the working-classes to believe that if they come in again some benefit will result to the workers above what the Tories have to offer them. They have, in fact, to win the vote of the ordinary working-men, not only those who professedly take interest in politics, but especially those who stand aloof from them, and that in Britain rather than in Ireland (since Ireland through its native leaders is theirs already), and especially in London, where there is so much to win. Now as long as the meeting in Trafalgar Square was 'a genuinely political meeting', that is a mere home rule affair, their presence and support was of little importance, since their good-will towards it might have been taken for granted. But when it became, as it did some days before the meeting, a protest against the repression of free speech, and was, whatever may be said to the contrary, a protest also on the part of the 'respectable' working-men of London against the maltreatment of their unemployed brethren, their support became of very great importance, at any rate to the future of the Liberal Party. It would have been accepted as a token of their sympathy with the popular cause, and would have gained them many thousands of votes which will now either be cast in favour of some Conservative of the 'dishing' kind, or will never be cast at all. In short, they would have won whatever of London could be won by them under any circumstances, and they would have lost nothing at all; for they may be quite sure that they have no chance of the votes of the shopocracy big or little; they have done enough to lose that, while they have done nothing to win what was to be won.

Their conduct gives a good measure of the utter political incapacity of the Liberal Party. It is quite likely that they may plead that their 'great and noble leader' is hard to move, that is, quite devoid of any perception of a dramatic situation; that at every crisis he has done all he could to discourage his friends and encourage his foes, but that is no excuse worth putting forward. The oracle of the Great Panjandrum was not needed to speak; even the next greatest panjandrums might have been dispensed with, *ie.*, Morley and Harcourt, and such like. If some dozen of Liberal MP's of the more respectable kind had given by some means their open support to the business, it would have been enough, and the assent of the 'leaders' would have been inferred, and the trick would have been done.

All this is now a thing of the past, and as a first consequence all people who can think at all must clearly see that the political Liberals look upon the Irish question simply as a mechanical matter to get them into office again. It is equally clear that freedom of speech for the people in general is no concern of theirs, except so far as they are afraid of the consequences of it if they were in power. No less clear [is] that they do not care a button for the unemployed so long as they can be kept quiet; and finally, that they have no foresight or plan for the future and [are] determined to shut their eyes resolutely to it. The result of all which will probably be, unless some blessed accident turns up to help them, that they will be exposed at the next election as the mere dregs of a beaten political party, a set of men afraid to proclaim themselves either Radicals or Reactionists; afraid of revolution, and (perhaps) ashamed of open reaction.

'Well, but what does all this matter to us?' a Socialist may say. Well, it is a matter of importance that the people should learn to know their friends from their foes; the people whom we still have to win over to our side – nay, whom to a great extent we still have to get to listen to us. Those Liberal members who have been crying out so loud about the wrongs of the Irish peasants and who so wholly blind to those of the London workmen, which are no less than those of their Irish brethren, have been teaching the lesson in question to the people sharply this time. They will understand that these champions of liberty are really saying: 'There is no political capital to be made of you, so we don't heed you: nay, since you are at our very doors, and are beginning to look dangerous, we are at heart glad that the muzzle is being clapped on to you.'

This is the meaning of the Liberal members standing aloof from the struggle for free speech in London; and used as people are to official poltroonery, they must see something of this meaning in it, and a heavy blow will be struck at the hope which some simple people still have in a change of ministry – it is called a change of parties, but it hardly amounts even to that. The people will in consequence begin to cry out for a party which does at least aim at being a popular one; which, however partially and ignorantly, does admit that the welfare and progress of the workers is the one necessary thing to be aimed at. In short, the orthodox Liberal party will visibly melt into the great reactionary party, and that very soon now in all probability; and though there will scarcely be a solid democratic party, yet at least there will be a great mass of ever-growing discontent. Both that of people who are increasingly suffering in their own persons from the progress of economical events and also of people of honest democratic instincts to whom all oppression is hateful when they see it, under whatever name it goes. This body of discontent it will not be difficult to penetrate with Socialist ideas, since it will no longer be able to hope anything from the vague bundle of makeshifts and evasions that passes under the name of a Liberal policy.

The gain, therefore, of the renunciation of the defence of freedom of speech by the Liberal leaders and their henchmen is all ours and the loss is theirs. The only possible reason for wanting a Liberal ministry in again is that the Irish question might be settled for the time. Against that possible gain is to be put tne (*sic*) certainty that the longer the question is delayed the more revolutionary the change will be. Nor is it so sure either that the Liberals would do much to settle it if they were in office, on the one hand, or on the other that the Tories may not dish them at last by doing pretty much the same as their opponents would do.

Anyhow the education of the Radicals ought to go on pretty fast, now that a strong Liberal minority pledged up to the eyes to resistance to coercion, and looking forward, rightly or wrongly, to winning at the next election, has stood by and looked on with half-approving eyes while the Tories were taking away from the people the right of meeting in open spaces in London with a high-handed violence worthy of the times of Castlereagh.

COMMONWEAL, VOLUME 3, NUMBER 98,
26 NOVEMBER 1887, P. 380

THE CONSCIENCE OF THE UPPER CLASSES

It seems to be universally admitted that the conference held on December 5th in the Memorial Hall, Farringdon Street, on the prevailing distress in London was the direct outcome of the unemployed agitation, for joining in which so many poor men have been sentenced with a spite at once so malignant and so petty that it fairly sickens an honest man to think of it. These rich and well-to-do persons were driven to meet together by a fear which I do not say they all felt in their own persons, but which is certainly permeating their class, a fear so easily aroused that a few hundred destitute, unarmed, peaceably behaved persons parading London streets could strike terror into the hearts of the well-to-do of the richest city of the most powerful empire in the world.

It is scarcely worth while to criticize the various schemes and opinions of the speakers at the meeting. In plain terms, the one person who said anything worth listening to was Cardinal Manning, and it is a curious sign of the times that a high official of the Catholic Church should give a lesson in sociology to Liberal and Radical politicians, humanitarian dissenting ministers, and professional philanthropists – the latter represented by Mr Arnold White, who, one might think, would be glad, if he dared, to advocate a battue of the useless foreigners and quick-breeding Britons of London, after the fashion of the Spartan Helot-hunts.

Of the Cardinal it must be said that he showed none of that base and cowardly hatred of the degraded poor (the poor whose degradation is caused by the exclusive 'refinement' of the rich) which is the ordinary feeling of the cultured classes, whether openly expressed or veiled under the pretext of poor-law-philanthropy. Said he: 'Thirty years ago I went into places where it was said the police dared not go, and found them very harmless.'

Again, as a Catholic prelate he was not concerned to support the cheerful commercial optimism (about other people's troubles) which is the lining, so to speak, of the moral pessimism of the well-to-do; and he exposed their miserable evasion of setting down the greater part of the unemployed demonstrators as criminals and loafers, and roundly accused 'society' of being responsible for their existence. Lastly he attacked, however mildly, the ferocity of the philanthropists about out-door relief. In fact it is clear that he could see nothing else for dealing with the present distress but that very out-door relief in some form or other, the horror of which a few years ago had established itself firmly in the hearts of all philanthropists as a kind of holy dogma not to be questioned; a piece of altruistic piety invented to take the place of the now obsolete 'Do unto others as you would have them do unto you'. There is a great deal of virtue in the Latinization of an English word: A Gods' name (or the Other One's) don't 'pauperize' people! But you may carefully keep them poor and feel none the worse for it!

The Cardinal wound up with what may be regarded as an official tag, about 'voluntary agencies', and the necessity of 'visiting the homes of the poor'. This was what his office compelled him to say and need not be noticed, if it were not of value as showing that we must not reckon on real help from the Catholic clergy. All that can be expected of them is the administration of charity in its less insulting and kindlier form, and the occasional startling of smug respectability from its after-dinner doze by the enunciation of some obvious social truth, which the genuine Catholic, with his contempt of human life on the earth except as a preparation for another, non-human life, finds it easy to see; but which is quite strange to the commercial religionist engaged in saving his own soul in this world and the next at everybody else's expense.

For the rest nothing was proposed except a mere bundle of evasions of the fact that our system of production is breaking down into ruin through its own triumph. Whatever middle-class rule has put before itself as an aim it has won; but the well-being of the worker was never its aim and could not be; his endurance and quietude only has been aimed at. But since the middle-class ideal is that there should be widely-spread comfort for those living wholly or partly on the labour of others, while those *others* should not be so sorely pinched as to rebel or refuse to work, the safeguards against the ruin of the system of wage-slavery have been disregarded; especially the chief safeguard, the organization of labour; the widening of the basis of spoliation by making it as easy as may be for the worker to pinch and screw himself out of his class into that of the robbers of labour, has been thought safeguard enough in this direction; but this safeguard is now yielding to the increase in the pace of competition; and we are face to face with the consequences of the wholesale *waste of labour* which is sure to happen in a society composed of rich and poor in an epoch well equipped with mechanical resources.

We have been forcing the great mass of the workers to make things of no use to the workers (or to any one else for that matter), and we have assumed that we shall always be able to find people willing to take these pieces of manufacture from us in exchange for food and other necessaries which are produced by the workers, and not by the buyers of the useless things. When we come to think of the fact, that these buyers of inutilities have nothing to buy them with except the necessaries which they steal from the workers, part of which they must dole out to them again as slave-rations under the modern name of 'wages', one need be no longer astonished that the scanty and seemingly harmless gatherings of the unemployed should have frightened the class that owns 'Society', and made them ask 'What's to be done now?' *They* will not find an answer, though the answer will come; because any attempt they may make to limit the waste of labour will but act as a lever for the destruction of the Society which they are so eager to *save*.

Commonweal, Volume 3, Number 101,
17 December 1887, p. 404

Contributions to *Commonweal*

1888

POLICE SPIES EXPOSED

There have always been found by the governments of all countries traitors ready to mingle in the ranks of every revolutionary party, including the Socialist, and by worming themselves into the confidence of the members, obtain their secrets to betray them, or by getting up dynamite plots and things of that kind, to arouse public feeling against the movement. Many other devices are there in the armoury of a tyrant, and in the days of the Third Empire they were carried, as men thought, to the utmost pitch of a devilish perfection. It has been left however for Bismark (*sic*) and his underlings to attain a yet higher (or lower) degree of skill and completeness of plan. Since the coming into effect of the anti-Socialist laws in Germany, 1879, police-spying, or the trade of head-monger and lie-smith, has become a recognized department of governmental work, an institution far more inwound with the existence of the State than even in the corruptest days of Napoleon the Little. Not only does Germany look after folk within her own borders, but provides them with careful friends in every city where Socialists are to be found; thus it is really an *international political secret police* that is maintained and worked from Berlin. Our well-known co-worker, the *Sozialdemokrat* of Zurich, has always been trying to get hold of the secrets of this organization, and has now and then succeeded in bringing facts to light, that spoiled some single plot, or exposed some spy. Of course it has had to bear the fate of the outspoken, and is often abused among a certain set as an organ of denunciation. Rather should it be praised for the courage with which it follows up a foe of the cause, and the skill with which it cuts open the disguise of a false friend, and shows the reptile underneath. *Der Socialdemokrat* deserves the thanks of all honest Socialists for its efforts in casting light upon a hideous host of vermin, and so depriving them of their power to betray. In its issue of December 24th is given a list of names of men who are *now* in the pay of the police-bureau. We assure our readers of the accuracy of the information.

The names are as follows:-

1. *Herm. Heinr. Sachs*, formerly lieutenant of the police at Berlin; author and professor. Police-spy in London (8 years in pay).
2. *Charles Theodore Reuss*, formerly theatrical impresario and concert-singer, now Bismark's (*sic*) political agent on the *Central News* of London and the *Cable News* of New York; contributor to the *Süddeutschen Presse* at Munich and the *Berliner Zeitung* at Berlin. Police-spy in London (2 years and 6 months in pay).
3. *Kaufmann* (alias Carl Morff), engineer, now partner in the 'City Club'. Police-spy in London (7 years in pay).
4. *Heinrich*, formerly engineer, now publican at Zurich.
5. *Karl Schroder*, insurance agent at Riesbach-Zurich (7 years standing).
6. *Christian Haupt*, agent at Geneva (8 years standing).
7. *Max Trautner*, formerly Bavarian officer, now journalist in Paris (previously at Brussels[)]. Military and political police-spy (8 years standing).
8. *Heinr. Oberwinder*, formerly one of the leaders of the Austrian Socialist movement, now journalist in Paris.
9. *H. Nonne*, teacher, formerly in London, now in Paris (At Berlin, for the time being).
10. *Ludw. Schweinhagen*, at Magdeburg.
11. *A. Wichmann*, agent at Altona (8 years in pay).
12. *Neumann*, carpenter at Hamburg.
13. *Herm. Nebel*, bookseller at Leipzig.

We need not further warn our readers against these despicable creatures, but may profitably add a word or two on those employed in London. Sachs has been for some time away doing some special political business in the South of France and on the Spanish and Italian frontiers. In London he specially took care of the German Communist Club (First Section); at the time of Most's arrest and conviction here he was a contributor to the *Freiheit*, and took away from the printing-office a lot of copy which had appeared in the paper; all of which duly reached the Berlin police. Reuss, among other things, caused the arrest of several Anarchists at Leipzig, Nürnberg, Augsburg and Berlin; was concerned in several so-called 'Anarchist' trials in Vienna; and with the aid of his accomplice, Joseph Peukert, carried out the infamous scheme by which our brave comrade, John Neve, was taken and condemned. In another line of business he has to work the press in order to manufacture 'public opinion' in favour of the extradition of political offenders and international repressive laws and treaties. During the late troubles in Trafalgar Square and Hyde Park, he was particularly active in this way. His blood-money is 450 marks a month (£22 10s.) It is interesting to know that he corresponds with his employer, Police-Councillor Krueger, Chief of [the] German Secret Police, directly at Kaiserin Augusta Strasse, 72, Berlin, or indirectly through either M. Fumagalli, Court Jeweller, 138, Leipziger-strasse, Berlin, or M. Hacke, formerly Chief of Police at Frankfort, now Police Councillor at Berlin, 31, Kulmstrasse. Kaufmann (or Carl Morff), an Austrian 'Anarchist', it was who furnished, from means provided him by the police, to Stellmacher and Kammerer the money needed for the notorious attempts at Vienna. After the death of his victims he was expelled from Switzerland. Ordered to London by his master, he has lived here ever since. For a time secretary of the Third Section, he is now partner in the 'City Club', a well-known rendezvous of Socialists, both English and German.

We may have to return to this theme again, but have said enough for the present.

Commonweal, Volume 4, Number 104,
7 January 1888, pp. 1–2

WHAT 1887 HAS DONE

The year 1887 is come to an end, a year in many respects eventful; what will it be chiefly known by in the future, when it has become mere history? To some it will be the Jubilee year; to some the central year of the great Tory ascendancy; to some, it may be, for a little while, the last of the thoroughly bad years of the depression of trade. Yet again it may be known hereafter as the last year of the European armed truce; and to others it will be remembered as the great year of Coercion. Which will it be? Another question can be our only answer. Is our future to be that of patient slaves bearing their hard lot apathetically, and idle and vacant lords who live by their labour, with no thought but for the follies and toys with which they kill the dragging and unhappy hours of their dull lives? Is the knowledge of the world still to bring us degradation, its wealth misery, its power slavery? If that is to be so let us remember the past year as the year of the Queen's Jubilee, and be mildly satisfied at the thought of the hundreds of thousands of slaves and slave holders who turned out into the streets to witness the symbolic procession of the triumph of Official Dishonesty, and let us note the year as the first of a new epoch of 'Resolute Government', the rule of tyrannous fools and pedants over helpless and unthinking cowards. But if, on the other hand, our future is to be the struggle of slaves to free themselves, however intermittent it may be; although that struggle be irresolute and unorganized, at whiles timid, at whiles rash – as, alas! the rebellion of slaves is but too apt to be, – if *rebellion* be our future, then we must look back at the past year with hope as one of the noteworthy landmarks on the road to revolution.

Let us briefly review the events of 1887, then, and see whether anything in them points to the conclusion that we shall be driven to forget our hopes, and accept the prospect of the immediate future as one of apathy and despair.

From the 'political' point of view the Irish Question has been the only one of the past year; and no doubt there will be many in these last days of 1887 who will both say and think that the Irish are further from reaching their goal than ever; that Resolute Government will keep the excitement under till from sheer weariness and despair people yield, and sit still in sullen discontent, and that the hopes of the Home Rulers, which were brightening in the early part of the year, are now clouded over. This opinion is not without some foundation in reason, and would be amply justified if the only point in the Irish Question were the establishment of an Irish Parliament in Dublin with more or less real authority over the Irish people; but, as has often been pointed out in these columns, the question goes much deeper than that, and necessity will compel either or both the political parties to act in a way more or less revolutionary, and to do some things which the Dublin parliament if established would have to do. For the question rests on the livelihood of the Irish peasants, and whether their landlords should be allowed for ever to squeeze their incomes in the shabbiest possible manner out of the poverty of these poor people, so that shelving the question is impossible; nor is it of any moment to Socialists or sensible people which of the two parties in the game of politics gives way and yields some practical measure of home rule as a step towards the attempt to deal with the question. Between a 'dishing' Tory measure and a compromizing Gladstonian one there will be little if any difference.

Meanwhile the Tories, in following out their natural course of upholding the shabby landlord tyranny in Ireland, have passed the Coercion Bill usual in dealings with that country. Under ordinary circumstances such a measure would have received little notice in England; but with the present revolutionary feeling that is in the air, its results have been much more telling than the results of such measures are used to be. Although the Gladstonians resisted it feebly enough in Parliament, and no determined protest was made against it except by the Socialists and extreme Radicals, yet the carrying out of its provisions in Ireland itself have as it were raised aloft the sufferings of the poor as a banner for all revolutionary-minded people to rally to. The imprisonment of Irish members and the Lord Mayor of Dublin, and the arrest of Mr Blunt, merely as a piece of arbitrary high-handedness, and the quashing of the case against the police murderers at Mitchelstown, have forced the dullest to see that Ireland is in rebellion against the Government, not the people, of England; and if anyone goes further to seek the cause for the rebellion, he cannot fail to find out that it is with the Irish landlord, as with the French seigneur before the Revolution, according to Carlyle's epigram: The widow is gathering three nettles for herself and her children, and two out of every three she has [to] yield up to the lord as *rent*. Is it too much to hope that the enquirer who has thus got to the bottom of the Irish question will follow the enquiry up as to the condition of the workman throughout civilization, and will get to know the meaning of *rent*, *profit*, and *interest*, and the way in which the proprietary class work them? Thus the Irish question will educate many in revolution, and the events of 1887 will certainly help on his education in this direction.

There is another series of events in which the past year has been rich, which must be lumped together as interference with the right of public meeting. In the beginning of the year these events seemed to most people to be of little importance except to the small body of men against whom they were immediately directed – the Socialists, to wit; and *they* have been for years accustomed to have their meetings attacked by the police on the specious grounds of public convenience. But the special point of all the attacks made on us this year had (*sic*) been their obvious malignity and vindictiveness, shown by the sentences on the men who fell into the power of the authorities. The game began with Justice Grantham's sentence on our comrades Henderson and Mowbray at Norwich, in which, as usual in such cases, the judge made himself an advocate for the prosecution. Then came the sentences on the members of the SDF and other men (not Socialists) who got entangled in the police-manufactured riot at the gates of Hyde Park in March. At this the general public kicked somewhat, and the magistrates sentences were impossible to be wholly upheld on appeal. But as the days wound round to the autumn, and it became clear that we were to have the usual unemployed demonstration in greater force than ever, the respectable classes took the alarm, and the police were set on to make the attacks on peaceable citizens who had committed the crime of being poor, which culminated in the shameful day of November 13th, and the still more shameful scenes in the police and law courts which followed it. This time the Socialists found themselves in alliance with the extreme Radicals, as in the affair of Dod Street. But the allies were deserted by everybody else, even by the Irish party (with the single exception, as far as I know, of Michael Davitt), although they are suffering from the same tyranny themselves. In fact this time the affair, as far as it has gone, has been an ominous flash from the smouldering volcano of class war which underlies modern sham-society. This has been so well felt that all respectability promptly sided with the attack on elementary political rights, and outside the definite Socialist organs we have had the whole of the press against us except the *Pall Mall Gazette* and *Reynolds*; while on the other hand no one who witnessed the sympathetic demeanour of the huge crowds that accompanied or looked on at Linnell's funeral procession could venture to deny that the *masses* in London are on our side.

To turn to the struggle of the workers in the net of capitalistic production. The year began with the abortive strike of the Lanarkshire miners, in which our comrades at Glasgow took a part at once bold and considerate, and thereby did much to forward the work of propaganda.

This was followed by the strike of the Northumbrian miners, which again was taken advantage of by Socialists, with most encouraging results. These have been the most typical instances of the direct labour struggle; but the whole year has been full of labour disputes, which is the more remarkable since up to the present time it has been a year of great depression; though just now there seem to be signs of a revival of business in several trades, which, if it turns out to have any endurance, will no doubt be hailed as a token of the stability of our present system of production, and the lasting glory of the British Empire which is not ashamed to live on the ruin of the Celtic peasants, and the desperate misery of the London slum-dwellers.

Abroad the American middle-classes have relieved their fear or satisfied their cold and stupid malice by the consummation of their revenge on the revolutionists who had the temerity to be actively on the workmen's side in a bitter Chicago labour struggle, – nor will they know till the revolution is upon them how dearly their revenge will cost them.

Bismarck has had one or two triumphs: won a huge majority in the spring; carries his army bill easily now; he has reduced the number of Socialist members to five, but has not succeeded in reducing the number of Socialists, which still goes on growing. He is engaged in strengthening the law against the Socialists, as a counter-stroke to the international congress which is to come off this year.

France having disappointed her enemies and the enemies of progress by avoiding a political revolution which could have been but political only, is still busily engaged by means of her bourgeoisie in contributing her share to the embroglio of corruption which must end at last in deadlock and the fateful outbreak and change.

In Russia the universities are closed in order to damp down the revolutionary fire spreading so swiftly among the students, and everything grows more and more unbearable.

And with all this the year has ended as it began with the terror of a great European war, concerning which Lord Salisbury, wishing to make the best of it, could say little more than that he didn't think it would come just yet.

Certainly it must be said that the past year has not been of such a kind as to give confidence to the upholders of the stability of the present system. Democratic ideas tending towards Socialism have been evolved from the Irish struggle, and men's minds have been familiarized thereby with resistance to authority; the precariousness of livelihood under the capitalist has been brought home more and more among the workers, and the preaching of Socialism has inspired them with hope to change all that; the special tyranny of the last two months has embittered the Radicals against the Government, and also shown them how little they can depend on their so-called leaders among the Liberals, and how powerless they are as an affix to the Liberal party; it has shown them that they as working men must be true to their class or be of no account in politics at all; the sentences passed on the so-called rioters, after evidence which one would have expected even a lawyer to reject, have shown the 'lower classes' that the boasted equality before the law is a gross sham; that the law is made *for* the rich man and the master and *against* the poor man and the worker, and that when the class-war rises to its height, no more mercy will be shown by the 'moral' smug British bourgeois than by any tyrant of modern or ancient times; that law and civilization are no protection for those who may frighten the proprietary classes, and that the strong arm only will help them. All this has been speedy education towards revolution, and will sink deep into the mind of the people. Doubtless the past year has been a landmark on the road to revolution, and the reaction of which the stupid Tories and their allies the pessimistic prigs of 'culture' make so much of is but a measure of the advance of the tide of the new social life. 'Progress' no longer means a political game in which these high personages could take a part without any danger to their position, or offence to their sensibilities: the 'common people' have now to be dealt with as real persons threatening real things, and respectability shrinks back before them, partly in fear, partly in hatred. This explains the recrudescence of Toryism, the apparent victories of reaction. Once again the class-war is becoming obvious to all, and 1887 has done a great deal to make it so.

COMMONWEAL, VOLUME 4, NUMBER 104,
7 JANUARY 1888, PP. 4–5

RADICALS LOOK ROUND YOU!

The Winchester election is, it must be admitted, a shabby text to preach from: given, a cathedral establishment, a military depot, a middle-class public school, a large class of the villa-dwellers, and a noble lord as owner of a greater part of the town, and the result of an election in such a place would seem to be certain – the return of the Tory candidate – even if he were not a local magnate, and his opponent a mere name: only an electioneering agent on the look-out for a job one would think could venture to encourage opposition to the winning colour under such circumstances. However, the Liberals have chosen to make a kind of test-case of this most trumpery faction-fight as to whether the tide is still continuing to flow back to them, as other bye-elections (*sic*) seemed to show it was doing, and, since it has gone against them so completely they are bound to admit, and really do admit the inference, that the tide has turned again, and the Tory ship has weathered the dangerous headland for the present. All this, which is but an affair of 'ins and outs', would be a matter of complete indifference to us if it were not that there is still a Radical tail hanging on to the official Liberal party, and that the Radicals have been making towards Socialism under the educational influence of the Irish rebellion, and the general force of circumstances which is driving them out of their barren negative position, and forcing them to consider whether there is any forward road for them except Socialism. To the Radicals one may preach a little from even such a contemptible text as the Winchester election, and ask them once more whether they are going to be dragged about through the mud by their Liberal allies, or are going to give free play to their aspirations towards the popular cause, and assert themselves as men who are sincerely trying to learn what is to be done to carry the country out of this shabby period of the rule of the dregs of the bourgeoisie, helped by the distinguished cowards, knaves, and fools, for whom no worse name can be found at present than that of 'superior persons' or 'men of culture'.

I would ask them to note, then, that it did seem true towards the middle of last year that the Tory or Irish coercionist party seems (*sic*) to be losing ground, and that there did seem a chance of the Gladstonites shortly coming into power again, and victoriously 'settling' the Irish question; in which case the Radicals would have felt a glow of triumph, as feeling that after all it was a Radical victory rather than a Liberal one, and that they had led the whole of that constitutional party to the wished-for goal. This was the outlook then; but it is very different now; whatever the chapter of accidents may do in the future, the Tory Government is steady enough at present; that is really felt by everyone, and in the constitutional contest of 'ins and outs' the Liberals are not showing any signs of solicitude for their Radical allies, but are quite prepared to shake them off if need be; and, in short, we would seem to be further than ever from a Radical triumph. How has it all come about?

Let us remember that whatever it may be elsewhere, in this country the Government is always a genuine Government of the middle-classes; whatever is done is done for them, even though it may sometimes take the guise of helping the working-classes; and that only means helping such and such groups to manage the human machinery necessary to their welfare; most middle class men, 'thoughtful' or unthoughtful, never realize the fact that there is a working-class; the artisans or labourers that they may come across are to them but aspirants towards the middle-class, or failures from it, mere accidents of society in short. As long as this mood of the middle-class is undisturbed, as long as they are blankly ignorant of the composition of modern society, they can quite calmly divide themselves into two parties, Conservative and Liberal, or whatever else you may call them, it being, of course, understood that the greater part take no interest, or only a very languid one, in politics. But the events of the last five or six years, the change that has been coming over the commercial outlook, has made some inroads into this ignorance, and the Irish question, founded as it is on the further question 'How are the Irish peasants to live?' has also at last sorely shaken them, though at first it was looked upon as a mere political matter on which there might be difference of opinion between 'respectable' persons. As the English, Scotch, and Welsh working-men became educated into friendliness and sympathy with the Irish peasant, so the middle-class became educated into hatred of him. To them he is no longer now a romantic survival of past times of a rebellion made beautiful by distance, carrying about a preposterous sentiment of nationality never to be realized save as a flavour to a few old ballads sung to melancholy ancient tunes; he is a working-man asking for some of the property of the proprietary classes, and not too nice as to the means by which to establish his claim. And as on the one hand, new development of the Irish question made it clear to the middle-classes that it was time not to play with progress any longer, so on the other the putting forward of it by Mr Gladstone gave them an opportunity for backing out with that ease and dignity which the British hypocrite manages to impart to the action of sneaking out through a back door. The upshot is the 'Tory Reaction', as real a reaction as any political reaction ever is. What has happened is this: amongst political middle-class folk, the clearer-sighted once-Liberals, who could see witherward things are tending, have, as aforesaid, taken the opportunity of Gladstone's new departure to rat formally, leaving behind a group of Gladstonites whom habit and clinging to a vague shadowy habitual idea of principle keep in the ranks at present. That means breaking up the Liberal party; but there is more at the back of that. There is the great body of middle-class non-politicals, who include a great many 'superior persons;' these who usually have nothing to do with the political game are, nevertheless, an enormously powerful body; they form, in fact, what the newspapers mean when they speak of 'the public'; and this 'public', which is fully equipped with votes, goes solid for the Tory reaction, and is, in fact, the central and really noteworthy part of it. This public has a blind and instinctive, but quite genuine hatred of the 'other public', the 'lower classes', whose misery it has made and lives upon: it usually only acts as a dead weight to keep them down, but from time to time takes vigorous action enough. It is the public which applauded Napoleon the Little and the Butchers of the Commune, smiled safe approval on the slaying of the Chicago martyrs, egged on the evictions of Irish tenants for the behoof of the shabby tyrants who rob their poverty, shut up Trafalgar Square, beat helpless prisoners in their cells, and makes the disgraceful pedant Stephen feel safe and comfortable on his seat of iniquity; it is the public which will make civil war inevitable as the claims of the workers rise, and are more distinctly formulated; it is, in short, the real danger to what of genuine society yet exists amongst us; the mass of blind wrong-doing led by 'superior persons' who know what is right and hate it, who have made wrong their right. Now it may be said, 'surely the Tories could always rely on the support of this criminal class, how is it that it was thought last summer that the present Government was tending towards its defeat on the Irish matter?' The answer is, the Tories were then only *threatening* coercion, and soft as the Gladstonites were fighting they seemed strong enough to deal with their political foes, considering the conversion of the working-men, which at least on the Irish question, was going on. We did not believe that the threat of coercion would be seriously carried out; but it seems that the Tories had estimated the relative voting power of the working-class, and the above-mentioned criminal class, better than we had, and knew that they were safe, and accordingly started fair on their new career of Resolute Government, which will carry them who can say where, but in the meantime has gained them the enthusiastic support of the whole non-political middle-classes. Let our Radical friends note that for the present, and until the times get 'quiet', these ordinary non-political people are turned into ardent politicians with one aim in view, the keeping down of the popular element amongst us, by whatever name it may be called, and that this support will keep the Tories in power for many a day, while all the political opposition they (the Tories) will meet with will come from a party pledged, it is true, to grant Home Rule in Ireland (a pledge which may be as easily evaded as other pledges have been), but so far from being pledged to help the whole people out of their misery, that they also, when events press hardly on them, will have to take obvious measures to keep the people down, and avail themselves of the support of that party of blind wrong-doing.

The Radical *party* is effaced from the Parliamentary record, because its education towards progress had been advancing. Let all true Radicals take advantage of that effacement by educating themselves yet further; let them set to work seriously to learn what those popular claims are which the Liberal leaders steadily refuse to consider, but which form the only politics worth attending to. It is true that if they do this they will soon find themselves Socialists and outcasts; but they will be recompensed for that when the time comes, as it soon will, when all distinctions of party will merge into the two camps, of the people and their haters, for they will then know clearly why they are on the right side, as they will have joined it consciously and not by mere compulsion. I believe that many Radicals are now taking this course, and I would encourage them to think that all these apparent Tory victories are only so many signs of the enlightenment of the workers of their own interests, and the consequent development of the middle-class hatred against them.

COMMONWEAL, VOLUME 4, NUMBER 105,
14 JANUARY 1888, PP. 12–13

ON SOME 'PRACTICAL' SOCIALISTS

The study of economics is no doubt necessary for militant Socialists; the more a man knows of them in all their details the more able he is to meet not only the sophistries of the 'educated' anti-Socialist, but, which is still more important, the awkward and hard-to-be-answered questions which people who have never thought of these matters at all sometimes stumble on.

Of course, that he should be able to make his knowledge of any use depends on whether he has understood what he has learned, especially in dealing with enquiring ignorance. The 'educated' man will sometimes be floored by a phrase, will retire abashed before 'surplus value', and refuse to tackle the iron law of wages, on the same grounds that the Oxford undergraduate declined to give his examiner any information about King David for fear he should be lugged all through the Kings of Judah and Israel; but the ignorant man may require information after he has got over the first shock of the unaccustomed enunciation of the big-worded dogma. So that our student of economy had best be careful to look to it that he can translate his phrases into a language 'understanded of the people'. But when our learner has really got to know something about economics; nay, when he has them at his fingers ends, he still has to beware of another trap, or rather of two more. He has (for as old a Socialist as he may be) to take care that he does not read the present into the future, to suppose that when the monopoly in the means of production has been abolished, and no one can any more live on the labour of others, but must do some recognized service to the community in order to earn his livelihood, yet, nevertheless, people's ways of life and habits of thought will be pretty much as they are now. The other trap generally besets the way of the same kind of Socialist who is apt to fall into the first-named; it is the too entire absorption in the economic view of Socialism, and the ignoring of all its other aspects.

The kind of Socialist who is most likely to be caught by these traps is he who considers himself as specially practical; although the due deduction from the last one at any rate would be the abstention from action of all kinds, and the acceptance of the position of an interested but helpless spectator. Your 'practical' man is (very naturally) anxious that some step towards Socialism should be taken at once, and also that it should be taken under definitely Socialist auspices, therefore, he really addresses himself to people who would be likely to be frightened into mere hostility by any apprehension of a large change in the life of Society; he is thinking entirely of the conservative side of human nature as the thing to be won over, and ignores that which exists justs (*sic*) as surely, its revolutionary side. The result is that the wolf of Socialism gets clad in the respectable sheeps-skin of a mild economic change; yet not with much success. I have been present on several occasions when this experiment has been tried, and have been much amused by the demeanour of the respectables, who trying to be convinced, or at least to appear to be, have nevertheless showed uneasiness, as if they detected the disguised animal, and noted his glistening teeth and red jaws peeping out from under the soft woolly clothing of moderate progress. Also, though it was less amusing, it was as instructive to note the look of those convinced but not fully instructed Socialists who were present, on whom the sight of the transmogrified sham amiable monster produced nothing but blank disappointment and dismay. Altogether, these occasions have been to me hours of humiliation and discouragement; and I think also that there was no gain in the humiliation; neither I nor the other comrades needed to undergo it. The opponents were not won over by it, they were only confused and puzzled, and made feel as if they had been laughed at.

But I do not mean to say that these one-sided Socialists are generally acting disingenuously, or merely trying to smooth down a hostile audience. I believe, on the contrary, that they do not see except through the murky smoked glass of the present condition of life amongst us; and it seems somewhat strange, not that they should have no vision of the future, but that they should not be ready to admit that it is their own defect that they have not. Surely they must allow that such a stupendous change in the machinery of life as the abolition of capital and wages must bring about a corresponding change in ethics and habits of life; that it would be impossible to desire many things which are now the main objects of desire; needless to guard against many eventualities which we now spend our lives in guarding against; that, in short, we shall burn what we once adored, and adore what we once burned.

Is it conceivable, for instance, that the change for the present wage-earners will simply mean hoisting them up into the life of the present 'refined' middle-classes, and that the latter will remain pretty much what they are now, minus their power of living on the labour of others? To my mind it is inconceivable; but if I could think such a prospect likely, I should join with Mr Bradlaugh (whose idea of the aims of Socialism is probably just this) in a protest against the dull level of mediocrity. What! will, *eg.*, the family of the times when monopoly is dead be still as it is now in the middle-classes, framed on the model of that of an affectionate and moral tiger to whom all is prey a few yards from the sanctity of the domestic hearth? Will the body of the woman we love be but an appendage to her property? Shall we try to cram our lightest whim as a holy dogma into our children, and be bitterly unhappy when we find that they are growing up to be men and women like ourselves? Will education be a system of cram begun on us when we are four years old, and left off sharply when we are eighteen? Shall we be ashamed of our love and our hunger and our mirth, and believe that it is wicked of us not to try to dispense with the joys that accompany procreation of our species, and the keeping of ourselves alive, those joys of desire which make us understand that the beasts too may be happy? Shall we all, in short, as the 'refined' middle-classes now do, wear ourselves away in the anxiety to stave off all trouble, emotion, and responsibility, in order that we may at last merge all our troubles into one, the trouble that we have been born for nothing but to be afraid to die? All this which is now the life of refined civilization will be impossible then.

I have often thought with a joyful chuckle how puzzling, nay inexplicable to the generations of freedom, will be those curious specimens of human ingenuity called novels now produced, and which present with such faithful detail the lives of the middle-classes, all below them being ignored except as so many stage accessories; amongst them all, perhaps, Dickens will still be remembered; and that because of what is now imputed to him as a fault, his fashioning a fantastic and unreal world for his men and women to act in. Surely here again all will be changed, and our literature will sympathize with the earlier works of men's imagination before they learned to spin out their own insides like silkworms into dreary yarns of their sickly feelings and futile speculations; when they left us clear pictures of living things, alive then and for ever. We shall not desire and we shall not be able to carry on the feverish and perverted follies of the art and literature of Commercialism.

I wonder that those who will insist in reading the life of the present into a world economically changed, do not see how they start wrong from the beginning; and I wonder all the more as they are often clear-headed and capable persons.

The competition of the profit-market forces us under our present system to turn our attention overmuch to producing wares with the least possible labour; our epoch is compelled to sacrifice everything to this necessity. Considering the aspect of London and our great manufacturing centres, for instance, it seems that if it were possible for us to go on for long at our present rate of sacrificing to this tyrant of cheap production, the time would come when having to choose between the greater part of us living in cellars and never seeing the sun again, and foregoing the cheapening of cotton cloth by a halfpenny a yard, we should be compelled to choose to submit ourselves to the former – inconvenience. This I say is our necessity at present, because the competition for profits, which is the master of production, is a system of mere waste, first as a war and next as a bonfire, so to say, for the consumption of the product of labour merely in the interests of the power of the proprietary classes. Or may we not say that the gentilities, the luxuries, the pomp of these classes in an ascending scale, from the small villa dweller to the great territorial magnate, are the necessary baits held out to the producing classes to ensure their 'content' with the present state of things. 'It is true', they proclaim, 'that you are in an inferior position now, because you belong to the useful class; but there is no legal disability preventing you from rising out of that class; by means of thrift, self-denial, and clever rapacity, you may attain to this nice stuccoed villa with its 'art objects' and nick-knacks, its smiling obsequious servants, and vacant wife and daughters dressed up to the nine; next, as you grow older and colder and stupider, this mansion awaits you with all the 'refinements of civilization,' flunkies, libraries, parties, seats in Parliament and the rest of it; and at last, when you have really come to believe in yourself as a benefactor to the human race, because you, once the robbed, have become a robber on the very largest scale, here is your park with its surrounding acres, and the state and majesty of a landed gentleman amongst the toilers afield who have even less than you began with when you were a useful man. There shall you found a family, take a peerage, and die universally respected.'

Expensive baits these! Yet necessary while classes last, since the lapse of time has evolved us out of the simpler systems of chattel slavery and serfdom.

I won't go into figures as to the cost of these two gulfs of waste necessary to the stability of our present system, the waste of commercial war, the waste of the supporting a proprietary class with all its camp-followers and hangers-on; nor do I suppose that we shall ever know how prodigious a waste we have saddled ourselves with in this matter; but it is clear that it *is* prodigious. Well, under the new conditions of Society commercial war will have died out, and with it the wasteful occupations that support it; and class-rule will have disappeared, so that its waste will have gone; labour will no longer be directed in the interest of the profit-grinder or the idler, and the task of the producers will be so easy, that the dogma which our pessimist friends now hold that men will always do their work in the way which gives them least trouble (understood whatever sacrifices they have to make for it), will cease to have any meaning; because there will practically be no longer any compulsion to work.

Mark Twain says, apropos of Tom Sawyer's white-washing, that work is labour that we are compelled to do, and pleasure labour that we choose to do, which we beg our economico-pessimist friends to remember.

Meantime, I hold that we need not be afraid of scaring our audiences with too brilliant pictures of the future of Society, nor think ourselves unpractical and utopian for telling them the bare truth, that in destroying monopoly we shall destroy our present civilization. On the contrary, it is utopian to put forward a scheme of gradual logical reconstruction of society which is liable to be overturned at the first historical hitch it comes to; and if you tell your audiences that you are going to change so little that they will scarcely feel the change, whether you scare any one or not, you will certainly not interest those who have nothing to hope for in the present Society, and whom the hope of a change has attracted towards Socialism. It is a poor game to play (though so often played in politics) to discourage your friends in order to hoodwink your foes for a brief space. And certainly the Socialists who are always preaching to people that Socialism is an economic change pure and simple, are very apt to repel those who want to learn for the sake of those who do not.

COMMONWEAL, VOLUME 4, NUMBER 110,
18 FEBRUARY 1888, PP. 52–53

A TRIPLE ALLIANCE

The struggle for the elementary right of freedom of speech, of which the events of Bloody Sunday formed such a dramatic episode, is taking a new development. The police onslaught of November 13th, and the subsequent reactionary tyranny of the Government, came as a surprise on the genuine Radicals who took part in the proceedings of that disastrous and shameful day: and it can hardly be doubted that the orthodox Liberals were also surprised at it; but their surprise took the form of striking them dumb as well as deedless. Comment has been made in these columns on the dastardliness of their behaviour, which, all things considered, was not astonishing, as well as on its stupidity, which really was almost astonishing. For here had the Tories put a weapon in their hands of a like nature to that which they were using so eagerly in Ireland, and yet they let it tumble to the ground and lie there; thus practically admitting their real alliance with the very men they are formally contending with in the Parliamentary game. So much for Mr Gladstone's British following, and, grievous as it is to say it, his Irish allies behaved no better. Here one has some right to be surprised: how could it be that they did not see the force of the argument ready to their mouths, 'You Englishmen, you Londoners, have coerced and gagged Ireland, with the result that you are coerced and gagged; join you with us, as we will with you, to get rid of coercion and gagging altogether, or else you will suffer along with us'?

And moreover, in joining heartily in our protest they would have been even formally pushing their own cause; the meeting on Bloody Sunday was called to protest against the wrong done to an Irishman and Ireland, and every man in the bludgeoned processions was an enthusiastic Home Ruler. Yet no one spoke or stirred, except, to be fair, Mr Bradlaugh, mindful of his old struggles in the Square. It was left for the Socialists only, helped in the press by the professed democratic and workman's paper, *Reynolds*, and the *Pall Mall Gazette*, which for the time at least became almost a Socialist journal.

Nevertheless, so fragrant was the case, so open was the intention to thrust forward the merest absolutism, so disgracefully unfair was the conduct of the courts that tried the 'rioters', and so savagely vindictive the sentences passed on them, that the conspiracy of silence has failed at least as far as London is concerned; and the Southwark election, which otherwise would have been a matter of little importance, showed, as is admitted on all sides, that the London workmen understand the subject of Trafalgar Square much better than their so-called 'leaders'.

This fact has at last penetrated the numskulls (*sic*) of the orthodox Liberals, and it [is] said that the wily old politician who 'leads' them is going to contribute his 'old stager' wisdom to the debate on Trafalgar Square, which is (perhaps) to come off on Thursday: nay, that the very dissentient Liberals themselves have taken the alarm, and are meditating a little dishing of the Glastonians.

Meantime, the meeting of Monday 20th, which was called to welcome Burns and Graham, became under these circumstances a demonstration of a triple alliance for freedom of speech between the Irish, the Radicals, and the Socialists. We are bound to hope that this alliance will give back Trafalgar Square to the people, and put the whole matter of open-air meeting on a better footing than it is at present; but it will only do so if the rank and file of the Irish and Radicals are determined to make a genuine alliance with their Socialist brethren, whatever the leaders may do: it is their business if they are in earnest in upholding freedom of speech throughout the country to look to it that the Liberals do not use it merely as a good electioneering cry for London, to be cast aside on the first opportunity. At the meeting of the 20th the Radical part of their audience were loud in their boast that they could win the right of free speech from the reactionists by the ballot box. So be it! They are certainly not prepared to win it by physical force or the threat of it; though for my part I must think that rather their shame than their glory; and also that it is impolitic to cry out to such an enemy as they are facing (if they are in earnest) 'Do what you will with us, if we cannot out-vote you, you are safe'. However, let that pass; they are *not* prepared to carry the matter by force, and they think they can by voting. Well, then, at least let them vote hard and not soft; let them exact a pledge from every candidate to support the freedom of speech in Trafalgar Square and open spaces generally, and refuse to vote for anyone who will not give this pledge unreservedly, whether he calls himself Liberal, Radical, or Home Ruler. If they do less than this they may be sure of one thing, that the attitude of the Liberals when they come into power will be pretty much that of the Tories; and they will find after all that they will be driven to use force if they really want to speak out their grievances in public. For after all, it will one day be just as inconvenient to the Liberals as to the Tories that the people should claim what they want by means of public meetings, and whatever opinions the majority in the House of Commons may profess, the Executive will always do its best to silence the people, unless it is repeating parrot-fashion the words put into its mouth by its masters.

As to whether the mass of the Radicals are prepared to assert themselves, and will pluck up heart of grace to beard their leaders, from all that is past one cannot help being very doubtful about that. If they are not, they are exciting themselves very unnecessarily about getting rid of the Tories, who will in that case answer all their purposes quite as well. They may make use of the Liberal party to carry on democracy to the point when it must melt into Socialism; if they do not, they will be made use of to get a party into office, which, as far as any practical purpose is concerned, is composed of leaders who will not lead, and of followers who have got nothing to follow.

Commonweal, Volume 4, Number 112,
3 March 1888, p. 68

DEAD AT LAST

The flood of cant and servility which has been poured out by the bourgeois press during the last few days, because the long-expected death of [Frederick III Emperor of Germany] a tyrant of the old type embedded in a modern type of tyranny, has at last happened, disgusts one so much that at first one is tempted to keep silence in mere contempt for such degraded nonsense. Court mourning is always a preposterous spectacle, but here is a case where it is more preposterous than usual. Conventional universal grief, when scarcely any one is grieved at the event, no one whose interests do not suffer by it, most people are profoundly indifferent, and a great many cannot help being glad, although the death of this man may make no immediate difference in the condition of the people who suffered from his life – what *can* one say of this?

Yet though silence may be best in the abstract, it may be misunderstood at a time when even democratic papers, which are busy advocating federalism, profess to share more or less in the sham sentiment of the day which weeps strange tears indeed over the death-bed of this tough specimen of the ancient absolutist lined by the modern centralizer. As a Socialist print, the *Commonweal* is an outlaw from the press, and its poverty and desolate freedom compels it to speech, though but of a few words.

For what the death of this sham mediæval tyrant calls our attention to is a weighty and serious matter enough in spite of the nothingness of the man himself. The ancient and obviously irrational absolutism is gone from Europe except for the tottering throne of the Czar of the Russias; but the house of Hohenzollern has gathered to itself whatever of dangerous and practical in absolutism still exists, and has built up of it a fortress of the new bureaucratic absolutism as a last refuge to the capitalistic civilization of our day, and has put a face of rationality and business capacity on it, so that the scarcely less grievous tyranny of constitutional bureaucracy under which we suffer might reach out a hand to it unashamed; and so helpful have our masters felt this fortress to be to the system which enables them to rob the people at home, that even the elevation by its builders of the Germans into a holy race of military and commercial conquerors which may one day swallow them up also, has not scared them from accepting their friendship.

Abundance of patience, energy, skill, almost genius, have been expended in this attack on the progress of humanity, but not only these qualities were needed, and the most has been made of persons who could serve as instruments towards it, although they had no qualities but the blindness and dogged hardness inbred by their position. Of these instruments the person just dead was as fit for his post as might be, just as Bismark (*sic*) and Moltke have been fit for theirs; though the German centralizing absolutism is modern, a monarch or figure-head of the modern type would not have suited it as well as what was ready to its hand for the purpose, a mere stupidly implacable soldier without any capacity for doubt or remorse. The man who began his career of 'glory' by the slaughter of citizens in the streets of Berlin in '48, was a proper tool for the statesmen who saw the necessity of the system, which had bred them, of 'educating' Germany by constant wars of ambition, and was not likely to shrink from the last success of a hideous race war, which will when all is said, lead to events that these pests of humanity were far from foreseeing.

Plainly then, the somewhat timid whitewashing by the Radical press of this figure-head of the most dangerous form of absolutism is a sorry business, and I must say sincerely that the German people are not likely to thank our press for it. Even the *Daily News* is compelled to allude to the Berlin massacres, though it speaks of them as an event to be lightly passed over, a venial offence, to be expected (as indeed it was) of a person in the position of its hero. But are the people of Berlin forgetting it? Are they really worshipping the memory of the pious hero of Sedan? If this is true of even a part of the population, it can only be said that it shows into what depths of degradation the vice of patriotism can lead people – of patriotism, that is, the cultivation of national rancour founded on the national development of selfish greed which is the basis of civilized society.

One thing, at least, we should not forget, and that is the protest of the German Socialists in the teeth of all the jingoism newly stirred up by the danger and excitement of the occasion, against the race-war which Bismark (*sic*) and his willing puppets were leading Germany into in the interests of law and order, to whom the death and suffering of hundreds of thousands of men, women and children, is a light matter, so only that the people may be kept down....

COMMONWEAL, VOLUME 4, NUMBER 114,
17 MARCH 1888, P. 81

A Speech from the Dock

Our comrade John Burn's speech before Mr Justice Charles has been printed in full. It is one of those documents which will one day be eagerly sought after as illustrating a remarkable period in the Social Revolution in which we are now all of us taking a part. It is called a speech in defence of the defendant, but in point of fact, considering the nature of the evidence brought forward in support of the ridiculous charges made against our friends Burns and Graham, no defence was needed, except against the legal quibble by which the defendants were found guilty of illegal assembly and sent to jail for having committed this crime. Under these circumstances Burns' speech really took the form of an indictment against the society which had been terrified by the meeting of a few of its victims under the name of the unemployed; and which in its terror, egged on by the bourgeois press, eager to make a sensation of anything that came handy, and the tradesmen of London who pretended to think their trade was in danger, got the meeting of the 13th November proclaimed and manufactured the riots of Bloody Sunday.

Socialists may well be glad this speech has been printed, in which Burns has clearly shown that this fear of the unemployed was the genuine cause of the closing of Trafalgar Square, since it has been the fashion of the half-hearted Radical, and no-hearted Liberal MP's who have been driven to take up the matter, to dwell on the point that the meeting on the 13th was a genuine political meeting and was on a different footing to those that had been held there before during last autumn. Whatever significance there was about that meeting was given to it by the previous meetings and the treatment they had met with;

and I repeat that a meeting merely to protest against Irish wrongs would not have been proclaimed. Burns and Graham went to jail on behalf of the unemployed, and for the matter of that for the employed also; those who are employed to produce wealth which their employers and not themselves enjoy. Our comrade did well then to keep their case so stoutly before the court, and to take coolly whatever might befal (*sic*) him from the partisan judge who tried him. All Socialists should be well acquainted with their comrade's defence, not of himself but of them.

Commonweal, Volume 4, Number 115,
24 March 1888, p. 93

SOCIALISM MILITANT IN SCOTLAND

Since a year may make a good deal of difference in the position of a party, even when it is being carried on by quiet propaganda, I give a brief account of my lecturing tour in Scotland and my impressions of the position of Socialism there. On the 21st March I lectured at Kilmarnock, a not very important town on the edge of the mining district. The chief industry in the town itself is that of the railway works – a tolerably good indication, by the way, of labour being cheap in the neighbourhood; accordingly I was informed that the iron-miners in the neighbourhood are earning about nine shillings a-week working four days a-week, and that the coal-miners in the neighbourhood are not much better off. I spoke in the church of Mr Forrest, my inviter. The audience was fair as to numbers; they were not demonstrative, and it was found impossible to get them to ask any questions; they were, however, very attentive, and showed their interest in the subject by buying over 10s. worth of literature. A large proportion of the audience seemed to me to be of the middle-classes. A branch of the Scottish Land and Labour League has just been formed here, but I was told that the town was hard to move.

The following Friday produced a failure. Our Edinburgh comrades had taken a large hall for my lecture in Leith (not being able to get a smaller one), but only five persons turned up besides the branch, who showed up well; so the money was returned and we gave it up. However, seeing plenty of people hanging about in the street as we went homeward rather sadly, we started an open-air meeting, and got together upwards of 200 persons, who listened for an hour and a half to me and some of the members of the branch, though the snow presently began to come down fast.

The next day I went to West Calder, a mining village some half-hour's railway ride from Edinburgh. We did not expect much of a meeting on a Saturday evening in such a place, especially as a very moderate amount of advertising had been used; but some of our Edinburgh comrades got down there, and did their best to get an audience by beginning in the open air; the bell-man – or rather, the bell-boy – was sent round also, and we got together some sixty persons, all work-men, into the room, which was thought very good considering the circumstances. They made an excellent audience as to attention and spirit. In the ensuing discussion, one person put forward as an objection a point which I see is made the most of by a well-known hand in *To-day* – to wit, that Socialism will produce wealth so abundantly and easily that we should not find work enough to do, and should deteriorate in consequence. The audience, mostly miners, obviously thought that this was an objection which might be passed over for the present, and were much tickled by the objector's persistency in his threats of a life of ease.

The Edinburgh Whig rag, the *Scotsman*, by the way, paid me the compliment of publishing a paragraph on this meeting, which implied that I could not get an audience and came away with nothing done; and when I wrote to contradict its statement, favoured its readers with an explanation which was a model of the suppression of truth and suggestion of untruth. It is a matter of course that this journal goes out of its way to treat our friends unfairly.

On Sunday I went to Glasgow; and here I had every reason to damn 'the nature of things' as heartily as Porson did when he hit his head against the doorpost; for it came on to snow at about one o'clock and snowed till the time of meeting harder than I ever saw it snow, so that by 7.30 [the] Glasgow streets were more than ancle-deep (*sic*) in half-frozen slush, and I made up my mind to an audience of fifty in a big hall; however it was not as bad as that, for it mustered over 500, who passed *nem. con.* a resolution in favour of Socialism. Owing to the weather, our comrades could not attempt the preliminary open-air meetings which they had intended to do; so I passed the day with them in their rooms in John Street, very much to my own pleasure, as without flattery they were, as I have always found them, hearty good fellows and thorough Socialists. All political parties in Glasgow have been depressed of late, they told me, and the Socialists have partly shared in this depression, though not as much as other bodies; but the knowledge of the movement and sympathy with it have grown very much, and our comrades are in good heart about it. The first novelty of the subject has worn off, and those who attend the meetings now are those who look upon the matter seriously. This is the view taken by our comrades wherever I went, and from all I could see I thought it the accurate one.

Perhaps the next day's meeting (Monday) at Edinburgh tended to show this. It was a miserable night again, and we did not expect an audience of dilettanti – and did not get it. It was about as numerous as I got last year under better circumstances, but differed from that in having scarcely any middle-class persons in it. As to quality, it was one of the very best audiences I ever spoke to, and missed no point in the lecture. In fact in Edinburgh at least I seem to have exhausted the sympathies (?) of those who came at first to amuse themselves over the eccentricities of a literary man, and only those are left who really want to take counsel about the one question worth considering – how to free our minds and bodies from capitalistic tyranny. We had the usual treat afforded us by one Mr Job Bone, who attends and opposes all meetings, and who used to be thought a nuisance, but is now accepted as a convenient shoeing-horn to a discussion, and whose malicious folly is useful in drawing out the lecturer to explain matters that might otherwise remain unnoticed.

The next day I went to Dundee, where I had much the same kind of audience, except that there were more middle-class persons amongst it, who made themselves useful by asking questions easily answered, but (I hope) in a way not satisfactory to them, though very much so to the working-men present. One of the questioners was the sub-editor of the Radical paper, and I answered an unfair question of his with some warmth, so I was not surprised at getting a very curt report next morning; whereas the Tory journal reported us fairly and well. The audience was very hearty and appreciative. There is a branch here of the Scottish Land and Labour League, manned by energetic workers, whose work, however, is difficult, because ordinary party politics run high in Dundee, and the Radicals there have not got further than the Gladstoneite programme, if it can be called a programme.

From Dundee I went to Aberdeen, where I found another branch of the SLLL, including some energetic and intelligent men, a good deal kept down, as might be expected, by the ordinary Radicalism of the place, and some of whom, I think I may say consequently, are rather eager to try parliamentary agitation. Another stormy and wretched evening made me expect a thin audience; but the hall, which was a small one, was filled. The audience was mostly middle-class here, and rather heavy to lift, though attentive and not disposed to carp. The press reported the meeting carefully and well next morning.

If I could have, I would have visited Carnoustie, a mere village between Aberdeen and Dundee, but which has a good branch; but time was getting on, and I had promised to assist at a social gathering of our Edinburgh comrades on Thursday evening. I had a pleasant and interesting evening with them; and so finished what I came to do.

On the whole, in spite of some poor audiences (though the weather largely accounts for that), I was very favourably impressed by the outlook for Socialism in Scotland. There can be no doubt that much progress has been made since last year, in the teeth of great difficulties. As aforesaid, the novelty has worn off; respectability is beginning to see what Socialism really means, and doesn't like the look of it at all; the press is deadly hostile, and not ashamed of any meanness in its treatment of the movement; those who are dependent on 'employers' need expect no mercy from them if they are spotted as Socialists; the traditional puritanism of the country throws additional obstacles in the way of propaganda, – and with all this the movement is gaining ground steadily, and has an appearance of solidity about it which is most encouraging. I saw most of our Edinburgh comrades, and they seem to me to have entered on a new stage of the movement, and to promise to be as staunch as may be. The progress they have made since last year is remarkable.

COMMONWEAL, VOLUME 4, NUMBER 117,
7 APRIL 1888, PP. 106–107

THE REACTION AND THE RADICALS

The other day a friend was remarking to me that the ordinary Liberal and Radical of the Parliamentary type was very slack in his resistance to the Tory supremacy in these days; and in spite of the brags of the Gladstonian press, it must be admitted that this is true, after making all the allowances that can be made for the apparently brisk conflict over Irish matters: for that conflict is really in the hands of the Irish themselves; Mr Parnell's causing the Irish vote to be cast in favour of the Tories in 1885 forced Mr Gladstone's hand. Up to that time the Liberals had reckoned on the general support of the Irish Parliamentary Party, but after it they understood that that support must be bought by the yielding to Irish demands; that is in the main the plain story of the Gladstonian conversion. And the terms of the bargain so made have to be kept, as the Irish are at hand to enforce them, and Mr Gladstone himself as usual puts considerable energy into the work which lies ready to his hand. Hence the appearance of a stout battle between the Ins and Outs in Parliament, which, however, as has often been said, is by no means to the taste of the greater part of the Liberal Gladstonites. They will be heartily glad when it is over, especially if, as is probable, and as Lord Randolph Churchill's conduct the other night indicated, it ends in a compromise.

But the Irish matters shelved for a time and the Liberals set free from their bargain, what is to follow as the immediate future of that respectable party? Who can answer that question that believes in the continued existence of a Liberal party in Great Britain? Mr Gladstone has in all probability taken his last forward step in politics; and Mr John Morley, who is considered (Lord help us!) to be the leader of the advanced (respectable) party, has already pretty much declared himself for the sign-post of democracy as it was understood twenty years ago. In fact the future, or indeed the present, of the Liberal party is now prefigured by those uninteresting sea-shores on the south coast of England, where the land having grown wheat and marigold and turnips, and having fallen into inferior pasture, is at last nothing but a flat waste of sand with a few tufts of useless herbs dotted here and there upon it, and so goes dwindling down into the sea in an undramatic inglorious fashion. Having performed mechanically the part that has been forced upon it in the Irish struggle, there is an end of it in mere barren officialism and the hopes of another term or two of do-nothing government. The great obstructionist party will swallow it up, regretted by no one.

Meantime, what about the few Radicals who at present hang on to it, and can hardly be called a party, since so many of them have gone through the same proceedings with the Liberals as the latter have done with the Tories, and been swallowed up by them? Well, the few that can still be called Radicals – that is, men who really wish to move forward if they only knew how – are being paralysed by the approaching death of the Liberal party, the tail of which they have hitherto formed. Their hope in that direction has vanished, and their occupation has gone with it; what have they to turn towards? Whether they are conscious of it or not, they are waiting for Socialism to take up the work of progress. They are not convinced Socialists; many of them probably have never taken the trouble to understand what Socialism means; but they are nevertheless waiting for its approach, and that is the reason why they are so unenergetic in the face of the Tory reaction, which reaction – a real thing enough – means the absorption of the Liberals into the party of obstruction: an obstruction which is modern and suitable to its date, and therefore does not put persons of cultivation and intellect, 'superior persons', to shame; which differs by the compulsion of surrounding conditions from the old compulsion, but not at all in spirit.

Well, these Radicals turned languid in action because of the circumstances in which they find themselves, are very decidedly waiting: they are still Radicals, and in theory can see no further than the old shibboleths; but they instinctively know that in practice all that is no longer of any use, and they are consequently expecting orders from Socialism. Their position is, that they wish to go on being Radicals, and to do Socialist work if they can only find out what is, without declaring for Socialism.

In short, the old democracy, whose watchword is the fullest liberty of 'free contract', is finding out that before its theory could be worked out to the utmost, Socialism has come upon it and thrown it out of date, although the obstructionists of the old type are still making a show of attacking it, as if it were yet alive. Radicalism proper can live no longer than the life of Toryism proper; when the obstructionists cease to attack 'the freedom of contract', or rather when they make it their own standing-ground, as they are now doing, the Radical loses his reason for existence – his function is at [an] end.

The obstructionists or Tories represent personal and political slavery, which was once, but a very long time ago, a necessity for progress; the Radicals represent the economical slavery of a class, joined to political freedom, which was also once a necessity for progress, but not so long ago; the Socialists represent progress itself with no temporary veil distorting its features.

Commonweal, Volume 4, Number 121,
5 May 1888, pp. 137–138

THE POLICY OF THE SOCIALIST LEAGUE

Since the Socialist League was founded to support the principles of International Revolutionary Socialism, and since there has been some difference of opinion amongst us as to the meaning of those words, the Council of the League thinks it its duty to point out what in its opinion that meaning is, as expressed by publications of the League, which at the time of their publication were not challenged by any of its branches or members; and in doing this the Council wishes to disclaim any narrowing of the principles of the League beyond what it believes has been recognized from the first as necessary to give it a reason for existence separate from that of other Socialist bodies.

The aim of the Socialist League, therefore, is the realization of a society based on equality of condition for all persons without distinction of race, sex or creed; a society which will not recognize the right of any privilege to interfere with that equality, whether such privilege rests its claim on birth, wealth or capacity in the individual.

The League holds that the necessary step to the realization of this society is the abolition of monopoly in the means of production, which should be *owned* by no individual, but by the whole community, in order that the *use* of them may be free to all according to their capacity: this we believe would necessarily lead to the equality of condition above-mentioned, and the recognition of the maxim '*from* each according to his capacity, *to* each according to his needs'.

It is necessary to explain here that some Socialists believe this first step, the abolition of monopoly in the means of production is the *end* of Socialism, and that the society so founded will admit of competition for the relative shares of the wealth produced for use; although it is obvious that success in such competition can only be attained by the successful at the expense of the unsuccessful, and thus new classes would be formed which would take the place of those destroyed by the abolition of monopoly. On this point, therefore, the Socialist League differs in its aim or ideal of society from some other Socialists.

Again, the League believes, when it speaks of *International* Socialism, that the word internationalism applies only to the present state of slavery, as expressing that the workers do not recognize the national distinctions made by their masters, and that in the society of the future, nations as political entities will cease to exist, and give place to the federation of communities bound together by locality or convenience. Here again the League differs from some Socialists who cannot see so far as the abolition of nationality, and this again implies a difference in ideal.

As to the means for the attainment of the abolition of the private ownership of the means of production, and through that to equality of condition for all persons, the League believes that the first and most indispensable of such means is the putting before the people its aims, ultimate and immediate, plainly and honestly, and has always acted on that belief; in the confidence that however strange these aims may be to the greater number of persons, the time will come when circumstances will force the workers to accept them as their own, and that it is no waste of energy meantime to familiarize them with these aims and thereby to quicken their desires and give something for their intelligence to seize hold of, and for their hope to feed on. The education of the vague discontent which (happily) is now so prevalent among the workers into a definite aim, is the chief business of the Socialist League; nor can this work ever be dispensed with even on the very eve of the first obvious and open steps towards revolution.

There are other Socialists, however, and they are numerous enough, who are not contented with the slow and patience-trying work of getting the workers to understand their position and the remedies for it. They cannot believe that anything is being done unless attempts are being made to get Socialists into Parliament, and other elected bodies; although it is clear that these bodies are the most direct expression of the power of our enemies, and their intention to put down all attempts towards the regeneration of society; and though the passing of a few palliative measures is the utmost that could be hoped from Socialists in Parliament until the time when the people are strong enough to destroy Parliament itself.

The Socialist League has declared over and over again its sense of the futility of Socialists wasting their time in getting such palliative measures passed, which, if desirable to be passed as temporarily useful, will be passed much more readily if they do not mix themselves up in the matter, and which are at least intended by our masters to hinder Socialism and not to further it. Over and over again it has deprecated Socialists mixing themselves up in political intrigues; and it believes no useful purpose can be served by their running after the votes of those who do not understand the principles of Socialism, and who therefore must be attracted by promises which could not be fulfilled by the candidates if by any chance such candidates were returned to Parliament. The two last Annual Conferences of the League have declared by large majorities of the delegates assembled that it was the policy of the League to abstain from parliamentary action, and have refused to allow any alteration of this policy.

The Council of the Socialist League therefore feels itself bound frankly to point out the impossibility of propaganda by electioneering coexisting with the educational propaganda *in the same body* to any good purpose. Those holding the two sets of ideas will and must mutually hamper each other, even where their root-principles do not differ widely; and this all the more as the advocates of propaganda by electioneering must feel how heavy their task is, and that they *must* begin at once with it and insist early and late on the necessity of turning all our attention to getting Socialists into Parliament by any means feasible. The Council of the Socialist League believes that there will for a long time be this difference of opinion as to the method of propaganda, and thinks itself justified not only in pointing out the evil effects of contesting the point within the League itself, but also in appealing to those Socialists who agree with the League and who now belong to other bodies, to join it, rather than impair their usefulness also by remaining in those bodies when they feel themselves out of harmony with their tactics.

At the same time, the Council wish it to be clearly understood that they have stated the differences between the League and other Socialists in no contentious spirit, but only to justify the continued existence of the League as a separate body, and to deprecate any alteration in its principles and tactics, which, if carried out would put it into a position of mere factious opposition to other Socialist organizations. The Council desires further to say that it thinks it the duty of the League and its members to co-operate in the most cordial way with other Socialists on all occasions when it can do so without loss of principle, and without prejudice to the form of propaganda which it has from the first believed it to be its duty to press forward.

COMMONWEAL, Volume 4, Number 126,
9 June 1888, p. 180

The Skeleton at the Feast

The consolation dinner to Mr Jesse Collings was rather a comical business in so far as it was a party coddling-up of the poor well-intentioned feeble gentleman who got practically turned out of the society which he himself had planted and watered so carefully; and the speeches delivered at this queer celebration would afford amusement enough to a cynical man with a good memory for things not worth remembering – to wit, the politics of the last three years. In days which people who have serious work on hand are forgetting speedily, Mr Collings manufactured a sort of stage landscape of a happy village, over which, as in other stage landscapes, shone a fatuous moon in the shape of three acres and a cow, a long way off: which (heaven knows why – or perhaps the election agents!) was so enticing to a great many members of parliament that rather than disturb it they gave an adverse vote against the then Tory Government and turned it out, it would seem to the great grief of Lord Hartington.

However, as might be expected, this beautiful scene became of little importance when the Outs had become Ins, and it was carried off to the lumber room – acres, cow and all. But again the Outs became Ins, and the new Ins with commendable prudence remembered that there would be another general election some day, and the votes of the field-labourers would then be of great importance to them; so they got up a new illusion scene, of which all that can be said is that it was somewhat more honest than the other in proclaiming itself an illusion; which, however, was not the reason why the Gladstonian Liberals turned their backs on it. Doubtless Mr Jesse Collings['] friends were right in asserting that the Gladstonians treated the whole matter from an electioneering point of view; and also doubtless their own impudence in implying that they were not at that very moment treating it in exactly the same way would be enough to stagger people not used, as unluckily we are, to parliamentary dodgers. Well, to go on with this stupid story, the Gladstonites turned Mr Collings out of the Allotments Association, and the Rural Labourers League (how many rural labourers are there in it, I wonder?) received him into its bosom, and there he sat the other night hugging his grievance, and drinking in the flattery of the friends of the ejectors of the Irish, and the Scotch crofters, perhaps at that moment the happiest man in Britain; probably not much disturbed at the fact that a French nobleman, turned on for the occasion, told him pretty plainly that his three acres and a cow was all rubbish, and that wholesale emigration was the real remedy for the diminishing numbers of the English field-labourers, as well as for the discontent of the Irish 'rebels'; while Mr Chamberlain promised him another ally, a Yankee Tory, one Mr Hurlburt, in his magnanimous hatred of the Irish peasant.

This *is* a scurvy story; and the worst of it is that I believe Mr Collings was once in real earnest in wishing to do a good turn to the English field-labourers; but parliament knocked all that out of him and at last has dragged him through the mud, and stuck a fool's cap on his head, while it has been using his poor little foolish scheme, of making the field-labourers work double tides to pay their own poor-rates, for electioneering purposes, not heeding him or anybody else in playing its Bedlamite game.

To think of it, that while this banquetting flavoured with the keen amusement of the game aforesaid is going on, there are the field-labourers actually existing! Rubbing through life toward the workhouse and the grave on ten shillings a-week. Go through the lovely country now in this 'leafy month of June', and if you turn your thoughts from the mere beauty of the earth or the memories of past history which the external aspect of the old buildings help you to, can you, if you think of it, even if you are not a Socialist (if any one but a Socialist ever thinks about these things at all), help feeling that everything there is *padlocked* against the use of man – the men who have *made it of use.* These are the men whose forefathers built our cathedrals, wrote our poems for us, fought for our liberties (such as they are!), kept alive the history which links us to the past: and they themselves it they had had anything approaching to decent treatment would have done as much or more. And then look at them, working in their allotments if you please, pinched and heavy and vacant-looking, too poor to look anxious even; forbidden to think or to hope; losing all the arts of life which used to make their lives endurable; grown to be mere appendages to the great centres of population which will swallow up so many of them. To the parliament gentry at St Stephens, what are they? *Votes,* – otherwise inconvenient, and to be emigrated out of the way if possible. And will either of our factions or all of them together do anything to unpadlock the wealth of the land for them? Certainly not; it will not, nay, it *cannot.* It is they themselves, with their brethren of the towns to help, who must knock off the padlock – or else what will happen? Sir Henry James, at that dismal tragic-farce of a consolation banquet, spoke of 'the danger in which our inexperienced democracy [O Lord! inexperienced!] stood at this moment'. What is the danger? He would say 'disruption of the empire', or some such twaddle; others would say 'revolution'. Is it not rather 'Starvation'? That is the skeleton sitting by the guests at the Whig feast.

Commonweal, Volume 4, Number 127,
16 June 1888, p. 188

PENTONVILLE PRISON

The following letter is worth reprinting entire as a really cheering sign of the times; and one can scarcely be wrong in thinking that such a letter could hardly have been written to the ordinary press or printed by it but for Bloody Sunday and all that followed it, which has dragged to light the horrors of the English prison system.

> *Sir*, – As foreman of a jury at Clerkenwell Sessions, on being discharged yesterday, after sitting six days, I with my fellow-jurymen (by order obtained of the judge) went over the above prison. We were much horrified and pained to see the brutal system under which torture is hourly inflicted upon many of the poor prisoners. We were told that for a month after entry the prisoners, as we saw them, are kept upon that abominable invention, the treadmill, their time of actual working on it being 5 1/4 hours daily. We were then shown the prisoners' cells, and the dreadful instrument of torture called the plank-bed. From the mill, aching in every limb, the poor prisoner, for a whole month, has to lie all night upon this slightly-raised platform, without a mattress or pillow. This is not punishment – its steps beyond it – it is deliberate torture. As an Englishman, and a ratepayer, I protest most earnestly against its longer continuance. The chapel in which the gospel of love and forgiveness is daily set forth to the prisoners we also visited, but I fail to see how any prisoner aching in all his bones from the plank-bed can obtain belief in such far-off possibilities. The system of silence which also prevails is against human nature, and productive of prison crime. Surely it is high time, if we mean really to be a civilized and

Christian nation, to sweep away the treadmill, the silent system, and the plank-bed altogether, and to treat prisoners as human beings entitled to our kindness whilst in durance, instead of driving them into a wearisome melancholy madness. Kindly dip your pen, Sir, into the ink, and say a strong word to our countrymen on this matter, cruel to their fellows, because ignorant of their sufferings. Your insertion of this letter will much oblige my fellow-jurymen and myself. – Yours truly,

John Parnell.

Chichester House, Rockley Road, West Kensington Park, London, W., June 13.

It is surely not too much to hope that the jury and its foreman, who take such a very unconventional view of our prisons, would be likely to take a similar view of what Mr Gladstone calls 'our admirable police', as they appear when giving evidence, and those noble specimens of the champions of impartiality and fair dealing, the British judges as they appear in directing a jury what verdict to give.

COMMONWEAL, VOLUME 4, NUMBER 128,
23 JUNE 1888, P. 195

COUNTING NOSES

Mr Chamberlain...believed that the experience of the United States and their own, so far as it had gone, went to show that when people were constantly being called on to vote, the whole matter fell into the hands of caucuses and machine politicians.

Thus the reporters of the House of Commons give us the present view of the once semi-Socialist agitator, the advocate of the ransoming of the upper-classes; and no one can wonder at the 'ironical cheers and laughter' of the opposition that followed this expression of opinion from the once darling of the caucuses, the once supreme leader of the midland-county machine politicians. 'That would lead', said this right honourable, 'to a state of things which had never existed in this country, and which he for one would extremely deprecate.' 'Renewed laughter' followed this brilliant joke, which seems to have taken by surprise even people so used to impudence as MP's are.

Perhaps, though, the laughter was not so much at what Mr Chamberlain *said* as at what he *meant* in reference to his present position; the Devil preaching a serious sermon on sin without himself laughing at his humbug is proverbially an amusing business, and Mr Chamberlain's contradiction of his first sentence by his second doubtless makes it more amusing; but except for that second sentence, in which he spoke of the reign of caucuses and machine politicians as a state of things which had never existed in this country, I think we may go some way in agreeing with him, even without attacking the nostrum of triennial or yearly parliaments which is so dear to Radical politicians.

It is true, indeed, that we are not very often called upon to vote for MP's at least, and that the majesty of the House of Commons and its elections has overshadowed the other kinds of voting so much that only a few very eager local politicians heed such occasions for voting, unless in the case of the School Board, in which the cumulative vote is enticing to some who otherwise would see clearly that they had no chance of getting their opinions represented.

But though we don't vote often, I really do not see how we could be 'machined' more than we are at present, even if we voted every day. In our centralized 'society' (if one must abuse that good word by using it for the thievish muddle ruled by the government clerk and the policeman) the whole political duty of man is to vote: that is at once the healing faith, and the fruits worthy of salvation put before us by our political church to-day, and the priests of that church are for ever engaged in bribing people to vote and intimidating them to vote, and cheating them into voting, and beseeching them to vote; and also in receiving their votes; and when the votes are received and the representative is elected by them, he then has to put his whole soul into squaring his conduct in accordance with the chances of the next election and the hopes of again obtaining votes.

Under this system how can any politician be other than mechanical? So far from his trying to abate party spirit, and try to be useful, it is his business carefully to push anything that has a tendency to become human and reasonable back into the lists where the battle of nose-counting is being fought. Administration becomes a joke, and the Metropolitan Board of Works the true image of official business. Worn-out party cries are allowed to shout down all suggestions of the true issues of political life. The leaders are obliged at any rate to profess ignorance (like Mr Morley the other day) of a great part of the events happening under their very noses, and as to their ignorance of ideas that are beginning to move all intelligent persons, they have no need to *profess* ignorance of them, for their ignorance on this head is so complete that it cries out for all men to take note of. In this coarse, blind, ignorant party warfare, the issues put before us are so futile and wide of the real point, that honest and thoughtful men are compelled to spit and pass by. Here, say the politicians, vote for *this* or for *that*. Is there no third course, you say, but to vote for a piece of reaction or a piece of inaction? None, they answer; your business is to have your nose counted on one side or other of the business that we nose-counters have made for you: if you object, you are a faddist, a crank, a person ignorant of 'practical politics'.

This is the way that 'representatives' are manufactured, that the 'great representative body' is manufactured; and after all it must be said that if it does not represent us, it represents our condition. It is said often that the House of Commons does little or nothing. Well, what in the name of patience *need* it do? There is the vast organization of commerce at work day by day, hour by hour, taking care that the war for riches amongst the members of the classes privileged to 'employ', shall be orderly, and that the members of the classes that *are* employed shall gain nothing more than bare subsistence by their competition with one another; turning to their own advantage, not only the work of the workers, but their love of pleasure and longing for ease which forbids them to take up consciously the class struggle which they *must* carry on unconsciously; their sense of justice and aspirations for a decent life, which make them averse to violence; nay, they can even turn the struggle for wages and the trades combinations to their advantage by using them as a warning to note how far they can venture to go in the robbery of the useful class; and their political aspirations the capitalist representatives can use in much the same way; they can discover by the vote-catching process what tune must be played in order to lull the workers to sleep while their pockets are being picked – of well-being and happiness.

They need do nothing else except keep a large force of policemen and a tolerable army on foot, together with the criminal courts and the due amount of middle-class jurymen in case the victims should wake up and get restive.

I say again if the Parliament manufactured by the nose-counting which is manipulated by caucuses, Primrose League, election agents, the last corruption of hero-worship, and the rest of it, does not represent *us*, it represents *our condition* – a privileged class robbing us, destroying, if not our lives, yet the reason for our lives; and a working class apathetic because it is used to the miserable life it leads. A class which does not know what happiness is, and therefore will not seek the means of obtaining it.

Surely the time will come when the mere struggle for bare livelihood will force on us the knowledge of the means not merely of obtaining bare livelihood but of happiness also, and then what a farce will seem to us that 'representation' founded on 'machine-politics' and the count of noses of unhappy people driven and cheated into voting for this or that form of the continuance of their own unhappiness.

Commonweal, Volume 4, Number 128,
23 June 1888, p. 196

THOUGHTS ON EDUCATION UNDER CAPITALISM

The other day I heard Mr Charles Leland (better known as Hans Breitman) speak on the teaching of the 'minor arts' (we wont trouble for the present as to what they are) and he told us he was engaged in carrying out a plan (in America) by which *all* children should be taught these arts and so gain an interest in handicrafts which he thought, and I heartily agree with him, would be a great gain to the art and consequently to the happiness of people generally. Mr Leland said that he had been engaged in this work of educating children's hands for many years, and he expected success to follow his efforts, a success which would mean, if it were worth speaking of, that the interest in sound workmanship combined with beauty would become general, and that a demand for such work would follow and compel the manufacturers to get such work turned out.

But such success is impossible even supposing that hundreds of persons were following Mr Charles Leland's laudable example. It would indeed be possible enough, nay it would be certain, if the capitalists the 'manufacturers' were the *servants* of society as they sometimes profess to be; but who shall force such a prodigious change upon them as success even in such a minor matter as this would indicate, so long as they are the masters of society, which is their real position? For Mr Leland's scheme means, if it were logically carried out, *ie.*, if it were successful, the substitution of handicraft for 'manufacturing' in all the wares of which art or beauty forms a party and which admit of being done by handicraft, in short to take us back to the Middle-Ages as far as these wares are concerned. But it is clear that the wares so produced will, if the labour on them is decently paid, cost so much more than the manufactured wares which they are intended to supplant, that only rich people with a whim for art will be able to buy them; they will not be produced in any great quantity, and if there should be a passing fashion for them, the 'manufacturers' would immediately imitate them by machinery and 'organized labour', and cheapen them out of existence; or indeed if the whim of rich people for the genuine article still went on, another process of cheapening would be resorted to; wholesale dealers in such articles would exploit the unfortunate handicraftsmen (or women, whose cheap work would certainly be largely used for such wares). They would take advantage of the competition for the most miserable livelihood between people in dire necessity to produce 'cheap art' for the swelling of their own purses; and if the thing grew it would be a favourite form of exploitation, as it would require little capital and little managerial capacity, and would have a dash of philanthropy and 'practical remedy' about it, which would help to make such sweating an honourable as well as pleasant occupation. Cheap art indeed – and nasty! But in all probability the fashion for such articles would be limited and transitory, and all that would happen to the persons educated into a capacity for and a pleasure in refined handicraft would be that they would have to be used up in the mere mechanical drudgery of commercial production.

But it is not the matter of art that I wish to illustrate by the mention of this feeble attempt of Mr Leland and others (for the kind of futility is common enough). It is rather the relation of our capitalistic system to general education. For just as the capitalists would at once capture this education in craftsmanship, suck out what little advantage there is in it and then throw it away, so they do with all other education. A superstition still remains from the times when 'education' was a rarity that it is a means for earning a superior livelihood; but as soon as it has ceased to be a rarity, competition takes care that education shall not raise wages; that general education shall be worth nothing, and that special education shall be worth just no more than a tolerable return on the money and time spent in acquiring it; and, mind you, such special education must be very carefully directed towards the one aim of commercial success in the speciality, or it will miss, and be thrown into the mass of general education which earns nothing.

As to the pleasure to be derived from education at present by hard-working men, a bookish man is apt to think that even the almighty capitalist can hardly take that away from his slave if he has really learned to enjoy reading and to understand books, and that whatever happens he must have an hour in a day (or if it were only half an hour) to indulge himself in this pleasure. But then *does* the average hard-working man (of any grade) really acquire this capacity by means of the short period of education which he is painfully dragged through? I doubt it. Though even our mechanical school system cannot crush out a natural bent towards literature (with all the pleasures of thought and imagination which that word means) yet certainly its dull round will hardly implant such a taste in any one's mind; and as for the *caput mortuum*, the dead mass of mere information which the worker comes away with when his 'education' is over, he will and must soon forget this when he finds out that it is of little use to him and gives him no pleasure.

I must say in passing that on the few occasions that I have been inside a Board-school, I have been much depressed by the mechanical drill that was too obviously being applied there to all the varying capacities and moods. My heart sank before Mr M'Choakumchild (*sic*) and his method, and I thought how much luckier I was to have been born well enough off to be sent to a school where I was *taught* – nothing; but *learned* archæology and romance on the Wiltshire downs.

And then supposing the worker to be really educated, to have acquired both the information and the taste for reading which Mr McChoakum-child's (*sic*) dole will allow to him under the most favourable circumstances, how will this treasure of knowledge and sympathy accord with his daily life? Will it not make his dull task seem duller? Will it not increase the suffering of the workshop or the factory to him? And if so, must he not rather strive to forget than strive to remember? Will not nature force him to that? I cannot help thinking that as a rule it must be so, unless he has joined the ranks of the discontented; in which case he will gain something of pleasure from mere bitterness and railing if he is not a Socialist, and how much more than that some of our readers know well, if he is one.

Now if I am told that this is *à priori* reasoning, I am prepared to fortify it by my own observation. I have often been told by working-men (Socialist and others) that they cannot read books; are too tired with the day's work to do so, and the like. Also amongst my middle-class acquaintances, who believe that they work hard, I meet with men who clearly *do* not read books, and therefore, I suppose, *cannot*; and I move in each case in a circle that has decided literary tendencies. So that other person's experiences will, I am sure, lead them to conclusions on this point not more favourable than mine.

Then there is the enormous mass of printed paper which is not books or literature, but which the public pays for every day, since I suppose a faculty once acquired produces a habit and must be exercised, even when it is the mechanical one of reading print. The quality of this joint product of paper-maker, compositor, and sub-editor, confirms my *à priori* reasoning remarkably, for no adventure in this kind of wares has any chance of success if it has more than the merest suspicion of a flavour of literature or thoughtfulness, as we have often been told when the prospects of the *Commonweal* have been under discussion. I will not say that the worse a periodical is the better chance it has of success, but that if it intends to succeed it must appeal to habits that are as much akin to the reasonable aims of education as is the twiddling of a bit of string by a fidgetty (*sic*) person.

I believe, indeed, it is thought by some that this habit of the consumption of newspapers is the first step in education. Good! the second step, I take it, will be the cessation of that habit.

All this betokens that the end towards which our sham Society directs the means, 'education' is the one end to which all its 'social' dealings are directed to, the sustaining and easy working of its usurpation of true Society. People are 'educated' to become workmen or the employers of workmen, or the hangers-on of the employers, they are not educated to become *men*. With this aim in view the conditions under which true education can go on are impossible. For the first and most necessary of them are leisure and deliberation; and leisure is a thing which the modern slave-holder will by no means grant to his slave as long as he grants him rations; when the leisure begins the rations end. Constant toil is the only terms on which they are to be had. Capitalism will not allow us the leisure, either for education or the use of it. Slave labour and true education are irreconcilable foes, for the latter means the continuous and duly balanced development of our faculties, whether in the school, the workshop, or the field, and how can that co-exist with the continuous, hopeless, mechanical drudgery of the man who whatever he produces will have all taken from him that exceeds a bare subsistence.

In short, our present education outside its uses to our enemies, the masters of Society, is good for one thing, the creation of discontent. I doubt it will serve us in no other way.

Commonweal, Volume 4, Number 129,
30 June 1888, pp. 204–205

SWEATERS AND SWEATERS

No. 1.– MATCHES BY THE FACTORY DRILL

The London Trades' Council having taken up the strike of the match girls, it did at any rate go on long enough to force the attention of even the stupidest of the capitalist class, and the girls have at least gained something out of the struggle; and surely nobody but the cruellest as well as the stupidest of bourgeois will grudge them that small gain. For the rest, like other strikes, it is a necessary incident in the war of capital and labour; whatever may be the fate of any particular strike, the whole mass of strikes forms one side of this great war: if there were no strikes but those which were likely to succeed in times like the present, the manufacturing capitalists would have an easy time of it, and would reduce the workers under their control to the very lowest point of misery; but as it is, even people in such a wretched condition as these poor match girls can make themselves felt temporarily, and can help to swell the mass of opposition to the manufacturers' ideal, to wit, human machinery which will give not more, but less, trouble than the machinery of mere dead matter, and will be as contented as that; so that Mrs Besant and the others whose exertions have made this strike possible have done and are doing good service.

It is curious, though, to see how the capitalist press have straightway set their backs up, and set to work to whitewash the extremely 'respectable' firm – company, I should say – who live on this miserable industry. What has become of the 'Bitter Cry' and all the fashionable slumming which followed it? Why, this industry, which is of such commercial importance to the world – of shareholders – is just the very thing that all that deedless sympathy was poured out on; and yet now we find the press, which was so 'interested' in the affairs of the East-end workers four years ago, is quite content to leave the match girls to the tender mercies of Messrs Bryant and May and other such benefactors of the human race; and if any attempt is set on foot to make these poor folk conscious of the fact that they are part of a great class which *must* struggle for existence and *should* struggle for a decent life, immediately we find the papers, to say the least of it, tender of the rich and harshly critical of the poor, scattering broadcast inuendoes (*sic*) against the disinterested people who really feel the 'Bitter Cry', telling mere lies about the events of the strike, chuckling over the slavery of the poor wretches who hug their chains and are angry with the strikers for making them risk the loss of the starvation wages which they are doomed to exist on. Such shabby people as these, and the public for which they write, who simply want to be mildly amused by other people's troubles, are not likely to note one lesson which would seem to be pretty clearly taught by the exposure of this manufacture to the light of day, and that is the utter helplessness of any philanthropic remedies for these miseries, or, indeed, any remedies but the one remedy of destruction of the whole system under which they are possible; still less are they likely to see that this flourishing and respectable company, the names of whose managers are a kind of household words, is a *reductio ad absurdum* of the competition for profits which is the 'bond of society' at present. The superstition of the 'cultivated classes' of to-day concerning the necessity of profit-grinding is as gross as ever superstition was. I take as an illustration a sentence from an article in the *Daily News* by a well-intentioned sort of person apparently, and read:- 'These poor people are really the victims, 'not of any exceptional greed or hard usage of Messrs Bryant and May' (close shavers, though, my friend!) but of that steady onward rush of the great industrial machine whose course is directed not by the needs and welfare of those immediately beneath its wheels, but of the community at large for generations to come.'

Well! that *is* tall talk. Let us pick this match-making business from 'the steady onward rush', and see what it means. It is a very simple story, and a very shabby one. A lot of helpless girls and women are driven by fear of mere destitution to hire themselves out at starvation wages to do mechanical and unhealthy work; they are cleverly drilled by a perfected system which aims at wasting nothing (except human life) and the result of their labour is sold at the lowest price possible in order that the money passing through the hands of the company may be turned as often as possible; and in order to do that even the wretched wages are clipped by fines, which have the double advantage of helping in the drilling as well as saving the wage outlay. That is the process; what is the gain that comes of it, beyond the keeping alive in misery a number of girls? Certain persons are able to live a luxurious and useless life without working, and matches are made so cheap that the public buy twice as many as they want of them and waste half. Here is a gain indeed for 'the generations to come'! Are we so helpless that this shabby story is to be told over and over again, and the sad fact always a-doing? Once more, a farthing box of matches is no great plunder to take from a 'victim' of the great industrial machine, and, on the whole, I think it would be better to try to direct it 'by the needs and welfare of those immediately beneath its wheels' – only you cannot, as long as the machine is composed of capital and wage-slavery. You can only help whatever tends towards upsetting the said machine. And all wise men will do so, and spread discontent till we make a better bargain than selling ourselves to the Devil – for nothing.

No. 2.– PASSING ON THE PINCH

It is noteworthy that we are to-day having the extreme form of the systems of the robbery of the worker dragged up before the public gaze. On the one hand there is this system of the complete merciless drill of the factory, obvious authoritative compulsion, and on the other the compulsion which passes through the links of the sweating system, in the last link of which mere obvious necessity of bread earning compels the poor sweater to compel. When the two systems are brought face to face it will be seen that there is little enough to chose between them, because after all there are plenty of links between the idle appropriator of the results of other people's labour and the workman in the factory system; the various managers, clerks, and foremen are the sweating machinery in this case, and many of these are of the working-class just as the sweating tailor is. It is true that the organized sweating system carries the misery a stage lower down, in spite of the shameless defence of it which is being made before the Lords' Commission, and the last link the poor sweater is a speciality of the system, and a disgrace even to our disgraceful sham society. But it must never be forgotten, and we must repeat it again here, that all capitalistic production which is not purely individual, as the work of the doctor or the artist, is done by means of sweating in some form or other. It is the knowledge, conscious or otherwise, of this fact which gives some of the witnesses before the Lords' Commission courage to stand up and represent their horrible industry as a benefit to humanity; they cannot help feeling that the sympathy of the lords and gentlemen on the Commission will be accorded to those respectable people who are performing the whole duty of modern man by making a profit, even if they are forced by circumstances to be the instruments of inflicting misery upon other people; for as our worthy friend in the *Daily News* on the match-girls sees, that is the necessary process of commercial production: in short, the respectable factory capitalist excuses the sweater, respectable or not. Doubtless the conclusion that will be expressed in the report of the Commission on Sweating will be that the evils of the system have been much exaggerated, that the worst form of it is not widespread, that the system, with whatever exaggerated evils belong to it, is necessary to civilization, nay, to humanity; all this probably in much these words, and as a practical rider to the conclusion, though *not* openly stated, that we the commission recommend that something be pretended to be done to keep the people quiet.

A friend of mine once expostulated with a hatter for the price he charged for his hats; the hatter had been dining, and wine inspired him to tell the truth. 'Mr —', said he 'how can I live in the style in which I do unless I charge you at least as high?'

This is really the conclusion which the Sweating Commission must come to. The misery of those who are sweated, whether by the drill of the factory or the many links of the sweating chain, is the high price that we pay for the glory of sustaining a class of idle rich men. Is the gain worth the price? Working men, it is for you to answer the question, and act according to your answer.

COMMONWEAL, VOLUME 4, NUMBER 132,
21 JULY 1888, PP. 225–226

SOCIALIST WORK AT NORWICH

I am sure our comrades generally will be glad to hear a little of the course of Socialist propaganda in Norwich and its neighbourhood, which for some reason or other has become a stronghold of the cause.

Our comrades had determined on a rally in Norwich, and invited several of us Leaguers, together with Mrs Besant and Herbert Burrows, to help them. Faulkner, Mrs Schack, Mainwaring, and Morris got down to the old city on Saturday evening, and were most cordially received by the Branch at the Gordon Hall, where there was singing and recitation, and agreeable converse generally.

On the Sunday morning Mainwaring went to Yarmouth, and addressed a large meeting on the beach. Mrs Schack went to Wymondham, and though the meeting in that quiet little place was not big, it was very attentive and serious. In the city itself, Faulkner spoke at St Mary's Plain and Morris, with Mowbray in the chair, in the Market Place. The meeting there was considerably over a thousand, and was attentive and sympathetic. Faulkner came up just before it was over, and gave a short address on the subject of Education; and the meeting held well together to the last.

In the afternoon a waggonette was drawn up under the bronze shadow of that very dull hero the Iron Duke (in bronze), and Mowbray was in the 'chair' there at 2.30, our comrades of the Branch being drawn round the platform. It was an exciting scene when we got there, the concourse being very large round the platform, in spite of the counter attractions of the fag end of the Salvation Army and the summons of the bells of the huge tower of St Peter Mancroft. The 'Army' having done speaking, moved away with its band, which presently came into the place, but with few followers, and the coming of another band of gospellers had no influence on the meeting except to swell it somewhat. Before 3 o'clock there must have been fully ten thousand persons closely packed round the waggonette. The comrades being called upon now sang 'No Master', in the midst of which Herbert Burrows and Mrs Besant came duly punctual, and the business began. A resolution in favour of the abolition of private property had been prepared, which was moved by Herbert Burrows, who began by telling the audience that some five years ago he lectured on Socialism in Norwich to an audience of five persons. His clear and telling speech was well received. Mrs Besant followed, and was received with much enthusiasm. Morris supported, and the resolution was put after an amendment had been called for without result, and four-fifths of the meeting or more held up their hands for and six hands against. Mrs Schack and Faulkner then spoke, and the meeting broke up, without the least disorder, except that one man, a stranger, got somewhat obstreperous (or rather the liquor in him did) and was run in by the police. This would not be worth mentioning if it were not that our comrades were vexed and indignant that the Norwich Nupkinses gave him a month next day, our comrades by no means wishing to bring the law down on their opponents for such trifles.

In the evening Burrows and Mainwaring spoke again in the Market Place to a large audience, and Morris lectured (on Monopoly) at the Gordon Hall, which was as full as it would hold. No opposition could be got, and it was clear that the whole audience were really Socialists.

On the Monday Burrows, Mainwaring, and Morris spoke in the Market Place in the dinner hour; the audience was again large for a week-day, and did not break up till 2.30, having listened eagerly all the time. Burrows and Mrs Besant spoke at Carrow, close to Colman's mustard works, in the dinner hour, and had a large and satisfactory audience, mostly composed of the workmen and girls, Mrs Besant telling her hearers of the illegality of fines. The last open-air meeting was in the Market Place at 6.30. Burrows, Mainwaring, and Morris speaking. One or two ill-conditioned persons attempted to get up a row on this occasion, but produced little or no effect on the crowd, who listened as attentively as before.

The meetings ended with Mrs Besant's lecture in St Augustine's School, a large room somewhat on the outskirts of the town, to which we had been driven by the refusal of the large halls in the town. This place was crammed by an eager audience, who took up every point in the lecture, which, though both eloquent and clear, would have been hard to follow by a non-Socialist who had not studied the question. The answering of the questions also which were put gave occasion to the audience to show that they appreciated the points, and certainly except for a few respectables who honoured us with their presence, there could have been but few present who were not thoroughly sympathetic.

The press, both Liberal and Tory, reported all our proceedings fully, and considering all things, quite as fairly as could be expected. In comparing the audiences there with others, one could not fail to be struck with an air of eagerness and receptiveness, which shows that the propaganda is doing its work. The audiences do not come to stare or loaf, but to listen.

The impression which Socialism has thus made in a place not very important, nor specially progressive, is the result of sheer hard work on the part of our comrades, who are all quite poor men, and have no influence but what their steadiness and enthusiasm in the Cause gives them. What has been done there can be done elsewhere if only men will devote themselves to the propaganda.

Our comrades are in trouble at Yarmouth. The week before this demonstration, comrade Poynts was summoned for speaking on the Church Plain in that town, though we had held meetings there for long, and though a religious meeting was being held at the same time as he was holding the Socialist one. Our comrade has been sent to prison for a month for this terrible 'offence' of free speaking, and as this is clearly a piece of mere persecution of opinion, it is to be hoped that all parties who have any feeling for freedom will back up our friends, who are fighting the battle of free speech for all honest men both in the present and the future.

COMMONWEAL, VOLUME 4, NUMBER 137,
25 AUGUST 1888, P. 268

A MODERN MIDAS

In one respect at least, we Socialists have an advantage over other people. The very simplest and rudest ideal that a Socialist can conceive of would bear realization well; a Socialist could only be discontented with such realization by ceasing to be a Socialist; and there are few creeds or causes of which this could be said. Some have discounted the usual ideals, so to say, and rejected them beforehand, like the old Scotch lady who declined to sacrifice her pleasure on earth for the chance of sitting on a damp cloud and singing psalms all day for ever in another world; others, like Swedenborg, have gravely (though in his case with much humour also) tried to reason devotees out of the more foolish parts of their ideal, and put heaven before them as little more than the realization of Socialism in a future state. Modern creeds, on the other hand, with characteristic cowardice, have generally evaded the difficulties that beset the realization of ideals by taking care to make them so vague that at no stage of the change could it be said whether they were realized or not.

One religion there is, however, whose ideal as a religion is simple and straightforward enough, and quite capable of realization, and indeed is often realized; that religion is the religion of money-making. To put yourself in such a position that no one could for a moment suppose that you need do or were doing anything useful, is, as we all know, the one thing to be striven after according to the Money-God; although the pursuit of this ideal is made easier by the pretence of having others, of the damp-cloud and psalm-singing nature. But the realization of this ideal does not always (it is said) bring satisfaction: 'to live the life of a gentleman' has been found irksome to many who have had in earlier days more exciting ways of life than that. Nay, one anecdote I know, which was told me as a fact by a business man of great respectability, which seems to show that a 'gentleman's' life has unexpected dangers. A man in business in a large Midland town, said my acquaintance (who knew the man), after a long struggle as an agent and broker and what not, carried on with that untiring energy and strength of mind which so distinguishes the English bourgeois (only, by the way, the man was a German) – this man at last grew rich, and 'lived like a gentleman'; and then very rich, and lived, I suppose, more like a gentleman. But here came the hitch: either he was so bored by the results of his triumph, his realized ideal, or his mind was so strong before that now it became weak, and he found that the only fun to be got out of his ideal was the pursuit of it. In short, this German representative of English industry went mad, and his madness took the form of his thinking that his ideal was still unrealized, and that he was poor and struggling still. He now grew so little like 'a gentleman' that he begrudged his own belly, his own back (and not other peoples') victuals and clothes. His friends (or hangers on) would come to him and say, 'So and so, the doctor has ordered you a mutton chop'; and he would answer, 'Well, the doctor had better send it me then, *I* can't afford it'. The case being urgent, and the man daily growing weaker, the 'friends' would say, 'Well, that's true; but look here, if you will have a mutton chop we will pay you for eating it'.

Then Midas, believing, as he naturally would, that the money which he had 'made' came from nowhere in particular, and that there was no reason why this miracle should not be again, and even continuously exhibited, would say with caution, 'Well, what will you give me?' and they, having command of an unlimited bogus cheque-book, would say, also with caution, 'Well, let us say £100'; but Midas would turn away with a snort of indignation, and the bidding would rise to £500. 'Come', Midas would say, 'make it £750! Eating chops is such expensive work'; and they after some demur would agree, the cheque would be solemnly drawn and signed, and Mr Midas would fulfil his part of the contract with all the probity of a British merchant. But of course the game had to be repeated at every fresh meal. The same comedy had to be played with the clothing of this pattern of industry. When he became visibly lousy, or perhaps a little before, there was the job to get him to change his shirt! He would manœuvre and dodge ahout (*sic*) to screw another £100 out of his bribers, as though he had got a treasure to sell them, which they could not bear to lose, and would chuckle over his bogus cheque with complete enjoyment.

I don't know how long this industrious apprentice lived in this condition; I unamiably hope a long time, for he must have been a great nuisance to his hangers on, or keepers, or what not, and they deserved it for not being Socialists. It must be observed that the man was admittedly mad, and not an ordinary miser, and had kept a plenteous house and great [e]state before he reverted to his original thrift and industry.

The moral is obvious enough not to need repeating: only perhaps some of our Fabian friends will not so much see Midas in the story, as a judgement called down on the man for neglecting to learn the true theory of rent in its various forms.

Indeed, I must unsay what I have just said, and end by asking our readers to look upon this true story, which does not stand by itself, as a type of our sham society, which inflicts so many miseries on others in order to be itself unhappy.

COMMONWEAL, VOLUME 4, NUMBER 141,
22 SEPTEMBER 1888, P. 300

In and About Cottonopolis

On Sunday the 2nd, I delivered my annual lecture to the Sunday Society at Ancoats to an audience larger than usual. These lectures are not followed by questions and discussion, so there was not much opportunity for finding out what the audience thought about Socialism. The audience seemed, as usual, much made up of the 'lower middle-class' and the 'aristocracy of labour'. But there was a sprinkling of our comrades of the SDF, with whom to help I engaged in a good private discussion at tea (which followed the lecture) with enquirers and carpers, which is also a usual feature of these gatherings. In the evening I went with comrade Hunter Watts to the rooms of the Manchester Branch of the SDF, where I addressed our comrades. The members of the branch were almost all of the non-aristocracy of labour, but many of them were as eager and earnest as could be desired. I take it that the above-said aristocracy of labour in Manchester are very shy of Socialism, though it is making very good progress among the labouring class even in Manchester itself. There is also a good deal of sympathy (as it is called) from the definitely well-to-do, who say here as elsewhere: 'We agree with you, but–.'

On Monday the 3rd, I went to Bolton and lectured (by request) on 'Art and Socialism'. The audience was fair only, the room not being full. The chairman was a middle-class man who really seemed in sympathy, and I think the audience was in the main socialistic. The condition of labour in Bolton is very instructive; business is brisk there, very brisk; but there are among the spinners at least 4,000 out of employment, and with no hope of it. Moreover, a great deal of the 'employment' that there is, is at starvation wages; the 'piecers' often fathers of families work for the noble reward of from 12s. to 13s. a-week! I was told that the engineers here were in a very depressed state of mind after last year's strike, with all its excitement, and were in an attitude of abject humility before their masters; which, dismal as it is, seems to be a natural consequence of defeat in a struggle which had no ideal in it, whose aim was the usual narrow one of strikes in this country.

On the 4th, I went to Blackburn and lectured in the Spinner's Hall, which was not quite filled; our comrade Sharman took the chair. The audience were very eager, and took up all the points well. One or two of the questions asked were to the point, but it seems that these were asked by Socialists. The others were of the usual type, questions asked by persons who expect the lecturer to say so-and-so, and are perhaps put out by his perversity, but nevertheless ask the question they had intended to ask before they heard him.

The open-air meetings have been very brisk in Blackburn, where there is a good open space in which no meetings are interfered with. The branch of the SDF is good here, and there is a strong branch of the SDF at the neighbouring town of Darwen.

On the 5th I had to address a very different audience to these; to wit, the ladies and gentlemen gathered together for the rather mild amusement of listening to artists talking about art. I was not able to get to Liverpool in the morning, and so missed hearing Walter Crane's address; but I was told that he spoke very plainly in condemnation of the present system of production. I myself had a large audience (in the Rotunda), and of course spoke nothing but Socialism. I challenged opposition, as I had heard that some of the capitalists were going to 'smash me up'; but I am sorry to say that they thought better of it; and the little that was said turned out to be of a discouraging feebleness, turning on the village-industry and technical education. The next day I heard a paper of Cobden-Sanderson on Craft-Ideals, in which he preached Communism pure and simple. Also an architect, not a Socialist, received applause for asking the question, What was the use of museums and art education if the social condition of the people remained what it is now? I shall have a few words to say about this same congress next week, so I will say no more now.

The evening of the 6th I went to Rochdale and lectured to an audience fair in numbers and otherwise good. It was followed by a long conversational debate, the questions being, as a matter of course, the usual ones, but, by the working men present, asked and stuck to with the pertinacity and in the good-natured bullying manner with which I am familiar in Lancashire and the North generally. Two or three middle-class opponents were of great use to me in enabling me to state my position again and again. One of these said that as far as Rochdale and the neighbourhood generally was concerned I had exaggerated the poverty of the workers! But this I conclude to be a conventional tradition, the birth of the history of the sham co-operation which began with the good intentions of the Rochdale Pioneers, and has now by the confession of very moderate people become a reactionary force, 'Divi' being the one thing looked to, and jobbing in 'Co-op' shares being a favourite occupation among the small capitalists created by the system.

Anyhow our comrades gave me a very different view of the 'prosperity' of the workers of Rochdale, and told me that wages were very low and hours very long there, and that in short the masters had it pretty much their own way. The branch of the SDF is strong in numbers, and has in it some very strenuous and sincere propagandists.

Altogether, except in Liverpool, where there is nothing doing, the SDF branches are doing well in S. Lancashire; the drawback to their usefulness is that they are giving so much attention to electioneering matters; a course of action which, whatever else may be said about it, *must* trench upon the time which they ought to be giving to learning Socialism thoroughly, so as to be able to hold their own in argument with the non-Socialists around them. I say this in spite of the fact that I talked with some of our comrades who had mastered the subject by dint of very hard work done in the 'leisure' which their slavery allows them.

COMMONWEAL, VOLUME 4, NUMBER 153,
15 DECEMBER 1888, P. 396

TALK AND ART

The Art Congress (or whatever is the proper name for it) at which I assisted last week, may easily be made a mark at which to shoot shafts of ridicule. The crowds of lion-worshipping ladies, the many worthy artists set up to speak about an art which is above all things a matter of the instructed eye and deft hand; and many of them into the bargain but poor speakers, in all senses of the word (small blame to them for that same, since above all things their craft is of *doing*). The bands of idle busy-bodies; the stock phrases bandied about by people who, if questioned about them, would have been able to give but a sorry account of their meaning; and which phrases, when repeated to a reasonable person for the fiftieth time, became at last difficult to reply to with the amiable grin expected on the occasion instead of an outburst of the fury within him. All this the outward manifestation of the set of fashion towards 'earnestness' in the minor arts is discouraging enough, and I thought I discerned in the faces of my Socialist friends whom I met there some of the shamefacedness which I myself felt. Nor did I wonder that the 'manufacturers' lay low under the storm of open denunciation and implied censure and scorn which was the leading feature of the Congress: nay, I had an uncomfortable sensation, as though I could feel them chuckling at our expense, as if they were saying, 'Well, after all, this fine gathering for talk, and all its materials, including the well-fed, well-clothed, well-housed artists who are abusing us, have passed through our hands before they got here, and by no means unfruitfully for us. You also, our friends the artists, are our slaves, though your tether may be somewhat longer than that of our factory hands; nor do we much heed your talk, for it and your Congress and your village industries do us no harm on the one hand, and are rather good for trade on the other. In short, we are the masters of the situation, and you cannot help it; and indeed the greater part of you would be very sorry to help it if you could, and sacrifice your comforts to disturbance in the present and severity of life in the future.'

That at first seemed to me to be the mocking echo of our talk at Liverpool; and no doubt not one cog or fly-wheel will be displaced in that horrible South Lancashire by all the murmuring sea of talk. Yet after all even this set of fashion against commercial production on one side of it, and the silence of the manufacturers under it, are tokens of the sickness of society and the change drawing near: an epoch whose system is healthy and flourishing does not protest against and is not conscious of any loss which it suffers from the necessary process of that system; it accepts without murmur the gains which the system has brought about, and only thinks of fresh gains to be obtained by the perfecting of the process which has been found necessary to the conditions of life of the passing day. Nor, in spite of their chuckling, are the manufacturers in as good a position as they boast themselves: *we* know that. They are driven by necessity to find work for the demon which they have created, and which threatens to eat them up. Perhaps it is the knowledge or suspicion of this fact that keeps them silent under the attack of the artists. Else one would have expected to have seen many utterances like a clever letter published the other day in the *Manchester Guardian*, the writer of which told the artists roundly that it was their business to paint and not to talk (meaning, of course, that they should forget that they, scrubs as they are, are citizens), taunting them with wrapping themselves up in the past and not heeding the present world-grief (he used the German word), and reminding people that a spinning-jenny was a much more important thing than a carved chest or an illuminated manuscript.

All this sounds at first sight like common-sense, and even seems to have some elevation of aim in it; but after all it is but clap-trap. Let us forget the grievance of the humbug and hypocrisy that always hangs itself on to every movement that shows discontent with the present, and see what it is that the artists are aiming at, those of them who are in earnest. Their aim, instinctive or conscious, is to make everybody an artist; whereas the aim of the *Guardian* letter-writer (signing himself 'P.') is to make everybody a 'manufacturer' or a manufacturer's 'dependent'. To him the spinning-jenny is glorious, not because it produces yarn which the public can use, but because it produces 'hands' whom the manufacturers can use; so no wonder that 'P.' wants the artists to glorify the modern world-grief, since it is the system which he and his live by and have created. 'P.'s' aim is to realize a world for the manufacturer of market-wares – *ie.*, manufacturers' profits – made without the will of the makers and in the teeth of their miserable toil.

And what for? That Manchester may be made. And why should Manchester be made? That market-goods bearing a profit may be made. What a lamentable vicious circle! But the artists' aim is that all men should be artists. Folly! cries 'P.', and perhaps also some of our readers. But wait a little! What is an artist? A man who works at useful work that is fit for him and according to his own will. Therefore the artists are right in their aim; for when work is so done the world will be happy, but not before. Here is a worthy aim indeed; whereas 'P.' and his brethren have *no* aim, nothing more than an instinct for going on living at the expense of the workers.

I say again, in wishing to make all people artists, the artists are absolutely right, whatever follies they may be entangled in while they are still unconscious of their aim and its meaning. But those of them who are worth anything will not long remain unconscious of their aim. They see through the hypocrisy about the world-grief, with which the Philistine tries to sentimentalize filth, stink, and hideousness; their senses as human animals have led them on the right road so far at least as to demand beauty and interest in life for themselves at anyrate, and they will soon find out that they cannot have this except by means of the co-operation of the labour that produces the ordinary wares of life; and that co-operation again they cannot have as long as the workmen are dependent on the will of a master. They must co-operate consciously and willingly for livelihood, and out of that free co-operation will spring the expression of individual character and gifts which we call art. Then those spinning-jennies which so affect 'P.'s' soul will be used for producing yarns which we want, and not yarns that we only want to sell.

Commonweal, Volume 4, Number 154,
22 December 1888, p. 404

CONTRIBUTIONS TO *COMMONWEAL*

1889

WHIGS ASTRAY[1]

A Dialogue Between Owen Marx Bakounine Jones, *an architect (unsuccessful), and – the* Rev. Swain Stride, *a Nonconformist parson, and* Mr Jeremiah Brown, *a business man – advanced Radicals.*

Scene – A comfortable batchelor-looking (sic) room in Mr Brown's *house, with tobacco and pipes and grog to the fore.* Mr Stride *and* Mr Brown *sitting on either side of the fire, looking important and self-satisfied. Enter to them* Mr Jones *with an ill-concealed grin on his face; after the usual greetings he sits down and says:*

Jones. Well, Mr Brown, here I am, ready to hear what you have to say to me, and eager to know what puts you into such good spirits this evening, as you obviously are in.

Brown. Well, we are; we have been talking about matters that make us hopeful.

J. I *am* glad of that. I see so many doleful faces nowadays, that it does me good to see two cheerful ones, especially as finials to two such pinnacles of the temple as a parson and a man of business.

Stride. I don't like you to call me a parson, Jones. I am none of your priests; and really I think you know me well enough not to set me down as a relation of Chadband. You know very well that what I'm really interested in is politics, and practical at that; and that I want them to be discussed without fear or favour; so knowing you for a

[1] The portions of this dialogue between the single 'quotes' are taken from a genuine document – 'A Radical's Creed', by John Page Hopps, in the *Pall Mall Gazette* of Dec. 10th, 1888.

cantankerous Socialist, I asked Brown to ask you to come here to-night.

J. Thank you for the compliment – and also for your company: you want to cheer me up, which is kind of you. But you know how curious I am; what *can* it be? It can't be politics, for things are looking rather blue for your side of the house. Is business beginning to boom, Brown? Have you been speculating in a gold-mine which is turning up trumps, Stride?

B. Well, perhaps business is a thought better. But that's not it. You see—

S. (*interrupting.*) It so happens that you are out about it's not being politics. Brown and I think matters are looking much more hopeful of late.

J. Indeed! And now I look at you, there is something portentous about your cheerfulness. What's up? Are you going to turn Tory-Democrats, the last refuge for the desperately hopeful? Or does the Salvation Army raise your spirits? Have you got another Gordon on hand to put a stop to war by cutting down the fruit-trees on which potential warriors live, and to put a stop to slavery by killing the niggers before they can be made slaves of? Are you civilizing Africa?

S. Now don't you be offensive about Gordon: you know I'm dead against the whole nigger-slaying business.

J. Yes, but somewhat in favour of the Christian-hero pest. But let that pass. Is Lord Salisbury dead? Don't be too glad of it; it won't do you Liberals much good. Vic can truly say with King Harry in 'Chevy Chase',

'I trust I have within my realm
An hundred good as he.'

S. (*laughing.*) Hear the spite of the Tory-Democrat!

J. (*severely.*) Don't call bad names, Stride!

B. (*anxiously.*) No, but ain't you a Tory Democrat, Jones? Stride always calls you one.

J. Yes, that comes of his innate wisdom, that does not need vulgar information. I am not a Tory-Democrat, Brown.

B. What are you then? Because –

S. (*interrupting.*) Come, let's be serious, Jones. You know I'm really a practical Socialist.

J. Indeed I did *not* know it. May I ask –

S. (*interrupting.*) No, please don't interrupt me! I say I am a practical Socialist; and yet I cannot be one of your hard-shell Socialists, with your impossible nostrums of the abolition of capital and railways, and your preposterous ideals of communism and equality; and your false political economy, dead in the teeth of all the accurate thinkers of the day, such as Mill and Tennyson and Ricardo and Swinburne, and – and – Lord Rosebury and Auberon-Herbert. But yet, you see, I was bothered that there should be no true Socialist party that I could work with heartily; and now I really think that we are getting one, and I've got out a sort of manifesto of it: indeed, there it lies on the table now.

J. And you have asked Brown to ask me here to cheer me up with it? How kind of you. Is it in print?

S. No; but any Radical paper will print it.

J. Well, well, things *are* getting on fast. And is Brown a member of the new party? Are you a Socialist, Brown?

B. Well, where's the harm of a name? Stride and I thought –

S. (*interrupting.*) We don't *call* ourselves Socialists, of course.

J. No, of course not.

S. We call ourselves Advanced Liberals or Radicals.

J. (*with preternatural gravity.*) Hah! But is that such a great invention in the way of names?

S. That's just the beauty of it.

J. I grant you the beauty of it must be there – or nowhere.

S. Pray be serious, and don't interrupt!

B. I assure you, Jones –

S. (*interrupting.*) *We* are Socialists who don't set class against class, which I think is downright wickedness.

J. (*softly.*) Let the galled jade wince, *my* withers are unwrung! The ages have done all that for me.

S. (*taking up a paper from the table.*) Nevertheless we have a clear, definite Creed, which I will now lay before you, Jones.

J. Ah, *now* I see what makes you look so happy! You are Radicals who have been searching for the planks of your platform, and you think you have discovered the necessary timber – (*sotto voce*) all out of your own heads.

S. (*hurriedly, and not listening.*) Yes, that's it. Now look here, this is the preamble. (*Reads.*) 'It is always foolish and wicked to set class against class, but the time has come for a resolute forward movement in favour of the toilers of our streets and fields. Legislation cannot do much to make the weak strong, to make the poor rich, to make the miserable happy; but it can keep off the greedy hand, and shield the helpless from oppression. It can help the poor to help themselves. It can break down legalized monopoly. It can clear the road by sweeping away many hindrances in the path of men without influence. It can give the poor "the benefit of the doubt". It can help the wage-earner to give his child a chance. It can provide something better than the workhouse for old men and women whose strength is spent and whose friends are gone.'

J. It is nicely written, Stride, and I'm sure that you mean well, so far as you know how to; but you are deceiving yourself. How can legislation do all these things with one hand, while with the other it is engaged upholding that very monopoly (do you know what monopoly is, my friend?) of which the poor and their terrible needs are a necessary result? It exists to support the greedy hand; it exists for oppression, and when ceases to oppress will cease to exist. This is a riddle you cannot rede till you know a little more.

S. Well, well, that's only the preamble. Wait a bit! Our first plank is, 'Government by the people, for the people, in the interests of the people'.

J. If the people govern themselves for themselves and in their own interest, there will be nothing but themselves: is that so? Can it be so while the present system lasts, reformed or not? Your first plank is not a plank, but a phrase, and a phrase without meaning. As long as there are rich men nursed up at the expense of the people they will govern us for their interest, whatever the machinery of their government may be. Meantime the people is but the material for the feeding of the rich.

S. Well, this next is a plank, at all events: 'The State should as far and as fast as possible delegate to each locality the rights of self-government, and should encourage and protect them in the use of such rights.' There!

J. County Councils, eh? A Tory measure; and properly so. Bodies with feeble administrative powers in themselves; mere machinery in the hands of the central government; good to strengthen that by doing its dirty work and appearing responsible for it, while in reality they are responsible for nothing. That is what you mean by self-government. If you were to mean more your plank would be a plank to be walked by the present society; for when the State has delegated all its powers what is the good of it, and what shall we do with it?

S. Hilloa! Since when have you turned Anarchist?

J. Don't use words you don't understand. But go on.

S. 'We should lift the burdens as far as possible from the shoulders of the struggling classes' –

J. Stop a bit! That's good! *as far as possible* is a good phrase. No Tory could object to that plank so far. Well, where are you going to put these burdens when you have lifted them as far as possible? I suspect back again.

S. We would 'put them to a greater extent on the shoulders of those who toil not, but without toiling have enough and to spare'.

J. Well, that I call a great invention; only it smacks somewhat of going about to get something out of nothing. For how the devil can those who toil not (*ie.*, produce nothing) have enough and to spare – unless they steal it? In short, your struggling classes are too poor to pay taxes; that you admit (and by the admission admit also that the whole of the middle-classes or well-to-do are thieves). So you are going to set the *other* classes to steal from the poor, in order that the taxes may be duly paid. That will bring about no new blessing for the struggling classes; they enjoy it already.

S. You needn't talk nonsense! 'We believe in a graduated income-tax and graduated death-dues.'

J. Just so: to be paid by those who have no income but what they steal. Here is a pretty outcome of 'the career open to talent', which I believe is still the great maxim of the Radicals. Certainly *I* need not talk nonsense.

S. Now listen! 'We are in favour of a reform of the poor-laws.'

J. Gently, gently!

S. 'It is of course necessary to watch carefully lest the path to the poor's purse or the poor's house should not become too easy.'

J. Stop! Do you know why it is necessary?

S. No.

J. Of course, no. Why (also of course), because the share of the national purse which the poor get by working hard is only just enough to give them a most miserable life. So that if you did not make the path to that palace of bliss, the poor-house, a hard one, that kingdom of heaven would be taken by storm.

S. Well, 'At any rate that is no reason why the hopelessly beaten in the battle of life should be penned up like criminals'.

J. Excuse me: it is *the* reason.

S. 'In any case the neglect of poor old people in England is almost our greatest sin and shame.'

J. The sentiment does honour to your heart: but you are too sensitive: there are plenty of sins and shames quite as bad; the neglect of worn-out workers is a natural consequence of *the career open to talent* according to the doctrine of private property.

S. Well, now I have begun, I suppose I must go on. But how cantankerous you are!

J. I flatter myself I am. But go on, pray.

COMMONWEAL, VOLUME 5, NUMBER 158,
19 JANUARY 1889, PP. 18–19

WHIGS ASTRAY[1]

A Dialogue Between Owen Marx Bakounine Jones, *an architect (unsuccessful), and – the* Rev. Swain Stride, *a Nonconformist parson, and* Mr Jeremiah Brown, *a business man – advanced Radicals.*

Scene – A comfortable batchelor-looking (sic) room in Mr Brown's *house, with tobacco and pipes and grog to the fore.* Mr Stride *and* Mr Brown *sitting on either side of the fire, looking important and self-satisfied. Between them* Mr Jones *with an occasional ill-concealed grin on his face.*

S. 'We are in favour of giving some relief by way of security of tenure to leaseholders who are exposed to enormous losses and ruin. It is true that this may only be in accordance with a contract voluntarily entered into; and it must be admitted that the evil is a difficult one to deal with.'

J. Yes, so difficult with your qualification tacked on to the remedy (as you think it) that you won't deal with it at all. It doesn't matter: a man who can have enormous losses must be rich: it is a question between two groups of capitalists. Pass on.

S. 'We are in favour of the State making some provision for employing men and women who are unable to find work. It is a matter requiring very careful treatment; but

[1] The portions of this dialogue between the single 'quotes' are taken from a genuine document – 'A Radical's Creed', by John Page Hopps, in the *Pall Mall Gazette*[,] Dec. 10th, 1888.

no one can believe that the State as the people's executive has exhausted its powers in this matter.'

J. Well, if it has, certainly exhaustion has come before effort; for it has never tried to give work to the rejected of the labour-market: and if it did try it could only do so at the expense of the workers generally.

S. Well, but you see, 'the work provided and the wages paid need only be sufficient to stave off hopeless poverty; but that at all events a wise and practical system of government might offer'.

J. Yes, indeed, only sufficient to stave off hopeless poverty: an easy job, isn't it? Man alive, do you know what hopeless poverty is? Live the life of it, and then you will know. And how many live such a life? – two thirds of all the workers? Nearer three thirds, I think. Your system of government need be wise and practical indeed to stave that off.

S. Let us hope it will be; for we say 'there ought not to be a single human being in the nation who can honestly stand up and say: I am willing to work, but I know not where to go to earn house-rent and daily bread'.

J. Of course there ought not, and I am glad to hear you say so; but what are you to do but cherish your sentiment as a pious opinion? Can't you see that if it were so, labour would be dear; the capitalist would have to compete for the workman, instead of the workman for the capitalist, as is now the case? The capitalist would be undone, and would cease to employ, unless by the aid of new machinery he could once more win the blessing of having a due amount of men willing and unable to work. And if the capitalist won't employ labour – *ie.*, workmen – how is it to be employed?

S. They must employ themselves, I suppose.

J. *I* suppose so. In that case, where are those non-producing classes that you are so tender of?

S. Well – gone, I suppose.

J. So do *I* suppose. And yet you have been speaking of them as though they and their necessary complement, the poor, were essential and eternal.

S. (*after a pause.*) For my part, Jones, I think you are trying to confuse the simplicity of true democratic ideas with your pedantic political economy. Let us come back to the point. Now please attend. 'We are in favour of making justice easy of access to all. The path to the judge ought to be the most easy; but it is the most difficult. Justice ought to be the cheapest commodity in the nation; and it is the dearest.'

J. The path to the judge is pretty easy for some people; and it strikes me that when they find him, they pretty often find an animal which is a cross between a baboon and a tiger. But do you know that I suspect that by *justice* you mean *law*; and I more than doubt if that wouldn't be dear at any price. For doesn't all civil law mean the enforcement of private contract, with all its intricacy, by the over-mastering violence of the executive, which doesn't trouble itself to consider whether the carrying out of the contract will be injurious to the private person or to the community, so long as it has been entered into legally?

S. I really don't understand you.

J. I fear not; and there are many in your case, who think that peace means the rule of law. So much the worse for all of us. I advise you to watch a civil process in a law court (if you haven't done so already), and then tell me what you think of it. If you then don't understand what I have been saying, it's no use trying to make you understand.

S. Well, listen to this! Now I think that you will agree with me: 'The Radical is in favour of a resolute reform of the Land Laws, with a view to getting the whole of the land into the hands of the community or the State. Our great towns, especially London, are getting dangerously congested simply because the countrymen who are pressing into them cannot get at the land; and they cannot get at the land because of laws and customs which were never made for tenants and labourers, but for landlords and aristocrats; and there will never be any hope for the labouring classes in the country districts until these bad old laws and customs are changed.'

J. I agree with what you *say*, and with what you might *mean*, but which I don't think you do mean, since you began by cursing those who set class against class.

S. Why! what do you mean?

J. Ain't the landlords and aristocrats a class?

S. Well – well – perhaps they are.

J. They are, when you have properly understood the meaning of the word aristocrat nowadays; to wit, a person privileged to live on the labour of others.

B. Of course he doesn't mean –

S. (*interrupting.*) Yes, yes, Brown, you're quite right. Of course, I don't mean that the land shall be taken for the landlords without compensation; though, perhaps, not full compensation.

J. Mr Brown, will you lend me a pound?

B. (*putting his hand in his pocket.*) With pleasure, my dear fellow.

S. (*laughing rather sulkily.*) Only he will require compensation.

J. Twenty shillings, eh?

B. Oh, silver will suit perfectly well.

J. Now I was thinking 15s. would do.

B. (*grinning.*) I see; an apologue. No, Mr Jones, I shall want the twenty shillings in full.

J. So will your landlords, friend Stride – if they can get it. Believe me, they will try for *more* if a Radical government should (the fancy is a wild one) try such a measure as 'getting the whole of the land into the hands of the community or the State'. And if they can't get *more*, I promise you they won't take *less* without fighting for their position.

S. I don't know; perhaps they will if the thing is done carefully, without frightening them. Of course they won't if you go hilloaing Socialism at them.

J. Well, if you like, we will grant that they will agree to the land nationalization which you propose to them. What are you going to do with the other capitalists?

S. The *other* capitalists! We shan't meddle with the capitalists at all.

J. Indeed! They will do what they like with their riches then?

S. Certainly; it would be mere slavery for them else.

J. And what are their riches?

S. Well – well – well –

J. I see you don't know, so I must tell you. So much privilege to make the producers of wealth pay for leave to live for no cause except the 'interests' of the taxers. That is what you have got to take away from the landlords and aristocrats. If you leave them that, whatever measure of land nationalization may be passed, whoever or whatever *owns* the land, they will monopolize the use of it. And how can you compensate people for taking away such a monopoly but by giving it back again to them?

B. (*gasping.*) But – why – Mr Jones, you are advocating the abolition of private property!

J. Mr Brown, you are a clear-headed man. Shake hands!

[Brown *seems rather doubtful, but* Jones *seizes his hand and shakes it enthusiastically.*]

S. Never mind, Brown, he doesn't mean half he says.

J. I wish I could say half I mean.

S. Now comes the really important and practical part of our platform. We 'are in favour of one man one vote...of equal suffrages for men and women...of a more democratic House of Commons...the candidate under certain conditions should be freed from the official conditions; and it might be good policy to offer a small annual payment to those MP's who need and desire it –'

J. Hold on, your qualifications and exceptions and cautions are muddling me sadly; but it don't matter.

S. We 'are in favour of making an end of the House of Lords as a house of hereditary legislators'.

J. Yes, so that you may have the Lords in the Commons; more qualifications. Well, go on; are you nearly at an end?

S. Yes, yes! I'm just at the end. 'When Ireland has its Parliament for Irish affairs, and Scotland has its Parliament for Scotch affairs, and Wales has its Parliament for Welsh affairs, the present House of Commons might be turned into the English Parliament; the House of Lords might then be converted into a great Imperial Parliament for Imperial affairs, in which there should be representatives from every part of the Empire at home and across the seas. This is the great Radical ideal.'

J. Well, that's a new way of abolishing the House of Lords, certainly! I don't think they will grumble much at it. At any rate, you wind up with a good thumping piece of nonsense. – Well, I must be off; that lecture will be half over by now, and I promised to go.

B. (*showing renewed energy after a tendency to sleep.*) Stop a bit, Mr Jones; I think I ought to explain to you that the earlier part of our programme –

S. (*interrupting*). Yes, Brown, yes; our friend understands. You see, Jones –

B. (*rather indignantly.*) I say, Stride, just let me have one word. Mr Jones, all that about land nationalization, and State works for the unemployed, and the old people at the workhouse, and all that – you musn't be too severe upon it; because, I say, it is put in – (no, Stride, let me go on!) – just to make people, or some people, help us in these suffrage matters, which is the thing we advanced Liberals or Radicals really care about; and I flatter myself we know something about it too.

J. Well, I must say I think you ought to, considering the number of years you have been hemming and hawing about it. But look here, gentlemen, I must go, I bet the lecturer is just in his peroration. But, I say, isn't 'Advanced Radicals' rather lengthy in spelling?

B. But, Jones, how would you spell it?

J. Try – it will save you some letters – try W-H-I-G-S - A - S-T-R-A-Y – it *means* the same thing if it don't *spell* it. Well, good-bye; I shall just be in time for question-time.

COMMONWEAL, VOLUME 5, NUMBER 159,
26 JANUARY 1889, PP. 26–27

DUCKS AND FOOLS

When I was in Iceland, I was told about the habits of the eider ducks, which breed in great quantities in the little islets scattered about the firths there, and also of their treatment. They, of course, get their own living; they are pretty good to eat, but not very good; so they are not allowed to be shot, because they produce valuable down, which can be got at by the following process: They make their nests on the ground in the above-mentioned islets; the duck half strips her breast of the down to line her nest; this down is at once collared from the nest by those who are privileged to do so according to law. Then the duck pulls off the rest of her down, as she is anxious to sit and hatch; comes the legal owner of the down, and takes that also. Then comes the drake and half strips himself; this also the legal owner takes, grumbling because the drake's down is coarser, and also because his game is over; for now the poor devils of ducks would not hatch their eggs unless the drake were allowed to line the nest with all that remains to him. *Therefore* this time the down is not taken; the eggs are allowed to be hatched, so that in due time they may fulfil the function of their lives, and produce down for others' use. *Moral*: Ducks are obliged to stand this from Icelanders; but why Englishmen should stand similar usage from Englishmen is a curious question.

Commonweal, Volume 5, Number 169,
6 April 1889, p. 107

CORRESPONDENCE

In answer to our comrade Blackwell's suggestion, and in default of someone else beginning that free discussion he speaks of, I wish to note down a few thoughts suggested by reading the clauses of the Anarchist Congress at Valentia, as stated by our comrade; premising that I do so in no polemical spirit, but simply giving my own thoughts and hopes for the future for what they may be worth.

I will begin by saying that I call myself a Communist, and have no wish to qualify that word by joining any other to it. The aim of Communism seems to me to be the complete equality of condition for all people; and anything in a Socialist direction which stops short of this is merely a compromise with the present condition of society, a halting-place on the road to the goal. This is the only logical outcome of any society which is other than a close company sustained by violence for the express purpose of 'the exploitation of man by man' in the interest of the strongest. Our present 'society' dominated by capitalism, the society of contract, is a form of this class-society which has been forced upon those who hold the slave ideal by the growth of knowledge and the acquirement by man of mastery over the forces of nature. The history of 'society' since the fall of feudalism has been the gradual freeing of class or slave society from the fetters of superstition, so that it might develope (*sic*) naturally within its prescribed limits of 'exploitation of man by man', and that stupendous and marvellously rapid growth in power and resources of modern slave society is due to this shaking off of superstition.

Communism also will have to keep itself free of superstition. Its ethics will have to be based on the recognition of natural cause and effect, and not on rules derived from *a priori* ideas of the relation of man to the universe or some imagined ruler of it; and from these two things, the equality of condition and the recognition of the cause and effect of material nature, will grow all Communistic life. So far I think I can see clearly; but when I try to picture to myself the forms which that life will take, I confess I am at fault, and I think we must all be so. Most people who can be said to think at all are now beginning to see that the realization of Socialism is certain; although many can see nothing further than a crude and incomplete State Socialism, which very naturally repels many from Socialism altogether. All genuine Socialists admit that Communism is the necessary development of Socialism; but I repeat, further than this all must be speculative; and surely in speculating on the future of society we should try to shake ourselves clear of mere phrases; especially as many of them will cease to have a meaning when the change comes that we all of us long for. And here I join issue with our Anarchist-Communist friends, who are somewhat authoritative on the matter of authority, and not a little vague also. For if freedom from authority means the assertion of the advisability or possibility of an individual man doing what he pleases always and under all circumstances, this is an absolute negation of society, and makes Communism as the highest expression of society impossible; and when you begin to qualify this assertion of the right to do as you please by adding 'as long as you don't interfere with other people's rights to do the same', the exercise of some kind of authority becomes necessary. If individuals are not to coerce others, there must somewhere be an authority which is prepared to coerce them not to coerce; and that authority must clearly be collective. And there are other difficulties besides this crudest and most obvious one.

The bond of Communistic society will be voluntary in the sense that all people will agree in its broad principles when it is fairly established, and will trust to it as affording mankind the best kind of life possible. But while we are advocating equality of condition – *ie.*, due opportunity free to everyone for the satisfaction of his needs – do not let us forget the necessary (and beneficent) variety of temperament, capacity, and desires which exists amongst men about everything outside the region of the merest necessaries; and though many, or if you will, most of these different desires could be satisfied without the individual clashing with collective society, some of them could not be. Any community conceivable will sometimes determine on collective action which, without being in itself immoral or oppressive, would give pain to some of its members; and what is to be done then if it happens to be a piece of business which must be either done or left alone? would the small minority have to give way or the large majority? A concrete example will be of use here, especially as it affects *my* temperament. I have always believed that the realization of Socialism would give us an opportunity of escaping from that grievous flood of utilitarianism which the full development of the society of contract has cursed us with; but that would be in the long run only; and I think it quite probable that in the early days of Socialism the reflex of the terror of starvation, which so oppresses us now, would drive us into excesses of utilitarianism. Indeed, there is a school of Socialists now extant who worship utilitarianism with a fervour of fatuity which is perhaps a natural consequence of their assumption of practicality. So that it is not unlikely that the public opinion of a community would be in favour of cutting down all the timber in England, and turning the country into a big Bonanza farm or a market-garden under glass. And in such a case what could we do, who objected 'for the sake of life to cast away the reasons for living', when we had exhausted our powers of argument? Clearly we should have to submit to authority. And a little reflection will show us many such cases in which the collective authority will weigh down individual opposition, however reasonable, without a hope for its being able to assert itself immediately; in such matters there must be give and take: and the objectors would have to give up the lesser for the greater. In short, experience shows us that wherever a dozen thoughtful men shall meet together there will be twelve different opinions on any subject which is not a dry matter of fact (and often on that too); and if those twelve men want to act together, there must be give and take between them, and they must agree on some common rule of conduct to act as a bond between them, or leave their business undone. And what is this common bond but authority – that is, the conscience of the association voluntarily accepted in the first instance.

Furthermore, when we talk of the freedom of the individual man, we must not forget that every man is a very complex animal, made up of many different moods and impulses; no man is always wise, or wise in all respects. Philip sober needs protection against Philip drunk, or he may chance to wake up from his booze in a nice mess. Surely we all of us feel that there is a rascal or two in each of our skins besides the other or two who want to lead manly and honourable lives, and do we not want something to appeal to on behalf of those better selves of ours? and that something is made up of the aspirations of our better selves, and is the *moral conscience* without which there can be no true society, and which even a false society is forced to imitate, and so have a sham social conscience, – what we sometimes call hypocrisy.

Now I don't want to be misunderstood. I am not pleading for any form of arbitrary or unreasonable authority, but for *a public conscience* as a rule of action: and by all means let us have the least possible exercise of authority. I suspect that many of our Communist-Anarchist friends do really mean that, when they pronounce against all authority. And with equality of condition assured for all men, and our ethics based on reason, I cannot think that we need fear the growth of a new authority taking the place of the one which we should have destroyed, and which we must remember is based on the assumption that equality is impossible and that slavery is an essential condition of human society. By the time that is assumed that all men's needs must be satisfied according [to] the measure of the common wealth, what may be called the political side of the question would take care of itself.

COMMONWEAL, VOLUME 5, NUMBER 175, 18 MAY 1889, P. 157

'LOOKING BACKWARD'

We often hear it said that the signs of the spread of Socialism among English-speaking people are both abundant and striking. This is true; six or seven years ago the word Socialism was known in this country, but few even among the 'educated' classes knew more about its meaning than Mr Bradlaugh, Mr Gladstone, or Admiral Maxse know now – *ie.*, nothing. Whereas at present it is fashionable for even West-end dinner-parties to affect an interest in and knowledge of it, which indicates a wide and deep public interest. This interest is more obvious in literature perhaps than in anything else, quite outside the propagandist tracts issued by definitely Socialist societies. A certain tincture of Socialism, for instance (generally very watery), is almost a necessary ingredient nowadays in a novel which aims at being at once serious and life-like, while more serious treatment of the subject at the hands of non-Socialists is common enough. In short the golden haze of self-satisfaction and content with the best of all possible societies is rolling away before the sun-heat bred of misery and aspiration, and all people above the lowest level of intelligence (which I take to be low gambling and statesmanship) are looking towards the new development, some timorously, some anxiously, some hopefully.

It seems clear to me that the reception which Mr Bellamy's 'Looking Backward' has received that there are a great many people who are hopeful in regard to Socialism. I am sure that ten years ago it would have been very little noticed, if at all; whereas now several editions have been sold in America, and it is attracting general attention in England, and to anyone not deeply interested in the social question it could not be at all an attractive book. It is true that it is cast into the form of a romance, but the author states very frankly in his preface that he has only given it this form as a sugar-coating to the pill, and the device of making a man wake up in a new world has now grown so common, and has been done with so much more care and art than Mr Bellamy has used, that by itself this would have done little for it: it is the serious essay and not the slight envelope of romance which people have found interesting to them.

Since, therefore, both Socialists and non-Socialists have been so much impressed with the book, it seems to me necessary that the *Commonweal* should notice it. For it is a 'Utopia'. It purports to be written in the year 2000, and to describe the state of society at that period after a gradual and peaceable revolution has realized the Socialism which to us is but in the beginning of its militant period. It requires notice all the more because there is a certain danger in such books as this: a twofold danger; for there will be some temperaments to whom the answer given to the question 'How shall we live then?' will be pleasing and satisfactory, others to whom it will be displeasing and unsatisfactory. The danger to the first is that they will accept it with all its necessary errors and fallacies (which such a book *must* abound in) as conclusive statements of facts and rules of action, which will warp their efforts into futile directions. The danger to the second, if they are but enquirers or very young Socialists, is that they also accepting its speculations as facts, will be inclined to say, 'If *that* is Socialism, we won't help its advent, as it holds out no hope to us'.

The only safe way of reading a utopia is to consider it as the expression of the temperament of its author. So looked at, Mr Bellamy's utopia must be still called very interesting, as it is constructed with due economical knowledge, and with much adroitness; and of course his temperament is that of many thousands of people. This temperament may be called the unmixed modern one, unhistoric and unartistic; it makes its owner (if a Socialist) perfectly satisfied with modern civilization, if only the injustice, misery, and waste of class society could be got rid of; which half-change seems possible to him. The only ideal of life which such a man can see is that of the industrious *professional* middle-class men of to-day purified from their crime of complicity with the monopolist class, and become independent instead of being, as they now are, parasitical. It is not to be denied that if such an ideal could be realised, it would be a great improvement on the present society. But can it be realized? It means in fact the alteration of the machinery of life in such a way that all men shall be allowed to share in the fulness of that life, for the production and upholding of which the machinery was instituted. There are clear signs to show us that that very group whose life is thus put forward as an ideal for the future are condemning it in the present, and that they also demand a revolution. The pessimistic revolt of the latter end of this century led by John Ruskin against the philistinism of the triumphant bourgeois, halting and stumbling as it necessarily was, shows that the change in the life of civilization had begun, before any one seriously believed in the possibility of altering its machinery.

It follows naturally from the author's satisfaction with the best part of modern life that he conceives of the change to Socialism as taking place without any breakdown of that life, or indeed disturbance of it, by means of the final development of the great private monopolies which are such a noteworthy feature of the present day. He supposes that these must necessarily be absorbed into one great monopoly which will include the whole people and be worked for its benefit by the whole people. It may be noted in passing that by this use of the word monopoly he shows unconsciously that he has his mind fixed firmly on the mere *machinery* of life: for clearly the only part of their system which the people would or could take over from the monopolists would be the machinery of organization, which monopoly is forced to use, but which is not an essential part of it. The essential of monopoly is, 'I warm myself by the fire which you have made, and you (very much the plural) stay outside in the cold'.

To go on. This hope of the development of the trusts and rings to which the competition for privilege has driven commerce, especially in America, is the distinctive part of Mr Bellamy's book; and it seems to me to be a somewhat dangerous hope to rest upon, too uncertain to be made a sheet-anchor of. It may be indeed the logical outcome of the most modern side of commercialism – *ie.*, the outcome that *ought* to be; but then there is its historical outcome to be dealt with – *ie.*, what *will* be; which I cannot help thinking may be after all, as far as this commercial development is concerned, the recurrence of break-ups and re-formations of this kind of monopoly, under the influence of competition for privilege, or war for the division of plunder, till the flood comes and destroys them all. A far better hope to trust to is that men having once got it into their heads that true life implies free and equal life, and that is now possible of attainment, they will consciously strive for its attainment at any cost. The economical semi-fatalism of some Socialists is a deadening and discouraging view, and may easily become more so, if events at present unforeseen bring back the full tide of 'commercial prosperity'; which is by no means unlikely to happen.

The great change having thus peaceably and fatalistically taken place, the author has to put forward his scheme of the organization of life; which is organized with a vengeance. His scheme may be described as State Communism, worked by the very extreme of national centralization. The underlying vice in it is that the author cannot conceive, as aforesaid, of anything else than the *machinery* of society, and that, doubtless naturally, he reads in to the future of society, which he tells us is unwastefully conducted, that terror of starvation which is the necessary accompaniment of a society in which two-thirds or more of its labour-power *is* wasted: the result is that though he *tells* us that every man is free to chose his occupation and that work is no burden to anyone, the *impression* which he produces is that of a huge standing army, tightly drilled, compelled by some mysterious fate to unceasing anxiety for the production of wares to satisfy every caprice, however wasteful and absurd, that may cast up amongst them.

As an illustration it may be mentioned that everybody is to begin the serious work of production at the age of twenty-one, work three years as a labourer, and then choose his skilled occupation and work till he is forty-five, when he is to knock off his work and amuse himself (improve his mind, if he has one left him). Heavens! think of a man of forty-five changing all his habits suddenly and by compulsion! It is a small matter after this that the said persons past work should form a kind of aristocracy (how curiously old ideas cling) for the performance of certain judicial and political functions.

Mr Bellamy's ideas of life are curiously limited; he has no idea beyond existence in a great city; his dwelling of man in the future is Boston (USA) beautified. In one passage, indeed, he mentions villages, but with unconscious simplicity shows that they do not come into his scheme of economical equality, but are mere servants of the great centres of civilization. This seems strange to some of us, who cannot help thinking that our experience ought to have taught us that such aggregations of population afford the worst possible form of dwelling-place, whatever the second-worst might be.

In short, a machine-life is the best which Mr Bellamy can imagine for us on all sides; it is not to be wondered at then that his only idea of making labour tolerable is to decrease the amount of it by means of fresh and ever fresh developments of machinery. This view I know he will share with many Socialists with whom I might otherwise agree more than I can with him; but I think a word or two is due to this important side of the subject. Now surely this ideal of the great reduction of the hours of labour by the mere means of machinery is a futility. The human race has always put forth about as much energy as it could in given conditions of climate and the like, though that energy has had to struggle against the natural laziness of mankind: and the development of man's resources, which has given him greater power over nature, has driven him also into fresh desires and fresh demands on nature, and thus made his expenditure of energy much what it was before. I believe that this will be always so, and the multiplication of machinery will just – multiply machinery; I believe that the ideal of the future does not point to the lessening of men's energy by the reduction of *labour* to a minimum, but rather to the reduction of *pain in labour* to a minimum, so small that it will cease to be a pain; a gain to humanity which can only be dreamed of till men are even more completely equal than Mr Bellamy's utopia would allow them to be, but which will most assuredly come about when men are really equal in condition; although it is probable that much of our so-called 'refinement', our luxury – in short, our civilization – will have to be sacrificed to it. In this part of his scheme, therefore, Mr Bellamy worries himself unnecessarily in seeking (with obvious failure) some incentive to labour to replace the fear of starvation, which is at present our only one, whereas it cannot be too often repeated that the true incentive to useful and happy labour is and must be pleasure in the work itself.

I think it necessary to state these objections to Mr Bellamy's utopia, not because there is any need to quarrel with a man's vision of the future of society, which, as above said, must always be more or less personal to himself; but because this book, having produced a great impression on people who are really enquiring into Socialism, will be sure to be quoted as an authority for what Socialists believe, and that, therefore, it is necessary to point out that there are some Socialists who do not think that the problem of the organization of life and necessary labour can be dealt with by a huge national centralization, working by a kind of magic for which no one feels himself responsible; that on the contrary it will be necessary for the unit of administration to be small enough for every citizen to feel himself responsible for its details, and be interested in them; that individual men cannot shuffle off the business of life on to the shoulders of an abstraction called the State, but must deal with it in conscious association with each other. That variety of life is as much an aim of true Communism as equality of condition, and that nothing but an union of these two will bring about real freedom. That modern nationalities are mere artificial devices for the commercial war that we seek to put an end to, and will disappear with it. And, finally, that art, using that word in its widest and due signification, is not a mere adjunct of life which free and happy men can do without, but the necessary expression and indispensable instrument of human happiness.

On the other hand, it must be said that Mr Bellamy has faced the difficulty of economical reconstruction with courage, though he does not see any other sides to the problem, such, *eg.*, as the future of the family; that at any rate he sees the necessity for the equality of the reward of labour, which is such a stumbling block for incomplete Socialists; and his criticism of the present monopolist system is forcible and fervid. Also up and down his pages there will be found satisfactory answers to many ordinary objections. The book is one to be read and considered seriously, but it should not be taken as the Socialist bible of reconstruction; a danger which perhaps it will not altogether escape, as incomplete systems impossible to be carried out but plausible on the surface are always attractive to people ripe for change, but not knowing clearly what their aim is.

Commonweal, Volume 5, Number 180,
22 June 1889, pp. 194–195

UNDER AN ELM-TREE; OR, THOUGHTS IN THE COUNTRY-SIDE

Midsummer in the country – here you may walk between the fields and hedges that are as it were one huge nosegay for you, redolent of bean-flowers and clover and sweet hay and elder-blossom. The cottage gardens are bright with flowers, the cottages themselves mostly models of architecture in their way. Above them towers here and there the architecture proper of days bygone, when every craftsman was an artist and brought definite intelligence to bear upon his work. Man in the past, nature in the present, seem to be bent on pleasing you and making all things delightful to your senses; even the burning dusty road has a look of luxury as you lie on the strip of roadside green, and listen to the blackbirds singing, surely for your benefit, and, I was going to say as if they were paid to do it, but I was wrong, for as it is they seem to be doing their best.

And all, or let us say most things, are brilliantly alive. The shadowy bleak in the river down yonder, which is – ignorant of the fate that Barking Reach is preparing for its waters – sapphire blue under this ruffling wind and cloudless sky, and barred across here and there with the pearly white-flowered water-weeds, every yard of its banks a treasure of delicate design, meadowsweet and dewberry and comfrey and bed-straw – from the bleak in the river, amongst the labyrinth of grasses, to the starlings busy in the new shorn fields, or about the grey ridges of the hay, all is eager, and I think all is happy that is not anxious.

What is that thought that has come into one's head as one turns round in the shadow of the roadside elm? A country-side worth fighting for if that were necessary, worth taking trouble to defend its peace. I raise my head, and betwixt the elm-boughs I see far off a grey buttressed down rising over the sea of green and blue-green meadows and fields, and dim on the flank of it over its buttresses [I] can see a quaint figure made by cutting the short turf away from the chalk of the hill-side; a figure which represents a White Horse according to the heraldry of the period, eleven hundred years ago. Hard by that hill-side the country people of the day did verily fight for the peace and loveliness of this very country where I lie, and coming back from their victory scored the image of the White Horse as a token of their valour, and, who knows? perhaps as an example for their descendants to follow.

For a little time it makes the blood stir in me as I think of that, but as I watch the swallows flitting past me betwixt hedge and hedge, or mounting over the hedge in an easy sweep and hawking over the bean-field beyond, another thought comes over me. These live things I have been speaking of, bleak and swallows and starlings and blackbirds, are all after their kind beautiful and graceful, not one of them is lacking in its due grace and beauty; but yesterday as I was passing by a hay-field there was an old red-roan cart-horse looking seriously but good-humouredly at me from a gap in the hedge, and I stopped to make his acquaintance; and I am sorry to say that in spite of his obvious merits he was ugly, Roman-nosed, shambling, ungainly: yet how useful he had been – for others. Also the same day (but not in the same field) I saw some other animals, male and female, with whom also I made acquaintance, for the male ones at least were thirsty. And these animals, both male and female, were ungraceful, unbeautiful, as ungainly as the roan cart-horse; yet they were obviously useful, for they were making hay before my eyes. Then I bethought me that as I had seen starlings in Hertfordshire that were of the same race as the Thames side starlings, so I had seen or heard of featherless two-legged animals of the same race as the thirsty creatures in the hay-field; they had been sculptured in the frieze of the Parthenon, painted on the ceiling of the Sistine Chapel, imagined in literature as the heroes and heroines of romance; nay, when people had created in their minds a god of the universe, creator of all that was, is, or shall be, they were driven to represent him as one of that same race to which the thirsty haymakers belonged; as though supreme intelligence and the greatest measure of gracefulness and beauty and majesty were at their highest in the race of those ungainly animals.

Under the elm-tree these things puzzle me, and again my thoughts return to the bold men of that very country-side, who, coming back from Ashdown field, scored that White Horse to look down for ever on the valley of the Thames; and I thought it likely that they had this much in common with the starlings and the bleak, that there was more equality amongst them than we are used to now, and that there would have been more models available amongst them for Woden than one would be like to find in the Thames-side meadows.

Under the elm-tree I don't ask myself whether that is owing to the greater average intelligence of men at the present day, and to the progress of humanity made since the time of the only decent official that England ever had, Alfred the Great, to wit; for indeed the place and time are not favourable to such questions, which seem sheer nonsense amidst of all that waste of superabundant beauty and pleasure held out to men who cannot take it or use it, unless some chance rich idler may happen to stray that way. My thoughts turn back to the haymakers and their hopes, and I remember that yesterday morning I said to a bystander, 'Mr So-and-so (the farmer) is late in sending his men into the hay-field'.

Quoth he, 'You see, sir, Mr So-and-so is short-handed'.

'How's that?' said I, pricking up my Socialist ears.

'Well, sir,' said he, 'these men are the old men and women bred in the village, and pretty much past work; and the young men with more work in them, they do think that they ought to have more wages than them, and Mr So-and-so, he won't pay it. So you see, he be short-handed.'

As I turned away, thinking over all the untold, untellable details of misery that lay within this shabby, sordid story, another one met my ears. A labourer of the village comes to a farmer and says to him that he really can't work for 9s. a week any more, but must have 10s. Says the farmer, 'Get your 10s. somewhere else then'. The man turns away to two month's lack of employment, and then comes back begging for his 9s. slavery.

Commonplace stories of unsupported strikes, you will say. Indeed they are, if not they would be easily remedied; the casual tragedy cut short; the casual wrongdoer branded as a person out of humanity. But since they are so commonplace –

What will happen, say my gloomy thoughts to me under the elm tree, with all this country beauty so tragically incongruous in its richness with the country misery which cannot feel its existence? Well, if we must still be slaves and slaveholders, it will not last long; the Battle of Ashdown will be forgotten for the last commercial crisis; Alfred's heraldry will yield to the lions of the half crown. The architecture of the crafts-gildsmen will tumble down, or be 'restored' for the benefit of the hunters of picturesque, who, hopeless themselves, are incapable of understanding the hopes of past days, or the expression of them. The beauty of the landscape will be exploited and artificialized for the sake of the villa-dweller's purses where it is striking enough to touch their jaded appetites; but in quiet places like this it will vanish year by year (as indeed it is now doing) under the attacks of the most grovelling commercialism.

Yet think I to myself under the elm-tree, whatever England, once so beautiful, may become, it will be good enough for us if we set no hope before us but the continuance of a population of slaves and slave-holders for the country which we pretend to love, while we use it and our sham love for it as a stalking-horse for robbery of the poor at home and abroad. The worst outward ugliness and vulgarity will be good enough for such sneaks and cowards.

Let me turn the leaf and find a new picture, or my holiday is spoilt; and don't let some of my Socialist friends with whom I have wrangled about the horrors of London, say, 'This is all that can come of your country life'. For as the round of the seasons under our system of landlord farmer and labourer produces in the country pinching parsimony and dulness (*sic*), so does the 'excitement of intellectual life' in the cities produce the slum under the capitalist system of turning out and selling market wares not for use but for waste. Turn the page I say. The hayfield is a pretty sight this month seen under the elm, as the work goes forward on the other side of the way opposite to the bean-field, till you look at the haymakers closely. Suppose the haymakers were friends working for friends on land which was theirs, as many as were needed, with leisure and hope ahead of them instead of hopeless toil and anxiety, need their useful labour for themselves and their neighbours cripple and disfigure them and knock them out of the shape of men fit to represent the Gods and Heroes? And if under such conditions a new Ashdown had to be fought (against *capitalist* robbers this time), the new White Horse would look down on the home of men as wise as the starlings in their *equality*, and so perhaps as happy.

Commonweal, Volume 5, Number 182,
6 July 1889, pp. 212–213

IMPRESSIONS OF THE PARIS CONGRESS

We delegates of the League met as agreed at London Bridge Station, and found an enormous crowd of people going our way. We got stowed into the carriages somehow, and whiled away the time in singing songs and selling a few numbers of *Commonweal* to divers good folk who had only a glimmering about the events that the French were going to celebrate on the morrow. Getting to the boats at Newhaven, we found that the clerk of the weather had provided us with a *sell* in the form of spring tides, so that the boats which were timed to start at 11 pm did not stir from the harbour till close on 3 am. And even then there was not enough water for us to get into Dieppe for an hour or two; so that, in short, instead of getting into Paris at 8 a.m. we did not start from Dieppe till 10, and got to Paris at 1.30, somewhat weary with the long journey.

We were met at the station by several old acquaintances, and made the best of our way to our headquarters, which is in the Montmartre district, the northern suburb of Paris. As a matter of course we thus missed the first sitting of the Congress at the Rue Petrelle, though I, having been put upon the committee, went down to the hall and saw our friend Lafargue and the members of the Organizing Committee; after which there was nothing left for us but to take our pleasure as we best could in wandering about the city and seeing what I should irreverently call the 'fun of the fair'.

The next morning, Monday, we went down to the Salle Petrelle, and found the delegates assembling; I found myself also appointed to verify the mandates of the English-speaking delegates, and had plenty of work to do. It was obvious from the first that the Salle Petrelle was not large enough for the Congress, as it would not hold 300 persons, and besides the delegates the public was admitted. Hasty arrangements were made for another hall, and we were presently on the way to a kind of theatre, called the Fantasies Parisiennes, in the neighbouring Rue Rochechouart, where we soon got to business, with Vaillant and Liebknecht in the chair. The first business was of course the roll-call of the delegates, which of itself was a somewhat imposing ceremony, considering the great number of them, and the trouble and even risk to which some of them had been put to come. The numbers of the delegates first taken were as follows: French, 180; Germans, 81, English, 21; Belgian, 14; Austrian, 8; Italian, 11; Russian, 6; Swiss, 6; Denmark, 3; Roumania, 4; Spain, 2; Poland, 4; Hungary, 3; America, 2; Portugal, 1; Greece, 1; Holland, 4; Sweden, 1; Norway, 1. In all, 353; but later comers made up the list to upwards of 400. The spirit of the Congress was good, the enthusiasm undoubted. As above said, the mere presence of so many Socialists come together from so many countries so earnest and eager was inspiriting and encouraging.

Little was done at this morning meeting except what might be called formal business; but it was clear from the first that there were two parties in the Congress, one of which was anxious almost at any price for fusion with the Possibilist Congress, and the other quite contented to let them hold their deliberations by themselves. Accordingly a meeting of the English delegates met on the Monday afternoon to decide upon their course of action, at which the delegates of the League were unanimous for keeping quite apart from the Possibilist Congress, which has no pretentions to being a Socialist Congress, and considering that Germany is quite unrepresented there, and that there is a distinct smack of jingoism about it, no *valid* pretensions to being international.

We expected that this question of fusion would come on in the evening sitting of Monday, but the whole time was taken up in settling various details of the constitution of the Congress, some of which excited angry feeling among the French delegates; the cause of which it was difficult, or impossible rather, for a stranger to understand. Underlying it all, however, was this question of fusion: for it must be understood that the Belgian, Dutch, and Italian delegates had a definite mission to bring about a fusion of the two congresses, and that many of them were very hot about it. The chairman (a Swiss) at this evening meeting, though apparently a straightforward sincere man, had no hold on the meeting, so that it got rather out of hand; and no doubt there was some of the usual police element present. However, amongst the genuine Socialists no harm was meant and none was done.

The next morning we received at our headquarters comrades Charles and J. and R. Turner, and at the Congress the ground was cleared for the settlement of this question of fusion. There were practically three resolutions before the meeting. Domela Nieuwenhuis spoke for the fusion in a speech which his obvious earnestness and good-will made very impressive; though he ignored the fact that as to the French party neither the Guesdists nor the Possibilists really desired it, and rightly so, as the breach was too great between them to be healed by a mere formality. Tressaud, the Marseilles delegate, in a speech quite straightforward and to the point, spoke against the fusion, and I followed him, and supported him with the full assent of our comrades of the League.

Liebknecht brought forward another motion which threw the onus of making the fusion on the Possibilists; and this was clearly the popular view among the French and German delegates. The propositions made, a long time was spent in a somewhat wearisome and very involved discussion as to how we were to vote, and at last it was settled that the voting should be by nations. Then the voting took place, and it became clear that if we voted for Tressaud's proposal, as we should have preferred to do and thus took our votes away from Liebknecht, we should risk giving the majority to those who wished for fusion on almost any terms, and thus should find ourselves sitting in a Congress which, as above said, was not a Socialist one. We therefore voted for Liebknecht's proposal, appending to our vote a statement that if Tressaud's had been brought up we should have voted for it; and we found that the French delegates had voted in the same way. There was a large majority for Liebknecht's motion; and a committee was appointed to confer with the Possibilists and see if anything practical in the way of fusion could follow from this motion, which expressed a wish for fusion, but only on the terms that there should be no submission on our part; and thus a long sitting came to an end.

The next morning (Wednesday) we heard that the Possibilists had accepted the fusion; but on condition that we should submit to having our mandates examined by the united Congresses, which it was clearly impossible for us to agree to, as even those who had been most eager in pressing on the fusion admitted. We answered the Possibilists therefore that we could not agree to these terms, and in the evening received an answer from them in return breaking off the negotiations for good and all.

We had thus wasted two whole days in discussing a matter which in the opinion of the delegates of the Socialist League ought never to have been discussed at all, since our Congress was open even at the last moment to the delegates of any genuine working-men's association, so that there was nothing to prevent any one from joining us who felt friendly towards us. And furthermore, the plain truth is that real union between the two French sections was impossible, and an artificial union would have produced worse quarrels, and have prevented any profitable discussion to say the least of it.

On Wednesday morning, with this matter of the fusion hanging unsettled over us, began the reading of the reports, Bebel leading off for Germany. These have lasted all to-day; but as we shall go to press before an account of the end of the Congress could be given, I will leave these for the present.

Our comrades should understand that whatever is said in the Congress, whether French, German, or English, has to be translated doubly; and the translations seemed on the whole to be very well done. Mrs Aveling acted as translator between German and French and English; Vollmar did the German part: the translators had their difficult task made more difficult by the buzz of conversation which arose as soon as the original speaker ended.

The earnestness and enthusiasm of the delegates was very impressive, and seems to have made some impression even on bourgeois observers; and whatever eagerness there was in debate, we all met out of debate with great friendliness and goodwill. A great many of the delegates have continually found themselves sitting at the same table for the meal after the session in the pleasantest and most fraternal manner in the cheaper restaurants round about the place of meeting.

I am sorry to say that I must finish this letter with mentioning a disagreeable affair, on which it is impossible to be wholly silent. In the discussion which took place in the Possibilist Congress anent the fusion, Mrs Besant allowed herself to say that the English delegates at our Congress represented nothing but themselves. We have in consequence offered our comrades here to give them every opportunity for the fullest scrutiny of our mandates; but it is quite clear that we owe no account of ourselves to a Congress for which we have received no mandate.

Thursday, July 18th, 1889.

COMMONWEAL, VOLUME 5, NUMBER 185,
27 JULY 1889, P. 234

IMPRESSIONS OF THE PARIS CONGRESS: II

On the Wednesday, after the introduction of a delegate from the far-off country of Finland, who was received with much enthusiasm, Bebel began the reading of the reports with a history of the German movement in more recent days. This took two hours in the delivery, I should think, and of course could not be translated; a short resumé was all that could be given in French and English, but even from that it was plain that the original was able and exhaustive. I should mention that most, if not all, of the reports have been handed in in writing and will be printed; so that we shall have the benefit of noting the views of the delegates as to the position of the movement in the various countries.

A Spanish delegate (I think) followed Bebel, and spoke in his native tongue, which was translated by Lafargue. His address seemed emphatic and pithy.

In the evening the veteran Lavroff read a long and interesting report from Russia. After which came a threatening of the repetition of the fruitless noise of Monday evening, for what cause I, as a stranger, am utterly unable to say. The chairman (Anseele), however, disposed of this pretty easily, though I think in England we should have thought him a little too ready to adopt the last resort of 'chucking out'.

Then Jules Guesde got up and delivered what as a speech must be considered as the speech of the Congress, and was certainly splendid oratory. It was hardly a report, however, and to some of us there seemed too strong a flavour of electioneering in it; which, considering the position of the French Social-Democrats, was of course to be expected.

Next morning, after some preliminaries, I was called upon to report for England. I should mention here that we

SL delegates were strongly of the opinion that Keir Hardie, who represented the Parliamentary side of English Socialism, should have an opportunity of speaking to that side, and that we pressed this on the Committee. In the light of what occurred later, I thing this ought to be noticed.

I was told that the time now pressed so much that the rest of the speakers of reports would be asked to keep within ten minutes, which I tried to do – and I think kept within twenty. I handed in my written report later on.

I was followed by Adler, for Austria, who by no means imitated my brevity (nor did any one else). Volders reported for Belgium; Italy, Holland, and Poland also reported. After these national reports came the special reports – *ie.*, for associations, etc. Keir Hardie spoke for the Scotch miners; I missed his speech, and chiefly remember a speech of the delegate for the Waiters' Association – very straightforward and to the point, complaining of the irrational contempt in which these luckless slaves of the well-to-do are held even by their working brethren: and also a speech of Madame Zetkin, who represented the working women of Berlin. This last was in fact a very clear and closely reasoned essay on the relation between the industrial position of women and Socialism. When printed it will be valuable as clearly establishing the difference in view between the Socialist and the 'Woman's Rights' women. It was received with as much applause as any other speech; more than any, I think, except Guesde's.

The fag-end of this sitting (a very long one) was devoted to short speeches by various delegates. Here Kitz, as a result of a great deal of pressing on my part, was allowed to read the text of a resolution condemning the privileged thieves of society for their brutal treatment of the 'criminals' who have been first manufactured and then punished by our robber sham-society. We understood that he would have an opportunity of moving this resolution; but the opportunity did not turn up.

Two or three Anarchists spoke in this sitting, and spoke well, though to my mind they did not put forward any distinctively Anarchist doctrines: they were well received by the mass of the delegates; who indeed throughout strongly applauded any revolutionary sentiments. The gibe of one Anarchist deserves to be noted. Apropos of palliation by legislation on labour, he said: 'When I was a Collectivist I was taught the Iron Law so well by Marx and Liebnecht, that I cannot forget it now I am an Anarchist.'

That evening (Friday) the Paris Municipality threw open the splendid public rooms of the Hotel de Ville to the delegates of both Congresses and their friends, and entertained them very handsomely after the generous 'custom of the country'. Also there was a friendly meeting held at our friend Maxime Lisbonne's Taverne dur Bagne, which is got up to simulate a prison, with (in all senses) fearful pictures on the walls: waiters dressed as convicts, and where for the consideration of 1 1/2 francs you can be solemnly ironed in public (I don't know what charge is made for taking off the irons). Here Louise Michel spoke, and there was much enthusiasm shown. I was not able to attend either of these entertainments, as I had to spend the night in writing out my report from my notes.

On Saturday morning we found Cunninghame Graham in the chair, and we expected that Bebel's propositions would be formally put, debated on, and (certainly) carried by a large majority; but this was not duly done. I must explain here that for three days past I had handed in a resolution of a wide Socialist character, so that the Congress might pledge itself definitely to Socialism, which all our English comrades thought necessary to be done, if it were only to give our Congress a reason for existence in opposition to the Possibilist Congress. The organizers said that the preamble of Bebel's propositions practically carried with it the sense of my resolution. This was true; but I pleaded that a separate resolution ought to be put, as there were delegates present who would vote against Bebel's propositions who would assuredly vote for a Socialist resolution, and that moreover the resolution would not have the same force imbedded in a preamble which would not be noticed alongside of its 'practical' deduction.

The organizers agreed therefore to the putting of a distinct resolution, and on this Saturday morning I spent some time in Conference with our French and German friends (including Bebel), and arranged for the modification of my resolution by the introduction of matter from the French and German preambles, which, however, did not alter the sense of the original resolution.

Coming back to the Congress Hall again nothing serious seemed doing, and knowing that the vast majority of the delegates were in favour of Bebel's propositions, believing also that nothing serious would be put forward in opposition, I left for Rouen after the morning session along with Kitz and Tarleton, and was therefore not a witness of the lamentable scene that followed; therefore, what I say of it is subject to correction by those of our comrades who were there.

It was clear that no discussion of the propositions was to be allowed, and the clôture was voted. Thereupon, our friend Merlino rose to protest against this proceeding, but was howled down; he was attacked in words by a delegate and accused of carrying on organized interruption, and his expulsion was ordered by the chairman. This was carried out with much brutal violence, against which the League delegates attempted to protect him. After his expulsion, Mrs Schack and Tochatti rose also to protest, and then all our delegates present left and handed in a written protest against the violence and the smothering of the discussion.

Now surely, short as the time for discussion was, time could have been found for two speakers at least to put forward the contrary to the very propositions which from the first we had been called together to discuss; and since the Congress (though undoubtedly in the main composed of Social Democrats) had distinctly invited Socialists of all kinds, it must be said to have stultified itself in refusing to listen to opinions which everybody knew were held by some of the delegates; and the intolerance of the majority must remain a serious blot on what was otherwise a successful demonstration at least.

On the Saturday morning, the delegates went to Pere la Chaise to hang a wreath on the Mur des Federés, the death-place of so many of the murdered men of the Commune. Cunninghame Graham and Tochatti spoke there amongst others, and so came to an end this great gathering.

Looking back on it, it seems clear that if the Congress had gone on with its business instead of trying to stand well with the public by discussing the possibility of a fusion, which almost all of us knew was impossible, we should have gained at least one whole day for debating the pros and cons on Bebel's propositions; and if, in addition, the reports of the different nations had been taken as read (since they are all to be printed) we should have had time enough for a debate which would have satisfied everybody, and sent the delegates of all shades away contented. Because in the course of that debate everything could have been said that was necessary about the movement generally.

Finally, the impression made on me by attendance at this International Congress is that such gatherings are not favourable for the dispatch of business, and their real use is as demonstrations, and that it would be better to organize them as such. I mean that two or three great public meetings should be held (after the due formalities of verification, etc., have been gone through), that opportunities should be given for the delegates to meet each other in social and conversational meetings, and that there should be no voting, no 'playing at Parliament'. This is my wisdom after the event; but I think it is worth considering, as no doubt there will soon be another International Socialist Congress.

COMMONWEAL, VOLUME 5, NUMBER 186,
3 AUGUST 1889, P. 242.

TRIAL BY JUDGE v. TRIAL BY JURY

The Maybrick case, of which we have been hearing so much, does not differ in essence from most other trials for murder. A man is killed; there is a certain amount of presumptive evidence against such and such a person; a coroner's jury find that this person is guilty of the murder. The presumptive evidence is after long delay brought before the Criminal Court; which delay, be it remarked, tends very much to increase the difficulty in getting at the truth, as lies and falsities have time to grow round the original kernel of fact, and make a (*sic*) regular problems for the solution of the professional dealers with other persons' misdoings – the lawyers and judge. In the Criminal Court the game begins. Each side has its theory for accounting for a series of events which are supposed to have taken place, and tries to establish that theory by piecing together of details, the cross-examination of witnesses, and so on. It must be said that in this game the defence, which has to prove a negative, is necessarily very much weaker than the prosecution.

Next, the theory on either side being complete, it is in practice submitted to the judgement of *one man*, the judge, who is of course a thoroughly practised and skilful lawyer, drilled into a knowledge of what is called the 'law of evidence' – *ie.*, a series of maxims, more or less arbitrary, as such theories must be, as to the credibility of statements of events more than half forgotten, misunderstood by the witnesses at the time they happened, confused by hearsay, corrupted by prejudice – in a word, mostly lies. This one man, the judge, may be a treasure of impartiality, though he is not likely to be, since he is a successful advocate, and therefore *must* have been in the habit of wresting appearances towards the side that he was conventionally interested in, however they might have showed to his real self. But, however impartial he may be, it is not in the nature of man for a person not to take sides in a dispute which he is obliged to listen to, and considering his official position, the side that this person is most likely to take is the official one – *ie.*, that of the prosecution.

In theory, however (as we all know), it is the jury and not the judge who have to make the final decision of the case, – but in theory only. For the jury are of necessity men of average intelligence, taken from the middle class; and they are in consequence deeply imbued with the middle-class prejudices of the day. Now the present-day middle-class theory of the jury has mistaken the function of the jury, and assumes that its business is, not to judge the case, as it was originally meant to do, but to correct any gross mistakes or partiality in the judge; to be, in short, a kind of censorship on the judge, and therein to represent the public generally. This being the case, as a matter of fact the jury almost always take their verdict from the judge's summing-up, and it is rare indeed that those who are watching a case need trouble themselves about the jury's decision when they have heard or read the judge's summing-up – unless, indeed, he is really puzzled over the matter, in which case, having no opinion, he kindly allows the jury to have one.

And now in the midst of this intricate game which is being played for the life or death of a fellow citizen, there is one person who is out of it all, and can only watch what is going on; and that person is the one who is principally interested. The mouth of the accused is shut until the decision is given. Whatever misunderstandings, falsifications, or wrong deductions take place must pass without challenge from his personality, although it is obvious that often a few words from the accused might explain the matter, and give a new course to the evidence either for or against.

In short, in an English Criminal Court sides are taken for and against the silent onlooking accused (who, in spite of all theories to the contrary, is always looked on as guilty from the first). The judge decides which of those two sides has the preponderating weight of evidence, and the jury formally ratifies his decision, unless it is so monstrously unfair that they are compelled to protest by expressing their own opinion. The 'criminal' either 'escapes' or is convicted and slaughtered; our 'cultivated classes' bless their stars they are not living in days of violence, and those of the working classes who are not Socialists at heart echo their cant in various degrees of *un*-cultivation, however miserably they may be living.

For the rest, this is that 'average' justice which is in complete harmony with the commercialism of the age, which declines to supply the public with anything choice; it is, like all machine-work, a make-shift. Such make-shifts people put up with without grumbling for a long time; but at last when some dramatic demonstration of their futility is given, when the shoe-sole comes off in the middle of a muddy road, or the hat melts in a heavy shower, they get angry, and express their anger – in a futile way indeed, because they are the slaves of the machine which they grumble at.

That we would fain hope, is the explanation of the popular ebullition of temper at Liverpool the other day; the people there were at last struck by the obvious *un*fairness of the whole proceeding, of the farce which thus trifles with the lives and liberties of the citizens. At all events they directed the expression of their anger rightly this time. The judge and his summing-up is the real centre of the whole iniquity[.] That is the head and front of the attack on Trial by Jury, which, as long as it was a reality, was a true defence of the liberties of the people.

That is the interest the Maybrick case has to us Socialists. The case itself was a wretched one, a mere exemplification of the unhappiness which springs from the corruption of a Society founded on robbery; an unhappiness which so often avenges the wrongs of the poor on those whose iniquitous position puts them beyond the reach of the special misery which they inflict on so many millions of people, as good as or better than themselves. Yet, indeed, it must be said once more that Mrs Maybrick's 'immorality' weighed heavily against her, helped the judge to get the conviction, and that if people are to be hanged for making mistakes in married life, there will be a large mortality amongst the upper and middle classes.

The remarks in the capitalistic papers on this case, a great part of which amount to a defence of the present system of dealing with circumstantial evidence in criminal cases, are curious, but are too numerous to go through. One, however, must be noticed, because it is the argument most often and most plausibly used. It is admitted, say these wiseacres, that this was a case of doubt; but in the teeth of the maxim that the jury should give the benefit of the doubt to the accused, if this were done, almost no criminal could be convicted, as all evidence is circumstantial, and in almost every case there is doubt.

What does this amount to but this? That so beautifully constructed is the machine of criminal law, that it gives us two overwhelming risks, either of the escape of the guilty, or the condemnation of the innocent. Unhappily, it is not doubtful which risk our Society will take hardened as it is by the daily and hourly practice of wrong against so many people.

In effect, it is a ghastly thing to note so many respectable persons sitting safe as home in luxury so convinced of the necessity for hanging some one, either the right or the wrong person, if a 'crime' is committed. How strange that persons not ill-natured, not specially stupid, should think it above all things necessary that a private murder should be remedied by a public one.

As to the Court of Appeal which is in every one's mouth at present, it would be a feeble protection against injustice; and if, as I suppose, it were to be a court of professional judges, it would tend to a further weakening of what is left of the jury system, and so do more harm than good.

Commonweal, Volume 5, Number 188,
17 August 1889, p. 257.

CORRESPONDENCE
COMMUNISM AND ANARCHISM

I have to excuse myself for being so long in answering our comrades. My journey to the Paris Congress, and business necessary to be done before and after that event, accounts for the greater part of the delay. I will now do what I can to answer our friends who have written to the *Commonweal.* I must premise, by the way, that I have let a typographical error of importance pass unnoticed: for '*moral* conscience' our friends should read '*social* conscience'.

And now I find that one difficulty in dealing with the friends who are discussing the matter is that, in all probability, I differ very little in theory from what they *think*, but considerably from what they *write* – *eg.*, comrade Armsden appears to meet my commonplace 'that you have a right to do as you like so long as you don't interfere with your neighbour's right to do as he likes' with a negative; which he cannot mean to do. Anyhow, I assert it again, and also assert that the *social* conscience, which being social is common to every man, will forbid such individual interference, and use coercion if other means fail: and also that without that there can be no society; and further, that man without society is not only impossible, but inconceivable. I may say that I perceive here that the unlucky misprint of *moral* for social has turned our friend's arguments beside the question.

Comrade H. Davis misunderstands my use of the word Communist in supposing me to use it as the Owenites did, as implying life in separate communities, whether those communities were mere scattered accidents amidst a capitalistic society or not; whereas I use it as a more accurate term for Socialism as implying equality of condition and consequently abolition of private property. In this sense, of course, you could not live Communistically unt[i]ll the present society of capitalism or contract is at an end. Equally of course, the living in small communities is not in theory an essential of this great change, though I have little doubt that it would bring about such a way of living and abolish big cities, which, equally with comrade Davis, I think much to be desired.

In his reference to Philip drunk and sober, comrade Davis does not of course really mean that any obnoxious person shall be allowed to tyrannize over the rest of the citizens without restraint from them; but that is what his words mean.

As to the matter of majority-rule, let us look at the matter again. All rule must be, as comrade Davis sees, majority-rule – *ie.*, of the *effective* majority. If at any time the minority rules, it is because they are better organized, better armed, less stupid, more energetic than the mere nose-counted majority: this effective majority therefore coerces the minority; and as long as it *can* coerce it, it *will*. The time may come, and I hope it will, when the social conscience will be so highly developed that coercion will be impossible, even on the part of the community: but then in those days the community will be composed of men who so thoroughly realize Communism that there will be no chance of any of them attacking his neighbour in any way. All reasonable men, whatever they may call themselves, would rejoice at such a change; and it is because I *know* that this cannot be brought about as long as private property exists, that I desire the abolition of private property, and am a Communist.

But I do not consider myself a pessimist because I am driven to admit that such a condition of things is a long way ahead. And what can we do in the meantime? I remember that the great traveller Dr Wolff, travelling in the eastern wastes, inhabited a tent alone with a stalwart Greek servant of his, who habitually got drunk on the feast-days of his church, and when drunk, habitually beat poor Wolff. The latter objected, and said to his servant (I quote his own words), 'You must either not get drunk, or when you get drunk you must not beat me'. But the servant said to Wolff, 'I *shall* get drunk, and when I am drunk I shall certainly beat you'. Wolff being the weakest physically, had to submit; but if there had been two Wolffs, I will answer for it that they would have had recourse to coercion, and if they had allowed the drinking, they would certainly have put a stop to the beating. And really I think we should all of us have done in likewise, and considered it pedantic to allow one man to beat two of us: and surely it will always be so, as long as the individual acts unsocially: in that case he has no right against the society, which *he himself* has cast off.

I must repeat practically also what I said in my first article: however much the unit of association may be divided, people will have to associate in administration, and sometimes there will be differences of opinion as to what should be done. *Eg.*, a community discuss the building of a bridge; some say Ay and some No, and persist in that opinion after all possible arguments have been exhausted: what is to be done? which party is to give way? Our Anarchist friends say it must not be carried by a majority; in that case, then, it must be carried by a minority. And Why? Is there any divine right in a minority? I fail to see it, although I admit that the opinion is held by the absolutists.

Or again, passing to matters of principle again. Supposing that a commune decides to re-introduce wage-slavery within its bounds. Is that to be allowed by the majority of communes? Are we not to deliver slaves from their masters? If not, why are we revolutionary Socialists to-day?

A friend under the signature of 'Anarchist' stumbles, I think, over voluntary and involuntary association. Where all men are equal, I believe 'the give and take' would have such influence over men's minds, that 'the authority of compulsory representative institutions', or whatever took their place, would be so completely at one with the Social Conscience that there would be no dispute about it as to principle, and in detail, as above, the few would have to give way to the many; I should hope without any rancour. The correspondent does not seem to be able to think himself out of the present state of things, and yet at the same time imagines a possibility of free association as things now are; a quite illusory hope, since those of us who are unprivileged are at the beck and call of the privileged.

Comrade Blackwell suggests that since the majority is no more likely to be right than the minority (which I admit) they might as well toss a copper for it. I don't object; but then there might be a difference of opinion on that method also, and how are we to settle that? It is curious that comrade Blackwell in suggesting that the larger of the two differing parties in a matter of administration should throw the matter over, cannot see that this would mean victory for the noes; or, in other words, that in any question which must be answered aye or nay, and one obstructive could always prevent any business being done, and could in such matters thereby establish the most complete minority rule conceivable.

The other side of comrade Blackwell's remedy is a system of perpetual compromise, which would be disastrous if it were possible, for it would so hinder all reasonable work or progress that it could not be submitted to.

Comrade Blackwell objects to my calling the 'Anarchist-Socialists' 'vague', but he himself furnishes a specimen of their vagueness in the platform of the Pittsburg Congress in 1883. He adds, 'Now I believe most members of the Socialist League agree to every one of these planks'. Exactly, and every other Socialist also; there is nothing distinctly Anarchist in them. And this I find is often the case with 'Communist-Anarchists'; they cannot differentiate themselves from the Communists. Their Anarchism consists in a somewhat exaggerated fear of a possible re-growth of some of the tyrannical methods of the destroyed Society, and a consequent distrust of the new Society have any definite form. On the other hand, I have met with Anarchists who were not at all vague, and who definitely opposed Communism. They had, indeed, this in common with militant Socialism, that they wished to abolish *organized* monopoly; but they supported unorganized monopoly, or the rule of the strongest individual, taking for their motto 'To each one according to his *deeds*', which means the upholding of private property with no association to uphold it, a position impossible and inconceivable.

Our friends who have been discussing this subject do not, I know, agree with this view, but intend to be Communists though they find stumbling-blocks by the way. As for me, I can only say that whatever will give us equality, with whatever drawbacks, will content me, and I find that at bottom this is the ideal of all Socialists. So I think the fewer party-names and distinctions we can have the better, leaving plenty of scope for the inevitable differences between persons of different temperaments, so that various opinions may not make serious quarrels.

COMMONWEAL, VOLUME 5, NUMBER 188,
17 AUGUST 1889, P. 261

The Lesson of the Hour

The labour revolt in the East-end, whatever the result of the dock-labourers' strike may be, will leave a lasting impression behind it, at least on the working men. The wiseacre Norwood, in his speech of Tuesday last, made the very remarkable discovery that 'the strike was aimed at capital and employers generally', and seemed to think that this *discovery* was a set-off against his other shortcomings.

As matter of fact, it is just this element of conscious or semi-conscious attack on the slave-drivers generally which distinguishes this strike from the ordinary trades-union bickerings. These latter, as individual struggles, have been usually little more than business disputes between the two parties to a contract, recognized as such by both parties to it. But this is a revolt against oppression: a protest against the brute force which keeps a huge population down in the depths of the most dire degradation, for the benefit of a knot of profit-hunters; and there is no doubt that nothing except the physical force of the executive which is, as it were, keeping the ring in this fight between the public and the shareholders, prevents the revolt from achieving far more success than the attainment of its immediate and declared aims.

In short, other strikes have been, on the surface, strikes of the business-accessories of the factory against its financial managers; this is a strike of the poor against the rich.

Let us hope that those of the respectable classes who have so loudly expressed sympathy with the strikers understand this: because if they do, it gives us a dawning hope that they will be prepared to meet us half-way when the crisis comes, when the workmen have come to understand definitely their full claim. For indeed they may be sure that this will be the only way to prevent those terrors which haunt the dreams of the the (*sic*) useless rich; it will be worth more to the pleasure of their lives than all the array of brute force, which they will certainly not always be able to depend upon; since, after all, that force is necessarily made up of men who are *workmen* forced by ill-luck into the ranks of the soldiery and the police.

As Burns hinted when the guards passed the meeting on Tower Hill the other day, they who are now hapless tools of the rich will presently become their hapless slaves once more, as they were before they put on their livery-coats.

Meantime, do not let us deceive ourselves as to the amount and quality of this respectable sympathy. We will not be ungenerous; we are quite sure that with many of the well-to-do the sympathy is genuine; that the horrible poverty of the East-end workers (and how many thousands outside the East-end) has touched their hearts; and these people will become Socialists of some kind before the end. But I fear they are in the minority among the respectables (or rather I know it) and that the rest have been rather *cowed* into silence, or into venting their irritation against the strike, by falling foul of Norwood and his gang; who, after all, are only following the necessary custom of the *whole gang*.

If this were not so, why do not the subscriptions to the strike fund amount to £20,000 or £30,000 instead of what they amount to now? They are workmen's pennies, somewhat eked out by contributions from a few of the better off; mostly those who can least afford it.

One word about the withdrawn manifesto of the Strike Committee. It was to have been expected that it would be attacked furiously by the capitalist press, but it was not to be expected that any calling themselves Socialists should have attacked it; and it is most lamentable that they should have done so, as they may perhaps see by the avidity with which their opinions were recorded by the capitalist press. For us surely the mere fact that it was thought possible to bring about a general strike in London remains the central point in the history of the strike; let us hope that the aspiration toward the use of such an effective weapon against Capital may remain in the minds of the more considerate of the workers and bring forth fruit before long.

'A good man will be contented fast enough if he be fed and clothed sufficiently; but if a man be not well fed and clad, he is a base wretch to be contented.' So says William Cobbett, and certainly the strikers might have one more banner with this inscription written on it. We have learned a good deal since William Cobbett's time, and some of us have become very 'refined' indeed; but still on this foundation of victuals and shelter without anxiety must you build 'refinement' and all.

Those who are 'discontented' on the grounds given by Cobbett, know all about the meaning of that phrase so often used, 'insufficiency of food and shelter'; and I am afraid it says little for the keenness of imagination at the present day, that those who have *not* suffered the insufficiency have so very little an idea of what it means. From that unimaginative content of the well-to-do comes all that covert hatred of the poor as inconvenient people, which is so common amongst us, and will one day (who can doubt it?) be so bitterly revenged.

This is the cause of the filling of the jails with manufactured criminals, a sort of criminal capital to be used for the production of more criminals; the preaching of thrift to people earning precarious starvation wages; the horrors of the workhouse, where poverty is punished for being poor; the horrors of the slum, which mocks the beauty of the earth outside the city, and the attempt to get rid of which is thrust aside as an insoluble problem; while all sorts of miracles, chemical, mechanical, and what not, are being invented for the benefit of capitalistic man, each one of them a million times more difficult than the due feeding and housing of all industrious persons. – *If* we could but once have the wits to cease oppressing others for our own discomfort.

One thing is to me certain, that anyone of the well-to-do class whose imagination is sufficiently touched for him to have a vision of poverty and to gain an inkling of what it means, must either become a Socialist of some sort, or else join Mr Justice Stephen's Religion of Inhumanity; and rather than that they had better, for their own sakes, have been knocked on the head while they were young enough to be innocent of cynicism at least. I say to all rich men, 'Once feel what poverty is, and you must either be a Socialist or a cruel tyrant conscious of your tyranny'. Are there such men? I should hope only a very few, and that the rest who sin against the people do so out of sheer stupidity.

The Great Strike does seem (as such things sometimes will) to have enlightened these last a little, to have touched their sluggish imaginations. If that could last, it would be something of a gain if there were no other. Yet I cannot help thinking that fear was an element of that enlightenment, at all events with many.

Meantime, surely a man of any imagination must have felt both puzzled and disgusted at the sentences on the men for intimidation. Here was the public sympathizing with the efforts of the men to gain a better livelihood, and scolding at their immediate tyrants the Dock Companies; and yet through their magistrates and police-courts these very same sympathizers were punishing the strikers for doing what was necessary to carry on the strike. And this although the capitalist papers – *eg.*, the *Daily News* – admitted that the intimidation was probably merely formal, and that the men were quite willing to accept the intimidation as an excuse for coming out. Certainly hypocrisy is a very useful – virtue – and one cannot wonder that it is so sedulously cultivated in the first commercial country, the *most practical* people in the world.

The recovery of trade, the cessation of depression, has been crowed over considerably of late; and some persons, both foes and friends, have seen in it the herald of the disappearance of Socialism; a most stupid assumption, and on the part of friends most cowardly, as has been pointed out in these columns a week or two back. But in any case a full recovery of trade to the period of Mr Gladstone's 'leaps and bounds' is a very unlikely event. Even now in the full flush of the 'recovery' we find the cotton-trade in a disastrous condition; Blackburn, *e.g.*, which but less than a year ago, was, as I was told when there, doing as brisk a business as might be, now shutting up mills on all hands.

By all means no fatalistic folding of the hands for Socialists! Let us go on with our work as briskly as possible, whatever temporary discouragements we may meet with. But this we may be sure of: first, that modern capitalism is doomed to destroy itself; and secondly, that no new form of capitalism can arise from its ashes: that nothing but Socialism can arise from them.

COMMONWEAL, VOLUME 5, NUMBER 191,
7 SEPTEMBER 1889, PP. 281–282

CONTRIBUTIONS TO *COMMONWEAL*

1890

FABIAN ESSAYS IN SOCIALISM[1]

This book is of importance as embodying the views of a society which has been so active in lecturing on behoof of the Socialist movement. Indeed, some time ago many of us thought and said that the Fabians should publish a volume of their lectures; and, without wishing to carp at the present expression of opinions from which we of the Socialist League dissent in some measure, I cannot help wishing that such a volume *had* appeared about three years ago: for such a book published at that date would have dealt almost wholly with the economical and practical side of the question, and would have formed a kind of text-book for Socialists of all shades of opinion; and illuminated, as it would have been, by the brilliant and attractive style of some of the present essayists, would have been a most useful weapon of attack on the capitalist position as long as the battle might last; whereas a large part of the present volume is given up to the advocacy of the fantastic and unreal tactic which the Fabian Society has excogitated of late, and which is at best tentative and temporary; is hardly constructed to last longer than the coming into power of the next Liberal government. The result is, that the clear exposition of the first principles of Socialism, and the criticism of the present false society (which latter no one knows how to make more damaging than Mr Bernard Shaw, *eg.*) is set aside for the sake of pushing a theory of tactics, which could not be carried out in practice; and which, if it could be, would still leave us in a position from which we should have to begin our attack on capitalism over again; a position, it may be said, which

[1] 'Fabian Essays in Socialism'. 233 pp. bound in cloth with designs by Walter Crane and May Morris. May be ordered from *Commonweal* Office at 6s. post free.

might be better or might be worse for us than our present one, as far as the actual struggle for the new society is concerned.

Mr Sydney Webb, to judge from this book, is the leader in this somewhat disastrous move. He seems to enjoy all the humiliations of opportunism, to revel in it, so to say; and, indeed, he would appear to drag some of his fellow-writers somewhat unwillingly behind his chariot wheels. In his hands the *argumentum ad hominem* becomes a rather dangerously double-edged weapon. He is so anxious to prove the commonplace that our present industrial system embraces some of the machinery by means of which a Socialist system *might* be worked, and that some of the same machinery is used by the present municipalities, and the bureaucratic central government, that his paper tends to produce the impression of one who thinks that we are already in the first stages of socialistic life, all the while that 'the poor we have always with us', and that the workers are worse off than they were under the feudal hierarchy. The retort of the enemy is obvious: 'If we are already all Socialists, be happy! for *we* are happy!'

I give Mr Sydney Webb all credit for sincerity in desiring the destruction of privilege; but it is strange that his rollicking opportunism should blind him to the fact that since he *is* sincere, the privileged will see through his attempt to hoodwink them into joining his attack on the privilege which is their life; while the discontented miserable workers will be discouraged by being practically told that they are already entering into the fruition of the Promised Land. They may well say: 'Is it to be like this society, or *something* like it? We thought Socialism would be quite unlike our present position; if it is not to be so –.' To avoid the disaster of gaining the doubtful alliance of the well to do at the expense of losing the support of the poor, it is surely necessary never to cease saying: The test of the realization of Socialism will be the abolition of poverty.

Let us be clear on this point, that if the municipal Socialism of Mr Sydney Webb were carried out and put in practice, though it should *logically* (perhaps) lead to the destruction of privilege and poverty, yet *historically* it may do nothing of the kind; and that at any rate it is *not* Socialism, as it would still admit of the existence of competing classes. We should remember (as a Socialist said to me the other day) that under the Roman Empire municipal administration reached a pitch which we are very unlikely to come to in England in our day; but it had no destructive effect on the society of that epoch, which was based on chattel slavery and a pauper proletariat fed by the doles of the rich.

Mr Sydney Webb takes in hand the 'historic' basis of Socialism; but he is not more historic than any other of the paper-writers, indeed, less so than Mr Shaw; his history only begins at the period just before the great industrial revolution of the eighteenth century. The industrial conditions of this period he treats too roughly; so roughly, indeed, as to be both inaccurate and misleading. It is true that some of the industries of the country were carried on in an individualistic way on the surface; but the greater part were under the rule of a most elaborate division of labour system, of which the mediæval workmen knew nothing; and even the Yorkshire weavers (as well described by Mr Illingworth), though they were masters of their tools, time, and materials within their workshops or houses, worked for a master (usually a neighbouring farmer) who exploited them, though mildly, and who in his turn sold the goods to a factor. The workmen had a world-market behind their backs though they were unconscious of it; the goods were made for profit, not primarily for use. In short, Mr Sydney Webb has ignored the transition period of industry which began in the sixteenth century with the break up of the Middle-Ages, and the shoving out of the people from the land. This transition is treated of by Karl Marx with great care and precision under the name of the 'Manufacturing Period' (workshop period we might call it), and some mention of it ought to have been included in Mr Sydney Webb's 'history'. I should not have felt bound to call attention to this blemish, however, if it were not, to my mind, another indication of the weak side of Mr Sydney Webb and his followers; their tendency, namely, to overestimate the importance of the *mechanism* of a system of society apart from the *end* towards which it may be used.

The great machine industries, though they have played an important part in the movement toward Socialism are not an essential condition of its existence; they may be used, as they are now, for the mere enslavement of the workers. They *will* be so used as long as they last, unless the workers in some form or other revolt against their slavery. On the other hand, as you may have a perfected system of co-operative production in a society of capitalism and wage-slavery, so you may have Socialism or Communism conjointly with a system of (so-called) individualist production. Nay, I feel certain that when the time comes, wherein we have forgotten the period of artificial poverty thrust upon us by capitalism and wage-slavery, the world will in a large measure return to the individual system which once produced *goods*; a word which our present system has deprived of three parts of its meaning. Fourier put forward his truly inspired doctrine of attractive industry to a world that *could* not listen to him, so sunken as it was in misery and slavery. In times to come we shall need no social philosopher to tell us that if we cannot make our work attractive we shall still be slaves, even though we have no master but Nature. But to-day the world is still so sunken in misery and slavery, that in this book, honestly devoted to the regeneration of society, the assumption is everywhere made that labour must for ever be unattractive.

It is through no disrespect to the other writers in this remarkable book that I have given so much of my space to the consideration of Mr Sydney Webb's paper, which is rather worse than better than the others, but simply because it shows most clearly the present position of the Fabian Society towards the Socialist movement.

Mr Clarke's paper, though not quite avoiding the historical mistake of Mr Sydney Webb, is clear and well written, and full of very valuable information; the latter portion, dealing with the special vagaries of American 'Commerce', will serve as a text-book for the subject 'until the times do alter'. At the same time, though we may well hope that the extravagance of exploitation and contempt of the public shown by these 'captains of industry' will lead us on toward Socialism, it is dangerous to *rest* our hopes on this development, as Mr Bellamy does in his 'Looking Backward'. It may, after all, be nothing but a passing phase of that capitalist organization of robbery, which surely must be attacked in front by the workers grown conscious of their slavery.

Mr Sydney Olivier's 'Moral Basis' is worth taking the trouble of careful reading. It is less obvious to the objections against the Fabian opportunism, partly no doubt because of the subject, but also partly, I think (judging from the paper), because of the turn of mind of the writer himself.

Mr Graham Wallas's 'Property Under Socialism' is clear and free from pedantry, and shows distinct sympathies with Communism; but it is confessedly dealing with the transitional period of Social Democracy, and consequently lacks the interest which a paper on more definite principles would have. There is, indeed, a tone of apology for the feebleness of Social Democracy running through it which might be sneered at by the bourgeois. One friendly objection I make to Mr Wallas – he allows himself to speak of Socialism as 'the system of property-holding which we call Socialism', and goes on to say that this is not necessarily the wished-for new life, 'any more than a good system of drainage is health, or the invention of printing, knowledge'. Here is a net statement of the exaggeration of the value of a mechanical system, which I have already complained of. Socialism is emphatically not merely 'a system of property-holding', but a complete theory of human life, founded indeed on the visible necessities of animal life, but including a distinct system of religion, ethics, and conduct, which, if put into practice, will not indeed enable us to get rid of the tragedy of life, as Mr Wallas hints, but will enable us to meet it without fear and without shame.

Mrs Besant's article on 'Industry Under Socialism' gives a sketch of State Socialism in practice in its crudest form, which, owing to the difficulty of the subject rather than from any shortcoming on her part, is not satisfactory,– could hardly be satisfactory to any one.

Mr Hubert Bland's paper, 'On the Outlook', is, for this book, a curious one, for it is a not very indirect attack on his optimistic democratic coadjutors. 'It is not so much to the thing which the state does, as to the end for which it does it', is stating again what I have already put forward in this article, and there is a good deal in Mr Bland's 'Outlook' to the same purport. For the rest, Mr Bland, of course, goes in for the Parliamentary struggle which we do not believe in; but he is too acute (his eye-sight being aided, I judge, by some traditional Tory instincts) not to see that the permeation of the Radicals by Socialism does not mean the creation of a Socialist-Radical Parliamentary party, but rather the absorption of the individuals of the Radicals, on the one hand, into the definite Socialist ranks, and, on the other, into the Whig phalanx; which latter, he, very rightly, looks on as a most formidable and enduring body of obstruction, capable of 'holding the fort' long after the intelligence of the nation has declared for Socialism, and of holding it in the teeth of the *logical* sequence of economical events. So goes history.

I have yet to mention Mr Bernard Shaw's two papers. Whatever I have to blame in them is comprised in the statement of my differences with the Fabian tactic which is so frankly condemned by Mr Hubert Bland. Yet, at least, Mr Shaw does not love opportunism for its own sweet self; for in his second lecture he definitely proclaims his shame of the course to which, as he thinks, circumstances have driven him; perhaps he only needs a little extra dose of Parliamentary tactics to disgust him so much as to force him to drop them altogether. Judging from the eloquence of the concluding part of his first paper, we can hardly suppose that that disgust will drive him into despair of the whole movement, and so deprive us of the services of one of the clearest heads and best pens that Socialism has got. As aforesaid, his criticism of the modern capitalistic muddle is so damaging, his style so trenchant, and so full of reserves of indignation and righteous scorn, that I sometimes wonder that *guilty*, *ie.*, non-Socialist, middle-class people can sit and listen to him. If he could only forget the Sydney-Webbian permeation tactic, even without putting any other in its place, what an advantage it would be to all of us! He would encourage his friends thereby; and as to his enemies – could he offend them more than he does now?

I have not had any space to quote passages from this book; I thought that there was no need to do so, as I assume that all Socialists will read it whether they agree with it or not.

Commonweal, Volume 6, Number 211,
25 January 1890, pp. 28–29

COAL IN KENT

The news that coal had been discovered in Kent, and that it would probably be found to be workable, has no doubt sent a shock of hope and expectation to some hearts and of terror to others. Amongst those who have anything to lose, those who are able to live in tolerably pleasant places without being too stupified by poverty to prevent their enjoying them, among the cultivated middle-classes in short, I should think the latter feeling prevails. The threat of the creation of a new black country on the ruins of the rural beauty of some of the most beautiful country in England, and close to London also, must impress most well-to-do people, who do not claim direct relationship with Mr Podsnap, as a real terror not to be compensated by the hope of that vague and somewhat doubtful advantage, additional commercial prosperity. This feeling shines pretty clearly through the conventional twaddle which is being written in the newspapers about the splendour of the discovery, and the splendid energy of that great and beneficent employer of labour, Sir Edward Watkin, whose virtues this grand discovery is advertising in a quite providential manner. We know pretty well that though a few capitalists may make fortunes over the job, and a few landlords fill their pockets with the royalties for working the coal-field, the discovery if it leads to anything serious will be to the well-to-do public a ghastly disaster, which will not be compensated by the possible reduction in the price of coal used for household purposes; a benefit which could be obtained at a much lower price by compelling the railways to carry the coals at reasonable rates. (I say nothing about the profits of the coal-masters and the royalties of the landlords of the existing coal-fields, as *they* should go to the miners and other workmen engaged in getting the coal and making it marketable).

But some of our working-men readers will perhaps cry out, 'O damn the well-to-do classes!' (a sentiment in which a knowledge of facts compels me to concur,) 'Won't this new discovery be a great benefit to the workers?'

Well, I don't think *Socialist* working-men are under any delusions on this point. I think they know pretty well that whatever loss they may suffer from the establishment of a new manufacturing hell in the south-east of England, will not be compensated to them by any amelioration in the lives of, for instance, the workers in London. They have learned by this time that Sir Edward Watkin and his pals will stick to whatever swag they may filch out of Kentish coal, which belongs to the people not to them, and will only yield to the workers what they are compelled to yield.

But to non-Socialist workers I must point out that whatever gains may be made will pass by them. The new coal-fields will give employment? Yes, but at no higher rate of wages than workmen receive now; that is, wages which just take the place of the slaves' housing and rations of ancient days; wages also subject to all the precariousness which curses the lives of all other workers at present. It will cheapen the price of coal to all London workmen? Well, if it does so permanently and generally, with such an article of necessity as coal, it will on the other hand reduce the wages of the workers throughout London. As a matter of fact, as far as the present condition of the London workers are concerned, it will leave them in the same condition as they are in now, and will but destroy the beauty of the country which will one day be theirs in reality, and not in name only as it is now. A few rich men will be richer; that is to say, they will waste more of the labour of the workers than they do now; but no poor man will have advanced one step nearer towards the attainment of wealth, that is, to a decent enjoyable life.

For the rest, surely a new manufacturing district is the thing of all others which England least needs. Double, treble, fourfold if you will (and I think you can) the yield of victuals from the fields of Kent, and you will have done some good; for though the profit-monger will in the present eat up the extra produce, and keep it from reaching those who need it, yet with the first days of the break-up of monopolist capitalism (*ie.*, class robbery) it would at once become real *wealth* to be *used* by our teeming population.

But fresh groups of manufactories for producing the inanities and abortions of civilization, what shall we say about them? This – in the present they are instruments for carrying on the robbery of the poor by the rich, for producing counters to be used in the gambling market, which at once dominates and supports the capitalistic system of production. That is one function of their production; and the other is the making of goods for poor people, which none but poor people (*ie.*, slaves) would buy. To make useless luxuries for the rich, and to force shoddy rubbish on the poor, will be the office of the manufacturing districts in the present if we are cursed with them. And in the future when we have become free, and no longer need the toys of the fool or the rags of the slave, what shall we do with them? They will be mere nuisances to be got rid of at the expense of labour and trouble.

Let us hope, then, that coal in Kent will turn out an empty scare; that is, *nothing but* a blatant advertisement for the worker's friend, Sir Edward Watkin.

COMMONWEAL, VOLUME 6, NUMBER 217,
8 MARCH 1890, P. 77

CORRESPONDENCE
CHRISTIANITY AND SOCIALISM

Mr Rickarby's letter, though written in a friendly and conciliatory spirit, requires, I think, some answer. Let it be admitted that Christianity, like all religions which include a system of morality, has something in common with Socialism. Let it also be admitted that many of the 'sneers and unjust charges' of which Mr Rickarby writes, are aimed at the stupidities and hypocrisies of the Christianity of the day, which no doubt men of Mr Rickarby's stamp sincerely condemn; granted this, yet if Christianity is 'a revelation *addressed to all times*' it can *not* be neutral as to political and social institutions, which, if they are to be binding on men's consciences, and not merely pieces of arbitrary coercion, must be founded on a system of morality; and that morality must not be founded on explanations of natural facts or a theory of life in which people have ceased to believe. At the risk of offending 'real Christians', however well-meaning or honest they may be, we must ask 'Is this *true?*'

Mr Rickarby's contrast between real and actual Christianity evades the point of difference; that real (I should call it ideal) Christianity has never existed at all. Christianity has developed in due historic sequence from the first, and has taken the various forms which social, political, economic circumstances have forced on it; its last form moulded by the sordid commercialism of modern capitalism being the bundle of hypocrisies which, as I have said, Mr Rickarby with other Christian Socialists condemns. When this beggarly period has been supplanted by one in which Socialism is realized, will not the system of morality, the theory of life, be all-embracing, and can it be other than the Socialistic theory? Where then will be the Christian ethic? – *absorbed in Socialism.* No separate system of ethics will then be needed; there will be no protest needed against the theory of life which will then be commonly held, we shall only have to guard the freedom which we have won.

Commonweal, Volume 6, Number 217,
8 March 1890, p. 77

THE GREAT COAL STRIKE

The great coal strike is ominous of coming changes, and cannot be looked on as even a great strike might have been a few years ago. The demands of the miners are so moderate, and so uncomplicated with any difficulties as to method of employment and the like, and moreover, the business facts on which the strike is based are so clear and so much in favour of the men, that it was expected in many quarters that the masters would give in at once, and in ordinary times they would have done so. The fact that they are preparing for an obstinate resistance shows that they are not so much thinking of the present strike as of their general position in [the] face of the awakening of Labour. The red spectre of Revolution looms threateningly in the distance before them, and instinctively they are prepared to fight.

Let us look at it from the same point of view, and understand that it is a battle, not a mere business dispute. If the miners act well together, and if they are supported by the sympathy of their brother workers, even those who will suffer by the strike, they will now for the first time understand their power, and a weapon for the hand of revolution will be fashioned, which will be irresistible; which can only be resisted by the brute-force in the hands of the upper classes – *ie.*, the army and police. This instrument, the striking-power of the coal miners backed by the assent of their fellow workers, being once ready, there will be nothing between us and revolution but a knowledge on the part of the workers *of what to claim*, which can be nothing short of an *abolition of the monopoly of the resources of nature – ie., the land and all that is on it, which is used for the reproduction of wealth.*

This, and not a pitiful rise in wages, is what in the long run lies before the strike of the coal miners: let us hope that the events of this strike will show them how necessary it is for them to make this claim, how feasible to get what they demand.

COMMONWEAL, VOLUME 6, NUMBER 219,
22 MARCH 1890, P. 91

LABOUR DAY

Is the demonstration of Labour Day a mere isolated demonstration, bearing no relation to anything but to the claim for a legal restriction of the hours of labour to the arbitrary figure of eight? Surely it is not so, whatever may be the wishes of some of those who may take part in it. On the one hand it points to what has taken place within the last few years, on the other to the coming events of the next few.

The great event in the history of labour of the last few years has been the growing comprehension of Socialism by the English workmen, as shown by the spirit underlying all the strikes which have lately taken place, and which has been quite different to that of the strikes of the decade before the revival of Socialism in this country.

That spirit is bred from a consciousness, or instinct perhaps, on the part of the workers that these strikes are a part of a definite *war* which the essential circumstances of their position force them to carry on against their employers; and the upshot of which must be, either the transformation of the workers in general into mere machines without any will at all; or the destruction of the position of the employers; or lastly, as Mr Giffen and some others try to persuade themselves, the creation of a large class of capable workmen, who, if not really well off, will be better off than ordinary workmen are now; and of a residuum beneath them of hopeless misery and brutality, whose numbers we shall try to reduce as much as we can, but whom we shall not otherwise heed, because they will be kept down by the great mass of the contented and well-to-do workmen.

Of these three conceivable outcomes of the labour war, it cannot be said that the first is really possible, although it is what may be called the high commercial ideal. For supposing the war between masters and men come to an end in the complete and hopeless subjection of the men, there would still remain the war between masters and masters, which, unrestrained by any possible struggle of the workers to free themselves, would at last reach such a pitch that it would bring the whole system to the ground, and result in mere disorganization and confusion.

Of the third, the outcome of the reasonable and enlightened employer – the contented honest workman and the residuum or helots of both, who don't like it, but can't help themselves – it must be said that it is the ideal of the rich man, who admits that the world is an ugly creation, but knows that he profits by its ugliness and misery, and is therefore content. Happily, it is a baseless dream; for so far from there being any likelihood of any such sharp distinction taking place between one class of workers and another, the whole set of the stream of modern production tends towards breaking down such distinctions. The contented and capable workmen would be very few, instead of being the great mass of workers, and would consist of foremen, sub-managers, and the like; the discontented would be very many, and *therefore* their discontent would be apt to take a practical form. Have the theorists who support this possibility forgotten the agricultural labourers? If so, they may one day be reminded of them in an uncomfortable manner. Their remains the revolutionary outcome; that is to say, the hope that the workers will set themselves free and become their own employers; that they will work, not as captives for a conquering enemy, but as neighbours for neighbours, exchanging labour against labour, without loss on either side, for each other's convenience and happiness.

At this outcome of the labour war is the only one which offers any betterment to the world, so most happily it is the only one which there is any chance of realising. As the war goes on, and therewith the value of the privilege of capital to compel labour without payment decreases, rent, profit, and interest will sink lower and lower, until they will scarcely be worth defending: the function of the employers will be gone, and necessity will compel the workers to push them out of their position of dignity in order that labour may be reorganized, so the world may not starve.

This, then, is the meaning of the unity of labour which the May Labour Day proclaims – that the workers must no longer be a class, but all society, or else there will soon be no society; and this new society they will certainly realize before long.

And how is it to be brought about? In the first place by the workers knowing that they are slaves and longing to be free. In the next place, by their learning that it is possible for them to be free. And lastly, by the enforcing of their will, so that they may become free.

Now, as to this last matter, Labour Day points out to us at least one instrument for the winning of freedom – to wit, an universal strike. The rich live on the labour of the workers in no way metaphorically, but really. Teach the rich this lesson practically, and their power, backed up by their armed slaves, is gone. The workers have shown that they have striking-power capable of victory on minor occasions: let them combine and organize their striking power – capitalise their resources, to borrow a word from the enemy – and how can they be resisted?

It is true that this idea of an universal strike was current amongst the Chartists and was given up by them as unfeasible: but in those days, near as they are to our own, labour was so much less elaborately organized, and the different trades so much less dependent on one another, that they assumed that a strike of a month (the Sacred Month, as they called it) would be necessary; whereas today if the coalminers struck with the full assent of the mass of the workers, would not three days be more than enough? The ruling classes would have either to give up or to attack the workers with the armed hand.

Would they do that? or rather, could they? Effectually, they could not; another Peterloo massacre would be the downfall of our present society, far more perilously balanced as it is now than it was in 1820. Some ineffectual sputter there might be; but if we make such a possibility a lion in our path toward freedom, we have degenerated from our forefathers' valiancy.

In short, the lesson of Labour Day is, first of all, consciousness of the unity of interests of labour; secondly, the necessity of the workers learning what it is that they can claim; and thirdly, unity once more in setting about the winning of the freedom of labour.

Commonweal, Volume 6, Number 225,
3 May 1890, p. 137

THE 'EIGHT HOURS' AND THE DEMONSTRATION

Now that the noise and clatter of the 4th of May demonstration are over, it may be profitable to consider what it was that that huge meeting was crying for, and whether it is likely to get it.

But first we must assume that the 4th of May demonstration did not aim at showing any expression of sympathy with labour generally throughout the civilized world. It was in fact an English trades-union meeting distinct from the meetings held on the Continent and in London on May Day, although it was only the agitation on the Continent that made it possible. The English workmen, if we may believe the *Star* (which is now a definitely reactionary paper) have got together a huge demonstration, which, while it was a mere hanger-on of the revolutionary meetings abroad, disclaims any solidarity with those who first began the movement, and allows the English press to insult them with jingo rot unrebuked.

The legal eight hours, then, is the thing claimed by the 4th of May. Of course, I do not deny that many who attended that meeting go much further than that; but then a great many more do not go as far, and only have very hazy ideas of what they want.

Furthermore, the spirit of that demonstration was a kind of missive to Parliament. It practically said: 'We want the eight-hours day: you, Parliament, must get it for us, and settle how it is to be.'

That this was its spirit is clear enough from the fact that no sort of hint has been given of any action to follow the demonstration. For instance, one would have thought that with such a definite and apparently small aim before them, the leaders of the movement would have called a congress of at least the London workmen to settle on some course of action to push the Parliament on toward some steps for giving effect to the workmen's wishes: but as above-said, nothing of the sort is being done, and the matter is to be allowed to go cold; and in the meantime the capitalist press is having *its* innings, and is showing with a mixture of truth and falsity peculiarly easy of employment under the circumstances, that the limitation of the hours of labour is impossible, and that if possible it would be of no advantage to the workers. Of course, these capitalist agents do not mean by this to put forth the matter from a Communist standpoint, as will have to be done here presently: all they mean is, that resistance wherever possible to the amelioration of the workers which is the great object of modern politicians.

Now let us look at this eight hours claim for a little and try to find out what it means. In the first place, no one who is not a slave-driver (and most middle-class persons are slave-drivers), would deny that it would be a good thing in itself for the maximum day's work to be reduced to eight hours; although on the other hand it would not in itself be even a step in advance towards Socialism. From that point of view it would be nothing more than an amelioration in the lot of – slaves; just as an increase in the wage-earner's wages is an increase in the slave's rations. Now, one must say that this kind of amelioration is just the thing which can only be gained by that species of 'self-help' which is called a general strike; and that if it were gained *in this manner*, *the manner* of gaining it would be so educational that the gain would have a very different and much greater significance than it would if thrown to the people by Parliament as a mere tub to the whale.

Now, as to the gain of an Eight Hours Bill, what would it amount to? In the first place, would it benefit the whole of the workers or only a part? Surely there can only be one answer to that question. For instance, how is such a Bill going to deal with the work of the agricultural labourers?

And I may notice in passing that this body of workers, at once the most useful and the most hardly used of all, are generally left out in the cold when it is a question of these partial 'ameliorations' – unless where it is obviously intended to 'work' them for some political plot. Many other instances of workers who would not benefit by an Eight Hours Bill will occur to any working man who thinks about the subject.

Again, the Bill passed, a struggle between masters and men will begin as to the *wages* to be paid for the shorter day's labour. Will Parliament deal with this difficulty, I ask? I will show presently what it will mean if it does. Meantime I assert that the men will have to deal with it by strikes – *ie.*, they will have to fight the whole battle over again. Once more, if the capitalists stand to lose by the change, they will strain every nerve to recover that loss; and the intensification of labour is one obvious means of doing this. Improved organization (*ie.*, slave-driving) in the workshop, improved machinery in the factory, will set the capitalist right again and force the workers to produce more in every hour – *ie.*, to *waste* their bodily and mental powers more.

Surely all these things must, in any case, be dealt with by the usual methods of a Labour war, and the mere machinery of a statute will have very little effect on that war. Why, then, when the workers must of necessity make the new bill work themselves, should they not save time and toil by making the unwritten custom themselves at first hand? Of what use will be the mere ornament of a legal enactment when they have got what they want without it? And let us also remember once more that every gain won by the combination of labour hastens the day when the odious distinctions of class will be abolished.

But some people will say, 'This may be true if we are to stop at a mere eight hours bill; we mean much more than this'. Quite true; every Social Democrat who knows the aims of his party, knows that a legal eight hours day will be unworkable without a legal minimum wage in each big trade (how about the little ones?), and that that again will be useless without the enactment of a maximum price of all general articles of consumption; and these enactments will make it necessary to establish national workshops in order to destroy the profit of the capitalists, *ie.*, the capitalists themselves. This means complete State Socialism, with which we Communists do not agree, because we believe that the difficulties besetting it are so great, that the realization of Communism would be no more difficult on the one hand, and on the other would mean a whole revolution, and not that most fertile parent of counter-revolution, a half revolution.

But apart from this, does any man in his senses suppose that any Parliament in England (or the world), on this side of civil war, would hesitate one moment between allowing an eight hours bill to become mere waste paper and accepting the logical consequences of it? Our artful Social Democratic friends would find they had done nothing with the small end of the wedge but jar their hands by hammering on it, and that they would have to begin all over again, unless they had force enough to *compel* the capitalist enemy to disgorge his ill-gotten gains for fear of worse.

We may be sure that whatever part of the Social Democratic claim Parliament yields to, will be given with the intention of its being either a nullity or a bait to quiet possible revolution.

One thing which the Demonstration of May 4th asked for they may get in a fashion, that is, the eight hours day in government factories; but it will be given, if at all, in the hope of its acting as a little bit of corruption. The price expected to be paid will be the quieting, the de-revolutionizing, of the workmen so employed. One may indeed hope that the price will not be paid. But this on the other hand is sure to happen, that the Parliamentary capitalists will think they have done a prodigious stroke of Socialist business, and will take care not to do any more Socialism till the Revolution is thundering at their doors, and no man cares a button what they do.

Meantime, one must use the thread-bare fable again, and say that when the *labouring* mountains have produced *this* ridiculous mouse, the music of his squeak will scarcely pay us for all our trouble and all our – shuffling. State Socialism? – I don't agree with it; in fact, I think the two words contradict one another, and that it is the business of Socialism to destroy the State and put Free Society in its place. But State Socialism in the hands of a bureaucratic department – that is indeed a strange birth of compromise and 'moderation'.

COMMONWEAL, VOLUME 6, NUMBER 227,
17 MAY 1890, P. 153

ANTI-PARLIAMENTARY

Most of those into whose hands this paper will fall know that as the organ of the Socialist League the *Commonweal* advocates abstention from Parliamentary action; that the Socialist League neither puts forward candidates, nor advises its members to vote for this that or the other candidate; that the readers of these columns will indeed find Parliament mentioned in them, but never with respect, and most commonly only to point the moral of the corruption of these latter days of capitalism. Our policy is, in short, abstention from all attempts at using the constitutional machinery of government, whereas to some Socialists this seems the only means of bringing us to the verge of the Social Revolution. Now this policy of abstention seems to some mere folly, and perhaps to others seems inexplicable. Let us, then, try to explain it, and leave others to call us fools if they needs must after having listened to our explanation.

What is the purpose of Socialist propaganda? Surely it intends to make it clear to all the working-classes that society (so-called) as it exists to-day, is founded on the robbery of the 'lower' classes by the 'upper', of the useful by the useless, of the many by the few; that so long as this privileged robbery goes on, those who do all the useful work that is done will be constantly deprived of the refinements of life which are supposed to make the difference between the civilized man and the savage; while their lives will be much more laborious and much more pleasureless than the lives of most savages. In short, thorough discontent with their position and a sense of its unfairness is the *first* thing we want to impress on the minds of the workers.

Next, we want to make it clear to them that this position of slavery, this unfairness which makes them so wretched and so bitter, is not a necessary condition for those who live by producing the wealth of the country (that is, the only people in it who have a chance of being honest); that these working-men and women could still work, live, and be useful if they were working for each other, that is to say, for their friends and not for their privileged masters, *ie.*, their enemies.

Again, we have to make it clear to the workers that this privilege of a few to compel the many to live miserably, is merely an explanation of the phrase, *The institution of private property*; that he who declares that he wishes to abolish privilege means to say that he wishes to abolish the Institution of private property; that he who defends the Institution of private property defends privilege, the gross inequality of rich and poor, the consequent misery of all genuine workers, and the consequent degradation of people of *all* classes. Let it be clearly understood that only two systems of society are possible, *Slavery* and *Communism*; all who know the A B C of Socialism know that this is so. Communism or the abolition of the individual ownership of property is our aim, the aim of all real Socialists.

Will Parliament help us towards the accomplishment of this aim? Take another question as an answer to that first question. What is the aim of Parliament? The upholding of privilege; the society of rich and poor; the society of inequality, and the consequent misery of the workers and the degradation of *all* classes.

Clearly if this is its aim, its reason for existence, it will only exchange *its* aim for *ours* if it be compelled to do so, or deluded into doing so.

Can it be forced? Well, Parliament is the master of the Executive; that is to say, of the brute force which compels the useful classes to live miserably; it will use that brute force to compel those classes into submission as long as it dares. When it no longer dares, it will practically no longer exist. Now I, for my part, say as I have always said, that in the last act of the Revolution the Socialists may be obliged to use the form of Parliament in order to cripple the resistance of the reactionists by making it formally illegal, and so destroying the power of the armed men on whom the power of the parliament and the law-courts really rests. But this can only come in the last act; when the Socialists are strong enough to capture the parliament in order to put an end to it, and the privilege whose protection is its object, the revolution will have come, or all but come. Meantime, it is clear that we cannot compel Parliament to put an end to its own existence; or, indeed, to do anything which it does not believe will conduce to the stability of Privilege, or the slavery of the workers.

Well, then, can we jockey Parliament into Socialism, into Communism? It seems to me a most hopeless enterprise. We shall not find it difficult, perhaps, to put so much pressure upon it as to make it pass measures for 'the amelioration of the lot of the working classes'. But what will that mean save the 'dishing' of the Socialists? – who, if they do not take care, will find that instead of *using* Parliament, they will be *used* by it. Let us remember, too, that the knowledge of Socialism is growing with tremendous rapidity, and that even MP's and their wirepullers will soon get to know what it means, and will then strain their ingenuity to take the sting out of any measures that look Socialistic on the outside; or at last, and perhaps before long, will stiffen themselves up into mere rejection of anything that looks like Socialism. The failure of the attempt to capture the *Star* for the parliamentary Socialists ought to be a sufficient lesson to them of the power of the reactionists, Liberal as well as Conservative, and the way in which they will refuse to be driven into a corner.

Well, then, if we cannot force Parliament to declare its function of safeguarding privilege at an end, when it is obviously in vigorous life; if we cannot jockey it into furthering the very thing which it hates most, and has most reason to hate – Socialism, to wit – what can we do?

'Nothing', say our parliamentary friends. I cannot see that. Is it nothing to keep alive and increase discontent with the vile slavery of to-day? Is it nothing to show the discontented that they can themselves destroy that slavery? Is it nothing to point out to them what lies beyond the period of struggle, and how workers can be happy when they are not robbed of all the pleasure of life by the idlers that live upon their labour?

Moreover, the events of the last twelve months are producing a different spirit in the mass of the workers, and they are now beginning to learn how to combine in earnest. It is now far more hopeful than it was five years ago to turn their attention from the Parliament of their masters to their own organization. In short, the true weapon of the workers as against Parliament is not the ballot-box but the *Boycott*. Ignore Parliament; let it alone, and strengthen your own organizations to deal directly with your masters in the present, and to learn how to manage your own affairs both now and for the future, and keep steadily in mind, and work for, the day when you will have to use the great weapon which your own wretched position of unrewarded toil puts into your hands, the weapon of *the general strike*. See to this, and let politicians elect politicians; let the upper and middle-classes by themselves choose for themselves members of the Committee for the Continuance of Slavery, which should be the name of the House of Commons, and you will see what terror you will inspire in the hearts of the canting hypocrites who call themselves statesmen. A terror which will be fully warranted by events; for such an anti-parliamentary boycott will show your determination to be free, and will give you the instrument of attaining your freedom.

COMMONWEAL, VOLUME 6, NUMBER 230,
7 JUNE 1890, PP. 180–181

Workhouse Socialism

'General' Booth no doubt does deserve his title; his conduct of the 'Army' shows that he is a general of no mean order. But like other people, he has the 'defects of his qualities' as the French phrase it, and a good general is not likely to be a good citizen; for it is the business of a general to sacrifice everything to immediate success, and I cannot help thinking that the Salvation General does not fall behind others of his kind in this respect.

Anyhow, his 'great scheme' as it is called, seems on the face of it to be meant as a bait to catch those who are looking open-mouthed for something to happen in the way of the improvement of life in this world, the reduction of some of the misery of modern civilization. Indeed, there are plenty of well-meaning people with money to spare willing to impart it to the setting on foot of a 'well-considered scheme' for the easing of their consciences by means of the amelioration of the lot of the poor; especially if such a scheme seems likely to dull the discontent now so rapidly rising all round about us, and which we hope will one day put an end to philanthropy by abolishing poverty. A *safe* scheme for the regeneration of society is likely to make rich people open their purses, and I think it is no injustice to the General to say that he knows this well enough. Otherwise he might have discovered any time these twelve years that before people can turn their attention to religion, or anything else than the satisfaction of their daily needs, 'they must be helped out of their present social miseries'.

Meantime, since Mr Booth is being proclaimed a new Socialist, and a prophet at that in some quarters, it may be as well to look for a minute at his scheme and see what it is worth, bearing in mind that it is put forward confessedly as a sort of shoeing-horn for a peculiarly degrading form of a worn-out superstition, which sees in the struggling world of men with all its aspirations and every changing succession of deeds, little more than an appendage and plaything of an irresponsible master, who neither asks nor allows mankind to understand him or his arbitrary commands.

For such a scheme of the universe, this social scheme of Mr Booth's for dealing with the world as it is, is perhaps good enough, but for anybody with manly hopes for finding himself one of a band of friends, with a God, if he has a God, who is also a friend, this scheme of reform is inexpressibly shabby and sordid.

Yet, in a way, we should thank him for the figure of speech under which he shows us the labour of modern civilization; or, to speak more plainly, the men who labour. Says he: 'The cab-horse has its charter of two points; work is found for it, with food and lodging sufficient to enable it to get through its daily task – that is the first; the second is that when it falls down, whether it be by its own fault, or by that of others, it is helped up again – all questions as to who was responsible for its fall being deferred until it is set upon its feet again!'

We have said something like this ourselves from time to time, only we were looking on this state of things as a condition to be struggled out of, while to General Booth it is an ideal which has to be attained to. We must needs thank the General for showing us so clearly that we have not yet reached the cab-horse stage of prosperity.

It is natural that General Booth from the standpoint of this cab-horse ideal should sneer at those who venture to hope that civilized men may one day become as happy as savages and somewhat more wealthy. Natural also that as a 'practical man' he should declare himself unable to wait any longer than the time necessary for effecting the smallest and most miserable of improvements. This is an old story that we are quite used to by this time; for we have seen on the one hand useless palliatives and blind-alleys of political trickery gone in for with enthusiasm, and on the other foolish pieces of rashness elevated into principles to be adored through thick and thin, all on the ground that we 'cannot wait'; when in good truth we *must* wait for all that is worth having till people's minds are sufficiently impressed by the coming change to allow us to take definite action.

As for the 'practical man' in question, the General: his practical scheme does not come to much; on the whole, it comes to less than any evasion of the real question which has been before the public. Whatever in it is not sheer nonsense – 'utilizing the waste of London', and so forth – seems to be taken from Mr Herbert Mills' workhouse colony plan, which itself was taken from the Dutch beggar-colonies scheme actually in operation.

In fact, this wonderful new scheme of Salvation Socialism will not save many bodies, whatever it may do for souls. It is a very low form of what may be called, for lack of a better name, Workhouse Socialism, which takes it for granted that the workers must be in the main paupers, and which casts about for devices at once to get them better rations and to lower the cost of keeping them to the capitalists. The professors of this kind of Socialism (save the mark!) can see only that part of the workers who have been so degraded by the vile system under which we live that they seem at least wholly unable to help themselves, and so are fit subjects to be trotted about and organized by those of the well-to-do who are afraid or ashamed of the huge mass of misery which they form. These gentlemen never take any count of whatever is self-reliant or thoughtful amongst the workers, believing them, perhaps, to be too respectable to be either unhappy or discontented – in short, dangerous to the stability of society. I think they are reckoning without their host, and that it is rather from the work-shops than the slums that the serious attack on 'civilized society' will come, though I admit it *may* come with sickening slowness. That is not so much our business as the making it sure, as we certainly shall.

Indeed, the real point of interest in General Booth's cab-horse Socialism is that he should have found it necessary to take up the miseries of the disinherited in order to keep his Army going and to advertise it. A few years ago such a move would not have been thought of. Now nothing is of any interest in politics, sociology, or religion which does not manage to pin itself to the subject of the impending change which is certainly coming on the world. The failure of civilization is manifest to everyone who takes the trouble to think at all, to everyone who is not fossilized by party political warfare. That gain at least we have won, and it is no small one.

Commonweal, Volume 6, Number 251,
1 November 1890, pp. 345–346

WHERE ARE WE NOW?

It is good from time to time for those who are engaged in a serious movement to look back and review the progress of the past few years; which involves looking around them and noting the way the movement is affecting other people. It is good to do so for this reason amongst others, that men absorbed in such a movement are apt to surround themselves with a kind of artificial atmosphere which distorts the proportions of things outside, and prevents them from seeing what is really going on, and consequently from taking due council as to what is best to do.

It is now some seven years since Socialism came to life again in this country. To some the time will seem long, so many hopes and disappointments as have been crowded into them. Yet in the history of a serious movement seven years is a short time enough; and few movements surely have made so much progress during this short time in one way or another as Socialism has done.

For what was it which we set out to accomplish? To change the system of society on which the stupendous fabric of civilization is founded, and which has been built up by centuries of conflict with older and dying systems, and crowned by the victory of modern civilization over the material surroundings of life.

Could seven years make any visible impression on such a tremendous undertaking as this?

Consider, too, the quality of those who began and carried on this business of reversing the basis of modern society! Who were the statesmen who took up the momentous questions laid before England of the nineteenth-century by the English Socialists! Who were the great divines who preached this new gospel of happiness from their pulpits?

Who were the natural philosophers who proclaimed their hope and joy at the advent of a society which should at last use their marvellous discoveries for the good of mankind?

There is no need to take a pen in hand to write their names. The traveller (*ie.*, the toiler) had fallen among thieves, and the priest and the Levite went by on the other side; or perhaps in this case threw a stone or two at the wounded man: it was but a Samaritain (*sic*), an outcast, an unrespectable person, who helped him.

Those who set out 'to make the revolution' – that is, as afore said, to put society on a new basis, contradictory to the existing one – were a few working-men, less successful even in the wretched life of labour than their fellows; a sprinkling of the intellectual proletariat, whose keen pushing of Socialism must have seemed pretty certain to extinguish their limited chances of prosperity; one or two outsiders in the game political; a few refugees from the bureaucratic tyranny of foreign governments; and here and there an unpractical, half-cracked artist or author.

Yet such as they were, they were enough to do something. Through them, though not by them, the seven years of the new movement toward freedom have, contrary to all that might have been expected, impressed the idea of Socialism deeply on the epoch. It is true that the toilers have not begun to reap benefit from that impression; but it was impossible that they should. No permanent material benefit *can* accrue to them until Socialism has ceased to be militant, and is merged in the new society. But as I said the other week, the movement has at least accomplished this, that no one who thinks is otherwise than discontented with things as they are. The shouts of triumph over the glories of civilization which once drowned the moans of the miserable (and that but a dozen years ago at most) have now sunk into quavering apologies for the existence of the horrors and fatuities of our system; a system which is only defended as a thing to be endured for lack of a better, and until we can find some means of packing it off into limbo: and the workers, who in the period of 'leap and bound prosperity' were thought to have reached the end of their tether, and to be fixed in a kind of subordinate heaven on earth, are now showing that they are not going to stop *there*, at any rate, and whatever happens. And the principles of Socialism are beginning to be understood, so that to some of ourselves, who are always hearing of them, they seem now mere commonplaces which need not be insisted on. Though with that view I can, as I shall show presently, by no means agree.

All this has come to pass. How and why? Was it by virtue of the qualities of those who have furthered it? That little band of oddities who fell in with Socialism during these last few years, did it turn out after all that they were so much better than they seemed? Well, they were (and are), most of them, human at least; but otherwise it cannot be said that great unexpected talent for administration and conduct of affairs has been developed amongst us, nor any vast amount of foresight either. We have been what we seemed to be (to our friends I hope) – and that was no great things. We have between us made about as many mistakes as any other party in a similar space of time. Quarrels more than enough we have had; and sometimes also weak assent for fear of quarrels to what we did not agree with.

There has been self-seeking amongst us, and vainglory, and sloth, and rashness; though there has been at least courage and devotion also. When I first joined the movement I hoped that some working-man leader, or rather leaders, would turn up, who would push aside all middle-class help, and become great historical figures. I might still hope for that, if it seemed likely to happen, for indeed I long for it enough; but to speak plainly it does not so seem at present.

Yet, I repeat, in spite of all drawbacks the impression has been made, and why? The reason for it has been given in words said before, but which I must needs say again: because that seemingly inexpugnable fabric of modern society is verging towards its fall; it has done its work, and is going to change into something else. That is the reason why, with all our faults, we have been able to do something; nor do I believe that there will ever be lacking instruments for bringing about the great change, exactly in proportion to the readiness of the solid elements in society – the workers, to wit – to receive that change, and carry on the new order to which it will give birth.

So much at least we have to encourage us. But are not some of us disappointed in spite of the change of the way in which Socialism is looked on generally? It is but natural that we should be. When we first began to work together, there was little said about anything save the great ideals of Socialism; and so far off did we seem from the realization of these, that we could hardly think of any means for their realization, save great dramatic events which would make our lives tragic indeed, but would take us out of the sordidness of the so-called 'peace' of civilization. With the great extension of Socialism, this also is changed. Our very success has dimmed the great ideals that first led us on; for the hope of the partial and, so to say, vulgarized realization of Socialism is now pressing on us. I think that we are all confident that Socialism will be realized: it is not wonderful, then, that we should long to see – to feel – its realization in our own life-time. Methods of realization, therefore, are now more before our eyes than ideals: but it is of no use talking about methods which are not, in part at least, immediately feasible, and it is of the nature of such partial methods to be sordid and discouraging, though they *may* be necessary.

There are two tendencies in this matter of methods: on the one hand is our old acquaintance palliation, elevated now into vastly greater importance than it used to have, because of the growing discontent, and the obvious advance of Socialism; on the other is the method of partial, necessarily futile, inconsequent revolt, or riot rather, against the authorities, who are our absolute masters, and can easily put it down.

With both of these methods I disagree; and that the more because the palliatives have to be clamoured for, and the riots carried out by men who do not know what Socialism is, and have no idea what their next step is to be, if contrary to all calculation they should happen to be successful. Therefore, at the best our masters would be our masters still, because there would be nothing to take their place. *We are not ready for such a change as that!* The authorities might be a little shaken perhaps, a little more inclined to yield something to the clamours of their slaves, but there would be slaves still, *as all men must be who are not prepared to manage their own business themselves.* Nay, as to the partial violent means, I believe that the occurrence of these would not shake the authorities at all, but would strengthen them rather, because they would draw to them the timid of all classes, *ie.*, all men but a very few.

I have mentioned the two lines on which what I should [consider] the methods of impatience profess to work. Before I write a very few words on the only line of method on which some of us *can* work, I will give my views about the present state of the movement as briefly as I can.

The whole set opinion amongst those more or less touched by Socialism, who are not definite Socialists, is towards the New Trades' Unionism and palliation. Men believe that they can wrest from the capitalists some portion of their privileged profits, and the masters, to judge by the recent threats of combination on their side, believe also that this can be done. That it could only very partially be done, and that the men could not rest there if it were done, we Socialists know very well; but others do not. Let that pass for the present. The Parliamentary side of things seems in abeyance, at present; it has given place to the Trade Union side. But, of course, it will come up again; and in time, if there is nothing to cut across the logical sequence of events, it will achieve the *legal* Eight Hours' Day – with next to no results either to men or masters.

For the rest, I neither believe in State Socialism as desirable in itself, or, indeed, as a complete scheme do I think it possible. Nevertheless, some approach to it is sure to be tried, and to my mind this will precede any complete enlightenment on the new order of things. The success of Mr Bellamy's utopian book, deadly dull as it is, is a straw to show which way the wind blows. The general attention paid to our clever friends, the Fabian lecturers and pamphleteers, is not altogether due to their literary ability; people have really got their heads turned more or less in their direction.

Now it seems to me that at such a time, when people are not only discontented, but have really conceived a hope of bettering the condition of labour, while at the same time the means towards their end are doubtful; or, rather, when they take the very beginning of the means as an end in itself, – that this time when people are excited about Socialism, and when many who know nothing about it think themselves Socialists, is the time of all others to put forward the simple principles of Socialism regardless of the policy of the passing hour.

My readers will understand that in saying this I am speaking for those who are complete Socialists – or let us call them Communists. I say for us *to make Socialists* is *the* business at present, and at present I do not think we can have any other useful business. Those who are not really Socialists – who are Trades' Unionists, disturbance-breeders, or what not – will do what they are impelled to do, and we cannot help it. At the worst there will be some good in what they do; but we need not and cannot heartily work with them, when we know that their methods are beside the right way.

Our business, I repeat, is the making of Socialists, *ie.*, convincing people that Socialism is good for them and is possible. When we have enough people of that way of thinking, *they* will find out what action is necessary for putting their principles in practice. Until we have that mass of opinion, action for a general change that will benefit the whole people is *impossible*. Have we that body of opinion of any thing like it? Surely not. If we look outside that glamour, that charmed atmosphere of party warfare in which we necessarily move, we shall see this clearly: that though there are a great many who believe it possible to compel their masters by some means or another to behave better to them, and though they are prepared to compel them (by so-called peaceful means, strikes and the like), all but a very small minority are not prepared *to do without masters.* They do not believe in their own capacity to undertake the management of affairs, and to be responsible for their life in this world. When they are so prepared, then Socialism will be realized; but nothing can push it on a day in advance of that time.

Therefore, I say, make Socialists. We Socialists can do nothing else that is useful, and preaching and teaching is not out of date for that purpose; but rather for those who, like myself, do not believe in State Socialism, it is the only rational means of attaining to the New Order of Things.

COMMONWEAL, VOLUME 6, NUMBER 253,
15 NOVEMBER 1890, PP. 361–362

Socialism from the Root Up

CHAPTER I
ANCIENT SOCIETY

In beginning this series on Socialism, we think it necessary to prelude the matter which may appear to interest more immediately us now living, by a brief allusion to the history of the past.

Our adversaries are sometimes forward to remind us that the present system with which we are so discontented, has been made by the growth of ages, and that our wills are impotent to change it; they do not see that in stating this fact they are condemning their own position. Our business is to recognize the coming change, to clear away obstacles to it, to accept it, and to be ready to organize it in detail. Our opponents, on the contrary, are trying consciously to stay that very evolution at the point which it has reached to-day; they are attempting to turn the transient into the eternal; therefore, for them history has no lessons, while to us it gives both encouragement and warning which we cannot afford to disregard. The hopes for the industrialism of the future are involved in its struggles in the past; which, indeed, since they have built up the present system, and placed us amidst its struggle towards change, have really forced us whether we will it or not, to help forward that change.

The modern civilized State has been developed by the antagonism between individual and social interests, which has transformed primitive Society into Civilization. The conditions of mere savage life recognized nothing but the satisfaction of the immediate needs of the individual; this condition of complete want of co-operation yielded to primitive Communism as the powers of man grew, and he began to perceive that he could do more than satisfy his daily needs for food and shelter. By this time he had found that he could aid nature in forcing the earth to produce livelihood for him; the hill and forest became something more to him than the place where berries and roots grew, and wild creatures lived, the land became pasture ground to him, and at last amid some races ground for tillage.

But the wealth of man still grew, and change came again with its growth; the land was common in the sense that it was not the property of individuals, but it was not common to all comers; primitive society was formed, and man was no longer a mass of individuals, but the groups of this primitive society were narrow and exclusive; the unit of Society was the *Gens*, a group of blood-relations at peace among themselves, but which group was hostile to all other groups; within the Gens wealth was common to all its members, without it wealth was prize of war.

This condition of war necessarily developed leadership amongst men; successful warriors gained predominance over the other members of the Gens, and since the increasing powers of production afforded more wealth to be disposed of above the mere necessities of each man, these warrior leaders began to get to themselves larger shares of the wealth than others, and so the primitive communism of wealth began to be transformed into individual ownership.

The Tribe now took the place of the Gens; this was a larger and more artificial group, in which blood relationship was conventionally assumed. In it, however, there was by no means mere individual ownership, although, as said above, Communism had been broken into; the tribe at large disposed of the use of the land according to certain arbitrary arrangements, but did not admit ownership in it to individuals. Under the tribal system also slavery was developed, so that class Society had fairly began (*sic*).

The Tribe in its turn melted into a larger and still more artificial body, the People – a congeries of many tribes, the ancient Gothic-Teutonic name for which – *theoth* – is still preserved in such names as *Theo*bald. This was the last development of Barbarism; nor was there much change in the conditions of wealth under it from those obtaining among the Tribe, although it held in it something more than the mere *germs* of feudalism.

Finally, ancient Barbarism was transformed into ancient Civilization, which, as the name implies, took the form of the life of the city. With these cities political life began, together with the systematization of the old beliefs into a regular worship. The religion of Barbarism was the worship of the ancestors of the tribe, mingled with fetichism, which was the first universal religion, and may best be described as a state of mind in which the universe was conceived of as a system of animated beings to be feared and propitiated by man. This was transformed into what may be called city patriotism, which summed up the whole religion of the city, and which was the real religion of the Greeks and Romans in their progressive period, and of all the then progressive races of mankind, including the Hebrew. In these cities slavery speedily developed until it embraced nearly the whole of industrialism, the main business of the free citizens being the aggrandizement of their city by war.[1] For the cities were as hostile to each other as the tribes had been.

The course of events towards further transformation was that in the East the cities formed federations which gradually fell under the domination of bureaucratic and absolute monarchies, of which China still remains as an example. The Greek and Latin cities carried on the progress of human intelligence, but did not escape corruption and transformation.

Amongst the Greeks the individual struggle for pre-eminence gradually broke down the city patriotism, and led the way towards the domination of mere military and political intrigue and confusion, till the independence of Greece was finally trampled out by the power of Rome,

[1] The Greeks added to this the practice of the higher arts and literature, neither of which the Romans possessed in their progressive period.

now corrupted also. For during this time in Rome the struggle of the plebeian order – or inferior tribes of which the city was composed – with the conservative oligarchy – that is, the three most ancient and consequently leading tribes – had developed a middle-class living on the profits derived from slave labour, which broke up the old city republic and led to the formation of a commercial and tax-gathering empire, founded on slavery, whose subjects were devoid of all political rights, and in which the triumph of individualism was complete. Indeed, this same struggle had taken place in one way or another in the Greek cities also. Thus was all public spirit extinguished. The natural greed of commercialism gradually ate up the wealth of the empire: even slave labour became unprofitable. The landlords were ruined; the taxes could not be paid; and meanwhile the Roman soldier, once a citizen religiously devoted to his city, became a bribed hireling, till at last no bribe was high enough to induce a civilized man to fight, and the Roman legions were manned by the very barbarians whose kinsmen were attacking the empire from without.

Thus was ancient civilization delivered over to the Barbarians, fresh from their tribal communism, and once more the antagonism of individual and common rights was exemplified in the two streams of Barbarian and Roman ideas, from the union of which was formed the society of the next great epoch – the Middle Ages.

Commonweal, Volume 2, Number 18,
15 May 1886, p. 53

CHAPTER II
MEDIÆVAL SOCIETY

We have now to deal with that Mediæval Society which was based on the fusion of ideas of tribal communism and Roman individualism and bureaucracy. The fullest, and one may say the most pedantic type of this society is to be found in the Mediæval German Empire; it was modified somewhat in other countries; in France by the fact that several of the other potentates, as, *eg.*, the Duke of Burgundy, were theoretically independent of the King, and practically were often at least as powerful. In England, on the contrary, the monarchy soon gained complete predominance over the great barons, and a kind of bureaucracy soon sprang up which interfered with the full working of the feudal system.

The theory of this feudal system is the existence of an unbroken chain of service from the serf up to the emperor, and of protection from the emperor down to the serf; it recognizes no absolute ownership of land; God is the one owner of the earth, the emperor and his kings are his vicegerents there, who may devolve their authority to their feudal vassals, and they in turn to theirs, and so on till it reaches the serf, the proletarian, on whom all this hierarchy lives, and who has no rights as regard his own lord except protection from others outside the manor that he lives and works on; to him his personal lord was the incarnation of the compulsion and protection of God, which all men acknowledged and looked for.

It is quite clear that this system was mixed up with religious ideas of some sort; accordingly, we find that the Middle Ages had a distinct religion of their own, developed from that early Christianity which was one of the forces that broke up the Roman Empire. As long as that Empire lasted in its integrity, Christianity was purely individualistic; it bade every man do his best for his future in another world, and had no commands to give about the government of this world except to obey 'the powers that be' in non-religious matters, in order to escape troubles and complications which might distract his attention from the kingdom of God.

But in Mediæval Christianity, although this idea of individual devotion to the perfection of the next world still existed, it was kept in the background, and was almost dormant in the presence of the idea of the *Church*, which was not merely a link between the earthly and the heavenly kingdoms, but even may be said to have brought the kingdom of heaven to earth by breathing its spirit into the temporal power, which it recognized as another manifestation of its own authority. Therefore, the struggles of the Temporal and Spiritual Powers, which form so large a part of the history of the Middle Ages, were not the result of antagonism of ideas between the two, but came of the tendency of one side of the great organization of Society to absorb the other without rejecting its theory; in short, on the one hand the Church was political and social rather than religious, while on the other the State was at least as much religious as it was political and social.

Such, then, was the theory of Mediæval Society; but apart from whatever of oppression on life and thought was inherent in it, the practice of the theory was liable to many abuses, to which the obvious confusion and misery of the times are mostly referable. These abuses again were met by a protest in the form of almost constant rebellion against Society, of which one may take as examples the organized vagabondage of Middle Europe, the Jacquerie in France, and in England what may be called the chronic rebellion of the Foresters, which produced such an impression on the minds of the people, that it has given birth to the ballad epic known by the name of its mythical hero, Robin Hood. Resistance to authority and contempt of the 'Rights of

Property' are the leading ideas in this rough but noble poetry.

Besides these irregular protests against the oppression of the epoch, there was another factor at work in its modification – the Gilds, which forced themselves into the system, and were accepted as a regular part of it.

The ideas which went with the survivals of the primitive communism of the tribes were, on the one hand, absorbed into the feudal system and formed part of it, but on the other, they developed associations for mutual protection and help, which at first were merely a kind of benefit societies according to the ideas of the times. These were followed by associations for the protection of trade, which were called the gilds-merchant. From these the development was two-fold: they were partly transformed into the corporations of the free towns, which had already began (*sic*) to be founded from other developments, and partly into the craft-gilds, or organizations for the protection and regulation of handicrafts – which latter were the result of a radical reform of the gilds-merchant, accomplished not without a severe struggle, often accompanied by actual and very bitter war. The last remains of these craft-gilds are traceable in the names of the city companies of London.

It should be noted that this tendency to association was bitterly opposed in its earlier days by the potentates of both Church and State, especially in those countries which had been more under the influence of the Roman empire. But in the long-run it could not be resisted, and at last both the gilds and the free towns which their emancipated labour had created or developed were favoured (as well as fleeced) by the bureaucratic kings as a make-weight to the powerful nobles and the Church.

The condition of one part of mediæval life industrial was thus quite altered. In the earlier Middle Ages the serf not only did all the field-work, but also most of the handicrafts, which now fell entirely into the hands of the gilds. It must be noted also that in their best days there were no mere journeymen in these crafts; a workshop was manned simply by the workman and his apprentices, who would, when their time was out, become members of the gild like himself: mastership, in our sense of the word, was unknown.

By about the year 1350 the craft-gilds were fully developed and triumphant; and that date may conveniently be accepted as the end of the first part of the Middle Ages.

By this time serfdom generally was beginning to yield to the change introduced by the gilds and free towns: the field serfs partly drifted into the towns and became affiliated to the gilds, and partly became free men, though living on lands whose tenure was unfree – copyholders, we should call them. This movement towards the break-up of serfdom is marked by the peasant's war in England led by Wat Tyler and John Ball in Kent, and John Litster (dyer) in East Anglia, which was the answer of the combined yeomen, emancipated and unemancipated serfs, to the attempt of the nobles to check the movement.

But the development of the craft-gilds and the flocking in of the freed serfs into the towns laid the foundations for another change in industrialism: with the second part of the mediæval period appears the journeyman, or so-called free labourer. Besides the craftsmaster and his apprentices, the workshop now has these 'free labourers' in it – unprivileged workmen, that is, who were nevertheless under the domination of the gild, and compelled to affiliation with it. The gildsmen now began to be privileged workmen; and with them began the foundation of the present middle-class, whose development from this source went on to meet its other development on the side of trade which was now becoming noticeable. In 1453 Constantinople was taken by the Turks; the art of printing was spreading; Greek manuscripts were being discovered and read; a thirst for new or revived learning, outside the superstitions of the mediæval Church and the quaint, curiously perverted and half-understood remains of popular traditions, was arising, and all was getting ready for the transformation of mediæval into modern or commercial society.

COMMONWEAL, VOLUME 2, NUMBER 19,
22 MAY 1886, P. 61

CHAPTER III
THE BREAK-UP OF FEUDALISM

The period of change from the feudal system into that of commerce is so important, and so significant to our subject, that it demands a separate chapter.

The beginning of the sixteenth century found, as we have said, the craft-gilds corrupted into privileged bodies holding within them two orders of workmen – the privileged and the unprivileged – the two forming the germ of a society founded on capital and wage-labour. The privileged workmen became middle-class; the unprivileged, proletarians.

But apart from the gilds, the two classes were being created by the development of commerce, which needed them both as instruments for her progress. Mediæval commerce knew nothing of capitalistic exchange; the demands of local markets were supplied by the direct exchange of the superfluity of the produce of the various districts and countries. All this was now being changed, and a world-market was being formed, into which all commodities had to pass; and a huckstering class grew up for the carrying on of this new commerce, and soon attained to power, amidst the rapid break-up of the old hierarchical society with its duly ordered grades.

The fall of Constantinople, which was followed in thirty years by the discovery of America, was a token of this great change. The Mediterranean was no longer the great commercial sea, with nothing beyond it but a few outlying stations. The towns of Central Europe – *eg.*, Augsburg, Nuremburg, Bruges, and the Hanse towns – were now sharing the market with Venice and Genoa, the children of Constantinople: there was no longer one great commanding city in Europe. But it was not only the rise in the commercial towns that was overturning feudal society. As they conquered their enemy, the feudal nobles, they fell into the clutches of bureaucratic monarchs, who either seized on them for their own possessions, or used them as tools for their projects on conquest and centralization. Charles V., *eg.*, played this game through South Germany, Austria, and the Netherlands, and with Venice, under cover of the so-called 'Holy Roman Empire', while at the same time he had fallen into possession of Spain by marriage; and disregarding his sham feudal empire, he bent all his efforts into turning these countries into a real bureaucratic State. In France the last liberties of the towns were crushed out. In England the plunder of the religious houses enabled Henry VIII to found a new nobility, subservient to his own absolutism, in place of the ancient feudal nobility destroyed by their late civil war.

Everywhere the modern political bureaucratic *nation* was being developed. In France the long and fierce wars of the Burgundian and Armagnac factions gave opportunity for the consolidation of the monarchy, which was at last effected by Louis XI, the forerunner of the most successful king of France and the last successful one – Louis XIV. In England the Wars of the Roses were not so bitter as the French wars, and the people took small part in them, except as vassals or the households of the contending nobles; but they nevertheless played their part in the disruption of feudality, not only by the thinning-out of the nobles slain in battle or on the scaffold, but also by helping directly to draw England into the world-market.

Under the mediæval system the workmen, protected and oppressed by the lords of the manor and the gilds, were not available for the needs of commerce. The serfs ate up the part of the produce spared them by their lords; the gild craftsmen sold the produce of their own hands to their neighbours without the help of a middle-man. In neither case was there anything left over for the supply of a great market.

But England, one of the best pasture countries of the world, had in her even then capacities for profit-grinding, if the tillage system of the manor and the yeoman's holdings could be got rid of. The landowners, ruined by their long war, saw the demand for English wool, and set themselves to the task of helping evolution with much of the vigour and unscrupulous pettifogging which has since won for their race the temporary command of the world-market. The tenants were rack-rented, the yeomen were expropriated, the labourers driven off the land into the towns, there to work as 'free' labourers, and England thus contributed her share to commerce, paying for it with nothing more important than the loss of the rough joviality, plenty, and independence of spirit, which once attracted the admiration of foreigners more crushed by the feudal system and their abuses than the English were.

Thus all over Europe commercialism was rising. New needs were being discovered by men who were gaining fresh mastery over nature, and were set free from old restraints to struggle for individual pre-eminence. A fresh intelligence and mental energy was shedding its light over the more sordid side of the period of change. The study of the Greek literature at first hand was aiding this new intelligence among cultivated men, and also, since they did but half understand its spirit, was warping their minds into fresh error. Art was no longer religious and simple – the harmonious expression of the thought of the people – but was growing more and more ambitiously individualistic and arrogant, and at the same time grew more and more retrospective and tainted with pedantry.

Amidst all this it is clear that the old religion would no longer serve the new spirit of the times. The Mediæval Church, the kingdom of heaven on earth, in full sympathy with the temporal hierarchy, in which also every one had his divinely appointed place, and which restricted commerce and forbade usury, such a Church was no religion for the new commercialism; its religion must have nothing to do with the business of this world; so the individualist ethics of Early Christianity, which had been kept in the background during the period of the Mediæval Church, were once more brought to the front and took the place of the corporate ethics of that Church, of which each one of the 'faithful' was but a part. Whatever base uses their enthusiasm was put to by cooler heads, this revived Christianity took a real hold on most of the progressive minds of the period, especially in the north; so that Protestantism became the real religion of the epoch, and even permeated Catholicism and gave it whatever true vitality it had; for its political part was an unreal survival from the Mediæval Church, and whatever of it was of any force became the mere ally of bureaucracy; a word which applies to the Protestant Churches just as much as the Catholic; and, in fact, everywhere the new religion became the useful servant of Commercialism, first by providing a new army of officials always subservient to the authority of government, and secondly by holding out to the people hopes outside their wretched life on earth, so as to quiet their discontent by turning their earthly aspirations heavenward. On the one hand like Early Christianity, it bade let the world alone to compete for the possession of privilege, and bade the poor pay no heed to the passing oppression of the day, which could not deprive them of their true reward in another world; but unlike Early Christianity, on the other hand it shared in the possession of privilege, and actively helped in the oppression which it counselled the oppressed not to rebel against. But, as a truly distinct and equal power beside the State, the Church was extinct; it was a mere salaried adjunct of the State. The story, moreover, of the robbery by private persons of the public property which the Mediæval Church once held, was a disgraceful one everywhere, but nowhere so disgraceful as in England.

But while modern Europe was developing for itself a new economy, a new religion, and a new patriotism, the change did not take place without a protest of the disappointed hopes of the people in the form of fresh rebellion; though it was little heeded amidst the furious wars for the place and power of kings, and the establishment of political boundaries of the newly made 'nations'. The Peasant War in Germany, and the revolt of the Anabaptists, are, so to say, the funeral torches of the Middle Ages. The first was much of the nature of other mediæval insurrections, except that it was fiercer and longer lived; it ends the series of outbreaks which had been so common in England during the first years of the century. The revolt of the Anabaptists was an attempt to realize the kingdom of God upon earth literally and simply in a Communistic Society based on supernaturalism, and was a protest of ignorant and oppressed men against the hardening of Christianity into bourgeois Protestantism, and of the hardening of feudal oppression into commercial exploitation.

Thus, then, was the feudal system broken down, to give place to a new world, whose government, under cover of carrying on the old monarchies and varied classes of feudality, was employed in one business only, the consolidation and continuance of the absolute property of the individual. It is true that in carrying out this function, the new society used the forms of the old, and asserted hereditary rights stiffly enough; but this was only in its transition from the old to the new. In truth the spirit of the Middle Ages was dead, and its theory of society and authority in Church and State was gone. The kingdom of heaven of the Mediæval Church had left the earth, and did not concern itself with its doings except so far as they constituted theological holiness or sins. God no longer owned the land allowing human beings to use it after a divinely ordained scheme. It was now the *property* of the absolute monarch, who might give it to whomsoever he would; and it was only for a brief space that a dim shadow of feudal responsibility clung to the landowner.

Serfdom was gone, and the gilds were now but close corporations of privileged workmen, or of employers of labour. The ordinary workman was now 'free'. That is to say he could work where and how he pleased, *if* he could find some one, who would set him to work at the price of taking from him a part of the produce of his labour; which labour was now a commodity to be bought and sold in the market as the body of the chattel-slave once had been.

Of the working of this new form of privilege and slavery we shall see more in our next chapter.

Commonweal, Volume 2, Number 20,
29 May 1886, p. 69

CHAPTER IV
MODERN SOCIETY: EARLY STAGES

By the beginning of the seventeenth century the centralizing, bureaucratic monarchies were fairly established: nay, in France at least, they were even showing the birth of modern party-government, which since – carried on, indeed, under the veil of constitutionalism – has been the type of modern government. Richelieu – the Bismarck of his time and country – begins the series of prime ministers or real temporary kings, who govern in the interest of class society, not much encumbered and a good deal protected by their cloaks, the hereditary formal sham kings. In England this prime-ministership was more incomplete, though men like Burleigh approached the type. Elizabeth reduced the Tudor monarchy to an absurdity, a very burlesque of monarchy, under which flourished rankly an utterly unprincipled and corrupt struggle for the satisfaction of individual ambition and greed. This grew still more rankly, perhaps, under James I, who added mere cowardice to all the other vices which are more common to arbitrary high place and power.

As to the condition of the people during the latter years of the sixteenth and beginning of the seventeenth century, the economical and religious revolution which had taken place had oppressed them terribly, and the 'free workman' had to feel the full force of the causes which had presented him with his 'freedom' in the interest of growing commerce. In England, on the one hand, the expropriation of the yeomanry from the land and the conversion of tillage into pasture had provided a large population of these free workmen, who, on the other hand, were not speedily worked up by the still scanty manufactures of the country, but made a sort of semi-vagabond population, troublesome enough to the upper and middle-classes. The laws made against these paupers in the reigns of Henry VIII and Edward VI were absolutely ferocious, and men were hanged out of the way by the thousand.

But in the reign of Elizabeth it was found out that even this was not enough to cure the evil, which of course had been much aggravated by the suppression of the religious houses, part of whose function was the housing and feeding of any part of the workmen temporarily displaced. A Poor Law, therefore, was passed for dealing with this misery, and strange to say, it was far more humane than might have been expected from the way in which the poor had been dealt with up to that time; so much so, indeed, that the utilitarian *philanthropists* of the beginning of this century felt themselves obliged to deal with it in a very severe way, which left us a Poor Law as inhumane – or let us say as cruel – as could well be. Toward the middle of the seventeenth century things began to improve with our working population: the growth of the towns stimulated agriculture, and tillage began to revive again, though of course under the new system of cultivation for profit. Matters were in fact settling down, and preparing the country by a time of something like prosperity for the new revolution in industry.

The condition of the people was on the whole worse on the Continent than in England. Serfdom was by no means extinct in France and, especially, in Germany, and that serfdom was far more burdensome and searching side by side with the exploitation of the market than it had been in the feudal period. Other survivals of the mediæval epoch there were also – *eg.*, in Germany the gilds had still some life and power, and the people were not utterly divorced from the land as in England, although the predominant competition of the markets prevented whatever good might linger in these half-extinct customs from acting for the benefit of the people. At the same time the populations were crushed by the frightful wars which passed over them – in all which religion was the immediate excuse.

The first of this series was the war carried on in Holland against the Catholic foreigners – the Spaniards – into whose hands they had been thrown by the family affairs of Charles V. Although noblemen took up the side of the rebels – *eg.*, Egmont and Horn, executed for so doing – this war was in the main a war of the bourgeois democracy on behalf of Protestantism, embittered by the feeling of a Teutonic race against a Latinised one. There is to be found in it even some foretaste of the revolutionary *sanscullote* element, as shown by the extreme bitterness of the ruder seafaring population, the men whose hats bore the inscription, 'Better Turk than Pope'.

In Germany the struggle known as the 'Thirty Years' War' was between the great vassals of the German empire, the shadow of whose former power was used for the aggrandisement of the house of Charles V, and also for the enforcement of Catholicism on the more northern countries. It must be remembered, by the way, that these countries were to the full as absolutist as those which obeyed the bidding of the Emperor. This miserable war, after inflicting the most terrible suffering on the unhappy people, who were throughout treated with far less mercy and consideration than if they had been beasts; after having crushed the rising intelligence of Germany into a condition from which it has only arisen in days close to our own, dribbled out in a miserable and aimless manner, leaving the limits of Protestant and Catholic pretty much where it had found them: but it also left the people quite defenceless against their masters, the bureaucratic kings and knights.

In France this religious struggle took a very bitter form, but it was far more political than in Germany. The leaders were even prepared to change their creed when driven into a corner – as Henry of Navarre at the time of the Massacre of St Bartholomew. In France the popular sympathy was by no means in favour of Protestantism: the Massacre of St Bartholomew, which inflicted such a terrible blow on the Hugenot (*sic*) cause, would otherwise have been hardly possible. It is true that the great Hugenot (*sic*) leader,

Henry of Navarre, became Hugenot (*sic*) king of France, but his accession did not carry with it a triumph as a consequence. Henry had to abjure Protestantism; a Protestant king of France was impossible.

The great struggle in England came later, and consequently probably the victory was more decided on the Puritan side. The enthusiasm with which Mary Tudor – 'Bloody Mary' – was received, and the Catholic insurrections in the reign of her successor, showed that there was at first some popular feeling on the Catholic side; but by the time of James I Catholicism was dead in England. The Book of Sports issued by his Government, which encouraged the people to play various games on Sunday, was widely received as an outrage on the feelings of the growing middle-class in town and country; and all was tending towards the irreconcilable quarrel which took place in the next reign between the Court and the Bourgeoisie, and which was nearly as much religious as political. For the rest, the Parliamentary party was on the advancing line of history both as regards politics and religion, and the King's party was simply reactionary; but the war was at furthest waged by a bourgeois democract, led at first by a constitutional oligarchy against a nobility inspired by a kind of romantic after-glow of mediæval chivalry. The successful outcome of the individual ambition of Cromwell extinguished whatever aspirations towards republicanism were cherished by a few purists, as well as the enthusiasm of the wild sectaries whose hopes of a rule of saints on the earth were tinged by some kind of communistic ideas; which were further fore-shadowed by the Levellers, though perverted by the mere asceticism which they held. Nevertheless, these men may be paralleled to the Anabaptists of Münster, although the latter were quite mediæval in spirit, and their fanatic religion had little in common with Puritanism; and though, also, the steady power of bourgeois rule concentrated in Cromwell's absolutism forbade them any opportunity of approaching even the most temporary realization of their idea.

Meanwhile England was unable to endure the weight of the absolute rule of Cromwell, lined with fully developed Puritanism, and a few plotters were allowed to restore the Stuart monarch, under whom the wild religion of the armed men – the victors over the nobility of England and their revived sham chivalry – sank into mere Quakerism, and the religious war was at [an] end, except for a few smouldering embers among the Cameronians in Scotland.

Meantime in France the last remnants of the old feudalism struggled in the party warfare of the 'Fronde' against Mazarin and his bureaucracy of simple corruption, till Louis XIV put the coping-stone on the French monarchy by forcing his nobility, high and low, into the position of his courtiers, while his minister Colbert developed the monarchy as a tax-gathering machine by the care and talent with which he fostered the manufactures of France, which just before his time were at a very low ebb; so that there was no need to touch the revenues of the nobility, who were free to spend them in dancing attendance on the Court: nay, were not free to do otherwise. The century began with the French monarchy triumphant over all its great vassals; it finished by reducing all its vassals, great and small, to the condition of courtiers, with little influence in the country-side, and diminished rents – mere absentee landlords of the worst type, endowed with privileges which could only be exercised at the cost of the starvation of the people and the exasperation of the Bourgeoisie, who furnished the funds for the Court glory. Everything in France, therefore, foreshadowed political revolution. What the advancing constitutionalism of England foreshadowed we shall have to speak of in our next chapter.

Commonweal, Volume 2, Number 21,
5 June 1886, p. 77

CHAPTER V
PREPARING FOR REVOLUTION – ENGLAND

The English seventeenth century revolution was from the first purely middle-class, and as we hinted in our last it cast off most of its elements of enthusiasm and ideality in Cromwell's latter days; the burden of the more exalted Puritanism was felt heavily by the nation and no doubt played its part in the restoration of Monarchy; nor on the other hand was England at all ripe for Republicanism; and so between these two disgusts it allowed itself to be led back again into the arms of Monarchy by the military adventurers who had seized on the power which Cromwell once wielded. But this restoration of the Stuart monarchy was after all but a makeshift put up with because the defection from the high-strung principle of the earlier period of the revolution left nothing to take the place of Cromwell's absolutism. The nation was quite out of sympathy with the Court, which was un-national and Catholic in tendency and quite openly debauched. The nation itself though it had got rid of the severity of Puritanism was still Puritan, and welcomed the Sunday Act of Charles II which gave the due legal stamp to Puritanism of the duller and more respectable kind. And though enthusiastic Puritanism was no longer dominant, it was not extinct. John Bunyan's 'Pilgrim's Progress' shines out, though a religious romance, amidst the dulness of the literature of the time. The Quakers who represented in their beginning the peaceable and religious side of the Levellers, arose and grew and flourished in spite of persecution; the Cameronians in Scotland, as we mentioned in our last chapter, made an ineffectual armed resistance to the dying out of enthusiasm; while across the Atlantic the descendants of the earlier Puritans carried on an almost theocratic government, which, by the way be it said, persecuted the Quakers most cruelly. Little by little, however, all that was not quite commonplace and perfunctory, died out in English Protestantism, and respectable indifferentism had carried all before it by the end of the century. Politics and religion had no longer any real bond of union, and the religious side of Puritanism, Evangelicalism, disappears here, to come to light again in the next century under the leadership of Whitfield.

Yet, such as English Puritanism had become, its respectable, habitual, and formal residuum was strong enough to resent James the Second's Papistry, and to make its resentment felt; while at the same time the constitutionalism which began the anti-absolutist opposition in Charles the First's time, and which had been interrupted by Cromwell's iron and Charles the Second's mud absolutism, gathered head again and began to take definite form. The Stuart monarchy, with its 'divine right' of absolute sovereignty, was driven from England in the person of James the Second, and a constitutional king was found in William of Orange, and constitutional party government began.

Thus, in spite of interruption, was carried out the middle-class revolution in England; like all other revolutions, it arrived at the point which it really set out to gain; but not until it had shaken off much which did at one time help forward its progress, and which was and still is mistaken for an essential part of it. Religious and Republican enthusiasm, although they (and especially the first) played their part in abolishing the reactionary clogs on the progress of the middle-classes, had to disappear as elements which would have marred the end proposed by that revolution; to wit, the creation of an all-powerful middle-class freed from all restrictions that would interfere with it in its pursuit of individual profit derived from the exploitation of industry.

Thenceforth, till our own times, respectable political life in England is wrapped up in Whiggery; tinged, indeed, on one side with the last faint remains of feudalism in the form of a quite unreal sentiment, involving no practical consequences but the acceptance of the name of Tory; and on the other by as faint a sentiment towards democracy, which was probably rather a traditional survival of the feeling of the old days of the struggle between King and Parliament, than any holding out of the hand towards the real democracy which was silently forming underneath the government of the respectables.

The first part of the eighteenth century, therefore, finds England solid and settled; all the old elements of disturbance and aspiration hardened into constitutional bureaucracy; religion recognized as a State formality, but having no influence whatever on the corporate life of the country, its sole reality a mere personal sentiment, not at all burdensome to the practical business of life. The embers of the absolutist re-action on the point of extinction, and swept off easily and even lazily when they make a show of being dangerous; the nobility a mere titled upper order of the bourgeoisie; the country prosperous, gaining on French and on Dutch in America and India, and beginning to found its colonial and foreign markets, and its navy beginning to be paramount on all seas; the working-classes better off than at any time since the fifteenth century. Art if not actually dead represented by a Court painter or so of ugly ladies and stupid gentlemen, and literature by a few word-spinning essayists and prosaic versifiers, priding themselves on a well-bred contempt for whatever was manly, passionate, or elevating in the wealth of the past of their own language.

Here then in England we may begin to see what the extinction of feudality was to end in. Mediæval England is gone, the manners and ways of thought of the people are utterly changed; they are called English, but they are another people from that which dwelt in England when 'forestalling and regratting' were misdemeanours; when the gild ruled over the production of goods and division of labour was not yet; when both in art and literature the people had their share, – nay, when what of both there was, was produced by the people themselves. Gone also is militant Puritanism, buried deep under mountains of cool formality. England is bourgeois and successful throughout its whole life; without aspirations, for its self-satisfaction is too complete for any, yet gathering force for development of a new kind, – as it were a nation taking breath for a new spring; for under its prosperous self-satisfaction lies the birth of a great change – a revolution in industry – and England is at the time we are writing of simply preparing herself for that change. Her prosperity and solid bureaucratic constitutional government – nay, even the commonplace conditions of life in the country, are enabling her to turn all her attention towards this change, and the development of the natural resources in which she is so rich. The fall of the feudal system, the invasion of the individualist method of producing goods, and of simple exchange of commodities, were bound to lead to the final development of the epoch – the rise of the great machine industries – and now the time for that development is at hand. The growing world-market is demanding more than the transitional methods of production can supply. In matters political prejudice is giving way to necessity, and all obstacles are being rapidly cleared away before the advent of a new epoch for labour; of which, indeed, we way say that if no great change were at hand for it in its turn, it would have been the greatest disaster which has ever happened to the race of man. In our next chapter we shall deal with the elements at work in preparing the transformation of the commercial system, for which this development of the great machine industry was so necessary and so mighty a servant.

Commonweal, Volume 2, Number 22,
12 June 1886, pp. 82–83

CHAPTER VI
PREPARATIONS FOR REVOLUTION – FRANCE

As we have said, Louis XIV succeeded in making the French monarchy a pure autocratic bureaucracy, completely centralised in the person of the monarch. This with an ambitious king like Louis XIV involved constant war, for he felt himself bound to satisfy his ideal of the necessary expansion of the territory and influence of France, which he looked upon as the absolute property of the king. The general success of Louis XIV brought with it the success of these wars of aggrandisment, and France became very powerful under his rule. Under the rule of his minister Colbert industrialism in France became completely commercialized. Colbert spared no pains or energy in bringing this about. Often, with more or less success, he drove an industry forward artificially, as with the silk and woollen manufactures. For he was eager to win for France a foremost place in the world-market, which he thought but the due accompaniment of her monarchial glory; and he knew that without it that glory would have died of starvation, since the taxes would not have yielded the necessary food. It is true that even in England growing commercialism was subordinate to constitutionalism, the English form of bureaucracy; but the idea was already afoot there that the former was rather an end than a means, whereas in France commercialism was completely subordinated to the glory of the autocratic monarchy – a mere feeder of it.

The religion of this period of the 'Grand Monarque' shows little more than an ecclesiastical struggle between Gallicanism on the one hand, which claimed a feeble spark of independence as regards Rome for the French Church, and is represented by Fénélon and Bossuet, and Jesuitry on the other hand, which was the exponent of Roman centralization. The leading intelligence of the time was on the Gallican side; but the king in the long run favoured the Jesuits, as being the readier instruments of his bureaucratic rule. Outside this ecclesiastical quarrel there was no life whatever in religion, except what was shown by the existence of a few erratic sects of mystics, confined to cultivated persons like the Quietists and Jansenists. The former of these may be said to have put forward the complete abnegation of humanity in the presence of God, while the latter attempted a revivification of the pietism of the Catholic Church.

The Regency which succeeded to the reign of Louis XIV saw the definite beginnings of the last corruption which betokened the Revolution. The wars of aggrandizement still went on but were now generally unsuccessful; the industrialism set a-going by Colbert went on steadily, but the profits to be gained by it did not satisfy the more adventurous spirit of the period, and the Regency saw a curious exposition of stock-jobbery before its time in the form of the Mississippi scheme of Law, which had its counterpart in England in the South-Sea Bubble. It was a financing operation – an attempt to get something out of nothing – founded on the mercantile theory of economy then current, which showed but an imperfect knowledge of the industrial revolution beginning under men's very eyes, and assumed that the wealth of a country consists in the amount of the precious metals which it can retain. This assumption, by the way, is curiously exemplified in the half-commercial half-buccaneering romances of Daniel Defoe, whose works we should have mentioned in our last chapter as a relief to the monotony of dulness of eighteenth century literature in England.

It is necessary to say something about the literature and art of this period that goes before the Revolution in France, because that country is the especial exponent, particularly in art, of the degradation which indicated the rottenness of society. As in England, literature was formal and stilted, and produced little except worthlessly clever essays and still more worthless verses that have no claim to be called *poetry*. The French verse-makers, however, aimed at something higher than the English, and produced works which depend on pomp and style for any claim to attention they may have, and for the rest are unreal and lifeless. Amidst them all one name stands forward as representing some reality – Molière, to wit. But the life and genuineness of his comedies serve to show the corruption of the times as clearly as the dead classicalism of Racine; for this, the one man of genius of the time, was driven into the expression of mere cynicism; though in one remarkable passage of his works he shows a sympathy for the ballad-poetry of the people, which, when noticed at all in England at the same period, and even much latter, received a kind of indulgent patronage rather than admiration. At the same time as there was a sham tragedy current at this time, so also there was a sham love of simplicity. The ladies and gentlemen of the period ignored the real peasants who were the miserable slaves of the French landlords, and invented in their dramas, poems, and pictures sham shepherds and peasants, who were bundles of conscious unreality, inane imitations of the later classics. This literature and art would be indeed too contemptible for mention, if it were not a sign of a society rotting into revolution.

The fine arts, which had in the end of the sixteenth century descended from the expression of the people's faith and aspirations into that of the fancy, ingenuity, and whim of gifted individuals, fell lower still. They lost every atom of beauty and dignity, and retained little even of the ingenuity of the earlier Renaissance, and became mere expensive and pretentious though carefully finished upholstery, mere adjuncts of pomp and state, the expression of the insolence of riches and the complacency of respectability. Once again it must be said of the art as of the general literature of the period, that no reasonable man could even bestow a passing glance at them but for the incurable corruption of Society which they betokened.

So the time wore away through the disgraceful years of the Regency and of Louis XV, till the accession of the once Dauphin, now Louis XVI, to the throne, which was hailed as a new era by the respectability of France; and was, indeed, the inauguration of a new era undreamed of by the actors in it. Of the conscious hopes and aims which came to the surface with this change, there were indications in the opposition of the higher bourgeoisie to the whimsical and scandalous courtesan-Absolutism, the rule of the Pompadours and Dubarrys, which was predominant under Louis XV, this opposition took the form, amongst others, of the assertion of the formal legal rights of Parliament so-called, which in France was but a privileged body of lawyers, representative of nothing but the crystalization (*sic*) of the abuses of a sham feudality, but which, nevertheless, both under Louis XV and his successor, found itself put forward as a champion of the respectability of Bourgeoisedom against the rampant corruption of the Court. But on the accession of Louis XVI this tendency of respectability to assert itself received fresh impulse, and took a more definite form, and became almost a party in the country, though it had no chance of exercising any direct influence on the government, which was a mere mass of abuses. This respectable reforming party, although for the most part outwardly orthodox, amongst themselves professed materialism and the worship of reason, and was inspired by a bourgeois humanitarianism which was its most genuine side, and which was largely fed, if not created, by the writings of Voltaire, and still more of Jean Jacques Rousseau and Diderot. This party was a most important element amidst the causes of the revolution; it rallied to it all who had any pretence to cultivated progress, and though it meant nothing but intelligent Conservativism, it formed a screen as it were behind which the true revolutionary forces could gather for the attack on privilege. Its formation was the last sign of the approaching end of the absolutist bureaucracy which was, so to say, propped up by the bodies of its former enemies which it had triumphed over, the feudal rights of the older nobility. That great French centralized monarchy had been a long time ripening, but once ripe it decayed very speedily, and no wonder since it was the corruption of a corruption.

Here, then, we have in France a contrast to the state of things in England. No constitutionalism here; an absolutism despised even by the privileged classes; unable to move in the direction of progress, even when, as in the case of Louis XVI, its head has a tendency to the intelligent conservatism above mentioned; bankrupt also amidst a people broken down, and a commerce hampered by the exactions of the hereditary privilege which is its sole support, discredited by unsuccessful wars, so that the door is shut to its ambition in that road; at home it has to face uneasily the new abstract ideas of liberty and the rights of men. These ideas are professed, indeed, by those who have an interest in preserving the present state of things, but are listened to and pondered by people who find that state of things unbearable. In short, while England, at peace at home and prosperous under reasonable conservatism, is forced to be seeking colonies and markets abroad, while within her own bounds industrialism is quietly developing toward the great change, France, driven back on herself, is forced face to face with the elements of violent change at home; on the one hand bankruptcy and deadlock, on the other intellectual activity directed wholly towards theories of material well-being of a well-to-do-class. And at the back of all a commercial bourgeoisie oppressed by privilege, and a miserable proletariat of mere starvelings. From such elements political revolution *must* be born.

Commonweal, Volume 2, Number 25,
3 July 1886, pp. 108–109

CHAPTER VII
THE FRENCH REVOLUTION: CONSTITUTIONAL STAGE

The bankruptcy towards which France was staggering under the régime of an untaxed privileged noblesse drove the Court into the dangerous step of attempting to do something, and after desperate efforts to carry on the old corruption by means of mere financing operations, under Calonne and others, aided by an assembly of the 'Notables', or kind of irregular taxing council, the Court was at last, on the 4th May, 1789, compelled to summon the States-General, a body which was pretty much analogous to a Parliament of our mediæval kings, that is a kind of taxing machine, but which attempted to sell its granting of taxes to the king for redress of certain grievances. This States-General had not met since 1614. Bickering between the three houses, Clergy, Noblesse, and Commons, immediately began, but the latter, which was middle-class in spirit though including some of the lower nobility, gave tokens of its coming predominance from the first. On the 20th of June the Court attempted a *coup d'état*, and the Third Estate held its celebrated session in the Tennis Court, and so broke with the old feudal idea, and became a constitutional 'National Assembly', the Court making but a feeble resistance at the time.

It, nevertheless, was contemplating forcible measures against what had now become the National Assembly, when on the 14th July came the first stroke of the *popular* insurrection which the bourgeois began by accepting as an ally of its revolution, which so far had gone wholly on constitutional lines; this was the taking of the Bastille by the people, and the slaying of De Launay the Governor, and Flesselles the Provost of the merchants. The Court gave way at once; the king visited Paris as a sign of submission, and certain of the higher nobility fled from the coming ruin. Two typical feudal fleecers, Foulon and Berthier, were afterwards hung by the people.

The ground thus cleared for it, the Constitutional Revolution went on apace; feudal titles were abolished, the Church reduced to a salaried official department; the very geography of the country was changed, the old provinces with their historic names abolished, and France divided into eighty-three departments named after the rivers and other natural features; everything was to be reduced to a pattern [of] constitutional centralized bourgeois bureaucracy.

But the other element of revolution was also stirring. The alliance of the mere starvelings could not be done without by the bourgeoisie, and they had it whether they would or no. A Jacquerie had arisen in the country, and armed peasants everywhere burned the chateaux or country-houses of the gentlemen, and hunted away their occupants. The Revolution was necessarily accompanied by the dislocation of all industry, and the scarcity was bitterly felt everywhere.

In the midst of this the Court, recovering from the first blow of the taking of the Bastille, began to plot counter-revolution, and devised a scheme for getting the king away from Versailles to Rouen or elsewhere, and putting him at the head of a reactionary army and an opposition reactionary assembly. A banquet given by the Court to a regiment supposed to be loyal, practically exposed this plot, and amidst all the terror and irritation which it gave rise to, a popular rising headed by the famous march of the women on Versailles, came to the aid of the Assembly, and forced the king to go to Paris and take up his abode at the Tuilleries (*sic*). In this affair the mere Sansculotte element became very obvious. It was stirred up by the artificial famine caused by the financial and stock-jobbing operations of the Court and of private persons; the popular middle-class Minister, Necker, having been the immediate cause of it by his issue of small paper money. And it was opposed by the Bourgeois soldiery, the National Guard, headed by Lafayette, who was the very embodiment of the Constitutional Revolution. This was followed by a further flight of the noblesse and higher bourgeoisie from France, which, as it were, gave a token of the complete victory of Constitutionalism over the Court party.

For some time the king carried on a struggle against the victorious bourgeoisie, apparently unconscious of its extreme hopelessness; while the bourgeois Government for its part was quite prepared to put down any popular movement, all the more as it now had a formidable army in the shape of the National Guard. But by this time there had arisen a kind of People's Parliament outside the Assembly, the famous Jacobins Club and the Cordelier Club to wit, and the sky was darkening over for triumphant Constitutionalism.

That triumph was celebrated by the great feast of the Champ de Mars, July 13th, 1790, when the king in the presence of delegates from all France swore to the Constitution. But Royalist plots went on all the same, and settled down at last into a fixed conclusion of the flight of the king to the northern frontier, where were the remains of what regular army could be depended on, with the threatening Austrian troops at their back. As a trial the king attempted at Easter to get as far as St Cloud, announcing his determination as a matter of course; but he was stopped by a mixed crowd not wholly Sansculotte, though Lafayette did his best to help royalty turned respectable, in the pinch. At last on the 20th June, the king and the royal family made the great attempt, in which they would most probably have succeeded, if they had not hampered themselves with all kinds of absurd appliances of wealth and luxury, and if they had had any idea of the kind of stake they were playing for. As it was in spite of, or perhaps partly because of, their having arranged for various detachments of troops to meet them on the way as escorts, they were stopped at the little town of Varennes and brought back again to Paris. It was a token of the progress of ideas, that by this time the king's presence in Paris was looked at from a two-fold point of view. By the pure constitutionalists as the necessary coping-stone to the Constitution, without which it could not stand; but by the revolutionists as a hostage held by the French people in the face of hostile reactionary Europe. Also now the word Republic was first put forward, and at last it became clear that there were two parties amongst those who were making the Constitution, the Constitutional Royalists and the Republicans.

The latter were supported by the people, who flooded the Assembly with petitions for the deposition of the king; the Assembly decided against it on the ground of the legal fiction familiar to the anti-Royalist party in our Parliamentary wars, that the king had been carried off by evil and traitorous councillors. But the split between the parties was emphasized by bloodshed. A Jacobin petition lay for signature on the Altar of the Country in the Champ de Mars, and great crowds were about it signing and looking on. In the evening Lafayette marched on the Champ de Mars with a body of National Guards, proclaimed martial law by the hoisting of the red flag, according to a recently made enactment, and finally fired on the people, killing many of them.

But in spite of this 'massacre of the Champ de Mars', as it was called, the Constitutionalists triumphed for the time. The National Assembly completed its work, and produced a Constitution wholly Bourgeois and even Monarchical, which was accepted by the King amidst one of those curious outbursts of sentiment of which the epoch was so fruitful, and which generally as on this occasion included the exhibition of the little Dauphin in the arms of his mother to the crowd. The National Assembly dissolved itself after enacting that none of its members could be elected to the new legislative body or first Parliament of the Revolution. Of this Legislative the bourgeois Republicans, the aristocracy of talent, became apparently far the most powerful party; whatever there was of talent that had frankly accepted the alliance of the Sansculottes was outside the Legislative. But another element was now added to the contest, that of foreign war, Austria beginning the attack. The obvious and necessary sympathy of the king and Court with what had now become their only chance of salvation, was met by the equally necessary terror and indignation of the revolutionists of all shades, which of course strengthened the extreme party, who had everything to lose from the success of a foreign invasion. In spite of this, the king driven into a corner was in constant contention with the Legislative, and used his constitutional right of veto freely, yet was driven to accept a revolutionary Ministry with Roland at its head: but as the hope of deliverance from the invasion grew on him he dismissed it again, and the Court found itself ticketted (*sic*) with the name of the *Austrian Committee.* On the 20th June, the populace expressed themselves clearly enough by invading the Tuileries itself, and for a brief space it seemed as if the monarchy was doomed to end there and then; but as there was no resistance it ended with a mere demonstration.

Nevertheless, the end of the Constitutional Revolution was at hand. Lafayette, quite misunderstanding his strength, left the army, and tried to stir up the Constitutionalists to attack the Jacobins, but failed ignominiously, and presently fled the country. The King once more swearing to the Constitution at the Feast of the Federates, wore armour underneath his clothes, and insurrection was obviously brewing. On the 10th August it came. Whatever Royalist force was available was collected in the Palace of the Tuileries, including the Swiss Guard; and a desperate resistance was prepared for with the faint hope of the king being able to cut himself out and reach the frontier; but those Constitutionalists who had any intention of supporting the king found their hearts failing them, and even the 'constitutional' battalions of the National Guard were prepared to take the popular side. The king and royal family left the Tuileries for the Legislative, leaving no orders to the unlucky Swiss, who with mechanical military courage stood their ground. The insurrectionary sections attacked the Tuileries and carried it, though not without heavy loss – 1200 killed, the Swiss being all slain except a few who were carried off to prison. On the 13th August, the king and his family were bestowed as prisoners in the Temple, and the first act of the Revolution had come to an end.

COMMONWEAL, VOLUME 2, NUMBER 28,
24 JULY 1886, PP. 130–131

CHAPTER VIII
THE FRENCH REVOLUTION: THE PROLETARIAN STAGE

The insurrection of the 10th August, which culminated in the final downfall of the monarchy and the imprisonment of the king and royal family in the Temple, was headed and organized by a new body definitely revolutionary, intended to be the expression of the power of the proletariat, the new Commune of Paris, the moving spirit of which was Marat, who even had a seat of honour assigned to him in the Council. Already, before the king had been sent to the Temple, the Girondin Vergniaud, as president, had moved the suspension of the 'hereditary representative' and the summoning of a national convention. Danton was made minister of justice; Robespierre was on the Council of the Commune. A new Court of Criminal Justice was established for the trial of the crimes of August 10th. The members of the Convention were chosen by double election, but the property qualification of 'active and passive citizens' was done away with.

While all this was going on, the movement of the reactionary armies on France was still afoot; and the furious flame of French national enthusiasm, which was afterwards used by the mere self-seeking conqueror Napoleon, was lighted by the necessity of the moment – not to be extinguished in days long after his. We mention this here because, in order to appreciate what follows, it must be remembered that an armed coalition of the absolutist countries was gathering together, threatening to drown the Revolution in the blood of the French people, and especially of the people of Paris; and that one of its armies, commanded by the Duke of Brunswick, a famous general of Frederick the Great, was already within a few days' march of the city; and that nothing was between Paris and destruction but undisciplined levies and the rags of the neglected army formed under the old régime; while at the same time the famous royalist insurrection had broken out in La Vendée. Every republican in Paris, therefore, had good reason to feel that both his own life and the future of his country were in immediate danger at the hands of those who did not care what became of France and her people so long as the monarchy could be restored.

Danton now demanded a search for arms, which was carried out on August 29th; and the prisons were filled with prisoners suspected of royalist plotting, and many of them surely guilty of it.

Verdun fell on the 2nd September, and the Duke of Brunswick boasted that he would presently dine in Paris; and on the same night insurrectionary courts of justice – Lynch-law, as we should call it now – were established at the prisons, and the prisoners were brought before them and judged. If found guilty they were turned out into the street with the words, 'Let the prisoner be enlarged', or, 'Let him be conducted to La Force' or 'the Abbaye', according to whether he was at one or the other. He was then immediately cut down and slain by a body of men waiting for him. If he was acquitted, the word went, 'Let him be enlarged', with the cry of 'Vive la nation!' and he went free. It should be noted, in order to show the hysterical excitement amidst which all this was done, that the acquittals were greeted with cries of joy, tears, and embraces on the part of the court and its sympathizers. It may be further noted that the watches, rings, etc., of the slain were brought to the town-hall by the slayers, who claimed each a louis (20s.) for their night's work. The number of the slain was one thousand and eighty-nine.

The next day a circular was issued by the Committee of Public Safety approving of the massacre, signed by Sergent, Panis (Danton's friend), and Marat, with seven others.

The Girondins in the Assembly and elsewhere kept quiet for the time, though they afterwards used the event against the Jacobins.

Meanwhile the French army, under Dumouriez, had seized on the woodland hills of the Argonne, checked Brunswick, defeated him at Valmy, and Paris was saved.

The Convention now met – on the 20th September – and the parties of the Girondins and the Mountain, or extreme revolutionists, were at once formed in it. It is noteworthy that while it declared as its foundation the sovereignty of the people and the abolition of royalty, it also decreed that landed and other property was sacred for ever. Apropos of which, it may here be mentioned that the bookseller Memoro, having hinted at something like agrarian law, and some faint shadow of Socialism, had to go into hiding to avoid hanging.

So far, therefore, we have got no further than the complete triumph of bourgeois republicanism; though, indeed, the possibility of its retaining its position depended, as the event showed, on the support of the proletariat, which was only given on the terms that the material condition of the workers should be altered for the better by the new régime. And those terms, in the long-run, bourgeois republicanism could not keep, and therefore it fell.

The Girondins or moderate party in the Convention, began their attack on the Jacobins on the subject of the September massacres, and also by attacking Marat personally (on the 21st September) – which attack, however, failed egregiously. The Girondins, as their name implies, leaned on the support of the provinces, where respectability was stronger than in Paris, and tried to levy a body-guard for the defence of the Convention against the Paris populace; but though they got the decree for it passed, they could not carry it out. In their character of political economists, also, they resisted the imposing a maximum price on grain, a measure which the scarcity caused by the general disturbance made imperative, if the proletariat were to have any share in the advantages of the Revolution. In short, the Girondins were obviously out of sympathy with the mass of the people – the only power that can support revolutionists; therefore, though they were posing as supporters of the rights of the people, they were bound to fall.

The trial of the king now came on, and tested the Girondins in a fresh way; they mostly voted his death, but as if driven to do so from a feeling that opinion was against them, and that they might as well have some credit for this. The king was beheaded on January 21st, 1793, and as an immediate consequence, England and Spain declared war. But this business of the king made a kind of truce between the parties, which, however, soon came to an end. Marat was the great object of attack, and on the 25th February, 1793, he was decreed accused on account of some passages in his journal approving of the bread riots which had taken place, and suggesting the hanging of a forestaller or two. On the other hand, on the 10th of March, the section Bonconseil demanded the arrest of the prominent Girondins. Meantime, Danton had been trying all along to keep the peace between the two parties, but on April 1st, the Girondins accused him of complicity with Dumouriez, who had now fled over the frontier, and so forced him into becoming one of their most energetic enemies. The position of the Girondins was now desperate. On the 24th March, Marat was acquitted and brought back in triumph to the Convention.

The Girondins got appointed a packed committee of twelve in the interest of the Convention as against the Paris sections. As an answer to this a central committee of the sections was formed, which on May 31st dominated the Municipality (not loth to be so dealt with) and surrounded the Convention with troops. After an attempt on the part of the Girondins to assert their freedom of action, the Convention decreed them accused and they were put under arrest. They died afterwards, some by the guillotine, some even more miserably, within a few months; but their party is at an end from this date. All that happened in the Convention from this time to the fall of Robespierre in 'Thermidor' was the work of a few revolutionists, each trying to keep level with the proletarian instinct, and each failing in turn. They had not the key to the great secret; they were still bourgeois, and still supposed that there must necessarily be a propertyless proletariat led by [the] bourgeois, or at least served by them; they had not conceived the idea of the extinction of classes, and the organization of the people itself for its own ends.

Marat's death at the hand of Charlotte Corday, on July 14th, removed the only real rival to Robespierre, the only man who might, perhaps, have made Napoleonism unnecessary.

The law of maximum was now passed, however, and a cumulative income tax, so that, as Carlyle remarks, the workman was at least better off under the Terror than he had ever been before; but without a direct attack on the root of exploitation there can be no true equality, and nothing that can be laid hold of as a principle of Society; the people cannot understand, and therefore cannot themselves organize themselves. Until labour is free, it has to be organized by those who are the masters of the labourers, and the revolutionists of this period were at once too good and too bad to be their masters; therefore, as above said, they could only drift on the current of events.

Robespierre, Danton, and the Herbertists were now what of force was left in the Convention, and doubtless the first of these had made up his mind to get the reins of power into his own hands. Meantime, a new calendar, in which the months were distinguished by names taken from the march of the natural drama of the year, was published, and an attempt was made to establish a new worship founded on Materialism; but, like all such artificial attempts to establish what is naturally the long growth of time, it failed. Chaumette, Hebert and their followers were the leaders in this business, which Robespierre disapproved of, and Danton growled at.

The Extraordinary Tribunal under Fouquier Tinville was now the Executive in Paris, and backed by the law of suspects, speedily got rid of all *obstacles* to the Revolution, and of many also who had worked according to their lights for its furtherance. Robespierre, it is hard to say how or why, became at last practical dictator.

The Herbertists under the name of the 'Enragés' (rabids) were accused at Robespierre's instance, found guilty and executed. Danton, giving way it would seem to some impulse towards laziness inherent in his nature, let himself be crushed, and died along with Camille Desmoulins on 31st of March, 1794, and at last Robespierre was both in reality and appearance supreme. On the 8th of June he inaugurated *his* new worship by his feast of the Supreme Being, but did not follow it up by any diminution in the number of batches for the guillotine; and ominous grumblings began to be heard. According to a story current, Carnot got by accident at a list of 40 to be arrested, among whom he read his own name. On the 26th July, Robespierre was met by unexpected opposition in the Convention. The next day he was decreed accused at the Convention, and Henriot deposed from the commandership of the National Guard; but there was a respite which a more ready man, a man of military instinct at least, might have used [but] Robespierre lacked that instinct; [and] Henriot failed miserably in his attempt to crush the Convention. The insurrectionary troops on being appealed to by the Convention, wavered and gave way, and Robespierre was arrested. In fact, Robespierre seems to have worn out the patience of the people by his continued executions. Had he proclaimed an amnesty after his Feast of the Supreme Being, he would have had a much longer lease of power; as it was he and his tail died on the 28th July.[1]

[1] A curious exemplification of the change in the speed of the transmission of news, is given by the fact that *The Times* published the first news of this fall of Robespierre three weeks after the event.

There was nothing left to carry on the Revolution after this but a knot of self-seeking politicians of the usual type; they had only to keep matters going till they were ready for the dictator who could organize for his own purposes people and army, and who came in the shape of Napoleon. The proletarians were no longer needed as allies, and disunited, ignorant of principles, and used to trust to leaders, they could make no head against the Society which they had shaken indeed, owing to its internal dissensions, but which they were not yet able to destroy.

One event only there remains to be mentioned; the attempt of Babœuf and his followers to get a proletarian republic recognized; it has been called an insurrection, but it never came to that, being crushed while it was yet only the beginning of a propaganda. Babœuf and his followers were brought to trial in April, 1796. He and Darthes were condemned to death, but killed themselves before the sentence could be carried out. Ten others were condemned to prison and exile; and so ended the first Socialist propaganda.

It is commonly said that Napoleon crushed the Revolution, but what he really did was to put on it the final seal of law and order. The Revolution was set on foot by the middle-classes in their own interests; the sentence which Napoleon accepted as the expression of his aims, 'la carrière ouverte aux talens' – 'the career thrown open to talent' – is the motto of middle-class supremacy. It implies the overthrow of aristocratic privilege and the setting up in its place of the money-aristocracy, founded on the privilege of exploitation, amidst a world of so-called 'free competition'. The Middle-class, the first beginnings of which we saw formed in the Middle Ages, after a long and violent struggle has conquered and is supreme from henceforth.

Commonweal, Volume 2, Number 29,
31 July 1886, pp. 138–139

CHAPTER IX
THE INDUSTRIAL REVOLUTION IN ENGLAND

In our last two chapters we had to deal with a revolution which was as rich in dramatic interest, and as obviously so, as any period in the history of the world. We have now to note a series of events the well-spring of which was Great Britain. This series is not usually connected by modern historians so as to be dignified by the name of a Revolution; but it is one nevertheless, and is at least as important in its bearing on the life of the modern world as that more startling and, on the surface, more terrible one in France.

In the last chapter wherein the condition of England was dealt with, we left it a prosperous country, in the ordinary sense of the word, under the rule of an orderly constitutionalism. There was no need here for the violent destruction of aristocratic privilege; it was of itself melting into money-privilege, and all was getting ready for the completest and securest system of the plunder of labour which the world had yet seen.

England was free in the bourgeois sense; that is, there were but a few checks, the survivals of earlier periods, to interfere with the exaction of the tribute which labour has to pay to property to be allowed to live. In a word, on the one hand exploitation was veiled; and on the other, the owners of property had no longer any duties to perform in return for the above-said tribute. Nevertheless, all this had to go on on a small scale for a while. Population had not increased largely since the beginning of the seventeenth century; agriculture was flourishing; one-thirtieth of the grain raised was exported from England; the working-classes were not hard pressed, and could not yet be bought and sold in masses. There were no large manufacturing towns, and no need for them; the presence of the material to be worked up, rather than the means for working it mechanically – fuel, to wit – gave a manufacturing character to this or that country-side. It was, for example, the sheep-pastures of the Yorkshire hill-sides, and not the existence of coal beneath them, which made the neighbourhood of the (*sic*) northern Bradford a weaving country. Its namesake on the Wiltshire Avon was in those days at least as important a centre of the clothing industry. The broadcloth of the Gloucestershire valleys, Devonshire and Hampshire kersies, Whitney blankets and Chipping Norton tweeds, meant sweet grass and long wool, with a little water-power to turn the fulling-mills, and not coal, to which material to be worked up was to be brought from the four quarters of the globe. The apparent condition of labour in those days seems almost idyllic, compared with what it now is: but it must be remembered that then as now the worker was in the hands of the monopolist of land and raw material; nor was it likely that the latter should have held his special privilege for two hundred years without applying some system by which it could be made the most of. Between the period of the decay of the craft-gilds and this latter half of the eighteenth century there had grown up a system of labour which could not have been applied to the mediæval workmen; for they worked for themselves and not for a master or exploiter, and thus were masters of their material and their tools and their time. This system is that of the Division of Labour; under it the unit of labour is not an individual man, but a group, every member of which is helpless by himself, but trained by constant practice to the repetition of a small part of the work, acquires great precision and speed in its performance. In short, each man is not so much a machine as a part of a machine. As, for example, it takes five men to make a glass-bottle: it is the group of these five men that makes the bottle, not any one of them. It is clear that under this system the individual workman is entirely at the mercy of his master the capitalist in his capacity of superintender of labour: in order not to be crushed by him, he must combine to oppose his own interests to those of his employer. It was by this system, then, that the demands of the growing world-market were supplied down to the end of the eighteenth century. The great political economist, Adam Smith, whose book was first published in 1771, marks the beginning of the transition between this system and that of the great machine industries; but his work implies throughout the Division of Labour system.

But that system was now to melt into the new one: the workman, from being a machine, was to become the auxiliary of a machine. The invention of the spinning-jenny by Hargreaves in 1760 is the first symptom of the beginning of this Industrial Revolution. From thence to the invention of steam as a motive-force, and thence again to our own days, the stream of invention has been continuous. The discovery that iron could be made with pit-coal removed the seat of the iron manufacture from the wooded countries of the south and west, where the old iron-works, called 'bloomeries', used to be carried on, to the northern and midland coal districts, and all manufacture of any importance flowed to the seat of fuel; so that South Lancashire, for instance, was changed from a country of moorland and pasture, with a few market towns and the ancient manufacturing city of Manchester, into a district where the 'villages', still so called, but with populations of fifteen or twenty thousand souls, are pretty much contiguous, and the country has all but disappeared. Of course a great part of this is the work of the years that have followed on the invention of railways; but even in the earlier period of this industrial revolution the change was tremendous and sudden and the sufferings of the working classes very great, as no attempt was made to alleviate the distress that was sure to be caused by the change from the use of human hands to machinery. Nor indeed could it have been made in a country governed by bourgeois constitutionalism until measures were actually forced on the government. In 1811 the prevailing distress was betokened by the first outbreak of the Luddites. These were organized bands of men who went about breaking up the machinery which was the immediate cause of their want of employment and consequent starvation. The locality where these riots were most frequent was the northern midland counties, where the newly-invented stocking-frames were specially obnoxious to them. The Luddites became the type of bodies of rioters who by a half-blind instinct throughout this period threw themselves against the advancing battalions of industrial revolution. In 1816, the year which followed the peace with France, the cessation of all the war industries threw more people still out of employment, and in addition the harvest was a specially bad one. As a consequence, this hunger insurrection was especially violent in that year. The riots were put down with corresponding violence, and the rioters punished with the utmost harshness. But as times mended somewhat this insurrection, which was, as we have said, a mere matter of hunger, and was founded on no principle, died out, although for a time riots having for their object destruction of property, especially of the plant and stock of manufacturers, went on through the whole of the first half of the century. The 'Plug Riots',[1] in the middle of the Chartist agitation, may be taken for an example of these.

It was a necessary consequence of the introduction of elaborate machinery that women and children should be largely employed in factories to diminish the number of adult males. This resource for the development of the profits of the new system was used by the manufacturers with the utmost recklessness, till at last it became clear to the bourgeois government that the scandal created by its abuse would put an end to its use altogether, unless something were done to palliate its immediate evils; and

[1] This meant destruction of boilers in factories, the rioters pulling out the plugs to ensure their bursting.

accordingly a series of Factory Acts were passed, in the teeth of the most strenuous and unscrupulous resistance on the part of the capitalists, who grudged the immediate loss which resulted in the hampering of the 'roaring trade' they were driving, even though it were for the ultimate benefit of their class. The first of these Acts which was really intended to work was passed in 1830, and they were consolidated finally in 1867. It should be understood that these Acts were not intended to benefit the great mass of adult workers, but were rather concessions to the outcry of the philanthropists at the condition of the women and especially the children so employed.

Meanwhile, in spite of all the suffering caused by the Industrial Revolution, it was impossible for the capitalists to engross the whole of the profits gained by it, or at least to go on piling them up in an ever-increasing ratio. The class struggle took another form, besides that of mere hunger riots and forcible repression, that of the Trade Unions. Although the primary intention of these was the foundation of benefit societies, as with the first guilds of the early Middle Ages, like them also they had soon to take in hand matters dealing with the regulation of labour. The first struggles of the trades' unions with capital took place while they were still illegal; but the repeal of the law against the combination of workmen in 1824 set them free in that respect, and they soon began to be a power in the country. Aided by the rising tide of commercial prosperity, which made the capitalists more willing to yield up some part of their enormous profits rather than carry on the struggle *à l'outrance*, they prevailed in many trade contests, and succeeding (*sic*) in raising the standard of livelihood for skilled workmen, though of course by no means in proportion to the huge increase in the sum of the national income. Further than this it was and is impossible for them to go so long as they recognise the capitalists as a necessary part of the organization of labour. It was not at first understood by the capitalist class that they did so recognize them, and consequently in the period of their early successes the trades' unions were considered mere revolutionists, and were treated to that kind of virulent and cowardly abuse and insult, which the shopkeeper in terror for his shop always has at his tongue[']s end.

The abolition of the corn-laws in 1847 and the consequent cheapening of necessary food for the workers, the discovery of gold in California and Australia, the prodigious increase in the luxury and expenditure of the upper and middle-classes, all the action and reaction of the commercial impulse created by the great machine industries, gave an appearance of general prosperity to the country, in which, as we have said, the skilled workmen did partake to a certain extent; and the views of middle-class optimists as to the continuance of bourgeois progress, and the gradual absorption of all the worthy part of the working-classes into its ranks seemed confirmed till within the last few years; all the more as the practical triumph of the Liberal party had ceased to make 'politics' a burning question. Nevertheless, as a sign that the underground lava had not ceased flowing, it was noticed that ever since the ripening of the great industries, in periods of about ten years came recurring depressions of trade; these were accounted for in various ingenious ways, but otherwise did not trouble the capitalist mind, which got to consider this also, because of its regular recurrence, as a sign of the stability of the present system, and merely looked upon it as a thing to be taken into the general average and insured against in the usual manner. But within the last few years this latest eternal bourgeois providence has failed us. The nations whom we assumed would never do anything but provide us with raw materials, have become our rivals in manufacture and our competitors in the world-market, while owing to the fact that America has enormous stretches of easily tilled virgin soil, which does not need manure, and that the climate of India makes it easy to support life there, those two countries supply us with such large amounts of grain, and at so cheap a rate, that raising it in England has become unprofitable; so that the farmers are poor, and the landlords cannot get the same rents for agricultural land as formerly. The exports have fallen off; towns where six years ago trade was flourishing and wages high, are now encumbered with a population which they cannot find employment for; and though from time to time there are rumours of improvement in trade, nothing comes of them, and people are obliged to await some stroke of magic which shall bring us back our old prosperity 'of leaps and bounds'.

The fact is that the commerce of the great industries has entered insensibly into its second stage, and mere cut-throat competition between the different nations has taken the place of the benevolent commercial despotism of the only nation which was thoroughly prepared to take advantage of the Industrial Revolution – Great Britain, to wit.

This second stage is doubtless preparing the final one which will end with the death of the whole bourgeois commercial system. Meanwhile, what is the real social product of the Industrial Revolution? We answer the final triumph of the middle-classes, materially, intellectually, and morally. As the result of the great political revolution in France was the abolition of aristocratic privilege, and the domination in the world of politics of the bourgeoisie, which hitherto had had little to do with it, so the English Industrial Revolution may be said to have created a new commercial middle-class hitherto unknown to the world. This class on the one hand consolidated all the groups of the middle-class of the preceding epoch, such as country squires large and small, big farmers, merchants, manufacturers, shopkeepers, and professional men; and made them so conscious of their solidarity, that the ordinary refined and thinking man of to-day cannot really see any other class at all, but only outside his own class certain heterogeneous groups to be used as instruments for the further advancement of that class. On the other hand, it has attained such complete domination that the upper-classes are merely adjuncts to it and servants of it. In fact, these also are now of the bourgeois class, as they are all engaged in commerce in one way or other: *eg.*, the higher nobility are all either house-agents or coal-factors, and would be of no importance without their 'businesses'. Moreover, striving ever to extend itself downwards as well as upwards, the middle-class has absorbed so much in that direction, especially within the last thirty years, that it has now nothing left below it except the mere propertyless proletariat. These last are wholly dependent upon it, utterly powerless before it until the break up of the system which has created it, the signs of whose beginning we have just noted, shall *force* them into a revolt against it. In the course of that revolt this great middle-class will in its turn be absorbed into the proletariat, which will form a new Society in which classes will have ceased to exist. This is the next Revolution, as inevitable, as inexorable, as the rising of to-morrow's sun.

COMMONWEAL, VOLUME 2, NUMBER 31,
14 AUGUST 1886, PP. 156–158

CHAPTER X
POLITICAL MOVEMENTS IN ENGLAND

During the French Revolution, especially during its earlier stages there was a corresponding movement in England. It made some noise at the time, but was merely an intellectual matter, led by a few aristocrats – *eg.*, the Earl of Stanhope – and had no sympathy with the life of the people; it was rather a piece of aristocratic Bohemianism, a tendency to which has been seen in various times, even our own. For the rest, there certainly was in England a feeling, outside this unreal republicanism – a feeling of which Priestly the Unitarian may be looked on as a representative; this feeling was of the nature of that felt by respectable and thoughtful Radicals of later days, and was distinctly bourgeois, as the other was aristocratic.

The French Revolution naturally brought about a great reaction, not only in absolutist countries, but also in England, the country of Constitutionalism; and this reaction was much furthered and confirmed by the fall of Napoleon and the restoration of the Bourbons in France. We may take as representative names of this reaction the Austrian Prince Mettternich (*sic*) on the Continent and Lord Castlereagh in England. The stupid and ferocious repression of the governments acting under this influence, as well as the limitless corruption by which they were supported, were met in England by a corresponding progressive agitation, which was the beginning of Radicalism. Burdett and Cartwright are representatives of the earlier days of this agitation, and later on Hunt, Carlile, Lovett, and others. William Cobbett must also be mentioned as belonging to this period – a man of great literary capacity of a kind, and with flashes of insight as to social matters far before his time, but clouded by violent irrational prejudices and prodigious egotism; withal a peasant rather than a bourgeois – a powerful disruptive agent, but incapable of association with others. This period of Radical agitation was marked by a piece of violent repression in the shape of the so-called Peterloo Massacre, where an unarmed crowd at a strictly political meeting was charged and cut down by the yeomanry, and eleven people killed outright.[1]

This agitation, which was partly middle-class and partly popular, was succeeded by the Chartist movement, which was almost exclusively supported by the people, though some of the leaders – as Feargus O'Connor and Ernest Jones – belonged to the middle-class. Chartism, on the face of it, was as much a political movement as the earlier Radical one; its programme was wholly directed towards parliamentary reform; but as we have said, it was a popular movement, and its first motive power was the special temporary suffering of the people, due, as we said in our last chapter, to the disturbance of labour caused by the growth of the machine industry; and the electoral and parliamentary reforms of its programme were put forward because it was supposed that if they were carried they would affect the material condition of the people directly: at the same time, however, there is no doubt that the pressure of hunger and misery gave rise to other hopes besides the above-mentioned delusion as to reform, and ideas of Socialism were current among the Chartists though they were not openly put forward on their programme. Accordingly the class-instinct of the bourgeoisie saw the social danger that lurked under the apparently political claims of the charter, and so far from its receiving any of

[1] The readers of *Commonweal* will find an article on this subject in the first number (Feb. 1885), by our comrade E. T. Craig, who was in Manchester at the time, though not an eye-witness. It is interesting to note that the scene of the massacre, St Peter's *Fields*, is now a mass of streets in the very centre of the city of Manchester.

the middle-class sympathy which had been accorded to the Radical agitation, Chartism was looked upon as *the* enemy, and the bourgeois progressive movement was sedulously held aloof from it. It is worthy of note that Chartism was mainly a growth of the midland and northern counties – that is, of the great manufacturing districts – and that it never really flourished in London. In Birmingham the movement had the greatest force, and serious riots took place there while a Chartist conference was sitting in the town. The movement gave birth to a good deal of popular literature; and it must be remembered that the press was very strictly controlled by the Government. No paper was allowed to be issued without a stamp, the expense of which prevented the issue of cheap papers; and one of the incidents of the struggle was the determined opposition to this law kept up by some courageous agitators, who published unstamped papers in the teeth of the certain imprisonment that awaited them.

The Chartist movement went on vigorously enough till the insufficiency both of its aims and of knowledge as to how to carry them out found out the weak places in it. The immediate external cause of its wreck was the unfortunate schism that arose between the supporters of moral force and physical force in the body itself. The fantastic folly of supposing that there can be any 'moral force' in matters political which does not rest on the resolution of a party to attain their end by the use of what 'physical force['] they may have, if it should become necessary to use it, does not call for much comment here; although some thoughtless persons may even at present *think* that they believe such a 'moral force' exists. On the other hand, it is clear to us now that a Chartist revolt had no chance of success at that time, and but for self-deception would have been clear to both leaders and rank and file of the party then.

It may here be mentioned that the trump-card which the Chartists were always thinking of playing was the organization of an universal strike, under the picturesque title of the Holy Month. In considering the enormous difficulties, or rather impossibilities, of this enterprise, we should remember that its supporters understood that the beginnings of it would be at once repressed forcibly, and that it would lead directly to civil war.

The truth is that there were two distinct groups in the party, one of which went about as far as our ultra-Radicals of the present day; and another which was at heart Socialist, only deficient in knowledge, and consequently without definite principles on which to base action; and these two groups pretty much corresponded to the division between the supporters of moral and physical force.

From 1842, when the schism came to a head, Chartism began to die out. Its decay, however, was far more due to the change that was coming over the economical state of affairs than even to its incomplete development of principle and ill-considered tactics. Things were settling down from the dislocation caused by the rise of the great industries. The workers shared in the added wealth brought about by [the] enormous expansion of trade, although in an absurdly small proportion to the share of the middle-classes; but those classes tended ever to become more numerous and more contented. The trades' unions began to be powerful, and improved the prospects of the skilled workmen. So-called co-operation began to flourish: it was really an improved form of joint-stockery, which could be engaged in by the workmen, but was and is fondly thought by some to be if not a shoeing-horn to Socialism at least a substitute for it; indeed Chartism itself at this time became involved in a kind of half co-operative half peasant-proprietorship land scheme, which of course proved utterly abortive.

As this improvement in the condition of the working-classes weakened that part of the life of Chartism which depended on mere hunger desperation, so the growing political power in the middle-classes and the weakening of the mere Tory reaction swallowed up the political part of its life.

Chartism, therefore, flickered out in the years that followed 1842, but its last act was the celebrated abortive threat at revolt which took place in April 1848. And it must be said that there was something appropriate in such a last act. For this demonstration was distinctly caused by sympathy with the attacks on absolutism then taking place on the Continent, and Chartism was always on one side of it a part of the movement which was going on all over Europe, and was directed against the reaction which followed on the French Revolution, and which was represented by the 'Holy Alliance' of the absolutist sovereigns against both bourgeoisie and the people.

On the fall of Chartism, the Liberal Party, a nondescript and flaccid creation of bourgeois supremacy, a party without principles or definition, but a thoroughly adequate expression of English middle-class hypocrisy, cowardice, and short-sightedness, engrossed the whole of the political progressive movement in England, and dragged the working-classes along with it, blind as they were to their own interests and the solidarity of labour. This party has shown little or no sympathy for the progressive movement on the Continent, unless when they deemed it connected with their anti-Catholic prejudice. It saw no danger in the Cæsarism which took the place of the corrupt sham Constitutionalism of Louis Philippe as the head of the police and stock-jobbing régime, which dominated France in the interests of the bourgeoisie, and hailed Louis Napoleon with delight as the champion of law and order.

Any one, even a thoughtful person, might have been excused for thinking in the years that followed on 1848 that the party of the people was at last extinguished in England, and that the class-struggle had died out and given place to the peaceable rule of the middle-classes, scarcely disturbed by occasional bickerings carried on in a lawful manner between the two parties to that false free-contract, which is the lying foundation on which Commercial Society rests. But, as we shall show in a future chapter, under all this, Socialism was making great strides and developing a new and scientific phase, which at last resulted in the establishment of the International Association, whose aim was to unite the workers of the world in an organization which should consciously oppose itself to the domination of middle-class capitalism. The International was inaugurated in England in 1864, at a meeting held at St Martin's Hall, London, and at which Professor Beesly took the chair. It made considerable progress among the Trades' Unions, and made a great impression (beyond indeed what its genuine strength warranted) on the arbitrary Governments of Europe. It culminated in the Socialistic influence it had, in the Commune of Paris, of which we shall treat in a separate chapter. The International did not long out-live the Commune, and once more for several years all proletarian influence was dormant in England, except for what activity was possible among the foreign refugees living there, with whom some few of the English working-men had relations. From this connection sprang, however, a new movement, which we must barely mention, though it cannot yet be considered a matter of history. In 1881, an attempt was made to federate the various Radical Clubs into a body, with a programme which, though for the most part merely Radical, had an infusion of Socialism in it, and which took the name of the Democratic Federation. The Radical Clubs, however, that had joined soon seceded, mostly from disagreement with the revolutionary attitude taken by the Federation on the Irish question. In 1883, the programme became more definitely Socialistic, and the next year the title was changed to that of the Social Democratic Federation; but in the last days of 1884 differences of opinion which had been developing for some time, chiefly centering on the questions of Parliamentary Opportunism and Nationalism, ended in a secession which founded the Socialist League as a definite Revolutionary Socialist body early in 1885.

At the present time the Socialist bodies, though relatively small, tend to attract various elements to them; the discontent of the workmen with an outlook of ever increasing gloom; that also of the Ultra-Radicals unable to make any real impression on the dense mass of mingled

Conservatism and Whiggery, which really governs the country. The aspirations of thoughtful people who have studied the works of the great Socialist thinkers; the permeation of Socialist feeling from its centres on the Continent; and lastly and chiefly the steady march of events towards a new state of Society, which is making itself felt even amongst those who are unconscious of the advance of Socialism, or hostile to it – all these causes combining together, are forcing even England, the stronghold of middle-class domination, to pay attention to the subject, and will certainly before long form a new and powerful Party of the People, whose outlook will be far more hopeful than that of any of those we have told of; since its aim will no longer be partial or one-sided, but will be the realization of a new Society with new politics, ethics, and economics, in short, the transformation of civilization into Socialism.

COMMONWEAL, VOLUME 2, NUMBER 33,
28 AUGUST 1886, PP. 170–171.

CHAPTER XI
REACTION AND REVOLUTION ON THE CONTINENT

When the great war which Napoleon waged against Europe came to an end by his defeat and ruin, France was once more handed over to the Bourbons, and Europe fell into the arms of reaction and sheer absolutism. The Holy Alliance, or union of reactionary monarchs, undertook the enterprise of crushing out all popular feeling, or even anything that could be supposed to represent it in the persons of the bourgeois.

But the French Revolution had shaken absolutism too sorely for this enterprise to have more than a very partial success even on the surface. The power of absolutism was undermined by various revolutionary societies, mostly (so-called) secret, which attracted to them a great body of sympathy, and in consequence seemed far more numerous and immediately dangerous than they really were. Still there was a great mass of discontent, mostly political in character, and by no means confined to the poorer classes.

This discontent went on gathering head, till in 1830, and again in 1848, it exploded into open revolt against absolutism all over Europe. This revolt, we must repeat, was in the main a mere counter-stroke to the reaction which was diligently striving to restore the aristocratic privilege which the French Revolution had abolished, and to sustain what of it had escaped its attack. In 1830 the revolt was purely bourgeois in character, and was in no sense social, but, as above said, political. In 1848 it had in some places a strong infusion of the proletarian element, which however was dominated by middle-class patriotism and ideas which led to the assertion and consolidation of nationalities. But a new element was present in these latter revolutionary movements, though at first it did not seem to influence their action much. This was the first appearance in politics of modern or scientific Socialism, in the shape of the Communist Manifesto of Marx and Engels, first published in 1847. The rise and development of this phase will be dealt with in detail further on; at present we can do no more than call attention to the steady and continuous influence of this last-born Socialism, compared with the rapid extinction of Babeuf's propaganda, although he had a numerous body of adherents; since this fact marks a very great advance in opinion since the end of the eighteenth century.

The general effect, however, at least as seen openly, of these insurrections was little more than the shaking of absolutism and the supplanting it in various degrees by middle-class constitutionalism; and also, as aforesaid, an added impulse to the consolidation of nationalities, which later on produced the unification of Italy and of Germany, and the assertion of the independence of the Hungarian nationality.

In France the outward effects of the insurrection were most obvious and lasted the longest; but the bourgeois republic which took the place of Louis Philippe's corrupt constitutional monarchy asserted itself tyrannically enough against the proletariat, and in consequence had no strength left to meet the political adventurer Louis Napoleon, whose plot against the republic received just as much resistance as gave him an excuse for the massacre of 4th of December 1851, by means of which he terrorized France for many years; although as to numbers it was quite insignificant compared with those which followed the taking of Paris by the bourgeois troops at the time of the fall of the Commune in 1871.

This successful stroke had really no relation to any foregoing reactionary dictatorship. It even professed to be founded on democratic feeling, though as a matter of fact it was the expression of the non-political side of bourgeois life – the social and commercial side – the ideal of the shopkeeper grown weary of revolutions and anxious to be let alone to make money and enjoy himself vulgarly. Accordingly France settled down into a period of 'law and order', characterized by the most shameless corruption and repulsive vulgarity. She got at last into full swing of the rule of successful stock-jobbery which had already been established in England, and carried it on with less hypocrisy than ourselves, but perhaps with more open blackguardism.

To sustain this régime various showy military enterprises were undertaken, some of which it was attempted to invest with a kind of democratic sentiment. It was also of some importance to make at least a show of giving employment to the working classes of France. This principally took the form of the rebuilding of Paris and the restoration, or vulgarization, of the mediæval cathedrals and public buildings, in which France is richer than any other country; so that this apotheosis of middle-class vulgarity has left abiding tokens of its presence in a loss which can never be repaired. But in spite of this militarism and the attempt to gain the support of the proletarians by gifts of 'bread and pageants', discontent of various kinds sprang up and steadily increased. Moreover, the new birth of Socialism was beginning to bear fruits; the Communistic propaganda got firm hold of the city proletariat of France. Socialism was steadily preached in Paris at La Villete and Belleville, which latter, originally laid out and built upon as an elegant suburb for rich bourgeois, proved a failure, and became a purely workman's quarter in consequence.

While all this was going on underground as it were, the Cæsarism of the stock-exchange was also beginning to get the worst of it in the game of statecraft; and at last the results of the consolidation of nationalities which was the chief aim of the bourgeois revolt became obvious in the revival of the old animosities between Germany and France. Bismarck, who had become the attorney-dictator of Germany, had got to know the weakness of the showy empire of Louis Napoleon, and had a well warranted confidence in that carefully elaborated machine the German army. He laid a trap for the French Cæsar, who fell into it, perhaps not blindly, but rather driven by a kind of gambler's last hope, akin to despair.

A great race war followed, the natural and inevitable outcome of which was the hopeless defeat of the French army, led as it was by mere selfseekers and corrupt scoundrels, most of whom lacked even that lowest form of honour which makes a Dugald Dalgetty faithful to the colours under which he marches. The Second Empire was swept away. The new Republic proclaimed after the collapse at Sedan still kept up a hopeless resistance to the unbroken strength of Germany – hopeless, since the corruption of the Empire still lived on in the bourgeois republic, as typified in the person of the political gamester Gambetta. Paris was besieged, and taken after a long resistance, which reflected infinite credit on the general population, who bore the misery of the siege with prodigious patience and courage; but no less disgrace on those who pretended to organize its defence, but who were really far more inclined to hand over the city to the Germans than allow it to gain a victory under the auspices of the revolution.

All this must be looked upon by us as Socialists as merely the prelude to the great drama of the Commune, whose aims and influence will form the subject of another chapter.

Commonweal, Volume 2, Number 35,
11 September 1886, p. 189

CHAPTER XII
THE PARIS COMMUNE OF 1871, AND THE CONTINENTAL MOVEMENT FOLLOWING IT

In dealing with the great event of the Paris Commune, we must take for granted a knowledge of the facts, which are in a brief form accessible to all since the publication by the Socialist League of its pamphlet on the subject.

As we have stated before, the International was founded in 1864, under the leadership of Beesley, Marx, and Odger. In 1869, at the Congress of Basle, Marx drew it into the compass of Socialism; and though in England it still remained an indefinite labour-body, on the Continent it became at once decidedly Socialistic and revolutionary, and its influence was very considerable.

The progress of Socialism and the spreading feeling of the solidarity of labour was very clearly shown by the noble protest made by the German Socialists[1] against the war with France, in the teeth of a 'patriotic' feeling so strong in appearance that it might have been expected to silence any objectors from the first. The result of the war seemed to offer at least a chance for action to the rapidly increasing Socialist party, if they could manage to take advantage of it, to get into their hands the political power; and under the influence of the Internationalists, the French Socialists determined to take action if an immediate opportunity offered. Neither did the opportunity fail. The final defeat of the French army at Sedan brought on the fall of the Empire, when Republican France might perhaps have made

[1] They also protested, at the end of the war, against the annexation of Alsace and Lorraine.

terms with the invaders, whom the men of the Empire had challenged. But a resistance was organized by Gambetta, at the head of a stock-jobbing clique, whose interests, both commercial and political, forbade them to let the war die out, lest they should find themselves face to face with a people determined to be fleeced no longer. This resistance, sustained by the success with which this clique played on the sham patriotic or jingo feelings of the general population, was always quite hopeless from a military point of view, and brought the country to the verge of ruin. It also necessarily involved the German siege of Paris, the result of which was to throw a great deal of power into the hands of the city proletariat, since they at least were in earnest in their resistance to the foreign enemy, and the theatrical resistance necessary to the ambition of the political adventurers who posed as their leaders could not have a decent face to put upon it without their enthusiasm. In October, while the siege was still at its height, a rising headed by Blanqui nearly succeeded in overthrowing the bourgeois domination; and after the siege the possession of arms, especially cannon, by the proletariat, in the face of the disarmed and disorganized army under the bourgeois, afforded the opportunity desired by the Socialists. On the failure of Thiers' attempt to disarm Paris – whether he expected it to succeed, or only designed it as a trap to enable him to fall with mere force of arms on Paris – on this failure the insurrection took place, and the Central Committee, largely composed of members of the International, got into their hands the executive power, a great deal of which they retained during the whole of the existence of the Commune. Their position was strengthened by the fact that, apart from their aims towards the economical freedom of the proletariat, in their aspirations towards genuine federalization they were, in appearance as (*sic*) least, in accord with the Radicals who wished to see an advanced municipalism brought about.

As the movement progressed, it became more and more obvious that if the resistance to Thiers and the attempt to establish municipal independence for Paris was to succeed, it must be through the exercise of Socialist influence on the p[r]oletariat: the Radicals, therefore, were forced by the march of events into alliance with the Socialists. The Socialist element therefore came to the front, and enactments of a distinctly Socialistic nature were passed, involving the suspension of contract and abolition of rents; and both in these matters and in the decentralization which was almost the watchword of the Commune, the advance from the proceedings of the earlier revolutionists is clearly marked. Also, although the opportunity for the establishment of the Commune was given by the struggle against foreigners, the international character of their aspirations was shown by the presence of foreigners in the Council of the Commune and in command of its troops. And though in itself the destruction of the Vendome Column may seem but a small matter, yet considering the importance attached generally, and in France particularly, to such symbols, the dismounting of that base piece of Napoleonic upholstery was another mark of the determination to hold no parley with the old jingo legends.

It should be noted that the risings which took place in other towns in France were not so much vanquished by the strength of the bourgeoisie, which at first found itself powerless before the people, but rather fell through owing to a want of fuller development of Socialism and a more vigorous proclamation of its principles.

The whole revolt was at last drowned in the blood of the workers of Paris. Certainly the immediate result was to crush Socialism for the time by the destruction of a whole generation of its most determined recruits. Nevertheless the very violence and excess of the bourgeois revenge have, as we can now see, tended to strengthen the progress of Socialism, as they have set the seal of tragedy and heroism on the mixed events of the Commune, and made its memory a rallying point for all future revolutionists.

However, the fall of the Commune involved that of the International. The immediate failure of its action was obvious, and blinded people to its indestructible principles. Besides, a period of great commercial prosperity visited the countries of Europe at this time. The French milliards which Germany had won as the prize of war were being turned over and over by the German bourgeois in their merry game of 'beggar-my-neighbour'. England was at the height of its period of 'leaps and bounds' – a period now called by the German middle-classes themselves the 'swindle period'. Even France, in spite of her being the plundered country, recovered from the condition into which the war had thrown her with a speed which made the plunderer envy her. In short, it was one of those periods which prove to the bourgeois exploiter that he is positively right, in which the bettermost workman grows quite unconscious of the chain which binds him, and is contemptuously regardless of that which lies heavy on the labourer below him, to whom the prosperity or adversity of the rest of the world make little or no difference.

Internal dissensions, also, were at work within the International, and at the Congress of the Hague in 1872 it was broken up; and though it still existed as a name for the next year or two, the remaining fragments of it did nothing worth speaking of.

In Vienna, in 1871, the movement in sympathy with the Commune became threatening, but was repressed by the authorities, and several of the prominent members of the party were imprisoned for the part they had taken in a Socialist demonstration – amongst others, Johann Most and Andreas Scheu.

For a while after the fall of the Commune the interest in the active side of the movement turns to Russia and Germany. In 1878 Nobiling and Hödel shot at the Emperor William; which event gave the occasion for the attack by Bismark (*sic*) on the rapidly increasing Socialist party in October 1878, when the repressive laws were enacted which have been in force ever since. The result of these laws, which suppressed meetings, papers, and other literature, has been to drive the movement into a purely parliamentary course. In spite of the repression, the party has not only succeeded in holding itself together, but has grown to large dimensions, numbering, according to official statements, 650,000.

In Russia the Socialist movement was, on the face of it, mixed up with nationalist and political agitation, which was natural in a country in the bonds of the crudest form of absolutism. Nevertheless the ultimate aim of the party is unmistakable, and the propaganda has been carried on with a revolutionary fervour and purity of devotion which have never been surpassed, if they have ever been equalled. The slaying of the Czar on March 13, 1881, with the tragic scenes that followed it, has been the most dramatic event which the Russian movement has given to the world; and it must be said of it that it has marked and initiated a new revolutionary period. Since that time the elements of Revolution have gathered force and cohesion; a sense of insecurity has come over the authority of 'law and order'; the sympathies of all people of honesty and good feeling have been attracted to the side of those suffering under mere open monstrous oppression; and men's minds generally have been opened to new ideas on the more insidious oppression under which labour groans in constitutionally governed countries.

The last stage of the great revolution inaugurated in France at the end of the eighteenth century seems destined to be reached at the end of the nineteenth – if, indeed, that thing of rags and patches called 'Constitutional Government' can keep itself alive so long.

COMMONWEAL, VOLUME 2, NUMBER 38,
2 OCTOBER 1886, P. 210

CHAPTER XIII
THE UTOPISTS: OWEN, SAINT SIMON, AND FOURIER

It is now necessary for us to turn for a while from the political progress of Socialism, to note the school of thinkers who preceded the birth of modern scientific or revolutionary Socialism. These men thought it possible to regenerate Society by laying before it its short-comings, follies, and injustice, and by teaching through precept and example certain schemes of reconstruction built up from the aspirations and insight of the teachers themselves. They had not learned to recognize the sequence of events which *forces* social changes on mankind whether they are conscious of its force or not, but believed that their schemes would win their way to general adoption by men's perception of their inherent reasonableness. They hoped to convert people to Socialism, to accepting it consciously and formally, by showing them the contrast between the confusion and misery of existing civilization, and the order and happiness of the world which they foresaw.

From the elaborate and detailed schemes of future Society which they built up they have been called the Utopists; the representatives of the different phases of their school are three most remarkable men, born within a few years of each other, whose aspirations and insight have done a very great deal to further the progress of Socialism, in spite of the incompleteness of their views.

Robert Owen was born at Newtown, Montgomeryshire, in 1771, of a lower middle-class family; he became a successful manufacturer through his own industry and quick-wittedness in the beginning of the rise of the Great

Machine Industries, when 'manufacturing' was advancing 'by leaps and bounds'. He was a born philanthropist in the better sense of the word, and from the first showed in all matters unbounded generosity and magnanimity. In the year 1800, when he was not yet thirty, he became the manager of the New Lanark Mills, and set to work on his first great experiment, which was briefly the conversion of a miserable, stupid, and vicious set of people into a happy, industrious, and orderly community, acting on the theory that man is the creature of his surroundings, and that by diligent attention to the development of his nature he can be brought to perfection. In this experiment he was entirely successful, but it was not in him to stop there, as the plain words he said of his success showed clearly enough: 'Yet these men were my slaves.'[1] He took part in all kinds of projects of a philanthropical nature, still founding all his action on his theory of the perfectibility of man by the amelioration of his surroundings, and became the first great champion of co-operation, although he did not suppose, as the co-operators of the present day do, that anything short of universal co-operation would solve the social question. In 1815, he pressed a meeting of Glasgow manufacturers to petition Parliament to shorten the hours of labour in the cotton mills, and the change which he experienced from the approbation of the governing classes to their reprobation, may well date from that proceeding of his, as a bourgeois biographer of his hints. But he still kept his position of a popular philanthropist, even after his declaration in favour of co-operation, until he at last cut himself off from respectability, by openly attacking Society through its received religions (August 21, 1816), from which date onward he was scouted by all that 'Society', of which he was now the declared enemy. But he was in nowise daunted. In 1823, he proposed Communistic villages as a remedy for the distress in Ireland; he

[1] Yet in 1806, when owing to the rise in cotton he could not continue manufacturing, he stopped the mills and paid his people their full wages till he could go on again in four months time, a prodeeding which cost him £7000.

established, in 1832, an exchange in Gray's Inn Road, in which labour was equitably exchanged against labour; and in 1825 he bought New Harmony from a community already established there (the Rappites), and made his great experiment in living in common; and late in life he published his 'Book of the New Moral World', which contains the exposition of his doctrine.

It will be thus seen that he was unwearied in practical experiments. His shortcoming was the necessary one of the utopist, a total disregard of the political side of progress; he failed to see that his experiments, useful as they were from that point of view, could never develope (*sic*) out of the experimental state as long as the governors of Society forcibly uphold the so-called 'rights of property', and he ignored the antagonism of classes necessarily existing under this system, and which in the long run must bring about the Socialism which he, the most generous and best of men, spent his whole life in attempting to realize. He died in 1858.

Saint Simon was born of a noble family at Paris in 1760. He acquired and ran through a fortune, deliberately experimenting in the various forms of 'life' from extravagance to abject poverty. There was in him none of that tendency to practical experiment in quasi-Socialistic schemes which characterized Robert Owen. His philosophy was mingled with a mysticism which had a tendency to increase, a tendency to form a new religion rather than to realize a new condition of life, and which was carried into the absurdities of a kind of worship by his immediate followers, more or less imitated by the Positivists of our own day, whose founder, Auguste Comte, was his most cherished disciple. His Socialism was of a vague kind, and admitted the existence of classes of talent as expressed by the motto of Saint Simonism, 'From each according to his capacity, to each according to his deeds'. In spite, however, of the tendency to mysticism, he showed singular flashes of insight in matters historical and economic, and intellectually was certainly ahead of Robert Owen. He may be said to have set himself the task of learning all life by whatever means and at whatever expense, in order to devote himself to the new religion, 'whose great aim is the swiftest possible amelioration of the moral and physical condition of the poorest and most numerous class'.

Frederick Engels well says of him: 'As early as his "Letters from Geneva", Saint Simon laid down that all men ought to work, and that the Reign of Terror had been the reign of the non-possessing masses. To face the fact in 1802 that the French Revolution was a struggle between the noblesse, the bourgeoisie, and the non-possessing classes was a discovery of genius. In 1816 he asserted that politics were but the science of production, and predicted their absorption by economy. The knowledge that economic conditions serve as the base of political institutions only shows itself here in the germ; nevertheless, this proposition contains clearly the conversion of the political government of men into an administration of things and a direction of the process of production; that is to say, the abolition of the State, of which such a noise has since been made.'

Internationalism also was clearly enunciated by Saint Simon. We quote Engels again: 'With an equal superiority over the views of his contemporaries, he declared in 1814, immediately after the entry of the allies into Paris, and again in 1815 during the war of the hundred days, that the sole guarantee of the peace and prosperous development of Europe, was an alliance between France and England, and of those two countries with Germany. Certainly it needed a courage by no means common to preach to the French of 1815 alliance with the victors at Waterloo.'

It is worth noting that one of the schemes of the Saint Simonians, which was most ridiculed at the time, was the cutting of the Isthmuses of Suez and Panama, and that M. de Lesseps was a Saint Simonian.

Saint Simon died in great poverty in 1825, with words of hope for the future of the party on his lips.

Charles Fourier was born in 1772 at Lyons; his father was a draper. He lost his property in the Revolution, and afterwards went into business as a broker. Amidst his dealings with Society, he was early struck by the shortcomings and injustices of individualism and competition. In his first book, 'The Theory of the Four Movements', he elaborates the proposition that human nature is perfectible through the free play of the appetites and passions, and asserts that misery and vice spring from the restraints imposed by Society. His criticism of modern Society is most valuable as anticipating that of scientific Socialism; unlike his contemporaries he has an insight into the historical growth of Society: 'He divides it into four periods of development, Savagery, Barbarism, Patriarchalism, and Civilization, meaning by the latter the Bourgeois Civilization.'[2] His saying, 'In civilization poverty is born even of superabundance', may well be noted in these days, and compared with Robert Owen's in 1816, 'Our best customer, the war, is dead'.

As a basis of the reconstruction of Society, Fourier advocated Industrial Co-operation; but here his Utopianism led him to the trap of formulating dogmatically an electorate scheme of life in all its details, a scheme which could never be carried out, however good the principlse (*sic*) on which it was based might be. His scheme arranges for phalanxsteries as the unit of co-operation, in which all life and all industry, agricultural and other, should be carried on, and all details are carried out by him most minutely, the number of each phalanxtery being settled at 1600 souls. His most valuable idea was the possibility and necessity of apportioning due labour to each capacity, and thereby assuring that it should be always pleasurable, and his dictum that children, who generally like making dirt-pies and getting into a mess, should do the dirty work of the community, may at least be looked on as an illustration of this idea, though laid down as a formal law. His system was not one of pure equality, but admitted distinctions between rich and (comparatively) poor; and advocated a

[2] Frederick Engels in 'Socialisme Utopique', and 'Socialisme Scientifique', as also the quotations above.

fantastic division of wealth between labour, capital, and talent. The abolition of marriage was a tenet of his doctrine.

In 1812, Fourier's mother died and left him some property, and he retired into the country to write his 'Treatise on the Association of Domesticity and Agriculture'. Afterwards he came to Paris again, became a clerk in an American firm, and wrote in 1830 his 'New Industrial World'. It is lamentable to have to relate that in 1831 he wrote attacking both Owen and St Simon as charlatans, in spite of the curious points of resemblance he had to either of them. He died in 1837, but not till he had founded a school, of which Victor Considerans, author of the 'Destinée Sociale', was the most distinguished member. The Fourierists started a paper in 1832, which expired in two years, but was revived in 1836, and finally suppressed by Government in 1850. A scheme for realizing the Phalanxtery experimentally was set on foot in 1832 by a deputy of France, but it failed for lack of funds; so that of the three great Utopists, Owen was the only one who had the fortune, good or bad as it may be considered, of seeing his schemes tried by experience. Cabet, indeed, a revolutionist of '48, founded a community in America under the name of Icaria, which was (and is, for it still exists) more nearly an approach to genuine Communism than any of the other communities which have owed their origin to Utopian Socialism. Of these communities there remains a word to be said as a warning to those who are young in Socialism. Although as experiments in association something may be learned from them, their conditions of life have no claim to the title of Communism, which most unluckily has often been applied to them. Communism can never be realized till the present system of Society has been destroyed by the workers taking hold of the political power. When that happens it will mean that Communism is on the point of absorbing and transmuting Civilization.

Commonweal, Volume 2, Number 42,
30 October 1886, pp. 242–243

CHAPTER XIV
THE TRANSITION FROM THE UTOPISTS TO MODERN SOCIALISM

Of the Socialist thinkers who serve as a kind of link between the Utopists and the school of the Socialism of historical evolution, or scientific Socialists, by far the most noteworthy figure is Proudhon who was born at Besançon in 1809. By birth he belonged to the working-class, his father being a brewer's cooper, and he himself as a youth followed the occupation of cowherding.

In 1838, however, he published an essay on general grammar, and in 1839 he gained a scholarship to be held for three years, a gift of one Madame Suard to his native town. The result of this advantage was his most important though far from his most voluminous work, published the same year, as the essay which the Madame Suard's scholars were bound to write: it bore the title of 'What is Property?' his answer being, Property is Robbery.

As may be imagined, this remarkable essay caused much stir and indignation, and Proudhon was censured by the Besançon Academy for this production, and narrowly escaped a prosecution. In 1841 he was tried at Besançon for a letter he wrote to Victor Considerant, the Fourierist, but was acquitted. In 1846 he wrote his 'Pholisophie de la Misère' (Philosophy of Poverty), which received an elaborate reply and refutation from Karl Marx.

In 1847 he went to Paris. In the Revolution of 1848 he showed himself a vigorous controversialist, and was elected Deputy for the Seine; he wrote numerous articles in several journals, mostly criticisms of the progress of the revolution: in the Chamber he proposed a tax of one-third to be levied on all interest and rent, which was, as a matter of course, rejected. He also put forward a scheme for a mutual credit bank, by which he hoped to simplify exchange and reduce interest to a vanishing point: but this scheme was also rejected.

After the failure of the revolution of '48, Proudhon was imprisoned for three years, during which time he married a young woman of the working-class.

In 1858 he developed his system of 'Mutualism' fully in his last work, entitled 'Justice in the Revolution and the Church'. In consequence of the publication of this book he had to retire to Brussels, but was amnestied in 1860, came back to France, and died at Passy in 1865.

Proudhon's opinions and works may be broadly divided into two periods: In his 'What is Property?' his position is that of a Communist pure and simple; but after this one clear development of a definite thesis we meet in his works, and we must add, in his political actions also, with so much paradox that it is next to impossible to formulate in brief any definite Proudhonian doctrine. At one time a Communist, at another the vehement opponent of Communism; at one time professing Anarchy, at another lending himself to schemes of the crudest State Socialism; at one time an enthusiastic Theist, at another apparently as strong an Atheist; in one passage of his works giving his eager adhesion to Auguste Comte's worship of women, in another a decided contemner of the female sex, – it is with a sense of confusion that one rises from the perusal of his works.

His connection with the Revolution of '48 seems to have been the turning point in the history; in his address to the electors of the Seine, in which he put forward the scheme for a credit bank backed by a number of decrees of a State-Socialistic nature, and strongly smacking of Bismarck, he announces himself as the man who said Property is Robbery, says that he still maintains that opinion, and then goes on to defend the rights of property which he had so successfully annihilated in his first work.

But as to his political career, the element he had to work in was an impossible one for the success of a man holding definite Socialistic ideas. On the one hand were the Jacobins with their archæological restorations of the ideas and politics of 1789; on the other Socialism showing itself and taking hold of people's minds, but attempting to realize its doctrines by crude dislocated and consequently hopeless schemes of action. Into all these affairs Proudhon looked shrewdly and with insight, and his bitter criticisms of the confusion of the period were shown by the event to have been well founded.

Proudhon defended the modern family and monogamy in its strictest sense, and does not seem to have troubled himself to study the history of those institutions even superficially: in short, he seems to have been singularly lacking in the the (*sic*) historical sense, and had not formed any conception of the evolution of society. Those who read his works will find themselves forced to return to his first essay, 'What is Property?' if they are seeking in him for any consistent series of ideas. He was an eager and rough controversialist, and his style is brilliant and attractive in spite of its discursiveness.

We may now mention the names of two men of no great importance in themselves, but worth noting as forerunners of the sentimental Socialists and Christian Socialists of the present day. Hughes Felicité Robert de Lamennais (born 1782, died 1854), is the type of the Christian Socialist: he was intended for a priest from the first, and duly took orders. He began by efforts to reform the Catholic Church, so as to make it an effective instrument for happiness and social morality and reform. He expected to be helped and encouraged by the clergy in these efforts, and at first, before they perceived their real tendency, he received some acknowledgement from them. At last, in his paper *L'Avenir* (the future), he took so decidedly a democratic turn that he incurred the animosity of the whole Church, especially of the then Pope, Gregory XVI. The signal for his complete rupture with the Church, however was the publication (in 1834) of his 'Paroles d'un Croyant' (words of a believer), which the Pope characterized as 'small in size but immense in perversity'. After that he became thoroughly democratic or even Communistic, as Communism was then understood. A series of political works and pamphlets followed, all in the sense of his new departure. He started, in 1848, two papers, one after another, which were suppressed. He sat in the Republican Constituent Chamber till the *coup d'etat*; and while Deputy drew up for the Left a plan of Constitution which was rejected as too revolutionary. He was buried by his own direction without ecclesiastical rites.

Pierre le Roux (born 1798, died 1871) was originally a disciple of St Simon. In 1840 he published his most important work, 'De L'Humanité', whence the name of his school, the Humanitarians. He joined George Sand and Niardof in a literary review, and it was owing to this connexion that the humanitarian tendencies of some of her novels are to be traced. In 1843 he set on foot a co-operative printing association, and started a journal advocating co-operation, or as he termed it, 'the pacific solution of the problem of the proletariat'. He also sat in the Republican Chamber of 1848: was exiled in 1851 and lived in Jersey, not returning to France till 1869. He died in Paris under the Commune, who deputed two of its members to attend his funeral, in the words of the *Official Journal*, 'not in honour of the partizan of the mystical ideas of which we now feel the evil, but of the politician who courageously undertook the defence of the vanquished after the days of June'. This is an allusion to the unpractical and non-political tendency of his teaching, which undertook to reform society by the inculcation of morality blended with mysticism, the result of which was to be the gradual spread of voluntary co-operation.

We finish this series with the well-known name of Louis Blanc, a personage more important than the last-named, and more definitely Socialistic in principles than either he or Lamennais, though his political career finished in a way unworthy of those principles, even if we accept the excuse that he never grasped the great truth that only through the class struggle can the regeneration of society be accomplished. He was born in 1813, of a middle-class family which, on the maternal side, was Corsican, and an incident of the relations between him and his brother Charles is said to have suggested to Dumas his famous novelette and play of the 'Corsican Brothers'.

In 1840 he published his 'Organization of Labour', the ideas of which he attempted to realize in his famous 'National Workshops', by which he is best known. In this work he put forward the genuine Socialistic maxim of 'From each according to his capacity, to each according to his needs' as the basis of the production of a true society.

He took an active part in the Revolutionary Government of 1848, and got an edict passed abolishing the punishment of death for political offences. And we ought here to notice that the common impression that his National Workshops failed from inherent defects is wrong; they were suppressed as dangerous by the Government, and their suppression was largely instrumental in causing the June revolution. We must, however, also note that this scheme was not founded on purely Socialistic principles, dangerous as it was thought to be at the time. In consequence of the events of June Louis Blanc was compelled to flee from France to England, where he wrote his 'History of the French Revolution'.

He returned to France [in] 1869, was elected to the legislative body, but played only a subordinate part in the stirring times that followed. It remains, indeed, an indelible stain on his character that he deserted the cause of the people in the days of March, leaving Paris to sit amongst the 'Liberals' in the reactionary Chamber at Versailles.

He died in 1883, having outlived his reputation and influence.

COMMONWEAL, VOLUME 3, NUMBER 56,
5 FEBRUARY 1887, PP. 42–43

CHAPTER XV
SCIENTIFIC SOCIALISM – KARL MARX

The foregoing chapters on modern Socialists may be regarded as leading up to the full development of the complete Socialist theory, or as it is sometimes called, 'scientific' Socialism. The great exponent of this theory, and the author of the most thorough criticism of the capitalistic system of production, is the late Dr Karl Marx.

He was born in 1818 at Treves, his father being a baptized Jew holding an official position in that city. He studied for the law in the University of Bonn, passing his examination with high honours in 1840. In 1843 he married Jenny von Westphalen, sister of the well-known Prussian statesman of that name. Philosophy and political economy, with especial reference to the great social problems of the age, were his special studies on leaving the university. These studies led him towards Socialism, the result of which was that he felt compelled to decline the offer of an important government post. About this time he left Treves for Paris, where he became co-editor with Arnold Rugé of the *Deutsch-Franzüsischen Jahrbücher*; and he also edited the Socialist journal *Vorwärts*; but in less than a twelvemonth he was compelled to leave France for Brussels. In March 1848 he was driven from Belgium and fled to Cologne, where the revolutionary ferment was at its height. He at once undertook the editorship of the *Rheinische Zeitung*, the leading revolutionary journal, which was suppressed on the collapse of the revolutionary movement in 1849.

We should mention that in 1847, in conjunction with his life-long friend, Frederic Engels, he put forward the celebrated 'Communist Manifesto', which subsequently served as the basis of the International Association.

After 1849 he went to Paris again, where he remained but a short time, and then left France for London, remaining there with brief intermissions till his death, which took place in the spring of 1883.

The principal part he took in political action during his sojourn in England was the organization of the International Association.

The most important among his works besides 'Das Kapital' are 'Die Heilige Familie', written in conjunction with Frederic Engels; the 'Misere de la Philosophie', the answer to Proudhon mentioned in our last article; '18 Brumaire', an anti-Napoleonic pamphlet; and 'Zur Kritik der Politischer Œconomic', which laid the foundation for his great work 'Das Kapital'.

The importance of this latter work makes it necessary for us to indicate the contents of the principal chapters, so as to form a brief sketch of the Socialist economy.[1]

Part I deals with Commodities and Money. The first chapter defines a commodity. A commodity according to Marx is briefly expressed as a socially useful product of labour which stands in relation to other similar useful products of labour. The *value* of such a commodity is primarily the amount of necessary social labour contained in it: that is to say, the average amount of labour carried through a certain portion of time necessary to its production in a given state of society. The young student must take special note that when Marx uses the word *value* by itself it is always used in this sense; *ie.*, to put it in a shorter form, as embodied average human labour. The term Use-value explains itself. Exchange-value means the relation of one commodity to another or to all others. The ultimate issue of the various expressions of Value is the money form: but in the words of Marx, the step to the

[1] We must remind the reader that we do not profess to offer more than some hints to the student of Marx. Anything approaching to an abstract of 'Das Kapital' would take up space far beyond the limits of the present little work.

money-form 'consists in this alone, that the character of direct and universal exchangeability – in other words, that the universal equivalent form – has now by social custom become identified with the substance gold'.

The second chapter deals with Exchange. Exchange, says Marx, presupposes guardians or owners of commodities, since these cannot go to market of themselves. A commodity possesses for the owner no use-value where he seeks to exchange it: if it did, he would not seek to exchange it. 'All commodities', says Marx, 'are non-use values for their owners and use values for their non-owners. Consequently they must all change hands. But this change of hands is what constitutes their exchange, and the latter puts them in relation with each other as *values*, and realizes them as *values*. Hence commodities must be realized as *values* before they can be realized as use-values.'

Commodities, then, find their universal value represented by one commodity from among them, which has in itself no use-value unless it be that of representing or of symbolizing the abstract quality of value.

Chapter III deals with the circulation of commodities under the money form. Here Marx very justly observes: 'It is because all commodities as values are realized human labour, and therefore commensurable, that their values can be measured by one and the same special commodity, and the latter be converted into the common measure of their value – *ie.*, into money. Money as a measure of value is the phenomenal form that must of necessity be assumed by that measure of *value* which is immanent in commodities, labour time.'

This long and important chapter proceeds to discuss the theory of circulating money or of currency at considerable length and in great detail. The subject is one of such importance and with respect to which so many fallacies are afloat, that we propose to devote our next article to an exposition of its leading features.

COMMONWEAL, VOLUME 3, NUMBER 59,
26 FEBRUARY 1887, PP. 66–67

CHAPTER XVI
SCIENTIFIC SOCIALISM – KARL MARX
II MONEY

We have now come to the point where it is necessary to consider the circulation of commodities; the first means to this circulation is the establishment of a *tertium quid*, or universal equivalent. And in order to have a really universal equivalent it is necessary that use-value should be eliminated from it, since such an equivalent is required to express not the diverse *qualities* of all the various commodities, but the relative *quantity* of embodied human labour which they severally contain.

Money as a mere measure of value is imaginary and ideal, but the bodily form of it must express quantitively equivalent abstract value – *ie.*, labour – and takes the form of the precious metals, finally of gold.

Gold has come to be the bodily form taken by the universal measure of value, partly because of its natural qualities – portability, durability, etc., but chiefly because the course of history has invested it with this function; and also because its value, instead of changing from, say, week to week, as is the case with other commodities, changes rather from century to century, so that its value may be considered stable relatively to them, just as one speaks of indigo as a permanent dye, which it is relatively to other dyes, although none are absolutely permanent.[1]

[1] As a deduction from this, we may say that while on the one hand there was no abstract necessity for the measure of value taking the form of gold, though there was a necessity for it to take a form embodying a certain definite amount of labour; on the other hand, since it has taken that form, labour notes, or mere promises to pay which are of no value in themselves, cannot as long as exchange lasts take the place of gold, which is a commodity having a value in itself and the particular commodity which has assumed that function through historical selection.

Paper money is promises to pay gold, which is directly exchangeable with all other commodities. Paper money, therefore, is merely a symbol of the exchange really effected by gold.

This universal equivalent takes the place of barter, which is the primitive and direct form of exchange,[2] and at which stage the distinction between buyer and seller has not arisen. It now gives place to the first form of indirect exchange, in which a third term is interposed between the articles which are to be parted with and acquired. Now for the first time the above distinction takes shape. The seller has a commodity which he does not propose to consume, and therefore he acquires with it money, with which money he buys in turn another commodity equal in quantity to that with which he has parted, but different from it in quality. Marx has formulated this transaction by the well-known and useful formula, Commodity, Money, Commodity: C – M – C.

The habit of hoarding which is common amongst ancient societies, and also among barbarous peoples, is a natural concomitant of this stage of exchange, and is the first germ of Capital. It is brought about by the arrest of the above process at its first phase thus, C – M – the seller of the commodity does not go on to buy. Under these conditions money becomes a social power; and being a commodity like other commodities, can be acquired by private persons, whom it invests with social power. Therefore in those states of society which had not outgrown their primitive social ethics, money was considered the embodiment of all evil.

This stage of exchange marks the pre-commercial use of money; after a while it tends to develope (*sic*) into another

[2] There are transitional stages between barter pure and simple and exchange operated by a universal equivalent, which only partly fulfiled (sic) this office: *eg.*, cattle, in the primitive ancient period, from which the name for money (*pecunia*) is derived; or ordinary woollen cloth, as in the curious and rather elaborate currency of the Scandinavians before coin was struck in Norway: which currency, by the way, has again, in the form of blankets, been used even in our own times in the Hudson Bay Territory.

stage, which carries the exchange a step further. The holder of a commodity which he does not propose to consume exchanges it for money, which he again exchanges for a commodity to be used, not for his personal consumption but to be exchanged once more for money. He would have no object in doing this if his aim were merely that of the simple exchanger (C. M. C.), namely, to obtain an article of consumption different in kind to that which he has exchanged, since in money there is no inherent difference of quality and therefore whatever difference there may be must be one of quantity. Accordingly the object of the exchanger in this second stage is amount, not kind. In going through his process of exchange (the formula for which may be stated thus:

C – M – C – M – C),

the second quantum of money must be more than the first, or else he will have failed in his object; will have made a bad bargain, as the phrase goes. On the other hand, though this form of exchange differs essentially it nevertheless connects itself with the earlier form, in which money occurs only as the middle term between commodity and commodity, thus distinguishing it from simple barter, because even in the later form the result of the merchant's transaction is a commodity with which he intends to begin a fresh transaction –

C – M – C – M – C.

This is the form of exchange which was the practice of the developed classical world in its commercial operations. The break up of the Roman Empire, and the confusion that followed, dislocated this commerce, and largely brought exchange back again to its earlier and simple form of the exchange of a commodity for money with which to buy another commodity to be consumed, which was for the most part the character of the exchange of the Middle Ages.

This second form of exchange leads without a break into the third or modern form of Capitalistic Exchange, in which the exchanger, beginning with money, buys a commodity in order to exchange it for money; which money, as in the foregoing stage, must be more in quantity than that with which he began, or his transaction will be a failure. This process differs from that of the last-mentioned stage of exchange in that the result of the transaction is always money, and not a commodity (that is, a use-value), the latter in the long-run appearing only nominally in the transaction.

To make this clearer, we may give concrete examples of the three forms of exchange:

In the first stage, illustrated by the proceedings of the Craftsman of the time of Homer, which were pretty much those of the Mediæval Craftsman also, the village potter sold his pots and with the money he got for them, which, possible trickery apart, represented just the *value* or embodied labour of the pots, he bought meal, oil, wine, flesh, etc., for his own livelihood and consumed them.

The merchant of the later classical period shipped, say, purple cloth from Sidon to Alexandria, sold his cloth there, and with the money bought gum-Arabic (from the Soudan) and frankincense (from Arabia), which he sold at Athens, where again he shipped oil for another market. He always handled the actual goods he professed to trade in, and the wares which he thus exchanged against the universal equivalent, money, were of various kinds. Similar commerce went on in the Middle Ages, as with the merchants of Amalfii, Venice, etc., side by side with the primitive exchange of the feudal manor, and the market-town with its corporation and gilds.

The modern man of Commerce necessarily begins his transaction with money. He buys, say, indigo, which he never sees, receives for it more money than he gave for it, and goes on steadily in this process, dealing (unlike the ancient carrier-merchant) with one class of goods only; and all the goods in which he deals represent to him so much money: they are only present in his transactions nominally. Money is the be-all and end-all of his existence as a commercial man.

This is an example of the pure form of capitalistic exchange, wherein money is exchanged for commodities, and these again for money plus an increment; the formula for which, as given by Marx, is M – C – M.

The next question we have to consider is how the surplus, the increment above-mentioned, obtained by this process of exchange is realized, – or, in plain language, where it comes from.

COMMONWEAL, VOLUME 3, NUMBER 61,
12 MARCH 1887, P. 82

CHAPTER XVII
SCIENTIFIC SOCIALISM – CONVERSION OF CAPITAL INTO MONEY

Says Marx: 'The circulation of commodities is the starting point of capital: the production of commodities, their circulation, and that more developed form of their circulation called commerce, these form the historical groundwork from which it rises. The modern history of capital dates from the creation in the 16th century of a world-embracing commerce and a world-embracing market.'

The great representative of this circulation is *money*, which is the first form in which capital appears. In history, *money* presents itself to us as opposed to *land*: the merchant is opposed to the landowner; an antithesis which struck people so much at one period that they expressed it by means of a double proverb – 'No land without a lord', and 'Money has no master'. This is, in fact, another way of stating the antithesis between the Mediæval basis of property, viz., *status*, a recognized position in the great feudal hierarchy, and *contract*, the commercial basis, on which is built the position of the modern exploiter.

We must now see how capital is born, and the manner in which it works after it has been born.

It is born out of the operation expressed by the formula M – C – M, which we had to take note of in our last chapter. The M in this operation, as we stated before, implies always quantity and not quality; the second M not representing merely the money the operation was begun with, but an increased sum, otherwise the operation would be meaningless. It remains to be seen how this increase has taken place.

It cannot have happened by the mere process of exchange; because that would mean that the whole capitalistic class was living by getting the better of the whole capitalistic class, which is impossible. The increase of money in the capitalistic process must come out of the labouring or productive class.

The *modus operandi* of this capital-making must now be noted. The labouring class is necessary to the production of capital, and the labouring class in a peculiar condition: the labourer, to be fitted for the purpose of the capitalist, must be submitted to the operation of the free competition of the capitalist in the market; that is, his labour-power must be; for with the *man* himself of course the capitalist has nothing whatever to do; neither will his own position as capitalist allow him to consider himself as a man; according to the well-known proverb 'Business is business'. This position of the labourer is what is understood by the phrase of a 'free labourer': his labour-power must be bought and sold in the market on the same terms as any other commodity; there must be no interference with his selling it at the price which it will fetch, a high price when the competition among the capitalists is brisk, a low price when it is slack; and as he has no other commodity to sell except his labour-power, he is *compelled* so to sell it – to be a 'free labourer'.

It is clear that this relation between the capitalist and the labourer is a conventional and not a natural one; nature does not produce men who from the first are possessors of money which it is their business to turn into capital, nor on the other hand does she produce men who are possessors of labour-power which they are compelled to sell in the free and open market to other men. As a consequence this relation is not common to all historical periods; but has developed from many economical revolutions, which have successively extinguished prior forms of social production.

It will be seen, then, that in the fully developed commercial period the capitalist, the reason for whose existence is the turning of money into capital, and who is the owner and the organizer of the whole of production, cannot carry on his business without having ready to his hand a class who are an adjunct of the machinery necessary to his business, and who, on their side, have no other reason for existence, so long as they are duly obedient to the system under which they live, save acting as such portion of this machinery.

We have now come to the subject of surplus-value, from which is derived profit, rent, and interest. This will form the subject of our next chapter.

COMMONWEAL, VOLUME 3, NUMBER 63,
26 MARCH 1887, P. 101

CHAPTER XVIII
SCIENTIFIC SOCIALISM – THE PRODUCTION OF SURPLUS VALUE – THAT IS, OF RENT, INTEREST, AND PROFIT

The problem to be resolved is as follows. The owner of money has to buy his commodities at their value, and to sell them at their value, and nevertheless at the end of the process to realize a surplus. This is the end and aim of his existence as a capitalist, and if he does not accomplish it, he is as a capitalist a mere failure. So that his development from the mere money owner to the full-blown capitalist has to take place at once within the sphere of circulation and without it: that is, he must follow the law of the exchange of commodities, and nevertheless must act in apparent contradiction to that law. This problem cannot be solved merely by means of the money which he owns, the value of which is, so to say, petrified. As Ricardo says, 'In the form of money, capital has no profit'. As money, it can only be hoarded.

Neither can the surplus originate in the mere re-sale of the commodity, 'which does no more than transform the article from its bodily form back into its money form'. The only alternative left is the change should originate in the use-value of the article bought with the money in the first instance and on which the capitalist has to operate.

'In order to be able to extract value from the consumption of a commodity, our friend Moneybags must be so lucky as to find within the sphere of circulation, in the market, a commodity whose use-value possesses the peculiar property of being a source of value, whose actual consumption therefore is itself an embodiment of labour, and, consequently, a creation of value. The possessor of money does find on the market such a special commodity in capacity for labour, or labour-power.'

By labour-power or the capacity for labour Marx understands the whole of the mental and physical capacities in a human being which are brought into action in the production of commodities; in short, the man and all that is in him as a wealth-producing machine.

Now in order that the possessor of money should find this necessity to the accomplishment of his end and aim – viz., labour-power as a commodity of the market, various conditions are requisite.

The man who is to exercise the labour-power for the capitalists' benefit – the labourer – must be 'free', that is, his labour must be at his own disposal, and also he must have nothing else to dispose of for his livelihood but his labour-power. On the other hand, any one who has to live by getting commodities other than labour-power must own the means of production, and also the means of subsistence while the commodities are being got ready for the market, and being converted into money.

As to the value of this article necessary to the life of the capitalist, this labour-power, it is estimated like the value of every other commodity by the average time necessary for its production or reproduction; that is the average time necessary in a given state of society; and in plain language this reproduction of labour-power means the maintenance of the labourer. 'Given the individual, the production of labour-power consists in the reproduction of himself – or his maintenance.'

Labour-power is realized only in action, that is, when it has become actual *labour*, and is producing a commodity; so that, 'the value of labour-power resolves itself into the value of a definite quantity of the means of subsistence. It therefore varies with the value of those means, or with the quantity of labour requisite for their production'.

The minimum limit of the value of labour-power is therefore determined by the value of these means. If the price of labour-power falls below that minimum it is destroyed: a higgling as to its price has to be gone through between the buyer and the seller, and the price is fixed by contract, though it is not realized until the article is consumed. From what is stated above, it will be seen that this contract is made between two parties; on the one hand the workman, or machine for production, who has no means of producing, on the other the possessor of money who has all the means necessary for working the machine and has therefore become a capitalist. 'He who was before the money-owner now strides in front as a capitalist: the possessor of labour-power follows as his labourer. The one with an air of importance, smirking, intent on business; the other timid and holding back, like one who is bringing his own hide to market, and has nothing to expect but – a hiding.'

The labour process necessary to Capitalism exhibits two characteristic phenomena: first the labourer works under the control of a capitalist, and secondly the product of the labourer is the property of a capitalist, and not of the labourer, its immediate producer. This product appropriated by the capitalist is a use-value, 'as for example yarn, or boots'; says Marx with a grin, 'but although boots are in one sense the basis of all social progress and our capitalist is a decided 'progressist', the capitalist does not for his special purpose look upon them as boots, or any other use-value. He has primarily two objects in view: first he wants to produce a use-value, not, again, for the sake of its use, but in order that he may exchange it; and next, in order that his exchange may be fruitful to him, he wants to produce a commodity the value of which shall be greater than the sum of the values used in producing it – that is, the means of production and the labour-power.'

This he is able to accomplish as follows. He buys the use of the labour-power of the workman for a day, while a certain duration of labour in the day is enough to reproduce the workman's expended labour-power – that is, to keep him alive. But the human machine is in all cases capable of labouring for more hours in the day than is necessary for this result, and the contract between the capitalist and the labourer as understood in the system under which those two classes exist implies that the exercise of the day's labour-power shall exceed this duration necessary for reproduction, and it is a matter of course that the buyer of the commodity labour-power should do as all buyers of commodities do – consume it altogether for his own advantage.[1]

It is on this industry, the buying of labour-power in the market, and the consumption of all the results of its exercise beyond what is necessary for its reproduction, that the capitalist lives, just as the industry by which the workman lives is the production of commodities.

Commonweal, Volume 3, Number 68,
30 April 1887, p. 141

[1] Says Mr Boffin in Dicken's 'Mutual Friend['], when he wants to make a show of striking a somewhat hard, but reasonable bargain: 'When I buy a sheep I buy it out and out, and when I buy a secretary I expect to buy him out and out', or words to that effect; and the reasonableness of the conditions are accepted on all hands.

CHAPTER XIX
SCIENTIFIC SOCIALISM – CONSTANT AND VARIABLE CAPITAL

Marx goes on to develope (*sic*) further the process by which the capitalist exploits the labourer under the present system of wages and capital.

We now come to the two instruments which the capitalist uses in his exploitation of labour, and which are named constant and variable capital; constant capital being the raw material and instruments of production, and variable the labour power to be employed in producing on and by means of the former.

The labourer, as we have seen, adds a value to the raw material upon which he works; but by the very act of adding a new value he preserves the old; in one character he adds new value, in another he merely preserves what already existed. He affects this by working in a particular way, *eg.*, by spinning, weaving, or forging, that is, he transforms things which are already utilities into new utilities proportionately greater than they were before.

'It is thus', says Marx, 'that the cotton and spindle, the yarn and the loom, the iron and the anvil become constituent elements of a new use-value.'

That is, in order to acquire this new value, the labour must be directed to a socially useful end, to a general end, that is, to which the general labour of society is directed, and the value added is to be measured by the average amount of labour power expended; *ie.*, by the duration of the average time of labour.

Marx says: 'We have seen that the means of production transfer value to the new product so far only as during the labour-process they lose value in the shape of their old use-value. The maximum loss of value that they can suffer in the process is plainly limited by the amount of the original value with which they came into the process, or in other words by the labour-time necessary for their production. Therefore, the means of production can never add more value to the product than they themselves possess independently of the process in which they assist. However useful a given kind of raw material, or a machine, or other means of production may be, though it may cost £150, or say 500 days labour, yet it cannot under any circumstances add to the value of the product more than £150. Its value is determined not by the labour-process into which it enters as a means of production, but by that out of which it has issued as a product. In the labour process it only serves as a mere use-value, a thing with useful properties, and could not therefore transfer any value to the product unless it possessed such value previously.'

The matter is succinctly put as follows: 'The means of production on the one hand, labour-power on the other, are merely the different modes of existence which the value of the original capital assumed when from being money it was transformed into the various factors of the labour process. That part of capital which is represented by the means of production, by the raw material, auxiliary material, and the instruments of labour, does not in the process of production undergo any quantitative alteration of value. I therefore call it the constant part of capital, or more shortly *constant capital*.'

At first sight it might be thought that the wear and tear of the machinery, and the seeming disappearance of part of the auxiliary material (as *eg*., the mordaunts used in dyeing cloth or yarn, or the gums, etc., used in textile printing) contradict this statement as to the alteration of value; but on closer view it will be seen that the above wear and tear and apparent consumption enter into the new product just as much as the visible raw material does; neither are really consumed, but transformed.

In the following chapters Marx enters into an elaborate and exhaustive analysis of the rate of surplus value, *ie*., of the rate at which the creation of surplus value takes place; and he also deals with the important subject of the duration of the working-day. But as this is after all a matter of detail, in spite of its very great interest and importance we must omit it, as it would carry us beyond the scope of these articles.

Marx distinguishes between *absolute* and *relative* 'surplus value'; the *absolute* being the product of a day's labour over and above the necessary subsistence of the workman, whatever the time necessary for the production of a definite amount of product may be. The *relative* 'surplus-value' on the other hand is determined by the increased productivity of labour caused by new inventions, machinery, increased skill, either in manipulation, or the organization of labour, by which the time necessary for the production of the labourer's means of subsistence may be indefinitely shortened.

It will be seen once again by all this, that whatever instruments may be put into the hands of the labourer to bring about a result from his labour, in spite of all pretences to the contrary, the one instrument necessary to the capitalist is the labourer himself living under such conditions that he can be used as a mere instrument for the production of profit. The tools, machinery, factories, means of exchange, etc., are only intermediate aids for putting the living machine into operation.

Commonweal, Volume 3, Number 75,
18 June 1887, pp. 196–197

CHAPTER XX
MARX'S DEDUCTION OF THE HISTORICAL EVOLUTION OF MODERN INDUSTRY

Capitalism cannot be said even to begin before a number of individual owners of money employ simultaneously a number of workmen on the same terms, that is to say before the development of a concert of action towards profit among the employers, and a concert of action towards production for the profit of the employers among the employed.

'A greater number of labourers working together at the same time in one place (or if you will, in the same field of labour) in order to produce the same sort of commodity under the mastership of one capitalist, constitutes, both historically and logically the starting-point of capitalist production.'

It differs from the mediæval system, that of the gilds and their craftsmen only by the greater number of the workmen employed; but this change to a new form of organization made at once considerable difference in the rate and manner of production: there was less comparative expense of the means of production, *ie.*, buildings, tools, warehouses, etc.[1] A consequence of this concentration of

[1] The master worker of the gild-system was not really a master at all even after he began to employ journeymen, because their number was limited very closely, and they were all sure to become masters in their turn: the real 'employer of labour' was the gild and the 'master' of that period was simply a foreman of the gild; the great change consisted in the breaking down of the position of the gild as employer, and the turning of its foreman into a real master or capitalist.

workmen under one roof was the development of the function of direction in the master as independent of his qualities as a craftsmen (*sic*), and the forcing on the system of this function as a necessary part of production. The master of the gild craftsman period held his place because he was a better workman and more experienced than his fellows; he did not differ from them in kind but in degree only; if he fell sick, for instance, his place would be taken by the next best workman without any disturbance in the organization of the workshop; but the master of even the earliest period of capitalism was from the beginning unimportant as a workman (even when he worked, as he often did at first) but all-important as a director of work.

'Simple co-operation', says Marx, 'is always the prevailing form, in those branches of production in which capital acts on a large scale, and division of labour and machinery play but a subordinate part.' This sentence leads to the next development of capitalism, that of the division of labour, which brings us into the system of manufacture, as the word is generally understood; though it has a final development, that of machinery and the factory. This period of the division of labour, more or less pure, extends from the middle of the 16th to the end of the 18th centuries, when it was brought to perfection; but it must be understood that these systems overlapped one another considerably.

The division-of-labour or manufacturing system starts under two conditions.

The first is where the employer collects into one workshop workmen of various crafts, the results of whose labours are finally combined into one article, as *eg.*, a carriage-maker's in which wheel-wright, coach-builder, upholsterer, painter, etc., work each at his own occupation, and their products are combined into the one article, a finished carriage.

The other is the system in which the employer collects his workmen under one roof, and employs the whole of them as one machine in the simultaneous production of one article which has to go through various processes, these processes being apportioned to various parts of the workman-machine. This system affords a distinct example of evolution by means of survival of the fittest; sudden increase of production seems to have been called for, and the work accordingly had to be reorganized by being apportioned to different workmen in order to save time. Thus this system is the reverse of that illustrated by the carriage-making, in which a number of crafts had to be combined into the manufacture of one article; whereas in this (pin or needle-making may be taken as an illustration) a number of processes which once formed portions of one craft, now become each of them a separate craft in itself.

From this follows the complete interdependence of each human being forming a part of the workman machine, no one of whom can produce anything by himself. The unit of labour is now no longer an individual, but a group.

But all these processes, however sub-divided, and however combined, were still acts of handicraft; the same necessities which forced the simple co-operation of the first capitalistic period into division of labour, now forced the latter system to yet further development; though, indeed, other causes besides merely economic ones were at work, such as the growing aggregation of people into towns and the consequent increasing division of labour in Society itself as to the occupations of its members. This final development was the substitution of the machine and the complete factory-system for the division of labour and workshop-system. Under the new system the group of workmen, every member of which by the performance of a special piece of handicraft turns out some special part of the article made, gives place to a machine which produces the results of all these manœuvres combined together; or to an association of machines acting in a group, as the workmen acted. The workman is no longer the principal factor in the work, the tools which he handled are now worked by a mechanism connected by another mechanism with the power, whatever it may be, which puts the whole in motion. This is the true machine of modern times, as contrasted with the mere tool-machine of the earlier period, which was an aid to the workman and not a substitute for him. Furthermore, the workshop gives place to the factory which is not a mere assemblage of machines under one roof, but rather a great machine itself, of which the machines are parts; as Marx says: 'An organized system of machines to which motion is communicated by the transmitting mechanism from a central automaton is the most developed form of production by machinery. Here we have in place of the isolated machine a mechanical monster whose body fills whole factories, and whose demon power, at first veiled under the slow and measured motion of his giant limbs, at last breaks out into the fast and furious whirl of his countless working organs.'

This is the machine which has produced the great revolution in production of our epoch. The workman once a handicraftsman, having all control over the article he produced, next became a part of a human machine, and finally has become the servant and tender of a machine; and by means of all this the fully developed modern capitalist has come into existence.

COMMONWEAL, VOLUME 3, NUMBER 80,
23 JULY 1887, PP. 234–235

CHAPTER XXI
SCIENTIFIC SOCIALISM: CONCLUSION

Marx now goes on to trace the development of the capitalist in the present epoch, indicating the latest phase of the class-struggle; he points out the strife of the workman with the machine, the intensification of labour due to the constant improvement of machinery, etc. He then gives what may be called a history and analysis of the Factory Acts, the legislation to which the employing class found themselves compelled, in order to make it possible for the 'free' workman to live under his new conditions of competition; in order, in short, to keep the industrial society founded by the machine revolution from falling to pieces almost as soon as it was established.

The point of the intensification of labour is so important that it demands a word or two in passing; the gist of the matter as put forward by Marx resolves itself into this: As the organization of production progresses towards perfection, the wear and tear of the workman in a given space of labour-time is increased; and this is true of the organization of the division of labour period, only it is limited by the fact that the man himself is the machine, and no such limitation exists in the period of fully developed machinery, in which the workman is an adjunct of the machine, which latter dictates to its supplement, the workman, in its constant craving for increasing productivity, the amount of wear and tear of his body in each hour's work. This emphasizes as plainly as possible the subjection of the man to the machine.

Marx also deals with [the] theory of compensation to the workman displaced by machinery; that is, the common view, that by the labour-saving of machinery, which at first sight would seem to tend to the lessening of the number of men employed, more capital is set free for employment.

But, says Marx: 'Suppose a capitalist to employ 100 workmen at £30 a-year each in a carpet factory. The variable capital annually laid out amounts therefore to £3,000. Suppose also that he discharges 50 of his workmen, and employs the remaining 50 with machinery that costs him £1,500. To simplify matters we take no account of buildings, coal, etc. Further, suppose that the raw material annually consumed costs £3,000 both before and after the change. Is any capital set free by this metamorphosis? Before the change the total sum of £6,000 consisted half of constant, half of variable, capital. The variable capital, instead of being one-half is only one-quarter of the total capital. Instead of being set free a part of the capital is here locked up in such a way as to cease to be employed in labour-power; variable has been changed into constant capital. Other things remaining unchanged, the capital of £6,000 can in future employ no more than 50 men. With each improvement in machinery, it will employ fewer.'[1]

And again: 'The labourers when driven out of the workshop by the machinery, are thrown upon the labour-market, and there add to the number of workmen at the disposal of the capitalists. In Part VII of this book it will be seen that this effect of machinery, which as we have seen, is represented to be a compensation to the working-class, is on the contrary a most frightful scourge. For the present, I will only say this: The labourers that are thrown out of work in any branch of industry, can no doubt seek for employment in some other branch. If they find it, and thus renew the bond between them and the means of subsistence, this takes place only by the intermediary of a new and additional capital that is seeking investment; not at all by the intermediary of the capital that formerly

[1] Constant capital, raw material, and the instruments of production; variable capital, money paid in wages.

employed them, and was afterwards converted into machinery.'

The remainder of this Part V of Marx deals with various questions connected with the great industry, and the changes produced by it on Society. Part VI deals with the transformation of the value or price of labour-power into wages; with time wages, price wages, and the national difference of wages. Part VII deals with the important subject of the accumulation of capital: First, with its simple reproduction, afterwards with the conversion of surplus value itself back into capital, and with the transition of the laws of property, that characterize the production of commodities into the laws of capitalistic appropriation. This part also contains a sarcastic refutation of the now exploded stupidity (scarcely to be called a theory) of 'abstinence' as the source of capital; it also deals with the old wages-fund theory and other fallacies of bourgeois economy. This part concludes with a long and elaborate chapter on the general law of capitalistic accumulation in its various aspects. The last Part (XIII) treats of the so-called primitive accumulation, of which Marx says: 'This primitive accumulation plays in political economy about the same part as original sin in theology. Adam bit the apple, and thereupon sin fell upon the human race. Its origin is supposed to be explained when it is told as an anecdote of the past. In times long gone by there were two sorts of people, one, the diligent, intelligent, and, above all, frugal *élité*; the other, lazy rascals, spending their substance and more in riotous living. The legend of theological original sin tells us certainly how man is to be condemned to eat his bread in the sweat of his brow; but the history of economic original sin reveals to us that there are people to whom this is by no means essential. Never mind! Thus it came to pass that the former sort accumulated wealth, and the latter sort had at last nothing to sell except their own skins. And from this original sin dates the poverty of the great majority, that, despite all its labour, has up to now nothing to sell but itself, and the wealth of the few that increases constantly although they have long ceased to work.... In actual history it is notorious that conquest, enslavement, robbery, murder, briefly *force*, play the great part. In the tender annals of Political Economy, the idyllic reigns from time immemorial. Right and 'labour' were from all time the sole means of enrichment, the present year of course always excepted. As a matter of fact, the methods of primitive accumulation are anything but idyllic.'

Marx then proceeds to give an instance of one important form of 'Primitive Accumulation', the expropriation of the peasants from the land, taking affairs in England as a type of this idyllic proceeding; as also the legislation at the close of the Middle Ages against vagrants, etc., that is, those who had been expropriated; and, besides, the enactments for the forcing down of wages. He then describes the birth of the capitalist farmer of modern times, and the reaction of the agricultural revolution on the town industry; the creation of the home market for industrial capital, etc. A chapter follows on the historical tendency of capitalistic accumulation to work out its own contradiction; it becomes necessary to quote a passage here as it bears reference to the future of Society: 'The capitalist mode of appropriation, the result of the capitalist mode of production, produces capitalist private property. This is the first negation of individual private property, as founded on the labour of the proprietor. But capitalistic production begets with the inexorability of a law of Nature its own negation. It is the negation of negation. This does not re-establish private property for the producer, but gives him individual property based on the acquisitions of the capitalistic era; *ie.*, on co-operation, and the possession in common of the land and of the means of production. The transformation of scattered private property, arising from individual labour,[2] into capitalistic private property, is naturally a

[2] It is important not to misunderstand this phrase as used here. The labour of the Middle Ages, though individual from its mechanical side, was from its moral side quite definitely dominated by the principle of association: as we have seen, the 'master' of that period was but a delegate of the Gild.

procession comparably more protracted[,] violent, and difficult, than the transformation of capitalistic private property, already practically resting on socialized production, into socialized property. In the former case we had the expropriation of the mass of the people by a few usurpers; in the latter, we have the expropriation of a few usurpers by the mass of the people.'

A chapter on the modern theory of colonization concludes the book, which it must always be remembered is but the first volume (in the original German issue) of a book intended to cover three volumes, but which, nevertheless, as a criticism of capitalistic production may be treated in most respects as an independent whole.

COMMONWEAL, VOLUME 3, NUMBER 82,
6 AUGUST 1887, P. 253

CHAPTER XXII
SOCIALISM MILITANT [PART 1]

We have now arrived at the most exciting part of our subject, since it has to do with what we may fairly call the practical politics of Socialism, with matters which all who call themselves Socialists must of necessity consider, unless they chose to relegate themselves to the position of theorists pure and simple. What lies in the scope of these chapters is the giving some idea of the relative position of the attack and defence in the passing time, when armies are definitely gathering for the battle, and it is beginning to be perceived that Socialism is the one serious question of the epoch, since it covers every interest of modern life.

Let us turn our attention first of all to the defence; and we use the word advisedly, since the present proprietary and dominant class has absorbed into itself its old enemy the feudal proprietary class, and, since it has now no longer anything to attack, has taken the position once occupied by the latter. This indeed has been the position of the victorious middle-class for some time, but it is now at last waking up to the fact, and can see the enemy which is advancing to the attack. The middle-class is speedily getting to be no longer democratic even in appearance: it once wore that guise because it was confounded with the working-classes, whose position was then entirely subordinate to it. This condition of things was the high-water mark of the French Revolution, though there were from time to time indications of the coming solidarity of labour; and it lasted through the revolutionary period of 1848. Up to that time the triumphant middle-class, trampling down the last embers of the feudal opposition, saw nothing before it but a continued career of success;

although the principles on which that success was founded were not of the kind that would allow it to have a definite aim beyond the point which it had already reached.

The first distinctive movement in England betokening a separate and aggressive community of feeling in the working-class itself, was the Chartist agitation; but this, as we have pointed out in preceding chapters, was swept away by the great wave of British commercial prosperity indicated by the success of the Cobden-Bright, or as it is called on the Continent, the Manchester School. The main result of this wave of prosperity was the enormous increase in the number and power of the middle-classes, and the corresponding rise in their standard of comfort. It is often alleged that the working-classes are in a better position than they were fifty years ago, and that this is the main work of the nineteenth century; but the improvement is doubtful and the inference drawn from it is false. The fact is, that the country fifty years ago was passing through a severe commercial revolution, that of the great machine industries, which, as before stated, brought for the time unexampled misery upon the workers, and that the settling down of this crisis did to a certain extent relieve this special and temporary misery. But apart from that the condition of even the aristocracy of labour is little if any better than it was. What has really happened is just that increase in the numbers and prosperity of the *middle-classes* above spoken of. But this great and overwhelming prosperity of theirs is now seriously threatened. The increasing severity of competition in the world-market, accompanied by a ceaseless and rapid increase in the productivity of labour, acting and reacting on one another, are bringing about a fresh commercial revolution which will extinguish the small capitalist by reducing his profits to the vanishing-point; so that none but huge concerns, joint-stock or otherwise, will be able to survive, and the once small capitalist will have to become a manager, a servant of the great one. This process is already far advanced, and is creating a fresh lower middle-class entirely dependent on the commercial aristocracy. Under these conditions that very rise in the standard of middle-class comfort has become a snare to the class as a whole. The difficulty of ordinary well-to-do families in finding a 'respectable' position for their children is now a sufficiently trite subject; all occupations endurable by a 'refined' youth are overstocked; education is cheap and common, and has lost its old market-value, and even at the ancient seats of learning it has grown to be a matter of commercial competition.[1] The lower ranks of art and literature are crowded with persons drawn to these professions by the pleasantness of the pursuits in themselves, who soon find out the very low market value of the ordinary educated intellect. These, together with the commercial clerks, in whose occupation no special talent is required, form an intellectual proletariat, whose labour is 'rewarded' on about the same scale as the lower portion of manual labour, as long as they are employed, but whose position is more precarious, and far less satisfactory.

On the whole, then, in spite of the rise in the standard of comfort of the middle-classes, it must be said that they have rather gained power than well-being, and that they are now being threatened with a loss of that power, their tenure of which, now that the working-classes are beginning to learn their solidarity, depends on the latter being apathetically contented with a position at the best inferior to that of the bourgeoisie.

But the bourgeois ideal of what that position of the workers might be at the best, has never been realized, nor ever can be; nor as above-said have the working-classes any special reason for being 'contented' at the present time. The class of unskilled labourers are still, as they always must be in a system which forces them to compete with

[1] A very old friend, who has been for many years engaged in tuition at Oxford, has told me that the pressure there has enormously increased since I was an undergraduate; that for instance the kind of man whose attainments would once have ensured him a mastership at Rugby or Harrow has now to put up with a place at a third-rate grammar school, and that the competition for quite insignificant posts is most severe. – W. M.

their fellows, in the position of earning a bare subsistence wage; and this class tends to increase more and more, as the introduction of fresh machines increases the productivity of skilled labour, makes it possible to substitute unskilled in its place, and thus drives the skilled artizan from his position and compels him to accept that of the unskilled labourer.

Elaborately arranged figures, therefore, by which [it] is sought to show that the workmen in general are steadily improving their condition, where in themselves correct, which is by no means always the case, are only applicable to certain groups of workmen, and even then frequently do not prove what they are intended to: *eg.*, the average wages will be stated at such and such, but it never happens in any trade that all the workmen receive the full amount of the wages stated after all deductions are made; few workmen indeed are in constant employment, even when trade is flourishing; the estimated prices are the full wage laid down by the trade unions, but most workers [are] unprotected by a union, and in bad times even men inside the union, often work for less than the full wage; some, as in the building trades, are never employed for a large part of the year; and in all trades it would be impossible to keep up the standard of wages without occasional strikes and lock outs. It must be remembered, too, that the workman is often taxed in the form of his subscription to his trades union or benefit society, which from one point of view means that he helps his master to pay his poor-rate. Moreover it is doubtful if the unions are strong enough pecuniarily to hold out against a continued depression of trade.

However, the question of this doubtful improvement in the position of the better-off workmen is by the way. The real point is, first, that there are many indications that this improvement cannot be sustained in the face of the continuous increase in the productivity of labour, and that the position of the skilled mechanic is a precarious one; and secondly, it is clear that however the workmen's position may have improved, they are growing discontented with it, since it is becoming manifest to them that it is one of inferiority, and quite unnecessarily so. And that especially since the management of *production* is less and less undertaken by the so-called manufacturers, who are more and more becoming mere financiers, or shareholders obviously living on the privilege of taxing labour, both that of the 'hand' and of the manager.

All this has been gradually dawning on the workmen of the Continent, and especially of Germany (so much more intellectually advanced than the British workmen) since the bourgeois constitutional revolution of '48.

COMMONWEAL, VOLUME 4, NUMBER 113,
10 MARCH 1888, PP. 76–77

CHAPTER XXII
SOCIALISM MILITANT [PART 2]

The movement was begun in Germany by Lassalle[1] about 1863 as a national movement; it grew in that form after his death for some years. Meantime 'the International' had been founded, and had gradually come under the guidance of Karl Marx and Frederic Engels, who won for themselves two energetic and able coadjutors in Liebnecht and Bebel, men untiring in gaining converts to the ideas of the International from the followers of Lassalle and of Schulze-Delitsch, the bourgeois co-operationist, to which latter party indeed Bebel himself once belonged.

The scope of this article prevents us from going into details as to the fortunes of the German party; it must be enough to say that the Marx party grew rapidly, and at the congress of Gotha in 1875 the Lassalle party amalgamated with them, formally renouncing the special tenets of Lassalle, notably the nationalist aims which formed a part of them. The party went on growing, and had a large newspaper press and some representation in the Reichstag. Then in 1878 came the 'attempts' on the Emperor by Hödel and Nobeling, followed by the repressive laws against the Socialists, which destroyed their press at one swoop, and extinguished all open agitation in Germany. Nevertheless the growth of the party was not perceptibly checked by these arbitrary measures; the headquarters of its direction were transferred to Zurich, where they yet remain. At the Congress held last October at St Gallen the revolutionary character of the party was sustained, in the teeth of some attempts at opportunism which came from a section of the

[1] Lassalle was killed in a duel in 1865.

representatives in the Reichstag. The temptation to this opportunism was the desire of some of the deputies to make the party felt in the Reichstag by forming alliances with other groups, whereas at present as a Socialist *party* they are quite powerless there. It may be added that there is a possibility in Germany, as in France, of a wave of 'patriotism', founded on fear of the danger of actual invasion, checking for a time the rapidity of the advance of Socialism; though in the party itself the feeling for internationalism is overwhelming and past all question.

France has for the present rather fallen back from her position of leader in the revolutionary movement. The party itself is somewhat split up into sections, though the differences between rank and file are not serious and mainly have to do with matters of tactics. Socialist ideas have permeated the whole mass of the town workmen, who are more separated from the peasantry than in any other European country. The fact is, therefore, that the movement in France, though unorganized, still expands, especially as it is spreading to all manufacturing centres. In France Socialism is not definitely attacked by the government as it is in Germany, but only suffers, as it does in this country, from the ordinary repressive police system.

In Holland the movement, which has now reached extraordinary dimensions, was begun in the year 1882. The propaganda has been mainly the work of Domela Nieuwenhuis, formerly a popular preacher in Amsterdam, released recently from a term of imprisonment. The police in Holland have gone so far in attacking the Socialists as to stir up mob violence against them, even to the extent of breaking into their meeting places and threatening the lives of their leaders.

In Belgium the movement is progressing vigorously, in the teeth of the two opposed parties, and the feeling of the workmen generally is very revolutionary, stimulated especially by the miserable condition of the mining population, who in 1886 broke out into riots that almost attained to the proportions of a revolt. The party supports a daily paper in Brussels.

In Denmark, the movement is so far advanced as to support two daily papers of large circulation, in spite of the smallness of the population. No doubt it is much helped there by the curious constitutional situation in which the Liberal majority and the Court party are holding each other at deadlock. This Danish movement has even penetrated to Sweden, and a Socialist party is growing up there.

In Russia, bureaucratic absolutism is blended with survivals of the mere barbaric absolutism, and as a consequence of the monstrous government which results from this, the movement seems now to be aiming at bringing about a constitutional revolution as a forerunner of the Social Revolution; and on the other hand this condition of things has so worked on the aspirations of the intelligent part of the people, that the movement there has been surrounded by a halo of personal heroism which has attracted universal admiration and respect even from its enemies.

In Austria, the faith of the masses generally is Socialism, but owing partly to the composite character of the Empire, which embraces such varied and rival races, and partly to the severity of the police measures of its Absolutist Government, there is no definite organization.

In Italy, the movement is progressing, although hampered by the tail of the democratic, and especially the Mazzinian, ideas, which can see nothing beyond the abolition of priest and king.

In Spain, the followers of Bakounine's Anarchism have had much influence, and the movement consequently is mostly Anarchist in colouring. The party supports several small weekly papers.

In America, the movement till recently has been entirely in the hands of the German immigrants; but of late years there has been a remarkable development of the class-struggle there. The result of numerous and most violent disputes between the capitalists and wage-earners has been the formation of an indigenous labour party, vague in aim and somewhat chaotic in action, but tending steadily towards a complete recognition of the solidarity of labour. The publication of Henry George's work, 'Progress and Poverty', which created such [a] sensation in this country, unsatisfactory as it was, has no doubt had its effect upon this movement, though its author in his quest for power and position has now practically recanted whatever opinions were of any value in it. One incident in the American movement is the formation of the gigantic trades' union called the Knights of Labour, which has more definite tendencies towards Socialism than those in this country; though Powderly's coquetting with the Catholic hierarchy has led to a split in the body, which leads to a hope that true Socialism may soon be generally accepted amongst the American working-classes. This will certainly be encouraged by the last act of the American capitalists, who in their dastardly fear of the possible combination of their wage-slaves, have murdered the Anarchist leaders at Chicago under the pretence of their being concerned in the throwing of a bomb-shell in the heat of a desperate labour-conflict in that city.

To get back again to this country, the movement is spreading much beyond the limits of the definite Socialist organizations, which are for the most part headquarters for knots of lecturers and speakers, and the publication of journals and pamphlets. In fact, it may be said that the strength of the movement here is on the intellectual side, and that organization for action of any kind is very defective. Nevertheless, Socialist opinion is making itself felt widely as well as deeply; this is very marked in the effect it is having on the Radicals, since it is detaching a constantly increasing number of them from their old position as the left wing of the Liberals, which whom and under whose orders they have hitherto acted since the time when Gladstone became the leader of the party. The Irish movement being at bottom a rebellion, and illustrating very strongly one side of the economical disabilities of the working-classes, has done much to widen the breach between the Democratic Radicals and the Liberal Radicals, and has made them much more ready to listen to Socialist doctrines. The Trades' Unions also, which have acted as a safety valve for the discontent born of the economical situation, have been much shaken by the attention which so many of their members have given to Socialism, and show signs of a growing inclination to change their position from being a mere appendage to capitalism to being organizations for a definite attack upon it. The dead weight of their leaders, who look upon this feeling with the utmost disfavour, and have done their best to smother it, hampers the possible development of the Trades' Unions in this direction; but it ever breaks through these and other obvious obstacles. They will become most formidable allies of Socialism in this country. It must be remembered in estimating the force of the movement in the British Islands, that all this is taking place in a country which, whatever its economical position may be, is politically, ethically, and intellectually generally the headquarters of reaction.

COMMONWEAL, VOLUME 4, NUMBER 114,
17 MARCH 1888, P. 82

CHAPTER XXIII
SOCIALISM TRIUMPHANT [PART 1]

It is possible to succeed in a manner in picturing to ourselves the life of past times: that is, our imaginations will show us a picture of them which may include such accurate information as we may have of them. But though the picture may be vivid and the information just, yet it will not be a picture of what really took place; it will be made up of the present which we experience, and the past which our imagination, drawing from our experience, conceives of, – in short, it will be *our* picture of the past.[1] If this be the case with the past, of which we have some concrete data, still more strongly may it be said of the future, of which we have none – nothing but mere abstract deductions from historic evolution, the logical sequence of which may be interfered with at any point by elements whose force we have not duly appreciated; and these are abstractions also which are but the skeleton of the full life which will go on in those times to come.

Therefore, though we have no doubt of the transformation of modern civilization into Socialism, yet we cannot

[1] The mediæval painters naïvely accept this position – *eg.*, in representing the life of a saint of the second century, they dress the characters in a costume but little altered from that of their own period; and it is worth noting that they gave up the attempt at archeology (*sic*) altogether with the more familiar characters – a carpenter or blacksmith will be just the craftsman that they had before their eyes every day; whereas the emperors, giants, and so forth, they do try to clothe in imaginative raiment. A further illustration may be given in the art of music: works such as Weber's der Freischutz or Wagner's Meister-singers, which seem to embody the spirit of past ages, nevertheless are in themselves thoroughly modern.

foretell definitely what form the social life of the future will take, any more than a man living at the beginning of the commercial period – say Sir Thomas More or Lord Bacon – could foresee the development of that period in the capitalism of to-day.

Nevertheless, though we cannot realize positively the life of the future, when the principle of real society will be universally admitted, and applied in practice as an everyday matter, yet the negative side of the question we can all see, and most of us cannot help trying to fill up the void made by the necessary termination of the merely militant period of Socialism. The present society will be gone, with all its paraphernalia of checks and safeguards: that we know for certain. No less surely we know what the foundation of the new society will be. What will the new society build on that foundation of freedom and co-operation? – that is the problem on which we can do no more than speculate.

No doubt some transition, the nature of which will be determined by circumstances, will take place between the present state of things, in which the political unit is a nation, and the future, in which a system of federalized communities will take the place of rival nationalities; but as this chapter has to do with the ultimate realization of the new society rather than with the transitional period, we need not speculate on this point.

We ask our readers to imagine the new society in its political aspect as an organized body of communities, each carrying on its own affairs, but united by a delegated federal body, whose function would be the guardianship of the acknowledged principles of society; it being understood that these two bodies, the township or community and the Federal Power, would be the two extremities between which there would be other expressions of the Federal principle, – as in districts that were linked together by natural circumstances, such as language, climate, or the divisions of physical geography.

It is clear that in such a society what laws were needed for the protection of persons and the regulation of inter-communal disputes, since they could be but the expression of the very root principles of society, would have to be universal, and the central regulating body would be charged with their guardianship, and at a last resort to carrying them out by force. Obviously no community could be allowed to revert to the exploitation of labour of any kind under whatever pretext, or to such forms of reaction as vindictive criminal laws. Such measures if allowed, even as local and spasmodic incidents, would undermine the very foundations of communistic society. This unity in Federation in short, appears to be the only method for reducing complexity in political and administrative matters to a minimum; and of ensuring to the individual, as a unit of society, the utmost possible freedom for the satisfaction and development of his capacities.

As to the methods of labour necessary to the existence and welfare of society, it would have to be co-operative in the widest sense. It would of course be subordinate to the *real* welfare of society; *ie.*, the production of wares would not be looked upon as the end of society (as the production of *profit-bearing* wares now is), but it would be regarded as the means for the ease and happiness of life, which therefore would never be sacrificed to any false ideas of necessity, or to any merely conventional views of comfort or luxury. For instance, in any society it is desirable that cotton cloth should be produced at the least expenditure of labour, but in a communistic society it would be impossible to condemn a part of the population to live under miserable conditions, conditions in any degree worse than that of others, as in a black country, in order to reduce the expenditure of labour for the community, which would have to pay the price for giving the weavers and spinners, etc., as good a life as anyone else, whatever that price might be.

Again, as to the conventional standard of comfort: we may here quote a good definition of a luxury, as given by a friend, as a piece of goods that the consumer would not have if he had in his own person to pay the full value of the work – *ie.*, if he had to make it himself, or to sacrifice an amount of his own labour equivalent to the making of it. As, *eg*., a lady of the present day would hardly consent to make a Mechlin lace veil for herself, or to pay for the due and proper livelihood of those who do make it; in order that she may have it, numbers of women and girls at Ypres and the neighbourhood must work at starvation wages.

To make the matter of production under Communism clearer let us consider the various kinds of work which the welfare of Communal Society would demand.

First, there would be a certain amount of necessary work to be done which would be usually repellant to ordinary persons; some of this, probably the greater part of it, would be performed by machinery; and it must be remembered that machinery would be improved and perfected without hesitation when the restrictions laid on production by the exigencies of profit-making were removed. But probably a portion of this work at once necessary and repellant could not be done by machinery. For this portion volunteers would have to be relied upon; nor would there be any difficulty in obtaining them, considering that the habit of looking upon necessary labour from the point of view of social duty would be universal, and that now, as then, idiosyncrasies would exist which would remove objections to work usually disliked.

Again, the greater part of this work, though not agreeable, would not be exacting on mental capacity, and would entail the minimum of responsibility on those engaged in it. We mention this as compensatory of the disagreeable nature of the work in itself.

As examples of this necessary and usually repellant work, we may give scavengering, sewer-cleaning, coal-hewing, midwifery, and mechanical clerk's work.

It must be remembered again that under our present system a great deal of this kind of work is artificially fostered for the sake of making business for interest-bearing capital, and that the competition for employment amongst the proletariat makes it possible to be so done; whereas in a Communal Society such work would be dispensed with as much as possible. Disagreeable work which a Communal Society found itself saddled with as a survival of past times, and which it found out not to be necessary, it would get rid of altogether.

Secondly, work in itself more or less disagreeable, and not absolutely necessary, but desirable if the sacrifice to be paid for it were not too great. This might be done if it could be made easy by machinery, but not otherwise; it would not be worth while to call for volunteers for the purpose of doing it, since the citizens would then have to make the sacrifice in their own persons. Before we leave the subject of work not generally pleasant, but which is either necessary or desirable, we may again call attention to the existence of idiosyncrasies which would make many people willing to undertake it, and still more to the variety of tastes which are so common that they could not be classed as idiosyncrasies, and which would help us out of many difficulties in this respect. There are, for instance, rough occupations involving a certain amount of hardship, which would be acceptable to many persons of overflowing health and strength, on account of the adventure and change which goes with them, and the opportunities which they afford for showing courage and adroitness and readiness; in a word, for the pleasurable exercise of special energies, such as sea-fishing, exploration of new countries, etc. Again, many people have so much love for country life and dealing with animals, that even hard work of this kind would not seem irksome to them. In short, we might go into great lengths on this subject, and every step we took on the road would show that the stimulus to exertion in production is much more various and much more complex than is usually thought in a period like our own, when everything is supposed to be measured by mere cash-payment.

Thirdly, we come to a kind of work which we may well hope will take a much higher position in communal life than it does at present; we mean work that has in it more or less of art; and we should here say that the very foundation of everything that can be called art is the pleasure of creation, which is, or should be felt in every handicraft. That even as things are it is very commonly felt, is proved by the craving that persons have for some occupation for their hands when they are debarred from their usual occupation, as very notably persons in prison. As to the matter of art as an occupation, we may divide it into *incidental* and *substantive* art. Incidental art is that which is subservient to some utilitarian function; as the designed form or added ornament in a knife or a cup, which is subservient to the cutting or drinking use of those things. What is commonly called decorative art comes under this heading. Substantive art is that which produces matters of beauty and incident for their own sakes, such as pictures or music, which have no utilitarian purpose. As to incidental art Commercial Society has nearly destroyed it by divorcing its exercise and the reward for it from the products which it should beautify; it has divided the producers of an ornamental article of use into the maker of the utilitarian article, the maker of the ornament for it, and the designer of the ornament, the two former being mere machines, and the latter being the producer of a marketable ware to be forced on the public in the same way that other wares are forced on them by commerce. In a Communal Society this division of labour will be recognized as impossible in a piece of goods of which the art of design formed an integral part, and that art itself will only be exercised in answer to an undoubted and imperative demand of the public; there will be no occasion to force a demand for it.

As to the substantive art that must always be on the surface the product of individual labour and skill, although at bottom it is a social product as much as or even more than any other production; since the capacity of the most original artist or author is really the result of tradition, and his work is the expression of a long social development of tendencies concentrated in the special individual.

A question may occur to some as to the probable future of the races at present outside civilization. To us it seems that the best fate that can befall them is that they should develope (*sic*) themselves from their present condition, uninterfered with by the incongruities of civilization. Those of them will be the happiest who can hold civilization aloof until civilization itself melts into Socialism, when their own natural development will gradually lead them into absorption in the great ocean of universal social life.

Commonweal, Volume 4, Number 121,
5 May 1888, pp. 140–141

CHAPTER XXIII
SOCIALISM TRIUMPHANT [PART 2]

It remains to say something on the religious and ethical basis of which the life of Communal Society may be called an expression, although from another aspect the religion may be said to be an expression of that life; the two together forming an harmonious whole.

The word religion has been, and is still in most minds, connected with supernatural beliefs, and consequently the use of the word has been attacked as unjustifiable where this element is absent. But, as we shall proceed to show in a few words, this is rather accessory to it than essential.

In the first instance religion had for its object the continuance and glory of the kinship – Society; whether as clan, tribe, or people, ancestor worship forming the leading feature in its early phases. That in such an epoch religion should have been connected with what we now call superstition was inevitable, since at that time no distinction was drawn between the human and any other form of existence, whether in animal life or in inanimate matters, all being alike considered conscious and intelligent.

Consequently, with the development of material civilization from the domination of things by persons to that of persons by things, and the consequent falling asunder of Society into two classes, a possessing and dominating class, and a non-possessing and dominated one, arose a condition of Society which gave leisure to the possessing or slave-holding class, the result of which was a possibility of observation and reflection amongst the upper class. As a consequence of this a process of reflection arose among this class which distinguished man as a conscious being from the rest of nature. From this again arose a dual conception of things: on the one hand was man, which was familiar and known, on the other nature, which was mysterious and relatively unknown. In nature itself grew a further distinction between its visible objects now regarded as unconscious things, and a supposed motive power which acted on them from behind, which was conceived of as manlike in character, but above mankind in knowledge and power, and no longer a part of the things themselves, but without them, and moving and controlling them.

Another set of dual conceptions arose along with this, firstly the distinction between the individual and Society, and secondly within the individual the distinction between the soul and the body. Religion now became definitely supernatural, and at last superstitious, as far as the cultured class was concerned, since they had gradually lost their old habit of belief in it.

At this stage there arose a conflict not only of belief but also of ethical conceptions; the ceremonies and customs based on the earlier ideas, on a nature composed of beings who were all conscious, became meaningless and in many cases repulsive to the advanced minds of the epoch; hence arose a system of esoteric explanation and the Mysteries.[1] An importance began to be attached to the idea of a future life for the individual soul, which had nothing in common with the old idea of a scarcely broken existence, founded not on any positive doctrine, but on the impossibility of an existing being conceiving of its non-existence; an idea naively expressed, for instance, in the burial ceremonies of all early races, in which food, horses, arms, etc., are buried with the dead man as a provision for his journey to the unknown country. These ideas, and the doctrines and

[1] The mysteries were nothing but a practice of the ancient rude ceremonies now treated as revelations to certain privileged persons of this hidden meaning which could not be understood by the vulgar: that is, people began to assume that the ancient rude and sometimes coarse ceremonies (belief in which directly as explanations of natural events now appeared to them incredible) wrapped up mystical meanings in an allegorical manner; *eg*., a simple sun-myth would be turned into an allegory of the soul and the divinity, – their relative dealings with a present and future life.

ceremonies embodying them, grow in number and body as the stream of history broadens down, till they finally issue in the universal or ethical religions (as opposed to the tribal or nature-religions) of which Buddhism and Christianity are the great historical examples, and in which the original ceremonies and their meaning have become fused with each other, and with the new ethics of these religions, and are supposed to express these ethics more or less symbolically. An illustration of what has here been said may be found in the fusion of the ancient notions of sacrifices in the doctrine of the Atonement.[2]

We have said that with the rise of civilization tribal society became divided into classes, owing to the growth of the individual ownership of property as opposed to its corporate ownership. The old relations of persons to society were thus destroyed, and with them much of the meaning of the old ethical ideas. In the tribal society, the responsibility of the individual to the limited society of which he formed a part was strongly felt, while he recognized no duty outside his tribe. In the new conception of morality which now arose he had, it is true, duties to all men as a man, irrespective of the community to which he belonged, but they were vague and could be evaded or explained away with little disturbance of the conscience; because the central point round which morality revolved was a spiritual deity who was the source of morality and directly revealed himself to the individual conscience. These two, the tribal ethics, the responsibility to a community however limited, and the universal or introspective ethics, or responsibility to a divinity to whom humanity was but a means of realizing himself, and to whom therefore the duties of man to man were of secondary importance[3] – are the two ethical poles. But

[2] See article 'Sacrifice' in the 'Encyclopædia Britannica' (9th Edition), by Professor Robertson Smith.

[3] 'Morality, thou dreadful bane,
What tens of thousands thou hast slain!'

(Protestant hymn.)

though the tendency was in this direction from the beginnings of civilization, it took historically many centuries to realize itself, and only reached its final development in Christianity; and has now under the influence of competitive economics taken the final form of the devil-take-the-hindmost doctrine and practice of modern society.

As regards the future form of the moral consciousness, we may safely predict that it will be in a sense a return on a higher level to the ethics of the older society, with the difference that the limitation of scope to the kinship society in its narrower sense, which was one of the elements of the dissolution of ancient society, will disappear, and the identification of individual with social interests will be so complete that any divorce between the two will be inconceivable to the average man.

We may say in conclusion that this new ethic is no longer a mere theoretical speculation, but that many thousands of lives are already under its inspiration. Its first great popular manifestation was given in the heroic devotion of the working-classes of Paris in the Commune of 1871 to the idea of true and universal freedom, which was carried on by the no less complete devotion of the little band of Russian revolutionists who made so little account of their individual lives in their engrossing passion for the general life of humanity.

Everywhere the same feeling is spreading, and even in England, the chosen home of bourgeois bureaucracy, which, with the instinctive cunning of a business country, gives every opportunity to well-to-do persons for forgetting the general welfare in that of the individual, it is getting more irrepressible every day. The wave of ethical feeling is no doubt the result of the development of the class struggle now rapidly approaching to the crisis which will abolish all classes: in fact, the mere hope, ever growing nearer to realisation, of an economical change which will make life easy and refined for all, is what has made this ethical idea possible, as the habits which the new economical system will engender will make any other form of ethics inconceivable: since once for all change in the economical system of society must always be accompanied by fresh ethical ideas.

We may be asked, since we have been putting forward the doctrine of evolution throughout these chapters, what Socialism in its turn will evolve. We can only answer that Socialism denies the finality of human progress, and that any system of which we can now conceive of as Socialism must necessarily give way to a new development of society. But that development is necessarily hidden from us by the unfinished struggle in which we live, in which for *us* the supreme goal is the Socialism we have been putting forward. Nor do we repine at this limitation of our insight; that goal is sublime and beautiful enough which promises to us the elevation of the whole of the people to a level of intelligent happiness and pleasurable energy, which at present is reached, if at all, only by a chosen few at the expense of the misery and degradation of the greater part of mankind; and even by those few, is held on such a precarious tenure that it is to them little better than a pleasant dream disturbed by fantastic fears which have their birth from the terribly real sufferings of the ordinary life of the masses on whom they live.

Commonweal, Volume 4, Number 123,
19 May 1888, pp. 154–155

Appendix

WILLIAM MORRIS'S JOURNALISTIC CONTRIBUTIONS TO *JUSTICE* AND *COMMONWEAL*: 1884–1890

Justice [1884].

1. *An Old Fable Retold,* Volume 1, Number 1, 19 January, p. 2.
   Signed 'William Morris'.
2. *The Principles Of 'Justice',* Volume 1, Number 1, 19 January, p. 4.
   Signed 'William Morris' jointly with 'H. M. Hyndman' and 'J. Taylor'.
3. *Cotton And Clay,* Volume 1, Number 2, 26 January, p. 2.
   Signed 'M'.
4. *Order And Anarchy,* Volume 1, Number 4, 9 February, p. 2.
   Signed 'William Morris'.
5. *The Bondholders Battue,* Volume 1, Number 4, 9 February, p. 4.
   Signed 'William Morris' jointly with 'H. M. Hyndman'.
6. *The Way Out: An Appeal To Genuine Radicals,* Volume 1, Number 7, 1 March, p. 4.
   Signed 'William Morris'.
7. *Art Or No Art? Who Shall Settle It?,* Volume 1, Number 9, 15 March, p. 2.
   Signed 'William Morris'.

8. *Chants For Socialists – No. 1: 'The Day Is Coming'*, Volume 1, Number 11, 29 March, p. 5.
Signed 'William Morris'.

9. *Henry George*, Volume 1, Number 12, 5 April, p. 4.
Signed 'William Morris'.

10. *Chants For Socialists – No. 2: 'The Voice Of Toil'*, Volume 1, Number 12, 5 April, p. 5.
Signed 'William Morris'.

11. *Why Not?*, Volume 1, Number 13, 12 April, p. 2.
Signed 'William Morris'.

12. *Chants For Socialists – No. 3: 'All For The Cause'*, Volume 1, Number 14, 19 April, p. 5.
Signed 'William Morris'.

13. *The Dull Level Of Life*, Volume 1, Number 15, 26 April, p. 4.
Signed 'William Morris'.

14. *A Factory As It Might Be*, Volume 1, Number 18, 17 May, p. 2.
Signed 'William Morris'.

15. *The Propaganda Fund*, Volume 1, Number 18, 17 May, p. 5.
Signed 'William Morris'.

16. *Individualism At The Royal Academy*, Volume 1, Number 19, 24 May, p. 4.
Signed 'William Morris'.

17. *Work In A Factory As It Might Be – II*, Volume 1, Number 20, 31 May, p. 2.
Signed 'William Morris'.

18. *Chants For Socialists – No. 4: 'No Master'*, Volume 1, Number 21, 7 June, p. 5.
Signed 'William Morris'.

19. *Work In A Factory As It Might Be – III*, Volume 1, Number 24, 28 June, p. 2.
Signed 'William Morris'.

20. *The Propaganda Fund,* Volume 1, Number 26, 5 July, p. 4.
    Signed 'William Morris. Treasurer of the Democratic Federation'.
21. *To Genuine Radicals,* Volume 1, Number 25, 12 July, pp. 4–5.
    Signed 'William Morris'.
22. *The Housing Of The Poor,* Volume 1, Number 27, 19 July, pp. 4–5.
    Signed 'William Morris'.
23. *Propaganda Fund,* Volume 1, Number 28, 26 July, p. 5.
    Signed 'William Morris'.
24. *Propaganda Fund,* Volume 1, Number 29, 2 August, p. 5.
    Signed 'William Morris'.
25. *Socialism In England In 1884*, Volume 1, Number 30, 9 August, p. 4.
    Signed 'William Morris'.
26. *Uncrowned Kings*, Volume 1, Number 34, 6 September, p. 4.
    Signed 'William Morris'.
27. *Social Democratic Federation To The Trades Unions,* Volume 1, Number 34, 6 September, p. 5.
    Signed 'William Morris' with others.
28. *The Hammersmith Costermongers,* Volume 1, Number 36, 20 September, p. 3.
    Signed 'William Morris'.
29. *An Appeal To The Just,* Volume 1, Number 39, 11 October, p. 4.
    Signed 'William Morris'.
30. *Literary Courtesy: To The Editor Of 'Justice',* Volume 1, Number 39, 11 October, p. 5.
    Signed 'I am, Yours fraternally, William Morris'.

31. *The Lord Mayor's Show,* Volume 1, Number 44, 15 November, p. 2.
Signed 'William Morris'.

32. *The Hackney Election,* Volume 1, Number 46, 29 November, p. 4.
Signed 'William Morris'.

33. *Philanthropists,* Volume 1, Number 49, 20 December, p. 2.
Signed 'William Morris'.

34. *Notices, Social-Democratic Federation,* Volume 1, Number 51, 3 January [1885], p. 5.
Signed 'William Morris' along with nine others.

Commonweal [1885].

35. *Introductory,* Volume 1, Number 1, February, p. 1.
Signed 'William Morris'.

36. *The Manifesto Of The Socialist League,* Volume 1, Number 1, February, p. 1.
Signed 'William Morris' with the rest of the Provisional Council of the Socialist League.

37. *The March Of The Workers,* Volume 1, Number 1, February, p. 4.
Signed 'William Morris'.

38. *[Untitled Appeal For Subscriptions],* Volume 1, Number 2, March, p. 12.
Signed 'William Morris'.

39. *The Message Of The March Wind,* Volume 1, Number 2, March, p. 12.
Signed 'William Morris'.

40. *The Worker's Share Of Art,* Volume 1, Number 3, April, pp. 18–19.
Signed 'William Morris'.

41. *The Pilgrims Of Hope – II,* Volume 1, Number 3, April, p. 20.
Signed 'William Morris'.

42. *[Untitled Review Of The First Edition Of The 'Anarchist'],* Volume 1, Number 3, April, p. 22.
Signed 'W. M.'.

43. *[Untitled Review Of 'Socialist Rhymes' By J. L. Joynes],* Volume 1, Number 3, April, p. 23.
Signed 'W. M.'.

44. *The Pilgrims Of Hope – III,* Volume 1, Number 4, May, p. 32.
Signed 'W. M.'.

45. *[Untitled Contribution To 'Sign Of The Times'],* Volume 1, Number 4, May, p. 35.
Signed 'W. M.'.

46. *[Untitled Review of 'Social Politics' By Charles Rowley],* Volume 1, Number 4, May, p. 35.
Signed 'W. M.'.

47. *[Untitled Report On An Anti-War Meeting],* Volume 1, Number 4, May, p. 36.
Signed 'W. M.'.

48. *Unattractive Labour,* Volume 1, Number 4, May, p. 37.
Signed 'William Morris'.

49. *The Pilgrims Of Hope – IV,* Volume 1, Number 5, June, pp. 44–45.
Signed 'William Morris'.

50. *Attractive Labour,* Volume 1, Number 5, June, pp. 49–50.
Signed 'William Morris'.

51. *[Untitled Paragraphs],* Volume 1, Number 5, June, p. 52.
Signed 'W. M.'.

52. *Notes On The Political Crisis,* Volume 1, Number 6, July, pp. 53–54.
Signed 'William Morris'.

53. *Socialists At Play,* Volume 1, Number 6, July, p. 56.
Signed 'William Morris'.

54. *Socialism And Politics,* Volume 1, Number 6, July, p. 61.
Signed 'William Morris'.

55. *First General Meeting Of The Socialist League,* Volume 1, Number 7, August, p. 65.
Signed 'William Morris' and 'Edward B. Aveling'.

56. *Report Of The Editors Of 'Commonweal',* Volume 1, Number 7, August, p. 66.
Signed 'William Morris (Editor), Edward Aveling (Sub-Editor)'.

57. *The Pilgrims Of Hope – V,* Volume 1, Number 7, August, pp. 68–69.
Signed 'William Morris'.

58. *Signs Of The Times,* Volume 1, Number 7, August, p. 72.
Signed 'W. M.'.

59. *Mr. Chamberlain At Hull,* Volume 1, Number 8, September, p. 77.
Signed 'William Morris'.

60. *[Meeting On The Recent Exposures],* Volume 1, Number 8, September, p. 78.
An article which includes a quote attributed to 'William Morris'.

61. *The Pilgrims Of Hope – VI,* Volume 1, Number 8, September, pp. 80–81.
Signed 'William Morris'.

62. *Appeal!,* Volume 1, Number 8, September, p. 84.
Signed 'William Morris' with 'E. Belfort Bax' and 'C. Theodor'.

63. *A New Party,* Volume 1, Number 8, September, p. 85.
Signed 'William Morris'.

64. *Answers To Previous Inquiries,* Volume 1, Number 8, October, p. 87.
Signed 'W. M.'.

65. *Ireland And Italy: A Warning,* Volume 1, Number 9, October, pp. 86–87.
Signed 'William Morris'.

66. *Signs Of The Times,* Volume 1, Number 9, October, p. 91.
Signed 'W. M.'.

67. *Inquiry Column. Answers,* Volume 1, Number 9, October, p. 92.
Signed 'W. M.'.

68. *Moves In The Game Political,* Volume 1, Number 10, November, p. 93.
Signed 'William Morris'.

69. *The Pilgrims Of Hope – VII,* Volume 1, Number 10, November, pp. 96–97.
Signed 'William Morris'.

70. *Free Speech And The Police,* Volume 1, Number 10, November, pp. 99–100.
Signed 'W. M.'.

71. *[Untitled Paragraphs],* Volume 1, Number 10, November, p. 100.
Signed 'W. M.'.

72. *On The Eve Of The Elections,* Volume 1, Number 11, December, p. 101.
Signed 'William Morris'.

73. *To Our Readers,* Volume 1, Number 11, December, p. 104.
Signed 'William Morris' and 'Edward Aveling'.

Commonweal [1886].

74. *The Morrow Of The Elections,* Volume 2, Number 12, January, p. 1.
Signed 'William Morris'.

75. *Notes,* Volume 2, Number 12, January, p. 4.
Signed 'W. M.'.

76. *The Pilgrims Of Hope – VIII,* Volume 2, Number 12, January, p. 4.
Signed 'William Morris'.

77. *'The Husks That The Swine Do Eat',* Volume 2, Number 12, January, p. 7.
Signed 'William Morris'.

78. *Notes,* Volume 2, Number 13, February, p. 12.
Signed 'W. M.'.

79. *The Commonweal,* Volume 2, Number 12, January, p. 8.
Signed 'William Morris' with 'E. Belfort Bax', 'H. H. Sparling' and 'Carl Theodor'.

80. *A Letter From The Pacific Coast,* Volume 2, Number 13, February, p. 13.
Signed 'William Morris'.

81. *The Commonweal,* Volume 2, Number 13, February, p. 16.
Signed 'William Morris' with 'E. Belfort Bax', 'H. H. Sparling' and 'Carl Theodor'.

82. *Our Policy,* Volume 2, Number 14, March, pp. 17–18.
Signed 'William Morris'.

83. *The Pilgrims Of Hope – IX,* Volume 2, Number 14, March, pp. 21-22.
Signed 'William Morris'.

84. *Notes On Matters Parliamentary,* Volume 2, Number 15, April, p. 28.
Signed 'William Morris'.

85. *The Pilgrims Of Hope – X,* Volume 2, Number 15, April, pp. 28-29.
Signed 'William Morris'.

86. *Socialism In The Provinces,* Volume 2, Number 14, April, p. 30.
Signed 'William Morris'.

87. *Editorial,* Volume 2, Number 16, 1 May, p. 33.
Signed 'William Morris' and 'E. Belfort Bax'.

88. *Independent Ireland,* Volume 2, Number 16, 1 May, p. 36.
Signed 'William Morris'.

89. *[Untitled Paragraph On The Socialist Trial],* Volume 2, Number 16, 1 May, p. 36.
Signed 'W. M.'.

90. *[Untitled Paragraph On The Pit-Brow Women],* Volume 2, Number 16, 1 May, p. 37.
Signed 'W. M.'.

91. *Concerning The 'Commonweal',* Volume 2, Number 16, 1 May, p. 38.
Signed 'W. M.'.

92. *[Untitled Paragraph On Mr Chamberlain And Ireland],* Volume 2, Number 16, 1 May, p. 38.
Signed 'W. M.'.

93. *Notes On Passing Events,* Volume 2, Number 17, 8 May, p. 41.
Signed 'William Morris'.

94. *Socialism In Dublin And Yorkshire,* Volume 2, Number 17, 8 May, p. 43.
Signed 'William Morris'.

95. *The Pilgrims Of Hope – XI,* Volume 2, Number 17, 8 May, p. 45.
Signed 'William Morris'.

96. *[Untitled Paragraph On Railway Monopoly],* Volume 2, Number 17, 8 May, p. 45.
Signed 'W. M.'.

97. *Notes On Passing Events,* Volume 2, Number 18, 15 May, pp. 49–50.
Signed 'William Morris'.

98. *Foot-note To 'The Commercial Hearth',* Volume 2, Number 18, 15 May, p. 50.
Signed 'W. M.'.

99. *Socialism From The Root Up: Chapter I,* Volume 2, Number 18, 15 May, p. 53.
Signed 'E. Belfort Bax and William Morris'.

100. *Notes On Passing Events,* Volume 2, Number 19, 22 May, p. 57.
Signed 'William Morris'.

101. *Socialism From The Root Up: Chapter II,* Volume 2, Number 19, 22 May, p. 61.
Signed 'E. Belfort Bax and William Morris'.

102. *Our Representatives,* Volume 2, Number 20, 29 May, p. 68.
Signed 'William Morris'.

103. *[Various Untitled Notes],* Volume 2, Number 20, 29 May, p. 68.
Signed 'W. M.'.

104. *Socialism From The Root Up: Chapter III,* Volume 2, Number 20, 29 May, p. 69.
Signed 'E. Belfort Bax and William Morris'.

105. *Notes And Queries: Practical Socialism,* Volume 2, Number 20, 29 May, p. 71.
Signed 'W. M.'.

106. *Branch Reports. Birmingham,* Volume 2, Number 20, 29 May, p. 72.
Signed 'W. M.'.

107. *Notes On Passing Events,* Volume 2, Number 21, 5 June, p. 73.
Signed 'William Morris'.

108. *The Pilgrims Of Hope – XII,* Volume 2, Number 21, 5 June, p. 75.
Signed 'William Morris'.

109. *Socialism From The Root Up: Chapter IV,* Volume 2, Number 21, 5 June, p. 77.
Signed 'E. Belfort Bax and William Morris'.

110. *Instructive Items,* Volume 2, Number 21, 5 June, p. 79.
Signed 'W. M.'.

111. *Notes On Passing Events,* Volume 2, Number 22, 12 June, p. 81.
Signed 'William Morris'.

112. *Socialism From the Root Up: Chapter V,* Volume 2, Number 22, 12 June, pp. 82-83.
Signed 'E. Belfort Bax and William Morris'.

113. *[Untitled Paragraph],* Volume 2, Number 22, 12 June, p. 83.
Signed 'W. M.'.

114. *Correspondence,* Volume 2, Number 22, 12 June, p. 86.
Signed 'W. M.'.

115. *Free Speech At Stratford,* Volume 2, Number 22, 12 June, p. 87.
Signed 'William Morris'.

116. *Notes On Passing Events,* Volume 2, Number 23, 19 June, p. 89.
Signed 'William Morris'.

117. *Whigs, Democrats, And Socialists,* Volume 2, Number 24, 26 June, pp. 97-98.
Signed 'William Morris'.

118. *Home Rule Or Humbug,* Volume 2, Number 24, 26 June, pp. 100-101.
Signed 'William Morris'.

119. *A Letter From Scotland,* Volume 2, Number 25, 3 July, pp. 105–106.
Signed 'William Morris'.

120. *Whigs, Democrats, And Socialists (Cont),* Volume 2, Number 25, 3 July, pp. 106–107.
Signed 'William Morris'.

121. *The Pilgrims Of Hope – XIII,* Volume 2, Number 25, 3 July, p. 107.
Signed 'William Morris'.

122. *Socialism From The Root Up: Chapter VI,* Volume 2, Number 25, 3 July, pp. 108–109.
Signed 'E. Belfort Bax and William Morris'.

123. *Notes On The Elections,* Volume 2, Number 26, 10 July, p. 113.
Signed 'William Morris'.

124. *The Sequel Of The Scotch Letter,* Volume 2, Number 26, 10 July, p. 114.
Signed 'William Morris'.

125. *Notes,* Volume 2, Number 26, 10 July, p. 116.
Signed 'W. M.'.

126. *Review: 'Modern Socialism',* Volume 2, Number 26, 10 July, p. 117.
Signed 'William Morris'.

127. *The Whig-Jingo Victory,* Volume 2, Number 27, 17 July, p. 121.
Signed 'Wm. Morris'.

128. *'An Empty Pocket Is The Worst Of Crimes',* Volume 2, Number 27, 17 July, p. 123.
Signed 'W. M.'.

129. *Review: 'Cashel Byron's Confession'*, Volume 2, Number 27, 17 July, p. 126.
Signed 'W. M.'.

130. *What Is To Happen Next?,* Volume 2, Number 28, 24 July, p. 129.
Signed 'William Morris'.

131. *Socialism From The Root Up: Chapter VII,* Volume 2, Number 28, 24 July, pp. 130–131.
Signed 'E. Belfort Bax and William Morris'.

132. *Free Speech In The Streets,* Volume 2, Number 29, 31 July, p. 137.
Signed 'Wm. Morris'.

133. *Socialism From The Root Up: Chapter VIII,* Volume 2, Number 29, 31 July, pp. 138–139.
Signed 'E. Belfort Bax and William Morris'.

134. *Political Notes,* Volume 2, Number 30, 7 August, p. 141.
Signed 'William Morris'.

135. *[Untitled Paragraphs],* Volume 2, Number 30, 7 August, p. 147.
Signed 'W. M.'.

136. *Mr Chamberlain's Leader,* Volume 2, Number 31, 14 August, p. 153.
Signed 'William Morris'.

137. *Notes On Passing Events,* Volume 2, Number 31, 14 August, p. 156.
Signed 'W. M.'.

138. *Socialism From The Root Up: Chapter IX,* Volume 2, Number 31, 14 August, pp. 156–158.
Signed 'E. Belfort Bax and William Morris'.

139. *The Abolition Of Freedom Of Speech In The Streets,* Volume 2, Number 32, 21 August, p. 161.
Signed 'William Morris'.

140. *Notes On Passing Events,* Volume 2, Number 32, 21 August, p. 164.
Signed 'W. M.'.

141. *Notes On Passing Events,* Volume 2, Number 33, 28 August, p. 169.
Signed 'William Morris'.

142. *Socialism From The Root Up: Chapter X,* Volume 2, Number 33, 28 August, pp. 170–171.
Signed 'E. Belfort Bax and William Morris'.

143. *Misanthropy To The Rescue,* Volume 2, Number 33, 28 August, p. 172.
Signed 'William Morris'.

144. *Notes On Passing Events,* Volume 2, Number 34, 4 September, p. 177.
Signed 'William Morris'.

145. *Notes On Passing Events,* Volume 2, Number 35, 11 September, p. 185.
Signed 'Wm. Morris'.

146. *The Paris Trades' Union Congress,* Volume 2, Number 35, 11 September, p. 187.
Signed 'William Morris'.

147. *Socialism From The Root Up: Chapter XI,* Volume 2, Number 35, 11 September, p. 189.
Signed 'E. Belfort Bax and William Morris'.

148. *An Old Story Retold,* Volume 2, Number 36, 18 September, pp. 197–198.
Signed 'William Morris'.

149. *Notes On Passing Events,* Volume 2, Number 37, 25 September, p. 201.
Signed 'William Morris'.

150. *The Reward Of 'Genius',* Volume 2, Number 37, 25 September, pp. 205–206.
Signed 'William Morris'.

151. *Socialism From The Root Up: Chapter XII,* Volume 2, Number 38, 2 October, p. 210.
Signed 'E. Belfort Bax and William Morris'.

152. *Notes On Passing Events,* Volume 2, Number 40, 16 October, p. 225.
Signed 'William Morris'.

153. *Notes On Passing Events,* Volume 2, Number 41, 23 October, p. 233.
Signed 'William Morris'.

154. *Notes On Passing Events,* Volume 2, Number 42, 30 October, pp. 241–242.
Signed 'William Morris'.

155. *Socialism From the Root Up: Chapter XIII,* Volume 2, Number 42, 30 October, pp. 242–243.
Signed 'E. Belfort Bax and William Morris'.

156. *Notes On Passing Events,* Volume 2, Number 43, 6 November, p. 249.
Signed 'William Morris'.

157. *Notes On Passing Events,* Volume 2, Number 44, 13 November, p. 257.
Signed 'William Morris'.

158. *A Dream Of John Ball,* Volume 2, Number 44, 13 November, pp. 257–258.
Signed 'William Morris'.

159. *The Moral Of Last Lord Mayor's Day,* Volume 2, Number 45, 20 November, p. 265.
Signed 'William Morris'.

160. *A Dream Of John Ball,* Volume 2, Number 45, 20 November, pp. 266–267.
Signed 'William Morris'.

161. *Mr. Jawkins At The Mansion House,* Volume 2, Number 45, 20 November, pp. 268–269.
Signed 'William Morris'.

162. *A Dream Of John Ball,* Volume 2, Number 46, 27 November, pp. 274–275.
Signed 'William Morris'.

163. *The Ten Commandments,* Volume 2, Number 46, 27 November, p. 276.
Signed 'W. M.'.

164. *Notes On Passing Events,* Volume 2, Number 47, 4 December, p. 281.
Signed 'W. Morris'.

165. *A Dream Of John Ball,* Volume 2, Number 47, 4 December, pp. 282–283.
Signed 'William Morris'.

166. *Notes On Passing Events,* Volume 2, Number 48, 11 December, p. 289.
Signed 'W. M.'.

167. *A Dream Of John Ball,* Volume 2, Number 48, 11 December, pp. 290–291.
Signed 'William Morris'.

168. *Notes On Passing Events,* Volume 2, Number 49, 18 December, p. 297.
Signed 'Wm. Morris'.

169. *A Dream Of John Ball,* Volume 2, Number 49, 18 December, pp. 298–299.
Signed 'William Morris'.

170. *Is Trade Recovering?,* Volume 2, Number 49, 18 December, p. 300.
Signed 'William Morris'.

171. *'The Law' In Ireland,* Volume 2, Number 50, 25 December, p. 305.
Signed 'W. Morris'.

172. *A Dream Of John Ball,* Volume 2, Number 50, 25 December, p. 307.
Signed 'William Morris'.

Commonweal [1887].

173. *Political Notes,* Volume 3, Number 51, 1 January, p. 1.
Signed 'William Morris'.

174. *A Dream Of John Ball,* Volume 3, Number 51, 1 January, p. 3.
Signed 'William Morris'.

175. *Editorial,* Volume 3, Number 51, 1 January, p. 4.
Signed 'William Morris. H. Halliday Sparling'.

176. *[Untitled Paragraph On Trafalgar Square],* Volume 3, Number 51, 1 January, p. 5.
Signed 'W. M.'

177. *Words Of Forecast For 1887,* Volume 3, Number 52, 8 January, p. 9.
Signed 'E. Belfort Bax and William Morris'.

178. *[Untitled Paragraph On The Czar],* Volume 3, Number 52, 8 January, p. 11.
Signed 'W. M.'.

179. *A Dream Of John Ball,* Volume 3, Number 52, 8 January, p. 13.
Signed 'William Morris'.

180. *Notes On News,* Volume 3, Number 53, 15 January, p. 17.
Signed 'W. M.'.

181. *The Political Crisis,* Volume 3, Number 53, 15 January, p. 20.
Signed 'William Morris'.

182. *A Dream Of John Ball,* Volume 3, Number 53, 15 January, pp. 20–21.
Signed 'William Morris'.

183. *Notes On Passing Events,* Volume 3, Number 54, 22 January, p. 25.
Signed 'W. Morris'.

184. *A Dream of John Ball,* Volume 3, Number 54, 22 January, pp. 28–29.
Signed 'William Morris'.

185. *Notes On Passing Events,* Volume 3, Number 55, 29 January, p. 33.
Signed 'William Morris'.

186. *Notes On News,* Volume 3, Number 56, 5 February, p. 41.
Signed 'W. M.'.

187. *Socialism From The Root Up: Chapter XIV,* Volume 3, Number 56, 5 February, pp. 42–43.
Signed 'E. Belfort Bax and William Morris'.

188. *Notes On News,* Volume 3, Number 57, 12 February, p. 49.
Signed 'William Morris'.

189. *Notes On News,* Volume 3, Number 58, 19 February, p. 57.
Signed 'W. M.'.

190. *Facing The Worst Of It,* Volume 3, Number 58, 19 February, pp. 60–61.
Signed 'William Morris'.

191. *Notes On News,* Volume 3, Number 59, 26 February, p. 65.
Signed 'W. M.'.

192. *Socialism From The Root Up: Chapter XV,* Volume 3, Number 59, 26 February, pp. 66–67.
Signed 'E. Belfort Bax and William Morris'.

193. *Fighting For Peace,* Volume 3, Number 59, 26 February, p. 68.
Signed 'William Morris'.

194. *Notes On News,* Volume 3, Number 60, 5 March, p. 73.
Signed 'W. M.'.

195. *Political Notes,* Volume 3, Number 61, 12 March, p. 81.
Signed 'W. M.'.

196. *Socialism From The Root Up: Chapter XVI,* Volume 3, Number 61, 12 March, p. 82.
Signed 'E. Belfort Bax and William Morris'.

197. *Notes On News,* Volume 3, Number 61, 12 March, p. 84.
Signed 'W. M.'.

198. *[The Ambleside Railway Bill],* Volume 3, Number 61, 12 March, p. 85.
Signed 'Ed'.

199. *Political Notes,* Volume 3, Number 62, 19 March, p. 89.
Signed 'W. M.'.

200. *Why We Celebrate The Commune Of Paris,* Volume 3, Number 62, 19 March, pp. 89–90.
Signed 'William Morris'.

201. *Notes On News,* Volume 3, Number 63, 26 March, p. 97.
Signed 'W. M.'.

202. *Socialism From The Root Up: Chapter XVII,* Volume 3, Number 63, 26 March, p. 101.
Signed 'E. Belfort Bax and William Morris'.

203. *Notes On News,* Volume 3, Number 64, 2 April, p. 105.
Signed 'W. M.'

204. *Law And Order In Ireland,* Volume 3, Number 65, 9 April, p. 113.
Signed 'William Morris'.

205. *The Revival Of Trade(?),* Volume 3, Number 65, 9 April, p. 115.
Signed 'W. M.'.

206. *[Untitled Paragraph On Flogging In Egypt],* Volume 3, Number 65, 9 April, p. 117.
Signed 'W. M.'.

207. *Notes On News,* Volume 3, Number 67, 23 April, p. 129.
Signed 'William Morris'.

208. *Notes On News,* Volume 3, Number 68, 30 April, p. 137.
Signed 'William Morris'.

209. *Socialism From The Root Up: Chapter XVIII,* Volume 3, Number 68, p. 141.
Signed 'E. Belfort Bax and William Morris'.

210. *Notes On News,* Volume 3, Number 69, 7 May, p. 145.
Signed 'W. M.'.

211. *Notes On News,* Volume 3, Number 70, 14 May, p. 153.
Signed 'W. M.'.

212. *Coercion For London,* Volume 3, Number 70, 14 May, pp. 153–154.
Signed 'William Morris'.

213. *The Reward Of Labour. A Dialogue,* Volume 3, Number 71, 21 May, p. 165.
Signed 'William Morris'.

214. *The Reward Of Labour. A Dialogue,* Volume 3, Number 72, 28 May, p. 170.
Signed 'William Morris'.

215. *Notes On News,* Volume 3, Number 72, 28 May, p. 172.
Signed 'William Morris'.

216. *How We Live And How We Might Live,* Volume 3, Number 73, 4 June, pp. 177–178.
Signed 'William Morris'.

217. *How We Live And How We Might Live,* Volume 3, Number 74, 11 June, p. 186.
Signed 'William Morris'.

218. *Notes On News,* Volume 3, Number 74, 11 June, p. 188.
Signed 'William Morris'.

219. *[Untitled Paragraph On The Indian Railways]*, Volume 3, Number 74, 11 June, p. 191.
Signed 'W. M.'.

220. *Notes On News,* Volume 3, Number 75, 18 June, p. 193.
Signed 'William Morris'.

221. *How We Live And How We Might Live,* Volume 3, Number 75, 18 June, pp. 194–195.
Signed 'William Morris'.

222. *Notes,* Volume 3, Number 75, 18 June, p. 196.
Signed 'W. M.'.

223. *Socialism From The Root Up: Chapter XIX,* Volume 3, Number 75, 18 June, pp. 196–197.
Signed 'E. Belfort Bax and William Morris'.

224. *'Common-Sense Socialism',* Volume 3, Number 75, 18 June, p. 197.
Signed 'W. M.'.

225. *The Labour Struggle. Belgium,* Volume 3, Number 75, 18 June, p. 198.
Signed 'W. M.'.

226. *How We Live And How We Might Live,* Volume 3, Number 76, 25 June, pp. 202–203.
Signed 'William Morris'.

227. *An Old Superstition – A New Disgrace,* Volume 3, Number 76, 25 June, p. 204.
Signed 'William Morris'.

228. *The North Of England Socialist Federation,* Volume 3, Number 76, 25 June, p. 205.
Signed 'W. M.'.

229. *How We Live And How We Might Live,* Volume 3, Number 77, 2 July, pp. 210–211.
Signed 'William Morris'.

230. *Notes,* Volume 3, Number 77, 2 July, p. 212.
Signed 'W. M.'.

231. *Notes On News,* Volume 3, Number 78, 9 July, p. 217.
Signed 'W. M.'.

232. *Notes On News,* Volume 3, Number 79, 16 July, p. 228.
Signed 'W. M.'.

233. *Socialism From The Root Up: Chapter XX,* Volume 3, Number 80, 23 July, pp. 234–235.
Signed 'E. Belfort Bax and William Morris'.

234. *Notes On News,* Volume 3, Number 80, 23 July, p. 236.
Signed 'W. M.'.

235. *The Boy-Farms At Fault,* Volume 3, Number 81, 30 July, p. 241.
Signed 'William Morris'.

236. *Notes,* Volume 3, Number 82, 6 August, p. 249.
Signed 'Wm. Morris'.

237. *Bourgeois Versus Socialist,* Volume 3, Number 82, 6 August, p. 252.
Signed 'William Morris'.

238. *Socialism From The Root Up: Chapter XXI,* Volume 3, Number 82, 6 August, p. 253.
Signed 'E. Belfort Bax and William Morris'.

239. *Notes,* Volume 3, Number 83, 13 August, p. 257.
Signed 'William Morris'.

240. *Notes On News,* Volume 3, Number 84, 20 August, pp. 265–266.
Signed 'William Morris'.

241. *Feudal England,* Volume 3, Number 84, 20 August, pp. 266–267.
Signed 'William Morris'.

242. *Notes On News,* Volume 3, Number 85, 27 August, p. 273.
Signed 'W. M.'.

243. *Feudal England,* Volume 3, Number 85, 27 August, p. 274.
Signed 'William Morris'.

244. *A Note On Passing Politics,* Volume 3, Number 85, 27 August, p. 276.
Signed 'William Morris'.

245. *Is Lipski's Confession Genuine?,* Volume 3, Number 85, 27 August, p. 276.
Signed 'E. Belfort Bax and William Morris'.

246. *Notes On News,* Volume 3, Number 86, 3 September, p. 281.
Signed 'W. M.'.

247. *Feudal England,* Volume 3, Number 86, 3 September, p. 282.
Signed 'William Morris'.

248. *Notes On News,* Volume 3, Number 87, 10 September, p. 289.
Signed 'W. M.'.

249. *Feudal England,* Volume 3, Number 87, 10 September, pp. 290–291.
Signed 'William Morris'.

250. *Artist And Artisan: As An Artist Sees It,* Volume 3, Number 87, 10 September, p. 291.
Signed 'William Morris'.
Published with a companion piece by Jim Allman entitled 'Artist and Artisan: As A Workman Sees It'.

251. *Notes On News,* Volume 3, Number 88, 17 September, p. 297.
Signed 'William Morris'.

252. *Notes On News,* Volume 3, Number 89, 24 September, p. 305.
Signed 'W. M.'.

253. *Notes,* Volume 3, Number 91, 8 October, p. 321.
Signed 'W. M.'.

254. *Free Speech In America,* Volume 3, Number 91, 8 October, p. 324.
Signed 'William Morris'.

255. *Notes,* Volume 3, Number 92, 15 October, p. 329.
Signed 'W. M.'.

256. *Notes On News,* Volume 3, Number 93, 22 October, p. 337.
Signed 'W. M.'.

257. *Notes On News,* Volume 3, Number 94, 29 October, p. 345.
Signed 'William Morris'.

258. *Practical Politics At Nottingham,* Volume 3, Number 94, 29 October, p. 349.
Signed 'William Morris'.

259. *Notes On News,* Volume 3, Number 95, 5 November, p. 353.
Signed 'W. M.'.

260. *Honesty Is The Best Policy,* Volume 3, Number 96, 5 November, pp. 356–357.
Signed 'William Morris'.

261. *Notes On News,* Volume 3, Number 96, 12 November, p. 361.
Signed 'W. M.'.

262. *Honesty Is The Best Policy,* Volume 3, Number 96, 12 November, pp. 364–365.
Signed 'William Morris'.

263. *London In A State Of Siege,* Volume 3, Number 97, 19 November, pp. 369–370.
Signed 'William Morris'.

264. *[Untitled Paragraphs],* Volume 3, Number 97, 19 November, p. 375.
First signed 'W. M.' the second 'Ed'.

265. *Notes On News,* Volume 3, Number 98, 26 November, p. 377.
Signed 'W. M.'.

266. *Insurance Against Magistrates,* Volume 3, Number 98, 26 November, p. 377.
Signed 'William Morris'.

267. *The Liberal Party Digging Its Own Grave,* Volume 3, Number 98, 28 November, p. 380.
Signed 'William Morris'.

268. *Notes On News,* Volume 3, Number 99, 3 December, p. 385.
Signed 'W. M.'.

269. *Notes On News,* Volume 3, Number 100, 10 December, p. 393.
Signed 'William Morris'.

270. *Notes On News,* Volume 3, Number 101, 17 December, p. 401.
Signed 'William Morris'.

271. *The Conscience Of The Upper Classes,* Volume 3, Number 101, 17 December, p. 404.
Signed 'William Morris'.

272. *Notes On News,* Volume 3, Number 102, 24 December, p. 409.
Signed 'W. M.'.

273. *Emigration And Colonisation,* Volume 3, Number 103, 31 December, pp. 417–418.
Signed 'William Morris'.

274. *[Untitled Reply To A Letter],* Volume 3, Number 103, 31 December, p. 421.
Signed 'Ed'.

Commonweal [1888].

275. *Notes On News,* Volume 4, Number 104, 7 January, p. 1.
Signed 'W. M.'.

276. *Police Spies Exposed,* Volume 4, Number 104, 7 January, pp. 1–2.
Signed 'Editors'.

277. *What 1887 Has Done*, Volume 4, Number 104, 7 January, pp. 4–5.
Signed 'William Morris'.

278. *Notes On News,* Volume 4, Number 105, 14 January, pp. 9–10.
Signed 'W. M.'.

279. *Radicals Look Around You!,* Volume 4, Number 105, 14 January, pp. 12–13.
Signed 'William Morris'.

280. *Notes On News,* Volume 4, Number 106, 21 January, p. 17.
Signed 'William Morris'.

281. *Notes On News,* Volume 4, Number 107, 28 January, p. 25.
Signed 'William Morris'.

282. *[Various Untitled Paragraphs],* Volume 4, Number 107, 28 January, p. 29.
Signed 'W. M.'.

283. *Notes On News,* Volume 4, Number 109, 11 February, p. 41.
Signed 'W. M.'.

284. *[Untitled Paragraph],* Volume 4, Number 109, 11 February, p. 43.
Signed 'Ed'.

285. *Notes On News,* Volume 4, Number 110, 18 February, p. 49.
Signed 'W. M.'.

286. *On Some 'Practical' Socialists,* Volume 4, Number 110, 18 February, pp. 52–53.
Signed 'William Morris'.

287. *Notes On News,* Volume 4, Number 111, 25 February, p. 57.
Signed 'W. M.'.

288. *[Untitled Paragraph],* Volume 4, Number 111, 25 February, p. 61.
Signed 'W. M.'.

289. *Notes On News,* Volume 4, Number 112, 3 March, p. 65.
Signed 'W. M.'.

290. *A Triple Alliance,* Volume 4, Number 112, 3 March, p. 68.
Signed 'W. M.'.

291. *Notes On News,* Volume 4, Number 113, 10 March, p. 73.
Signed 'W. M.'.

292. *Socialism From The Root Up: Chapter XXII,* Volume 4, Number 113, 10 March, pp. 76–77.
Signed 'E. Belfort Bax and William Morris'.

293. *Dead At Last,* Volume 4, Number 114, 17 March, p. 81.
Signed 'W. M.'.

294. *Socialism From The Root Up: Chapter XXII (Cont),* Volume 4, Number 114, 17 March, p. 82.
Signed 'E. Belfort Bax and William Morris'.

295. *Notes On News,* Volume 4, Number 115, 24 March, p. 89.
Signed 'W. M.'.

296. *A Speech From The Dock,* Volume 4, Number 115, 24 March, p. 93.
Signed 'W. M.'.

297. *Notes On News,* Volume 4, Number 117, 7 April, p. 105.
Signed 'W. M.'.

298. *Socialism Militant In Scotland,* Volume 4, Number 117, 7 April, pp. 106–107.
Signed 'William Morris'.

299. *Notes On News,* Volume 4, Number 118, 14 April, p. 113.
Signed 'W. M.'.

300. *Notes On News,* Volume 4, Number 119, 21 April, p. 121.
Signed 'W. M.'.

301. *[Untitled Verses],* Volume 4, Number 119, 21 April, p. 129.
Signed 'W. M.'.

302. *Notes On News,* Volume 4, Number 129, 28 April, p. 129.
Signed 'W. M.'.

303. *Notes On News,* Volume 4, Number 121, 5 May, p. 137.
Signed 'W. M.'.

304. *The Reaction And The Radicals,* Volume 4, Number 121, 5 May, pp. 137–138.
Signed 'William Morris'.

305. *Socialism From The Root Up: Chapter XXIII,* Volume 4, Number 121, 5 May, pp. 140–141.
Signed 'E. Belfort Bax and William Morris'.

306. *Notes On News,* Volume 4, Number 122, 12 May, pp. 145–146.
Signed 'W. M.'.

307. *Notes On News,* Volume 4, Number 123, 19 May, p. 153.
Signed 'W. M.'.

308. *Socialism From The Root Up: Chapter XXIII (Cont),* Volume 4, Number 123, 19 May, pp. 154–5.
Signed 'E. Belfort Bax and William Morris'.

309. *Notes On News,* Volume 4, Number 124, 26 May, p. 161.
Signed 'W. M.'.

310. *Notes On News,* Volume 4, Number 125, 2 June, p. 169.
Signed 'W. M.'.

311. *The Policy Of The Socialist League,* Volume 4, Number 126, 9 June, p. 180.
Signed by the 'Council Of The Socialist League'.

312. *Revolutionary Calendar: Wat Tyler,* Volume 4, Number 126, 9 June, p. 182.
Signed 'W. M.'.

313. *Notes On News,* Volume 4, Number 127, 16 June, p. 185.
Signed 'W. M.'.

314. *The Skeleton At The Feast,* Volume 4, Number 127, 16 June, p. 188.
Signed 'William Morris'.

315. *Notes On News,* Volume 4, Number 128, 23 June, p. 193.
Signed 'W. M.'.

316. *Pentonville Prison,* Volume 4, Number 128, 23 June, p. 195.
Signed 'W. M.'.

317. *Counting Noses,* Volume 4, Number 128, 23 June, p. 196.
Signed 'William Morris'.

318. *Notes On News,* Volume 4, Number 129, 30 June, pp. 201–202.
Signed 'W. M.'.

319. *Thoughts On Education Under Capitalism,* Volume 4, Number 129, 30 June, pp. 204–205.
Signed 'William Morris'.

320. *Notes On News,* Volume 4, Number 130, 7 July, p. 209–210.
Signed 'W. M.'.

321. *The Revolt Of Ghent,* Volume 4, Number 130, 7 July, p. 210.
Signed 'William Morris'.

322. *Notes On News,* Volume 4, Number 131, 14 July, p. 217.
Signed 'W. M.'.

323. *The Revolt Of Ghent,* Volume 4, Number 131, 14 July, pp. 217–218.
Signed 'William Morris'.

324. *Sweaters And Sweaters,* Volume 4, Number 132, 21 July, pp. 225–226.
Signed 'William Morris'.

325. *The Revolt Of Ghent,* Volume 4, Number 132, 21 July, pp. 226–227.
Signed 'William Morris'.

326. *Notes On News,* Volume 4, Number 132, 21 July, p. 228.
Signed 'W. M.'.

327. *[Untitled Paragraph On The Match Girls' Strike],* Volume 4, Number 132, 21 July, p. 229.
Signed 'W. M.'.

328. *Notes On News,* Volume 4, Number 133, 28 July, p. 233.
Signed 'W. M.'.

329. *The Revolt Of Ghent,* Volume 4, Number 133, 28 July, p. 234.
Signed 'William Morris'.

330. *Notes On News,* Volume 4, Number 134, 4 August, p. 241.
Signed 'W. M.'.

331. *The Revolt Of Ghent,* Volume 4, Number 134, 4 August, pp. 242–243.
Signed 'William Morris'.

332. *Notes On News,* Volume 4, Number 135, 11 August, p. 249.
Signed 'W. M.'.

333. *The Revolt Of Ghent,* Volume 4, Number 135, 11 August, p. 250.
Unsigned.

334. *Footnote To 'Death Of W. Stanley Jevons',* Volume 4, Number 135, 11 August, p. 251.
Signed 'S. W. – W. M.'.

335. *Notes On News,* Volume 4, Number 136, 18 August, pp. 257–258.
Signed 'William Morris'.

336. *The Revolt Of Ghent,* Volume 4, Number 136, 18 August, pp. 258–259.
Signed 'William Morris'.

337. *Notes On News,* Volume 4, Number 137, 25 August, p. 265.
Signed 'W. M.'.

338. *Socialist Work at Norwich,* Volume 4, Number 137, 25 August, p. 268.
Signed 'William Morris'.

339. *Notes On News,* Volume 4, Number 139, 8 September, p. 281.
Signed 'W. M.'.

340. *Notes On News,* Volume 4, Number 140, 15 September, p. 289.
Signed 'W. M.'.

341. *Notes On News,* Volume 4, Number 141, 22 September, p. 297.
Signed 'W. M.'.

342. *A Modern Midas,* Volume 4, Number 141, 22 September, p. 300.
Signed 'W. M.'.

343. *Notes On News,* Volume 4, Number 143, 6 October, pp. 313–314.
Signed 'W. M.'.

344. *Notes On News,* Volume 4, Number 146, 27 October, pp. 337–338.
Signed 'W. M.'.

345. *[Untitled Article On The Chicago Anarchists],* Volume 4, Number 148, 10 November, pp. 353–354.
Signed 'Editors'.

346. *Notes On News,* Volume 4, Number 148, 10 November, p. 356.
Signed 'William Morris'.

347. *Notes On News,* Volume 4, Number 149, 17 November, p. 361.
Signed 'W. M.'.

348. *Notes On News,* Volume 4, Number 151, 1 December, p. 380.
Signed 'W. M.'.

349. *Notes On News,* Volume 4, Number 152, 8 December, p. 385.
Signed 'W. M.'.

350. *In And About Cottonopolis,* Volume 4, Number 153, 15 December, p. 396.
Signed 'William Morris'.

351. *Notes On News,* Volume 4, Number 153, 15 December, p. 397.
Signed 'W. M.'.

352. *Notes On News,* Volume 4, Number 154, 22 December, p. 401.
Signed 'W. M.'.

353. *Talk And Art,* Volume 4, Number 154, 22 December, p. 404.
Signed 'William Morris'.

354. *Notes On News,* Volume 4, Number 155, 29 December, p. 409.
Signed 'W. M.'.

Commonweal [1889].

355. *Notes On News,* Volume 5, Number 156, 5 January, pp. 4–5.
Signed 'William Morris'.

356. *Notes On News,* Volume 5, Number 157, 12 January, p. 12.
Signed 'W. M.'.

357. *Notes On News,* Volume 5, Number 158, 19 January, pp. 17–18.
Signed 'W. M.'.

358. *Whigs Astray,* Volume 5, Number 158, 19 January, pp. 18–19.
Signed 'William Morris'.

359. *Notes On News,* Volume 5, Number 159, 26 January, p. 25.
Signed 'W. M.'.

360. *Whigs Astray,* Volume 5, Number 159, 26 January, pp. 26–27.
Signed 'William Morris'.

361. *Notes On News,* Volume 5, Number 160, 2 February, p. 33.
Signed 'W. M.'.

362. *Notes On News,* Volume 5, Number 161, 9 February, p. 41.
Signed 'W. M.'.

363. *Notes On News*, Volume 5, Number 163, 23 February, p. 57.
Signed 'W. M.'.

364. *Notes On News*, Volume 5, Number 164, 2 March, p. 65.
Signed 'W. M.'.

365. *Mine And Thine (Poem),* Volume 5, Number 164, 2 March, p. 67.
Signed '*Translated by* William Morris'.

366. *Notes On News*, Volume 5, Number 165, 9 March, p. 73.
Signed 'W. M.'.

367. *Notes On News*, Volume 5, Number 166, 16 March, p. 81.
Signed 'W. M.'.

368. *All For The Cause (Poem)*, Volume 5, Number 166, 16 March, p. 85.
Signed 'William Morris'.

369. *Notes On News,* Volume 5, Number 167, 23 March, p. 89.
Signed 'W. M.'.

370. *Apology For Missing The Paris Commune Celebrations,* Volume 5, Number 167, 23 March, p. 91.
Signed 'William Morris'.

371. *To Manchester Friends,* Volume 5, Number 167, 23 March, p. 93.
Signed 'Eds'.

372. *Notes On News*, Volume 5, Number 168, 30 March, pp. 97–98.
Signed 'W. M.'.

373. *The Society Of The Future,* Volume 5, Number 168, 30 March, pp. 98–99.
Signed 'William Morris'.

374. *Notes On News,* Volume 5, Number 169, 6 April, p. 105.
Signed 'W. M.'.

375. *Ducks And Drakes,* Volume 5, Number 169, 6 April, p. 107.
Signed 'W. M.'.

376. *The Society Of The Future,* Volume 5, Number 169, 6 April, pp. 108–109.
Signed 'William Morris'.

377. *Notes On News,* Volume 5, Number 170, 13 April, p. 113.
Signed 'W. M.'.

378. *The Society Of The Future,* Volume 5, Number 170, 13 April, pp. 114–115.
Signed 'William Morris'.

379. *Notes On News,* Volume 5, Number 171, 20 April, p. 121.
Signed 'W. M.'.

380. *Notes On News,* Volume 5, Number 172, 27 April, p. 129.
Signed 'W. M.'.

381. *Statement Of Principles,* Volume 5, Number 173, 4 May, p. 137.
Signed 'Council Of The Socialist League'.

382. *[Untitled Paragraph]*, Volume 5, Number 173, 4 May, p. 137.
Signed 'W. M.'.

383. *Notes On News,* Volume 5, Number 173, 4 May, p. 140.
Signed 'W. M.'.

384. *Notes On News,* Volume 5, Number 174, 11 May, p. 145.
Signed 'W. M.'.

385. *Notes On News,* Volume 5, Number 175, 18 May, p. 153.
Signed 'W. M.'.

386. *Correspondence,* Volume 5, Number 175, 18 May, p. 157.
Signed 'William Morris'.
NB: A letter opposing the Anarchists.

387. *Notes On News,* Volume 5, Number 178, 8 June, p. 177.
Signed 'W. M.'.

388. *Notes On News,* Volume 5, Number 179, 15 June, p. 185.
Signed 'W. M.'.

389. *Notes On News,* Volume 5, Number 180, 22 June, p. 193.
Signed 'W. M.'.

390. *'Looking Backward',* Volume 5, Number 180, 22 June, pp. 194–195.
Signed 'William Morris'.

391. *Notes On News,* Volume 5, Number 181, 29 June, p. 201.
Signed 'W. M.'.

392. *Notes On News,* Volume 5, Number 182, 6 July, p. 209.
Signed 'W. M.'.

393. *Under An Elm-Tree,* Volume 5, Number 182, 6 July, pp. 212–213.
Signed 'William Morris'.

394. *Impressions Of The Paris Congress,* Volume 5, Number 185, 27 July, p. 234.
Signed 'William Morris'.

395. *Notes On News,* Volume 5, Number 186, 3 August, p. 241.
Signed 'W. M.'.

396. *Impressions Of The Paris Congress,* Volume 5, Number 186, 3 August, p. 242.
Signed 'William Morris'.

397. *Trial By Judge v. Trial By Jury,* Volume 5, Number 188, 17 August, p. 257.
Signed 'William Morris'.

398. *Correspondence: Communism And Anarchism,* Volume 5, Number 188, 17 August, p. 261.
Signed 'William Morris'.

399. *Notes On News,* Volume 5, Number 189, 24 August, p. 265.
Signed 'W. M.'.

400. *The Lesson Of The Hour,* Volume 5, Number 191, 7 September, pp. 281–282.
Signed 'W. M.'.

401. *Notes On News,* Volume 5, Number 192, 14 September, p. 289.
Signed 'W. M.'.

402. *Notes On News,* Volume 5, Number 193, 21 September, p. 297.
Signed 'W. M.'.

403. *Notes On News,* Volume 5, Number 194, 28 September, p. 305.
Signed 'W. M.'.

404. *[Untitled Note],* Volume 5, Number 195, 5 October, p. 315.
Signed 'Ed'.

405. *Notes On News,* Volume 5, Number 197, 19 October, p. 329.
Signed 'W. M.'.

406. *Notes On News,* Volume 5, Number 198, 26 October, p. 337.
Signed 'W. M.'.

407. *Notes On News,* Volume 5, Number 200, 9 November, p. 356.
Signed 'W. M.'.

408. *Notes On News,* Volume 5, Number 201, 16 November, p. 361.
Signed 'W. M.'.

409. *Notes On News,* Volume 5, Number 202, 23 November, p. 369.
Signed 'W. M.'.

410. *A Death Song (Poem),* Volume 5, Number 202, 23 November, p. 371.
Signed 'William Morris'.

411. *Notes On News,* Volume 5, Number 203, 30 November, p. 377.
Signed 'W. M.'.

412. *Notes On News,* Volume 5, Number 204, 7 December, p. 385.
Signed 'W. M.'.

413. *Monopoly,* Volume 5, Number 204, 7 December, pp. 388–389.
Signed 'William Morris'.

414. *Notes On News,* Volume 5, Number 205, 14 December, p. 393.
Signed 'W. M.'.

415. *Monopoly,* Volume 5, Number 205, 14 December, p. 394.
Signed 'William Morris'.

416. *Monopoly,* Volume 5, Number 206, 21 December, pp. 401–402.
Signed 'W. M.'.

417. *Notes On News,* Volume 5, Number 207, 28 December, p. 409.
Signed 'W. M.'.

Commonweal [1890].

418. *News From Nowhere: Chapters I & II,* Volume 6, Number 209, 11 January, p. 9.
Signed 'William Morris'.

419. *News From Nowhere: Chapter II (Cont),* Volume 6, Number 210, 18 January, p. 18.
Signed 'William Morris'.

420. *News From Nowhere: Chapter III,* Volume 6, Number 211, 25 January, p. 25.
Signed 'William Morris'.

421. *Fabian Essays In Socialism,* Volume 6, Number 211, 25 January, pp. 28–29.
Signed 'William Morris'.

422. *Notes On News,* Volume 6, Number 212, 1 February, p. 33.
Signed 'W. M.'.

423. *News From Nowhere: Chapters III & Chapter IV,* Volume 6, Number 212, 1 February, p. 34.
Signed 'William Morris'.

424. *Notes On News,* Volume 6, Number 213, 8 February, p. 41.
Signed 'W. M.'.

425. *News From Nowhere: Chapter V,* Volume 6, Number 213, 8 February, p. 42.
Signed 'William Morris'.

426. *Notes On News,* Volume 6, Number 214, 15 February, p. 49.
Signed 'W. M.'.

427. *News From Nowhere: Chapter VI,* Volume 6, Number 214, 15 February, p. 49.
Signed 'William Morris'.

428. *Notes On News,* Volume 6, Number 215, 22 February, p. 57.
Signed 'W. M.'.

429. *News From Nowhere: Chapter VII,* Volume 6, Number 215, 22 February, p. 58.
Signed 'William Morris'.

430. *News From Nowhere: Chapter VIII,* Volume 6, Number 216, 1 March, p. 66.
Signed 'William Morris'.

431. *News From Nowhere: Chapter IX,* Volume 6, Number 217, 8 March, p. 74.
Signed 'William Morris'.

432. *Coal In Kent,* Volume 6, Number 217, 8 March, p. 77.
Signed 'William Morris'.

433. *Christianity And Socialism,* Volume 6, Number 217, 8 March, p. 77.
Signed 'William Morris'.

434. *News From Nowhere: Chapter IX (Continued),* Volume 6, Number 218, 15 March, p. 82.
Signed 'William Morris'.

435. *Notes On News,* Volume 6, Number 219, 22 March, p. 89.
Signed 'W. M.'.

436. *News From Nowhere: Chapter IX & Chapter X,* Volume 6, Number 219, 22 March, p. 89.
Signed 'William Morris'.

437. *The Great Coal Strike,* Volume 6, Number 219, 22 March, p. 91.
Signed 'William Morris'.

438. *News From Nowhere: Chapter X (Continued),* Volume 6, Number 220, 29 March, p. 98.
Signed 'William Morris'.

439. *Notes,* Volume 6, Number 220, 29 March, p. 100.
Signed 'W. M.'.

440. *Notes On News,* Volume 6, Number 221, 5 April, p. 105.
Signed 'W. M.'.

441. *News From Nowhere: Chapter X (Concluded),* Volume 6, Number 221, 5 April, p. 105.
Signed 'William Morris'.

442. *News From Nowhere: Chapter XI,* Volume 6, Number 222, 12 April, p. 113.
Signed 'William Morris'.

443. *Notes On News,* Volume 6, Number 222, 12 April, p. 116.
Signed 'W. M.'.

444. *News From Nowhere: Chapter XII,* Volume 6, Number 223, 19 April, p. 121.
Signed 'William Morris'.

445. *News From Nowhere: Chapters XIII & XIV,* Volume 6, Number 224, 26 April, p. 130.
Signed 'William Morris'.

446. *Labour Day,* Volume 6, Number 225, 3 May, p. 140.
Signed 'William Morris'.

447. *Notes On News,* Volume 6, Number 225, 3 May, p. 140.
Signed 'W. M.'.

448. *News From Nowhere: Chapter XV,* Volume 6, Number 225, 3 May, p. 141.
Signed 'William Morris'.

449. *News From Nowhere: Chapters XV & XVI,* Volume 6, Number 226, 10 May, p. 145.
Signed 'William Morris'.

450. *The 'Eight Hours' And The Demonstration,* Volume 6, Number 227, 17 May, p. 153.
Signed 'William Morris'.

451. *News From Nowhere: Chapters XVI & XVII,* Volume 6, Number 227, 17 May, p. 156.
Signed 'William Morris'.

452. *Notes,* Volume 6, Number 227, 17 May, p. 157.
Signed 'W. M.'.

453. *News From Nowhere: Chapter XVII (Continued),* Volume 6, Number 228, 24 May, p. 161.
Signed 'William Morris'.

454. *News From Nowhere: Chapter XVII (Continued),* Volume 6, Number 229, 31 May, p. 169.
Signed 'William Morris'.

455. *News From Nowhere: Chapter XVII (Continued),* Volume 6, Number 230, 7 June, p. 179.
Signed 'William Morris'.

456. *Anti-Parliamentary,* Volume 6, Number 230, 7 June, pp. 180–181.
Signed 'William Morris'.

457. *News From Nowhere: Chapter XVII (Concluded),* Volume 6, Number 231, 14 June, p. 186.
Signed 'William Morris'.

458. *Notes On News,* Volume 6, Number 232, 21 June, p. 192.
Signed 'W. M.'.

459. *News From Nowhere: Chapter XVIII,* Volume 6, Number 232, 21 June, p. 195.
Signed 'William Morris'.

460. *Notes On News,* Volume 6, Number 233, 28 June, p. 204.
Signed 'W. M.'.

461. *News From Nowhere: Chapter XIX,* Volume 6, Number 233, 28 June, p. 205.
Signed 'William Morris'.

462. *News From Nowhere: Chapters XIX, XX & XXI,* Volume 6, Number 234, 5 July, p. 209.
Signed 'William Morris'.

463. *Notes On News,* Volume 6, Number 234, 5 July, p. 212.
Signed 'W. M.'.

464. *News From Nowhere: Chapter XXII,* Volume 6, Number 235, 12 July, p. 220.
Signed 'William Morris'.

465. *The Development Of Modern Society,* Volume 6, Number 236, 19 July, pp. 225–226.
Signed 'William Morris'.

466. *News From Nowhere: Chapter XXII (Concluded),* Volume 6, Number 236, 19 July, p. 229.
Signed 'William Morris'.

467. *News From Nowhere: Chapter XXIII,* Volume 6, Number 237, 26 July, p. 233.
Signed 'William Morris'.

468. *Notes On News,* Volume 6, Number 237, 26 July, p. 235.
Signed 'W. M.'.

469. *The Development of Modern Society,* Volume 6, Number 237, 26 July, p. 237.
Signed 'William Morris'.

470. *News From Nowhere: Chapter XXIV,* Volume 6, Number 238, 2 August, p. 242.
Signed 'William Morris'.

471. *The Development Of Modern Society,* Volume 6, Number 238, 2 August, p. 244.
Signed 'William Morris'.

472. *News From Nowhere: Chapter XXIV (Concluded),* Volume 6, Number 239, 9 August, p. 250.
Signed 'William Morris'.

473. *The Development Of Modern Society,* Volume 6, Number 239, 9 August, p. 253.
Signed 'William Morris'.

474. *News From Nowhere: Chapter XXV,* Volume 6, Number 240, 16 August, p. 257.
Signed 'William Morris'.

475. *The Development Of Modern Society,* Volume 6, Number 240, 16 August, pp. 260–261.
Signed 'William Morris'.

476. *News From Nowhere: Chapter XXVI,* Volume 6, Number 241, 23 August, p. 266.
Signed 'William Morris'.

477. *News From Nowhere: Chapter XXVI (Continued),* Volume 6, Number 242, 30 August, p. 274.
Signed 'William Morris'.

478. *News From Nowhere: Chapter XXVI (Concluded),* Volume 6, Number 243, 6 September, p. 284.
Signed 'William Morris'.

479. *News From Nowhere: Chapter XXVII,* Volume 6, Number 244, 13 September, p. 292.
Signed 'William Morris'.

480. *News From Nowhere: Chapter XXVIII,* Volume 6, Number 245, 20 September, p. 298.
Signed 'William Morris'.

481. *News From Nowhere: Chapter XXIX,* Volume 6, Number 246, 27 September, p. 306.
Signed 'William Morris'.

482. *News From Nowhere: Chapter XXX,* Volume 6, Number 247, 4 October, p. 314.
Signed 'William Morris'.

483. *Workhouse Socialism,* Volume 6, Number 251, 1 November, pp. 345–346.
Signed 'William Morris'.

484. *Where Are We Now?,* Volume 6, Number 253, 15 November, pp. 361–362.
Signed 'William Morris'.

THE WILLIAM MORRIS SOCIETY

The life, work and ideas of William Morris are as important today as they were in his lifetime. *The William Morris Society* exists to make them as widely known as possible.

The many-sidedness of Morris and the variety of his activities bring together in the *Society* those who are interested in him as designer, craftsman, businessman, poet, socialist, or who admire his robust and generous personality, his creative energy and courage. Morris aimed for a state of affairs in which all might enjoy the potential richness of human life. His thought on how we might live, on creative work, leisure and machinery, on ecology and conservation, on the place of the arts in our lives and their relation to politics, as on much else, remains as challenging now as it was a century ago. He provides a focus for those who deplore the progressive dehumanization of the world in the twentieth-century and who believe, with him, that the trend is not inevitable.

The *Society* provides information on topics of interest to its members and arranges lectures, visits, exhibitions and other events. It encourages the reprinting of his works and the continued manufacture of his textile and wallpaper designs. It publishes a journal twice a year, free to members, which carries articles across the field of Morris scholarship. It also publishes a quarterly newsletter giving details of its programme, new publications and other matters of interest concerning Morris and his circle. Members are invited to contribute items both to the journal and to the newsletter. *The William Morris Society* has a world-wide membership and offers the chance to make contact with fellow Morrisians both in Britain and abroad.

Regular events include a Kelmscott Lecture, a birthday party held in March, and visits to exhibitions and such places as the William Morris Gallery, Red House, Kelmscott Manor and Standen. These visits, our tours and our short residential study courses, enable members living abroad or outside London to participate in the *Society's* activities. The *Society* also has local groups in various parts of Britain and affiliated Societies in the USA and Canada.

For further details, write to:
The Hon. Membership Secretary
Kelmscott House
26 Upper Mall
Hammersmith
London W6 9TA